The German 1918 Offe

Based on original German records not analyzed in depth for more than sixty years—including recently discovered records previously thought lost in the bombing of Potsdam during World War II—this book is the first study of the German 1918 offensives to focus on the "operational level of war" and on the body of activity known as the "operational art," rather than on the tactical or strategic level.

In the first half of 1918 a series of large-scale offensive operations designed to defeat Britain and France before the arrival of American troops produced stunning tactical gains, previously thought impossible in the gridlock of trench warfare. David T. Zabecki shows that the reasons these victories failed to add up to strategic success are to be found not at the tactical level of warfare, but rather at the operational level, a distinct realm of military activity that was only beginning to mature at the beginning of the 20th century.

He presents his findings here, with a thorough review of the surviving original operational plans and orders and offers a wealth of fresh insights into the German offensives of 1918 and into the planning and decision-making processes of the German General Staff of World War I.

For the first time, David T. Zabecki clearly demonstrates how the German failure to exploit the vulnerabilities in the BEF's rail system led to the failure of the first two offensives, and how inadequacies in the German rail system determined the outcome of the last three offensives. This is also the first study in English or German of Operation HAGEN, the planned but never launched final offensive of the campaign.

This book will be of great interest to all students of World War I, the German Army and of strategic studies and military theory in general.

David T. Zabecki started his military career as an enlisted infantryman in Vietnam and served during the 1968 Tet Offensive. He has been Commanding General of the U.S. Southern European Task Force (Rear) and has served as the U.S. Department of Defense Executive Director for all World War II 60th anniversary commemoration events in Europe. In 2003 he was the Senior Security Advisor on the U.S. Coordinating and Monitoring Mission in Israel. The Editor of *Vietnam* Magazine, he has a PhD in Military Science from the Royal Military College of Science, Cranfield University.

Routledge series: strategy and history

Series Editors: Colin Gray and Williamson Murray
ISSN: 1473-6403

This new series will focus on the theory and practice of strategy. Following Clausewitz, strategy has been understood to mean the use made of force, and the threat of the use of force, for the ends of policy. This series is as interested in ideas as in historical cases of grand strategy and military strategy in action. All historical periods, near and past, and even future, are of interest. In addition to original monographs, the series will from time to time publish edited reprints of neglected classics as well as collections of essays.

The German 1918 Offensives

A case study in the operational level of war

David T. Zabecki

LONDON AND NEW YORK

First published 2006
by Routledge
2 Park Square, Milton Park, Abingdon, Oxon OX14 4RN

Simultaneously published in the USA and Canada
by Routledge
270 Madison Ave, New York, NY 10016

Routledge is an imprint of the Taylor & Francis Group, an informa business

Transferred to Digital Printing 2009

Typeset in Times by Wearset Ltd, Boldon, Tyne and Wear

British Library Cataloguing in Publication Data
A catalogue record for this book is available from the British Library

Library of Congress Cataloging in Publication Data
A catalog record for this book has been requested

ISBN10: 0–415–35600–8 (hbk)
ISBN10: 0–415–55879–4 (pbk)

ISBN13: 978–0–415–35600–8 (hbk)
ISBN13: 978–0–415–55879–2 (pbk)

To my wife, Marlies Schweigler, for her never-ending patience and support of my military career and my academic pursuits

Contents

12 Conclusions 311

Tables

Maps

Foreword

One of the great ironies of 20th-century historiography has been the fact that it has only been in the last two decades that historians have actually begun to unravel the full complexity of the most disastrously influential war in human history. In effect, the conflict of 1914 to 1918 saw the invention of modern war—tactical and operational concepts that were still valid in the Tigris–Euphrates Valley in the spring of 2003. Its strategic and political consequences were to live on until the fall of the Berlin Wall and the collapse of the Soviet Union.

How is one to explain the fact that it has taken so long to understand the learning processes and adaptations that occurred on the battlefields of the Western Front? Part of the problem undoubtedly has had to do with the fact that World War II intervened at precisely the point when historians were beginning to examine the Great War through new perspectives. And when World War II finally ended, historians found themselves involved in examining what appeared to be a more interesting and vital conflict. Thus, the myths of the first conflict, typified by the "lions led by donkeys" school of history, remained to dominate the historical landscape.

Further complicating the difficulties that historians confronted was the fact that the RAF in its effort to pulverize the Third Reich managed to destroy much of the archival material pertaining to the German Army in World War I—or so we thought.

In fact there was another source available for at least the last year of the war. Ironically, as perhaps a reward for American support for German efforts to distort the history of what had happened during World War I, during the inter-war period the Germans allowed a team of American Army historians to examine and copy most of the records of the German Army's high command, army groups, armies, and corps dealing with the conduct of operations on the Western Front in 1918. This treasure trove of the day-to-day conduct of the German offensives then sat in various U.S. Army depositories over subsequent decades, unexamined and unused until David Zabecki, the author of this book, discovered them. With that discovery he was then able to write this book, the first account based on actual records, since the appearance of the last volume of the German government's official history—which was scheduled to appear in 1944, but which finally appeared in 1956.

This then is an account of that decisive year in world history, when the Germans managed to achieve outstanding tactical successes on the battlefield, but completely failed to translate tactical success into operational victory. In the case of their tactical successes, the Germans broke new ground. But the flawed operational execution of the spring 1918 offensives almost takes one's breath away for the level of incompetence and arrogance the Germans displayed. Quite simply put, Ludendorff not only had no strategic objective in mind, but no operational goal. It was, as he put it to Crown Prince Rupprecht of Bavaria, simply a matter of punching a hole in British lines and seeing what turned up. And the results were not hard to predict. At huge cost in terms of manpower and materiel they could not afford, the Germans seized large amounts of useless ground that proved harder to defend than the positions they abandoned when they began their advances.

Thus, this study breaks entirely new ground in the history of World War I. In many respects it is the most important monograph on the history of the war to appear in the past two decades, precisely because it rests on original sources that historians had believed had been completely destroyed in April 1945. General Zabecki has turned the new archival material into a brilliant account of how and why the German offensives of spring 1918 failed so disastrously and completely. His account represents an extraordinary contribution to the historiography of World War I; it provides the expert as well as the neophyte with a clear direct account of the turning point in World War I, for when the "Ludendorff" offensives failed, catastrophic collapse of Germany was the inevitable result. How and why these offensives failed, then, is Zabecki's story, and it is one that provides an entirely new perspective of the first German bid for world hegemony. It will represent the standard account for the German spring offensives for the foreseeable future. And it establishes General Zabecki as one of the major historians of World War I.

Williamson Murray
Fairfax, Virginia

Acknowledgments

The following individuals deserve my sincere thanks for their help and support during the researching and writing of this monograph: Prof. Richard Holmes, Dr. Chris Bellamy, and Ms. Steph Muir of the Royal Military College of Science, Shrivenham, Cranfield University; Prof. Duncan Anderson, Royal Military Academy, Sandhurst; Prof. Emeritus Williamson Murray, Ohio State University; Marlies Schweigler and Claudia Schweigler-Thom, Freiburg, Germany; Dr. Donald Frazier, Abilene, Texas; Lt. Col. (ret.) Lewis S. Sorley, U.S. Army; Oberstleutnant a.D. Hans J. Sommer, Bundeswehr; Lt. Col. (ret.) Tom Bower, U.S. Army; Lt. Col. (ret.) Roger Cirillo, U.S. Army; and Major General (ret.) Jonathan Bailey, British Army.

Special thanks to Cranfield University, the copyright holder of my doctoral dissertation, for granting permission to publish this modified version in book form. The staffs of the following institutions were also most helpful in facilitating access to the material in their collections: Bundesarchiv/Militärarchiv, Freiburg, Germany; Bayerisches Kriegsarchiv, Munich, Germany; Combat Arms Research Library, U.S. Army Command and General Staff College, Ft. Leavenworth, Kansas; U.S. Army Military History Institute, Carlisle Barracks, Carlisle, Pennsylvania.

Any errors in fact or interpretation in this study are solely mine.

David T. Zabecki
Freiburg, Germany

Glossary of acronyms and military and foreign terms

AAA Antiaircraft artillery
Absicht Commander's intent
AEF American Expeditionary Force
AK *Armeekorps* (German standard corps)
AKA *Artilleriebekämpfungsartillerie* (German counter-battery artillery units)
All Arms (British) *See* combined arms
Angriffsdivision German attack division
AOK *Armee Oberkommando* (German numbered army headquarters)
Arko *Artillerie Kommandeur* (German artillery headquarters)
A-Staff Adjutant General's Staff (British)
Aufklärung Reconnaissance
Aufmarsch Deployment
Battle A series of related tactical engagements.
BEF British Expeditionary Force
Bewegungskrieg Mobile warfare
Blue Cross German artillery shell marking indicating non-lethal, non-persistent vomiting gas.
Bombengeschwader German bomber wing
Bombenstaffeln German bomber squadrons
Buntkreuz German technique of simultaneously firing Blue Cross and Green Cross artillery shells at the same target.
C2 Command and Control
C3 Command, Control, and Communications
C3I Command, Control, Communications, and Intelligence
C4I Command, Control, Communications, Computers, and Intelligence
Campaign A series of related military operations designed to achieve one or more strategic objectives within a given time and space.
CB Counter-battery fire.
Center of gravity The hub of all power and movement upon which everything depends. That characteristic, capability, or location from which enemy and friendly forces derive their freedom of action, physical strength, or the will to fight.
Combined arms The synchronized application of two or more arms (infantry,

artillery, armor, cavalry, engineers, aviation) in which the strength of one of the arms either complements the strengths of the other arms, or compensates for their weaknesses.

Commander's intent A concise expression of the purpose of an operation, the desired objective, and the manner in which it will be achieved.

Culmination The point in time and space when the attacker's combat power no longer exceeds that of the defender, or when the defender no longer has the capability to resist successfully.

Decisive point A point, usually but not always geographic in nature, that when obtained or retained provides a commander with a marked advantage over his opponent. Decisive points can also include other physical elements such as enemy formations, command posts, or communications nodes.

Depth The concept of extending military operations against an enemy in both space and time.

Destruction A firepower effect designed to render a target completely combat-ineffective.

Durchbruch Breakthrough

Einbruch Break-in

Entscheidungsstelle Decisive point

FEKA *Fernkämpfartillerie* (German long-range artillery units)

Feuerwalze Creeping barrage

Firepower The projection of kinetic energy force against an enemy for the purpose of suppressing, neutralizing, or destroying him. One of the primary elements of combat power.

Fliegerabteilung Aviation reconnaissance and liaison detachment

Fliegerabteilung-A Artillery observation aviation detachment

Fliegeraufklärung Aerial reconnaissance

FO Forward observer

FOFA Follow-on forces attack

FOO Forward observation officer (British)

Friction The accumulation of chance errors, unexpected difficulties, enemy actions, and confusion in battle.

Fussartillerie Foot artillery, the German heavy artillery

Gegenangriff Deliberate counterattack

Gegenstoss Hasty counterattack

Generalstab General Staff (German)

GHQ General headquarters (British and American)

GQG *Grand Quartier Général* (French General Headquarters)

Green Cross German artillery shell marking indicating lethal, non-persistent choking gas.

G-Staff General Staff (British)

Hauptwiderstandslinie Main line of resistance

HE High explosive

Hgr. DKP *Heeresgruppe Deutscher Kronprinz* (Army Group Headquarters of German Crown Prince Wilhelm)

Hgr. KPR *Heeresgruppe Kronprinz Rupprecht* (Army Group Headquarters of Bavarian Crown Prince Rupprecht)

Ia German General Staff officer in charge of operations

IBB *Infantriebegleitbatterien* (German accompanying artillery batteries)

Ic German General Staff officer in charge of intelligence

IGB *Infantrie-Geschuestzbatterien* (German infantry gun batteries)

IKA *Infantriebekämpfungsartillerie* (German direct support artillery units)

Initiative The ability to set or change the terms of battle.

Intelligence In the military sense, the product resulting from collecting, processing, integrating, analyzing, evaluating, and interpreting information concerning an enemy force.

Interdiction Actions to divert, disrupt, delay, or destroy the enemy before it can affect friendly forces.

Jagdgeschwader German fighter wing

Jagdstaffeln German fighter squadrons

Jäger German light infantry units (literally hunters)

Kagohl *Kampfgeschwader*

Kampfstaffeln German bomber squadrons (original name)

Kogenluft *Kommandierender General der Luftstreitkräfte* (commanding general of air forces)

KTB *Kriegstagebuch* (war diary)

Landser Common German soldier

Landsturm Germany's second tier reserve force

Landwehr Germany's first tier reserve force

LC Line of contact

LD Line of departure

Liaison The contact or intercommunication maintained between elements of military forces to ensure mutual understanding and unity of purpose and action.

Line of operation A directional orientation that connects the force with its base of operations and its objective.

LOC Lines of communications, all routes (land, water, and air) that connect an operating military force with its base of operations, and along which supplies and military forces move.

Logistics The system of planning and executing the movement and sustainment of forces in the execution of military operations.

Maneuver Battlefield movement to gain positional advantage. One of the primary elements of combat power.

Materialschlacht Battle of attrition

MW *Minenwerfer* (trench mortars)

Neutralization A firepower effect designed to render a target temporarily combat-ineffective for a specific period.

OB Order of battle

Oberost German general headquarters on the Eastern Front

Offizierstellvertreter Temporary officer (usually an NCO acting as a platoon leader, and sometimes as a company commander)

OHL *Oberste Heeresleitung* (German general headquarters)

OODA Observe, Orient, Decide, Act (also known as the Boyd Loop)

Operational art Military planning and execution actions at the operational level of war.

Operational level of war The distinct level of warfare between the tactical and the strategic.

Operatives Ziel Operational objective

OPSEC Operational security

Q-Staff Quartermaster General's Staff (British)

Reach The distance over which a military force can project its combat power in sufficient concentration to achieve its objective.

Reconstitution Actions taken by higher headquarters to rebuild combat-worn units to a level of effectiveness commensurate with mission requirements and available resources.

RK *Reservekorps* (German reserve corps)

Schlachtstaffeln German ground attack squadrons

Schutzstaffeln German ground attack squadrons (original name)

SCHWEFLA *Schwerste Flachfeuerartillerie* (German heavy flat-firing artillery units)

Schwerpunkt Center of gravity, although the Germans used the term as synonymous with main effort, rather than the way Clausewitz meant center of gravity.

Siegfriedstellung Siegfried Position, called the Hindenburg Line by the Allies

Stellungsdivision Trench division

Stellungskrieg Trench warfare

Stollen German deep bunkers

Stosstrupp Storm troop company

Strategy The art and science of employing armed forces and other elements of national power during peace or war to secure national objectives.

Sturmabteilung Storm troop detachment

Sturmbattalion Storm troop battalion

Suppression A firepower effect designed to temporarily disrupt the capability of enemy forces in the target area from delivering effective fire on friendly forces.

Tactics The art and science of employing available means to win battles and engagements.

Tempo The rate of a military action. Controlling or altering tempo is a necessary means to initiative.

Vernichtungsschlacht Battle of annihilation

Vollmacht Authority delegated to a staff officer to issue orders in the name of the commander

Weisungsführung Command by directive

Wilhelmgeschütze Wilhelm Guns. Also known as the Paris Guns. Widely but incorrectly called Big Berthas.

Yellow Cross German artillery shell marking indicating lethal, persistent mustard gas.

1 Introduction

Why do we still bother with World War I?

> With regard to operational history, it becomes too easy to lose sight of battles and campaigns as means to higher ends and to overlook alternative paths not taken which might have led to very different outcomes.[1]
>
> Colonel Richard M. Swain

"Why bother with World War I? What's the point?" I frequently get this question from junior officers, and quite often from more senior ones. Why indeed? In the broader context, of course, there is very little question about the historical significance of World War I. The war marked the death of an entire way of life in Europe, and the true beginnings of the modern era. When World War I ended, four of the world's five great empires were dead, and the fifth was mortally wounded. The war marked the start of the shift of global power from the center of Europe to America and Russia on the flanks. In his 2001 book, *Forgotten Victory*, Gary Sheffield called the Great War "the key event of the twentieth century, from which everything else flowed."[2]

Yet despite its social, political, and economic significance, popular history has given the military aspects of World War I a very bad reputation. The conventional image of that war is one of a senseless blood bath—a dull and grinding war of attrition conducted by incompetent, even criminally stupid generals, without a trace of strategic thought or tactical innovation. Thus, many today believe that World War I has nothing to teach the modern soldier, especially in comparison to World War II, with its fast-moving armored and airborne divisions. Any detailed study of World War I seems largely irrelevant by comparison.

Much of the existing image of World War I is based on the vivid descriptions of contemporary poets and popular writers, many of who experienced directly the horrors of the Great War. The writings of Erich Maria Remarque (*All Quiet on the Western Front*), Robert Graves (*Good-bye to All That*), Siegfried Sassoon (*Memoirs of an Infantry Officer*), Vera Brittain (*Testament of Youth*), and especially C.S. Forester (*The General*) have left a lasting imprint on the popular mind, and to some extent have influenced the scholarly mind as well. With few exceptions, the most notable being Germany's Ernst Jünger (*Storm of Steel*), the

World War I writers and poets cast their own experiences in a largely anti-heroic light, which profoundly influenced the way people looked at war in general for the remainder of the 20th century.[3] As Professor Brian Bond has pointed out, the literary writers either ignored, or failed to address convincingly, the larger historical, political, and strategic questions of the war. What was it about and why was it fought?[4]

The observations of the military historians and theorists who wrote during the 1920s and 1930s were even more critical of the Great War's significance and conduct. In his 1987 book, *The Killing Ground: The British Army, the Western Front and the Emergence of Modern Warfare, 1900–1918*, Tim Travers identified two basic British schools of thought that had emerged by the 1930s. Although Travers referred specifically to the evaluation of the British Expeditionary Force (BEF), his model applies to the historiography of the entire war.[5]

The "Internal Factor," or "Mud and Blood" school of thought, holds that the slaughter on the Western Front was caused by the incompetence of the generals, with their bloody-mindedness, their physical and intellectual distance from actual front-line conditions, and their Victorian-era insensitivity. Among the most influential books of this school are Liddell Hart's *The Real War* and Lloyd George's *War Memoirs*. More recent contributions from this school include John Ellis' *Eye-deep in Hell: Trench Warfare in World War I*, and Lyn Mac-Donald's *They Called It Passchendaele* and *To the Last Man: Spring 1918*. The approach of this school is appealing because it is easy to understand in human terms. It is also far too simplistic, too pat. The notion that Germany, Britain, France, Austria-Hungary, and Russia all simultaneously produced complete higher-officer corps full of idiots requires too much of a stretch.

The "External Factor" school blames the Western Front deadlock on a combination of inexperienced staff officers, the technical difficulties of mastering new technology, the impressive tactical fighting ability of the Germans, and the interference of political leaders in strictly military affairs. The significant contributions from this school include the fourteen volumes of the British official history edited by Sir James Edmonds, and John Terraine's *Douglas Haig: The Educated Soldier*. But the arguments of this school are overly simplistic as well, and serve as apologists for the genuinely incompetent commanders the war did produce.

The past thirty years have seen the emergence of a third school of thought, which Travers calls the "Realists." The writers of this school take a more balanced approach to the study of World War I. The general thrust of their argument holds that the clash between old ideas and new weapons and technology, combined with the huge scale of the war and a lack of combined arms coordination, caused serious tactical and operational problems on all sides. While the new technology was an external factor, the inability to integrate the new weapons was an internal flaw.

In *The Killing Ground*, Travers also describes the paradigm shift from muscle-powered warfare to machine-powered warfare that is perhaps the most recognizable characteristic of World War I. It was a paradigm shift that occurred so fast that most military commanders and staff officers were unable to come to grips with it within the course of the war. Moreover, it was a shift that occurred unevenly, and this more than anything else caused the deadlock on the Western Front.

The two basic elements of combat power are fire and maneuver. Throughout military history the two have been locked in a constant struggle for dominance. Rarely has one gained the upper hand, or held it for very long. Yet by 1914 firepower technology was far ahead of mobility technology. Machine guns and rapid-firing artillery had truly mechanized firepower by 1914, but battlefield mobility was still based primarily on human and horse muscle power. This would begin to change by 1918, with the emergence of combat aircraft, the tank, and increased use of motor vehicles; but for most of World War I firepower retained the upper hand.

The writers of the Realist school point out just how difficult it was for even the most talented and intelligent of the Great War's military planners to come to grips with these changes that came on a "future shock" scale. They also argue that by 1918 the tactical and technical solutions were starting to emerge. World War I ended in exhaustion before the new solutions could be brought to fruition, but they formed the seedbed for the mobile tactics and operations of World War II.

One of the strongest and most concise arguments for the significance of World War I in the history of warfare can be found in Jonathan Bailey's 1996 pamphlet *The First World War and the Birth of the Modern Style of Warfare*. Bailey argued that between 1917 and 1918 "a Revolution in Military Affairs (RMA) took place which, it is contended, was more than merely that; rather it amounted to a Military Revolution which was the most significant development in the history of warfare to date, *and remains so*."[6]

Bailey built a strong and logical argument to support this seemingly radical thesis. He drew a sharp distinction between a *revolution in military affairs* and a *military revolution*. According to one definition, an RMA is "a discontinuous increase in military capability and effectiveness arising from simultaneous and mutually supportive change in technology, systems, operational methods, and military organizations."[7] A *military revolution*, according to Bailey, "embodies a more fundamental and enduring transformation brought about by military change."[8] The key distinction is that a military revolution introduces an entirely new concept in warfighting, rather than just quantum improvements in current ways of operating.

Bailey argued that the period on the Western Front from 1917 to 1918 introduced such a military revolution that brought about the birth of the *modern style of warfare*, "with the advent of three dimensional artillery indirect fire as the foundation of planning at the tactical, operational, and strategic levels of war." The result was something fundamentally different and new in warfare—operations in three dimensions and in depth.[9]

Essentially then, Bailey argued that the World War I paradigm shift was far more extensive than the muscle to machine shift described by Travers. Bailey suggested that the 1917–1918 shift to the *modern style of warfare* was so revolutionary that the subsequent introductions of armor, air power, and information-age technology have amounted to no more than complements to it. These advances have been incremental, technical improvements to the efficiency of the conceptual model of the modern style of warfare.

Bailey also argues it was the *indirect fire revolution* that grew out of the experimentation in the years just prior to World War I that made possible the conceptual leaps to three-dimensional warfare and deep battle. The supporting technologies of 1917–1918, however, were not up to the potentials of the indirect fire model. Specifically, transportation capabilities were inadequate for artillery to move forward rapidly and be re-supplied over rough terrain, and communications were inadequate to maintain decentralized command and control of the fire plan once an operation started. As a consequence, contemporary popular wisdom accepts that artillery dominated the battlefield in World War I. Few really understand, as Bailey argued, that artillery fire was the key to maneuver rather than the agent of stalemate. The technical solutions to these problems emerged in the years between the World Wars and proved themselves on the battlefields of World War II and since. As Bailey noted, "Clearly between 1914 and 1918 something of extraordinary historical profundity and enduring military significance had happened."[10]

According to Bailey, the RMA we are experiencing today is essentially an echo of World War I and hardly revolutionary by comparison. Key elements of today's RMA include: precise standoff strikes; real-time Command, Control, Communications, Computers, and Intelligence (C4I); information operations; and non-lethality. In 1917–1918 terms these would have been called: accurate indirect fire; improvement in command and control and intelligence; the means of acting upon it; and the munitions and techniques of neutralization and suppression.[11]

Other works from the "Realist" school include Gary Sheffield's *Forgotten Victory: The First World War Myths and Realities*; Shelford Bidwell's and Dominick Graham's *Fire-Power: British Army Weapons and Theories of War 1904–1945*; Bruce Gudmundsson's *Stormtroop Tactics*; Jonathan Bailey's *Field Artillery and Firepower*; Rod Paschall's *The Defeat of Imperial Germany, 1917–1918*; Bill Rawling's *Surviving Trench Warfare: Technology and the Canadian Corps, 1914–1918*; and my own *Steel Wind: Colonel Georg Bruchmüller and the Birth of Modern Artillery*.

The German 1918 offensives as a model

World War I also witnessed the first truly modern appearance of the Operational Level of War, which is the central topic of this book. It is not the primary objective of this study, however, to speculate on ways in which the Germans could have won World War I, or even could have achieved some sort of a battlefield victory in 1918. Rather, the primary objective is to use German offensive operations and planning in 1918 as a laboratory to examine and analyze the Operational Level of War. In the course of this analysis, alternative courses of action will be considered as a means to explore the flaws in German operational planning and execution.

The central purpose of the German military effort between March and July 1918 was Erich Ludendorff's attempt to stage a knockout victory in the west. In four of the five offensives the Germans launched, however, impressive tactical gains failed to lead to operational results, much less strategic success. In the fifth operation, the Germans failed to achieve even tactical success. After the failure of Operations MICHAEL and GEORGETTE, the subsequent offensives were supposed to set the conditions for the planned but never launched Operation HAGEN. Operationally, first MICHAEL, then GEORGETTE, and then HAGEN were supposed to knock the British out of the war, which would then lead to the strategic result of an Allied collapse in the west before enough fresh American forces could arrive to tip the strategic balance.

Ludendorff's ultimate strategic objective, however, was to achieve a decisive and unconditional military victory over the Western Allies, rather than establish a position of relative strength from which to negotiate a conclusion to the hostilities that would be favorable to Germany on the balance sheet. Most historians agree that such a decisive military victory was far beyond Germany's capabilities and resources in 1918. This, perhaps, was the fatal flaw or "disconnect" between the strategic and operational levels that doomed Ludendorff's offensives from the start. With more realistic strategic objectives and better operational design, however, Germany just might have been able to conduct a series of operationally successful campaigns and end the war in a far better strategic position than it actually did.

The tactical outcomes of Ludendorff's offensives are well known. The objective here is to compare the results with the plans and the process at the operational level, to identify the flaws, and to explore possible alternatives. This study attempts to answer the following questions:

1   What were the German planners and decision makers thinking, and what did the operations orders say?
2   How did the execution vary from the plans, and what impact did this have in the short and long term?
3   Given that the operational objectives did not support the strategic realities of 1918, could the German strategic and operational objectives have been modified to improve the chances of success?
4   Did the operational design maximize the tactical realities of 1918?
5   Why did each (and all combined) of the Ludendorff offensives fail to set the conditions for HAGEN?
6   Were the failures ones of planning or of execution?
7   What were the objectives and details of the HAGEN plan?
8   With the proper conditions, could HAGEN or any of the other offensives have succeeded—and if so, how?
9   At the operational level, what lessons did Germany learn or mis-learn from 1918?

Question Number 7 is especially intriguing. To the best of my knowledge, no scholarly study has ever been made of the HAGEN plans.

Scope and methods

This book focuses on German offensive operations and planning on the Western Front from November 1917 through July 1918. The discussion includes the Eastern Front, defensive operations in 1918, and overall operations in 1914–1917 only insofar as necessary to explain the plans and actions of the Ludendorff offensives. I have conducted the analysis from the point of view of the Germans. I have, of course, considered and described the responses of the Western Allies—the British, French, and Americans—but I have neither analyzed their plans nor critiqued their actions.

The main purpose of this study is to analyze the 1918 offensives at the operational level of war. In order to establish the framework for the analysis, I have devoted a considerable amount of discussion to the theory and development of Operational Art. I have also examined Operational Art as it was understood in the German Army before and during World War I. It is impossible to divorce completely the operational from the strategic and tactical levels. Thus I have also considered the German strategic situation in 1918 and the tactical and technical realities of World War I.

In conducting this analysis, I have relied on both primary and secondary sources. I have consulted published books, magazine and journal articles, official histories, and both contemporary and present-day doctrinal manuals. I have also examined all of the surviving German plans and records of the five Ludendorff offensives, and the planning files for Operation HAGEN. As described in the section below on primary sources, most of those records are in German.

In attempting to reconstruct the German decision-making and planning process, I have applied many of the tools and techniques of the military intelligence officer—a field in which I have some practical experience. Both the military historian and the military intelligence officer face similar challenges, and in many cases they use similar analytical tools. While the military historian tries to reconstruct and understand the past, the military intelligence officer works in the opposite temporal direction in an effort to predict future actions. Both, however, are concerned with identifying the capabilities, intentions, institutional culture, leadership, and courses of action of a military force. Both work at these tasks from a distance, and both are faced with the similar challenge of working from partial, often conflicting, and sometimes intentionally misleading information from a wide variety of sources of varying accuracy and reliability. The ultimate objective for both is to produce the best possible analysis from the best information available. This process can be as much an art as it is a science.

In analyzing the Ludendorff offensives at the operational level, I have focused on the systems and assets that intelligence analysts rely upon to develop an enemy's operational signature. In World War I these would have included air power, long-range and heavy artillery, and rail transport. Artillery is an especially important element of this analysis because it was in World War I that artillery firepower first acquired an operational role. By 1918 the Germans had a clear understanding of the difference between the close and the deep battle and the need to coordinate the two.

I have also considered the operational options, the plan, the preparations, and the execution for each of the operations. In assessing these operations, it is necessary to evaluate them against a model of a framework of the Operational Art. Unfortunately, no universally agreed upon framework exists. Even to this day the doctrinal manuals of a single country are often in conflict. Furthermore, many of today's operational concepts would not have been understood by commanders in 1918. For these reasons, in the following chapter I will develop and propose a Framework of the Operational Art for use throughout this study.

The primary sources

Since the end of World War I a great deal has been written about the German offensives of 1918. This is particularly true of the first and last offensives, Operation MICHAEL (21 March–5 April) and Operation MARNESCHUTZ–REIMS (15–18 July). The three middle operations, GEORGETTE (9–29 April), BLÜCHER (27 May–13 June), and GNIESANAU (9–13 June) have not been covered as extensively. The thoroughly planned but never launched Operation HAGEN only receives passing mention in the existing literature.

Much of this analysis has focused on the tactical level of war; on the planning, the conduct, and the results of the battles themselves. Several writers have placed the Ludendorff offensives in the strategic context, showing very clearly the impossibility of the German situation in 1918, despite what happened on the battlefield. To date, there has never been a thorough analysis at the operational level of war—that vital link between the strategic and the tactical. Some of the previous writings touch on various elements of the Operational Art, and some describe German planning and decision making at the operational level. None, however, have conducted a systematic analysis at the operational level, nor has there been a consideration of possible alternatives within a framework of more realistic German strategic objectives.

Much of what has been written in English about the German side in 1918 has been based on secondary sources, and much of that was published originally in German. Researching the German records today is a challenging proposition. The German Army in World War I kept fairly complete and accurate records. At the conclusion of the war, however, not all the records went to the *Reichsarchiv* in Potsdam. The records of Bavarian Crown Prince Rupprecht's Army Group, including those of the Sixth but not the Fourth Army, were sent instead to the *Bayerisches Kriegsarchiv* in Munich.

In 1944 many of the original World War I records in the *Reichsarchiv* were destroyed in a fire when Potsdam was bombed. After World War II, the bulk of the surviving World War I records became part of the *Bundesarchiv* collection in Koblenz. Some of the surviving records in Berlin, however, fell into Soviet hands and wound up in the *Kriegsarchiv* of the German Democratic Republic (DDR). In the 1960s, all the West German-held military records were relocated to the newly established *Bundesarchiv/Militärarchiv* (BA/MA) in the southwestern university town of Freiburg.

After the reunification of Germany, the records in the DDR *Kriegsarchiv* were consolidated with those of the BA/MA in Freiburg. Fortunately, the records in the *Bayerisches Kriegsarchiv* survived the World War II bombing of Munich, and they remain in that city. These records include Rupprecht's units in Operation MICHAEL, virtually all of GEORGETTE, and all of the planning files for HAGEN. During the course of my research, I spent several weeks in the *Bayerisches Kriegsarchiv* and almost five months in the *Bundesarchiv/Militärarchiv* studying the records in their collections.

The BA/MA also holds several important collections of personal papers (*Nachlass* in German). Some collections, including the professional papers of Colonel Georg Bruchmüller, were lost in the Potsdam fire. Bruchmüller's personal papers (N/275) survived, however, and are currently in Freiburg. Other important collections in the BA/MA relevant to the 1918 offensives include the papers of Hans von Seeckt (N/247); Friedrich Graf von der Schulenburg-Tressow (N/58); Hermann Geyer (N/221); Hans von Haeften (N/35); and Joachim von Stülpnagel (N/5).

Although many of the key original documents were destroyed in 1944, copies of some of those records have survived. Under the terms of a bilateral agreement between Germany and the United States, both sides had unrestricted access to the other's World War I military records until well into the 1930s. Between 1919 and 1937, the U.S. Army War College Historical Section maintained a senior American officer and a small locally hired clerical staff in Potsdam, transcribing selected records. The first officer assigned to this duty was Major Walter S. Krueger.[12] Born in Germany and fluent in German, Krueger would later command the U.S. Sixth Army in the Pacific in World War II. Other officers assigned as Representatives of the Historical Section included Colonel Lewis S. Sorley (1922–1926); Major Bertram Cadwalader (1926–1928); Lieutenant Colonel C.H. Müller (1928–1932); Major J.O. Wagner (1932–1936); and Major J.P. Ratay (1936–1937). Ratay closed the mission and left Potsdam in December 1937—almost five years after Hitler came to power. I am especially grateful to Lieutenant Colonel Lewis B. Sorley (U.S. Army, Retired) for sharing with me the section of his grandfather's unpublished reminiscences that deal with his time as head of the Potsdam mission.[13]

The American effort focused almost exclusively on the Western Front from about mid-1917 through the end of the war—the period of direct American involvement. As a result of these efforts, many of the most important German records of the Ludendorff offensives and the later 1918 battles have survived. The records of many significant Eastern Front battles, such as Riga in September 1917, were not copied by the Americans and were lost forever in the 1944 fire.

The American team in Potsdam did not translate any documents. They transcribed them word-for-word in the original German, typewritten with multiple carbon copies (at least two copies), using the brownish, semi-transparent, brittle copy paper of the day. After the transcribed documents were sent back to the Army War College, then located in Washington, they were split into two groups. Almost all the records from Operation BLÜCHER on were sent to Fort Leavenworth. There they were translated into English and used for lesson plan material throughout the 1920s at the U.S. Army Command and General Staff College. In 1923 some of the documents relating to Operation MARNESCHUTZ–REIMS were published by the General Service Schools Press at Fort Leavenworth in a book titled *The German Offensive of July 15, 1918 (Marne Source Book).*

The plan may have been to translate the records prior to BLÜCHER at some later date, but that apparently did not happen. The copies of the transcribed records eventually went to the U.S. National Archives and Records Administration (NARA), where they form the core of Record Group 165. This entire record group is now on microfilm. During the 1970s, the NARA gave the BA/MA what appears to be a complete set of carbon copies of the transcribed documents to help rebuild the collection lost in 1944. Copies of the translated documents, however, are not in the BA/MA. As near as I have been able to determine, the U.S. NARA does not have copies of the documents that were translated into English at Fort Leavenworth.

As of 1997, some copies of the translated documents were still in the Combat Arms Research Library (CARL) at Fort Leavenworth. At the time, they were part of an uncatalogued collection of World War I material sitting on a shelf at the back of the library. From my earlier work on the book *Steel Wind: Colonel Georg Bruchmüller and the Birth of Modern Artillery*, I recognized immediately that many of these records did not exist in the BA/MA in Freiburg. I believe I have been successful in obtaining photocopies of all the existing translated records at CARL with the kind cooperation of the staff. Of the slightly more than 900 documents I used for this analysis, some 200 of them, especially from Operations BLÜCHER and GNEISENAU, are from the CARL holdings. To the best of my knowledge they existed nowhere else until I donated a set of the copies to the BA/MA in December 2004.

Research limitations and risks

One of the most serious errors in historical analysis is to impose current thinking and values on the past. Yet the very concepts of the *operational level of war* and the *operational art* are relatively recent constructs. The Soviets coined the term "operational art" in the 1920s, and the U.S. Army only recognized the operational as a distinct level of war in 1982.

On the other hand, there has long been an understanding of certain distinct military activities that existed either at the high end of the tactical spectrum, or at the low end of the strategic. The term *"grand tactics"* was in vogue for some time. Likewise, many of the specific concepts we now associate with the Operational Art have been understood and appreciated for many years. *Culmination* and *center of gravity*, for example, are Clausewitzian notions, while both Jomini and Clausewitz discussed *decisive points*. Even Clausewitz's narrow definition of *military strategy* comes very close to what we would today call operational art: "the use of engagements for the purpose of the war."[14]

Although not necessarily called the "operational level of war," the German Army first started to pay serious attention to this category of activities from about the time of Moltke the Elder. Thus the challenge of this study has been to evaluate the six operations against a framework of operational art as it would have been understood by the Germans in 1918. As German historian Hans Delbrück noted, the history of every military institution should be written within the context of its national history.[15]

2 The operational art

I object to the word "operations." We'll just blow a hole in the middle. The rest will follow of its own accord.[1]

General of Infantry Erich Ludendorff

As noted in the Introduction, the concepts of the "operational level of war" and the "operational art" are constructs that started to evolve in the late 19th century and were only fully accepted in the West within the last thirty years. There remains today, moreover, a considerable amount of discussion among military theorists as to what these ideas really mean, what their components are, and how they fit into the scheme of the much older notions of strategy and tactics.[2] During the period of World War I, most armies in varying degrees had some understanding of many of the basic components of the operational art, but they all lacked an overall conceptual framework.

Prior to analyzing the German 1918 offensives at the operational level, therefore, it will be necessary to consider exactly what operational art is; its evolution in military thought and practice; and how it was understood and practiced in the German Army up through 1918. In order to develop a full understanding of the operational art, it also will be necessary to discuss briefly its development and evolution since World War I and up through the present. Finally it will be necessary to review the key elements of the operational art as they are currently understood and practiced today. From these elements we will construct a framework to analyze the 1918 German offensives.

The tactical–strategic link

The purpose of tactics is to win battles. The purpose of strategy is to win wars. The purpose of the operational art is to win the campaigns, which are based upon battles and which in turn contribute to strategic victory.[3] Put quite simply, then, the operational art is the vital link between tactics and strategy. The U.S. Army Command and General Staff College employs a simple graphic device to illustrate this point. The entire spectrum of warfighting activity is likened to a medieval morning star. The spiked ball that delivers the blow represents tactics.

The wooden handle that directs the blow represents strategy. The flexible chain that connects the two represents operational art.

It is a useful analogy, but it is one that comes apart if pushed too far. While in most cases tactical successes form the building blocks of operational success, and successful operations lead to strategic victory, this is not always the case. Nathaniel Greene's 1784 Southern Campaign in the American Revolution provides a clear example of a general who lost every battle but still won the campaign. In more recent history, the U.S. Army won virtually every one of its battlefield engagements in Vietnam, yet America still lost the war. This, then, indicates that the relationships and the linkages among tactics and the operational art and strategy are all very dynamic and situationally dependent.

For that reason, "operational art" remains a far better name for this category of activities than does "operational science." Shimon Naveh wrote that it is only at the operational level that the extremes of the abstract strategic and the mechanical tactical can be fused. This, in turn, generates a certain amount of dynamic tension.[4] The 1918 Ludendorff offensives offer one of the starkest yet most complex examples of a string of stunning tactical successes that led nowhere.

This still does not answer the question of what exactly the operational art is. The manual *ATP 35 NATO Land Forces Tactical Doctrine* defines the operational level of war as

> The operational level provides the vital connection between the military strategic objectives and the tactical employment of forces on the battlefield through the conception, planning, and execution of major operations and campaigns.[5]

The 1993 edition of the U.S. doctrinal manual *FM 100-5, Operations* defines the operational art as

> The employment of military forces to attain strategic and/or operational objectives within a theater through the design, organization, integration, and conduct of theater strategies, campaigns, major operations and battles. Operational art translates theater strategy and design into operational design which links and integrates the tactical battles and engagements that, when fought and won, achieve the strategic aim. Tactical battles and engagements are fought and won to achieve operational results. No specific level of command is solely concerned with operational art.[6]

The last sentence is particularly significant. Operational art was once thought to describe battlefield actions of the corps and higher levels. The real focus, however, is on the linkage to strategic aims. The size and nature of the war itself also have some bearing on where the operational level begins. In the Vietnam War, American divisions mostly functioned at the operational level; while in the last years of World War I on the Western Front and World War II on the Eastern Front most actions below the army-group level were tactical.

As most contemporary military theorists argue, the very nature of the operational art is significantly different from tactics. General Donn A. Starry, one of the leaders of the post-Vietnam American military reform, suggested that "one goal of the Operational Battle must be to lessen the probability of prolonged military operations." This point has a special resonance when considering the operational art during World War I. Starry also suggested that the operational art should seek to deny the enemy access to the objectives he seeks; deny the enemy's follow-on reinforcement; and find the opportunity to seize the initiative by destroying the integrity of the enemy's operational scheme.[7] Naveh advanced a similar argument by maintaining that the aim of the operational art should be the disruption of the enemy's system.[8]

James Schneider suggested that the dominant characteristic of the operational art is the "distributed free maneuver of forces in a theater of operations." Distributed free maneuver leads to the dispersion of combat force in space and time. This is opposed to the dominant feature of military operations up to the time of Napoleon—"concentrated maneuver of forces in a theater of operations culminating in a single decisive battle."[9] Like Schneider, Naveh asserted that operational thinking is a significant departure from the Clausewitzian notion of the destruction of the enemy's force. (More on this line of thought in the following sections.) Naveh also introduced the concept of "Interactive Cooperation." He defined this as the interaction between the holding element and the striking element of a force, with the relationship between the two varying from the operational offensive to the operational defensive. In the operational offense the striking element is superior in weight, length, and velocity. In the operational defense the superiority in weight and resources are on the side of the holding element, with the striking element having a thin and shallow vector. In both situations, decision is ultimately attained by the dynamic action of the striking force.[10] Note the similarity between Naveh's concept of the operational defense and Clausewitz's "shield of blows."

Richard Simpkin stressed the importance of synergism at the operational level, where the whole of the operation must have a greater effect than the sum of its parts. In the modern context, operational synergy includes the integration of air, land, and sea forces. During World War I, however, military planners wrestled with the problem of synergy on the even more fundamental tactical level. By 1918, only a limited number of those planners were beginning to understand fully the intricacies of combined arms (also called all arms) warfare that synchronized the tactical effects of infantry, artillery, armor, air attack, engineers, and the supporting services. Each possesses a distinctive tactical quality—effect, dimension, range, duration, etc. The strength of one compensates for the weakness of the others, while at the same time complementing the strengths of the others.[11]

There are a number of specific elements and components that constitute the operational art and which military planners must consider when developing the overall campaign plan. These will be discussed in detail in the concluding section of this chapter. But before a military commander or planner can begin to deal with that level of detail, a group of far more basic considerations must be addressed. These considerations are identified in the current version of U.S. *Joint Publication 3-0, Doctrine for Joint Operations*. These considerations are so fundamental that they can be used to evaluate virtually any military action at the operational level of war.[12]

The necessary military conditions: What is the definition of success? What is the desired end state? What are the goals? Without operational goals there is no basis for operational planning or decision making.

The necessary sequence of events: In most circumstances it is unlikely that a strategic goal can be achieved with a single operational stroke. What, then, are the stepping-stones to get there? Because of the dynamics of the battlefield, these steps cannot be fixed. What, then, are the branches and sequels to the operational plan? This recalls Moltke's famous dictum: "No operations plan will ever extend with any sort of certainty beyond the first encounter with the hostile main force."[13] As A.S.H. Irwin noted, it is the sequencing of operations that constitutes the precise difference between a battle and a campaign.[14]

The necessary resources: This includes both the combat power (manpower, weapons capabilities, etc.) and the major logistical component (supplies, transportation, maintenance, etc.) of the plan. At the operational level of war, the logistical realities dictate the combat possibilities far more than at the tactical level. As an intelligence indicator, the direction of the logistical tail more often than not points directly to the striking point of the combat teeth.

These three key considerations equate exactly to the three elements of the general military strategy model developed by Colonel Arthur Lykke of the U.S. Army War College. According to Lykke, military strategy consists of balancing the equation[15]

$$ENDS = WAYS + MEANS$$

Compared to *Joint Publication 3-0*, Lykke's Ends equate to the necessary military conditions; Ways equate to the necessary sequence of events; and Means equate to the necessary resources.

Even with all these considerations, it can still be very difficult to determine exactly where the tactical level ends and the strategic level begins. The three levels of war, in fact, are not discrete, and a fair degree of overlap occurs from situation to situation. Writing in 1993, Irwin suggested three key tests to identify the operational level of war. A "yes" to one or more of these tests indicates that the actions are at the operational level.[16]

First, is there a political dimension? Simpkin noted that an operational mission should be only "one remove from the strategic objective."[17] In the case of the 1918 offensives, Ludendorff wanted to collapse French resolve by knocking Britain out of the coalition.

Second, does the action have a possibility of achieving a decision that will materially alter the situation in terms of the overall campaign? In 1918 Ludendorff wanted to eliminate the BEF before American troops arrived in force and tipped the strategic balance.

And third, does the action have a possibility of achieving a decision that will materially assist in achieving the strategic goals? Rather than ending the war with a negotiated peace, Ludendorff believed that he could actually achieve a decisive military victory that would leave Germany in control of the strategic Belgian coast.

The evolution of the concept of the operational art

Strategy and tactics have long been identified as distinct albeit connected spheres of military theory and action. The notions of the operational art and the operational level of war are of far more recent origin. The military theories underlying the operational art did not evolve uniformly; rather they progressed in stages over the course of the last two centuries. Among many of the world's great armies during this period, major defeats provided the impetus for intellectual advances in doctrine. This is particularly true of Prussia following Jena; the Soviet Union following Warsaw in 1920; Germany following World War I; and the United States following Vietnam.[18]

These particular examples line up nicely with the four key landmarks in the evolution of operational theory suggested by Naveh. The first is the period of 19th-century military thought, which Naveh called the "roots of operational ignorance." This period ended in the 1920s and was characterized by an "attempt to manipulate tactics on a major scale." Soviet Deep Operations Theory followed, which broke with the Clausewitzian paradigm of the battle of annihilation (*Vernichtungsschlacht*). Then came the German so-called *Blitzkrieg*, which Naveh and others have argued lacked the fundamentals of true operational thought. And finally, American AirLand Battle, which formed the basis of the overwhelming Allied success in the 1991 Gulf War.[19]

19th-century military thought

The operational art is a distinct product of the modern age, with roots imbedded firmly in the Industrial Revolution. As the range and lethality of modern weapons increased, the battlefield expanded by necessity. Technological improvements made it increasingly less necessary to achieve massed effects with massed formations of troops. Simultaneously, those same improvements in weapons transformed the tightly packed massed formations of old into far more vulnerable and lucrative targets. As armies grew, modern warfare also became increasingly dependent upon the will and resources of the entire populations of nations.[20]

Although there is no rigid connection between unit size and the operational level of war, the operational art is clearly concerned primarily with the deployment, movements, and actions of larger units. Large-scale battlefield operations in the modern sense first emerged with the *levée en masse* and Napoleon's mass armies. Some would even argue that Napoleon actually created the prototype of the operational art with his maneuver of multiple corps formations on a grand scale.[21] The structure and organization of armies were never the same after Napoleon. Throughout the 19th century and into the 20th, large armies continued to be regarded as one of the principal factors for success in war. Writing on the eve of World War I, General Friedrich von Bernhardi noted: "Numbers seem to the present generation the decisive factor in war;" and, "all states of Europe are dominated by the mania for numbers."[22]

In the years following Napoleon his two major interpreters, Antoine Henri Jomini and Carl von Clausewitz, contributed much to the foundations of the operational art as we understand it today. Jomini hinted at an intermediate level of war, and he used the term "Grand Tactics" to describe it. His description of grand tactics is very close to the modern notion of the operational art: "The art of making good combinations preliminary to battles, as well as during their progress."[23]

Clausewitz emphasized the distinction between strategy and tactics, but a close reading of *On War* suggests that when Clausewitz spoke of "policy" he was speaking of what we now call strategy; and when he spoke of strategy he was really talking about what we now call operations. As he noted: "According to our classification then, tactics teaches *the use of armed forces in the engagement*; strategy *the use of engagements for the object of the war*" (emphasis in the original).[24] In one passage in *On War* Clausewitz clearly identified three distinct levels of war in both time and space: "The concepts characteristic of time—war, campaign, and battle—are parallel to those of space—country, theater of operations, and position."[25]

Historians are split on whether or not Clausewitz really had a clear grasp of the operational as distinct from the tactical and strategic. Bradley Meyer noted: "Clausewitz, like Moltke, used the term strategy to describe a phenomenon that would generally be described as operational art today."[26] Naveh, on the other hand, contended that, while Clausewitz recognized an intermediate sphere of military activity that synthesized mechanics with cerebration, he never understood the distinctive problems of the operational level of war. He thus, according to Naveh, relegated the operational level to an auxiliary one, designed to give tactical battle some of its technical requirements.[27]

Naveh's criticisms of Clausewitz's operational thinking often seem to take on a post facto character, almost as if Clausewitz should have been writing with fully developed 20th-century military technology in mind. Naveh, for example, criticized Clausewitz for placing greater value on operational destruction than on mobility.[28] And Clausewitz did in fact write: "Destruction being a more effective factor than mobility, the complete absence of cavalry would prove to be less debilitating to an army than a complete absence of artillery."[29] In Clausewitz's day, however, there was a great deal of truth to this.

Technology is clearly a major factor that influenced the development of operational theory. Improvements in battlefield mobility and communications have made possible speed and maneuver on vast scales while simultaneously maintaining control of units over a wide area. As technological capabilities evolved, operational theory evolved with them. The military use of the railway was perhaps the most influential technological change in the second half of the 19th century. Railways made possible rapid movement of large masses of troops and equipment; the correspondingly shortened transit time reduced feeding and billeting requirements; troops and horses arrived in relatively fresh condition; and improved logistical support enabled the sustainment of mass conscript armies in the field. The first operational use of military railways occurred in 1849, when a Russian corps moved from Warsaw to Vienna to protect the city from Hungarian rebels.[30] During the American Civil War, two Union corps—more than 20,000 troops, their equipment, and horses—moved 1,230 miles by rail in just eleven days in September 1864.[31] Moltke made a careful study of the lessons of the American Civil War, and in 1870 the Germans made far more masterful use of their rail system than did the French.

There is some debate, however, on the influence of railways on the operational art. Naveh suggested that the railways were a means of strategic movement, but not of operational maneuver. He further argued that efforts to use rail in the service of a strategic offense resulted in such distortions that operational maneuver could not be applied. These distortions were caused by the technical limitations of the rail system, which imposed its broad linear patterns on any deployment, thereby dooming true operational maneuver.[32] Moltke himself believed rail was an inflexible instrument, its effective use based on strict timetables. While this may have been true in 1870, European trackage tripled between 1871 and 1914. At the start of World War I the rail network in Europe was so dense that there was a far greater amount of flexibility in its use. By 1913 Germany had twelve kilometers of track for every 100 square kilometers of territory; France had ten; Austria-Hungary had seven; and Russia had only one.[33]

Advances in communications technology also made possible command and control of units spread across the battlefield on a scale previously unimaginable. First the electric telegraph, then the telephone, and then radio made real-time control possible over great distances; but these innovations also generated a false illusion of absolute control. In 1870 Germany had 1,000 telegraph stations; by 1911 it had 637,000. Early electronic communications technology, however, also had something of a retarding effect on operational maneuver. Permanent telegraph lines to a German Army headquarters in the field could be laid at the rate of only five miles per day—which could almost never keep pace with the rate of advancing units. And the ability to communicate often led directly to a tendency to over-control and micro-manage—a problem that most armies still grapple with at the start of the 21st century. By 1917 the average British field army's daily communications traffic averaged something like 10,000 telegrams, 20,000 telephone calls, and 5,000 messenger-delivered dispatches.[34] How much of that volume, one wonders, was really necessary for the planning and conduct of battlefield operations?

By the final decades of the 19th century, the Napoleonic concept of the "strategy of a single point" had given way to Moltke's concept of the "extended line"—which in turn finally reached its logical conclusion in the extended trenches of World War I. As battle lines expanded, the ability to control them directly decreased. Even with the improvements in communications technology, command and control increasingly became more indirect, through added layers of subordinate echelons.[35] At the start of the 20th century the Russo–Japanese War provided a brief foreshadowing of the technological "future shock" and the resulting tactical and operational problems that would come in World War I. The battlefield in Manchuria assumed previously unimagined levels of breadth and depth. The main problem became one of conquering space and time to bring about a concentration of combat power at the decisive point.[36] In 1904 the available technical means of mobility, communications, and control were not equal to the demands of the battlefield—nor would they be ten years later.

Although we will later discuss in detail German operational art in World War I, it is necessary here to fit the Great War briefly into the overall discussion. World War I in general, and the Western Front in particular, present a problem for the student of the operational art. After Germany's failure to win a quick and decisive victory, the Western Front fell into a stalemate that lasted almost until the end of the war. Until 1918, the operational art "had more to do with orchestration than with maneuver."[37]

The experience of World War I dramatically demonstrated that single operations no longer guaranteed the successful outcome of a campaign, and that cumulative tactical success was no guarantee of strategic success. Decisions could only be brought about by "successive operations linked by intent, location, allocation of resources, and concerted action."[38] This, however, only became clear after the end of the war. Between 1914 and 1918, most military leaders surrounded by the fog of war repeatedly tried to plan and conduct single battles of annihilation that would produce decisive strategic results.[39]

Writing in the years immediately after World War I, J.F.C. Fuller made one of the most significant contributions in the West to the evolution of the theory of the operational art—which Fuller called Grand Tactics. According to Fuller: "This is the duty of the grand tactician; he takes over the forces as they are distributed and arranges them according to the resistance they are likely to meet."[40] Fuller was also one of the first military theorists in the West to articulate clearly that the primary targets of the operational plan should be the enemy's plan and the will of the enemy commander. For Fuller, the object of grand tactics was the "destruction of the enemy's plan."

Fuller also believed that it was an error for the grand tactician to think only in terms of destruction. He argued that when Clausewitz wrote about destruction of the hostile force, he meant it as a means to enforcing policy. Fuller believed that this key point was glossed over by most of Clausewitz's followers, with the result that destruction became an end in itself, rather than a means. Fuller further noted that, while an objective of destruction was useful at the tactical level, at the level of "grand tactics" it was a serious error. The decisive point, he concluded, was not the body of an enemy's army, but rather it was "the will of the enemy's commander." "To paralyze this will we must attack his plan, which expresses his will—his reasoned decisions. Frequently, to do so, we must attack his troops, but not always."[41]

The grand tactician does not think of physical destruction, but of mental destruction, and, when the mind of the enemy's commander can only be attacked through the bodies of his men, then from grand tactics we descend to minor tactics, which, though related, is a different expression of force.

We see, therefore, that grand tactics is the battle between two plans energized by two wills, and not merely the struggle between two or more military forces.[42]

Soviet deep operations theory

In the years following World War I Soviet theorists made many significant contributions to the evolution of the operational art as we know it today. Even prior to World War I, Russian military writers around 1907 introduced the concept of *Opertika*.[43] Following the disastrous defeat of the Red Army at Warsaw in 1920, two opposing schools of thought emerged among the Soviets. One was led by Marshal Mikhail N. Tukhachevsky, the Red Army front commander at Warsaw. Tukhachevsky, who read Fuller's works, became the champion of the "annihilation" school of Soviet military thought. Annihilation depended upon the ability to conduct large-scale, immediate, decisive operations. It required a war industry in being, and a large standing army.[44] In 1924 Tukhachevsky delivered a paper on *Maneuver and Artillery* that had a strong influence on the Frunze Reforms of 1924–1925. Those ideas were later formalized in the *Field Service Regulations* of 1927.[45]

The opposing school of thought was led by Major General Aleksandr A. Svechin, a Soviet General Staff officer. In his influential 1926 book, *Strategy*, Svechin advocated the doctrine of "attrition," which relied more on Russia's traditional deep resources of space, time, and manpower. Svechin also introduced the concept of operations as distinct from strategy and tactics. He argued that tactics made up the steps from which operational leaps were assembled, "with strategy pointing out the path."[46] Within a year of Svechin introducing the concept, the Soviets established a Chair on the Conduct of Operations within the Department of Strategy at the Military Academy of the Red Army.[47]

Both Svechin and Tukhachevsky were murdered in Stalin's purges of the 1930s, but their opposing theories were synthesized by Vladimir K. Triandafillov in his book *The Nature of the Operations of Modern Armies*. Published in 1929, the book was one of the seminal works in Soviet military thought. Triandafillov too had read the works of many of the post-World War I Western writers, and his own view on the operational use of artillery was influenced at least indirectly by the ideas of Germany's Georg Bruchmüller.[48]

Triandafillov was the first to introduce the "planning norms" that became one of the benchmarks of Soviet operational planning. He also laid out the theory of successive operations and deep operations (*glubokaia operatsiia*), with the result that several successive operations were linked into one single continuous deep operation. Thus, the point of Napoleon and line of Moltke gave way to the vector in depth, with its multiple effects—both sequentially and simultaneously—in three dimensions. Another important concept introduced by Triandafillov was operational shock (*udar*), which echoed Fuller's ideas of striking at the enemy's system and plan.[49]

Although the operational art emerged during the inter-war years in the Soviet Union as a vibrant new field of military study, many of the operational concepts associated with it were stillborn or only partially developed. As David Glantz pointed out, the Red Army would learn this hard truth and suffer accordingly during the Winter War with Finland and in 1941 during the opening months of the war with Germany. Soviet operational art only reached its highest level of development through trial and error in the crucible of World War II. And yet for all its final sophistication, the Soviets never fully developed the air and naval components of their operational art.[50]

Blitzkrieg

The widely held popular belief is that what the West called *Blitzkrieg* represented the most highly developed form of the operational art at that time. Many historians, however, have argued that *Blitzkrieg* was at best a deeply flawed expression of the operational art. Naveh described it as a "mechanized manipulation of tactical patterns;" a "simplistic attempt to magnify the tactical patterns of infiltration and encirclement;" and a tactical response to Hitler's incoherent strategy.[51] Menning described *Blitzkrieg* as a theory of combined-arms tactics aimed at achieving rupture through the depth of an enemy's tactical deployment. Following the rupture, rapidly moving armored forces were to exploit the tactical penetration by driving into operational depth. Thus, while *Blitzkrieg* exhibited many of the features we now associate with the operational art, it focused too heavily on annihilation and rapid decision by a single bold stroke.[52]

Despite these criticisms of *Blitzkrieg*, the post-World War I German Army had a clear albeit imperfect understanding of a level of war between the tactical and the strategic. Writing in 1920, General Hugo Freiherr von Freytag-Loringhoven noted that among German General Staff officers, the term *Operativ* was increasingly replacing the term *Strategisch* to "define more simply and clearly the difference from everything tactical."[53] The 1933 edition of *Truppenführung*, the primary German warfighting manual of World War II, distinguished clearly between tactical and operational functions.[54] *Truppenführung*'s principal author, General Ludwig Beck, considered *Operativ* as a subdivision of strategy. Its sphere was the conduct of battle at the higher levels, in accordance with the tasks presented by strategic planning.[55] Naveh even admitted that *Truppenführung* was the "best evidence confirming the existence of operational cognition prior to the year 1938."[56] Tellingly, when U.S. Army intelligence made a rough translation of *Truppenführung* just prior to World War II, the term *Operativ* was translated throughout as "strategic."[57]

AirLand Battle

Post-World War II American military doctrine focused almost exclusively at the tactical level. Although the U.S. Army and its British ally had planned and executed large and complex operational campaigns during the war, the mechanics of those efforts were largely forgotten by the early 1950s.[58] Nuclear weapons cast a long retarding shadow over American ground combat doctrine, and the later appearance of "battlefield nuclear weapons" seemed to render irrelevant any serious consideration of maneuver by large-scale ground units. The Soviets, meanwhile, continued to study and write about the operational art and the operational level of war. And while the American military intelligence community closely monitored and analyzed the trends in Soviet doctrine, American theorists ignored or completely rejected these concepts. Because of its dominant role in NATO, America's operational blinders were adopted for the most part by its coalition allies.

In the early to mid-1970s American thinking began to change. The three major spurs to this transformation were the loss in Vietnam; the stunning new weapons effects seen in the 1973 Middle East War; and the increasing need to fight outnumbered and win against the Warsaw Pact.[59] Initially, American sights remained fixed at the tactical level—"Win the First Battle"—with little consideration beyond that battle.[60] The first result of this re-thinking was the 1976 edition of *FM 100-5 Operations*, which introduced the notion of "active defense," a rather questionable substitute for the tested concepts of mobile defense and defense in-depth. The 1976 edition was wildly controversial even before it had been fully distributed to the field. The resulting debate, however, was uncannily similar to the robust German doctrinal debate of the 1920s, and sparked something of a renaissance in American military thinking. The reactions to the 1976 edition included the notion of follow-on-forces attack (FOFA), which in turn led to recognition of the operational depth of the battlefield.

The concept of the operational level of war entered the debate when the influential defense analyst Edward Luttwak published the article "The Operational Level of War" in the winter 1980–1981 issue of the journal *International Security*.[61] About the same time, Colonel Harry Summers' book, *On Strategy: The Vietnam War in Context*, sparked a parallel renaissance in strategic thinking and the rediscovery of Clausewitz by the American military. The U.S. Army formally recognized the operational level of war with the publication of the 1982 edition of *FM 100-5*, which also introduced the concepts of AirLand Battle and Deep Battle.[62] The operational art was first defined in the 1986 edition, along with the concept that commanders had to fight and synchronize three simultaneous battles: close, deep, and rear. The idea was that one's own deep battle would be the enemy's rear battle, and the converse. The close battle would always be strictly tactical, but the deep and rear battles would have operational significance.[63]

American conduct of the 1991 Gulf War was based on the 1986 edition of *FM 100-5*, which is arguably the best official formulation of American operational thinking to date. The 1993 edition of *FM 100-5* actually shifted the emphasis away from operations toward strategy and Operations Other than War. Even the term "AirLand Battle" was dropped in favor of "Army Operations," but this was more the result of bureaucratic infighting between the army and air force. A new edition of *FM 100-5* in 1998 was supposed to shift the emphasis back to the operational art, but the final coordinating draft caused considerable internal controversy. The new manual was finally issued in June 2001 under a new numbering system as *FM 3-0 Operations*.

The British recognized the operational level of war in 1989. Current British doctrine distinguishes four levels of war, with strategy being split into grand strategy followed by military strategy.[64] Actually, American thinking about the strategic level of war remains a bit confused. Although they recognize only the strategic above the operational level, the Americans periodically issue separate documents for *National Security Strategy* and *National Military Strategy* that closely parallel the British notions of grand and military strategy. Furthermore, various American doctrinal manuals mention something called "theater strategy" that really sounds more operational than strategic. At the dawn of the 21st century, theories of the operational art and the operational level of war are still evolving.

German operational art

Military historians are in general agreement on their evaluations of the German Army at the tactical and strategic levels. Between 1870 and 1945, the Germans set the standard for tactical excellence on the battlefield. Many of the innovations they introduced during that period are still with us today. Simultaneously, the pre-1945 German Army had serious problems dealing with the strategic level of war. This was partially the result of their belief that strategy, especially national or grand strategy, lay in the political realm and was not the proper concern of the professional soldier. The course of instruction at the *Kriegsakadamie* reflected this bias, and that august institution produced generation after generation of German General Staff officers ill equipped to deal with strategic issues. When a political leader of Bismarck's capabilities was at the helm of the German state, this handicap did not necessarily prove fatal. But when incompetents or a madman were in control of strategy, as in World Wars I and II, the German military had no counterbalance to offer. The German officer education system was simply not designed to produce generals like Alanbrooke, George Marshall, or Colin Powell. Moltke the Elder was probably the closest the German Army ever came.

The middle ground of the operational level of war produces far greater division among historians. Naveh dismissed almost all German operational art as merely tactical manipulation on a massive scale, while Jehuda Wallach pointed to the overemphasis on—or the misreading of—Clausewitz's annihilation principle (*Vernichtungsprinzip*) as the source of German operational failure. Meyer, Simpkin, and Roland Foerster, on the other hand, have argued that the German

Army had a significant, if somewhat imperfect, understanding of the operational level from at least the time of Moltke the Elder.

Germany conducted seven operational-level campaigns between 1864 and 1918: Denmark in 1864; Austria in 1866; France in 1870–1871; France in 1914; France at Verdun in 1916; Russia and Romania in 1916–1917; and France and Britain in the first half of 1918. Six of the seven were against first-class opponents. Four of the seven succeeded and two came close. Verdun was a radical departure from German practice, where they tried to win through firepower and attrition.

In his book, *The German Army*, Herbert Rosinski wrote that German military theory alternated between stressing either operations or tactics. Scharnhorst emphasized tactics. Moltke balanced the two, although there was a significant operational component to his thought. Schlieffen tipped the balance heavily toward operations. And Ludendorff, with whom we are most concerned in this study, returned to the thinking that tactics took precedence over both the operational art as well as strategy.[65]

Moltke the Elder

Modern notions of the operational art developed under Moltke from the 1850s on, and its evolution was concurrent with the growth of the first modern General Staff system.[66] Rosinski maintained that under Moltke the operations to set up the conditions for the battle and the tactical outcome of the battle were seen as separate entities. But recognizing the increased firepower of modern weapons in the defense, Moltke's objective was to achieve decision in war by operational rather than by tactical means.[67] Foerster and Christopher Bellamy noted that Moltke clearly distinguished the relationship between strategy, operations, and tactics in his 1871 work, *Über Strategie*—although Moltke resisted defining the concepts too sharply.[68] Michael D. Krause argued that "Moltke's concept of operational direction was the beginning of the operational level of war."[69] John English, on the other hand, suggested that Moltke seems to have used the concept *Operativ* almost exclusively in the sense of the movement of bodies of troops for the purpose of combining forces for decisive battle.[70] Simpkin likewise noted that for Moltke, the purpose of the operational plan was to ensure that the initial contact between the main bodies of the opposing forces occurred under the most favorable of circumstances, at which point tactics took over.[71]

Meyer advanced what is perhaps the most forceful argument that Moltke "was a practitioner of operational art as the term is understood today."[72] Meyer identified three main elements of the operational art as practiced by Moltke: a clearly defined goal or objective for the campaign; the selection of goals to which the operations would be directed; and mastery of the mechanics of the operation at hand.[73]

Moltke was one of the first to understand that the battle, the campaign, and the war all had different, though related, aims. He also clearly understood that he was operating in an age of increasing firepower. The increased strength of the tactical defense, therefore, made it necessary to avoid frontal attacks—at least at the operational level. To accomplish this, Moltke's formula was one of "Fix, Encircle, Destroy" (*Umfassen, Einschliessen, Vernichten*). Moltke's operational concept involved rapid deployment along exterior lines exploiting rail movement, and a converging march of separated parts aimed at unification on the field of battle. As Moltke stated it, "march separated, fight concentrated" (*Getrennt marschieren, vereint schlagen*). The first arriving elements of the force would be used to fix the enemy frontally, while the movements of the still separated elements of the force would be directed to the enemy's flanks. If a unit's action contributed directly to the course of action of the campaign, then its action was operational. If the action of a unit did not have the potential to affect the course of the campaign, then the action was tactical, regardless of the size of the action.[74] As Moltke himself wrote, "Many important purposes of war can be attained without battles, through marches, through the choice of positions, in short, through operations."[75]

Schlieffen and the battle of annihilation

German operational thinking after Moltke and through the start of World War I was dominated by Schlieffen's focus on Cannae and his notions of envelopment on a grand scale combined with rapid decision through a decisive battle of annihilation. Less well remembered than Schlieffen's concept of the *Vernichtungsschlacht*, however, is his notion of the total battle (*Gesamtschlacht*). The latter provided the rationale for the former. According to this concept, the dynamics of operational forward movement would create the center of gravity and escalate into the annihilation of the enemy's force. The *Gesamtschlacht* combined separate actions and locations into an integrated operation in one joint and continuous movement. In so doing, Schlieffen replaced the arithmetical concept of operations that added battles up into a campaign with one of integrated, continuous, and expanding motion.[76]

Schlieffen took an opposite approach to Moltke, opting for a grand master plan to carry from mobilization right through to strategic victory. In so doing, he subordinated strategy to operations. By the time he retired in 1905, Schlieffen had developed a view of operations in which mobilization, deployment, and maneuver all flowed one from the other.[77] But when Bismarck had been in control of diplomacy and national strategy, the German General Staff did not have to worry about fighting a two-front war. Bismarck's skillful diplomacy also managed to keep Germany's opponents diplomatically isolated. Yet while Bismarck had sought quick victories to his wars to forestall the intervention of other powers, the German war plans based on Schlieffen's principles virtually guaranteed that intervention.

By 1914, eight years after Schlieffen's retirement, Germany still had only one basic war plan, despite the varied political circumstances that might bring it into war. This perhaps is the clearest of indicators of the German disconnect between operational and strategic thinking. During World War I, Germany for the first (but not for the last) time faced a coalition with greater resources than itself. Nonetheless, the German General Staff responded with an operational variation of the Wars of German Unification. The Germans tried to defeat the coalition one member at a time through operational campaigns. Although the strategic framework was entirely different, the operational approach never varied from the tried and true path. The traditional German operational solution focused on achieving a quick victory, and the General Staff never seemed to come to grips with the fact that they were in a long-term war. As Meyer noted: "The General Staff did not fight a four-year war, they fought four one-year wars."[78]

In *The Dogma of the Battle of Annihilation*, Wallach argued that the key distortion in German operational thinking resulted from Schlieffen misreading Clausewitz and placing far too much emphasis on achieving military decision through the rapid annihilation of the enemy force.[79] Naveh, on the other hand, argued that Schlieffen read Clausewitz correctly, for the most part, and that the so-called Schlieffen Plan "derived from Clausewitzian conceptual origin."[80] But in his book, *After Clausewitz*, Antulio Echevarria argued that Wilhelmine military theory "had clearly broken free of the Napoleonic paradigm by the end of the Russo–Japanese War."[81] The question remains, then, what exactly did Clausewitz mean by his *Vernichtungsprinzip*?

In *On War* Clausewitz wrote: "The fighting force must be destroyed: that is, they must be *put in such a condition that they can no longer carry on the fight*. Whenever we use the phrase 'destruction of the enemy's forces' this alone is what we mean" (emphasis in the original).[82] Is it really necessary, then, to annihilate a force to put it in a condition that it "can no longer carry on the fight"? Neutralization of an enemy force might accomplish this just as well. Schlieffen and his followers, however, drew the conclusion that it was not enough to be decisive, the enemy had to be annihilated. For Schlieffen this complete destruction could only be achieved by encirclement, and he therefore totally rejected the concept of breakthrough. But even Clausewitz himself was not exactly consistent on this point. In Book 1 of *On War*, the emphasis is clearly on destruction. Yet by Books 7 and 8, the emphasis seems to shift to one of dislocation of the enemy.[83]

In analyzing German military thought, it is all too easy to try to build too much of a case on what Clausewitz may have meant on a given point, or how he may or may not have been misinterpreted. The views of the pre-World War I German General Staff were more often in line with Jomini than with Clausewitz.[84] The German Army actually rejected some of Clausewitz's most important concepts, such as the relationship between war and policy and the idea of defense as the stronger form of war.[85] In his book, *How Germany Makes War*, Bernhardi bluntly wrote, "Clausewitz considers the defensive the stronger form of conducting war. I do not share this opinion."[86] Ludendorff himself went to the farthest extreme in rejecting the theories of the Philosopher of War, arguing for the primacy of war over politics.[87]

Both Rosinski and Wallach have offered explanations of why the pre-World War I German Army progressively turned away from the ideas of Clausewitz.

Rosinski pointed out that increasingly after 1871, materialism, glorification of science and technology, and admiration of wealth and power replaced traditional German humanistic values. The consequence was an ever narrower and less intellectual officer corps. While the officers of the era of Scharnhorst, Gneisenau, and Clausewitz were cultivated men with a wide range of intellectual interests, the generations between 1871 and 1914 tended to be technicians of power, with little interest in non-military matters. Thus, Schlieffen's "mechanical schematism," and his creation of simple dogmas carried far greater appeal for German soldiers of the Wilhelmine era than did Clausewitz's cerebral reflections on the nature of war.[88]

Schlieffen was by no means the sole source of German military thought in the years preceding 1914. For almost thirty-five years before World War I officers of the General Staff and military historian Hans Delbrück engaged in a *Strategiestreit* (strategy debate) over Clausewitz's distinction between absolute and limited war. Delbrück argued that this duality corresponded to two broad types of strategy: *Vernichtungsstrategie* (strategy of annihilation), which aimed for the complete defeat of the enemy; and *Ermattungsstrategie* (strategy of attrition), which had more limited goals. According to Delbrück, battle was the only means of *Vernichtungsstrategie*, but both battle and maneuver were the means of *Ermattungsstrategie*. Delbrück, the civilian professor, irritated the members of the General Staff by arguing that Frederick the Great had pursued a strategy of attrition rather than annihilation.[89]

General Sigismund W. von Schlichting was an interpreter of Moltke and a theoretical competitor and critic of Schlieffen. In his turn-of-the-century book, *Taktische und Strategische Grundsätze der Gegenwart*, Schlichting emphasized the importance of using operational (*Operativ*) maneuver to achieve the purposes of war. But he also argued that breakthrough battles would be impossible to avoid, and that the necessity to combine forms of maneuver such as penetrations and envelopments required a less mechanistic approach to command. Following the Russo–Japanese War, Schlichting's works were translated into Russian in 1910 and studied at the Russian General Staff Academy.[90]

Friedrich von Bernhardi was another independent thinker whose writings demonstrated a definite understanding of operational issues. In *How Germany Makes War* Bernhardi noted: "The tactical and strategic importance of reserves and the importance of the operative element in war must be minutely weighed."[91] In the chapter titled "Time, Space, and Direction," he wrote: "The art of war reckons with time and space, which have a distinct reciprocal effect upon each other."[92] This sentence shows a clear understanding of the multidimensional character of the modern battlefield—a distinct departure from Napoleon's point and Moltke's line.

Ludendorff and World War I

Many of the technical battlefield problems that came to characterize World War I were foreshadowed in the Russo–Japanese War, and to some degree in the

Balkan Wars of 1912 and 1913. The major European armies studied those conflicts closely, but the Great War started before most of the lessons could be
understood and integrated into existing force structure and doctrine. The
changes since Moltke's day were significant, indeed. As modern firepower had
increased, it took a smaller force to cover a given length of front with fire. The
armies themselves were much bigger, and armies with broader fronts were much
harder to flank. As World War I progressed, army groups made their first
appearance on the battlefield. As previously noted, World War I also saw the
advent of three-dimensional warfare, with both time and space acquiring a
dimension of depth.

This, then, became the overriding operational problem of the Great War on
the Western Front. The front was the easiest part of the enemy's force to attack,
not the flanks or rear. After the German failure at the Marne and the subsequent
"Race to the Sea," there were no longer any operational flanks to go around. The
sea itself constituted a strategic flank. The only solution apparent to both sides
was to attempt somehow to achieve and then exploit a tactical breakthrough of a
strongly defended front. But as those fronts solidified to great depths, a breakthrough became almost impossible—although a break-in could always be
achieved. The mobility and transportation technology of the day could not
support the speed and distances required for a successful breakthrough and
exploitation to operational depths. Contemporary firepower technology, on the
other hand, was quite capable of producing the volume, mass, and reach necessary to counter any attempted breakthrough. Thus, the technological imbalance
between fire and maneuver capabilities combined temporarily to produce a
period of both tactical and operational deadlock.

The German General Staff began World War I seeking an operational
decision in the west. When that failed, the Germans went on the strategic and
operational defensive in the west and sought a victory in the east. In the 1916
campaign in Romania, both Falkenhayn and Mackensen performed brilliantly.
That campaign showed dramatically that, when given a field of maneuver and
the opportunity to exercise the traditional tactics of open warfare, the Germans
had no equal.[93] In September 1917 at Riga, General Oskar von Hutier achieved a
tactical breakthrough that led to clear operational results. And the follow-up
amphibious attack against the Baltic Islands was one of military history's first
great examples of a successful joint campaign executed by naval, land, and air
forces. When the Germans finally succeeded in the east, they turned back to the
west and once again sought an operational victory there. The only exception to
this overall pattern of the war was Verdun in 1916, where under Falkenhayn the
Germans tried to achieve victory through attrition. But being the power with the
more limited manpower resources, attrition was the one method the Germans
could not afford to pursue for long.[94]

With their traditional emphasis on achieving a decision through a single bold
stroke, the Germans had a general inclination to opt for short-term solutions.
They accordingly based their planning assumptions on the short term. More than
once in the Great War this focus on achieving victory through a single stroke led

to longer-term strategic effects the Germans neither anticipated nor desired. In 1914 they invaded France through Belgium, accepting the entrance of Britain into the war on the assumption that the campaign would be over before Britain could mobilize and react. In 1917 the German leadership pushed for unrestricted submarine warfare, even though such a move was sure to bring America into the war. The assumption—more like wishful thinking—was that the submarine campaign would knock Britain out of the war before America could bring its weight to bear. After the Russian collapse in 1917, the German leadership also rejected the idea of a strategic defensive in the west coupled with a negotiated peace that might have preserved German gains in the east. They opted instead for an all-out offensive in the west, designed to produce victory in one swift strike before the U.S. Army could arrive in sufficient numbers to influence events on the battlefield.[95]

Ludendorff was undoubtedly one of the better battlefield tacticians of World War I. Typical of the wide majority of German officers of his era, he had little understanding of strategy. (The German strategic problems in World War I will be discussed in greater detail in Chapter 4.) As a practitioner of the operational art, Ludendorff presents a far more complex and contradictory picture. After Hindenburg and Ludendorff took charge at *Oberste Heeresleitung* (OHL), the First Quartermaster General did display some flashes of operational brilliance. These included the management of the Romania campaign and the sequencing of operations in 1917 culminating with the victories at Riga, Caporetto, and in the Baltic Islands. Operation ALBERICH in 1917 was a masterpiece of operational surprise in the defense. In April of that year units of Bavarian Crown Prince Rupprecht's Army Group withdrew from a 120-kilometer-wide sector between Arras and Vailly-sur-Aisne. The German troops fell back twenty-five to forty kilometers to prepared positions on the Siegfried Line. The move was carried out with great secrecy and speed and caught the Allies by surprise. ALBERICH shortened the overall German front by fifty kilometers and freed up thirteen divisions, which were added to the German reserve.[96]

The shortened lines gave the Germans a very strong position from which they could have stood on the defensive while attempting to negotiate a peace in the west with the war-weary French and British. Tactically and operationally that might have made perfect sense, but Ludendorff's strategic blindness and his belief in a military victory through a single bold stroke made it impossible for him to accept such an outcome. Thus, when the Germans went over to the operational offensive in March 1918, one of their major problems was caused by a result of the ALBERICH operation. In the course of that withdrawal, the Germans had carried out a scorched-earth campaign to leave nothing in the area to the Allies. During the MICHAEL offensive eleven months later, German units had to attack over this same torn-up and barren ground.[97]

Under Ludendorff, the German Army shifted to the thinking that tactics took precedence over operational considerations, and even over strategy. Ludendorff himself developed such an obsessive focus on tactics that he all but ignored the operational level on the Western Front. Bavarian Crown Prince Rupprecht, during one of the early planning conferences for the March 1918 attack, asked Ludendorff what the operational objective of MICHAEL was. Ludendorff responded with his famous quip about blowing a hole in the middle and the rest following of its own accord. At another conference at Rupprecht's headquarters on 21 January 1918, Ludendorff said:

> We talk too much about operations and too little about tactics. I have been involved in many operations. I never knew before, however, how an operation in fact turned out. Decisions had to be made on a daily basis. It cannot be predicted whether you will be able to direct a thrust in the desired direction or if you will be forced to change your course to somewhere else. It is not even predictable three or four days in advance. Meanwhile, the picture can change so much that the original intent cannot be implemented. Thus I warn you to commit your thoughts to one certain direction, the best one. That is why all measures have to concentrate on how to defeat the enemy, how to penetrate his front positions. *Follow-on measures are in many cases a matter of ad hoc decisions.* Then the decision must be correct. I therefore advise you to deal more with tactical problems.[98]
>
> (Emphasis added.)

Despite Ludendorff's apparent dismissal of the operational level, and the general German blindness for the strategic level, the German Army of World War I clearly recognized a body of warfighting activity that was neither tactical nor strategic. It did not necessarily think in terms of levels of warfare, as we would today. German doctrine of the era envisioned troops being mobilized and assembled for combat (the *Aufmarsch*), and eventually meeting and defeating the enemy (the *Schlacht*). Everything in between those two points fell to the realm of operations, in which the commander maneuvered his forces across the countryside in order to engage the enemy on the best terms possible.[99] But there was far more to the German concept of *Operativ* than mere maneuvering and positioning prior to battle. Many German operations orders and staff studies in the last two years of the war identify separate and distinct tactical and operational objectives ("*taktische und operative Ziele*").[100] In their post-war memoirs, many of the senior German commanders frequently used the term *Operativ* in a manner similar to the way a modern commander would use the term. Among them were Rupprecht, Lossberg, Hindenburg, and even Crown Prince Wilhelm. Almost without exception, however, the term came out as "strategic" in any contemporary English translation.

Tellingly enough, Ludendorff himself almost never used the word *Operativ* in any of his writings. In his own post-war memoirs, Ludendorff noted: "Tactics had to be considered over pure strategy [*Strategie*], which it is futile to pursue unless tactical surprise is possible."[101] Although Ludendorff's position and responsibilities in the German Army of 1918 made him one of their key operational decision makers, his mind and focus, at least on the Western Front, remained down in the trenches, at the level of a regimental or a divisional commander.

The framework of the operational art

There does not exist in the West today a single authoritative listing of the elements and components of the operational art. Even the doctrinal manuals of a single country, such as U.S. *FM 100-5* and *Joint Publication 3-0* give differing lists and emphasize different operational considerations and functions. For the purpose of this analysis, then, I have assembled a composite list, which is further divided into the two broad categories: elements of operational design; and elements of operational power. As we address each of these elements, we will also consider how military commanders would have understood them in 1918.

The elements of operational design

Center of gravity

The center of gravity (*Schwerpunkt*) is one of the most enduring ideas of Clausewitz. Almost quoting from Clausewitz verbatim, the 1993 edition of *FM 100-5* defines the center of gravity as "The hub of all power and movement upon which everything depends. It is that characteristic, capability, or location from which enemy and friendly forces derive their freedom of action, physical strength, or will to fight."[102] In theory, the destruction or neutralization of an enemy's center of gravity is the most direct path to victory.[103]

According to *FM 100-5*, the essence of the operational art lies in being able to mass combat effects against the enemy's main source of power—his center of gravity. At any given point in time, however, the true center of gravity might not be immediately discernible, nor will it be easy to attack.[104] Since an enemy will seek to protect his own center of gravity at all costs, it most likely will be the most difficult and costly point of direct attack. Very rarely will the center of gravity be a vulnerable point—a point easily accessible to attack. Vulnerable points can offer indirect pathways to gaining leverage over the enemy's center of gravity. Through the accumulation of operational circumstances, the creation of an operational vulnerability implies the identification of a situation inviting the delivery of a strike that in turn will threaten the enemy system's ability to accomplish its mission.[105]

In the course of this analysis I will argue that the Allied center of gravity, at least up to June 1918, was the British Army. Because of the correlation of forces in the field and Germany's overall strategic situation, a direct attack on the British stood little chance of success. On the other hand, a focused attack on a key vulnerability could very well have led to operational success. I will also argue that the British logistics system in general, and the BEF's rail system in particular, constituted just such a vulnerability. The German failure to exploit that vulnerability fully may well have been their single greatest operational failure in 1918.

Decisive points

Both Clausewitz and Jomini discussed the notion of the decisive point (*Entscheidungsstelle*). In *On War* Clausewitz wrote: "It follows that as many troops as possible should be brought into the engagement at the decisive point."[106] And: "the forces available must be employed with such skill that even in the absence of absolute superiority, relative superiority is attained at the decisive point."[107]

In Jomini's *The Art of War* he states as his third and fourth maxims for the fundamental principle of war:

3 On the battlefield, to throw the mass of the forces upon the decisive point, or upon that portion of the hostile line which is of the first importance to overthrow.
4 To so arrange that these masses shall not only be thrown upon the decisive point, but that they shall engage at the proper times and with ample energy.[108]

During the early period of operational reawakening in the West, there was a great deal of misunderstanding over the concepts of center of gravity and decisive point. The term "*Schwerpunkt*" was very much in vogue and often used interchangeably for the two ideas. The 1986 edition of *FM 100-5* even confused and combined the two.[109] Actually, the Germans themselves did not and still do not use the term *Schwerpunkt* quite as Clausewitz defined it. Hindenburg once noted that an attack without a *Schwerpunkt* was like a man without character. Decisive point would seem to fit better here than center of gravity. And the 1933 edition of *Truppenführung* used the two terms interchangeably, much in the same way that *FM 100-5* would do fifty-three years later.[110] The subsequent 1993 edition of *FM 100-5* stated clearly: "Decisive points are not centers of gravity, they are the keys to getting at the centers of gravity."[111]

Decisive points are only decisive in relation to the center of gravity. Although the enemy can have only one center of gravity, multiple decisive points are possible.[112] In designing an operation, planners must analyze all potential decisive points and identify those that enable eventual attack of the enemy's center of gravity. Furthermore, a decisive point may or may not be a vulnerability. The key geographic features or important enemy functions and capabilities identified as decisive points become the objectives for a given phase of an operation, and commanders must allocate resources to seize, neutralize, or destroy them. In all cases, the main effort of an operation must be directed at a decisive point. If the BEF's shallow rail system was one of its key vulnerabilities in 1918, then the German decisive points in successive order might have been the rail centers at Amiens, Hazebrouck, Abbeville, Abancourt, and finally St.-Omer. As we shall see, one of the greatest flaws in the MICHAEL plan was the failure to clearly designate Amiens as the operation's objective.

Culmination

Culmination is the third major Clausewitzian concept in modern operational art.[113] In the attack, culmination occurs at the point in time or space when the attacker's effective combat power no longer exceeds that of the defender, or the attacker's momentum is no longer sustainable, or both. Beyond the culminating point, the attacker becomes increasingly vulnerable to counterattack and risks catastrophic defeat. In the defense, the defender reaches culmination when he no longer has the capability to shift over to the counteroffensive or to restore cohesion to the defense. The defensive culminating point occurs where the defender must withdraw to preserve his force.[114]

Culmination is closely linked to another Clausewitzian concept—"friction." As Clausewitz described it, friction on the battlefield works in the same way that it works against the forward momentum of inertia in a mechanical system. The art of the attack at all levels, then, is to secure the objective before reaching culmination.[115] At the operational level that objective must be one that produces operationally decisive results. The Germans failed to do this in 1918. In each of five large-scale offensives they reached culmination and their stunning tactical gains led nowhere. After the fifth of those offensives, the position they were forced to defend was so overextended that they were in a state of defensive culmination even before the Allies counterattacked.

Lines of operations

Lines of operations define the orientation of the force in both space and time in relation to the enemy. According to *Joint Publication 3-0*, the two basic variations are interior lines and exterior lines.

> A force operates on Interior Lines when its operations diverge from a central point and when it is therefore closer to separate enemy forces than the latter are to one another. Interior Lines benefit a weaker force by allowing it to shift the main effort laterally more rapidly than the enemy. A force operates on exterior lines when its operations converge on the enemy. Successful operations on exterior lines require a stronger or more mobile force, but offer the opportunity to encircle and annihilate a weaker or less mobile opponent.[116]

Lines of operations constitute another of Jomini's concepts that would have been familiar to World War I commanders. The definitions in *Joint Publication 3-0*, however, are not quite the same as those defined by Jomini. In addition to interior and exterior lines, Jomini also identified concentric and divergent lines. In *The Art of War* Jomini wrote:

> Interior lines of operations are those adopted by one or two armies to oppose several hostile bodies, and having such a direction that the general

can concentrate the masses and maneuver with his whole force in a shorter period of time than it would require for the enemy to oppose to them a greater force.

Exterior lines lead to the opposite result, and are those formed by an army which operates at the same time on both flanks of the enemy, or against several of his masses.

Concentric lines of operations are those which depart from widely separated points and meet at the same point, either in advance of or behind the base.

Divergent lines are those by which an army would leave a given point to move upon several distinct points. These lines, of course, necessitate the subdivision of the army.[117]

Thus, the *Joint Publication 3-0* definitions seem to combine Jomini's interior and concentric lines, and his exterior and divergent lines. But as Jomini defined them, interior and exterior lines run to the friendly side of the line of departure, while concentric and divergent lines run from the enemy side of the line of departure. As we shall see, the German 1918 offensives in terms of Jomini's definitions were operating on interior, but divergent lines.

Depth

As already noted, the recent reawakening of the operational art in the West grew out of the need for follow-on forces attack and the recognition of the depth of the battlefield in both space and time. This brought with it the understanding that the immediate close battle might not necessarily be where the decision would be achieved. A corollary to depth is the abandonment of linearity and the adoption of non-linear tactics and operations. Simultaneity is a key feature inherent in the modern concept of deep operations. The intent is to bring force to bear on the enemy's entire structure in a near simultaneous manner that is within the decision-making cycle of the opponent.[118] According to Simpkin, the Soviets regarded two actions as exerting simultaneous pressure if one followed the other within the enemy's response time, or his "decision loop."[119]

The "decision loop" is a relatively recent construct as well. Lieutenant Colonel John Boyd, U.S. Air Force, first introduced it in the West in the early 1970s. Boyd's model suggested that any fighting element, from a single tactical aircraft to an army group, goes through a distinct cycle of four steps in order to react to a change in the situation.[120] In general, smaller elements can cycle through the steps of Observe, Orient, Decide, and Act much faster than larger elements. A platoon on the battlefield can almost always react faster than a division or a corps. Advances in technology have also reduced the cycle time of the so-called "Boyd Loop" or "OODA Loop." In Moltke's time, a deployed field army dependent upon telegraph communications might take weeks to complete the cycle. During World War II, field armies using radio could complete the cycle in days. By the 1991 Gulf War, major allied units using near-real-time satellite C3I systems could react within hours.

The concepts of simultaneity and the decision loop would not have been familiar to World War I commanders. Military planners of that era generally thought in terms of either single, or at best sequential operations. Depth and non-linearity, on the other hand, were concepts just starting to be understood in the last years of the war. In the defensive, the Germans had pioneered the flexible defense and the defense-in-depth. In the offensive, German infiltration or "Stormtroop" tactics were a clear abandonment of linearity—at least at the tactical level. Certain features of the 1918 German offensives also clearly addressed the issue of operational deep attack. These included German artillery task groupings whose sole mission was to attack Allied deep targets. These units were among the first to appear on the emerging modern battlefield with a specific deep attack mission.[121]

Timing, tempo, and sequencing

Proper timing enables a commander to dominate the action, remain unpredictable, and operate beyond the enemy's ability to react.[122] Operational tempo is a concept first adopted from the Soviets by Richard Simpkin. In the Soviet model tempo is a complex set of seven elements, all interacting, and all subject to Clausewitz's "friction." These include: physical mobility; tactical rate of advance; quantity and reliability of information; command, control, and communications (C3) timings; times to complete moves; pattern of combat support; and pattern of logistic support.[123]

A phase in an operation represents a period during which a large portion of the force is involved in similar or mutually supporting activities. A transition to another phase indicates a shift in emphasis. Branches are options built into the basic plan. Such branches may include shifts in priorities, changes in unit task organization, or even changes in the very nature of the operation itself. Sequels are subsequent or follow-on operations based on the possible outcomes of the current operation.[124]

This group of concepts, especially sequential operations, is central to the modern notion of the operational art. As noted, however, tempo is a relatively recent idea. Military commanders of 1918 would have had a basic understanding of timing, phases, and sequencing. As we shall see, timing was a major factor in the German decision-making process. Likewise, Ludendorff initially considered sequenced operations, and then rejected that option on the basis that the Germans had only enough combat power for one great operation—one decisive knockout blow. When that failed, the Germans returned by default to sequential operations and somehow found enough combat power to launch four more major attacks. Even as the fifth offensive was failing, Ludendorff still clung to the belief that he could launch yet one more big push—Operation HAGEN. What would the results have been if the resources and power that the Germans squandered in five only haphazardly linked operations had been synchronized into one seamless operational sequence?

Reach

Reach is the distance over which military power can be directed and concentrated decisively, the capability to operate at depth. Reach affects the ability to conduct deep operations and it is influenced by the geography surrounding and separating the opponents.[125] Reach has a significant technological component. During World War I, the battleship was the only weapon system with strategic (global) reach. Today, satellites, nuclear missiles, manned bombers, nuclear submarines, and aircraft carriers all have strategic reach—some more rapid than others. At the start of World War I, the railway was perhaps the only military system with operational reach, but it was a fixed and relatively rigid system. By 1918, aircraft and some artillery systems were capable of operational reach, and the tank was just beginning to give hints of its potential. Operational mobility, however, was still largely limited to rail.

The elements of operational power

Firepower and maneuver have long been accepted as the two primary elements of combat power. Maneuver is the movement of combat forces to gain positional advantage, and firepower is the destructive force essential to defeat the enemy's ability and will to fight. At various times, military organizations have added other elements to this list, usually in order to reinforce a point of current doctrine. The 1993 edition of *FM 100-5* added protection and leadership to the list.[126] The 2002 edition of *FM 3-0* adds yet another element, information.[127]

Leadership may well belong on the list, but it is certainly unquantifiable, highly volatile, and situationally dependent. The addition of protection might be regarded as reinforcing the current American fixation on "force protection." Simpkin, however, had a very solid argument for why it belongs on the list— except that he used the term survivability. Simpkin defined combat in pure mechanical terms as "an exchange of energy." Firepower is the ability to transfer energy to the enemy, while maneuver is the means of bringing firepower to bear, or of avoiding enemy firepower and maneuver. Survivability—or protection—is the capability to absorb enemy fire or to withstand the effects of enemy maneuver.[128]

Firepower, maneuver, protection, information, and possibly even leadership may well constitute the primary building blocks of combat power at the tactical level, but do they at the operational level? Since the operational art is of a fundamentally different nature than tactics, I would suggest a slightly different listing of elements of warfighting power at the operational level. Each of these elements has a strong technological component.

Operational maneuver

At the tactical level the purpose of maneuver is to gain positional advantage. At the operational level its purpose is the unhinging of the enemy's entire operational plan.[129] As defined in *Joint Publication 3-0*, the function of operational maneuver is to concentrate forces at decisive points to achieve surprise, psychological shock, and physical momentum.[130] At the operational level, the scheme of maneuver is described in the broadest terms of forms of the offense, patterns of the defense, or types of retrograde.

There is a widely held belief that true operational maneuver did not appear on the battlefield until World War II, because up until then military technology had not delivered the prerequisites of mechanization. This view, however, is too simplistic and deterministic. Examples of operational maneuver prior to 1939 include Wellington in the Peninsular Campaign; Moltke in the second half of August 1870; the Germans in Romania in 1916, and at Riga and in the Baltic Islands in 1917; and Allenby's march through Palestine in 1917–1918.[131]

Nonetheless, the peculiarities of the Western Front did combine to make that theater of war far more dependent than other theaters upon technological solutions to achieve operational maneuver. All armies entered World War I considering mounted (horse) cavalry units as their primary instrument of high mobility on the battlefield. These units by their very nature, however, had relatively little hitting power—especially in relation to modern weapons. The first months of the war also showed that these lightly armed units were extremely vulnerable to the new firepower. By 1918 the German Army had all but abandoned the use of horse cavalry on the Western Front, although horses continued to be the primary transport motive power from the front lines forward. The British, on the other hand, clung to some of their mounted divisions in the vain hope of creating the breakthrough for them to exploit. This role would be taken over by tanks in later years; but in World War I the Germans had almost no tanks, and Allied tanks lacked the mechanical reliability to conduct sustained deep operations.

Although the railroad was a fixed and relatively inflexible means of transport, it nonetheless was a major operational system in World War I. It was the key means of logistical support, of course, but it also played a role in what operational mobility was achieved on the Western Front. Both sides had well-developed and dense rail networks behind their lines; but the British rail system in Flanders had much less depth, and it had the additional complexity of having to tie into sea ports along the BEF's strategic lines of communications (LOCs). The German system, on the other hand, had far greater depth, very few if any significant choke points, and it ran straight back to the national base without having to link into sea ports. The whole system was far more robust and less vulnerable.

The Germans in 1917 and 1918 used rail for both strategic and operational mobility. Between November 1917 and the start of Operation MICHAEL on 21 March 1918, the Germans shifted by rail forty-eight divisions from the Eastern Front to the Western Front. From the start of January 1918 until the end of October, the Germans made an incredible 566 divisional moves from one point to another on the Western Front. This does not include the divisions that were transferred from one army to another because of a boundary shift. Many of the better divisions moved seven and eight times, and the 20th Infantry Division moved ten times.[132] Thus, rail clearly was a major factor in German operational maneuver—at least in the period up to the start of the tactical battle.

Although technology is the great enabler of operational maneuver, it does not guarantee its success. From July 1918 until the end of the war, the Allies enjoyed increasing superiority over the Germans in both aircraft and especially tanks. Despite these great technological advantages on the battlefield, the Allies never came as close to achieving operational maneuver as the Germans had in the first half of 1918. More recently, of course, the Americans lost in Vietnam despite having overwhelming mobility and technical supremacy.

Operational fires

Modern operational fire assets include both fixed and rotary wing aircraft, cruise missiles, artillery rockets, and some limited models of tube artillery. In littoral operations or operations against sea lines of communications, naval gunfire and mining operations also are included. At the operational level, firepower has three key functions: facilitate maneuver to operational depth; isolate the battlefield by interdiction; and destroy enemy functions and facilities having operational significance.[133]

In the West there has been a long-standing general agreement that firepower by itself can never be decisive—at least on the tactical level. The Soviets, on the other hand, have long believed that artillery by itself can be decisive.[134] Some analysts in the West have argued that firepower can be decisive at the operational level. Naveh suggested that fire was actually an integral part of operational maneuver, producing what he termed "Operational Striking Maneuver."[135] According to modern operational theory, operational fires are not the same as fire support, and operational maneuver does not necessarily depend on operational fires. Operational fires can be used to achieve a single operational objective.[136] In that sense, then, fires can prove decisive.

During the final years of World War I only aircraft, longer-range tube artillery, and in certain situations naval assets were capable of delivering fires to operational depths. Aircraft were capable of striking far deeper but, because of their limited fuel capacities, high vulnerability to ground fire, dependence on weather conditions, and small load capacities, they could produce only limited effects over relatively small areas of the battlefield. During the 1918 offensives, the Germans made good use of their tube artillery within the ranges of the guns. In some cases they even achieved limited operational effects through the interdiction and destruction of key Allied functions and facilities, but that effort was not focused.

Facilitating maneuver to operational depth was a major problem. The mobility limitations of 1918 weighed far more heavily on the artillery than it did on the infantry. Moving over torn-up ground at the speed of a man, the infantry was at least able to advance. With no roads, cratered ground, few motor vehicles, and even a shortage of horses, the artillery could hardly advance at all. As soon as the maneuver elements advanced beyond the supporting range of their artillery, the possibility of maneuvering to operational depths diminished rapidly.

Operational sustainability

Operational sustainability hinges on the "tyranny of logistics." At the operational level the various courses of action are either enabled or constrained by logistics to a far greater degree than at the tactical level. The synchronization of logistics with combat operations can forestall culmination and help the commander to control the tempo of his operations. The sustainment must be carried out in depth, both in space and time.[137]

World War I was the most prolonged period of massive and sustained military operations in history up to that time. The logistical effort to support the forces involved was nothing like any army had ever experienced before. Entire logistics systems and infrastructures had to be established rapidly, starting from almost nothing. With their limited national resources and their traditional focus on rapid decisions and short operations, the Germans never developed the logistics system their army required. Despite their superior rail network behind the lines, the German forces in the field never enjoyed the quantity or the quality of sustainment support as the Allies did. This general weakness for logistics also carried over to the German Army of World War II. The Allies, on the other hand, had very robust logistical systems but, as already noted, the British in particular had several key vulnerabilities in their system that the Germans never fully exploited.

Operational intelligence

Simply put, knowledge is power. This is especially true on the battlefield. The three key components of military information, or "situational awareness," are: information about the enemy; information about friendly forces; and the ability to communicate that information. The modern rubric for this collection of activities is C3I (Command, Control, Communications, and Intelligence.) Another term recently introduced in American military circles is Information Operations.

Although the first forms of modern communications technology emerged during World War I, only those communications over very short distances came close to approaching what we would now call "real time." Orders issued from a field army headquarters often took more than twenty-four hours to reach the front-line companies. Likewise, enemy and friendly information flowing back up from the front lines took just as long.

Operational intelligence looks deeper—both in time and space—than does tactical intelligence. Rather than focusing on the immediate contact battle, it focuses more on the enemy's overall intent within the framework of his capabilities. The target of operational intelligence is the mind of the enemy commander. The objective is to create a picture of defeat in the other commander's mind. As Simpkin noted, "The outcome turns . . . on the pictures in the opposing commanders' minds."[138]

Going into World War I, commanders gained tactical intelligence by developing the situation once contact with the enemy was established. When trench warfare set in and a semi-permanent state of contact became the norm, commanders had to rely more and more on their reconnaissance and surveillance assets. Military intelligence came of age in World War I. At the start of the war, most armies regarded intelligence as an additional staff function, not a military specialty that soldiers trained in and studied. By the end of the war, all armies had developed huge staff sections to collect, analyze, and disseminate intelligence from multiple sources. These included human intelligence from patrols and prisoners of war; signals intelligence from radio and telephone-line intercepts; imagery intelligence from aerial photographs; and counter-battery target acquisition from sound and flash ranging stations and from shell crater analysis. Initially the intelligence focus was purely tactical but, as technologies improved, assets like aerial photography and sound and flash ranging began to acquire capabilities to operational depths.

Operational deception

Deception is the enabler of surprise. Operational deception differs from tactical deception in target, timing, and scale. Operational deception must usually be sustained for protracted periods. Operational intelligence and deception are reciprocal functions, and the primary target of both is the mind of the enemy operational commander. Deception has both a passive and an active component. In today's terms, the passive component of deception is called operational security (OPSEC). The Soviets too had a concept they termed "*Operativnaya Maskirovka.*"[139]

World War I commanders had a solid appreciation of deception, even at what we would today call the operational level. The preparations for the German 1918 offensives included a number of well-planned and intricate deception operations. For the five offensives launched between March and July, German passive deception measures were extensive and elaborate.

Writing after the Great War, Fuller identified two different types of surprise at the operational level. Moral surprise he defined as a situation where the enemy does not know exactly where and when the attacker is coming. Material surprise is a situation where the enemy knows the attack is coming, but can do nothing to stop it. Material surprise is what we would term today as "turning within the enemy's decision loop."[140] The Germans achieved materiel surprise over the Allies in the first three of the 1918 offensives—MICHAEL, GEORGETTE, and BLÜCHER. They failed to achieve surprise at all in the last two— GNEISENAU and MARNESCHUTZ–REIMS. Furthermore, the Allies achieved moral surprise over the Germans when they launched their counterattack of 18 July.

Summary

To summarize, military commanders in 1918 had a clear understanding, if not a fully developed one, of the level of warfighting between the tactical and the strategic. And the evidence suggests strongly that, despite Ludendorff, the Germans had a better grasp of the operational level than their opponents. Most of what we have described here as the elements of operational design were known and understood. These included centers of gravity, decisive points, culmination, lines of operations, timing, and sequencing. Furthermore, the concepts of depth and to a lesser extent reach were just beginning to be understood. The elements of operational power as we would define them today were less well understood. German commanders in particular, however, had a good understanding of maneuver and deception at the operational level. Operational intelligence and sustainability were concepts that only began to emerge during the Great War. By the start of 1918 some German commanders also had a good grasp of operational fires.

3   The tactical realities of 1918

No matter how farseeing any regulations are constructed in their inception, they become obsolete after a time. . . . Emperor Napoleon measured that time to be ten years.[1]

Lieutenant General William Balck

It is in any case very difficult, if not impossible, to picture now what form a modern war in Europe would take.[2]

General Helmuth von Moltke the Younger

Although this study focuses on the operational level of war, a brief overview of the basic World War I tactical problem and the tactical realities of 1918 is necessary to understand the possibilities and the limitations the Germans faced in planning their great 1918 offensives. With a few notable exceptions, all the tools and techniques that we associate with modern 20th-century warfare were present in 1918, but many of them were in a relatively immature state. Tacticians on both sides were still grappling with the implications of the emerging technologies as the war moved into its final year.

The tactical problem

The key problem facing attackers in World War I was not so much achieving a break-in of the enemy's positions. That could almost always be accomplished if the attacker was willing to commit the necessary resources. The key problem was what to do next.[3] Once the break-in was achieved, there were two basic options. One was to attempt a breakthrough and a subsequent exploitation. The other was to consolidate the gains made at that position, and then hit the enemy again somewhere else, repeating this sequence over and over again until the cumulative effects of the attacks began to overwhelm the enemy.

The former was a tactical approach on a large scale, the latter was the beginning of an operational approach. The Germans in the first half of 1918 opted for the former; the Allies after July 1918 succeeded with the latter. Still trying to achieve the battle of annihilation, the Germans continually sought to gain the fastest possible results at the decisive point.[4] The problem with this approach was that nobody had sufficient mobility to make it work. The technology of fire-power had temporarily outreached the technology of maneuver, and that was the primary cause of the tactical gridlock of World War I.[5]

Fire and maneuver

Prior to 1914 the tactical doctrines of most major armies generally stressed combat operations consisting of vast sweeping maneuvers and meeting engagements. And while neither side planned for a long and drawn-out static war on the scale that actually developed, many military thinkers did recognize the problems of modern warfare. In a five-volume book published in 1899 under the direction of Jan Bloch, the Polish civilian banker argued that modern weaponry was making offensive maneuver all but impossible.[6] But while some military thinkers believed that the new technologies reinforced the inherent superiority of the defense, others believed that they favored the offense. There seemed to be no immediate solution to the problem of fire and maneuver, and tactical thinking on all sides remained in a state of flux. Many planners, likewise, understood that any war on the Continent would more than likely not be a short one, although that was what everyone hoped for.[7] Despite the German emphasis on the battle of annihilation, Ludendorff as early as 1912 wrote that any future war would be "a long-drawn out campaign with numerous difficult, long-lasting battles, before we can defeat any one of our enemies."[8]

At the start of the war the density of forces along the German, French, and Belgian borders became so great that there was little room for maneuver and open flanks rarely existed. Added to that problem were the vastly increased volume, range, and lethality that technology had given to the new generation of weapons that had appeared in the previous forty years. The Wars of German Unification ended in 1871. From then until 1914 there were no major wars in western or central Europe. During that same period a vast technological revolution produced entirely new types of weapons: smokeless gunpowder, recoiling and quick-firing artillery, magazine-fed repeating rifles, and the machine gun. All these weapons represented large-scale improvements in range, accuracy, volume of fire, and lethality that placed the soldier in the open at a distinct disadvantage to the soldier fighting from a protected position. Soldiers on all sides hated the spade, but the new firepower forced them to dig.[9]

Tactics are closely related to technology, and these new weapons should have radically altered the tactics of the day. But most of the European armies of 1914 had little recent combat experience against which to evaluate their old tactics. The indicators were there, however. During the Boer War the British got a taste of future warfare; and the Russo–Japanese War should have shown the Russian Army the wave of the future. The experiences of both conflicts were discounted to some degree, however, because the opposing combatants were not considered proper European armies. As World War I approached, the series of flare-ups in the Balkans also gave some hint of the future; but they came too close to 1914 to be analyzed and understood completely.

Most of the major armies entered World War I with some variation of the linear tactics that had been in use since Napoleon's day. Since the German experience in the summer of 1870, however, the density of the attacking formations tended to shift back and forth between open and close order in reaction to new experiences and the appearance of new weapons. Tacticians saw the problem as one of trying to maintain a balance between formations dispersed enough to increase survivability, yet close enough to maintain cohesion and control of the mass conscript armies.[10] At the start of the war typical skirmish lines moved forward with one to three meters between soldiers. As World War I dragged on the interval progressively widened until it reached five meters. (The French retained the one-meter interval until as late as 1916.)[11]

The early battles of August and September 1914 were characterized by a great deal of maneuver. But as both sides jockeyed around searching for that ever-illusive open flank, firepower took its grim toll. By the end of 1914 the Western Front had evolved into two roughly parallel lines of foxholes and hasty trenches running from the Swiss border to the North Sea. As time dragged on these defenses became more sophisticated and semi-permanent. With firepower technology gaining the upper hand over maneuver tactics, the result was trench warfare. The Eastern Front never quite got bogged down into the static and rigid network of trenches and fortifications that characterized the Western Front. But the flat terrain and wide open spaces in the east, combined with the increased firepower yet limited mobility of the World War I armies, produced the Eastern Front's own special brand of stagnation.

Many professional soldiers continued to believe that an aggressive spirit was the only chance the attacker had of overcoming the greater firepower. The cult of the offensive was especially strong in the French Army, with its doctrine of *attaque à l'outrance*, advocated by Colonel Loyzeaux de Grandmaison and Brigadier General Ferdinand Foch. According to Lieutenant Colonel Pascal Lucas, writing after the war, "Our officers had absorbed the theory of the offensive to the point where it had become a disease."[12] Firepower and its advocates, like Colonel Henri Pétain, were largely ignored. The cult of the offensive had become something of a substitute for any real body of doctrine.[13]

Commanders on all sides came to regard the static lines of fixed fortifications as an unnatural and temporary situation. They spent most of the war looking for a way to break through the enemy's defenses and restore the natural condition of maneuver warfare. The key flaw in this approach was that the military tacticians of the period failed to comprehend that the central paradigm of war itself had shifted. Rather than a contest between two opposing forces of blood, muscle, and bayonets, war had become a contest between two armies consisting of machines, where man's most important roles were the operation and direction of those machines. Muscle power had been replaced with mechanical power. Most of World War I, however, was taken up with trying to prevail with manpower in history's first truly mechanized war.[14] More importantly, the new technologies made coordination among the various arms more critical than ever. Gone were the days when large infantry units could win battles on their own. By the end of

World War I the foundations of combined-arms warfare would emerge, with infantry, artillery, and even armored fighting vehicles and airplanes complementing each other's strengths.

Indirect fire techniques and increased range of the guns, combined with the still primitive communications systems, made close support of the infantry very difficult the farther artillery moved from the attack line of departure. Radio was still in its infancy. In defensive situations the telephone worked reasonably well, but in the attack requests for fire and corrections had to be conveyed by messenger, which sometimes took hours. One solution to the problem was to move the artillery fire forward on a precise schedule, controlled by phase lines on the map. That eventually evolved into the creeping or rolling barrage, with the advancing infantry trained to follow closely behind the moving wall of their own fire. Shrapnel, the projectile of choice in these barrages, burst in the air sending most of the blast effect forward along the line of the shell trajectory. The infantry, therefore, could follow very closely behind it, often as close as fifty meters. Infantry commanders were encouraged to keep their troops as close to the barrage as possible, even though they might take some casualties from friendly fire.

The main problem with the creeping barrage and phase line techniques was that they wholly subordinated the infantry advance to the artillery schedule.[15] This in turn reinforced the use of the rigid linear tactics. Tactical decisions were centralized at higher and higher levels, which meant slower response times because the communications technologies could not support the greater centralization of control. Thus, front-line infantry commanders ignored terrain in their planning, came to have less and less control of the tactical situations around them, and soon even forgot how to maneuver their forces on the battlefield.

By the middle years of the war attack planning had been almost reduced to fixed sets of mathematical formulae—so many heavy guns per yard of front in the primary attack sector; so many machine guns; so many riflemen; so many rounds in the artillery preparation, etc. The enemy's first positions could always be taken, and usually his second positions—if the attacking commander was willing to pay the price in casualties and ammunition. The real problem came when attempting to move deeper into enemy territory. By that stage of the attack the initial infantry force was totally depleted and the supporting artillery was probably at the maximum limit of its range.

To advance, therefore, fresh infantry units had to be brought up and the artillery had to be displaced forward to extend its range. That took time, especially since those forces had to move over shattered terrain, blocked with the refuse of war. Such movements were always by foot, with sporadic horse transport. The defender, meanwhile, could reinforce the threatened area much more quickly by taking advantage of the roads and rail networks in his own rear area. Motor vehicles generally could operate in the rear areas without problem, but not in the cratered and muddy morass of no-man's-land. The essence of the problem, then, was that the defender's strategic mobility worked against the attacker's lack of tactical mobility.

Attack formations varied greatly during the war, but the principle was essentially the same. In some armies the regiments attacked in echelon, with two battalions in the first echelon, and one or two in the second. In other armies whole regiments were committed to the first wave, while additional regiments made up the second and succeeding waves.[16] Most armies, however, attacked using some variation of the wave system. The attacking soldiers moved across the torn-up terrain, through barbed wire, and against enemy fire carrying heavy loads. Each man in the first five waves typically carried his rifle, bayonet, gas mask, ammunition, wire cutters, a spade, two empty sandbags, flares, and two grenades. A soldier's individual kit weighed up to seventy pounds. The troops in the carrying platoons had it even worse. These men essentially were human pack animals. In addition to their individual kits, they carried heavy loads of ammunition, barbed wire, duckboard, and construction materiel to help fortify the objective.[17]

During the early years of the war defensive tactics focused on rigid defenses with the bulk of combat power concentrated in the forward trenches—a concept known as forward defense. As the human cost of taking ground increased, it seemed almost sacrilegious to yield even a few inches of it. Thus the defensive credo became one of holding "at all costs," regardless of the actual tactical situation. Allied commanders in particular felt that allowing units to withdraw under pressure (even when that made the most sense tactically) would be bad for morale and an inducement to mass cowardice. The fatal flaw of the forward defense, however, was that it was suicidal. It placed the bulk of the defender's combat power in densely packed areas well within the range of the attacker's artillery. Being on the defensive in the west, the Germans were quicker to recognize the problem, particularly as a result of their heavy losses on the Somme.

By mid-1917 many Allied commanders had realized the decisive penetration was not to be. Pétain, among others, began advocating limited objective attacks, designed to eat away at an enemy's position in small chunks.[18] Other tacticians, however, had bolder ideas. In May 1915 French Captain André Laffargue wrote a pamphlet suggesting that specially trained teams of skirmishers precede main attacks. Armed with light machine guns and grenades, these teams would infiltrate into the German lines ahead of the main attack, locate and neutralize the German machine guns, and even penetrate deeply enough to attack the German artillery positions. The British and French largely ignored Laffargue's pamphlet; but the Germans captured a copy during the summer of 1916, translated it, and issued copies to their front-line units.[19]

Cavalry was a special problem in World War I. In the days before the advent of the motor vehicle, it was the primary source of mobility and high-speed maneuver on the battlefield. Its three principal missions were reconnaissance and security before the battle; shock action during the battle; and exploitation and pursuit after the battle. By the start of World War I, however, many military leaders understood that modern firepower made cavalry shock action impossible.[20]

The Germans were quick to grasp that the days of horse cavalry were over, at least on the Western Front. They disbanded almost all their cavalry divisions and used the horses for much-needed transport. The German troopers were converted to infantry. The British, on the other hand, held on to their cavalry divisions until the end, hoping to use them as the exploitation force for the breakthrough that never came. As Lucas pointed out immediately after the war, none of the doctrinal publications issued under Ludendorff made any provisions for cavalry to exploit any of the decisive breakthroughs envisioned in the 1918 offensives.[21] John Terraine also criticized the Germans for launching the attacks without any cavalry to exploit. "Yet feeble as it was, the cavalry was the only exploiting arm that existed. To launch an offensive intended to win the war with none at all was not just foolish, it was criminal."[22] As we shall see later in this analysis, Operation MICHAEL might have turned out differently if the Germans had had a mobile exploitation force, especially on 26 March. The fact remains, however, that by 1918 the Germans did not have the horses to mount cavalry units, even if they had wanted to.

Trench warfare

Trench warfare was basically an extension of old-style siege warfare.[23] Trench works were not new in World War I. They had appeared in certain static situations in the American Civil War, and somewhat more prominently in the Russo–Japanese War. But for the most part they had been exceptions to the rule, temporary emplacements until the normal flow of warfare could resume. Writing before the war, General Friedrich von Bernhardi stated bluntly, "There can, of course, be no question of sapping in active operations."[24] Yet in World War I on the Western Front the trench line became the dominant physical feature of the battlefield. As Gary Sheffield pointed out, what was new on the Western Front was the "force-to-space ratio"—the sheer numbers of forces and advanced weapons crammed into a relatively restricted section of Belgium and northern France.[25]

The earliest trench systems were simple lines of fighting positions and slit trenches. In some areas where the ground water level was high, the soldiers put up birms and parapets above ground level. As the tactical situation on the Western Front became more static, the defenses were improved, reinforced, and became more elaborate. Allied commanders tended to push their lines as far forward as possible, believing that control of terrain mattered most. The Germans were generally more careful to place their trenches in the best positions to maximize concealment, fields of fire, and observation.[26] Before the start of the war French and British soldiers had received almost no training in the construction of defensive positions, and their supply trains carried almost none of the required materials. In the French Army, only the pre-war engineer manual contained any detailed defensive information.[27] The Germans were a little better off. Although their pre-war doctrine had overwhelmingly stressed the attack as well, they did train a little bit in defensive techniques—perhaps as a result of the reports from the extensive network of observers they sent to the Balkan Wars.

By 1917 the fully mature trench systems had evolved. On the British side trench systems had three basic zones. The Forward Zone was a thinly held string of strong points and early-warning positions, held together in some areas by connecting trenches, but usually not forming a continuous line. Two to three kilometers to the rear the Battle Zone consisted of three and sometimes more sets of roughly parallel trenches, reinforced with periodic strong points, and holding up to two-thirds of the artillery. Through the spring of 1918 the Allies kept up to two-thirds of their combat power packed into the Battle Zone. Six to ten miles behind the Battle Zone was the Rear Zone, which held the counterattack forces and also provided the final line of defense for the artillery positions.[28] The French system, based on Pétain's Directive Number 4 of 20 December 1917, was essentially the same with minor variations.[29] (The German system will be discussed below.)

The space between the forward edges of the opposing sets of trench lines (anywhere from fifty to 3,000 meters) was no-man's-land. Extending out into this area the front of the trench system was covered by massive entanglements of barbed wire to impede the forward movement of any attacker. Wire complexes were designed with carefully concealed paths, to allow friendly patrols in and out. These paths were always covered by observation and fire, usually by machine guns.[30]

Trench warfare also produced its own specialized weapons, some of which are still in use today. The mortar, a small, high-trajectory, short-range artillery weapon, had been around for hundreds of years, but was almost extinct by the time World War I started. With trench warfare the mortar came back into its own. Since it fired only at high angles, and all its recoil was directed into the ground, the mortar was an ideal source of heavy firepower for the forward trenches. Throughout the course of the war both sides built up large trench mortar organizations.[31] In some armies these trench artillery units were part of the artillery; in some they were part of the infantry; and in the German Army they were part of the pioneers (combat engineers). The early World War I mortars bore little resemblance to the mortars of today, until the British introduced the Stokes Mortar, the forerunner of all modern "stovepipe"-type mortars.

Flamethrowers and hand grenades were weapons of trench warfare that are still very much a part of modern arsenals. At first only specially trained soldiers called bombers were allowed to throw grenades. During an offensive every soldier in an attack wave might carry several grenades, but they were to be passed to the unit's bomber for actual use. As the Germans evolved their assault tactics, every soldier in the elite storm troop units carried and threw grenades.[32] The grim hand-to-hand combat that trench fighting sometimes produced also resulted in a grisly assortment of more primitive weapons for quick and silent killing. A wide array of trench knives, blackjacks, and knuckle-dusters were fabricated right in the trenches and carried by most men. A form of mace even appeared, a weapon not seen on the battlefield since medieval times.

The trench raid was a favorite nighttime operation of both sides. Trench raids were sent out to locate enemy machine guns and artillery, capture prisoners for interrogation, and just simply to terrorize the enemy. Some soldiers excelled as trench raiders, and specialized in that one activity. Some enjoyed working as lone operators, and some, no doubt, came to take a perverse pleasure in the killing. The size of a raid could be anything from a few men to an entire company, depending on the mission.

Units did not remain in the trenches for months on end. Normally units were rotated in and out of the line on a routine basis. When out of the line a unit was supposed to relax and refit; but most of the time was taken up with intensive training on new weapons and tactical methods. Sometimes a soldier was able to get more rest in the line than out of it, but his living conditions out of the line were generally better.

In wet periods the trenches filled with water and mud making life miserable for the soldiers. The primitive sanitary facilities in the front, combined with the ever-present (but none too clean) water, produced serious health problems: frostbite, trench foot, trench mouth, dysentery, etc. Complicating the health problems, the garbage, waste, and decaying and hastily buried bodies drew fleas and rats. Even during quiet periods a typical battalion while in the line might expect to take up to sixty casualties per month from wounds and disease—a phenomenon known as "trench wastage." As in all previous wars, the armies of World War I took more casualties through disease and sickness than through combat action.[33]

Technology

The Germans in World War I had selective blind spots for technology, and that hurt them at both the tactical and operational levels. World War I was history's first high-tech war. As James Corum noted, it "constituted the most rapid period of technological change in history."[34] Between 1830 and 1910 two technological waves completely altered the face of battlefield tactics. In the first wave came breech-loading, rifled weapons; in the second wave came smokeless powder, repeating rifles, machine guns, rapid-firing artillery, and the internal combustion engine. The cumulative effect of these two waves was to make coordination between the various arms absolutely necessary for success on the battlefield.[35] With the culmination of these waves came Travers' paradigm shift from the muscle-powered, psychological battlefield to the machine-dominated, technological battlefield.

Despite the impressive tactical and organizational innovations of the German Army (discussed below), the Germans never managed to overcome their blind spot for many of the technical possibilities, and pursued instead largely tactical solutions to many of the battlefield problems.[36] As Holger Herwig put it: "In short, the Germans ignored technical innovation and mass production in favor of the hallowed concept of 'bravery in battle.' In the process, they denied themselves mobility and flexibility at the operational level."[37] To a large degree this streak of technophobia was exacerbated by the inter-branch feuding that characterized the pre-war German Army.[38]

Writing immediately after the war, even as talented a tactician as William

Balck still clung to the old paradigm when he noted: "Nothing could be worse than to place our reliance principally on technical means. The moral forces in the breast of the commander and in the soul of the entire people are the qualities which have finally turned the scales in war."[39]

Nonetheless, other German analysts correctly identified the problem. Colonel Kurt Theobeck, writing for one of the study commissions established immediately after the war by General Hans von Seeckt, criticized the German General Staff for being full of tacticians but having no technicians. It had no weapons specialists who really understood the limitations and tactical effects of technology, thus compounding the institutional blind spot.[40] As a result of the von Seeckt reforms of the 1920s, the *Reichswehr* and later the *Wehrmacht* embraced military technology with a passion—at least at the tactical level.

The Germans were not completely blind to technology and new weapons systems, of course. In some areas they held their own with the Allies and in some areas they were significantly ahead. Most of those areas fell into the firepower column—field artillery, heavy artillery, mortars, machine guns. The mobility column was where they seem to have had the most problems, which is somewhat ironic considering their earlier embrace of the railroad.

Artillery and gas

Artillery and gas were two of the most powerful elements of the German tactical system of 1918. But in the years prior to the start of World War I field artillery on both sides had focused on mobility to the exclusion of almost everything else. Horse-drawn batteries trained to charge into action at some critical moment, fire off a few rounds of direct fire, and then rush off to some other decisive point on the battlefield. The basic forms of indirect fire, counter-battery work, and meteorological corrections were possible in the years just prior to World War I, but the actual techniques were cumbersome and thus largely ignored as being incompatible with fast-moving maneuver warfare.[41]

Once the war started all forms of firepower quickly gained the upper hand over maneuver and trench warfare set in. Artillery quickly became the primary means of prosecuting the war. As Ian V. Hogg noted, "The war of 1914–1918 became an artillery duel of vast proportions."[42] In a remarkable series of articles published in the 1920s in the *Journal of the Royal Artillery*, Lieutenant Colonel Alan F. Brooke (later Field-Marshal Lord Alanbrooke) identified four general phases of artillery employment experienced to varying degrees by all sides in the Great War: Inadequacy; Experimentation and Build-up; Destruction; and Neutralization.[43]

Inadequacy 1914

Most armies entered the war regarding artillery as strictly an auxiliary arm whose job was to assist the infantry in the attack. There had always been a great deal of talk about the notion of coordinating infantry and artillery actions, but very little real effort. During the early months of the war the results were dismal, with artillery firing on its own infantry all too often.[44]

Napoleon had convincingly demonstrated the power of massed artillery; but in 1914 most armies continued to believe that mass firepower could only be achieved by physically massing guns well forward on the ground. The experiences of the Russo–Japanese War had proved both the value and the practicality of indirect fire to many artillerymen; but the idea was strongly resisted by the maneuver branches of most armies.[45] They believed infantrymen needed the psychological reinforcement of seeing their own artillery right on the front line with them, instead of hiding behind a hill somewhere in the rear. But when World War I combat operations started, artillery turned out to be all too vulnerable to the new forms of small arms, especially the machine gun. As the Russian Army had learned in Manchuria, the firepower of these new weapons quickly drove artillery off the front line, increasing the distance between the gun and the target. The gunners were thus forced to resort to indirect fire.

Aside from the nebulous concept of the "artillery duel," there was very little systematic counter-battery doctrine before the war. The French High Command, and especially the French Infantry were hostile to the very idea of a set-piece artillery duel, seeing it as a waste of firepower better spent in support of the infantry's attack. The French Field Service Regulations issued in 1913 specifically forbade their artillery from engaging in artillery duels.[46]

In 1914 there was very little real centralized command and control (C2) of artillery. In almost all armies the division was the highest level of artillery C2. The British Army did not introduce a divisional-level artillery commander until 1912, and the Royal Artillery entered the war with no experience in coordinating and controlling fires above the level of the artillery battalion (which the British at the time called artillery "brigades"). In most armies of 1914 corps-level artillery existed only as a pool of assets, to be allocated among the divisions as the mission required. The senior artillery officers at corps levels and above were merely advisors, rather than commanders. Even as late as 1917, the senior gunner in General Sir Hubert Gough's Fifth Army was not consulted on the plans for the Passchendaele attack.[47]

The pre-war doctrine of high mobility required that the guns used by field artillery be mobile, which meant light. All nations were armed primarily with light flat-firing field guns. But the German 77mm, the Russian 76.2mm, the American 3-inch, the British 18-pounder, and the famous French 75mm were all too light to have any real effect against well-prepared field fortifications.[48] Once these guns were forced to move back off the front lines, they lacked the higher trajectories necessary for indirect fire, especially in rougher terrain.

Experimentation and buildup 1915

As the stalemate on the Western Front set in, all sides spent most of 1915 scrambling to develop new ordnance and new fire support techniques. But before those issues could even be addressed, all the belligerents ran into a more immediate and critical problem—ammunition. Despite the evidence from recent conflicts, all armies entered World War I with far too little artillery ammunition. During the Russo–Japanese War the Russian Army averaged 87,000 rounds for each month of combat operations in 1904. By the First Balkan War in 1912, the Bulgarian Army was shooting 254,000 rounds per month.[49]

Nonetheless, the French Army started World War I with less than five million rounds on hand. The Russians were in a little better position with about twelve million rounds. The Germans seemed to be in the best shape with slightly more than twenty million rounds, but that had to be split between the two fronts. French plans called for an average consumption of 100,000 rounds per month; but the actual monthly average for 1914 was close to 900,000 rounds. By 1916 the French were shooting 4.5 million rounds per month; and by 1918 the Germans were averaging eight million rounds. Industry could not keep up with the ever-growing demand, and the ammunition crises caused political scandals in Britain, Russia, and France. Throughout most of 1914 and 1915 tactical plans were held hostage to the supply of artillery ammunition.[50]

Shrapnel was the standard round for the light field gun in 1914. Howitzers and heavier guns primarily fired high explosive (HE). Up until nearly the end of World War I the HE round produced very little fragmentation and was used principally for its blast effect. The shrapnel round was packed with steel balls and a bursting charge that was triggered by a hand-set, powder-burning time fuze. When the round went off in the air the bursting charge blew the nose cap off the front of the round and shot the balls forward—something like a huge airborne shotgun. Under the control of a skilled observer, shrapnel could be deadly against troops in the open. But it was ineffective against dug-in troops, and virtually worthless against fortifications. Thus HE increasingly became the round of choice. By the end of the war the metallurgical and chemical compositions of the HE round and its filler had been perfected to the point where an air burst of HE was as effective as properly adjusted shrapnel. After World War I the shrapnel round passed from the scene.

Another source of early problems was the distinction that existed in most armies between the different branches of artillery. The U.S. Army had Field Artillery and Coast Artillery, and the British artillery was divided into the Royal Horse Artillery, Royal Field Artillery, and the Royal Garrison Artillery.[51] The German Army had a similar distinction between the Field Artillery and the Foot Artillery. German Field Artillery was mounted, armed with light field guns, and supported the maneuver forces. Foot Artillery units had little organic mobility and used heavy howitzers and siege mortars. Like the U.S. Coast Artillery and the Royal Garrison Artillery, the German Foot Artillery manned coastal defenses; but it also manned the guns of interior fortifications and was responsible for conducting set-piece sieges in the field should such operations become necessary. The reduction of the Belgian forts along the Meuse River in 1914 was primarily a foot artillery operation.

Although the difference between these two major categories of artillery seemed logical enough on paper, the distinctions started to blur during World

War I, as the heavier guns of the foot and garrison branches were increasingly called upon to give direct support to combat operations. In most armies the two branches were barely on speaking terms. Field artillery emphasized speed and mobility, while heavy artillery stressed precision and technical applications.[52] In the German Army the foot and field branches even had gun sights calibrated in different units of angular measurement.[53] Field gunners in all armies tended to look down upon their garrison and foot colleagues as "Dugout Artillerymen."

The French started the war with almost no heavy artillery. Their pre-World War I doctrine rejected the howitzer entirely. They put all their faith in the M1897 75 mm field gun. This remarkable weapon was the world's first truly modern artillery piece. But the French believed it could accomplish any artillery mission on the battlefield. Whatever the gun lacked in hitting power could be more than compensated for by its high rate of fire (twenty to thirty rounds per minute). This was a very curious notion, considering the French entered the war with only 1,300 rounds for each of their 75 mm guns—almost all of it shrapnel.

By the end of the war the French view of heavy guns had changed drastically. In August 1914 they had 3,840 75 mm guns; but they had a grand total of only 308 guns larger than 75 mm. By November 1918 the French artillery had 4,968 field guns and 5,128 guns and howitzers above 75 mm. Although the total size of the French artillery increased by two-and-a-half times during the war, the increase in heavier guns was something on the order of 1,700 percent.[54]

The Germans paid closer attention to the results of the Russo–Japanese and Balkan Wars and entered World War I with a higher ratio of howitzers and heavy guns. The famous gun works of central Europe, including Krupp and Skoda, conducted aggressive research and development programs in heavy artillery prior to the war. By 1914 Germany had 5,086 77 mm field guns and 2,280 howitzers and larger pieces—outnumbering the French heavy hitters by more than seven to one. But even German heavy artillery grew during the war at a faster rate than the light field guns. By 1918 the German Artillery had 6,764 field guns and 12,286 artillery pieces above 77 mm—still outnumbering the French heavies by more than five to one.[55]

The British had learned the value of the howitzer in their relatively recent Boer War. As a result, they had a higher proportion of howitzers and heavier guns than almost any other army. Throughout the war their ratio of light guns to howitzers and heavier guns changed only slightly. In 1914 the British Army as a whole had 1,608 light guns and 1,248 howitzers and heavies. Unfortunately, the ill-equipped British Expeditionary Force landed in France with a total of only eighty-nine mediums and heavies, which included twenty-four old siege guns. By 1918 the British Army in France had 3,242 light guns and 3,195 howitzers and heavies.[56]

In the early part of the war the fire direction procedures for indirect fire were cumbersome and slow. As the various armies expanded, their pools of trained manpower also shrank through attrition. The gunnery problem grew technically more complex, but the large numbers of poorly and hastily trained replacements required even simpler methods. One solution to the problem was the establishment of phase lines on the ground to control the shifting of fires. The system was slow and rigid, but it worked. Requests to lift fires from one phase line to another often had to be carried by runner, and sometimes took hours to accomplish.

Fire on the objective took the form of standing barrages along the enemy's trench lines. As the attackers overtook the leading trench line, the standing barrage would shift onto the next trench line back. The Germans quickly learned to counter the standing barrages by taking some of their machine guns out of the trenches and placing them on the ground between the trench lines. This led to the requirement for the artillery to sweep the intervening ground with fire as it moved from one standing barrage to the next.

By 1916 on the Western Front (and most likely earlier on the Eastern Front) the standing barrages and the sweeping fire between them evolved into the creeping barrage (also called a rolling barrage), with the advancing infantry following closely behind a steadily moving wall of friendly artillery fire. But, as already noted, over-reliance on artillery phase lines and creeping barrages had an adverse effect on maneuver tactics. Infantry commanders at all levels began to ignore terrain and the old linear tactics returned in a new guise.[57]

Destruction 1916–1917

As the war moved into its third year the Western Front settled into a pattern of tactical stagnation. During this phase of the war artillery on both sides became a blunt instrument for indiscriminately pounding large sections of ground. The main functions of artillery on the battlefield had become destruction and annihilation—destroy the attacking enemy before they reached friendly lines, and destroy the defending enemy before attacking friendly troops reached the hostile positions. Special emphasis was placed on obliterating the enemy's fortifications, with artillery expected to cut his barbed wire. This only added to the steadily increasing rate of ammunition consumption. The prevailing philosophy of this third period became: "The artillery conquers, the infantry occupies."[58]

The dominance of artillery on the battlefield naturally gave rise to counter-battery (CB) operations. Here the destruction philosophy dominated too, and CB work became almost the exclusive domain of the heavier guns. Counter-battery planning was carried out according to rigid mathematical formulas.[59]

The key offensive fire support technique during this period became the artillery preparation. The first large-scale preparation of the war took place during the British attack at Neuve Chapelle on 10 March 1915. In what was the greatest artillery bombardment in military history to that time, 354 British guns fired on the German positions for thirty-five minutes.[60] As the war progressed through 1916 and 1917 the artillery preparations grew longer and longer, lasting days and even weeks. Military leaders on both sides convinced themselves that the more HE shells they dumped on an objective, the easier the infantry's job would be. In truth, however, the long preparations accomplished very little and actually caused more problems for the attacker. In the first place, a long preparation sacrificed surprise; it told the defender exactly where the attack was coming. The longer the preparation, the longer the defender had to take counter-measures. Quite often a defender was able to withdraw his front-line infantry entirely from the area being shelled, reinforce it, and re-insert it when the fire lifted.[61]

The long preparations generally did an uneven job of cutting the defender's barbed wire; but they were most effective in tearing up the terrain the attacker had to cross.[62] That made the ground not only difficult for the infantry to attack over, it made it almost impossible for the artillery to follow in support. That, in turn, practically guaranteed an attack would falter as soon as the infantry advanced beyond the range of their own stalled artillery. Destroyed road net-works to the front also made it more difficult to bring up logistical support for any advance that might be made. The long destructive preparations actually created more obstacles for the attacker then they cleared.

The massive preparations also caused an enormous logistical drain that slowly bled the national economies of the belligerents. By mid-1916 the Great War had degenerated into a dull grinding war of attrition—the *Materialschlacht* the Germans had feared most. The destruction by artillery doctrine reached its zenith (and finally demonstrated its own bankruptcy) during the apocalyptic battles of later 1916 and 1917 on the Western Front.

In July 1916 the British Army started its attack at the Somme with a seven-day preparation, during which 1,537 guns fired 1,627,824 rounds. The British Army, nonetheless, took 57,470 casualties that first day, including 19,240 killed.[63] After fighting five months on the Somme the Allies had taken only about 125 square kilometers of ground. The British tried the same sort of attack on a large scale again at Passchendaele in July 1917. This time the size of the artillery preparation was doubled. Over the course of thirteen days 3,168 guns of the Royal Artillery threw 4.3 million rounds at the German positions. By the end of the five-month-long Third Ypres campaign British losses ran to nearly 400,000.

Neutralization 1917–1918

Throughout the course of the war leaders on both sides and at all levels searched for ways to improve tactics and break the deadlock. For artillery tactics, the most aggressive experimentation took place first on the Eastern Front. The key to the new fire-support thinking was a belief that artillery fire was more effective when its tactical effect was neutralization rather than destruction. This idea, which meshed nicely with the evolving attack doctrine, was actually a return to pre-war tactical concepts.[64]

The most influential artillery tactician of the war was Colonel Georg Bruch-müller, a previously obscure, medically retired German officer recalled to active duty for the duration. It is necessary to review his tactical system thoroughly, because of the key role he played in fire planning for all of the 1918 German offensives.[65] Bruchmüller eventually received the *Pour le Mérite* with Oak

Leaves, which were awarded only 122 times, and only twice to "higher artillery commanders." General Max Hoffmann called Bruchmüller "an artillery genius,"[66] and Ludendorff called him "one of the most prominent soldiers of the war."[67]

Starting on the Eastern Front as early as 1915 and culminating in the 1917 Battle of Riga, Bruchmüller experimented with various fire-support methods that were radical departures from convention. Bruchmüller was one of the first to advocate a return to the principles of neutralization. He understood the counter-productive nature of the long, destruction-oriented preparations. Thus while the preparations in the west were lasting weeks, Bruchmüller planned and executed preparations in the east lasting only a few hours, yet achieving better effect. His preparations may not have been long, but they were incredibly violent—designed not to obliterate a defending enemy, but to stun him sense-less. In his own words, "We desired only to break the morale of the enemy, pin him to his position, and then overcome him with an overwhelming assault."[68]

Bruchmüller was one of the first to organize artillery preparations into dis-tinct phases, with each phase intended to accomplish a specific tactical purpose. The typical Bruchmüller preparation had three main types of phases: a short sur-prise strike (*Feuerüberfall*) on command and control and communications targets; a period of reinforced fire against the enemy artillery; and attack in depth of the defender's infantry positions. Bruchmüller concluded the last phase with a short sub-phase of saturation fire against the leading enemy infantry posi-tions. It did not take those on the receiving end long to realize that the saturation fire on the front line was the signal for the start of the infantry assault. As a counter, Bruchmüller inserted varying numbers of dummy saturation sub-phases into the first and second phases. That way, the defenders never really knew for sure when the German preparation was over.[69] Both the U.S. and Soviet/Russian Armies still use variations of the Bruchmüller preparation model to this day.

Bruchmüller was noted for his innovative use of gas, which was the perfect neutralization weapon. He was one of the first to match the effects of various types of gas against specific types of targets to get specific results. He used lethal, persistent mustard ("Yellow Cross" markings on German shells) gas to screen the flanks of attacks and contaminate enemy artillery positions, thus taking the guns out of action for the duration of the fight. Most gas masks of World War I were effective against lethal, non-persistent "Green Cross" (choking) gas, but ineffective against non-lethal, non-persistent "Blue Cross" (vomiting) gas. Bruchmüller's technique was to fire a mixture of both, which he called *Buntkreuz* (mixed-color cross), against the same target. The Blue Cross gas would penetrate the mask, forcing the wearer to remove it in the presence of the lethal Green Cross.[70]

Despite some claims to the contrary, Bruchmüller almost certainly did not invent the creeping barrage (*Feuerwalze*), but he did develop some interesting variations on it. On the Eastern Front he introduced the double creeping barrage, with the first wave of fire consisting of non-persistent gas, followed by a second wave of shrapnel and HE. The gas was timed to dissipate just before the attacking infantry reached the objective. It was the first time that gas was ever used in direct support of attacking troops.

At Lake Narotch in April 1916 Bruchmüller became the first in the German Army to plan and coordinate fires above the divisional level.[71] One of his greatest innovations was a system of task-tailored artillery groups, each with a specific mission to perform on the battlefield. The main mission of the counter-artillery groups (*Artilleriebekämpfungsartillerie*, or AKA) was to neutralize the enemy's artillery. While almost everyone else was using howitzers and heavy guns for counter-battery work, Bruchmüller used mostly light field guns, because of their high rates of fire and the plentiful supply of gas ammunition for them. This was another application of the neutralization principle. It was not necessary to destroy the enemy guns, it was sufficient to neutralize them by temporarily eliminating their crews and contaminating the equipment. The use of gas also required far less accuracy in the locations of the enemy batteries.

The counter-infantry groups (*Infantriebekämpfungsartillerie*, or IKA) struck at the enemy infantry positions. During the reinforced counter-battery phase of the preparation, however, the counter-infantry guns joined in with the counter-artillery guns to overwhelm the enemy batteries. Although not strictly artillery assets, Bruchmüller's fire planning also included the fires of the trench mortars (*Minenwerfer*, or MW). In the German Army at the time, the trench mortars were manned by pioneers.[72]

Bruchmüller was one of the earliest advocates of centralized fire planning and C2. The counter-infantry units were controlled by the divisions, the counter-artillery units were controlled by corps. At the field army level, Bruchmüller established special heavy artillery groups (*Schwerste Flachfeuerartillerie*, or SCHWEFLA). These units fired destruction missions against critical targets, like rail centers, bridges, and concrete-reinforced command posts. At the corps level, Bruchmüller also set up long-range artillery groups (*Fernkämpfartillerie*, or FEKA), whose mission was interdiction against reserves and other deep targets. Bruchmüller's long-range groups were among the first units to appear on the modern battlefield with a specific deep-battle mission, and were the first tube artillery units to deliver operational fires.

Accuracy in artillery fire was, and still is, a problem. The primary way to achieve accuracy is to fire a registration against a target with a precisely known location. By comparing the "should-hit" firing data to the "did-hit" data a set of corrections can be derived and applied against future targets. The system works something like zeroing a rifle. The only problem is that in registering, an artillery battery gives away its position, and it usually becomes an instant counter-battery target in the process. Also, hundreds of batteries suddenly registering in a given area give a clear indicator that a major attack is in the works.

On the Eastern Front Bruchmüller experimented with various methods to eliminate or abbreviate the registration and thereby avoid telegraphing the attack. When he came to the Western Front in late 1917, Bruchmüller became the principal champion of a newly developed technique to "predict" registration corrections from careful measurement of weather conditions and muzzle-velocity characteristics of each gun tube. The system, developed by Captain Erich Pulkowski, required precise calibration data from each gun tube to determine its velocity error, which the Germans called "special influences." The gun, however, did not need to be fired in the line to obtain this data. It could be done in a rear area, where the calibration firing could not be observed by the enemy. The special influences were then algebraically combined with the weather, or "daily influences." The Germans used a limited version of the "Pulkowski Method" in Operation MICHAEL, and the full version of the system in the remaining four of the 1918 offensives. They achieved stunning tactical surprise in the process.[73] The basic mechanics of the Pulkowski Method are still used by all NATO armies today, albeit computerized.

Bruchmüller was not the only artillery innovator of the war, of course; nor did he personally develop all of the techniques he used so effectively. He did, however, perfect many of them on the battlefield, and he was the first to make them all work in a comprehensive system. French artillerymen, for the most part, were always several steps behind the Germans. They were slow to accept a return to neutralization, and to understand the value of surprise. Several British Gunners, on the other hand, had been advocating many of the same principles as the war progressed. Foremost among that group were Lieutenant-General Sir Noel Birch, Major-General Sir Herbert Uniacke (known in Royal Artillery circles as "the British Bruchmüller"), and Brigadier-General H.H. Tudor. For the most part, they were held back by Haig's prejudices on artillery, and the more rigid British staff system. The British attack at Cambrai actually pre-dated the Germans in the use of a system to predict artillery corrections without registering. Technical errors in the application, however, produced mixed results.

Air power

Perhaps no other weapon system ever went through a steeper growth curve than the aircraft in World War I. At the start of the war airplanes were used for reconnaissance only. By the end of the war, all sides had purpose-built aircraft for reconnaissance, bombing, and air superiority roles. In 1917 the Germans introduced the Junkers J-1, armed with three machine guns and a bomb load. It was both the world's first all-metal aircraft, and the first one specifically designed for ground attack. The Germans later introduced the Hanover C–III, another ground attack model.[74]

In September 1915 aircraft losses on both sides of the Western Front totaled thirty-seven. By August 1918 that figure totaled 832 for both sides. Throughout the war the Germans produced some 47,637 aircraft of 150 types. The Allies produced 138,685.[75] At any given time the Germans were outnumbered 2:1 in the air by the Allies, but until the last months of the war the Germans were able to achieve local air superiority over the battlefield when they needed it. The Germans consistently shot down between two and three Allied aircraft for each of their own losses. Training deaths accounted for 25 percent of the total

German pilot losses, while in the Royal Flying Corps the figure was closer to 50 percent.[76]

The Germans countered Allied numerical superiority by forming larger units and concentrating their forces in the sectors where they needed local air superiority. By the fall of 1916 they had established a central headquarters (*Kommandierender General der Luftstreitkräfte* or *Kogenluft*). By the start of 1918, the German air forces were organized into four basic types of units.[77]

Fliegerabteilung and *Fliegerabteilung-A*: The primary mission of these units was reconnaissance, liaison, and aerial photography. The *Fliegerabteilungen* designated *-A* also performed artillery aerial observation. The standard *Flieger-abteilung* had six aircraft, the *Fliegerabteilung-A* had nine. *Fliegerabteilungen* were allocated on the basis of one per front-line division, and three to four per front-line corps. The Germans, however, seldom had sufficient assets to allocate on the standard basis. The *Fliegerabteilungen* accounted for roughly 49 percent of all German aircraft.

Schutzstaffeln, later called *Schlachtstaffeln*: The *Schutzstaffeln* were origin-ally established as security flights for the *Fliegerabteilungen*. As the ground-attack role increased in importance and aircraft specially designed for that role were introduced, their designation was changed to *Schlachtstaffeln*. Each squadron had six aircraft. By the start of 1918, some 10 percent of German air-craft were in the *Schlachtstaffeln*. An entire section of the new German attack doctrine issued in January 1918 was devoted to air support for the ground forces.[78] That doctrine was amplified further by a document issued on 20 Febru-ary 1918, specifically dealing with the *Schlachtstaffeln* and their control under divisional command in the initial stages of the attack.[79] The new doctrine also stressed ground attack by multiple aircraft in formation, rather than by indi-vidual planes. The Second Army air orders for MICHAEL required an entire *Schutzstaffeln* to attack in lines, two waves to a line. The first wave was to attack enemy artillery positions, and the second wave was to support the infantry attack.[80]

Jagdstaffeln: These were the standard air superiority and air defense fighters. Each squadron had fourteen aircraft. Four *Jagdstaffeln* were organized into a *Jagdgeschwader*. Both the *Schutzstaffeln* and the *Jagdstaffeln* were controlled at the field-army level. The *Jagdstaffeln* accounted for about 34 percent of the German aircraft.

Kampfstaffeln, later called *Bombenstaffeln*: These were the long-range bombers, accounting for roughly 5 percent of the German aircraft. Each squadron had six aircraft, with three *Bombenstaffeln* organized into a *Bombengeschwader*. One specialized unit, *Kampfgeschwader* 3 (*Kagohl* 3) was dubbed the "England Wing." Flying from five air fields around Ghent in the Fourth Army area, *Kagohl* 3 on 25 May 1917 initiated the bombing campaign against England with a raid on Folkestone. Operating directly under the control of OHL, *Kagohl* 3 flew the huge Gotha bombers with their 500-kilogram payload.

Tanks

The tank was either the most decisive weapon of World War I, or the most over-rated. Almost ninety years after the end of the war the debate continues. What is clear is that the Germans were slower than the Allies to recognize the potential of the new weapon system, and a number of factors contributed to this. Even before the start of the war the Germans had conducted trials with armored cars armed with light guns and machine guns. Bernhardi dismissed the whole thing, writing, "no serious military value can really be attached to these experi-ments."[81] The British used tanks for the first time on the Somme on 15 Septem-ber 1916. Committed in small numbers, they produced some initial surprise effect, which did not last long. The French first used them on 16 April 1917, but the results were bad because of poor terrain.

The initial poor results led Ludendorff and many others at OHL to conclude that the tank was little more than a nuisance weapon that could be countered with the right tactics. They responded with special training for artillery crews, the construction of antitank obstacles, and the introduction of a 13 mm antitank rifle that required a crew of two to operate. The first German manual on tank operations, published in January 1918, declared that the tank was an auxiliary weapon that could not decide battle on its own. Its primary mission was to assist the infantry in reaching its objectives. Ludendorff saw their primary value as reducing enemy wire and overrunning machine gun positions.

Many at OHL, however, began to see the tank in an entirely different light after the British committed them in mass for the first time at Cambrai on 20 November 1917. And after the Allied counterattack of 18 July 1918, spear-headed by 759 tanks, OHL staff officer Colonel Albrecht von Thaer commented in his diary that "even Ludendorff" should now understand the power of the tank.[82] Nonetheless, in his post-war memoirs Ludendorff continued to insist:

> The best arms against tanks are the nerves, discipline, and intrepidity. Only with the decline in discipline and the weakening of the fighting power of our infantry did the tanks in their mass employment and in conjunction with smoke gain a dangerous influence on the course of military events.[83]

Writing after the war Balck made the excuse that German industry could only have produced tanks at the expense of artillery, aircraft, and submarines.[84] Ludendorff claimed, with some justification, that the priority for German indus-try had to be the production of motor vehicles to relieve the horse shortage.[85] By October 1918, as the Allies were using tanks in greater and greater numbers, the *Reichstag* asked the War Ministry and OHL why they had not requested tank development in late 1917. OHL responded that it had looked into the issue and concluded that German industry was too heavily committed to higher priorities to be able to deliver tanks in any significant numbers before the summer of 1918.[86]

Actually, OHL had made a request to the War Ministry for the development of tanks as early as October 1916. In 1917 construction started on 100 "caterpillar vehicles." Only twenty were meant to be armored fighting vehicles, the rest were to be front-line transport vehicles. The result was the monstrous and cumbersome A7V. It was twenty-four-feet long, weighed thirty tons, and had a crew of eighteen. It was armed with a 57 mm main gun and six machine guns. It had a speed of five miles per hour on level surfaces, and a range of only fifteen miles. Five A7Vs were delivered to the army in January 1918, and another ten in March. The fifteen A7Vs and seventy-five captured tanks were the only German tanks to see combat in World War I.[87] By the end of the war, the British had built 2,636 tanks and the French had built 3,900. Thousands more were on order for the 1919 campaign.[88]

A question remains as to just how effective the tank was. J.F.C. Fuller argued that the Germans would have won in early 1918 had they focused all their manufacturing resources on field guns and tanks.[89] Even General Hermann von Kuhl wrote that the March 1918 offensive would have succeeded "if 600 tanks had cleared the way for our infantry."[90] Ludendorff made the rather odd comment; "[Tanks] were *merely an offensive weapon*, and our attacks *succeeded* without them."[91] (Emphasis added.)

Major-General Hubert Essame once posed the question that if tanks alone had been the panacea for victory in 1918, then how did the Germans manage to penetrate so much deeper without them than the Allies did with them?[92] And Terraine pointed out that the number of tanks the Allies could mass on the first day of an attack mattered little, regardless of how spectacular the results that day might seem. What really mattered was how many tanks were available for action on the second and subsequent days. Tanks in 1918 still had huge mechanical reliability problems and, as their experience against tanks increased, the German antitank measures became more sophisticated and effective.

During the counterattack of General Charles Mangin's French Tenth Army on 18 July 1918, 346 tanks were available; 225 actually got into action; and 102 were knocked out. On the following day, 195 were available; and fifty were knocked out. By the third day the French had only thirty-two tanks available. During the British counterattack at Amiens on 8 August 1918, Ludendorff's "Black Day of the German Army," 414 tanks were available for action on the first day; 145 on the second day; eighty-five on the third day; thirty-eight on the fourth day; and by 12 August the British had only six tanks in action.[93]

These attrition rates raise serious questions about just how effective an exploitation weapon the tank would have been even if the Germans had mass numbers of them. The fact remains, however, that the Germans did not have tanks in 1918, and our analysis of their operational plans must focus on what was possible with what they had.

Command, control, and communications

Communications provide the vital link that ties together fire and maneuver and facilitates the coordination and synchronization of many elements over a wide area. Effective, secure, and rapid communications are an essential prerequisite for the successful prosecution of war at the tactical and operational levels. In many ways, they are even more important at the operational level. While the operational level can often move almost as fast as the tactical level, the size, scope, and number of diverse elements are far greater. Command, Control, and Communications systems (C3) are what tie them all together.

The real-time and near real-time communications systems modern soldiers take for granted did not exist during World War I. Wire was fairly well developed, but radio was in its infancy. All armies made extensive use of non-electronic communications systems that had been in use for hundreds, if not thousands of years. The faster electronic systems were more effective in the defense; the older and slower manual systems were more effective in the offense. This made responsive fire support especially difficult, as artillery observers moved forward with the advancing infantry.

At the start of the war all forms of wire communications (voice and tele-graph) were fairly well developed. Induction intercepts were technically feasible at distances up to three kilometers, and the Germans used this intelligence-gathering tool to good effect against the Russians at Tannenberg. By May 1917 the Germans had laid some 515,000 kilometers of wire in the west, and 349,000 kilometers in the east. Wire was very vulnerable to all sorts of enemy as well as friendly hazards, and the Germans required sixty-two kilograms of wire to main-tain one kilometer of the Western Front for one month. At the start of the war radio transmissions were mostly Morse code, but by the end of the war radio voice transmissions had a range of up to sixteen kilometers. By the end of the war each German division had a wireless battalion. The growing use of intercep-tion as an intelligence-gathering tool led to the increased use of code and the introduction of deceptive transmissions.[94]

The more primitive communications techniques were much slower, but also tended to be more reliable under combat conditions. Messengers, both foot and mounted, had the highest casualty rates of any job in the war, but they were fairly reliable under fire—especially when used with redundancy. Carrier pigeons and messenger dogs were widely used by both sides. The dogs were very reliable within a two-kilometer radius. The pigeons were relatively uninflu-enced by fire and gas, but they required clear weather and were only good for front-to-rear communications. Early in the war the Germans abandoned the use of signal flags, but the use of signal lamps and flares proved fairly effective in combat situations.[95]

All sides tried various ways to exercise effective command and control over a wide area with the primitive and slow communications technology of the day. The Allies generally tried to centralize both planning and execution at the highest levels, which in the end robbed subordinate commanders of all initiative and made it almost impossible to exploit rapidly tactical opportunities as they arose.[96] The Germans, on the other hand, retained a fairly high level of central-ized planning, but pushed the execution down the chain of command as far as possible—at least at the tactical level.

Contrary to the rigid and hierarchical nature of militaries in general, and German society in particular, the German Army developed and practiced several innovative and flexible command and staff techniques that many other armies have since tried to copy, but almost none have mastered. *Weisungsführung* (command by directive) allowed great latitude to higher-level subordinate commanders at the field army and in some situations at the corps level. Rather than issuing explicit and detailed orders, the OHL issued generalized statements of its intentions, which then provided the framework for independent initiative by the subordinate commanders. This technique capitalized on the local commander's superior knowledge of the situation to his front, and also compensated for the slow and unreliable communications systems of the day.

Weisungsführung could only work if the commanders and their staffs at all levels operated on the same set of principles and worked through the tactical decision-making process with the same set of intellectual tools. The General Staff officers at each echelon of command provided the common link to ensure that happened. Many critics over the years have dismissed this system as nothing more than groupthink on a huge scale; but such an assessment is far too simplistic and misses the main point entirely. The system did not produce perfect solutions every time, but it almost always produced workable solutions. And it produced them more quickly, which almost always gave the Germans a huge tactical advantage over their opponents.[97] As Bernhardi put it, "Acting with self-reliance in the sense and spirit of General Headquarters, and of the uniform plan of battle known to us, is the decisive factor in modern battle."[98]

Closely allied with *Weisungsführung* was the concept of *Vollmacht*, an authority usually delegated to a staff officer to issue orders and shift units without first consulting with the commander. This technique too compensated for slow communications, and placed great faith on the staff officer on the spot to make the correct decisions. *Vollmacht* was an emergency procedure, normally only used in a crisis situation. Most often a staff officer was specifically delegated *Vollmacht*, but in some rare situations he assumed and exercised it based on the situation. Military historians to this day still debate whether Lieutenant Colonel Richard Hentsch had *Vollmacht* or if he was just carrying a *Wiesung* (directive) to the First Army during the First Battle of the Marne in 1914.[99]

Following World War I, the Germans pushed the concept of *Weisungsführung* farther down the chain of command by expanding on the pre-war concept of *Auftragstaktik*. One of the most important military concepts of the 20th century, the term can be translated loosely to "mission-type orders," but there is no real English equivalent that adequately conveys the full meaning. *Auftragstaktik* is based on the principal that a commander should tell his subordinates what to do and when to do it by, but not necessarily tell them how to do it. In accomplishing their missions, subordinate commanders are given a wide degree of latitude and are expected to exercise great initiative.[100] Where *Weisungsführung* only entrusted commanders down to the field army or sometimes the corps level with broad discretionary powers in the execution of their missions, *Auftragstaktik* extended that principal down to the lowest squad leader and even, when necessary, to the individual soldier.

For *Auftragstaktik* to work, a subordinate leader or even a common soldier given a mission must fully understand his commander's intent (*Absicht*)—and in most cases, the intent of the next higher commander. This, of course, implies that the subordinate leader must understand "why." If he doesn't understand, he has the obligation to ask. Conversely, the superior leader issuing the order has the obligation to explain. Such a process does not fit the popular stereotype of military organizations in general, nor is it especially characteristic of German society. Although traditional German deference to higher authority and preference for well-defined procedures are the very antithesis of *Auftragstaktik*, the post-World War I German Army made it work to a degree unsurpassed by any other army in history—and its roots were deeply embedded in the institutional culture of the World War I German Army.

Another concept that was completely alien to most military hierarchies, and especially to class- and status-conscious German society, was the notion that function overrode rank.[101] The Germans routinely appointed officers to command and staff positions far above the actual rank they held. Once in the position, however, the officer functioned with the full authority of the position, regardless of the nominal ranks and pay grades of his functional subordinates. Corps chiefs of staff, who may have been lieutenant colonels, routinely passed orders unchallenged to general officers commanding subordinate divisions. During the final offensives in May through July 1918, Bruchmüller, though only a colonel, was designated as the artillery commander of the entire Western Front, while at the same time the typical army group artillery commander was a lieutenant general. Ludendorff himself never wore more than three stars.

German combat effectiveness

Conventional wisdom has long held that the attacker must achieve a three-to-one superiority over the defender, at least at the decisive point. Yet there was no way that the Germans could have achieved this level of superiority over the Allies in 1918—at least in terms of the raw numbers. In *On War* Clausewitz noted: "superiority of numbers admittedly is the most important factor in the outcome of an engagement so long as it is great enough to counterbalance all other contributing circumstances."[102] But then he also said: "Superior numbers, far from contributing everything, or even a substantial part, to victory, may actually be contributing very little, depending on the circumstances."[103] Thus, as Clausewitz indicated, raw numbers by themselves do not necessarily translate directly into relative combat power. His "other contributing circumstances" include factors such as weapons effectiveness, terrain, mobility, morale, and training.

There have been many attempts over the years to reduce all such factors to quantifiable variables or constants that can be applied to various formulae that would predict the outcome of a battle. Early in the 20th century aeronautical engineer Frederick W. Lancaster introduced his Linear and Square Laws on the principle of concentration in combat-aircraft design.[104] Fuller, among others, attempted to turn Lancaster's Equations into a more general model of combat. But Fuller added the caveat: "Superior moral or better tactics or a hundred and one other extraneous causes may intervene in practice to modify the issue, but this does not invalidate the mathematical statement."[105] Expressing frustration that Lancaster's Equations could not be made to fit any actual historical data, Trevor N. Dupuy went on to develop his highly controversial Quantified Judgement Model.[106] Somewhere in between Clausewitz and Dupuy lie the Soviet concepts of planning norms and correlation of forces, and the later Cold War NATO notions of force multipliers.

Although the outcome of combat still continues to defy precise mathematical prediction, few historians would deny that there was something especially effective about the German Army between 1870 and 1945—at least at the tactical level. Many books have been written on the subject, including Dupuy's *A Genius for War* and Martin van Creveld's *Fighting Power*, a comparative study of the German and U.S. armies between 1939 and 1945. In applying his Quantified Judgement Model to Operation MICHAEL in 1918, Dupuy concluded that the Germans were 78 percent more effective than the defenders in the phase of the battle that ran from 21 to 26 March; and 27 percent more effective than the defenders in the 27 March to 4 April phase.[107]

Why then was the German Army so tactically effective during a period stretching over almost seventy-five years? In popular myth the Germans in general, and the Prussians in particular, have a peculiarly warlike and militaristic national character. Dupuy challenged that myth by arguing that in the 130 years following the Napoleonic wars Germany was involved in six wars. France was involved in ten. Russia was involved in thirteen. Britain was involved in at least seventeen. And even the United States was involved in seven.[108] A corollary myth holds that the Prussian system, based on harsh discipline, produced soldiers who were efficient, but unimaginative and completely inflexible. That myth falls apart under even the most cursory level of historical scrutiny. In trying to answer why the Germans were so tactically innovative in World War I, Tim Travers identified four competing theories.[109]

One theory holds that Germany had more than its share of great tacticians and talented staff officers, among them Georg Bruchmüller, Hermann Geyer, Fritz von Lossberg, Max Bauer, Willy Rohr, and Georg Wetzell. This is a central argument in Wynne's *If Germany Attacks*, and is a variation on the "great man" theory of history. Another theory argues that doctrinal development in the German Army was a corporate process, supported by institutional excellence deeply ingrained in the German Army's culture. This is a central argument of Timothy Lupfer's *Dynamics of Doctrine* and many of Dupuy's books. Yet a third theory centers on the notion that necessity is the mother of invention. The Allies pursued a war of attrition based on their overall manpower and resources advantages. The Germans were forced by necessity into a policy of scarcity and therefore had to be more resourceful. This is an argument advanced by Norman Stone.[110]

Finally, Michael Geyer advanced a theory based on the relationship between the German Army, ideology, and society. The fundamental change in warfare became very clear around 1916 and coincided with the arrival of Ludendorff and the "machine culture" technocrats at OHL. But the German Army at that point was "locked into a procurement system, centered around heavy industry, that was hostile to new weapons systems, like tanks. . . . In the end, it proved easier to change the army than to crack the system of weapons procurement."[111] Geyer's theory supports Travers' basic arguments and there is a great deal of validity to what Geyer has to say about the German industrial system. What is debatable—especially in light of the 1920 report of Colonel Theobeck's commission—is the degree to which OHL actually converted to the technological/machine power paradigm of warfare.

There are elements of validity in all four of these theories. The Germans most certainly were forced by necessity to do things the Allies never had to. And as I argue in my book *Steel Wind*, Bruchmüller had a far greater (but by no means exclusive) influence over German artillery tactics than Lossberg, Geyer, or Rohr individually had over infantry tactics. Yet it was the corporate culture of the German Army and especially its General Staff system that allowed the lessons of war to be absorbed quickly and the doctrine and training to be changed accordingly.

For the Germans, the key test of doctrine was what worked on the battlefield. They saw doctrine as a means to an end, and not as an end in itself. Methodology was the key to the doctrine process. They paid close attention to cause-and-effect relationships and they did not cloak fuzzy doctrine in fancy terms and catch phrases.[112] As Corum pointed out, the very word doctrine (*Doktrin*) is not at all common in the German language; and when used it does not imply the sense of the "proper way to do things," as Americans tend to apply it to tactics.[113] Doctrine was not some sort of sacred talisman, as *attaque à l'outrance* was for the French. Prior to launching his disastrous offensives in 1917, French General Robert Nivelle triumphantly proclaimed, "We have the formula!"[114] In his war diaries published after the war, Crown Prince Rupprecht of Bavaria wrote: "There is no panacea. A formula is harmful. Everything must be applied based on the situation."[115] Despite his reputation as the ultimate Prussian, stiff-necked, rigid, and unimaginative, Ludendorff was a flexible and innovative tactician who presided over one of the most remarkable doctrinal transformations in the history of war. It was even more remarkable for the speed with which it was carried out, the training necessary to make it all work, and the fact that the whole process was executed amidst the chaos of the greatest war in history up to that time.

Despite Ludendorff's overpowering personality, he did not monopolize or dominate the process of tactical reform. Rather, he encouraged and fostered a spirit of corporate effort and tolerated a remarkable degree of dissent within his group of talented staff officers.[116] In the end, however, the Germans in World War I were never able to escape the long shadow of the *Vernichtungsprinzip*—and it cost them dearly at the operational level.

German defensive tactics

Although this study focuses on the great German offensives of 1918, a brief review of the development of German defensive tactics will prove beneficial for several reasons. First, it provides insight into the German process of tactical doctrine revision that started first with the defensive, and then moved to the offensive. Second, Allied errors in applying the new defensive tactics, despite having grappled with them throughout much of 1917, contributed significantly to the German success in the March, April, and May offensives. Third, by June and July 1918 the Allies had almost completely adopted the German defensive tactics, which contributed in no small measure to the failure of the last offensive, MARNESCHUTZ–REIMS.[117] And fourth, any evaluation of the HAGEN attack plan must be made on the assumption that the British would have been using the new defensive tactics.

While he was chief of the General Staff at OHL, General Erich von Falkenhayn pursued a ruthless strategy of exploiting the Allies' tactical doctrine of conducting rigid defenses with the bulk of their forces packed into the forward trenches. In those positions they became just so many targets for German firepower. Oddly enough, Falkenhayn himself followed the same defensive doctrine, insisting that German commanders hold the front line at all costs. There were two schools of thought among the staff officers at OHL, however. The debate revolved around where the defensive battle should actually be fought—at the front line or behind it? Many of the junior officers at OHL, including Bauer and Geyer, favored a flexible defense fought behind the front line. Lossberg favored the rigid defense fought at the front line.[118] As one of the few officers at OHL with direct combat experience, Lossberg believed his OHL colleagues were too prone to overestimate the capabilities of combat units and underestimate the problems of front-line combat.[119]

When the British attacked on the Somme in 1916, OHL posted Lossberg as chief of staff of the German Second Army (later re-designated the First Army). During his time on the Somme, Lossberg determined that it took anywhere between eight and ten hours for a message to travel one way in either direction between a divisional headquarters and the front line. The tactical situation usually changed drastically in the time that it took for information to flow up and the corresponding orders to flow back down. Lossberg concluded that the only way to improve tactical responsiveness was to give the front-line battalion commanders total control of their own sectors. The higher headquarters, then, had the obligation to support the front-line commanders' decisions. The battalion commander would also have operational control of any reinforcements committed to his sector, regardless of the size of the reinforcing unit or its commander's rank. This approach ensured continuity of command and exploited the front-line battalion commander's superior knowledge of the terrain and the situation.[120]

Lossberg's innovations effectively shortened the chain of command. Under this system, the regimental commander became a manager of reinforcements and logistical support. At the next higher levels the role of the divisional commanders mirrored that of the front-line battalion commanders. The divisions controlled everything in their sectors without having to get permission from the corps. When a reinforcing division was committed, it came under the operational control of the commander of the reinforced division.[121]

When Ludendorff arrived at OHL in late 1916 he immediately initiated a complete review of the way the German Army fought. The resulting reform process incorporated many of Lossberg's innovations. On 1 December 1916, OHL published the German Army's new defensive doctrine as *Principles of Command in the Defensive Battle in Position Warfare (Grundsätze für die Abwehrschlacht im Stellungskrieg)*. The manual was based on lessons learned and actual practice, and it was compiled and written primarily by Bauer and Geyer.[122] As early as September 1916, several months before the new manual was in print, the Germans were conducting a special month-long course in the new tactics for company and battery commanders.[123]

The new doctrine can best be described as flexible defense, or flexible defense-in-depth. It rested on three key principles: Flexibility, Decentralized Control, and Counterattack. While the command and control of the Allied attacks became centralized at ever-higher levels, German commanders in the defense had an impressive amount of autonomy. A front-line battalion commander had the authority to withdraw from forward positions under pressure as he saw fit. More importantly, he had the authority to order the remaining battalions of his regiment (positioned to his rear) into the counterattack when he judged the timing right.

The Germans recognized two distinct types of counterattacks. The hasty counterattack (*Gegenstoss*) was immediate and violent, designed to hit the attacking enemy immediately, before he had a chance to consolidate his newly won position or move up reinforcements. Locally planned and executed, the *Gegenstoss* was launched on the initiative of the front-line battalion commander. The deliberate counterattack (*Gegenangriff*) was centrally planned and more methodically prepared. It was only used when a *Gegenstoss* had failed or was unfeasible. Most importantly for our study, the counterattack tactics developed during this period had a great influence on the later development of the offensive tactics.

The Germans organized their positions into three zones. The Outpost Zone (*Vorfeldzone*) was 500 to 1,000 meters in depth, and manned with sparsely located early-warning positions. The Battle Zone (*Kampffeld*), was up to 2,000 meters deep. And the Rearward Zone (*Hinterzone*), was where the reserves and counterattack units were held, often in deep, reinforced bunkers. The leading edge of the Battle Zone was the Main Line of Resistance (*Hauptwiderstandslinie*), with three or more successive trench lines. Between the Battle Zone and the Rearward Zone came another line of multiple trenches that served as the protective line for the artillery. The Germans also decreased the strength of the forward positions. While the French were putting two-thirds of their combat strength into the first two lines, the Germans put only 20 percent into the same positions. The Germans even came to regard their forward-most trenches as useful only in quiet periods. During an artillery bombardment prior to an Allied attack, the forces in the rear would move into their deep protected bunkers to ride out the storm. The troops in the thinly held Outpost Zone would slip out of their trenches and take cover in nearby shell-holes—while the Allied artillery pounded the empty trenches.[124]

When the Germans withdrew to the Hindenburg Line (which they called the *Siegfriedstellung*) in early 1917, they added a new twist to the flexible defense-in-depth. The Germans planned this withdrawal very carefully, and made extensive preparations of their new positions before occupying them. In as many places along the line as possible, the trenches of the main line of resistance were sited on high ground on the reverse slope facing away from the Allies. The concept of reverse-slope defense ran counter to tactical conventional wisdom of the time because it did not make optimal use of the maximum range of the machine gun. Actually, the technique gave the defender significant advantages. It placed his positions out of the line of sight of the attacker's base position, thereby complicating the attacker's communications and the coordination of his artillery. At the same time, those positions remained within the line of sight of the defender's rear positions and artillery, giving the defending commanders the advantage in knowing where and when to move reserves and to counterattack.[125]

By the latter half of 1917 the Germans started distinguishing between two types of divisions with different tactical functions. The defensive positions in the line were manned by "trench divisions" (*Stellungsdivisionen*). Farther back in the operational rear the Germans positioned their "attack divisions" (*Angriffsdivisionen*) to conduct the larger-scale, deliberate counterattacks. When the Germans went over to the offensive in 1918 this distinction played a key role, with an entire attacking corps moving up into a sector of the line that had been held by a single trench division.[126]

German offensive tactics

As previously noted, Captain André Laffargue's May 1915 pamphlet, *The Attack in Trench Warfare*, advocated many of the tactical techniques that later came to be associated with German storm troop, or infiltration tactics. The Germans, however, did not capture and translate a copy of the pamphlet until the summer of 1916, well after they had started their own experiments with new attack tactics.

Captain Willy Rohr was one of the earliest leaders in the development of the new offensive tactics. In August 1915 Rohr took command of the recently formed storm troop assault detachment (*Sturmabteilung*) on the Western Front. Under Rohr the assault detachment conducted very successful counterattacks, using non-linear tactics drawn from the traditional tactics of the German *Jäger* units. The basic unit for such operations was the assault squad (*Stosstrupp*). Armed with grenades, automatic weapons, trench mortars, and flamethrowers, their tactics and techniques were very similar to those suggested by Laffargue.[127]

Rohr's detachment eventually grew into a *Sturmbattalion*. After the initial attacks at Verdun, the Fifth Army started using Rohr's battalion as a training unit during the lulls in the fighting. In May 1916, at Bauer's suggestion, Falkenhayn directed selected Western-Front units to spend fourteen days training with Rohr's battalion. When Ludendorff arrived at OHL he expanded the program. By January 1917 each German field army had an assault company. By the end of 1917 each field army had an assault battalion that functioned as a training cadre.[128]

These special assault units became known as storm troops (*Stosstruppen*). The storm battalions were one of the earliest forms of a true combined-arms task force. Typically their structure included: three to four infantry companies; a trench mortar company; an accompanying artillery battery; a flamethrower section; a signal section; and a pioneer section.[129] Meanwhile, by March 1917 the standard German infantry squad was restructured around a seven-man team as a maneuver element, and a four-man light machine gun team as the fire element.[130]

By 1917 Rohr's infiltration tactics became the official counterattack doctrine on the Western Front. In September 1917 the Germans made their first attempt to apply the tactics to a large-scale offensive operation—on the Eastern Front at Riga. Instead of the typical attack formations of rigid lines, the German Eighth Army of General Oskar von Hutier attacked in fluid leaps and bounds, with one element moving forward while another element provided fire cover. Then the two elements would reverse roles and leapfrog each other. The forward-most units completely bypassed the defender's strong points, isolating them and leaving them for heavier follow-on forces to eliminate. Reserves were only used to reinforce success, rather than being thrown in where the attack was faltering.

Riga was also the first time the new infantry tactics were combined with the new artillery tactics developed by Bruchmüller on the Eastern Front. The Germans also used similar tactics during their successful attack at Caporetto the following month. The new tactics, or more precisely their results, shocked the Western Allies. The French, in particular, looked for a single tactical mastermind as the source of the new tactics and settled on Hutier. Thus they somewhat erroneously dubbed the new German tactics "Hutier Tactics."[131]

The Cambrai counterattack on 30 November 1917 was the first large-scale use of storm troop tactics on the Western Front. The twenty-division counterattack was almost as successful as the British mass tank attack ten days earlier. On 1 January 1918 OHL formally issued the new offensive doctrine, *The Attack in Position Warfare (Der Angriff im Stellungskrieg)*, with Geyer again as the principal compiler.[132] The new manual followed very closely the after-action report issued by Crown Prince Rupprecht's Army Group, *Lessons of the Cambrai Counteroffensive*.[133]

The new doctrine envisioned the attack in two main phases: first, a methodical assault against the enemy's organized positions, which required detailed preparation and centralized control; and then an aggressive continuation of the attack to prevent the enemy's ability to reorganize and respond. The second phase was characterized by decentralized execution and initiative on the part of the subordinate commanders. This phase began in the intermediate zone, beyond the range of the creeping barrage. In the attack, as opposed to the defense, the higher echelons maintained tighter control of the follow-on forces.[134]

The flanks of the attacking elements would be secured by speed and depth. The immediate objective of the attack was to penetrate as far as possible into the enemy positions, at a minimum reaching and overrunning the enemy's artillery positions on the first day. The new doctrine stressed infantry–artillery coordination and the need to move artillery forward to sustain the attack. Artillery neutralization fire was emphasized over destruction. The intent was to disrupt the enemy's communications, and bypass and isolate his strong points. The new doctrine marked a key conceptual shift from destruction to large-scale disruption—which is one of the basics of the operational art.[135]

While the Allies attacked in successive waves, in order to relieve the pressure on their lead units, the Germans continued to press the attack with the lead units in order to maintain momentum. This, of course, burned out the lead units quickly.[136] Thinking in terms of the *Vernichtungsschlacht*, this approach might have made sense. But within a framework of sequential operations, it was counter-productive and had serious consequences for the Germans after March 1918.

The Germans never lost sight of the chaotic nature of warfare or the need for front-line initiative and leadership. Thus *The Attack in Position Warfare* contained passages that would be the basis for what later evolved into *Auftragstaktik*, and passages that would be reproduced almost verbatim in the 1933–1934 German operations manual *Truppenführung*.[137]

> Every attack offers the opportunity for initiative and decisive action at all levels down to the individual soldier.[138]

> Everything depends on rapid, independent action by all echelons within the framework of the whole.[139]

The Germans considered the division the basic unit capable of conducting independent battlefield operations. In 1916 they reconfigured all their divisions from the square to the more flexible triangular structure. As noted above, they started distinguishing between trench and attack divisions in 1917. The *Angriffsdivisionen* started out as counterattack units, and eventually evolved into the principal units for the 1918 offensives. The best trained and best equipped of the attack divisions were classified in 1918 as mobile divisions (*Mob. Divisionen*).[140] Essentially they became entire storm troop divisions, but their standards and training were not as high as original assault battalions. Divisions were converted by being pulled out of the line and put through three to four weeks of special training at Sedan or Valenciennes.[141] Only half the heavy machine gun units of the *Angriffsdivisionen* were horse-drawn because of the shortage of animals. By March 1918 only fifty-six out of 192 German divisions on the Western Front were classified as attack divisions. Ludendorff later came to regret the decision to have two different divisional structures.[142]

4   The strategic reality

Superiority of numbers in a given engagement is only one of the factors that determine victory.

The forces available must be employed with such skill that even in the absence of absolute superiority, relative superiority is attained at the decisive point.[1]

Major General Carl von Clausewitz

All the theories of Clausewitz should be thrown overboard. Both war and politics are meant to serve the preservation of the people, but war is the highest expression of the national will to live, and politics must, therefore, be subordinate to the conduct of war.[2]

General of Infantry Erich Ludendorff

By the end of 1917 almost no level of tactical or operational virtuosity could have saved Germany from military defeat. Going into World War I, the German military had a deeply flawed understanding of the strategic level of war, and that view became even more muddled when Ludendorff came to power. Germany's basic geopolitical disadvantage, combined with its Byzantine and incompetent internal political institutions and structures, resulted in shifting and incoherent war aims throughout the conflict. As the war entered its final year, the Germans made the decision to shift to the strategic and operational offensive in the west, resulting in the Ludendorff offensives.

German concepts of strategy

Clausewitz unambiguously stated that war is an instrument of national policy.[3] That fundamental concept, however, was resisted by many German soldiers in the 19th century—to the point where the second edition (1853) of *On War* was deliberately changed.[4] Although German operational thinking may have been "realist" in its approach, it was built on a strategic foundation that flowed from early 19th-century philosophies about war and the state. The German approach to strategy depended on the autonomy of the military as distinct and separate from civilian society. Strategy remained separate from military doctrine, which established the guidelines for the best use of weapons and troops. The former was the domain of politicians, the latter the domain of soldiers. Such strategic thinking, however, increasingly came under pressure with the rise of mass armies.[5]

Moltke the Elder saw things a little more clearly. Understanding that in 1871 Germany had achieved only a semi-hegemony on the Continent, Moltke did not believe that future wars could be decided by single battles. Any level of military victory would require political diplomacy to re-establish peace. Agreeing with Clausewitz, Moltke stated firmly that war and strategy served politics.[6]

Schlieffen, on the other hand, rejected the concepts of Moltke. Schlieffen believed that France was the most immediate threat to Germany, and therefore had to be the target of a quick knockout blow. This also meshed with the belief of the military élites of all countries at the time that war had to be limited, and thus controlled. That, of course, kept war in the professional domain. Schlieffen's solutions were the concepts of *Vernichtungsschlacht* and *Gesamtschlacht*.[7] (See Chapter 2, "The Operational Art.")

The so-called Schlieffen Plan of 1905 was not in fact a war plan, rather it was a memo to his successor that Schlieffen penned upon leaving office. In keeping with the practices of the German General Staff, the actual war plan in effect when Schlieffen retired was revised and modified every succeeding year as the strategic and diplomatic situation shifted. Schlieffen's successor Moltke the Younger has been severely criticized for tampering with this supposed master plan. The truth is that the plan of 1905 would not have addressed the realities of 1914.[8]

Nonetheless, the German war plan that existed in 1914 was still firmly grounded in Schlieffen's principles and assumptions. The German plan, however, was not a comprehensive plan for war, covering all political, military, and economic aspects. Rather, it was a large-scale mobilization and deployment plan for German ground forces only. The plan's rigid timetable left no flexibility for diplomacy, and it also pitted the German weakness of lack of motor transport against the enemy strength of interior rail lines. It also ignored Moltke's famous dictum that no plan survives first contact with the enemy. The plan showed Schlieffen's disregard for the consequences of violating Belgian neutrality, which he assumed would be violated by France or Britain first. The plan also seemed to ignore the importance of the British Empire and its major instrument of military policy, the Royal Navy.[9]

The German war plan appears to have been developed by the Great General Staff almost in a vacuum. There had been no coordination with the Foreign Office, even over the tripwire issue of violating Belgian neutrality. Displaying the same ineptitude for coalition warfare that would continue to plague the Germans in World War II, there was no real effort to integrate Germany's strategy with that of its Austro-Hungarian ally, with each side assuming the other would bear the major burden in dealing with Russia.[10] Nor was there any real coordination with the German Navy. Admiral Tirpitz apparently never even studied the possibility of basing the High Seas Fleet in the French Atlantic ports if the "Schlieffen Plan" had succeeded. In 1914 the Royal Navy moved eight

British divisions across the Channel without any attempt at interference from the German Navy.[11] Referring to the overall influence of German naval power on the strategic situation, Admiral Reinhard Scheer wrote in his post-war memoirs: "But so far as can be seen from the course of the war, no material change was made in the fundamental principles underlying our strategic operations on land."[12]

The two years following the failure of the "Schlieffen Plan" were character-ized by a general lack of purpose in military operations.[13] Once it became clear that a decisive victory was beyond their grasp, German military planners were at a loss as how to use the manpower and weapons at their disposal. Any approach to German strategy was made more complex by the Byzantine world of German military administration, which divided command functions and administrative responsibilities among the Prussian War Ministry, the Kaiser's Military Cabinet, and the Great General Staff. Add the head of government, the Chancellor, to the equation and it was a recipe for chaos. In theory, any differences of opinion over policy fell to the King-Emperor to resolve.[14] In the case of Frederick the Great the system might have worked. But in the case of Wilhelm II it was a disaster waiting to happen, especially when Ludendorff stepped onto center stage in the autumn of 1916.

Ludendorff and strategy

Despite the many books that have been written declaring Ludendorff to be something of a military genius, he fell far short of that level. As Holger Herwig wrote, "The truth is that Ludendorff never rose above the intellectual level of a regimental colonel commanding infantry."[15] Ludendorff was a direct reflection of the institutional strengths and weaknesses of the Imperial German Army. He was intelligent, disciplined, driven, and focused. Yet he also represented every-thing negative that the older generation of German officers saw in the rising gen-eration at the turn of the century: he was bourgeois by birth, specialist by training, and boorish and materialistic by instinct. Yet he was also ambitious.

In August 1916 Hindenburg was appointed the chief of the General Staff at OHL in the west, and Ludendorff went with him as his deputy with the title First Quartermaster General. Despite their formal titles, they were the de facto com-mander and chief of staff of the German Army in the field. Yet, despite his stiff-necked and rigid personality, Ludendorff between late 1916 and early 1918 presided over a complete overhaul of German tactical doctrine.[16] There can be no doubt that Ludendorff was a gifted tactician. His abilities and performance at the operational and strategic levels are an entirely different matter, however. Ludendorff apparently believed that a local tactical victory, merely breaking the enemy's line somewhere, was all that was necessary for the Allied armies to dis-integrate and then surrender.[17] He was bewildered by the storm of criticism that greeted his post-war comment that "Tactics had to be raised above pure strat-egy."[18] Thus Ludendorff and Hindenburg ushered in a period in which German strategic thinking declined, while strategic expectations grew. Tactics reigned supreme, and operational planning and strategy were reduced to the management of weapons, men, and resources.[19]

In the attempt to exercise increasingly tighter control over all aspects of Germany's wartime economy and society, Ludendorff and his close circle at OHL forced through three successive measures that not only failed to achieve their stated intent, but actually caused greater chaos, inefficiency, and losses at the time when Germany could least afford them. The measures also established and extended Ludendorff's "Silent Dictatorship" over the German nation.

Almost as soon as Hindenburg and Ludendorff arrived at OHL, one of their first steps was an attempt to bring Germany's already chaotic war production under control. Introduced on 31 August 1916, the Hindenburg Program expanded munitions production by calling for a 100 percent increase in ammunition and trench mortars and a 300 percent increase in artillery and machine guns by the spring of 1917. The program also required substantial increases in aircraft and antiaircraft artillery; the culling of the labor force for military service; and tighter controls over production and raw materials. The Prussian War Ministry had previously blocked similar programs that OHL's Colonel Max Bauer attempted to push through.[20]

Enthusiastically supported by heavy industry, the Hindenburg Program amounted to a virtual end to civil government in Germany.

Industry's only complaint was that it did not have the necessary manpower needed to carry out the program. Hindenburg responded by offering to release large numbers of skilled workers from the army. By the winter of 1916–1917, some 125,000 soldiers had been released from the front lines. The result was a decline in the average strength of a front-line infantry battalion from 750 to 713.[21]

The major flaw in the Hindenburg Program was the inability of OHL or any other organization to exercise the necessary controls. The decision to direct all available resources to conventional artillery and machine gun production closed off the development potentials of the tank and antitank weapons. The program did nothing to rationalize weapons production. In 1914 German factories were producing fourteen different models of artillery. By April 1917 they were producing seventy-seven models; and by January 1918, 100 different models.[22]

On 1 November 1916 the control of all raw materials, labor, and munitions was brought under the General War Office (*Allgemeines Kriegsamt*), headed by General Wilhelm Groener. The War Office was established essentially to manage the Hindenburg Program. Although Ludendorff wanted the War Office to report directly to OHL, he lost that battle and it came under the Ministry of War. But at Ludendorff's insistence, the Minister of War was replaced by General Hermann von Stein, who was under Ludendorff's thumb.[23] The War Office proved to be little more than another layer on top of Germany's already chaotic bureaucratic structure. It was a Prussian institution and it had no real authority over the non-Prussian War Ministries. Bavaria, Saxony, and Württemberg all set up their own independent War Offices and sent representatives to the Prussian War Office.[24]

As the war progressed, Ludendorff became increasingly obsessed with the

problem of the "cohesion of the people," and in harnessing all Germany's physical and psychological resources to the war effort. In December 1916 Ludendorff introduced the draft of the Auxiliary Service Law (*Hilfsdienstgesetz*) to the
government and insisted on its prompt passage. Drafted by Groener, the law
made every German male between the ages of seventeen and sixty liable for
some form of involuntary wartime service.[25] Groener did convince Ludendorff
to drop his initial demands for compulsory female labor, but by June 1918
Ludendorff was again renewing those demands.[26] In October 1917 Ludendorff
pushed his control over civilian labor a notch higher by notifying Chancellor
Theobald von Bethmann Hollweg that it was essential to begin restricting the
freedom of movement of civilian workers. The mechanism to enforce the new
restrictions would be the 1851 Law of Siege.[27]

These measures all failed to produce their intended results, and even Ludendorff came to recognize the Auxiliary Service Law's negative effects: "not
merely insufficient but positively harmful in operation."[28] The number of soldiers freed for duty at the front by the Auxiliary Service Law never equaled the
number of soldiers released from the front required by the Hindenburg
Program.[29] Ludendorff's entire life to that point had been focused on military
matters to the exclusion of almost all else. He had the German military officer's
traditional total disdain for politics, either internal or external. It can be little
wonder, then, that he displayed a stunning ineptitude from late 1916 on whenever he meddled in internal or external political affairs. Almost everything he
touched in the political, economic, or technical arenas turned to ashes.

The shifting German war aims

A coherent strategy is impossible without a clearly defined end state, yet the
German government entered World War I without specific aims. After the initial
German military victories in the east, expansionist elements in Germany began
pushing for wide-ranging war aims. For most of the war, however, the government purposely left the question of war aims vague, hiding behind the fiction of
a defensive war that no one really believed. At first, Chancellor Bethmann
Hollweg actually believed that clearly defined war aims would restrict Germany's
freedom of action. Later, he came to believe that ambiguous war aims would
facilitate a negotiated peace. This lack of clearly defined war aims flowed from
Germany's deeper and most critical domestic problem, the need for internal
governmental and social reform.[30]

By the middle of 1917, the direction of foreign policy had slipped completely
away from the political leadership and into the inexperienced hands of Ludendorff
and OHL. After Ludendorff assumed power, German war aims remained out-
wardly ambiguous, but there was little doubt about his expansionist outlook.
Ludendorff firmly believed that the average German soldier would keep fighting
only for expansive war aims. He also believed that control of the Belgian coast
was vital to Germany's strategic survival. But Belgian independence was as
important a war aim for Britain as regaining Alsace and Lorraine was for France.[31]

By the winter of 1917 German politics were completely polarized. The parties of the left and labor supported a "Schiedemann Peace," without annexations or reparations. The parties of the right, OHL, and the monarchy demanded a "Hindenburg Peace," with vast annexations and large indemnities. In the east, Ludendorff rejected any moderate settlement, demanding a peace that would dismember Russia and annex its border states. He believed this would better position Germany for a future war in the east; provide settlement and expansion areas for Germans; and provide a buffer against the Slavic hordes.[32]

The basic position of OHL was stated in an estimate of the situation published on 30 September 1917.[33] Written by Major Georg Wetzell, the head of OHL's Operations Section, the position paper focused not so much on the present war, but on Germany's need to position itself for a future war. "When one surveys this political situation in its larger aspects, it develops that, from a military viewpoint, we cannot come out of this peace strong enough by any means." Wetzell clearly saw Britain as the major threat of the future. "If England does not emerge from the war as the victor, then we have the first basis for a decisive future war between Germany and England." Although he was off by some seventy-five years, Wetzell predicted the construction of a Channel tunnel—perhaps two—linking Britain to the Continent. Seen primarily as a means to move military forces, Wetzell estimated that a four-track tunnel was capable of moving 160 trains, or one corps, in a twenty-four-hour period.

In order to respond to any military threat to its west, Wetzell wrote, "The German Army must be in a position to concentrate on the line Ostend–Metz–Strasbourg, with the center of gravity behind the right wing. (Upper Alsace should be defended by fortifying the Voges.)" Thus, "Our future military needs would not be satisfied if Belgium should remain a free state in any form, and we should perchance be restricted to the line of the Meuse." This led to the conclusion: "It is absolutely necessary that we force through the military requirement that we be able to use Belgium as a concentration area."

Wetzell is one of the more controversial figures of the last half of the war, and opinions on him were and are deeply divided. For a long time Ludendorff placed great faith in Wetzell, but Kuhl had a low opinion of his skills as a military planner.[34] Nonetheless, Wetzell's 30 September assessment was the basis for Ludendorff's war aims in the west, at least up until the failure of Operation BLÜCHER in May 1918. After that point, Ludendorff seemed to indicate to OHL's liaison officer at the German Foreign Office, Colonel Hans von Haeften, that he was willing to compromise on Belgium.[35] But because of Ludendorff's obsession with holding on to all of Germany's military gains, he never seriously considered using Belgium or Alsace and Lorraine as bargaining chips in return for a free hand in the east.[36]

Germany's overall strategic posture in World War I

Germany entered World War I burdened by many serious strategic handicaps. Some of these handicaps were beyond Germany's control, the result of geography, demographics, economics, and technology in the first decades of the 20th century. Many of Germany's handicaps, however, were self-inflicted. Both categories of handicaps became exacerbated as the course of the war progressed.

Germany's geopolitical handicap

Many historians argue that by any application of the principles of economics, international politics, and military history, Germany never stood a chance of winning World War I. Liddell Hart, on the other hand, believed that, with Germany's strong position in central Europe, there was little France, Britain, and Italy by themselves could have done to impose a military defeat. Even the British naval blockade, he argued, would have been of only limited effectiveness without American involvement in the war.[37] Nonetheless, Germany stood against a large portion of the world, only supported by three weak allies, Austria-Hungary, Turkey, and Bulgaria. While Germany's population outnumbered that of France by sixty-seven million to forty million, the combined Allied population totaled 378 million.[38]

With limited access to the sea, Germany was fighting a war on two fronts—or even three, counting Italy, the Balkans, and the Middle East. Because of Germany's and Britain's relative positions to the sea, Britain could impose a naval blockade on Germany without causing undue harm to neutrals. Germany could not do the same. France and Britain could carry on trade with the United States, Germany could not. Correlli Barnett argued that geography was the determining factor in which side America eventually would fight: "Pro-Allied sentiment alone would not have brought her in."[39]

Unrestricted submarine warfare and the German Navy

The German Navy and its High Seas Fleet are one of the great "what ifs" of World War I. Unfortunately for the German Navy, World War I started eight years too early. Admiral Alfred von Tirpitz's master plan to challenge the Royal Navy was programmed out through 1922.[40] Even if the building program had been completed, the High Seas Fleet would have had great difficulty challenging the Royal Navy globally. The majority of the German Navy's ships were designed for a decisive engagement in the North Sea, and thus did not have the range to sortie beyond the Dover Straits. Lacking the ability to refuel at sea, they would have had to anchor somewhere near Scotland, Norway, or the Faeroes to have the fuel aboard for combat or to escape when operating west of Great Britain, much less in the North Atlantic.

The design of the German ships was driven by the assumption that in time of war the British would impose a traditional close blockade. Instead, the British opted for a far blockade using patrolling cruisers. Geography favored the British. By closing the sea entrances in the Channel, the North Sea, and the narrow straits north of the British Isles, Germany could be isolated effectively.[41] The naval blockade in turn meant that, despite her strong central position,

Germany could not remain on the defensive indefinitely. Without some sort of military decision, the naval blockade increasingly dominated the military situation. As Liddell Hart put it, "The all-pervading factor of the blockade intruded into every consideration of the military situation."[42]

Prior to the end of the 19th century, Prussia/Germany had never been known as a sea power and had little naval tradition. But after Wilhelm II succeeded to the throne, Germany in the 1890s began an aggressive program of naval expansion clearly intended to challenge the supremacy of Britain. The resulting Anglo-German Naval Arms Race was one of the principal causes of World War I. As late as the 1880s, Germany and Britain had been on fairly good terms. But as Otto von Bismarck had predicted, a German naval buildup quickly pushed Britain into an alliance with France.

The German naval buildup consumed vast amounts of national resources. The German Navy's budget grew from 20 percent of the Army's in 1898, to 53 percent in 1911. But once World War I started and the Germans realized that the High Seas Fleet was incapable of directly attacking the blockading forces, they were also unwilling to risk a direct confrontation with the Grand Fleet. Thus, the German Navy spent most of World War I as a mere "fleet-in-being."[43] This, in turn, tied up vast resources that could have been put to better use in other sectors of the war effort, especially steel and manpower. Germany continued to build battleships and other large fleet units right to the end of the war, when it should have been apparent after Jutland that other than U-boats, no new naval construction was needed or justified. The last battleship (*Württemberg*) was launched in June 1917; the last battlecruiser (*Graf Spee*) was launched in September 1917; and the last light cruiser (*Frauenlob*) was launched in October 1918. On 1 October 1918, forty-two days before the end of the war, the German Navy initiated the Scheer Program, which was supposed to be a naval equivalent to the Hindenburg Program.[44]

As early as 1912 Winston Churchill accurately called the German Navy the "Luxury Fleet." How many tanks could have been built instead of a battlecruiser, or even a light cruiser? That is a question that would not make much sense today, because of the vastly different manufacturing technologies involved in shipbuilding and armored combat-vehicle production. In 1917 and 1918, however, the manufacturing technologies for the two types of weapon systems were not all that different. Even in World War II the construction of a Tirpitz-class battleship required 8,000 tons of armor plate, enough to equip a Panzer division. Perhaps the most useless of the High Seas Fleet's units were its twenty-one pre-Dreadnought battleships. Their combined crews alone (728 officers and 13,205 men) could have filled an additional army division. (Germany finished the war with nineteen Dreadnoughts.)[45]

The requirements of coastal defense alone did not justify the size of the High Seas Fleet. In 1914 the German Navy had 80,000 officers and men, enough to man six to seven army divisions.[46] As the war progressed the German Navy had almost as many men tied up in coastal defenses as it did in the fleet. Germany maintained heavy fortifications along its North Sea coast, and from 1915 it heavily fortified the Belgian coast, garrisoned by three divisions of naval infantry.[47]

As the war on the Continent developed, Britain's "contemptible little army" became the backbone of the Allies' fighting power. Yet Britain itself remained largely invulnerable to direct attack. German military leaders increasingly came to see indirect attack through unrestricted submarine warfare in the Atlantic as the solution to that problem. With an apparent strategic stalemate both on land and at sea after Jutland, the submarine campaign also seemed the only way of averting defeat by slow starvation.[48] Bethmann Hollweg opposed the submarine campaign because he was sure it would bring America into the war. Admiral Henning von Holtzendorff, chief of the Admiralty Staff and one of the main proponents of the campaign, informed OHL in October 1916 that the campaign would decisively defeat Britain within six months, well before America could influence the war on land.

During the debate the German Navy argued (quite incorrectly) that America did not have sufficient shipping of its own to transport its forces, and would have to rely on British shipping, which was already stretched to the limit. Ludendorff believed that it would take America at least a year to train and deploy even five or six divisions, and he generally dismissed the combat capabilities of American units.[49] Betraying his characteristic political and strategic ineptitude, Ludendorff later wrote that he regretted that the internal debate over the submarine campaign had become a political issue, because he considered it "a purely military matter."[50]

The campaign started on 1 February 1917. The U-boats sank 436,000 tons of shipping in February, 603,000 tons in March, and 841,000 tons in April.[51] On 6 April America declared war. President Wilson skillfully used the incredible German mishandling of the Zimmermann Telegram to overcome the traditional isolationism of many Americans. In May the British initiated convoy procedures, and the sinkings started falling. By the summer they were down to 350,000 tons per month. By November 1917 the United States had 100,000 troops in France. Despite claims by Holtzendorff that the United States could at best have only 300,000 troops in Europe by the end of 1918, the U.S. actually had 1.98 million on the Continent by the end of the war. The U-boats had not managed to sink a single American troop ship.[52]

The submarine campaign was a total failure. As early as 20 June 1917 Wetzell concluded in a staff study that the U-boats would not seriously restrict the arrival of American troops.[53] Rather than winning the war for Germany, the U-boat campaign turned into another sinkhole for precious resources. First priority on the supply of raw materials had gone to submarine construction, but by 1918 U-boat loss rates were rising.[54] Average U-boat life expectancy was only six patrols. During the war the Germans built 344 U-boats, but by mid-1917 150 had been lost.[55]

Despite a successful amphibious operation against the Russian-controlled Baltic islands of Moon, Ösel, and Dagö in October 1917 (Operation ALBION), there was little that the High Seas Fleet could contribute to the war effort by

1918. Sailors on some of the High Seas Fleet's capital ships mutinied in August 1917. They would do so again in late October 1918, triggering the final chain of events in Germany's collapse. By 1918 the High Seas Fleet had only limited capability to interdict the British Army's Channel ports. British convoys crossed the Channel in two to four hours and had airship and aircraft support. Convoys were heavily escorted and protected behind a triple-layer minefield.

After 1916 submarines, mines, coastal artillery, and naval aviation were the German Navy's only effective weapons in the west. Had these assets been directed against the BEF's lines of communications (LOCs) in the Channel in coordination with a focused ground attack against the BEF's rail network, the British might well have been forced to withdraw from the Continent. The German submarine threat against their sea LOCs was a constant concern to the British, and one of the objectives behind the bloody battle of Passchendaele was to clear the Channel coast of the U-boat bases.[56]

German mines in the Channel could have been delivered by air or by submarine. The Navy's Freidreichshafen bomber was capable of carrying and dropping 750-kilogram naval mines. One such mine, in fact, sank a Russian destroyer during the Baltic Islands operation. Submarines were the other way to lay mines, with the UC-class boats specifically designed as minelayers.[57] By the start of 1918, the Germans had forty-two operational fleet U-boats; sixty-six operational coastal U-boats (UB-class); and thirty-three operational UC-class minelayers. The British, of course, had the Channel heavily mined, which increased the hazards of any U-boat operations.[58] The Germans, nonetheless, had a capability to lay mines in the Channel and at least disrupt that leg of the BEF's LOCs.

On 14 February 1918, the German Navy did launch one major and largely successful surface raid against British defenses between Dover and Calais. The Heinecke Torpedo Boat Flotilla sank twenty-eight British picket ships and other vessels, including an older cruiser. That raid, however, was never followed up. Nor had it been coordinated with OHL, rather it had been launched at the request of the naval corps in Flanders.[59] Even after the failure of Operation MICHAEL in March 1918, General Ferdinand Foch still thought that increased submarine operations in the Channel posed a serious threat to cutting off the BEF.[60]

Finally, German naval artillery could have been turned against the BEF's channel ports. The three so-called Paris Guns (*Wilhelmgeschütze*) were actually manned by naval crews. With a maximum range of 127 kilometers, they had the reach to hit the BEF's three primary northern Channel ports (Boulogne, Calais, and Dunkirk) and even Dover, if the guns had been positioned in the Fourth Army sector. But between 16 and 30 March 1918, during Operation MICHAEL, they did not fire in support of the attacking Seventeenth, Second, or Eighteenth Armies. Rather, the guns were positioned in the Seventh Army sector, delivering pointless terrorizing fire against Paris.[61] At least two German coastal batteries in Flanders were capable of hitting Dunkirk and could have fired in support of ground forces during Operation GEORGETTE. But *Batterie Deutschland* (four 380 mm guns) never fired against land targets, and *Batterie Pommern* (one

380 mm gun) delivered only occasional fire against Dunkirk and the major British base at Poperinghe. A third battery, *Batterie Tirpitz* (four 280 mm guns), had the range to hit targets in the northern quarter of the Ypres salient, but it too never fired in support of ground operations.[62]

Military–political conflict within the German leadership

Germany's weak political and rigid social institutions were arguably its greatest handicap in World War I—certainly the one that made the development of a coherent strategy virtually impossible. As opposed to past wars, this time Germany did not have a Frederick the Great or an Otto von Bismarck. Instead, she had only Wilhelm II and a weak and vacillating string of Chancellors: Theobald von Bethmann Hollweg; Georg Michaelis; Georg Graf von Hertling; and Prince Max von Baden. They were opposed on the Allied side by men like David Lloyd George, Georges Clemenceau, and Woodrow Wilson. Nor on the military side did Germany have another Helmut von Moltke the Elder.

On his arrival with Hindenburg at OHL on 20 August 1916, Ludendorff immediately began pushing for a ruthless mobilization of all German resources that eventually led to the Silent Dictatorship. Supported by Hindenburg, Ludendorff increasingly meddled in political affairs. Curiously enough, Ludendorff rejected the idea of an outright military dictatorship, despite having the chancellorship almost thrust upon him.[63] Nonetheless, by the last months of the war Ludendorff wielded close to absolute power. Yet in his post-war memoirs he complained: "Unfortunately, the government did not state clearly and emphatically in public that it, and not General Ludendorff, was governing."[64]

The question of unrestricted submarine warfare became one of the first fault lines that split the civilian and military leadership. Although Bethmann Hollweg finally acquiesced, his relationship with the military went steadily downhill. He further infuriated Hindenburg and Ludendorff when he eventually convinced the Kaiser to reform Prussia's three-class voting system. In June 1917 Ludendorff forbade German commanders even to talk to Bethmann Hollweg during the Chancellor's visit to the front.[65] The last straw was the Chancellor's inability to derail the Peace Resolution being debated by the Reichstag. Ludendorff countered by ordering patriotic instruction (*Vaterländischer Unterricht*) for all troops. He and Hindenburg then forced Bethmann Hollweg to resign by threatening the Kaiser with their own resignations.

Bethmann Hollweg resigned on 13 July 1917. The next day, the colorless Michaelis was appointed Chancellor with the support of OHL, but over the objections of the majority parties in the Reichstag. Nonetheless, the Reichstag passed the Peace Resolution on 19 July, and Michaelis quickly lost the support of the military. He was forced out of office on 31 October and replaced with the aging Hertling. Although Hertling remained in office for almost one year, he spent most of his efforts trying to placate OHL, which further weakened any effectiveness he might have had in the Reichstag. On 8 January 1918 Wilson announced his Fourteen Points, eight of which echoed war aims of the Entente.

Few, if any, German statesmen and soldiers even bothered to read the Fourteen Points, although Hertling criticized the peace proposal in the Reichstag.[66]

OHL continued to exercise its heavy hand in political affairs right until the end of the war. After the failure of Operations BLÜCHER and GNEISENAU in May and June 1918, Foreign Minister Richard von Kühlmann made a major foreign policy speech in the Reichstag, stating that the war could no longer be won by purely military means and calling for a negotiated peace. Hindenburg and Ludendorff reacted violently, demanding he be replaced. Kühlmann resigned and was replaced by Rear Admiral Paul von Hintze, a retired naval officer turned diplomat. Much to OHL's chagrin, however, Hintze continued to follow the moderate policies of his predecessor.[67]

Germany's strategic situation in 1918

In a sense, 1918 was like 1914 all over again for the Germans. Instead of facing two sets of enemies separated by space (France/Britain and Russia), they were now facing two sets of enemies separated by time (France/Britain and America). And although Germany and France/Britain were almost burned out by more than three years of war, America was coming in fresh, albeit inexperienced. Yet even Ludendorff could see that, despite any military shortcomings American soldiers and units might have, they would sooner or later arrive in numbers so massive that the strategic scales would have to tip. Time was not on Germany's side.

The situation in the air

Germany lagged behind the Allies in aircraft production throughout the war. Recognizing the significance of the shortfall, Ludendorff on 23 June 1917 requested an increase in production rates to 2,000 aircraft and 2,500 engines per month.[68] This was the so-called America Program (*Amerikaprogramm*) that was supposed to establish forty new fighter squadrons and seventeen new airforce regiments in a matter of months.[69] By the start of Operation MICHAEL Germany was still outnumbered 3,670 to 4,500 aircraft of all types.[70] Nonetheless, the Germans used their air assets with efficiency and effectiveness. Through at least the end of May 1918 they managed to achieve air parity and even local air superiority over the battlefield wherever they needed it.[71] The comparative air loss statistics claimed in the German official history for March through September 1918, however, do not correlate with Allied statistics.[72] See Table 4.1.

On 25 May 1917 the Germans started a strategic bombing campaign against Britain, which they thought would prove strategically decisive in conjunction with the submarine campaign. The main instrument of the strategic bombing campaign was *Kagohl* 3, operating directly under the control of OHL and flying the Gotha G.IV bomber with a payload of 500 kilograms. Like the earlier Zeppelin raids, however, periodic terror was the primary effect produced by the strategic bombing campaign. London was the main objective, and there was

Table 4.1 1918 Western Front claimed aircraft losses

	German	Allied
March	159	451
April	136	283
May	198	425
June	155	506
July	131	528
August	174	658
September	116	650

some effort to target the national-level command and control centers (Parliament, War Office, Admiralty, etc.), but the volume and the level of accuracy were just not sufficient to achieve significant effect. OHL halted the strategic bombing campaign in May 1918.[73]

After the raids against London were suspended, German bombers in May, June, and July 1918 were finally directed against British and French rail yards and shipping in the English Channel.[74] By then, however, it was too little too late. Whatever damage these raids did to the British LOCs was done in isolation. The major British rail nodes on the Continent remained under interdiction fire through the end of July, but were never again threatened seriously after the failure of Operation GEORGETTE at the end of April.

Weapons, ammunition, and materiel

As with aircraft, the Allies at the start of 1918 had more artillery than the Germans. Yet as with aircraft, the Germans used their artillery far more effectively, especially under the brilliant direction of Colonel Georg Bruchmüller.[75] Despite the general failure and chaos of the Hindenburg Program, the German Army was not chronically short of guns, small arms, machine guns, trench mortars, ammunition, or field engineering materials at the start of 1918. In March 1918 OHL had an ammunition reserve of 2,840 railroad trains. By October that reserve still stood at 1,632 trains. The field gun production rate was originally set at 3,000 per month, and later lowered to 750. Yet in March 1918 German industry produced 2,327 artillery pieces. The monthly production rates for rifles and machine guns stood at 75,000 and 6,000 respectively.[76]

Transportation

The world had never seen such a period of massive and continuous military consumption as World War I. Logistics rapidly grew to take on a level of significance that came to determine what was possible and not possible on the battlefield, particularly at the operational level. As the war progressed, all nations expanded exponentially the production/acquisition component of their logistical systems. The distribution component did not grow as fast, or in as many different directions, because it was tied directly to the existing transportation infrastructure, which could be expanded only incrementally.

Ports were important to all nations at the level of their national economies, hence the significance of the British blockade against Germany and the threat imposed by the German submarine campaign. As a Continental power, however, Germany did not have to rely on sea ports to move military units and war materiel. Initially, France too was not very dependent on ports for military movement and re-supply, except for the shifting of some colonial units. Ports became far more important to France after America entered the war.

As an island nation, Britain was absolutely dependent on ports to project and supply its armies. By February 1917, some 800,000 tons of supplies for the BEF arrived every month in France through six Channel ports.[77] North of the Somme, Dunkirk, Calais, and Boulogne received almost half the BEF's supplies. South of the Somme, Rouen, Le Havre, and Dieppe received the other half.[78] They were critical choke points in the British logistics system that should have been, but never were, decisive points in German operational thinking.

Railways (also discussed in Chapter 2) were one of the most important means of strategic and operational movement during World War I. Prior to 1914 the Railroad Department was the largest section of the Great General Staff, and the entire execution of the Schlieffen Plan (in all its variations) depended heavily on rapid and precise rail movements. In August 1914 the Germans had 26,300 troops assigned to either constructing or operating rail lines. By June 1917 that number had grown to 201,300, and OHL's chief of the Field Rail Service estimated he would need an additional 80,000 to support future operations.[79]

Both France and Germany started the war with a dense, high-capacity, and interconnecting rail network. Furthermore, the Germans were fortunate in that the rail grid was about the same behind the front lines of the areas of France and Belgium they occupied. The German system had great depth. Judging from the rate at which the Germans shifted their divisions around in 1917 and 1918, they had no serious shortage of rail motive power and rolling stock. It took sixty trains to move a single division by rail. One train averaged forty-nine cars, or 2,940 cars per division.[80] Between 15 February and 20 March 1918, the German military rail system operated day and night to run 10,400 trains moving men and supplies—an average of 306 trains per day.[81]

In October 1917 the German Army made seventy-three divisional moves. For the purpose of this analysis, divisional moves from one field army to a directly adjacent field army are not considered, since such shifts could have been accomplished by marching, or by redefining army boundaries. The capacity and robustness of their rail system gave the Germans a great deal of flexibility in shifting combat forces around, but that flexibility also had a downside. The movements took time, and while the divisions were moving they were out of the line. It took four hours to load, and somewhat less than that to unload a single train. Even though the Germans had very large and efficient marshalling yards that allowed the loading or unloading of many trains simultaneously, it took at least a day to load and a day to unload a division under the best of conditions.

Once the division detrained, it still had to march to its new sector in the front lines, which on average took two days. Once at the front line, it took a division another three days to occupy its new positions. The pass time for a single division was four days for an intra-theater move, and six to eight days for an inter-theater move.[82] General Fritz von Lossberg estimated that a typical divisional move by rail took eight to ten days.[83]

Using a very conservative estimate of an average of six days out of action per division per move by rail, Table 4.2 shows the number of divisional moves per month during the last year of the war; the number of divisional days and divisional months out of combat; and the percentage of total non-available combat power for that month (based on 250 divisions, until July 1918).[84] Note the non-availability percentages for the critical months of March (MICHAEL) and April (GEORGETTE).

The BEF was far less fortunate with the rail network in its sector. The British position in Flanders had no depth at all. North of the Somme, the British front lines averaged only about ninety kilometers from the coast. Rail was the BEF's primary means of moving supplies and troops from the ports. The rail network was adequate at best, with most of the lines running east–west. By 1916, the British had to operate 250 trains per day to keep the supplies moving along an overstrained rail system.[85] The entire British transportation system was on the verge of collapse until Sir Eric Geddes was brought in to reorganize it at the end of 1916.[86] In April 1918, during the last phases of Operation MICHAEL and during Operation GEORGETTE, the British ran 725 ammunition trains to their front.[87]

There were two key choke points in the British rail grid. Almost everything that came in through the three northern ports had to go through Hazebrouck. Almost everything that came in through the three southern ports had to go through Amiens. Furthermore, 80 percent of the north–south traffic went

Table 4.2 German divisional movements by rail

Month	Divisional moves	Divisional days	Divisional months	Percentage of unavailable combat power
November 1917	21	126	4.2	1.7
December 1917	32	192	6.4	2.6
January 1918	14	84	2.8	1.1
February 1918	24	144	4.8	1.9
March 1918	67	402	13.4	5.4
April 1918	98	588	19.6	7.8
May 1918	62	372	12.4	5.0
June 1918	46	276	9.2	3.7
July 1918	65	390	13.0	5.2
August 1918	104	624	20.8	8.6
September 1918	130	780	26.0	11.3
October 1918	105	630	21.0	9.4

through or skirted Amiens. In early 1918 the north–south traffic averaged 140 trains per day, including forty-five coal trains from the Béthune coalfields for French munitions factories in the south. "Strategic movements," i.e. shifting reserves and other large forces, could add an additional twenty-four to seventy-two trains per day, resulting in a surge requirement of 212 per day. Haig's Q-Staff estimated that if the Allies lost Amiens, all possible bypasses could only handle ninety trains per day. If Abancourt, forty kilometers southwest of Amiens fell as well, the only remaining north–south link would be the Dieppe–Eu–Abbeville Line, with a capacity of only eight trains per day.[88] (Map 1.)

During Operation MICHAEL the British were very worried about losing Amiens. On 27 March the town came under German artillery fire. The day before, Haig's Quartermaster-General, Major-General Travers Clarke, convened a meeting to consider the possible courses of action if the Germans succeeded in separating the British and the French, thereby cutting the BEF off from its southern LOCs. On 31 March the Q-Staff issued Scheme X. That quickly evolved into Scheme Y, which had options for evacuating (a) Calais and Dunkirk in the north, or (b) Abbeville, Albancourt, and Dieppe in the south. By April, the Q-Staff issued Scheme Z, a plan for abandoning the entire area north of the Somme. The evacuation plan would require twenty-eight days to execute, with 85 percent of the existing supplies north of the Somme being destroyed in place.[89] British contingency planning for losing key segments of their rail network continued through mid-July because Amiens and Hazebrouck both remained subject to German interdicting fire. As we shall see later, that fire appears to have never risen much above the harassment level.

In mid-January 1918, General Sir Henry Wilson, the British representative to the Allied Supreme War Council at Versailles, had used his staff to wargame a 100-division German attack at the British–French juncture, driving toward Amiens.[90] Rejecting the results of Wilson's wargame, Haig continued to deploy the main weight of his forces behind his center and northern wing.[91] Nonetheless, the British did understand just how fragile their transportation network was, and once Operation MICHAEL started, they were quicker than the Germans to recognize the critical vulnerability at Amiens. So was Marshal Ferdinand Foch, who wrote in his memoirs: "From the outset all were unanimous in recognizing that Amiens had to be saved at all costs, and that the fate of the war depended on it."[92] After he took command of the Fifth (re-designated as the Fourth) Army, General Sir Henry Rawlinson wrote to Wilson: "There can be no question but that the Amiens area is the only one in which the enemy can hope to gain such a success as to force the Allies to discuss terms of peace."[93] The Germans seem never to have really understood that until it was too late—if they ever really saw it at all.

While the Germans did not have to worry about vulnerable ports or rail centers, the weak link in their transportation system was from the forward railheads to their own front lines, and then beyond. The Germans had only about 30,000 trucks to the Allies' 100,000.[94] The Germans were also critically short of fuel and rubber, and were heavily dependent on Romania for petroleum. German

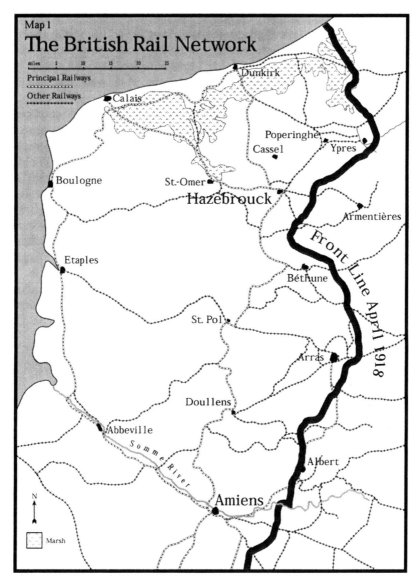

Map 1 The British sector and rail network (source: Map by Donald S. Frazier, Ph.D., Abilene, Texas, based on sketches and notes provided by David T. Zabecki).

trucks had to run on iron tires, which tore up the roads, creating further mobility problems.[95] On the other hand, the Allies' numerical advantage in trucks was offset somewhat by the lack of good roads, especially in the BEF sector. Had the capacity of the British rail been seriously degraded, truck transportation could not have provided much relief. It took 150 trucks to replace one train, and as one British staff officer noted, "good roads for lorry work were few and far between."[96]

Although the Germans had dismounted almost all of their cavalry units early in the war (except for some units in the east), horses still remained the primary means of motive power in the forward areas. Unfortunately for the Germans, the horse replacement situation was bleak at the start of 1918. In December 1917 the German Army was some 43,000 horses short of its required level of 690,000. An additional 15,000 replacement horses were required each month just to keep even with the losses. The horses the Germans did have were underfed and below standard because of low stocks of forage. In March 1918 the Germans transferred some 14,500 horses from the Eastern Front, rendering thirteen divisions there immobile. Even so, only the attack divisions for the MICHAEL offensive were brought up to their authorized horse levels.[97]

The shortage of trucks, the heavy dependence on horses, and even the shortage and low standards of horses all combined to restrict German battlefield mobility. That in turn limited the depth to which any German attack could be pushed and sustained.

German manpower

Schlieffen's Plan of 1905 required ninety-four divisions to execute. Germany at the time had scarcely sixty. Schlieffen's solution to this problem was to include mobilized reserve units in the first-line order of battle. This was a risky approach that meant Germany would have no general reserve. Moltke also recognized all the other problems that would come with the early commitment of reservists. (The U.S. Army has been wrestling with the same problems since adopting a similar manpower strategy following Vietnam.) By the time the war started, German and Austria–Hungary were able to field 136 divisions, against 182 divisions of the three Entente powers.[98]

From a total population of sixty-seven million, Germany mobilized eleven million men and suffered 7.2 million casualties (dead, wounded, missing, and prisoners). The total figures for the Central Powers were 22.8 million mobilized and 15.2 million casualties. The Allied and Associated Powers, with a combined population of 378 million (not including the French and British colonies) mobilized 42.2 million, and suffered 21.8 million casualties.[99] Thus, each mobilized Central Powers soldier on average inflicted one casualty on the Allies, while it took almost three Allied soldiers to inflict a casualty on the Central Powers. Nonetheless, Germany's manpower situation was already becoming critical by the summer of 1917.

On 17 December 1917 OHL estimated the monthly replacement requirements at 150,000, of which returning convalescents only contributed 60,000 per month.[100] As of 1 January 1918 there were 2,154,387 German men directly in the war industry, 1,097,108 of whom could be classified as fit for field service.[101] Unfortunately, most of that group could not be touched unless the German government was willing to extend compulsory war work service to women. That was one measure even Ludendorff was never able to force through.

Complicating the replacement problem, the Germans were starting to suffer from high numbers of deserters, mostly from the infantry.[102] Returning POWs from Russia "were contaminated politically and opposed to serving on the Western Front." The last possible manpower draw, 637,000 men born 1899–1900, was probably insufficient to continue the war, and they would not be ready to enter service until the autumn of 1918.[103]

High officer casualties, especially among the best officers, also hurt the Germans. Ludendorff actually wanted to draw officer replacements from the most capable NCOs, without regard to social background. The selection of officers, however, was one of the sole remaining prerogatives of the Military Cabinet, which insisted on maintaining pre-war social standards. The only solution was the creation of many temporary officers (*Offizierstellvertreter*), who would have to revert to the ranks at the end of the war.[104] By mid-March 1918 German Army strength was distributed as shown in Table 4.3.[105] Actual trench strength in the west was 1,232,000. The Germans still had more than one million troops (410,000 combat troops) garrisoning the east to enforce Ludendorff's expansionist goals. A large percentage of those troops, however, were over the age of forty, and some 85,000 were from Alsace or Lorraine—considered politically unreliable for service in the west.

Between 1 November 1917 and 21 March 1918, the Germans transferred forty-eight divisions from the Eastern Front to the Western Front (and two from the Western Front to the Eastern Front), and eight divisions from Italy to the west. From 22 March to the end of May eleven more divisions transferred from east to west, but three more went back to the east.[106] On the eve of Operation MICHAEL the 243 German divisions were deployed as shown in Table 4.4.[107]

In the west the Germans had more divisions than the Allies, but the numerical strength of those units was lower. As the war ground its way through 1918, the trench strength of their front-line units progressively declined. In April 1918 average infantry battalion strength was 766; by June it was down to 718; and by September it was down to 570. The Germans were finally forced to eliminate the fourth company in the battalion to maintain company strength.[108]

Table 4.3 German strength March 1918

	Officers	*Enlisted*	*Horses*
West	136,618	3,438,288	710,827
East	40,095	1,004,955	281,770

Table 4.4 Deployment of German divisions on 21 March 1918

West	191 divisions
East and southeast	47 divisions
Balkans	2 divisions
Zone of the interior	3 divisions

Not all German divisions were equal, of course. As noted in Chapter 3, the Germans distinguished between their attack divisions and trench divisions. Allied intelligence order of battle sections also closely monitored the capabilities and state of readiness of all the German divisions. The Intelligence Division of the American Expeditionary Force (AEF) put the German divisions into four classes, with Class 1 being the most capable, and Class 4 being the least. For the most part, those divisions the AEF rated as Class 1 in 1918 were the attack divisions. Class 2 consisted of some attack divisions and the better trench divisions, with the remainder of the trench divisions in Class 3. The divisions the AEF rated as Class 4 were the *Landwehr* divisions, for the most part. By March 1918 there were only two Class 3 divisions on the Eastern Front; all the rest were Class 4.[109] As an AEF intelligence report reproduced in the American official history noted:

> On March 21, Germany had 45 divisions on the western front rated as first class battle divisions. The plan, more or less closely followed, has been to make large use of such divisions for offensive operations. When the objective of a given operation is reasonably well attained these divisions are withdrawn, rested, reconstituted, and prepared for further use.[110]

The previously discussed analysis of divisional moves also showed clearly that the higher-class divisions made more moves between January and October 1918, and they were committed to action more often. Most of the Class 1 divisions were in at least two of the five major offensives, some were in three, and many were earmarked for Operation HAGEN. The average number of moves per division was the same for the Class 2 and Class 3 divisions; higher for the Class 1 divisions; and lower for the Class 4 divisions. These differences are statistically significant at the 99 percent level of confidence.[111] See Table 4.5.

Table 4.5 1918 divisional movements by class

	Number of divisions	Total number of moves	Average moves per division	Standard deviation
Class 1	45	208	4.6	1.813
Class 2	61	212	3.5	1.812
Class 3	72	250	3.5	1.928
Class 4	43	70	1.6	1.732

Allied manpower

At the end of 1917 the British and French had 3,700,000 troops on the Western Front. The 175 Allied divisions had a trench strength of 1,480,000. Twelve Belgian divisions held the extreme north of the Allied line. Then came fifty-seven British and two Portuguese divisions, organized into four armies. The ninety-nine French divisions were organized into three army groups, North, Center, and East. In the French sector were also four huge American divisions. With 28,000 troops, each was about twice the size of a European division.[112] The Allies at that point still did not have a unified command structure. Pétain kept sixty of his ninety-nine divisions in the main line; fifteen covering the Vosges sector in the south; and twenty in reserve behind the main French sector. He also earmarked four divisions to support the British in the north, if necessary. Haig held only eight divisions in general reserve, and he refused to provide any for a central Allied Reserve.[113] Pershing infuriated the French by insisting on keeping the American divisions under his own command, rather than allowing them to be broken up and fed piecemeal into the line as reinforcements.[114]

When America entered the war in April 1917, the U.S. Army consisted of approximately 130,000 regular soldiers and some 70,000 National Guardsmen. In a period of nineteen months, America raised an army of more than four million, and managed to send about half that number across the Atlantic. In May 1917, however, the Americans had only 1,308 troops in Europe. That month OHL estimated that, based on the British experience, the U.S. Army would need at least ten months to organize, equip, and train any of its major units. And, in fact, although there were seven American divisions in France by March 1918, only one was ready for combat. But then the numbers started to increase almost exponentially (see Table 4.6).[115]

Table 4.6 American cumulative strength

Month	Total American troops
May 1917	1,308
June 1917	16,220
December 1917	183,896
January 1918	224,655
February 1918	245,378
March 1918	329,005
April 1918	434,081
May 1918	667,119
June 1918	897,293
July 1918	1,210,708
August 1918	1,478,190
September 1918	1,783,955
October 1918	1,986,618
November 1918	2,057,675

The large jump in May 1918 (233,038) was accomplished in part by leaving equipment behind and linking the troops up with excess stocks already in France. The large increase in the arrival rate of the Americans from May on caught OHL by surprise.[116] From March to July the Americans put 956,000 troops into Europe—in the same period that the Germans lost 973,000.[117] By the time the French launched their counteroffensive on 18 July they had nine American divisions. By the end of the war, forty-three American divisions were in France, and twenty-eight of those were either in or ready for combat.

In their assessment of the Americans, the Germans committed one of the deadliest sins of warfare—underestimating the enemy. Ludendorff initially dismissed the Americans out of hand. As late as December 1917 an OHL intelligence summary noted: "The officer corps is not trained for the exigencies of major warfare. For this reason alone it will be impossible for a time to employ American units of any size under their own command in difficult situations."[118] Even the usually astute General Hans von Seeckt underestimated the influence of American entry into the war. He thought it would prolong it, but not decide it.[119]

The German home front

By 1917 the war was costing Germany 3 billion marks per month, and the cumulative cost had reached 111 billion marks by March 1918.[120] Thanks to the British blockade the food situation in Germany was grim. The winter of 1916–1917 was called the "Turnip Winter," and that spring Germany was short two million tons of breadstuffs.[121] German infant mortality in 1917 was up 49.3 percent over what it had been in 1913.

Germany depended heavily on its occupied zones for food supplies, which somewhat justified Ludendorff's continued commitment of forces in the east. In 1918 German civilian adults had a diet of only 1,000 calories per day. Early that year the food supply system collapsed completely. Industrial firms had to compete with municipalities for food for their workers, and both were forced to resort to the black market.[122] The food shortage also affected the German soldiers, whose daily caloric intake had fallen from 3,100 in August 1914 to 2,500 by early 1918.[123] On 15 June 1918, army commanders were informed that until the next harvest, there would be no more deliveries from Germany of corn or potato fodder for the horses, and only limited potatoes for the troops.[124]

After three and a half years of war German national morale was low. The war hysteria of 1914–1916 was gone, and the left-wing and pacifist fervor that had swept France in 1917 was now sweeping Germany. In 1917 there were over 500 strikes involving more than one million war workers.[125] On 28–30 January 1918, 400,000 workers went on strike in Berlin. Additional strikes quickly followed in Bremen, Hamburg, Leipzig, and Essen. The strikers demanded immediate peace with no annexations and no indemnities; an improvement in the food supply; the end of military control of the factories; and the release of political prisoners.

On 30 January Ludendorff sent a message to the Chancellor demanding the arrest of the strike leaders. With army support, the police closed down labor newspapers. Some 50,000 munitions workers were recalled to active duty and sent to the front, but that only served to infect the front lines with more revolutionary agitators.[126] Nonetheless, the army effectively broke the strikes. After that, the period from March to July 1918 was one of relative calm in Germany, as the people waited with renewed hope, but ultimately in vain, for the promised military victory of Ludendorff's offensives.[127]

The situation in the east

On 15 December 1917 Germany and Russia agreed on an armistice, but it turned out only to be a ceasefire. Negotiations with Russia broke down over the terms of the Treaty of Brest-Litovsk—terms mostly dictated by Ludendorff. Meanwhile, Germany on 9 February signed a separate peace treaty with the newly independent Ukraine. But anarchy broke out almost immediately, and by 16 February most major Ukrainian towns and rail centers were in the hands of the Bolsheviks. On 18 February 1918, OHL broke off negotiations with the Russians and ordered the twenty weak divisions of Army Group Eichhorn to regain control of the Ukraine. The Germans reached Kiev on 1 March, Odessa on 12 March, and Kharkov by April. On 7 March the Ukrainian government re-established itself in Kiev. That government was overthrown on 24 April, but its replacement recognized the economic agreement with Germany and promptly asked for German troops to help get the harvest in.[128] Only by abandoning the Ukraine would it have been possible to free up significant numbers of troops for Operation MICHAEL. Yet Germany absolutely had to retain its control over the Ukraine, which was a vital source of critically needed grain, meat, and horses.[129]

On 3 March Lenin finally agreed to the terms of the Treaty of Brest-Litovsk, including the recognition of Ukrainian independence. Brest-Litovsk, of course, was every bit as draconian as the Treaty of Versailles would turn out to be. Russia lost 89 percent of its coal mines; 50 percent of its industry; 73 percent of its iron production; 33 percent of its rail lines; and 32 percent of its population.[130] The Bolshevik government remained very hostile to Germany, and stepped up its efforts to export the communist revolution to the land of Karl Marx's birth.

The Russians agreed to terms only eighteen days before the Germans launched Operation MICHAEL in the west. In the early months of 1918, when he should have been focusing all his attention on MICHAEL, Ludendorff was obsessed with the Treaty of Brest-Litovsk, sketching the future borders of the map of Europe.[131]

The decision to attack[132]

By late 1917 Hindenburg and Ludendorff had come to the conclusion that the war would be lost or won on the Western Front.[133] This was the very proposition of Falkenhayn's they had argued against from 1914 through 1916. But even during the preparations for the defensive battles of 1917, OHL began to realize that they had miscalculated Germany's military situation.[134] The senior German military leadership in the west was divided on the issue. The two principal army group commanders, Crown Princes Wilhelm and Rupprecht, were convinced that Germany could no longer win a military victory. They wanted to make peace before the offensive, even if it meant giving up Belgium.[135] In his post-war memoirs, however, Wilhelm expressed a somewhat different attitude than he expressed at the time to his chief of staff, General Friederich von der Schulenburg.[136]

> If the war could not be ended otherwise than by a military decision, and the statesmen could find no diplomatic method of leading the parties to the negotiating table, there was no other choice but to take the offensive.[137]

Rupprecht's chief of staff, Kuhl; the chief of staff of the Fourth Army, Lossberg; and Ludendorff's replacement as chief of staff on the Eastern Front, General Max Hoffmann, were arguably the best field chiefs of staff of the war. All three saw no alternative. Lossberg wrote to Ludendorff at the time: "The war can be decided in our favor only through an offensive."[138] After the war Kuhl wrote: "The enemy's numerical superiority, enhanced by the prospective arrival of American contingents, rendered the defensive hopeless in the long run." "There was no other choice."[139] In his personal War Diary, however, Kuhl in November 1917 expressed a slightly different point of view, noting that neither a major offensive nor a protracted defense held any prospect for success. Instead, Germany should conduct a strategic withdrawal from Flanders, followed by a series of powerful counterattacks.[140] In Hoffmann's post-war memoirs he wrote: "From the point of view of a military critic, nothing can be said against the decision to attack."[141]

Ludendorff continued to reject any peace through negotiation. While OHL continued to debate whether or not to attack, and if so where, none of Germany's political leaders had a voice in the decision.[142] On 19 September 1917 Ludendorff told the army group and army chiefs of staff that a major attack in the west was out of the question.[143] On 30 September Wetzell issued his previously discussed strategic estimate of the situation that focused on the next war. On 23 October Wetzell produced another estimate of the situation in which he argued that the only viable strategy was "to deliver an annihilating blow to the British before American aid can become effective." Wetzell estimated that the offensive would require thirty divisions, which could be freed up in two ways: first, by shortening Army Group Crown Prince Wilhelm's front by withdrawing to the Gudrun Line, which would free up fifteen divisions; and second, by withdrawing fifteen more divisions from the east.[144] Ludendorff approved the concept within twenty-four hours.

On 25 October Rupprecht sent Ludendorff an estimate of the situation that argued against a major offensive and recommended only limited counterattacks, possibly in the Armentières area.[145] On 9 November Wetzell produced a revised staff study. While still continuing to argue for a major offensive, Wetzell reversed himself from his 23 October staff study. He now considered a direct attack against the British as too hard, and argued instead for an attack against the French by cutting off the Verdun salient.

> Beyond all doubt our toughest and most stubborn, but at the same time our clumsiest opponent is the Englishman, and next spring, in my opinion, the most dangerous one will again be the Frenchman, tested in war, more skillful, and reinforced by the Americans.[146]

Ludendorff decided the Germans had to attack, he just wasn't sure where, how, or when. His key advisors were even more divided on those questions than on the primary question of whether or not to attack. On 11 November he met at Rupprecht's headquarters in Mons with Wetzell, Bauer, Kuhl, and Schulenburg. They did not reach a decision. Ludendorff then ordered the development of an entire set of courses of action, and he issued his basic planning guidance. The decision on where, how, and when would be made later.

Given the strategic box the Germans had put themselves in, was the decision to shift to the strategic offensive the correct one? There really were only two other options—the strategic defensive and negotiation. Noting that the Allies never did make the kinds of breakthroughs the Germans made in 1918, Correlli Barnett argued that the defensive policy would have been no more disastrous in the long run, and not as risky.[147] Perhaps, but one of the most critical elements of a successful defense is time, and that was the one resource the Germans were the shortest of. On 20 December 1917, General Henri Pétain, Commander in Chief of the French Army, issued a directive that made the Allied strategy quite clear:

> The Entente Powers will reach numerical superiority only when sufficient American troops can enter the line. Until that time it will be necessary for us, unless we wish to use up our forces irretrievably, to assume a waiting attitude, with the express purpose of taking up the offensive as soon as we are able to do so; for only the offensive will bring us final victory.[148]

By the end of 1917 negotiation was probably the best way out. The Germans actually did attempt a "Political Offensive," but Ludendorff's intransigence on Belgium doomed that course of action to failure every step of the way. On 11 February 1918 Germany's political leaders sent Ludendorff a memorandum pointing out the increasing unrest at home and the economic weakness of the Central Powers, and urging as rapid a peace as possible. They also strongly urged that the coming military offensive should be preceded by a political offensive. A month earlier, on 14 January, OHL's liaison to the Foreign Office, Colonel Hans von Haeften, had given Ludendorff an elaborate proposal for just such a political offensive.[149] Ludendorff actually forwarded Haeften's memorandum to the Chancellor, after first removing the key element—the demand for a clear statement on Belgium.[150]

On 9 March 1918, Haeften briefed Ludendorff on the results of his talks at The Hague with President Wilson's delegate, Jacob Noeggerath. The Americans refused to budge on Belgium, but throughout March and April, during Operations MICHAEL and GEORGETTE, Ludendorff continued to insist on German domination over Belgium.[151] On 3 June, after the failure of Operation BLÜCHER, Haeften gave Ludendorff a second proposal that pushed the idea of Germany as the world's champion against eastern Bolshevism.[152] But that plan too sidestepped the issue of Belgium. Writing after the war, Hoffmann noted:

> On the very day on which OHL gave the order to cease the attack on Amiens, it was their duty to notify the government that the time had arrived to proceed to peace negotiations, and that there was no longer any prospect of finishing the war with a decisive victory on the Western Front.[153]

The offensive was the only real option Ludendorff and OHL allowed for Germany. But as Wetzell stressed in his 9 November estimate, "it must have a far-reaching strategic objective." As we shall see, it did not. Driven by the German fixation on the *Vernichtungsschlacht*, Ludendorff continued to believe until the end that a decision could only be achieved by directly attacking the enemy's strength. It apparently never occurred to him to take an indirect approach by attacking a key vulnerability, like the BEF's logistics system. Thus the most serious question facing the planners was whether, after executing a breakthrough, the field force would be sufficiently mobile to exploit it.[154] Given Germany's shortage of horses, inadequate forage, shortage of trucks, scarcity of fuel, scarcity of rubber for tires, and lack of tanks, the answer was No.

Most of the key German military leaders went into the 1918 offensives believing they had no other viable course of action, yet somehow understanding that the whole thing was a gamble, one huge roll of the dice. Writing in his post-war memoirs, Crown Prince Wilhelm noted:

> Even if we could confidently anticipate a great tactical success, our operational success remained uncertain. We could only conjecture on how far it could be developed into something that would decide the campaign.[155]

And in his memoirs, Hindenburg wrote:

> Even with the advantage of numbers on our side, it was not a simple matter to decide on an offensive in the west. It was always doubtful whether we should win a great victory.[156]

5   The operational decision

11 November 1917 to 21 January 1918

> From a military standpoint, it didn't make much difference whether we directed
> our first offensive against the French or the British.[1]
>
> Field Marshal Paul von Hindenburg

The decision-making process

Once OHL made the decision to attack, they then had to decide where, when,
and how. The decision against whom was a function of the decision where. The
process of making the decisions on where and when played out over a period of
ten weeks. It involved three major conferences and a large number of estimates
and memorandums circulating among OHL and the army and army group headquarters. During that period, a number of course of action analyses were also
initiated to address the specifics of how the offensive would be carried out. That
process continued up through mid-March.

The Mons Conference[2]

As noted in the previous chapter, Ludendorff met with Kuhl, Schulenburg,
Wetzell, and Bauer at Mons on 11 November 1917. Typical of the German
Army at that time, it was a meeting strictly with chiefs of staff and key General
Staff officers. No commanders were present, but all were presumably later
briefed by their respective staff chiefs.

Kuhl argued strongly for an attack in the north, in the direction of Bailleul-
Hazebrouck, with the left flank anchored on the La Bassée Canal. The objective
of the attack would be to cut the British in half by echeloning on the left wing.
The key drawback would be having to wait until April for the ground in the Lys
valley to dry sufficiently. Ludendorff generally favored the northern option, but
he insisted on attacking no later than the end of February.[3] (See Map 2.)

Schulenburg advocated an attack against the French center on both sides of
Verdun—from the region in and to the east of the Argonne Forest, and from
St. Mihiel westward. Schulenburg argued that while Britain could probably
survive a military disaster, France would be broken by one.[4] That option,
however, counted heavily on the assumption of French psychological collapse.

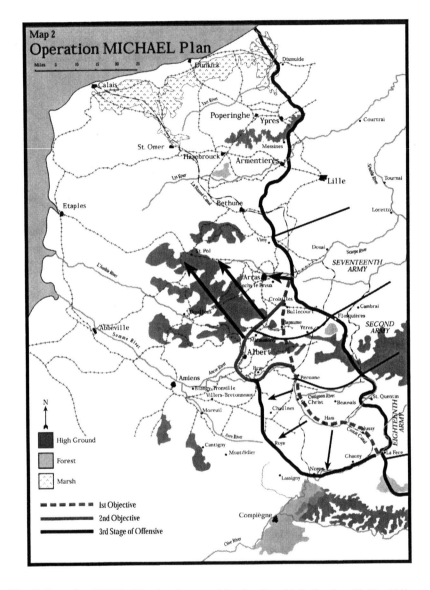

Map 2 Operation MICHAEL plan (source: Map by Donald S. Frazier, Ph.D., Abilene, Texas, based on sketches and notes provided by David T. Zabecki).

Schulenburg was supported by Wetzell and his 9 November staff study (see Chapter 4), but Ludendorff countered that there was no major incentive for the British to send reinforcements to the French at Verdun. That meant the Germans would still have to fight the British later in Flanders. He also believed that the relative inactivity in that sector had allowed the French Army to reconstitute its strength partially.

Ludendorff then asked if Rupprecht's Army Group could attack farther to its south, near Arras or St. Quentin. Ludendorff noted:

> It would seem that an attack near St. Quentin offers promising prospects. After reaching the line of the Somme between Péronne and Ham it might be possible, by resting the left flank on the Somme, to advance the attack still farther in a northwestern direction, and thus eventually roll up the British front. For the success of this operation it would be especially necessary to render useless the various rail centers by means of long range artillery and bombing squadrons. That would create difficulties for the timely arrival of the enemy's strategic reserves.[5]

This appears to be one of the few times that Ludendorff paid any attention to the BEF's transportation system. In this case, however, he was focusing narrowly on the movement of reserves, rather than more broadly on the BEF's entire lines of communications.[6] Kuhl objected to the plan, pointing out its two major drawbacks. The Germans would have to attack over the terrain that had been devastated by the 1916 Somme battles, and by their own Operation ALBERICH withdrawal to the Siegfried line in 1917. Also, the left wing of such an attack would by necessity come into contact with the French and draw in their reserves that much faster.

Despite Ludendorff's strong leanings, no final decision was reached at the Mons Conference. He ordered further staff studies and the course of action development of five principal operational options: ST. GEORG centered on Hazebrouck; MARS centered on Arras; ST. MICHAEL centered on St. Quentin; CASTOR north of Verdun; and POLLUX east of Verdun. Ludendorff concluded the conference by issuing the principles that would be the basis for future staff planning:[7]

1 The situation in Russia and Italy will probably enable us in the new year to strike a blow on the Western Front. The relative proportion of strength of the belligerents will be approximately equal. For an offensive it will be possible to make available approximately 35 divisions and 1,000 pieces of heavy artillery. *These resources will be adequate for one offensive only. A second, large diversionary attack will not be possible.*
2 Our general situation requires an attack as early as possible, at the end of February or start of March, before the arriving American forces tip the scales.
3 The British must be knocked out of the war.

(Emphasis added.)

In analyzing the previous Allied offensives, German planners concluded that they had failed because of a lack of adequate diversionary attacks. Yet

Ludendorff decided that the Germans did not have sufficient forces to mount major diversionary attacks. Rupprecht later also noted that he thought Ludendorff was vastly underestimating the toughness of the British.[8] As Correlli Barnett pointed out, it was the Schlieffen Plan all over again—a gamble under acute time pressure, making use of a temporary superiority that was not really overwhelming.[9]

The very next day, Crown Prince Wilhelm's Army Group fired off the first of a long string of staff studies, this first one strongly advocating the Verdun option. Schulenburg argued that Britain would not end the war because of a partial defeat of its army. Only the complete collapse of the French would cause the British to make peace. The St. Quentin option would surely draw in both French and British reserves, and surprise in the St. Quentin area would be almost impossible to achieve. Only the destruction of the French forces around Verdun, he concluded, would eliminate any possibility of an Allied offensive.[10]

On 16 November Wilhelm's Army Group issued planning guidance to its subordinate armies.[11] Already assuming that OHL was leaning toward one of the options in Rupprecht's Army Group sector, Wilhelm's Army Group told the Seventh, First, and Third Armies that they could not count on reinforcements in the case of an Allied counterattack. The army group also issued specific instructions for yielding ground. Three days later the army group requested permission from OHL to initiate the withdrawal to the Gudrun Position starting 15 December.[12]

Sometime in November, Lossberg sent a detailed course of action analysis to Ludendorff addressing three key questions:[13]

Timing of the offensive: Lossberg thought there was a very low probability that the Allies would attack the Germans first. They would most likely wait for a German attack, or wait until the arrival of the Americans gave them an overwhelming superiority. The Americans would take time, but as soon as the German offensive was launched, they would accelerate their preparations. If the offensive was not operationally and decisively successful, the Germans would then be forced to transition to the operational defensive, facing an enemy superior in numbers and strength. The later in the year the Germans would be forced to do this, the better, because the autumn and following winter weather would work to their advantage in the defense. Thus, Lossberg concluded the offensive should not start until mid-May. That also would allow the ground to dry out thoroughly, especially in the Lys valley, and it would provide time to move more divisions from the east. Even if those were low-quality units, they could be used to release higher-quality divisions from other positions in the line.

Method of attack: Their good rail net and especially their superiority in motor vehicles gave the Allies the ability to reinforce threatened sectors faster than the Germans could during the Allied offensives. Thus, the Allies first should be forced to commit and tie down their reserves through a series of about four limited diversionary attacks. The diversionary attacks should average fifteen kilometers in width and seven to ten kilometers in depth—to the Allies' first line of artillery. Each attack should be conducted by five attack divisions with three in reserve. Each attack should be able to destroy three enemy divisions and tie down five more committed to reinforce that sector, plus another five in reserve. Twenty German attack divisions, then, should be able to destroy twelve Allied divisions, and tie down another forty.

Location of the offensive: Lossberg stressed that the objective of the offensive should be a tactical and operational breakthrough (*taktischen und operativen Durchbruchs*) and a subsequent roll-up of the enemy front. He was vague, however, on the precise location, only noting, "The choice of the location of the offensive must allow for an obvious operational success (*operativen Erfolg*)." After Ludendorff made his final decision for a single great strike, Lossberg proposed a two-phase offensive: first phase, attack north of Lens, in order to take the well-fortified defensive zone of Arras from the rear; and second phase, continue to Amiens. Lossberg specifically recommended against a frontal attack against Arras (MARS). He also strongly recommended against an attack across the old Somme battlefield, because the condition of the shell-cratered ground would make follow-on support and sustainment extremely difficult.

Crown Prince Rupprecht's Army Group followed up with its own very detailed staff study on 20 November.[14] The study was based on fact that Russia was still at war with Germany. Disagreeing with Lossberg, Kuhl argued that the attack should be made as early as possible, considering the arrival of the Americans. The Germans also had to assume that the British would continue their offensive in Flanders. Kuhl then went on to examine the three options in Rupprecht's Army Group sector, ignoring the Verdun option completely.

ST. GEORG: Kuhl still primarily advocated the attack in the region of Armentières, against the flank and rear of the large British force in the Ypres salient. The main attacking forces would be General Friederich Sixt von Arnim's Sixth Army, supported by General Ferdinand von Quast's Fourth Army. Kuhl also noted the two weak Portuguese divisions in the attack sector as an exploitable vulnerability. He laid out two alternative courses of action for GEORG: the first as a decisive attack, and the second as a diversionary attack to relieve pressure elsewhere.

Bailleul-Hazebrouck was the main direction of advance for GEORG as a decisive attack. The British forces packed tightly into their northern flank would have great difficulty maneuvering. They would have the sea on their left flank as well as their rear. The objective would be to take the British in the flank and rear, cut off their retreat, and defeat the main body. The attack would also protect the German U-boat bases in Flanders. Kuhl argued that the ground conditions in the Lys valley would actually work to the attacker's advantage by giving the defenders a false sense of security. The left flank of the German attack would push the British across the La Bassée Canal and anchor on that terrain feature. The canal would provide a defensive line against French reinforcements moving up from the south—although strong reserves had to be held to counter such a thrust. Kuhl cautioned that the Germans must avoid committing heavy forces to a set-piece fight for the high ground around Mount Kemmel. GEORG as a decisive attack would require forty divisions and 400 to 500 heavy batteries.

GEORG as a diversion to relieve pressure elsewhere would also attack across the Lys and Lawe in the direction of Bailleul-Hazebrouck, but to far less depth. The attacking force would consist of twenty to twenty-five divisions, a force naturally too small to engage the British main force.

MARS: Kuhl devoted only a few paragraphs of discussion to the options in the northern end of the sector of General Georg von der Marwitz's Second Army. He thought MARS would be far too difficult because the Allies held Vimy Ridge and other key high ground with large concentrations of artillery, especially Monchy le Preux, just east of Arras. (See Map 2.) Kuhl estimated that an attack between the La Bassée Canal and the Scarpe would require nineteen divisions in the first line, nineteen divisions in the second line, twelve divisions in reserve, and 600 heavy batteries. He also noted the possibility of an attack on both sides of the Scarpe, but he did not provide a force estimate.

MICHAEL: Although the British defenses in the MICHAEL sector were far less well prepared, Kuhl argued that the area devastated by Operation ALBERICH was too much of an obstacle for the attacker. The Second Army, which as of November 1917 held most of the proposed MICHAEL sector, was so far away from the main British force in Flanders that the operational objective of the attack could not be that force. The objective of MICHAEL, then, would have to be "to break through the enemy front and in warfare of movement against the enemy reserves to achieve the most decisive result possible"—whatever that was. Kuhl never spelled it out.

Kuhl thought the turn-and-pivot maneuver to accomplish the roll-up after the breakthrough was far too complex. The Second Army's front ran from northwest to southeast, and the basic direction of the exploitation phase ran to the northwest. A ninety-degree turn of an attacking force in motion is one of the most difficult of all battlefield maneuvers. Kuhl also argued that MICHAEL would require far more forces than GEORG—fifty-five divisions and 600 heavy batteries. Because of MICHAEL's position closer to the French, it would be harder to block the movement of their reserves. He didn't believe that Ludendorff's plan to disrupt the movement of the enemy reserves by attacking the transportation system would be effective. To support that argument, he noted that the effectiveness of the air units in any such attacks would be heavily dependent on weather. He also noted that, during their own attacks of the previous year, the British had not seriously interdicted the German rail lines. Kuhl's argument, however, overlooked the overall fragility of the BEF's rail network, and the fact that the German rail network had no significant choke points the equivalent of Amiens or Hazebrouck. Kuhl concluded his assessment:

> After examining all the operations that can possibly be staged within the zone of this group of armies, I have come to the conclusion that the decisive offensive ST. GEORG constitutes the most advantageous operation we can undertake in 1918. *The important thing is not to commit our main forces against the enemy too soon, but rather to let the situation develop.*

Despite the objection, raised during the conference in Mons on 11

November, that the offensive cannot be launched soon enough, I should like nevertheless to propose the ST. GEORG operation again.

During the coming spring an exceptionally favorable operational situation (*operative Lage*) will develop for us.

Our naval offensive—the U-boat campaign—will force the Briton to continue his offensive in Flanders. To this end, he will be obliged to mass his main force in Flanders at the extreme northern wing of the entire hostile front, with the sea at his flank and rear. Along the south of the British front there are wide stretches of lightly held positions, consisting mainly of earthworks above ground, which will permit a rapid breakthrough in a direction that will be most effective operationally (*operativer Richtung*).[15]

(Emphasis added.)

The key weakness in Kuhl's assessment was the lack of a well-defined objective or end state. Kuhl was also wrong about the effectiveness of the U-boat campaign, and he was wrong about a resumption of the offensive in Flanders by the BEF. Haig wanted to continue the offensive, but the BEF was far too short of manpower to do it. The replacements were available, they were just not in France.[16] War Office returns for 1 January 1918 showed 38,225 officers and 607,403 men in Britain, fit for duty. Just 150,000 would have brought Haig's divisions up to full strength.[17] This was something that German intelligence apparently missed completely. Kuhl, therefore, may have correctly assessed his enemy's intent, but not his capability.

On 7 December Rupprecht's Second Army submitted a plan for the MICHAEL option based on a breakthrough on a broad front by attacking on both banks of the Somme. The main effort would be farther to the south, in the direction of Ham. That had been the southern limit of Ludendorff's initial focus. The plan continued with a push as far as possible toward Amiens, with the left wing based on the Oise as a barrier to the anticipated French counterattacks.

Wetzell produced another staff study on 12 December, arguably his most important.[18] He noted that France in 1918, with a rested army and reinforced by the Americans, would have freedom of maneuver. The Germans estimated that as of that time on the Western Front, 106 British and French divisions opposed $118\frac{1}{2}$ German divisions in the line, with sixty-two Allied and forty-two German divisions in reserve. By the end of February the Germans would have seventy divisions in reserve. Moreover, after the British 20 November attack at Cambrai and the German counterattack, the British forces were more evenly distributed. The French forces were strongest on their left wing, opposite General Hans von Boehn's Seventh Army.

Wetzell still considered the offensive at Verdun as the most decisive option. That attack would require some thirty divisions. Wetzell also admitted that the GEORG option, which would require forty divisions, had its advantages, but GEORG was not likely to achieve decisive results by itself. Wetzell expressed doubts about attempting a breakthrough on a large scale. He pointed out that the difficulties in achieving a breakthrough in the west were so immense that it was impossible to achieve the goal by attacking in one place only. He also doubted that it was even possible to achieve tactical surprise.

Wetzell did not believe that an attack in the St. Quentin area could produce decisive results by itself either. The Allied rail network in that sector gave them the capability to reinforce from both the north and the south. "*Therefore, we will succeed in gaining truly decisive results only by a skillful combination of multiple attacks having highly reciprocal effects.*" (Emphasis added.) This statement was one of the clearest examples of German operational cognition in 1918. If Ludendorff, then, was determined to attack at St. Quentin, Wetzell proposed a two-phase operation against the British, "using the railways for the rapid transfer of [German] troops."

The first phase would be a two-pronged attack in the St. Quentin sector by the Second and Eighteenth Armies to draw in the large British reserves from Flanders. (Although not yet in the German line, General Oskar von Hutier's Eighteenth Army was scheduled to be inserted between the Second and Seventh Armies within a week.) That attack would require twenty-two divisions.

a. With 12 divisions from a line of departure on both sides of Bullecourt in the direction of Bapaume, for the purpose of reaching the Bapaume–Cambrai railroad, the principal supply line of the British Cambrai front.
b. With ten divisions between the Somme and the Oise, as well as from the direction of La Fére, in order to gain possession of the Crozat Canal.
c. This double attack will merge two days later into the main attack with 20 divisions from St. Quentin and the region north of it in the direction of Péronne, for the purpose of closing the gap between the attacks a. and b. and reducing the Cambrai Salient.

As to the purpose and objective of the combined attack, Wetzell wrote:

> The two attacks on the wings, a. and b., are to fix the British and French local reserves located in front of our Second and Eighteenth Armies, and thus establish favorable conditions for the rapid and deep thrust of the later main attack from St. Quentin and the area north of it.

The second phase of the offensive would follow about two weeks later, conducted by thirty divisions. Wetzell estimated that eight to ten divisions should be able to be released from the Second Army after the St. Quentin phase, and an additional four to six divisions could be shifted from German Crown Prince's Army Group. Most of the artillery and trench mortars used in the first phase would have to be used in the second as well. The Fourth Army would attack north of Armentières in the direction of Kemmel-Bailleul; and the Sixth Army would attack south of Armentières in the direction of Estaires. "Principal direction for both attacks: Hazebrouck." The objective of the second phase:

To penetrate the British front in Flanders—now stripped of its reserves—by means of an attack in the direction of Hazebrouck (the GEORG offensive proposed by Rupprecht's Group of Armies); to strike the British front in the flank and rear, shattering the entire British line, rolling it up from the north.

Wetzell's plan had a great deal of merit, and might just possibly have worked if executed as he envisioned it. He did recognize the importance of the rail lines, but he was only thinking at tactical depth in this case—cutting the Bapaume–Cambrai line into the Cambrai salient (which the British called the Flesquières salient), instead of cutting the rail network at operational depth at Amiens. Hazebrouck was the objective of the second phase, but there is no mention in his assessment of the importance of the rail center there.

Ludendorff did not adopt Wetzell's plan, because he was already fixed in his mind to a single great attack—a Schlieffenesque Battle of Annihilation—rather than a sequenced operation with cumulative effects. Nonetheless, Wetzell's plan almost certainly influenced Ludendorff's decision to continue contingency preparations for an attack in Flanders should the attack at St. Quentin fail. As we shall see, the major operational errors Ludendorff committed during the planning and especially during the execution of Operation MICHAEL made it impossible for the Germans to attack in Flanders later with any hope of achieving decisive effect. As the British official history put it:

> Fortunately for us, Lieut.-Colonel Wetzell's proposals were not accepted, although, in the end, after the first offensive had come to a standstill, Ludendorff, bearing them in mind, did order the second act—too late.[19]

On 15 December Rupprecht's Army Group submitted a new assessment to OHL based on the change in the strategic situation following the suspension of hostilities with Russia. With the loss of Russia Kuhl now agreed with Lossberg and thought the Allies would sit on the defensive until at least summer. That meant the British would not mass in Flanders for their own offensive, but rather better deploy their defenses. That also would make an attack against them much harder. The prospects, Kuhl conceded, now looked better for success farther south, in the Sixth and Second Army sectors. Kuhl again emphasized that the previous Allied offensives had failed because of lack of supporting attacks to tie down the German reserves, and he seconded Lossberg's earlier recommendation for diversionary attacks against the French around Verdun, and against the British around either Ypres, or better, Cambrai. The diversionary attacks should start 1 March, followed by major demonstrations (troop movements, etc.) in the areas of Verdun and Cambrai. The main attack [GEORG] should start in mid-April, its objective would be to "administer to the Briton a severe blow, but also hit him hard by the capture of the Channel coast near Dunkirk and by threatening Calais. If this operation succeeds, it will be possible to roll up the British front toward the south."[20]

This was a course of action that clearly focused on the importance of the

British logistics system, rather than focusing solely on attacking the British main force. The key question is: did the Germans have the forces and the mobility to penetrate all the way to the Channel in a single operation? The answer almost certainly is no. Kuhl also stressed the necessity of starting the offensive with a short, violent, surprise artillery preparation, of the type artillery expert Georg Bruchmüller was then advocating.[21]

On 19 December OHL ordered the insertion of Hutier's Eighteenth Army into the line from St. Quentin to the Oise River, effective 1200 hours, 27 December. The same order also assigned Bruchmüller and his Arko 86 staff to the Eighteenth Army.[22]

On 21 December Rupprecht's Army Group issued another MICHAEL course of action analysis.[23] Kuhl now argued that the Cambrai battle had altered the situation. With the British having strongly reinforced the area, the MICHAEL option would be even more difficult. GEORG, therefore, should be the option selected for the offensive. Kuhl recommended, however, that the Second and Eighteenth Armies should still continue to make all the preparations to conduct MICHAEL. Those preparations alone would serve as an effective deception measure to cover for GEORG. And, if GEORG failed, MICHAEL could still be launched as a follow-up. In that case, the Second Army should attack in the general direction of Bapaume.

Wetzell issued another operational assessment on 25 December, continuing to push for an attack against the French.[24] He cited the estimated British strength at sixty-seven divisions along 180 kilometers of front, with twenty divisions in reserve. That resulted in one British division in line per 2.9 kilometers and one division in reserve per five kilometers. French strength was estimated at 105 divisions on a front of 510 kilometers, with thirty-five divisions and three American divisions in reserve. That resulted in one French division in line per five kilometers, and one division in reserve per fourteen kilometers. With their much broader front, it would also be more difficult for the French to mass their reserves at a threatened point.

Wetzell also noted that eight French reserve divisions had recently moved behind the British north of the Oise. He stressed that an abortive attack on the British could destroy any possibility of a future attack on the French, and thereby condemn Germany to losing the war. "[The British] we can defeat but not destroy. If we defeat the Frenchman, it will mean destruction for him: first of all, the fall of the government, and probably the end of the war." Oddly enough, this was the last assessment Wetzell issued until 19 April, well after Operation MICHAEL had died, and Operation GEORGETTE was in its final death throes.

On 25 December Rupprecht's Army Group also issued planning guidance for simultaneous preparations of MICHAEL and GEORG.[25] Once the decision had been made for one option, the continuation of the preparations for the other would be a necessary deception measure. The importance of deception was stressed throughout the document. The army group also noted that the requirement to prepare both offensives simultaneously would require the establishment of an additional field-army headquarters to take over part of the Second Army's sector, despite the fact that the Eighteenth Army had just been inserted into the line. The instructions also included initial planning guidance for rapidly regrouping from GEORG to MICHAEL, or vice versa.

The Krueznach Conference[26]

Ludendorff held his second major planning conference with the army group chiefs of staff at Krueznach on 27 December 1917. Again, no final decision was made, but Ludendorff emphasized that the balance of forces in the west would be in Germany's favor by the end of February, making it possible to attack in March. At the conclusion of the conference OHL issued a directive to the army groups to plan and start preparing a complete array of operations spanning almost the entire German front. The completed plans would be due on 10 March 1918.[27]

Rupprecht's Army Group was directed to plan GEORG II in the Ypres sector; GEORG I in the Armentières sector; MARS in the Arras sector; MICHAEL I in the direction of Bullecourt–Bapaume; MICHAEL II north of St. Quentin toward Péronne; and MICHAEL III south of St. Quentin toward La Fére. Both Rupprecht and Kuhl had serious misgivings about GEORG II from Mt. Kemmel toward Bailleul, because of the heavily cratered ground in the Ypres sector. Both also considered MARS virtually impossible.[28]

Crown Prince Wilhelm's Army Group was directed to plan ACHILLES, an attack by the First Army west of Reims; and HECTOR, an attack by the Third Army in the Argonne. Wilhelm's and Gallwitz's Army Groups were directed to plan jointly CASTOR, west of Verdun; and POLLOX, south of Verdun. Alberecht's Army Group was directed to plan STRASSBURG in the direction of the Breusch Valley; and BELFORT, a diversionary operation in the south.

On 1 January 1918 Ludendorff admitted to Kuhl in a phone conversation that the attack would be against the British.[29] That same day OHL issued its new tactical doctrine, *The Attack in Position Warfare* (discussed in Chapter 3). On 3 January 1918 Rupprecht's Army Group issued further planning guidance to its field armies.[30]

The Fourth Army was directed to develop the GEORG II option, the attack against Ypres salient. The estimated forces required were two to six divisions. The Sixth Army was directed to develop two alternative options. The first was the GEORG I attack against Armentières, breaking through in the direction of Hazebrouck, with further objectives Calais and Dunkirk. The estimated forces required were thirty to forty divisions. The second was MARS, an attack from Loretto Heights—Arras to Vimy, then rolling up the British front from either the north or the south. The estimated forces also were thirty to forty divisions.

The Second Army was directed to develop two simultaneous options. The first was MICHAEL I, an attack from the Cambrai front in the direction of Bullecourt–Bapaume. The second was MICHAEL II, an attack from the left wing of the army in the direction of Péronne and then north. The objective of both attacks was to cut off the enemy forces in the Cambrai salient, then continue the attack northwesterly to roll up the British. The estimated forces required were twenty to twenty-five divisions.

The Eighteenth Army was directed to develop MICHAEL III, an attack on both sides of St. Quentin to throw the enemy back over the Crozat Canal in the Péronne–Ham sector; then cover the flank of MICHAEL II. The estimated forces required were twenty divisions. The supporting attack was being planned for almost as many forces as the main attack.

On 8 January Ludendorff again cautioned Kuhl not to become too committed to GEORG.[31] On 9 January 1918 Rupprecht's Army Group sent a message to the Fourth Army telling them that, although GEORG II would be a supporting attack, they should be prepared to shift it to the main attack if the situation changed.[32] In such a case, its objective would be to cut off the British in the Ypres salient and break through toward Cassel. The following day the army group issued a new assessment, stressing that preparations for both options should continue simultaneously, with the decision made as late as possible.[33] Despite the fact that Ludendorff had long since ruled out strong diversionary attacks, Rupprecht's staff again recommended that whichever course of action was accepted, the other should become a diversionary attack. GEORG I was still recommended as the best course of action, with GEORG II as the supporting attack.

By late January, German intelligence was starting to get indicators that the British would extend their southern wing, taking over the sector of the French line that would be attacked by MICHAEL III. Haig, in fact, had agreed with Pétain on 17 December to extend the British southern wing to the Oise by the end of January.[34]

The Aresens Conference

As a preliminary to the Aresens Conference, Ludendorff, accompanied by Kuhl and Schulenburg, made a tour of the front, visiting army group and army head-quarters.[35] On 18 January they held a conference on GEORG II at the Fourth Army headquarters. On 19 January, they met on GEORG I and MARS at the Sixth Army headquarters.[36] Ludendorff continually stressed the importance of moving artillery forward to support the attack. "The whole matter depends on the advance of the artillery, and that depends on terrain." All the participants agreed that the MARS attack got more difficult the farther it advanced, and that a quick and deep breakthrough was not possible.

On 20 January they met with the Second Army and Eighteenth Army staffs at Marquette and Bussigny.[37] Ludendorff noted that the formula for the German attacks would be to handle the reserves economically and advance the artillery forcefully. The participants discussed the use of non-persistent Blue and Green Cross gas in the creeping barrage. Ludendorff noted that if the German troops hesitated to go through their own gas the attack would stall. There was also a lot of discussion about horse replacements and a proposal to rate divisional combat readiness based on their horse strength. All the meetings leading up to the

Aresens Conference focused almost exclusively at the tactical level. According to the meetings' minutes, Kuhl raised the only real operational issue when he started a discussion on whether the MICHAEL attacks should be conducted simultaneously or sequentially.

Ludendorff announced his final decision at the Aresens Conference on 21 January 1918.[38] Setting the tone for the entire meeting, Ludendorff made his famous "We talk too much about operations and too little about tactics," comment.[39] Summarizing the various options, Ludendorff ruled out GEORG as too dependent on the weather. A late spring in the area might delay the start of the attack until May, which was far too late for Ludendorff. He also said he thought it necessary to take Mount Kemmel and the southern Béthune hills, which added to the difficulty of the operation. In his memoirs after the war Ludendorff wrote: "Strategically the northern attack had the advantage of a great but limited objective. It might enable us to shorten our front if we succeeded in capturing Calais and Boulogne."[40] It was odd that Ludendorff thought that capturing Calais and Boulogne would only produce the limited effect of allowing the Germans to shorten their lines, rather than the much wider-ranging effect of possibly collapsing the BEF's logistics system.

MARS was too difficult all the way around. MICHAEL, then, on both sides of St. Quentin was the decision. "Here the attack would strike the enemy's weakest point, the ground offered no difficulties, and it was feasible for all seasons."[41] Ludendorff, however, decided to extend MICHAEL's northern wing to the Scarpe. Supporting attacks in the south by the Seventh Army were ruled out for the time being because, while such attacks might tie down the local reserves, they also would pull in the Allied strategic reserves that much faster.

Ludendorff planned to have eighty-five to ninety divisions in reserve in the west by the end of March. He saw the problems with the MICHAEL option, but he also saw the advantages of splitting the British and the French.

> The center attack seemed to lack any definite limit. This could be remedied by directing the main effort [Ludendorff used the term *Schwerpunkt*] between Arras and Péronne, toward the coast. If the blow succeeded the strategic result [*strategischer Erfolg*] might indeed be enormous as we should separate the bulk of the English army from the French and crowd it up with its back to the sea.[42]

Rupprecht, Kuhl, Wilhelm, and Schulenburg all pushed Ludendorff to set specific ground objectives for the attack.[43] Ludendorff countered, "In Russia we always merely set an intermediate objective, and then discovered where to go next."[44]

Ludendorff also announced that General Otto von Below's Seventeenth Army (formerly the Fourteenth Army from Italy) would be inserted into the line between the Second and Sixth Armies, effective 1 February. At the same time, the Eighteenth Army was to be detached from Rupprecht's Army Group and assigned to the German Crown Prince's Army Group.[45] Rupprecht naturally objected to this obvious violation of the unity of command, and Lossberg strongly opposed it as well.[46]

The Eighteenth Army's mission was to provide flank security for the attacks of the Second and Seventeenth Armies. The Eighteenth Army would advance to the line of the Somme between Péronne and Ham, and to the Crozat Canal. The initial Eighteenth Army plan was to attack south of the Somme on the first day of the operation, and to start the attack north of the Somme the next day.[47] During the meeting Hutier's newly appointed artillery chief, Bruchmüller, argued against that on the basis that the enemy would too easily anticipate the northern attack. That would allow them to attack preemptively the densely packed masses of artillery and ammunition in position to support the northern attack.

The Second and Seventeenth Armies would make the main attack. Ludendorff told Rupprecht's Army Group to continue making preparations for GEORG, but the Germans would attack in Flanders only if MICHAEL failed.[48] But failed to do what? That question was never answered. OHL issued the operations orders for MICHAEL on 24 January, 8 February, and 10 March. (Discussed in detail in the following chapter.)

Assessment: was the BEF the right objective?

On the day of the Aresens Conference Rupprecht noted in his diary that he did not expect the German offensive in the west to succeed. He actually thought the attack should be launched in Italy, to take the Italians out of the war and to force the British and French to divert resources.[49] Hindenburg was ambivalent, and Wetzell, Schulenburg, and Crown Prince Wilhelm insisted that the French had to be attacked first. But most of Ludendorff's key advisors, including Kuhl and Lossberg, agreed that Britain had to be taken out first. In terms of sheer force numbers on the Continent, Britain was the weakest member of the coalition, and in March 1918 that coalition suffered from a lack of a central command authority, or even a central reserve.[50]

As Brigadier-General James Edmonds put it in the British Official History, "Two main objectives seemed at [British] GHQ to present themselves to the enemy, either Paris or the Channel ports."[51] An attack against Paris might not necessarily result in the decisive defeat of the French armies. They could still withdraw behind the Loire and later support Haig when the Germans turned on the British. Paris was some eighty miles from the front lines, and during any thrust toward the French capital the Germans would have to reinforce their right flank heavily to protect their own lines of communications against British counterattacks.

On the other hand, "An attack towards the Channel ports would, if successful, be disastrous for the British armies." The Channel ports were only fifty miles from the German lines, and only about forty miles from effective heavy gunfire. The British had no depth in Flanders, which closed off the option of an elastic defense. Besides, the British had been trained for the offense, and all their recent experience was in offense. Also, there was much resistance in BEF to adopting defense-in-depth tactics. As one anonymous regular NCO is widely quoted as saying at the time, "It don't suit us. The British Army fights in line and won't do any good in these bird cages."[52]

Nonetheless, the British were far stronger and less vulnerable on their northern wing than on their southern, even if it would be easier for the French reserves to reach the British southern wing. The British themselves made several decisions that made things easier for the Germans. The first was the decision to keep the BEF short of replacements and its divisions under-strength, specifically to prevent Haig from resuming the offensive in Flanders. Although the assumption for many years has been that this was a deliberate policy of British Prime Minister David Lloyd George, historian Timothy Travers has shown evidence that suggests Chief of the Imperial General Staff General Sir William Robertson was behind that decision.[53]

Regardless of who was behind the decision, it compounded the effects of the second decision made by the British War Cabinet in January 1918, ordering the BEF to take over an additional sector of the French front. A provision for compensating reinforcements was not part of that decision, which meant that the British line had to be weakened somewhere. The issue of British manpower also ties to the question of an adequate reserve. If Haig had the forces to contribute, an effective Allied central reserve might have been available in March 1918. Edmonds later argued that if the BEF had had a robust enough reserve force, the MICHAEL offensive could have been defeated by a counterattack.[54]

As the result of the extension of the British line to just south of the Oise, General Sir Hubert Gough's Fifth Army found itself in new, very poorly developed positions. That forced the troops to spend a lot of time on labor details at the expense of training. By 21 March the Fifth Army's Battle Zone had no dugouts and was incomplete between St. Quentin and the Oise.[55] The Rear Zone consisted of a single trench line marked out on a map. The Fifth Army also consisted of only New Army and second-line territorial divisions. It had no regular, first-line territorial, or Empire divisions.[56] And finally, of all the BEF's armies, the Fifth had the most thinly held line (see Table 5.1).

The generally accepted explanation for Haig's decision to keep the Fifth Army weak is the assumption that Gough had the depth to fall back into, and there was nothing critical in his rear—except Amiens, which was at a greater

Table 5.1 BEF March 1918 frontal densities[57]

Army	Average divisional fronts
Second	1.92 miles
First	2.36 miles
Third	2.00 miles
Fifth	3.23 miles

Source: Middlebrook, p.71.

depth than most World War I commanders would have believed to be vulnerable.[58] And, based on a 7 March agreement between Haig and Pétain, the French were to put a reserve of six divisions immediately behind Gough on Haig's request. Travers, however, argues convincingly that this is a post facto rationalization to cover the fact that Haig and GHQ were slow to recognize the threat at the southern end of their line, and that for several days into the battle they believed the main danger was on the northern end of the MICHAEL attack.[59] The irony here is that that certainly was the original German intent. The "open space" explanation also ignores the critical danger of a Franco–British rupture.

Gough was only too well aware of the vulnerability of his position and, as the date of the German attack drew closer, he was increasingly convinced that the main blow would fall on the Fifth Army. On 4 and 9 February GHQ gave Gough specific instructions that in the event of a major attack, he was to stand and fight if he could, and then conduct a fighting withdrawal, but no farther back than the line of the Somme. He was also to maintain the connection with the Third Army at all costs.[60]

By striking at the British at their juncture with the French, the Germans would be following the Napoleonic formula for defeating a coalition: Attack the weakest member at its weakest point, and then defeat the other members in detail. With the German troops trained for infiltration tactics, the shattered ground of the Somme area, with its maze of trenches, ditches, craters, and cellars, actually worked to the advantage of the attacking infantry—but not of course to the advantage of the following artillery and logistical support. The critical flaw in the German plan was that it was still conceived as a force-on-force operation—a *Vernichtungsschlacht*—rather than a wedge between the coalition partners and a focused attack on the very vulnerable logistics system of the numerically weaker but more resilient partner. Ironically, Hindenburg in his post-war memoirs clearly identified the logistics vulnerability that Ludendorff never seemed to recognize:

> Had we reached the Channel coast, we would have touched Great Britain's very life-cord. By so doing, we not only would have been in the most favorable position for interfering with her communications, but we would also have been able thence, by means of our heaviest calibers, to bombard a portion of Great Britain's southern coast.[61]

6 Operations MICHAEL and MARS

21 March to 5 April 1918

We indeed hope that it may succeed, but it is impossible for us to guarantee. If we were stronger, if matters were different, but with the available forces it will be very difficult.[1]

Bavarian Crown Prince Rupprecht

We can now deploy our entire strength in the West. To be sure, that is our last card.[2]

Colonel Albrecht von Thaer

Plans (21 January–20 March)

Even before Ludendorff made his decision on 21 January, the Eighteenth Army chief of staff, General Traugott von Sauberzweig, sent Wetzell a memo on 16 January proposing that the Germans exploit the recent southern extension of the British line by heavily weighting the left wing of the Eighteenth Army attack.[3] Sauberzweig estimated that the Eighteenth Army would have a fairly easy time of it and could reach the line of the Somme and Crozat Canal in two to three days. This line would not be crossed. Once reached, all reserves would be oriented to the northwest toward Péronne to support the Second Army. As Sauberzweig noted, "The more forces the enemy introduces east of the Somme and the Crozat Canal, the more decisive will be his defeat if our breakthrough is successful and we continue to advance."[4] (See Map 2.) Three days later Rupprecht's Army Group sent a rather testy response to the Eighteenth Army noting: "The attack of the Eighteenth Army does not have a purpose of its own, rather in the scheme of the total MICHAEL operations its mission is to cover the flank of the Second Army." And, "The main effort of the MICHAEL operations is on the left flank of MICHAEL II."[5] Already fault lines in the MICHAEL plan were forming along the army group boundaries.

On 24 January, OHL issued the order assigning the boundaries,[6] and another order laying out the basic planning guidance. The MICHAEL offensive had to be ready to go about 20 March, with the Seventeenth Army conducting MICHAEL I; the Second Army conducting MICHAEL II; and the Eighteenth

Army conducting MICHAEL III. A supplemental order further stated: "The MICHAEL offensive will rupture the enemy front with the line La Fére–Ham–Péronne as its objective; thereafter, the offensive is to be advanced, in conjunction with the Operation MARS left wing, beyond the line Péronne–Arras."[7] MARS would only be launched south of the Scarpe (MARS-SÜD), a few days after the start of MICHAEL, after the artillery was regrouped and shifted. The attack north of the Scarpe (MARS-NORD) was cancelled because of insufficient forces. Even by this stage there was no clear purpose to the MARS operation, aside from the goal of achieving some sort of vague tactical success in the first phase of the operations to provide a guide for the second phase.

Preparations were to continue for Operations GEORG I (Armentières) and GEORG II (Ypres), but without hindering the preparations for MICHAEL. The GEORG operations had to be ready to go by the beginning of April, but only thirty divisions were now available for GEORG I. OHL put Operations HECTOR and ACHILLES east of Reims on hold, but did not cancel them. Operations CASTOR and POLLUX on both sides of Verdun were cancelled. Planning was to continue for Operations STRASSBURG and BELFORT on the southern end of the German line. OHL also added two new operations for planning purposes: ROLAND, an attack by the Third Army farther to the east in the Champagne area; and ERZENGEL (ARCHANGEL), an attack by the Seventh Army to support the Eighteenth Army by striking south of the Oise to take the high ground east of the Oise–Aisne Canal.[8] The Seventh Army initially planned ERZENGEL for eleven divisions controlled by four corps.[9]

Although Ludendorff decided on the MICHAEL option on 21 January, that decision was tightly held for security purposes and not widely disseminated. Thus, the working staffs at the different echelons continued to plan and develop the various courses of action as modified by OHL's 24 January order. Two days later Rupprecht's Army Group ordered its armies to start the preparations for the GEORG, MARS, and MICHAEL options. If GEORG did not become a main attack it would become a supporting attack for MICHAEL, called KLEIN-GEORG (SMALL-GEORG).[10]

The Second Army, meanwhile, was developing its plan for MICHAEL II. The planning guidance sent to the subordinate corps stated:

> The purpose of Attack MICHAEL II is to cut off, in conjunction with the attack operations of the Seventeenth and Eighteenth Armies, the British forces stationed in the Cambrai Salient, and to continue the advance westward via Péronne and north thereof.[11]

The Second Army's planners estimated their force requirements at eighteen attack and eight trench divisions; 198 light and 186 heavy artillery batteries; and twenty-one observation, eighteen attack, and nine fighter squadrons, and two bomber wings.[12] In the end, they got more artillery than their original estimate, but fewer divisions and air units.

OHL held another planning conference at Mons on 3 February. Ludendorff once again emphasized the primacy of tactics by stating: "It is the impression of OHL that the preparation phase for the attacks places too much emphasis on surprise and too little on tactical effect."[13] Ludendorff reiterated that MICHAEL was the main attack, supported on the flanks by ERZENGEL and MARS. If these attacks failed, then either ROLAND or GEORG would be launched as soon as the supporting heavy artillery could be shifted.[14] The key point, however, was that available heavy artillery and not divisions was the pacing factor. After the meeting Rupprecht expressed some relief that Wetzell's original plan of alternating hammer blows finally seemed to have achieved limited acceptance at OHL.[15] Kuhl, on the other hand, thought that if Ludendorff continued to listen to Wetzell, the German Army would wind up delivering a series of pointless attacks all up and down the Western Front.[16]

During the 3 February meeting Below also pressed to extend his Seventeenth Army's attack as far north as the Scarpe. Ludendorff, however, held firm that Seventeenth Army would attack only from Croisilles, some twelve kilometers south of Arras. After the artillery was regrouped, the MARS attack would go in. It was important to keep the weight of the main effort at the junction of Second and Seventeenth Armies. Ludendorff wanted to keep three OHL reserve divisions at Denain, some thirty-five kilometers to the rear. From there they could be committed to reinforce either the Seventeenth or the Second Army.[17] Thus, at the same time Rupprecht's Army Group was saying the main effort was on the left of MICHAEL II, OHL was saying the main effort was on the right of MICHAEL II. On 3 February OHL also conducted a conference at Maubeuge on artillery technical and tactical matters. Despite some lively discussion, no final decision was reached on the question of firing without registration.[18]

OHL finally transmitted the formal decision for MICHAEL in an operations order issued on 8 February.[19] The order mostly contained tactical planning guidance resulting from the 3 February Mons Conference. That same day Schulenburg sent a memo to OHL stating that the main effort of the Eighteenth Army's attack should be in the north.[20] Two days later OHL issued an order designating Flanders as only a diversionary sector, owing to a lack of forces.[21] All the German efforts and resources were lining up behind the MICHAEL offensive. Yet, in a meeting with the Kaiser and Chancellor at Homburg on 13 February, Ludendorff made a comment that betrayed his own belief in the German ability to conclude the war with a single masterstroke. "We must not believe that this offensive will be like those in Galicia or Italy. It will be an immense struggle that will begin at one point, continue at another, and take a long time."[22] It was a rather uncharacteristic comment from the man who could not stand the word "operations."

On 14 February Rupprecht's Army Group sent the Seventeenth Army a message indicating that the main effort of MICHAEL I should be more on the pivot of the right wing against Arras, rather than on the left wing in cutting off the Cambrai salient and linking up with MICHAEL II.[23] Two days later OHL overruled the army group planners in a message re-emphasizing the relationship of MICHAEL and MARS. According to OHL, the main effort of the

Seventeenth Army attack had to be on the left wing initially, in the direction of Bapaume and to the west. OHL also stated: "The execution of the MARS attack depends solely on the complete success of the MICHAEL (I–III) attacks. Therefore, the decision [to launch MARS] cannot be left to the Seventeenth Army. The decision will remain with OHL."[24]

Ludendorff met again with the chiefs of staff at Charleville on 24 February. The entire meeting was devoted almost entirely to artillery issues. Bruchmüller was present and he defended the efficacy of the Pulkowski Method. Bruchmüller and Ludendorff also spent much time debating about whether the creeping barrage should make 100- or 200-meter shifts. Ludendorff also decided that ammunition would have transportation priority over rations once the German forces started moving forward.[25]

Not all the planners were convinced that MICHAEL would be a complete success. On 26 February Rupprecht's headquarters issued preliminary planning guidance for the regrouping of forces from MICHAEL-MARS to GEORG. Throughout the document the operation was still called GEORG, rather than KLEIN-GEORG. The order contained the remarkable statement: "It must be assumed that the MICHAEL operations will be halted because of operational considerations." This could occur when the Germans reached the line Croisilles–St. Leger–Bapaume–Coumbles–Clery–Somme. Extensive use of land marches would be necessary to ease the load on rail traffic and to execute the regrouping as rapidly as possible. Units from the Seventeenth Army were to march to the Sixth Army area, and units from the Second Army would move by train to the Fourth Army area.[26]

Rupprecht's Army Group issued specific targeting instructions against rail installations for air and super-heavy artillery units (SCHWEFLA). The priority targets were the rail centers at Béthune, St. Pol, Doullens, Amiens, Longueau, Montdidier, and Compiègne and the lines connecting those points. Bomber Wing 3 (based in the Fourth Army area) was assigned to attack Béthune and St. Pol, augmented by the fire of the super-heavy batteries in the Sixth Army area. Bomber Wing 5 (based in the Seventeenth Army area) was assigned Doullens; and Bomber Wing 7 (in the Second Army area) was assigned to attack Amiens and Chaulnes.[27] The Germans did recognize the necessity to interdict the Allied lines of communications; but the primary purpose of these attacks was to prevent the Allies from moving their reserves, rather than strangling the Allied logistical system. OHL estimated that during the first eight days of the operation the Allies could not move up more than forty divisions in reserve, while the Germans could move up at least fifty.[28]

About three weeks before the start of the attack, more indications surfaced that the staff of the Eighteenth Army had somewhat different ideas about Operation MICHAEL. Major Klewitz, an OHL liaison officer, reported on 28 February that the Eighteenth Army sent a request to Crown Prince Wilhelm's Army Group for one division from the Seventh Army to be placed in position to support if the situation arose where the Eighteenth was ordered to advance beyond the Crozat Canal to the Oise.

On 3 March, Ludendorff noted in a telegram:

> Agreed. It is most desirable for the rapid and favorable course of the MICHAEL attack that the left wing of the Eighteenth Army should press forward well beyond the canal. For this purpose, as many divisions as possible of the Seventh Army should be brought forward via La Fére.

Although he was agreeing to the preparations to exploit the contingency, he did not agree to extend the Eighteenth Army's initial objectives beyond the Crozat Canal. That question, he said, would be would be settled at a conference with the chiefs of staff at Mons on 7 March.[29]

Wilhelm's Army Group responded on 6 March that any push toward La Fére would do little good if MICHAEL III remained a limited objective attack. If the Eighteenth Army were allowed to attack beyond the Somme, it might produce significant results. It was necessary, then, to secure the bridgeheads west of the Crozat Canal at Tergnier and Jussy as soon as possible to facilitate any counterattack against French reserves moving up.[30]

Several days earlier the Eighteenth Army sent Wilhelm's Army Group a message explaining its initial lineup of forces. Noting that the main effort of MICHAEL III was in the north, the message stated: "The commitment of forces in the first line at the start seems contradictory—five divisions for the north attack, six divisions for the south attack." The Eighteenth Army justified this because the starting width of the northern attack was narrower that in the south. A sixth division would be committed in the north after that front broadened as it advanced. Despite this rationale, it was a rather odd way to weight the main attack.[31]

Ludendorff had made it very clear from the outset that a large-scale operation would only be possible if the Cambrai salient were cut off "on the first day."[32] Rupprecht's Army Group, therefore, forced the Second Army to modify its plans for its main effort. The Second Army had wanted to put its main effort sufficiently far from the Cambrai salient to avoid the British reserves stationed close by. Rupprecht's Army Group pointed out that this would not support the left wing of the Seventeenth Army that was supposed to push to Etray, and then link up with the right wing of the Second Army in the vicinity of Equancourt no later than the first day. Thus, the right wing of the Second Army attack (XIII Corps) would have to be strengthened considerably. But then the same order also betrayed the deeply rooted suspicion that the Eighteenth Army might be fighting its own separate campaign:

> It had been expected that the Eighteenth Army, after capturing Holon Woods, would jump into action across Omignon Creek [the inter-army boundary] in order to facilitate the advance of the left of the Second Army. However, according to the intentions of the Eighteenth Army as made known here, one can no longer count on that. Should the current intentions of the Eighteenth Army remain in effect, the Second Army will have to help

itself, and turn over to the LI Corps [the left flank corps] the forces that are absolutely necessary.[33]

So in the same order the Second Army was told to strengthen both flanks at the same time. The next day Second Army came under more pressure to strengthen its left wing. "OHL has decided that the left wing of the Second Army . . . is to attack without regard to any advance on the part of its neighboring units."[34] It seemed that even OHL recognized that the Eighteenth Army might go off on its own tangent.

Rupprecht's Army Group also issued specific guidance for the synchronization of MICHAEL I and II.

> The prime objective of MICHAEL I and II is the cutting off of the British forces in the Cambrai Salient and the achievement of a major tactical victory thereby. For this purpose, it is necessary that the Seventeenth and Second Armies, with strong interior wings and without regard to losses, advance in one bound as far as possible on Ytres and Equancourt respectively.[35]

The interior wings of the two armies were not supposed to pivot too early. In order to facilitate the attack, the two divisions on the extreme right of the Second Army would conduct a frontal holding attack to pin down the British forces in the salient. After cutting off the salient, the German forces were to continue to move in a westward direction, but with no specific objectives designated.

> In reference to the further course of operations, only the following can be stated regarding the general plan. Besides, everything is dependent on circumstances. In general, the Seventeenth Army will have to continue the attack in a northwesterly direction, enveloping the adjacent front; and the Second Army in a westerly direction, its left wing protected by the Somme.[36]

Ludendorff met the army and army group chiefs of staff on 7 March at Mons. It was the last time he saw them before the start of the offensive. Ludendorff agreed to the Eighteenth Army's proposal to take the bridgeheads over the Crozat Canal, but he rejected all suggestions to expand the Eighteenth Army's attack until the tactical situation developed. Ludendorff also expressed the hope that subsequent operations in the Fourth and Sixth Army sectors would be possible if MICHAEL made good progress in the north. He further thought that if the attacks went well, there would be little to fear from an Allied attack in some other sector.[37] Rupprecht, however, wrote in his diary that even if the main mass of their reserves were drawn into the MICHAEL attack, the Allies could still attack other sectors with massed tanks, without an extensive artillery preparation, much as they had done at Cambrai.[38]

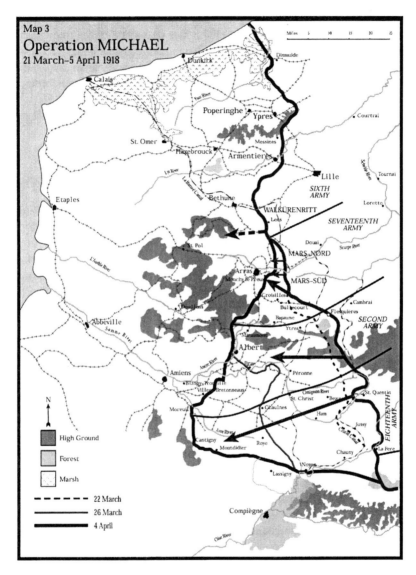

Map 3 Operation MICHAEL (source: Map by Donald S. Frazier, Ph.D., Abilene, Texas, based on sketches and notes provided by David T. Zabecki).

On 9 March the Second Army issued an order assigning missions to its supporting air units. The fighter squadrons had the mission of preventing Allied aerial observation and protecting German aerial observation. The first priority for the attack squadrons was the Allies' artillery. After the German infantry passed the line of the enemy artillery the priority of targets became: Allied reinforcements moving up, Allied artillery and tanks moving up, and any moving Allied motor vehicles. On the night of the first day, the bomber units were to bring the rail centers at Amiens and Longueau under constant attack. They were also to attack individual trains moving between Amiens and Albert, and Amiens and Chaulnes. Their follow-on mission would be attacks against the Péronne rail installations.[39]

OHL issued the main operations order for MICHAEL on 10 March. Its complete text bears repeating here:

His majesty commands:

1   The MICHAEL attack will take place on 21 March. Units will break into the enemy's first positions 0940 hours.

2   The Group of Armies of Crown Prince Rupprecht will, as their initial important tactical objective, reduce the Cambrai Salient now held by the British, and thereafter advance to the north of Omignon Creek to the line Croisilles–Bapaume–Péronne and the confluence of Omignon Creek and the Somme. In the event that the attack of the right wing makes favorable progress, the Seventeenth Army will advance it beyond Croisilles. The group of armies has the further mission to push forward in the direction of the line Arras–Albert; to hold with its left wing on the Somme at Péronne; and by shifting its main effort to the right wing, to force the British back across the front of the Sixth Army, thus releasing for the advance additional forces hitherto engaged in positional warfare. To this end, all divisions now in the rear of the Fourth and Sixth Armies will be committed should the contingency arise.

3   The Group of Armies of the German Crown Prince will first of all gain the line of the Somme and the Crozat Canal to the south of Omignon Creek. In the event of the Eighteenth Army making rapid progress, it will capture the passages across the Somme and the Canal. In addition, the Eighteenth Army will be prepared to extend its right wing to Péronne. The Group of Armies will reinforce the left wing of the Eighteenth Army with divisions from the Seventh, First, and Third Armies.

4   The 2nd Guard Division, 26th Württemberg Division, and 12th Division remain in OHL reserve.

5   Based on the progress of operations, a decision will be made later on the MARS and ERZENGEL attacks. Preparations for those attacks must continue without interruption.

6   The armies not participating in the attack will follow the instructions in order Ia 6925 dated 4 March. Crown Prince Rupprecht's Army Group will secure the right flank of MARS-MICHAEL against British counterattack. The Seventh, First, and Third Armies of the German Crown Prince's Army Group will fall back in the face of major French attacks, except in the sector for ERZENGEL. In the sectors of Gallwitz's and Duke Albrecht's Army Groups, there is no immediate decision on the

response in case of a major French attack. Divisions from those army groups may be shifted to support the main battle.[40]

The basic operational scheme was a departure from Ludendorff's original concept, broadening the attack rather than focusing it. The main objective, however, was still the defeat of British forces north of the Somme. The scheme of maneuver was not a frontal attack but rather a penetration followed by an attempt to cut across the British rear with the Seventeenth Army, using the Second Army and Eighteenth Army in supporting efforts to hold the French in the south, and then reinforcing the breakthrough on the right.

The Seventeenth Army had the most difficult mission. The reduction of the Cambrai salient required it first to advance to the southwest on Bapaume. After that, it had to turn northwest to reach the line Arras–Albert. The Seventeenth Army's maneuver would be restricted on its right by Arras and the high ground around Monchy. Like Below, Kuhl wanted to extend the Seventeenth Army's attack to cover Arras and the Scarpe from the start, which would have greatly facilitated the rolling up of the British line later. Kuhl asked OHL to reinforce the Seventeenth Army at the expense of the Eighteenth, but OHL refused.[41]

In its initial attack, then, the Seventeenth Army had to divert resources to cover itself from Allied reaction from Arras until the heavy artillery could be shifted to support the launching of MARS. This in itself would be an extremely difficult task. The artillery would have to move laterally across the lines of communications for MICHAEL I. The artillery grouped for MICHAEL had the advantage of being able to move into position under conditions of relative security. The artillery re-positioned for MARS would have to enter a battle under way, moving into position without the benefit of surprise.

The Second Army mission was somewhat easier. Initially it had to attack to the west. As soon as the Seventeenth and Second Armies reached the line of Croisilles–Bapaume–Péronne, the Second Army would continue its advance toward Albert, anchoring its left flank on the Somme. From that point its mission would be to support the Seventeenth Army in rolling up the British.

The Eighteenth Army had the easiest mission. After reaching the Somme, it would extend its right wing as far north as Péronne. The operations order contained no follow-on mission for the Eighteenth Army after it reached the line of the Somme and the Crozat Canal. The sole purpose of its attack was to capture the river crossings and the canal.

On 11 March, ten days before the start of the attack, the Second Army reported evidence of increased British artillery strength opposite its sector.[42] As a result of the Second Army's reports, Ludendorff started to consider the possibility of a much slower advance by Second Army, and also the possible necessity for a deep inward swing by the Seventeenth and Eighteenth Armies.[43] The next day Rupprecht's Army Group sent OHL another memo on MICHAEL and MARS. Noting that the heavy artillery from MICHAEL would be available for transfer to MARS on the evening of 21 March, Rupprecht's headquarters stressed that MARS should be launched as early as 22 March. "A MARS offensive executed only some days later will be more difficult and more bloody than an immediate roll-up of the front after the first great breakthrough." It also recommended that the reserve divisions for MARS, including those under direct OHL control, should be positioned as close as possible to facilitate their immediate commitment.

> If the OHL divisions are still at Bouchain on the afternoon of the 21st, then they will not be able to arrive before the evening of the 23rd, and cannot attack before the morning of the 24th. Therefore, they must be in the area south of Douai on the morning of the 21st if they are to be available when needed. The earliest they could attack then would be the 22nd.[44]

These OHL divisions were the ones referred to in Paragraph 4 of the main operations order. Rupprecht's headquarters also reminded OHL that: "The Seventeenth Army cannot provide from its MICHAEL forces such a strong reserve for the right wing that it would still be able to continue the attack in the direction of Arras under its own power." Because of the requirements of the deception plan (cited in Paragraph 6), more divisions could not be withdrawn from the Fourth and Sixth Armies until at least 21 March.

On 12 March OHL also issued an order reconfirming 21 March as D-Day (*Y-tag*) for the attack.[45] Crown Prince Wilhelm's Army Group issued its operations order on 14 March.[46] Strong reserves were to be brought up close to the rear of the right wing of the Eighteenth Army. Their mission was to attack in the flank and rear (northwest) any enemy forces opposing the Second Army. After the attack succeeded, the Eighteenth Army had to be prepared to extend its right flank as far as Péronne. The Seventh Army had the mission to secure the left flank of the German attack with Operation ERZENGEL. Bomber units assigned to the Eighteenth Army were ordered to attack Allied headquarters and air fields. From the evening of 21 March the priority target was the rail net between Ham, Amiens, Creil, Verberie, Compiègne, and Noyon.

The following day, only six days before the start of the operation, Hutier submitted a proposal to Wilhelm's Army Group calling for a significant expansion of the Eighteenth Army's mission far beyond the line of the Crozat Canal. Its key passages included:

> 1 If the enemy is driven back over the Somme and the Crozat Canal by the Eighteenth Army, he will try to hold that line to secure the commitment of his reserves against the Second and Seventeenth Armies via Roye–Amiens. Therefore, this sector must be seized quickly. Any loss of time on our part will enable the enemy to strengthen his defenses.
> 2 Having crossed the Somme and the Crozat Canal, it will be the mission of the Eighteenth Army to draw in its direction the French reserves intended to reinforce the British, to defeat these reinforcements, and interrupt the communications between the British and the French.
> ...

It must be assumed that the French will bring up more reinforcements over the railroad lines Roye–Chaulnes and Montdidier–Amiens, in order to commit to action below Péronne against the flank of the Second Army and in front of the Eighteenth Army.

. . .

Even in the event of a major offensive against their own front, the French will still provide local support to the British. In order to secure their own flank, they will probably push additional forces forward via Chauny–Noyon, and over the Compiègne–Noyon railway.

. . .

The troop movements will begin as soon as our combat activities on the inactive fronts are recognized as feints. They will probably occur on the second day of the offensive at the latest.

. . .

The mission of the Eighteenth Army requires, therefore, fast and decisive action, not only during the forcing of the line of the Somme and Crozat, but during further advances as well. The earlier the Eighteenth Army reaches the line Chaulnes–Roye, the better will be the chances of meeting the French while they are in the process of concentration, the more favorable will be the prospects for mobile warfare.[47]

On 18 March, Wilhelm's Army Group forwarded Hutier's proposal to OHL with the following endorsement:

The more the French reaction is directed toward Rupprecht's Group of Armies, the more effective will be the proposed operation to strike the French. The enemy will soon become aware of its ominous significance and of the menace to his capital. We must therefore expect him to react very forcefully. It is for this reason that we should undertake this operation with strong forces.[48]

OHL made no changes to the orders it already issued, noting that the possibility of the Eighteenth Army advancing beyond the Crozat Canal had already been established with the order to seize the crossings. Nonetheless, the plan of attack for the Eighteenth Army had already grown far more ambitious than Ludendorff had envisioned originally. From a supporting attack controlled by the same army group that was making the main attack, MICHAEL III had grown into a distinct attack of its own, with no fixed objectives, controlled by a separate army group, with a potential to engage the French on open ground.

On 16 March Rupprecht's Army Group issued its operations order for the attack. Emphasizing that the MARS attack could only be launched after the Second and Seventeenth Armies achieved "a great tactical success," OHL would make the final decision on launching MARS, but those attack forces had to be positioned so they could exploit the advantage immediately by rolling up the British front north of Fontaine lez Croisilles. The whole purpose of MARS was to facilitate the pivot of the Seventeenth Army. The Sixth Army, in the sector north of the La Bassée Canal, had to be prepared to pursue the enemy and prevent the escape of his forces "in case he has to retreat from the pressure of MICHAEL."[49]

On 18 March Ludendorff and Hindenburg, along with an augmented Operations Division, established an OHL forward command post at Avesnes. The next day, OHL finally bowed to the continuous pressure from Rupprecht's Army Group and the Seventeenth Army and agreed to move the three OHL reserve divisions in the Douai area behind the Seventeenth Army's right flank by the evening of 21 March.[50] Their commitment, however, depended entirely on the success of MICHAEL.

On 20 March OHL issued the launch order for the next day, informing the subordinate commands that the Kaiser himself had come to the front to assume personal command.[51] That same day Ludendorff, in a telephone conversation with Kuhl, talked about his concept for the exploitation and follow-on objectives in the event that MICHAEL proved a major success. The Eighteenth Army would move toward the line Bray–Noyon; the Second Army on Doullens–Amiens; and the Seventeenth Army in the direction of St. Pol. The result would be a divergent attack. Ludendorff stressed that such a divergent operation would only be feasible if the Allies were defeated along the entire front. Even then, it would depend on whether the necessary forces were available at that point.[52] This, of course, would represent a significant change in the original operational concept. And as we shall see, it is almost exactly what Ludendorff tried to do, but without first achieving his stated conditions for success.

Preparations

The German buildup and preparations for MICHAEL were a masterpiece of staff work. For the most part they were representative of the preparations for all of the 1918 offensives. At this point, therefore, we can consider the MICHAEL preparations in some detail, and then consider only the significant differences for the subsequent operations. Although much of what is considered in this section traditionally constitutes the "boring bits" of military history, they are nonetheless the fundamental building blocks of the operational level of war.

Main preparations

Even before the final decision was made, on 25 December Rupprecht's Army Group issued general preparation guidelines establishing two main preparation phases: a general phase lasting approximately six to eight weeks, and a close phase lasting four weeks. The plan established the requirements for extension of road networks and narrow-gage field rail networks; extension of communications nets for the various headquarters, the artillery, and aviation; establishment of routes of approach, march tables, assembly areas, and divisional zones of action; establishment of command posts and observation posts; establishment of forward air fields and the pre-positioning of required tentage; and establishment of artillery and trench mortar firing positions and the pre-positioning of ammunition.[53]

During the final phase, units would be moved up and emplaced in the following order of priority: first, corps headquarters, artillery headquarters, and communications units; second, divisional staff advanced parties, artillery staffs, engineer staffs, ammunition trains, and motorized trains; third, artillery units, air defense units, labor and road construction companies, aviation companies, and balloon detachments; and fourth, divisional combat units, horse depots, bridge trains, subsistence trains, medical units, and field hospitals.[54]

Security, surprise, and deception

At this point, strategic surprise was impossible to achieve, but the Germans went to extreme measures to achieve operational surprise. Their basic approach is best summarized in the words of a security order issued by the Second Army on 22 January:

> Not a single man in the army must have any doubt in his mind that the fight has already begun, the fight for secrecy and for concealment of our preparations. Every one must realize that he himself stands in the midst of this battle and that he must employ the weapons of caution and reticence in order to win out.[55]

German troops and even subordinate-level commanders were kept ignorant of the actual plan for as long as possible. As previously noted, OHL made the attack option decision on 21 January, but the armies were not notified until the operations order of 8 February. To ensure the strict adherence to security procedures, OHL established a network of special security liaison officers with broad enforcement powers. These officers were augmented with motor transport, aerial observers, balloon observers, and photoreconnaissance resources. During the preparation and buildup the security restrictions mandated that no orders or information were to be disseminated to the trenches; no movement was to be made during daylight; all detraining must take place as far to the rear as possible; special controls were to be established on all incoming and outgoing personal mail; telephone discipline was to be strictly enforced; all new positions required overhead concealment; route discipline was to be enforced to avoid cross-country vehicle tracks observable from the air; and increased air activity was to be avoided in the planned attack sector.[56]

German intelligence reported on 5 February that the prevailing assumption among the French was that the German attack would come in the direction of Nancy, while the British were convinced the attack would occur on their front.[57] On 18 February OHL issued its main deception plan, designed to convince the French that they would be the objective of the main attack, either by the First and Third Armies in the Champagne area, or by the Fifth Army north of

Verdun.[58] OHL also issued a supplemental deception plan designed to make it look like OHL itself was relocating to the vicinity of Strasbourg on or about 1 April.[59]

On 28 February Rupprecht's Army Group issued the orders for its own deception operations under the codename GEORGEPLAN. Based on the GEORG and KLEIN-GEORG operations, GEORGEPLAN was designed to convince the British that the main blow would fall on their front in the Flanders sector. The deception activity also had the advantage of laying the groundwork for a subsequent KLEIN-GEORG operation, should it be necessary. The Fourth Army was allocated three divisions to carry out the plan, the Sixth Army got four divisions. An equal level of activity was supposed to be maintained along the army group front until about 5 March. After that point the GEORGEPLAN preparations were to become more obvious than the MICHAEL preparations.[60]

A follow-on OHL deception order required the First and Third Armies of Crown Prince Wilhelm's Army Group to launch diversionary attacks against the French in the Champagne sector starting 19 March and continuing through 24 March. Starting the morning of 21 March, feint artillery preparations would be fired in the GEORG and ERZENGEL sectors simultaneously with the MICHAEL artillery preparations.[61] For the most part, the troops and the subordinate leaders carrying out the deceptive measures were kept in the dark themselves and actually believed that they would be making the main attack. This added to the realism of the deception measures that were so effective that, two days into MICHAEL, the French still believed it was a diversion for the main attack in Champagne.

Artillery preparations

As discussed in the chapter on the tactical realities of the Great War, the fire planning for the 1918 offensives was influenced greatly by Colonel Georg Bruchmüller. After the battle of Riga Bruchmüller transferred to the Western Front along with the rest of Hutier's staff to take over the Eighteenth Army. In early November 1917, Bruchmüller, his chief assistant, Major Wilhelm Marx, and other key tactical leaders from the Eastern Front met at Le Cateau for a debriefing session conducted by OHL. It was a frustrating meeting for Bruchmüller. For the most part the Western Front staff officers dismissed the experiences of their Eastern Front colleagues. One OHL staff officer made the statement: "We just don't have enough experience with offensive operations in trench warfare. We should be looking at the Russo–Japanese War." Bruchmüller later wrote in exasperation: "And that in spite of Toboly and Galicia, in spite of Riga and Jacobstadt!"[62]

A small circle of Western Front General Staff officers did take the experiences of the imports from the east seriously. This group included Kuhl, Wetzell, Bauer, Geyer, and Ludendorff himself. In early December 1917 Bruchmüller met with Kuhl at Rupprecht's headquarters in Mons. Kuhl was acutely aware of the tactical disadvantages of artillery registration, and he wanted to hear more about Bruchmüller's abbreviated registration techniques in the east. Later that month Bruchmüller and Marx met with Captain Erich Pulkowski at Maubeuge. Pulkowski had been working under OHL orders on his new fire direction technique since the spring of 1917, but he was having a hard time getting anyone at OHL to take it seriously. The system was seen as useful only in static defensive situations. Bruchmüller quickly saw it as the answer to the dilemma of registration versus surprise during the attack. But the precision registration was a procedural icon on the Western Front, a mindset reinforced by the long period spent in a defensive posture. The new *Attack in Position Warfare* manual of 1 January 1918 still required all firing units to register, even the infantry accompanying batteries. The new doctrine was quite clear on the importance of accuracy versus operational security: "Even if the registration alerts the enemy to an impending attack, that still is not as bad as an invalid registration."[63]

Bruchmüller argued that precise registrations conducted over a period of time were impossible because of the changing effects of the weather. That left two options. All registrations could be fired immediately preceding an attack—but that amounted to handing the enemy a copy of the operations plan. The other option was to spread the registrations out for days and even weeks prior to the attack, and then continually update the correction factors for the changes in the weather. This required the guns to be in final position well before the attack, making them all that more vulnerable to detection. Bruchmüller reasoned that the Pulkowski Method could produce the same results with less effort and far less chance of compromising security.

Bruchmüller nonetheless had a hard time getting his ideas accepted. Early in January Bruchmüller, Marx, and Pulkowski met with Kuhl and won his support. On 10 January 1918 Prince Rupprecht's Army Group sent a request to OHL to be allowed to use the Pulkowski Method in combat operations. OHL refused. Meanwhile, Pulkowski had written a memo to Geyer on 7 January urging adoption of the system. Geyer supported the system and wrote a memo to Bruchmüller noting, "The procedure is theoretically unquestionable and more secure."[64] Geyer forwarded the memo and Pulkowski's letter to Bauer who first briefed Ludendorff, and then arranged an extensive test firing at Maubeuge for 2 and 3 February and later at the Artillery Test Board Range at Jueterbog. Bruchmüller was present at the Maubeuge test firings. The results were mixed, however, and the War Ministry in Berlin decided squarely against the Pulkowski Method. That was not the end of the issue, however.

The operations staff at OHL evaluated other Bruchmüller concepts that were resisted strongly by many officers on the Western Front. They opposed his taskgroup organization, which shifted the counter-battery mission to the corps artillery as being a violation of the principle of unity of command. There was little understanding of the reinforced counter-battery phase in the preparation. Bruchmüller's concept of positioning all guns as far forward as possible also ran against Western Front practice, where two years of almost continuous defensive operations had laid stress on positioning artillery in depth. There was also a great resistance to the synchronized use of non-persistent gas in close support of attacking infantry troops, despite the results obtained at Riga. Finally, there was widespread resistance to using medium and heavy calibers in the creeping barrage, although this too had proved successful in the east.

OHL issued the basic order on artillery preparations on 25 January.[65] The following day key members of the operations staff and the army artillery chiefs of Rupprecht's Army Group met to discuss the new tactics and techniques. Bruchmüller also attended the meeting, representing the Eighteenth Army. The result was an eight-page memorandum issued on 29 January that covered twenty key points, including the call for the elimination of registrations, artillery organization for combat, and the optimum length of preparations. Not all the participants were in agreement and the memorandum included various dissenting opinions. The artillery chiefs of the Sixth and Seventeenth Armies recorded dissenting opinions on several key points, including the elimination of the registration and placing the counter-battery groups under corps control. For the most part, however, the meeting was an affirmation of the methods Bruchmüller had already proved in the east.[66]

Following the 24 February Charleville meeting, OHL on 28 February issued a new set of artillery instructions formally adopting many of the techniques proposed in the 29 January memorandum. Despite the urgings of Kuhl and Rupprecht and the support of Geyer and Bauer, the Pulkowski Method was not adopted; but OHL did allow the use of the abbreviated registration procedures. Specifically, OHL required the verification of the guns' angle of lay in all cases, and also registration for range in cases where there were doubts about the accuracy of firing-position locations or gun calibration.[67] It was a partial victory for Bruchmüller, but the 28 February instructions were not at all popular and they were opposed by many artillery and General Staff officers right up to the start of MICHAEL. But OHL, strongly backed by Ludendorff, stuck to the new concepts.[68] According to Wetzell, it was Bruchmüller who almost single-handedly pushed the German Army into making these radical changes in fire-support doctrine.[69]

Bruchmüller had seven weeks to work out and implement the plans of the Eighteenth Army's artillery support. There was no overall artillery coordination among the three armies, but all were to follow the general guidelines of the 28 February memo, including the counter-battery organization and the abbreviated registrations. The duration of the preparations for the Eighteenth and Second Armies was set down by OHL. Rupprecht's Army Group was allowed to establish the preparation length for the Seventeenth Army.[70]

The new artillery concepts still met with stiff resistance, especially in the Seventeenth Army. On 3 March Ludendorff had to order the Seventeenth Army in writing to modify its artillery plan in accordance with the new principles. He even suggested very strongly that the Seventeenth Army adopt the specific procedures of the Eighteenth Army.[71] But many German artillery officers just could not bring themselves to abandon the precision registration, with its sacred fifty-meter bracket. Just prior to the start of the attack one of the armies sent the following message to Rupprecht's headquarters: "The army urgently requests permission to conduct a precision registration prior to the attack." Kuhl replied: "If a registration is necessary the army group will not attack."[72]

The artillery preparations required painstaking and systematic organization of the battlefield. Well prior to an attacking corps moving into a sector of the line held by a trench division, the commander and staff of the trench division's artillery initiated the planning. The trench division artillery commander personally managed the counter-battery planning and he eventually assumed command of the corps' counter-artillery group when it was formed. The divisional artillery command post of the trench division became the command post of the corps' counter-artillery group. Other senior artillery officers of the trench division initiated the preparations for the direct support batteries, and eventually became commanders or primary staff officers of the counter-infantry groups and subgroups that supported the attack divisions of the corps. The commander of the trench division's heavy artillery battalion usually became the commander of the attacking corps' long-range group. The idea was that these officers from the trench divisions were already in position and were most familiar with the situation and the terrain of the forward area.

The preparation activities included the reconnaissance of firing positions, observation posts, supply routes, approach routes, and ammunition facilities. Each corps required an artillery ammunition depot, and each attack division needed a forward ammunition dump and a rear ammunition supply point. In the Eighteenth Army sector alone 2,978,436 rounds of artillery ammunition, including 479,286 gas rounds, were placed in position prior to the opening of the attack.[73]

Once the positions were reconnoitered, the artillery staffs of the trench divisions started the initial preparations. Preliminary survey work was done, including establishing orienting lines at the firing positions. Telephone lines were installed as far down as sub-group command posts. When the attacking corps' firing units later moved into position they completed the internal communications circuits. As the preparations proceeded, the advanced parties and support troops of the attacking corps' artillery moved up and assumed the tasks in progress. The topographic section of the corps' survey battalion produced firing charts on a common grid. The flash and sound ranging sections located active enemy batteries and started the counter-battery target lists.[74]

The guns themselves moved into position using infiltration techniques. In most cases the majority of the batteries moved up into their firing positions only hours before opening fire. Those positions were prepared well in advance of the occupation, camouflaged, stocked with ammunition, and hooked into the telephone nets. Battery commanders and fire-direction personnel moved into the positions well ahead of the guns to prepare the firing charts. Since a huge number of guns that close to the front was sure to draw the enemy's attention sooner or later, the insertion of the batteries was carried out in three groups:[75]

Class I: Positions with cover and concealment available: these batteries occupied their positions immediately upon arriving in the attack sector. Very few batteries ever fell into this class.

Class II: Hiding places (barns, haystacks, ruins, etc.) available in the general vicinity of the firing positions: these batteries infiltrated into the hiding places during the nights preceding the attack. The night of the start of the preparation the guns were moved by hand into their firing positions. Most batteries fell into this category.

Class III: No concealment available anywhere near the positions: these guns were brought up from the rear and moved into position on the night of the attack. Horses were used exclusively for motive power.

Air preparations

The air buildup started in early March and was complete by 20 March. On 7 March there were eighty-two squadrons in the sectors of the three attacking armies. By 21 March there were 125. Air units were assembled far behind the front, beyond the range of enemy reconnaissance. It was not possible to construct all the required hangers beforehand, but tents were pre-positioned at reconnoitered positions for use as expedient hangers. Units were moved up piecemeal and the aircraft were hidden in barns and under horse tents. New balloon units were brought up under cover but not inflated until just before the start of the artillery preparation fire. The new squadrons were not allowed into the air until the day of the attack. The attack squadrons conducted training in formation attacks far behind the front. By forty-eight hours before the start of the attack all ground support units were at their forward air fields making the final preparations. By twenty-four hours before the attack, all the aircraft had flown in by infiltration.[76]

Supply and transportation

The German Army in the 20th century generally gets low marks from historians in the area of logistics, and supply failures are considered to be among the major causes of the collapse of the 1918 offensives. Ludendorff himself contributed to that belief in the message he sent out terminating MICHAEL on 5 April: "The supply situation does not allow the continuation of the attack...."[77] Not all of Ludendorff's contemporaries necessarily agreed with him on that point. In the several versions of his own monograph on the offensives, Kuhl described a relatively well-planned and -executed, albeit strained, supply and support system. Early in 1930, the former General Staff officer Ib (supply) of the Seventeenth Army, Colonel Fritz Jochim, deposited in the Reichsarchiv a remarkably detailed rough manuscript explaining the Seventeenth Army's logistics planning and execution for MICHAEL. Near the end of his manuscript Colonel Jochim specifically said that in his opinion MICHAEL failed because of operational, rather than supply-system failures.[78]

In preparation for offense the Germans shifted from a pull to a push supply system. During the buildup the daily supply requirement was 25,000 tons, or sixty standard trains.[79] The Eighteenth Army alone required 650 troop trains and

500 supply trains for its buildup.[80] The planners recognized that transportation and forward movement would be the critical factors in sustaining the momentum of the advance. In terms of total tonnage, one of the most critical supply items was gravel for road construction, which was shipped as far forward as possible by canal. Each attacking corps was assigned an engineer battalion with a road-building company.[81] One of the Second Army's orders stated: "All forward movement must proceed without interruption. The infantry of the first and second lines will clear the roads for vehicular traffic, primarily for ammunition and supply vehicles and for artillery. The infantry will march alongside the roads." All wagons of the field trains above the authorized number were to be left behind.[82]

In the Second and Seventeenth Army sectors the advance would have to proceed through the old Somme battlefields, with ground chewed up from years of shelling. Forward transportation through the crater fields was the immediate problem. Conducting experiments in a crater field in its rear area at the end of February, the Seventeenth Army concluded that rolled mats of duckboard with earth packed into the craters beneath was the best solution. Aerial photography was used to determine the shortest paths across the crater fields in each corps sector. Movements through the crater fields proceeded in the following priority:

1 Ammunition columns of the infantry regiments;
2 Accompanying artillery with double ammunition carriages;
3 Elements of the field and heavy artillery of the first-line divisions;
4 Field and heavy artillery of the second-line divisions;
5 Combat, ammunition, medical, and baggage columns of the first-line divisions;
6 Corps-level trench mortars and heavy artillery;
7 Combat, ammunition, medical, and baggage columns of the second-line divisions;
8 Army-level artillery units;
9 Field and heavy artillery of the third-line divisions;
10 Combat, ammunition, medical, and baggage columns of the third-line divisions.[83]

Once through the crater area, the Germans planned to capture and use the Allies' front-line narrow-gage rail network, and then eventually sectors of the main rail network. Thus, great quantities of rail construction material had to be positioned in readiness, along with sixty railroad construction companies supported by forty-eight labor companies. Each attacking corps had a narrow-gage rail network in its own forward areas. The Second Army identified the critical Allied rail lines in their forward area that would have to be put back in service as soon as possible. The planners estimated that it would take fourteen days to restore the Cambrai–Roisel–Péronne and Epehy–Fins–Maricourt lines to service. Until then, the Second Army's main rail supply line would be the Cambrai–Bussigny–Bohain line, which ran parallel to the front, from ten to twenty-five kilometers behind it.[84]

One of the most interesting sections in Colonel Jochim's manuscript concerns the use of tracked re-supply vehicles by the Seventeenth Army. The few that were available were used to transport ammunition through the worst of the crater areas. According to Jochim, they proved valuable, even though they broke down quite often.[85] This is a point to which we will return when we discuss the allocation of the few available tanks in the German order of battle.

Training, organization, and equipment[86]

The Germans faced an enormous challenge in totally converting three armies from defensive to offensive configuration and posture in a very short period of time. In each army a special corps headquarters was established to coordinate training. The fifty-two attack divisions had to be brought up to full strength for men, horses, and transportation equipment, most often at the expense of the trench divisions. Starting in late December 1917 the attack divisions and the OHL-level field and heavy artillery units were all withdrawn from the front and billeted far to the rear, where they received four weeks of rest, rehabilitation, and training. In the Eighteenth Army Major Marx and Captain Pulkowski trained over 6,000 officers in the new fire-direction techniques—including the still not fully approved Pulkowski Method. All the new batteries assigned to reinforce the Eighteenth Army were sent immediately to a gunnery range in the rear to re-calibrate.[87]

For the infantry units, a myriad of details had to be worked out and coordinated, including: assignment and transportation of light trench mortars and light machine guns; assignment of accompanying artillery; assignment of grenadiers (a critical specialty); ammunition basic loads; infantry ammunition wagons; hand grenades and flares; reduction of the infantryman's basic pack; composition of combat trains and field trains; draft animals for the train vehicles; and boards, bridging sections, and other material for crossing shell-holes and obstacles. The artillery units had their own special technical requirements, which included ammunition vehicles and organization of ammunition trains; organization of field trains; draft animals for supply vehicles; assignment of flash and sound ranging detachments; and assignment of accompanying engineer detachments to help the artillery move forward.

Finally, the attack divisions had to be augmented with specialist units that turned each of them into a combined arms organization that closely approximated what we now think of as a modern divisional organization: engineer companies, telephone and radio detachments, medical collecting companies, ammunition trains, subsistence trains, and road repair and labor companies.

Reconnaissance and intelligence

Between 10 and 20 March the weather was good for both operational and tactical aerial reconnaissance (*operative und taktische Fliegeraufklärung*). According to the intelligence estimate of 17 March, there was increased Allied trenching activity in front of the sectors of the three attacking armies, especially in the second and third positions. There were, however, no abnormal increases in rail cars and locomotives at the major rail centers of Albert, Amiens, Beauvais, Compiègne, or Noyon; in motor traffic along key roads; or in numbers of aircraft or air fields. Deep reconnaissance indicated that the Allied reserves and counterattack divisions had not been assembled in depth behind the main attack sector. The assessment, therefore, was that, although the Allies had reinforced their defenses at the local level, their reserves were not in position, nor could they be for at least three days, to interfere with the German attack.[88]

Allied actions

It was not exactly hard for Allied intelligence to figure out that a major German attack would come in 1918. But with no unified Allied command, both Haig and Pétain made their own preparations based on their own priorities. Haig, most concerned with covering the Channel ports, kept 30 percent of his divisions in reserve, with eight in general reserve. Pétain, who was more concerned with protecting Paris and the heart of France, kept thirty-nine of his ninety-nine divisions in reserve: nineteen between the Argonne and the Vosges; eighteen behind the French center in Champagne; four west of Soissons behind the British Fifth Army; and two behind the Belgians in Flanders.[89]

The British defenses were poorly prepared and organized, compared to those of the Germans in 1917. In late 1917, the British had started studying defensive methods for the first time since 1914. On 14 December 1917, BEF GHQ issued its first set of instructions on defense layout and tactics.[90] The instructions copied the German defense methods, but only in form, not in spirit. The British still relied heavily on the notions of static defense. In the German defensive system, two-thirds of the force was kept far to the rear, available for counterattack and maneuver. In the British system of early 1918, at least two-thirds of the total strength was within range of the initial German artillery preparation.[91] The situation in the Fifth Army area was made worse by forced southward extension of its line to just below the Oise, where it took over former French positions that were in terrible shape.

The British were also somewhat slow in understanding the new German attack tactics; although the September 1917 attack at Riga had drawn wide attention, and the Germans had used their infiltration tactics to great effect during the counterattack at Cambrai. In a certain sense, the Cambrai counterattack was a dress rehearsal for MICHAEL. In early January 1918, General Jan Smuts issued a warning that the Germans could be expected to use similar tactics in an attack on a much larger scale. That warning, however, was largely ignored in the BEF.[92]

In December 1917, Pétain and Haig tentatively agreed to provide mutual support in the event of a German attack. Pétain agreed to put the French Third Army (five infantry divisions and a cavalry corps) at Clermont for action in the British zone either between the Oise and the Somme, or north of the Somme.[93]

In January and February, meanwhile, the Allied Supreme War Council continued to wrangle over the question of establishing a general Allied reserve, where it would be positioned, and who would command it and have the authority to commit it. At that point the newly arriving American Expeditionary Force (AEF) was the only general reserve.

On 1 February Gough sent GHQ an assessment accurately predicting that the main German attack would come between the Scarpe and the Oise, and pointing out the inadequate state of the Fifth Army defenses.[94] Three days later GHQ sent the Fifth Army a memo titled "Principles of Defence," in which Gough was instructed to fight east of the Somme if possible, but he was authorized to fall back to the line of the Somme if absolutely necessary.[95] On 9 February GHQ also told the Fifth Army that it should join with the Third Army in defending the Péronne bridgehead.[96]

On 2 March the BEF intelligence estimate noted: "There is strong indication that the enemy intends to attack on the Third and Fifth Army fronts, with the objective of cutting the Cambrai salient and drawing in our reserves."[97] That same day Haig wrote in his diary, "I was only afraid that the enemy would find our front so very strong that he will hesitate to commit his Army to the attack with the almost certainty of losing very heavily."[98] On 10 March the BEF weekly intelligence summary estimated that none of the German attacks would be south of St. Epehy, roughly the boundary between Third and Fifth Armies. A week later BEF intelligence now estimated that the German attacks would reach as far south as St. Quentin. GHQ still didn't know where the main attack was coming, and still regarded an attack in the north against the Channel ports as the most dangerous enemy course of action.[99]

On 20 March a British XVIII Corps trench raid captured German prisoners who pinpointed 21 March as the start of the attack. Gough tried to have the two GHQ reserve divisions nearest to him moved up closer to his line. Haig's chief of staff rejected the request and, when the attack fell, Gough's closest support was almost twenty-five miles from the front.[100]

German order of battle

Various sources give slightly different figures for the German starting order of battle on the morning of 21 March. For this analysis we will use the information cited in the German official history, which matches the surviving records. Although the Seventeenth Army had the highest starting density of first-line divisions for the width of its attack sector, that density would diminish drastically as soon as the MARS attack south of the Scarpe added another ten kilometers to the sector width. Although the Germans had an overall force superiority of 2.6:1 in divisions, it is difficult to see from Table 6.1 below any significant weighting of the main attack.

In addition to its divisions committed to MICHAEL I, the Seventeenth Army had two trench divisions in the first line and one attack division in the second line south of the Scarpe earmarked for MARS-SÜD; and another two trench

Table 6.1 German divisions on 21 March 1918[101]

	First line	Second line	Third line	Total divisions	Sector width
Seventeenth Army	7 Attack 4 Trench	5 Attack 1 Trench	5 Attack*	17 Attack 4 Trench	20 km
Second Army	6 Attack 3 Trench	4 Attack 1 Trench	2 Attack 3 Trench#	12 Attack 7 Trench	40 km
Eighteenth Army	8 Attack 5 Trench	8 Attack 1 Trench	5 Attack§	21 Attack 6 Trench	42 km
	21 Attack 12 Trench	17 Attack 3 Trench	12 Attack 3 Trench	50 Attack 17 Trench	103 km

Source: *Der Weltkrieg*, Vol.14, Appendix 38a.

Notes
*3 OHL reserve divisions earmarked for MARS.
#1 OHL reserve division.
§1 OHL reserve division.

divisions in the first line and one attack division in the second line north of the Scarpe in the MARS-NORD sector. Three of the five attack divisions in the third line belonged to the OHL reserve, presumably for commitment to MARS. The other two attack divisions formed the army reserve.

Not actually counted in the MICHAEL order of battle, the Second Army had two trench divisions on its extreme right flank, facing the front of the Cambrai salient. Their mission was to conduct a holding attack to pin down the British forces in the salient. There was only one OHL reserve division behind the Second Army, and that was a trench division. The Second Army itself had the largest army reserve, with one attack and one trench division in the second line, and two attack and two trench divisions in the third line. The sixty-seven attacking divisions were controlled by thirteen corps headquarters. See Table 6.2.

All the divisions in the Eighteenth Army sector were committed directly to MICHAEL. OHL had one attack division in reserve behind the Eighteenth, and the army-level reserve consisted of four attack divisions. The Eighteenth Army, then, had the largest number of attack divisions in army reserve (see Table 6.3).

The weighting of the main attack was even less clear for artillery. Although the Eighteenth Army was making a supporting attack, it had more field guns and significantly more heavy guns than the other two armies. The three armies combined had 48 percent of the German Army's artillery pieces, and 40 percent of its trench mortars. Overall, the Germans had a tube superiority ratio of 2.5:1. Prior to the attack Allied intelligence underestimated German artillery strength at approximately 4,000 guns.[102] Immediately following the attack, the ferocity of the artillery fire led British intelligence to overestimate the number of German guns that had fired on them at 8,067.[103] See Table 6.4.

Table 6.2 German Corps on 21 March 1918[104]

| | *(North to south)* | | |
	Corps	Commander	Attacking on 21 March
Seventeenth Army		Below	
	I Bavarian Reserve	Fassbender	No
	III Bavarian	Stein	No
	IX Reserve	Dieffenbach	No
	XVIII	Albrecht	Yes
	VI Reserve	Borne	Yes
	XIV Reserve	Lindequist	Yes
	XI	Kühne	Yes
Second Army		Marwitz	
	XXXIX Reserve	Staabs	Holding
	XIII	Watter	Yes
	XXIII Reserve	Kathen	Yes
	XIV	Gontard	Yes
	LI	Hofacher	Yes
Eighteenth Army		Hutier	
	III	Lüttwitz	Yes
	IX	Oetinger	Yes
	XVII	Webern	Yes
	IV Reserve	Conta	Yes
	Group Gayl	Gayl	Yes

Source: *Der Weltkrieg*, Vol.14, Appendix 38a.

Table 6.3 Reserve divisions on 21 March 1918[105]

	Army reserve	OHL reserve
Seventeenth Army	3 Attack	3 Attack
Second Army	3 Attack	1 Trench
	3 Trench	
Eighteenth Army	4 Attack	1 Attack

Source: *Der Weltkrieg*, Vol.14, Appendix 38a.

Table 6.4 Guns and trench mortars on 21 March 1918[106]

	Field guns	Heavy guns	Super-heavy guns	Total guns	Trench mortars
Seventeenth Army	1,408	801	25	2,234	1,197
Second Army	1,034	704	13	1,751	1,080
Eighteenth Army	1,568	1,028	27	2,623	1,257
	4,010	2,533	65	6,608	3,534

Source: *Der Weltkrieg*, Vol.14, Appendices 38a and 39a.

The artillery commander (*General von der Artillerie*) in each army was responsible for the detailed fire planning, including the number of guns required. Bruchmüller's assignment to the Eighteenth Army may partially explain the weighting of guns in that army's favor. He clearly was a far more innovative fire planner than his two colleagues at Second and Seventeenth Armies. On the other hand, the Eighteenth Army also received a larger allocation of the heavy artillery batteries controlled directly by OHL (see Table 6.5).

Although the Germans were outnumbered in aircraft 3:1 overall, they managed to mass 1,070 planes against 579 British aircraft in the MICHAEL attack sectors. The Second Army received slightly more attack squadrons than the other two armies, and the Eighteenth Army got two bomber wings as opposed to one each for the Second and Seventeenth. This made some sense given the mission of those units to interdict the French reinforcements moving up from the south over the rail lines. See Table 6.6.

The final curious point about the German order of battle is the assignment of the few tanks the Germans had. All nine of the German tanks were assigned to two corps of the Eighteenth Army, both in Hutier's center. The four German-built A7V tanks were assigned to XVII Corps, and five captured Mk IV tanks

Table 6.5 OHL heavy artillery batteries on 20 March 1918[107]

Army	OHL batteries
Fourth	99
Sixth	80
Seventeenth	228
Second	199
Eighteenth	251
Seventh	57
First	52
Third	66
OHL reserve	118
Other army groups	149
	1,399

Source: OHL, II 78685, "OHL Heavy Batteries in Position by 20 March," (26 February 1918), Bundesarchiv/Militärarchiv, File PH 3/259.

Table 6.6 German squadrons on 21 March[108]

	Observation	Attack	Fighter	Bomber	Total
Seventeenth Army	17	7	13	3	40
Second Army	16	11	10	3	41
Eighteenth Army	16	9	12	6	44
	49	27	35	12	125

Source: Reichsarchiv, "Historical Study of Air Forces 1918," (12 April 1926), Bundesarchiv/Militärarchiv, File RH 2/2195.

were assigned to IX Corps.[109] Why did the army making the supporting attack get the tanks? One argument might be that the more open and even ground in the area south of the Somme was better suited for armored vehicles. That argument might make sense today, or even with World War II-era tanks, but not for the tanks of World War I with their limited, speed, range, and mechanical reliability. Recall also Colonel Jochim's comments about the effectiveness of the tracked supply vehicles in helping to get through the crater fields of the Seventeenth Army's attack sector. In the end, nine tanks would most likely not have helped the Seventeenth Army significantly, but this represents another example of the German failure to weight the main attack.

British order of battle

The British held 126 miles of front with fifty-seven infantry and five cavalry divisions, either in front lines or in army-level reserve. A cavalry division was about the size of an infantry brigade. This amounted to an average of one division per 2.2 miles. Eight divisions were in general reserve, with two of those behind the Fifth Army. The thinly spread Fifth Army had five divisions facing the German Second Army, and seven divisions facing the Eighteenth Army. Nineteen of the twenty-one divisions in the Fifth and Third Army front lines had been involved in the Passchendaele battles. See Table 6.7 for British order of battle.

Execution (20 March–5 April)

20 March   On the morning of 20 March, Hindenburg, Ludendorff, and the key members of the OHL staff met to decide whether or not to launch the offensive on the following day. The German artillery preparation relied heavily on gas for its effect, which in turn was heavily dependent on wind direction and weather conditions. The previous day had been rainy and windy, not the best conditions for gas. At 1100 hours Ludendorff got a meteorological report indicating that the weather the following day would not be perfect, but adequate for the attack. At noon Ludendorff made the decision to attack the next day, and OHL sent out the launch order. By 2100 hours that night, a heavy fog had settled in on top of the British Third and Fifth Army positions.[110]

Table 6.7 British order of battle in the MICHAEL sector 21 March 1918[111]

	Infantry divisions	Cavalry divisions	Army reserve	Heavy guns	Total guns	Sector width
Third Army	14	0	4 Inf	461	1,120	45 km
Fifth Army	12	3	1 Inf 1 Cav	515	1,566	68 km

Source: Edmonds, *1918*, Vol.I, pp.114–115.

21 March By 0200 hours on the morning of the attack the thick fog along the front had reduced visibility to just a few yards. At 0330 hours British artillery began sporadic interdiction fire against the German trenches and road junctions. The German artillery opened fire at 0440 hours. The preparation fire lasted for five hours. The Eighteenth Army preparation had seven main phases (see Table 6.8). Three sub-phases built into Phases 5 and 6 each put brief periods of heavy fire on the ground between the defender's trenches. Bruchmüller did this in case the British infantry tried to use the German technique of crawling out of the trenches and taking cover in nearby shell-holes. Despite the obligatory abbreviated registrations for the counter-infantry units in Phases 2, 3, and 4, the Eighteenth Army apparently did not fire abbreviated registrations for the other firing units. In 1922 Bruchmüller hinted in a book that he had used the Pulkowski Method for these units without the OHL's knowledge or permission. In a 1935 letter to Wetzell he admitted as much.[112]

Table 6.8 Eighteenth Army artillery preparation 21 March 1918[113]

Phase	Start time	Duration	Mission
1	0440	120 mins	Time-on-target with HE followed by counter-battery and fire against C3 targets with gas and HE at a 4:1 ratio. Trench mortars (MW) slacken fire after first 20 minutes.
1a	0530	10 mins	Surprise shift by all MWs and guns (except SCHWEFLA) onto infantry lines, with no counter-battery fire. HE against the 1st defensive positions. *Buntkreuz* against the 2nd defensive positions.
2	0640	10 mins	IKAc batteries shift onto their targets in the 2nd defensive positions to verify firing data. All other batteries continue firing on Phase 1 targets.
3	0650	10 mins	Same as Phase 2, with IKAb batteries verifying data on targets in the rear of the first defensive position.
4	0700	10 mins	Same as Phases 2 and 3, with IKAb batteries verifying data on targets in the intermediate defensive position.
5	0710	70 mins	AKA, FEKA, and SCHWEFLA continue firing on their assigned targets. All IKA units shift onto enemy trenches. IKAa verifies data on front of first defensive positions.
5a	0740	15 mins	IKAa sub-groups (howitzers) sweep ground between the trench lines in the first defensive position.
5b	0740	10 mins	IKAb sub-groups (howitzers) shell defensive strong points.
5c	0740	10 mins	IKAc sub-groups (field guns) shell ground between 1st and 2nd defensive positions with *Buntkreuz*.
6	0820	75 mins	Repeat of Phase 5 (including sub-phases) with slight variations in targets.
7	0935	5 mins	All artillery and trench mortars deliver saturation fire on enemy's front-most positions.

Source: Bruchmüller, *Die Artillerie beim Angriff*, (1926), pp.101–103.

The MICHAEL preparation was the greatest artillery bombardment in history to that time. The sound of the firing could be heard as far away as London. The Germans fired 3.2 million rounds on the first day of the battle. Approximately one-third of that total was gas, with the Yellow Cross inflicting almost 12,000 Allied casualties and the *Buntkreuz* accounting for 3,000 more.[114]

At 0940 hours the creeping barrage started to move forward followed closely by the German infantry. The heavy fog until late that morning favored the attackers and tended to prolong the effects of the German gas. Bruchmüller did note that the poor visibility had an adverse impact on the effectiveness of the creeping barrage. The accompanying artillery units followed closely behind the infantry and by the afternoon of the first day they were exchanging direct fire rounds with the guns of the Royal Artillery.

By 1400 hours the Germans were up to the Fifth Army's battle zone and preparing to attack it. About that same time Rupprecht's Army Group ordered the Seventeenth Army to start planning to move forces to both sides of the Scarpe, including two divisions from the Sixth Army.[115] By end of day, the Fifth Army's III Corps and 36th Division of XVIII Corps were fighting in the rear of their own Battle Zone.[116]

Despite the seemingly stunning results, the senior German commanders were somewhat disappointed. The results were far from even, with the Eighteenth Army making the greatest advances, and the Seventeenth Army the least. The Germans had hoped to overrun all the British artillery positions on the first day, but even the Eighteenth Army had captured only eighty guns. Rupprecht concluded at the time that the British Fifth Army had been caught in the act of a voluntary withdrawal to the Crozat Canal.[117] Crown Prince Wilhelm, on the other hand, thought "the way was opened for exploitation of the breakthrough."[118] His chief of staff, Schulenburg, believed that the offensive would achieve substantial results, but in the end Germany's position would be worse than ever.[119]

At the end of the first day the Seventeenth Army was stuck in front of the British Battle Zone, having advanced only four to five kilometers. It was still some seven kilometers short of its objectives for the day, the British artillery line, and had already committed sixteen of the eighteen divisions under its control.[120] The Second Army's right had not progressed well either, but its left wing had made better progress. The Second had committed fourteen of its divisions by end of day.[121] Both the Second and Seventeenth Armies had taken heavy casualties. The Eighteenth Army had broken into the British Battle Zone all along its front. It had committed only two of its second echelon divisions, and now had fourteen in the front line with twelve following.[122]

Ludendorff later wrote that the main problem with the Seventeenth Army was that its creeping barrage had outrun the advancing infantry.[123] Lieutenant Ernst Jünger, whose 111th Infantry Division was near the far right flank of the Seventeenth Army attack, gave a somewhat different account:

> A little before the edge of the village [Vraucourt], we were brought to a stop by our own artillery, which had the stupidity to go on shooting at the same

spot until the next day.... As I learned later, the artillery had orders to go on shooting at their longest range. This incomprehensible order took the finest fruits of victory from our grasp.[124]

Astride the boundary between the Seventeenth and Second Armies the British forces in the Cambrai salient still held out, but that was not necessarily an advantage for the British. Third Army commander General Sir Julian Byng had ordered his V Corps holding the salient to withdraw only 4,000 yards to an intermediate defensive line.[125] But GHQ had clearly ordered that the Flesquières salient (as the British called it) only be held as a "false front." As a result, the Third Army had twenty-one battalions packed into ten miles of front facing MICHAEL I in the Flesquières salient, as compared to eleven battalions on a similar length of the Fifth Army front.[126] In theory, this made a very strong defensive sector. In fact, it provided the German artillery with a densely packed zone of targets.

Despite Ludendorff's pronouncement of 6 March, the Cambrai salient had not been cut off on the first day. The basic operational concept was already slipping.[127] Ludendorff now had a choice between opportunism and consistency of purpose.[128] He could reinforce his right wing in order to push through his original intent, or he could shift reserves to exploit Hutier's success on the left. Reinforcing success and not reinforcing failure is generally a sound practice at the tactical level. At the operational level such shifts are not that easy to make, and they usually have greater consequences in terms of second- and third-order effects.

Ludendorff decided for opportunism. On the evening of 21 March, OHL committed no fresh forces to the Seventeenth or Second Armies, but ordered six new divisions to start moving to the Eighteenth Army, even though the Eighteenth had the best reserve posture. One division came from the First Army, two from the Third Army, and one from the Fifth Army, all of which were to the left of the Eighteenth Army.[129] OHL did not, on the other hand, start shifting northward the heavy artillery that would be needed to support an immediate launching of MARS, as Rupprecht's Army Group had considered so essential.[130]

About 2150 hours Ludendorff also ordered "strong forces" of the Seventh Army to move to the Oise in preparation to support the left flank of Eighteenth Army.[131] At 2300 hours Wilhelm's Army Group ordered the Eighteenth Army to continue attacking throughout the night.[132] The left wing of the army was to seize the crossings over the Crozat Canal, but prepare to defend east of the canal. The Seventh Army was ordered to neutralize the Allied artillery south of the Oise. Despite the order to attack throughout the night, the Fifth Army was able to fall back relatively unmolested.[133]

Around 1100 hours Haig received first official report of the attack. He ordered three divisions from the First and Second Armies to the Fifth and Third Army sectors. By the end of the day GHQ had ordered five divisions from the north to assist the south, but the first four went to the Third Army.[134] Haig also requested three French divisions from Pétain who, even before receiving the request for assistance, ordered five divisions from the French Third Army to be ready to move by 1200 hours on 22 March. They were concentrated in the Noyon area, twelve to fifteen miles behind the right flank of Fifth Army. Because of transport lag time, they would not be able to influence the action before 27 March.[135] French intelligence, meanwhile, had concluded that the German main objective was Amiens.[136]

22 March   There was heavy morning fog again on 22 March. On the first day, the fog had not hampered the German artillery too much, because the British positions had all been located accurately before the start of the attack. On the second day, after the Germans had moved forward, they had to rely more on observed fires, which the fog severely hampered. The fog also restricted the German air operations, but it did provide concealment for the attacking infantry.

That morning British sappers blew the three rail bridges over the Crozat Canal. (See Map 3.) One, however, remained standing and passable for infantry. At 1045 hours Gough issued an order to his corps to "fight rear-guard actions back to the forward line of the rear zone, and, if necessary, to the rear line of the rear zone."[137] Around noon, British XVIII Corps initiated a withdrawal to the line of the Somme. That in turn exposed the left flank of the southernmost III Corps, and facilitated the German rupture of the British line.[138] Wilhelm's Army Group issued the orders at 1345 hours to cross Crozat Canal but advance no farther than the bridgeheads. The first Eighteenth Army troops crossed the canal shortly thereafter. By the end of 22 March the Eighteenth Army was on the Somme and Crozat Canal.[139] The Fifth Army had lost its entire Battle Zone, and remnants of its XVIII, XIX, and III Corps were reeling back.[140]

In the north, the Seventeenth Army was ordered to continue attacking on its left wing in coordination with the Second Army to eliminate the Cambrai salient. The Seventeenth Army's right wing was stuck south of Arras. The Second Army was also stalled on its right wing, but its left wing was moving with the Eighteenth Army. Both the Seventeenth and Second Armies were ordered to take the objectives that had been assigned to them for 21 March. By the end of the 22nd most of the Second Army had broken into the British third positions, but the Cambrai salient still held, despite the concentric German attack.[141] The British V Corps, however, had received orders to fall back from the salient that night.[142]

OHL originally intended that the Eighteenth Army would shift its main effort to supporting the Second Army on reaching the Crozat Canal in the south and the British third position in the north. But now, Wilhelm's Army Group started arguing that the Eighteenth could best support the Second by pushing forward. At 2140 hours the Eighteenth Army received the orders to continue its advance.[143]

At 1845 hours Ludendorff spoke to Kuhl by telephone. He ordered the Seventeenth Army to exploit the success of the Second Army by attacking toward Bapaume—in other words, to drive more south than west as in the original plan. OHL also ordered preparations for attacks on *both* sides of the Scarpe, despite

Kuhl's and Rupprecht's views of the difficulty of MARS-NORD, and the fact that the northern attack had been cancelled as far back as 24 January because of insufficient forces.[144]

At 1900 hours Rupprecht's Army Group issued the orders. The inner wings of the Second and Seventeenth Armies were to avoid pivoting too early, with the lead elements of the inner attack wings aiming for Ytres (Seventeenth) and Equancourt (Second). The Seventeenth also was ordered to be prepared to execute MARS, now on both sides of the Scarpe.[145] Rupprecht's Army Group also ordered the Sixth Army to start planning and preparing an operation to be called WALKÜRENRITT (RIDE OF THE VALKYRIES), an attack north of MARS-NORD, against the Loretto Ridge. This would extend the attack as far north as Lens. OHL, however, had retained for another day the artillery needed for MARS in both the Second and Seventeenth Army sectors.[146]

At 2000 hours Gough notified Haig that the Germans had broken through the Fifth Army's reserve line. Haig approved the fall back to the Somme, contingent on holding the Péronne bridgehead. At 2330 hours GHQ ordered the Third Army to maintain contact with the left of Fifth Army.[147] By this point Pétain had seven divisions from the French Third Army preparing to move up to the line of the Somme and Crozat Canal. That night Haig also wrote to his wife that he still expected the main German attack to come in the north toward Arras.[148]

23 March   On 23 March, the left wing of the Second Army reached the Somme between Péronne and St. Christ. The right wing of the Second Army and the left wing of the Seventeenth Army lagged behind, east of Bapaume. Overall, the Germans had achieved a breach almost forty miles wide in the Allied line, but fatigue was starting to take its toll. That morning Marwitz complained to Kuhl about the lack of bridging trains in the Second Army sector, stressing that his initial orders had not required him to cross the Somme.[149] German deep reconnaissance from Dunkirk to Calais via Aire to Amiens and to Montdidier showed little significant Allied traffic on the main lines. On 23 March the *Wilhelmgeschütze* in the Seventh Army sector opened fire on Paris for the first time.[150]

At 0045 hours the British V Corps in the Cambrai salient was ordered to fall back farther still. It was its third withdrawal order in less than twelve hours; but V Corps had stayed in the salient too long. When it was finally forced out, it had to withdraw to the northwest, away from the Fifth Army's VII Corps on their southern flank. That exacerbated the gap that was opening up between the two armies.[151] At 0930 hours OHL issued new orders:

> The Seventeenth Army will attack vigorously in the direction of Arras–St. Pol, left wing moving on Miraumont. The Second Army will advance in the direction of the line Miraumont–Lihons. The Eighteenth Army echeloned in depth will march on the line Chaulnes–Noyon, at the same time sending forward strong forces via Ham.[152]

The war diary of Rupprecht's Army Group noted with alarm that the attacks were starting to diverge. Rupprecht himself thought the new OHL orders would work "only if the enemy remains in full retreat," to which all indicators seemed to point. Rupprecht still believed that the British were in the process of withdrawing to their old pre-July 1916 Somme positions, where they would then wait for the French counterattack against the German flank. In such a situation, the British should be given no rest. Rupprecht thought that the weight of the attack should be concentrated behind the Second Army, putting pressure on the British withdrawal, while the southern wing of the Eighteenth Army should consolidate its positions in preparation for the French attack. At some future point the Second Army could proceed along the line of the Somme.[153]

At 1300 hours the Seventeenth Army was ordered to complete breaking through the British third position, take Bapaume with its left wing, and then begin to wheel northwest toward St. Pol. The advance to the northwest would take the strong British positions at Vimy from the rear. Preparations for MARS-SÜD were to continue without additional forces.[154]

That afternoon Ludendorff met with Kuhl and Schulenberg in Avesnes. Stating that "a considerable part of the British force has been defeated," Ludendorff estimated their remaining strength to be about fifty divisions. He also thought it no longer probable that the French would be in a position to launch a relief offensive. With only about forty divisions at their disposal, the French would be forced to concentrate south of the MICHAEL sector. Based on that wildly optimistic estimate of the situation, Ludendorff continued:

> The objective of the operation now is to separate the British from the French by means of a rapid advance on both sides of the Somme. The Seventeenth and Sixth Armies, to be joined later by the Fourth Army, will attack the British to the north of the Somme and drive them into the sea. They will, therefore, attack again and again in new places (MARS, WALKÜRENRITT) in order to force back the entire British front. The Seventeenth Army will make its main effort in the direction of St. Pol and with its left wing will push forward by way of Doullens toward Abbeville. To the south of the Somme, the operation will take the form of an attack against the French, which will be accomplished by occupying the line Amiens–Montdidier–Noyon, and by means of a further advance thence in a southwestern direction. To this end, the Second Army will advance on both sides of the Somme by making its main effort toward Amiens, and maintaining close contact with the Eighteenth Army. If this operation succeeds, the left wing of the Eighteenth Army will have the mission of attacking southward across the Oise between Noyon and Chauny, and combine with the Seventh Army to throw the French over the Aisne.[155]

At this point, the conditions for exploitation described by Ludendorff in his 20 March phone conversation with Kuhl did not exist. This was also a complete departure from the original operational plan. Previously, the attacks of the

Second and Seventeenth Armies against the British constituted the main effort. Now the objective was to separate the British from the French and to attack both simultaneously. This required a significant shift to the left. No longer on the north side of the Somme only, the Second Army's mission was now to advance straight ahead in the direction of Amiens—on both sides of the Somme. The Seventeenth Army's mission was now to attack the British in a northwest direction, with a deep objective line of St. Pol–Abbeville. The Eighteenth Army mission was no longer to screen the Second Army on the line of the Somme. Its mission now was to cross the Somme and the Crozat Canal between St. Christ and La Fére, then attack the approaching French in a southwesterly direction.

Thus the Germans launched off on diverging attacks: northwest, west, and southwest. The original operational concept of massing forces in one sector for a decision while adopting the defensive and economy of force measures in all other sectors was dead. Instead of the original concept of a main effort against the British carried by the Seventeenth and Second Armies; instead of the thrust along the Somme that Rupprecht's Army Group recommended; instead of the free rein for the Eighteenth Army that Wilhelm's Army Group wanted, Ludendorff decided to do all three. His forces now had three different missions: separate the French and British; defeat the British; and defeat the French reserves. It is also important to note here that, although Amiens was now designated as a direction of advance for the Second Army, the vital rail center was still not an operational objective.

The Seventh Army was ordered to send three more divisions (it had already sent three) to the Eighteenth Army.[156] Ludendorff was dissipating his reserves, assuring that he would not have them in position to exploit any break that did occur. The indicators to that point, however, did not come close to supporting Ludendorff's grandiose scheme. The total artillery bag for the first three days had been about only 400 guns, which should have been captured by the first day. This was hardly indicative of an army retreating in full rout. By the end of the third day, the Germans had committed fifty-nine divisions to the attack.[157]

About 2300 hours Wilhelm's Army Group ordered the Eighteenth Army to cross the Somme, advance in a southwesterly direction between Noyon and Chauny, and then proceed south over the Oise. It was supposed to keep strong reserves behind its left wing and, in coordination with the Seventh Army, throw the French back across the Aisne.[158]

Late that afternoon Pétain and Haig met at Dury. Haig asked for a large concentration of twenty French divisions in the vicinity of Amiens. Saying that he still expected a major German attack in the Champagne sector, Pétain agreed to take over the British line as far as Péronne. He then ordered another six French divisions to prepare to move forward. With the gap between the Fifth and Third Armies growing wider by the hour, Haig was faced with the decision of sacrificing the Fifth Army to hold the rest of the BEF together. About 1700 hours GHQ ordered: "Fifth Army will hold the line of the Somme River at all costs. There will be no withdrawal from this line.... The Third and Fifth Armies must keep in closest touch ... and must mutually assist each other in maintaining Péronne as a pivot."[159]

24 March   Rupprecht's Army Group tied the Seventeenth Army's intended wheel to the northwest to the Second Army's right wing objective of Miraumont, some ten kilometers away. The Eighteenth Army no longer had to extend north to cover the Second Army; rather the Second now had to extend south to cover the Eighteenth. Thus the Second Army's front was diverging from its initial operational boundaries. The Second and Seventeenth Armies did gain some ground that day, but the Second Army was still seven miles short of its daily objectives. The two armies finally established contact that evening at Beaulencourt.[160]

At 1330 hours Rupprecht's Army Group reported to OHL that it anticipated capturing Bapaume that day, and would drive past it to the west. The divisions on the left of the Seventeenth Army that would be squeezed out by the convergence of the front would pass into the second echelon. The Seventeenth Army would then advance to facilitate the crossing of the Ancre by the Second Army. The deep objective for the Seventeenth Army was St. Pol, to the northwest.[161]

At 1630 hours OHL changed the direction of the Seventeenth Army attack, ordering it to push hard to the west, toward Doullens.[162] The success of that attack might make the MARS attack unnecessary. Nonetheless, OHL was now planning a grandiose series of operations based on the mistaken assessment that the British had been broken completely. The new attacks included: MARS-SÜD on 27 March, to drive the British back from Arras and push beyond; MARS-NORD on 28 March, to roll up the British on Vimy Ridge from the southeast; WALKÜRENRITT on 29 March, to support MARS-NORD; and KLEIN-GEORG in about eight days if all the British reserves were drained south. The operational objectives (*Operationsziel*) were Boulogne for the Sixth Army; Doullens–Abbeville for the Seventeenth Army; and Albert–Amiens for the Second Army.[163]

In the south, the Eighteenth Army pushed across the Somme. Chaulnes was to be captured on 24 March, and Royon on 25 March. The British III and XVIII Corps disintegrated in front of the Eighteenth Army as it pushed forward. By end of day, however, most of Hutier's units had advanced only four kilometers instead of the assigned twelve. The Eighteenth Army was starting to slow from fatigue and supply strain, even though it had been reinforced with a total of eight divisions in the first three days of the operation.[164] The *Wilhelmgeschütze* also fired thirty-four rounds into Paris on 24 March.[165]

Despite reports of French forces pouring toward Noyon on the southern extreme of the German advance, Ludendorff wanted the reinforced left wing of the Eighteenth Army to seize the heights above Noyon that day and then prepare to push across the Oise. The Seventh Army, meanwhile, was ordered to be ready to attack with Operation ERZENGEL across the Ailette. OHL also ordered heavy air attacks on the Compiègne rail center.[166]

Ludendorff was now adding additional objectives north and south to an already diverging operation. On the Allied side, Haig still faced the decision of whether to abandon the Fifth Army and pull the Third Army back to the north, or to try to hold the line between the two armies. At a QMG conference on the

24th, the decision was made to prepare contingency plans to abandon the Fifth Army.[167] The British Third Army, meanwhile, continued to withdraw its right flank in an attempt to maintain contact with the Fifth Army.

All day long on 24 March French infantry units had been thrown into the battle as soon as they detrained. Often they were committed without communications equipment or supporting weapons. French *Grand Quartier Général* (GQG) realized that the only way to restore the situation between the Somme and the Oise was to establish a prepared defensive position and then let the Germans come to it. GQG ordered the French First Army to move to the Montdidier area and be prepared either to intervene on the British right or to support the French Third Army. The British Fifth Army was to withdraw to the line of the Avre between Montdidier and Amiens. The Germans were still thirty kilometers from the Avre at that point, but the French First Army could not be in position before 26 March.[168]

At 0900 hours Pétain issued a new order to the French armies identifying his primary and secondary objectives in the battle: first, keep the French armies together and not allow Army Group Reserve to be cut off; and second, maintain, if possible, the link with the British forces.[169] Pétain still feared a major German attack in Champagne and he was worried about a possible threat to Paris. Thus, the maintenance of the unity of the French Army became Pétain's primary mission. He would continue to support the British only so long as he could hold together his own forces.

Haig and Pétain met again at BEF headquarters about 2300 hours. Pétain informed Haig that if German progress continued along the line toward Paris, he would be forced to withdraw French reserves to cover the capital.[170] As dismayed as he was by that news, Haig did agree to place the Fifth Army and the line south of the Somme under the command of General Marie Fayolle's Army Group Reserve. With twelve infantry and five cavalry divisions and twelve regiments of heavy artillery, Fayolle was now responsible for the battle between the Somme and the Oise.[171] Haig, nonetheless, immediately reported what he considered to be Pétain's unreliability to London and he requested that Sir Henry Wilson, the new Chief of the Imperial General Staff, come to France and help arrange the establishment of a unified supreme command to take central control of the battle.

25 March On the morning of 25 March, Ludendorff and Kuhl met at Avesnes to discuss both MARS attacks, WALKÜRENRITT, and KLEIN-GEORG I. WALKÜRENRITT was the most difficult and would need the most preparation. OHL could supply only three or four fresh divisions for KLEIN-GEORG I, but if the Arras attacks were successful, KLEIN-GEORG might not be needed. If that attack were launched, the deep objective for the Sixth Army would be Boulogne. Doullens–Abbeville remained the main axis of advance for the Seventeenth Army, but elements of the Seventeenth would probably have to support the advance of the Sixth Army on Boulogne. The Second Army remained oriented on Amiens. Ludendorff was now following almost the same general plan advocated earlier by Kuhl, except that, while the Second, Seventeenth, and Sixth Armies were now going to attack the British, the Eighteenth and Seventh Armies were also attacking the French.[172]

The Eighteenth Army, meanwhile, was still not at line Noyon–Chaulnes, although it had to insert a new corps headquarters (XXV Reserve Corps) into the line to control all the extra divisions it was receiving.[173] Wilhelm's Army Group ordered the Seventh Army to prepare to advance its right-wing trench divisions to the Ailette in order to plug the gap on the Eighteenth Army's left.[174] Wilhelm also recommended to OHL that the left wing of the Eighteenth should not go beyond Noyon–Roye, and that the main weight should be shifted to the right wing to support the Second Army in taking the line from Caix to the Avre valley.[175] Wilhelm later wrote in his memoirs:

> My chief of staff and I were of the opinion, and remained so during the next few days, that our principal mission was to split the French and the English completely by continuing to drive west. And then, but not until then, we would press to the southwest and south.[176]

By that evening the Eighteenth Army had succeeded in separating the British Fifth and French Third Armies and was beginning to envelop the French flank northeast of Roye. The two French cavalry divisions assigned to cover this flank were not yet in position.[177] Writing in his post-war memoirs, Ludendorff stated:

> Strategically we had not achieved what the events of the 23rd, 24th, and 25th had encouraged us to hope for. That we had also failed to take Amiens, which would have rendered communications between the enemy's forces astride the Somme exceedingly difficult, was especially disappointing. Long-range shelling of the railway installations of Amiens was not a good equivalent.[178]

This is another post facto justification. In the German plans and orders up through the 25th, Amiens had only been identified as a direction of advance, but never as a key objective of the operation.

On the Allied side, French forces were starting to move up from the south. By the morning of 25 March the French Third Army, under General Georges Humbert, was moving into position with a strength of seven divisions behind the British XVIII and III Corps. The French First Army, under General Marie Debeny, also was moving toward the area with six divisions.[179] Later in the day the British Third Army was ordered to withdraw to the line Noyon–Montdidier.[180]

Haig ordered the British Third Army to withdraw to the Ancre, telling its commander Byng that all further withdrawals must be to the northwest, and that he should no longer rely on the French or the British Fifth Army. The mission of the Third Army was now to protect the southern flank of the BEF.[181] The British Q-Staff also prepared to fall back to the north, and started to develop *Scheme X* and then *Scheme Y* to increase the supply flow through the northern ports, while shutting down the southern line of communications. (See Chapter 4.) The QMG also decided to let the French take over the logistics operations up to the line of the Somme and absorb the logistics structure of the Fifth Army.[182]

Later in the day Haig met Foch's chief of staff, Colonel Maxime Weygand, at Abbeville. Haig repeated his request for the immediate concentration, "astride the Somme, west of Amiens, of at least 20 French divisions for the purpose of acting against the flank of the German attack on the British Army." The French took this to mean that the British had decided to defend west of Amiens, and intended to fight falling back slowly to cover the Channel ports. As Foch saw the situation:

> Two distinct battles were being fought by the Allies: a British battle for the ports, and a French battle for Paris. They were carried on separately and farther and farther away from one another. The Allied commanders thus tended to emphasize the separation of their armies, the primary objective of the German operations.[183]

26 March   On the morning of 26 March Kuhl issued telephone orders to the Seventeenth and Second Armies to continue to drive hard to the west toward Doullens–Amiens, keeping their inner wings linked.[184] As mobile warfare conditions started to break loose, the British communications system, hardwired in place for trench warfare, began to break down. Even the usually realistic Rupprecht now began to believe the Germans would succeed in splitting the British in two and driving them back to the bridgehead position of their ports.[185] Hope ran high among the Germans that the British would not make a stand on the Ancre, even though it was the last natural line of defense before the sea.[186]

About 0820 hours the Eighteenth Army captured Roye and Noyon, outflanking elements of the French Third Army moving up. The Eighteenth Army formed a defensive front along the Oise from Chauny to Noyon, and Wilhelm's Army Group ordered it to advance its right wing, in coordination with the Second Army, past Chaulnes to take the old French trenches of 1916.[187]

By 1700 hours that afternoon the Second Army finally took Albert. Proceeding through the town, some German officers lost control of their troops as they stopped to loot the unbelievable wealth they found in the British depots.[188] Nonetheless, the fall of Albert cut the double-tracked Amiens–Albert–Arras line and severely restricted Allied lateral rail communications to Arras. Lateral rail transport was now limited to the double-tracked line Amiens–Doullens–St. Pol, with single-track lines running into Arras. The loss of that line, however, did not cut too badly into the Allied capacity to shift reserves from north to south.

About 1930 hours, a frustrated Ludendorff called Rupprecht and said he was considering relieving Below's chief of staff, Konrad Krafft von Dellmensingen.[189] Always looking for tactical reasons for success or failure, Ludendorff believed the main reason for the Seventeenth Army's failure was "apparently because it had fought in too dense formation."[190]

By that evening the right flank of the British Fifth Army was being forced back toward Nesle and Amiens, instead of toward Roye and Montdidier. That movement eventually would create a twelve-mile gap between the British and French.[191] The left wing of Seventeenth Army had passed Miraumont and was approaching Hebuterne, while the Second Army was trying to negotiate the "trackless crater-fields of the Somme."

In the south, the right wing of the British Army seemed to have been crushed. Nonetheless, German intelligence reported heavy troop concentrations moving north into Compiègne and beyond it toward Noyon, combined with heavy road traffic moving east and southeast from Amiens. Elements of six French divisions arrived by the 26th, and the French First Army was starting to form in front of Amiens. Ten British and eight French divisions were now in front of the Eighteenth Army, and two more French divisions were moving up. The French Sixth Army under General Denis Duchêne was forming a defensive front south of Noyon with five French divisions and the remnants of two divisions from the British III Corps.[192]

At 2200 hours OHL issued new orders.[193] The Seventeenth Army retained its mission to advance in the direction of the line Doullens–St. Pol, keeping its left wing above the Nievre River, and moving its right wing toward St. Pol, using Arras as a pivot. The Seventeenth's attack would be extended on the right by MARS-SÜD and -NORD. Instead of being launched a day apart as originally planned, both MARS attacks would now be launched on the same day. The following day the Sixth Army would launch WALKÜRENRITT, extending the attack as far north as Lens, with the completely unrealistic deep objective of Boulogne. But the Seventeenth's main effort was now on its left wing, which calls into question the whole reason for the northern group of three attacks.

The Second Army was to make its main effort south of the Somme, its left wing advancing toward the Avre in a southwesterly direction, with Moreuil as the left boundary. The right wing was to cross the lower Somme at Airaines, and the center was to capture Amiens ("*nimmt Amiens...*"). The follow-on objective for the left wing would be Bréteuil. Thus, the Second Army was being required to execute a complex two-phase maneuver. It was supposed to keep its right wing north of the Somme and its left wing south of the Somme until past Amiens, and then swing southwest. Combined with the Eighteenth Army, the maneuver would be a massive swing away from the Somme, to face the French.

The Eighteenth Army was to make its main effort southwestward to the Avre to seize the crossings, but not to cross the river without specific orders from OHL. The Eighteenth's deep objective was Compiègne, with a strongly echeloned left wing. Despite the fact that Amiens was now designated for the first time as an actual objective, the new orders focused more on executing the southwest swing than on taking Amiens. The right wing of the Eighteenth Army in this maneuver would pass eighteen miles south of Amiens, leaving it entirely to the Second Army.

On the extreme left wing of the German attack the Seventh Army was to advance toward the junction of the Oise and the Aisne. The overall concept now was that the Seventh, Eighteenth, and Second Armies would form a barrier facing southwest against the French, while the Seventeenth and Sixth Armies would deal with the British, and the Fourth with the Belgians. Nowhere did the new orders consider covering the twenty-kilometer gap that would open up between the Second and Seventeenth Armies from Airaines to Doullens.

The war diary of Rupprecht's Army Group noted: "Everything depends on the breakthrough in the direction Doullens–Amiens."[194] But as Kuhl later wrote, the new scheme of maneuver was "a renewed widening of the already widely stretched frame of operations...." And, "The offensive power of the armies soon proved insufficient for all these tasks."[195] Some French writers have suggested that Ludendorff intended to drive on Paris, but as Edmonds correctly pointed out, nothing in the German orders suggests this.[196] In his own memoirs Ludendorff wrote:

> The original idea of the battle had to be modified and the main weight of the attack vigorously aimed in this direction [Amiens]. I still hoped we should get through to open warfare and followed this perspective in my instructions to the armies. But the Seventeenth Army was not moving; the Second and the Eighteenth were still gaining ground. I continued my efforts toward reinforcing the left wing of the Second Army and to direct it and the Eighteenth on Amiens.[197]

The situation, however, was nowhere nearly as clear in the orders he issued on the evening of 26 March. Rather than narrowing the scope of the attack and focusing the main effort along the Somme toward Amiens, as he implies in his memoirs, Ludendorff continued to try to grab for everything at once. The German official history called the orders of the 26th a "logical amplification" (*folgerichtige Erweiterung*) of the orders of the 23rd.[198] But the three-pronged attack of the 23rd had now become a two-pronged advance against the British and French simultaneously.

At 2240 hours Rupprecht's Army Group issued the orders to the Second and Seventeenth Armies to complete the breakthrough toward Amiens and Doullens.[199] The Seventeenth Army's main effort was on its left wing, which was supposed to push forward "as far as possible" in coordination with the right wing of the Second Army. The Seventeenth Army's right wing was supposed to take Mercatel. But after six days of fighting, that objective was still less than a mile behind the rear of the original British Battle Zone, which indicates the lack of progress in the north.

By this stage in the battle the tyranny of logistics was starting to impose itself on the Germans. The German infantry was outdistancing its own artillery, while the artillery was outrunning its ammunition trains. The Eighteenth Army already was fifty-six kilometers away from its forward railheads. On 25 March the III Corps had been forced to cut its artillery ammunition supply rate in half.[200] And while the German supply and transport systems were being stretched thinner and thinner, the British at the same time were falling back on their own logistics base. Many of the German attack divisions were burned out. By the end of 26 March, eight of the thirty-seven divisions in the front line were back in action for a second time. The Eighteenth Army had committed thirty divisions to the fight, and OHL was getting ready to send it four more.[201]

On 26 March the Allied conference at Doullens became one of the pivotal events of the last year of the war. After years of bickering about it, the Allies finally establish a unified command. At that point, however, it was only for the conduct of the immediate battle. Foch was given the authority to coordinate and synchronize the Allied response. Foch was not yet designated actual Commander in Chief of the Allied armies. That would come later, on 14 May. Foch later wrote: "From the outset all were in unanimous agreement in recognizing that Amiens had to be saved at all costs and that the fate of the war depended on it. I made some strong remarks in this sense."[202] Ironically, Foch saw clearly what Ludendorff did not. Foch wasted no time. As he later wrote:

> Before the close of this same day, the 26th, I had thus explained my intentions to all the commanders whose troops were in action. In the evening, moreover, General Pétain cancelled his instruction of March 24th and ordered General Fayolle to cover Amiens and to maintain contact with Field Marshal Haig's forces. In addition, he directed that ten divisions and four regiments of artillery be withdrawn from other groups of armies and moved towards the reserve group.[203]

27 March   The Eighteenth Army's orders for the day called for crossing the Avre from La Neuville, drive past Montdidier, and push southeast to Lassigny. Around 0745 hours Ludendorff called to supplement his previous orders. The Eighteenth Army's follow-on advance to Compiègne, he cautioned, would probably not take place until 30 March. He also reemphasized the importance of the right wing completing the southwest pivot and reaching the line Montdidier–Lassigny to hold the French. Montdidier absolutely had to be taken by the 27th and the blocking positions established, but the Eighteenth Army was not to cross the objective line even if there was an opportunity for exploitation. Sauberzweig recommended that the Eighteenth be allowed to press forward, but Ludendorff refused. Then Ludendorff made a most uncharacteristic comment for the man who could not stand the word "operations." He said that it was no longer the time for battles, but for operations ("*nicht mehr gekämpft, sondern operiert werden*").[204]

The Eighteenth Army attack jumped off at 1000 hours. Progress was slow initially. Between Rosieres and Noyon, Hutier had eleven divisions in his front line; three divisions along his southern flank on the Oise; twelve divisions in his second line; and six in his third line, including three in OHL reserve.[205] In support of the attack, the bomber units in the Eighteenth Army sector dropped 11,000 kilograms of bombs on the rail center at Soissons.[206]

By noon the Eighteenth Army's right wing was making good progress and closing in on Montdidier. Newly arriving French units put up poor resistance against the Germans in that sector. The gap started to widen between the British Fifth and the French Third Armies, and a gap of more than five miles developed between the French Third and First Armies. Still operating under Pétain's original orders, the French poured all their resources into plugging the gap between their two armies.

In the German center the Second Army made very little progress in face of stiff British resistance. The right wing of the Second tried to cross the Ancre in force and to expand the bridgeheads at Albert and Aveluy. The Ancre, however, proved to be a death trap. That tributary of the Somme was shallow and only twenty to thirty feet wide, but it was bounded by marshes and flood plains 200–300 meters wide. The crossings were limited and plainly visible. The British artillery on the west bank sat on high ground from where it had good observation and clear fields of fire.

The Second Army's left wing, south of the Somme, was too weak to advance the attack on Amiens. Even though Ludendorff had designated it as the main effort, Marwitz had only three front-line and three second-line divisions on that axis. As Crown Prince Wilhelm later wrote, "the left wing for this very preferable undertaking was not strong enough."[207] From 25 to 27 March the front of the Second Army had fanned out from twenty-five to almost forty kilometers.[208] Although the Second didn't capture Amiens, it did get close enough to put the rail center under fire with 150 mm guns.[209]

The Seventeenth Army made only minor progress. In two days of fighting it had advanced only 1.5 kilometers.[210] In the middle of the day the Seventeenth Army attack halted temporarily to wait for MARS. At 1355 hours Rupprecht's Army Group issued the final orders to the Seventeenth, Sixth, and Fourth Armies for MARS and WALKÜRENRITT.[211] Between 1400 and 1500 hours, Rupprecht requested that OHL commit three of its reserve divisions to support the right wing of the Seventeenth Army. OHL refused, and when Rupprecht learned that OHL had already diverted those three divisions to the sector south of the Somme, he commented, "Now we have lost the war."[212] Rupprecht's chief of staff, however, was starting to feel more optimistic. Late that night Kuhl sent a message to OHL, "We're pulling through." (*"Ich habe den Eindruck, dass wir durchkommen."*)[213]

Although the Germans certainly gained more ground south of the Somme on the 27th, they committed roughly equal forces in both sectors on that day: thirty-six divisions in the north, with fifteen in the front line; and twenty-eight divisions in the south, with sixteen in front line.[214] The Eighteenth Army started entering Montdidier about 1930 hours, cutting one major rail line over which the French reserves were moving. The French, meanwhile, were in the process of closing the gap between their Third and First Armies, but the gap between the British and the French remained.[215]

Later that evening Wetzell had a phone conversation with the chief of staff of Wilhelm's Army Group. Schulenberg said: "Ludendorff does not place great importance on Schoeler's attack. After the capture of Montdidier it will be necessary to position strong reserves on the right wing."[216]

Schoeler was the commander of VIII Corps, another corps headquarters recently inserted on the extreme left flank of Eighteenth Army to control the ever-growing number of divisions.[217] Wetzell told Schulenberg:

> After capturing Montdidier, march straight along the Avre valley to Amiens. Take advantage of the success at Montdidier, advance toward Amiens, then come around. Wait for further orders reference the attack in the southeast. Again, Eighteenth Army to advance with its right wing; Second Army to advance with its left wing in order to exploit the advantage gained at Montdidier. [218]

28 March   Shortly after midnight the commander of the French First Army reported to Foch that he could do no more with the British.[219] The Eighteenth Army had accomplished the splitting of the French from the British. The road to Amiens was open from the south, and the main rail line from Paris to Calais along which the French reserves were moving was only twelve miles away. Hutier had at least five divisions (including four assault divisions) available for commitment. Two were in the second and third lines of the XXV Reserve Corps, and three were in the second and third lines of the IX Corps. But eleven hours later Wilhelm's Army Group reported to OHL, "The Eighteenth Army is not in a position to advance to Amiens."[220]

Rupprecht and many other Germans considered 27–28 March the turning point of the offensive.[221] Wetzell too saw that MICHAEL was dead. Seventeen years after the war, Wetzell, by then a retired lieutenant general, wrote: "the failure of OHL to recognize and exploit fully the gap in the French front at Montdidier was one of the principal causes of the failure of the great offensive."[222] Wetzell recommended to Ludendorff that MICHAEL be broken off and the forces shifted north for a strong GEORG attack, not merely the reduced KLEIN-GEORG. Rupprecht, on the other hand, thought that the low levels of ammunition would preclude launching even a modified version of GEORG for at least ten days. Ludendorff refused, hoping that the MARS and WALKÜREN-RITT attacks would re-energize MICHAEL.[223]

OHL issued new orders.[224] The Seventeenth Army and right and center of the Second Army were to stand fast and be prepared to exploit the success of MARS. The left wing of the Second Army and the right wing of the Eighteenth Army were to continue the drive toward Amiens. Ludendorff also approved an Eighteenth Army recommendation for its right flank corps to shift to the northwest and drive toward Moreuil. This is the first indication of Ludendorff focusing seriously on Amiens. But even still, it was a half-hearted effort. The main thrust of the Eighteenth Army continued to pivot toward the south.[225] By this point in the battle, the Eighteenth Army had been reinforced with a total of ten divisions, and one more was enroute.[226] The British, meanwhile, had already cleared their ordnance depot at Amiens, and were developing plans to blow up the ammunition dumps on their southern line of communications.[227]

At 0300 hours 1,250 guns started firing the artillery preparation for both MARS attacks, and the infantry jumped off at 0730 hours. The Seventeenth Army attacked with only nine divisions, one corps north of the Scarpe, and two south of the river. Only five of the divisions were attack divisions. Even the German official history noted that the attacks were executed shoulder to shoulder, with no hint of the infiltration tactics that had been so successful in the early stages of MICHAEL.[228] The Germans encountered well-prepared British defenses. North of the Scarpe MARS made no progress at all; south of the Scarpe it made only slight progress.

Even in the early stages of MARS, Ludendorff at 0815 hours told the Second Army that their main effort was south of the Somme. At 0905 hours the Second Army's chief of staff told Kuhl of the difficulty of moving ammunition columns forward. He estimated that half his losses had come from enemy aircraft. By 1400 hours OHL was reporting to Second Army that MARS was a failure.[229] By 1700 hours both MARS attacks were at a standstill with heavy losses. Rupprecht's Army Group, nonetheless, was convinced that victory between Albert and Arras was still possible, and requested additional divisions to resume the attack. OHL refused.[230] Wilhelm's Army Group, meanwhile, was stressing to OHL the importance of capturing the rail center at Amiens.[231]

At 1855 hours OHL ordered the Second Army to drive hard on Amiens from south of the Somme. Amiens was now the principal objective of the Second Army, but its main axis of advance was also now toward the southwest. The Second Army's left wing was to push forward to reach beyond the Avre by 30 March.[232] To accomplish these missions the Second Army would be reinforced by two divisions from the Seventeenth Army.[233] In his memoirs Ludendorff later claimed: "I continued my efforts to strengthen the left wing of the Second Army and to direct it with the Eighteenth Army on Amiens."[234]

OHL issued new orders for the other armies at 2345 hours.[235] MARS and WALKÜRENRITT were cancelled. The Seventeenth Army was now given the mission of containing the British with local attacks and supporting the Second Army with its right wing. Operation GEORG or even KLEIN-GEORG were no longer possible because of the resources squandered in MICHAEL. An even more reduced version, renamed GEORGETTE I, was ordered for the right wing of the Sixth Army in eight to ten days, depending on the weather.[236]

The Eighteenth Army, meanwhile, would receive four more divisions, but it was not supposed to cross the Avre without specific orders. Essentially, the Eighteenth was supposed to mark time for two days while the Second Army completed its pivot to the southwest and took Amiens.[237] After taking Amiens, everything seemed to center on a vague hope of some great success by the Eighteenth Army. At OHL Ludendorff said: "In the next few days it must be done by the Eighteenth Army."[238]

29 March   Late on 28 March General John J. Pershing made the few ready American divisions in France available to Foch. By 29 March strong French reserves were beginning to mass in the vicinity of Beauvais.[239] The force consisted of the French Fifth and Tenth Armies, with six infantry and three cavalry divisions in the first echelon.

At 0600 hours Wilhelm's Army Group sent a message to OHL recommending that, if the attacks of 30 March did not draw in heavy French forces, then the interior flanks of the Seventh and Eighteenth Armies should launch a strong enveloping attack on the enemy to their front, with a possibility of extending the objective to the east. Ludendorff approved the recommendation.[240]

Later that morning in a phone conversation with Kuhl, Ludendorff ordered the Seventeenth Army to go over to the defensive.[241] The Germans at that point held Bapaume, Albert, Péronne, Nesle, Ham, Chauny, Noyon, Roye, and Montdidier. They were also approaching the outskirts of Villers-Bretonneux and were able to shell sections of Amiens, only ten miles away. That meant that almost all the British Fifth and Third Army's forward railheads had been overrun. British GHQ decided to reduce tonnage at the southern ports of Le Havre and Rouen by 60 percent and to increase Calais by the same figure.[242]

That afternoon Ludendorff issued further orders by phone.[243] The attack beyond the line Chauny–Noyon–Montdidier was to be continued with the left wing of the Second Army, the Eighteenth Army, and the right wing of the Seventh Army. The rest of the Second Army and the Seventeenth Army would later join in the attack north of the Somme, to support the drive on Amiens. OHL also ordered strong reserves pushed up behind the Eighteenth and Second Armies. Rupprecht's Army Group responded by ordering three more divisions from the Seventeenth to the Second.[244]

OHL's orders at 1800 hours made another change.[245] Despite the heavy actions of the inner wings of the Second and Eighteenth Armies, the attack now had to be pushed as far as the Noye, five miles west of Moreuil. The left wing of the Second Army had the objective of the Amiens–St. Fuscien–Ailly road, and the right wing of the Eighteenth Army had La Faloise as an objective. In order to deny the French the time to make an orderly deployment, Ludendorff cancelled his orders of the previous day requiring the Eighteenth Army to stand firm until the Second Army had completed its pivot to the southwest and had reached Amiens. In the British official history, however, Edmonds seems not to have understood the significance of Amiens when he wrote: "So now Ludendorff's grandiose schemes for the capture of the British Armies were dwindling down to the scale of a local operation to seize a railway centre, Amiens."[246] That rail center should have been the operational objective from the start.

At 2235 hours OHL again stressed to the Second Army that its left wing must advance the next day.[247] Two corps of Seventh Army, meanwhile, started preparations to launch Operation ERZENGEL on 2 April.[248] The Eighteenth Army by this point had grown so large and unwieldy that the VIII Corps on extreme left flank of the Eighteenth Army was transferred to the Seventh Army.[249]

On the Allied side, five more fresh divisions had reached the French First Army, which already had relieved the entire British XVIII Corps.[250] That allowed Haig to reconstitute his reserves and reorganize the Fifth Army (now re-designated as the Fourth Army) without pulling it out of the line.

30 March The German attacks resumed on 30 March, but they generally stalled all along the line. The Second Army took the Avre crossing at Moreuil, but the French continued to pour in reserves. By that morning the German Second and Eighteenth Armies had a total of forty-one divisions (twenty-two in the front line), and four more moving up. The British Fourth and French First and Third Armies had thirty-three infantry and six cavalry divisions (twenty in the front line), and five moving up.[251] The attack had reached culmination. By 1800 hours the Germans broke off all their attacks. An after-action analysis of the day's attacks conducted by Wilhelm's Army Group two months later concluded:

> OHL was of the opinion that the attack should only be executed from the north, whereas the Army Group wanted to launch it from the north and south. The Army Group thought that the entire enemy artillery could have been wiped out in this way. This attack would have required a longer preparation period, but probably could have been launched within a short period of time.[252]

At 1845 hours OHL sent Rupprecht's Army Group a warning order that GEORGETTE would be executed. OHL also issued the orders to start shifting the artillery northward.[253] At 2200 hours Ludendorff ordered the Second Army to continue attacking the next day along its whole front, even if its left wing did not make any headway. Second Army protested that it could not do that without adequate preparation and additional resources. Ludendorff backed down, and the attack was postponed.[254] Wilhelm later wrote in his memoirs: "My chief [of staff] and I saw in the general attack from the first only an attempt to bring the faltering operation once more into motion."[255]

31 March Ludendorff had two basic options at this point. He could break off MICHAEL immediately and prepare to launch another major attack somewhere else. The best possibility would be an expanded version of GEORGETTE, which in its current form had been designed as either a diversion or a supporting attack. The second option was to resume the MICHAEL attacks after giving the troops a few days' rest and fresh reinforcements. Ludendorff chose the latter.[256]

That morning OHL ordered all units to transition temporarily to the defensive.[257] Then at midday OHL issued new orders for continuing operations. The Eighteenth Army was ordered to reorganize to repel any French attacks, but its right wing had to be prepared to attack west of Moreuil to reach the line Thory–Ailly. That attack would be supported by the Second Army, with the inner wings of the two armies reinforced by six divisions. The Second Army was also ordered to continue its drive on Amiens, but transferring the main weight of that attack south of the Somme, where the terrain favored offensive operations. The renewed attacks were scheduled for 4 April. Meanwhile, the Seventh Army's ERZENGEL attack was rescheduled tentatively for 8 April.[258]

1 April   Ludendorff met in St. Quentin with the chiefs of staff of both army groups and the Second and Eighteenth Armies. Kuhl recommended: "The main objective is the British. Therefore, the Second and Seventeenth Armies should attack north of the Somme." Ludendorff responded that the main objective was to split the British and the French, then the next objective could be the defeat of the British. This would be done with the GEORGETTE attack by the Sixth Army, supported by the Seventh Army's ERZENGEL attack in the south.[259]

After the meeting OHL issued the new orders. Offensive operations would resume on 4 April south of the Somme toward Amiens, with the left wing of Second Army and the right wing of the Eighteenth Army. One day later, the attack would resume north of the Somme with the right wing of the Second Army and the left wing of the Seventeenth Army, with pressure in the direction toward Amiens. On 5 April the Seventh Army also would attack the salient near Amigny as a preliminary operation for ERZENGEL. The Sixth Army would follow up with the GEORGETTE attack on 7 or 8 April.[260]

2–3 April   The Germans conducted only local attacks on 2 and 3 April, concentrating on the preparations for the resumption of operations on 4 April. At 1150 hours on 2 April Kuhl confirmed to the chief of staff of the Second Army that Ludendorff wanted the main effort on the army's left wing, but now north of the Somme. This was a contradiction of the orders issued on 31 March and 1 April.[261] About 1900 hours on 3 April the Second Army's chief of staff complained to Kuhl about the shortage of ammunition on his left wing.[262]

The Allies, meanwhile, had almost completed sealing off in depth Hutier's penetration in the south. Fayolle's Army Group now had twenty-seven infantry and five cavalry divisions, with 1,344 guns and some 700 aircraft. (The Germans at this point had 822 aircraft, the result of reinforcements added to the squadrons supporting MICHAEL.) By 3 April the French had extended their line an additional three miles, with two French divisions relieving two of the British Fourth Army's divisions. To the north, the British Third Army had fifteen divisions in its first line, facing thirty-one of Rupprecht's divisions.[263]

4 April   German artillery started a seventy-five-minute preparation at 0515 hours. The infantry jumped off at 0630 hours in persistent rain. Fourteen divisions were committed to the attack, but only four were fresh. The attack was intended to reach the line Chirmont–Blangy Tronville, and if possible cross the Noye and establish a bridgehead north of Ailly. That modest objective line did not include Amiens itself, but it would put the Germans within 12,000 meters of the critical rail center. The more ground the Germans gained, the more effective their shelling would be against the main rail station and the rail bridge over the Somme west of Amiens.[264]

As the day's fighting dragged on, the Eighteenth Army reported that it could not push the Allies across the Noye. The Eighteenth did make a slight improvement in its Avre bridgehead, but it was difficult to keep its artillery on the far bank supplied with ammunition. Just south of the Somme the Second Army reached the outskirts of Villers-Bretonneux, which sat on a key piece of high ground overlooking Amiens, only ten kilometers away. At 1700 hours, a desperate counterattack by one Australian and one British battalion halted the 9th Bavarian Reserve Division only 400 meters short of the town. Within an hour the Germans had been driven back 2,000 meters.[265]

Wilhelm's Army Group recommended not continuing the attacks on 5 April because of the increasingly strong Allied counterattacks. Nonetheless, OHL ordered the resumption of the attacks for the next day.[266] Kuhl, on the other hand, wrote in his diary that Germany's last chance to strike a decisive blow against the British had just passed. The shortages of reserves, ammunition, and especially horses would make it impossible to launch another offensive on such a large scale.[267]

5 April The Second Army and the left wing of the Seventeenth Army attacked north of the Somme, but now the objective was more to prevent the Allies from shifting forces north against GEORGETTE. The attack started at 0900 hours, but by noon it had failed. In the south, the Eighteenth Army was too exhausted to make any headway, and in fact had to fend off counterattacks from five French divisions along the line from Cantigny to Castel.[268]

By end of day, all of the army and army group chiefs of staff were recommending the termination of MICHAEL. At 1925 hours OHL sent out Ludendorff's message: "The supply situation does not allow the continuation of the attack by the Second and Eighteenth Armies. The attack is henceforth temporarily discontinued..." except "...where an improvement of the local situation demands it."[269]

6 April The day after the termination of MICHAEL, the Seventh Army launched Operation ERZENGEL with six divisions. The operation had originally been intended as a diversion in support of MICHAEL. But after the Eighteenth Army had pushed farther south than originally planned, ERZENGEL became an operation to reduce the salient between the inner wings of the Seventh and Eighteenth Armies. The attack centered on Coucy le Château, and its primary objective was the high ground east of the Oise–Aisne Canal.

The artillery preparation started at 0425 hours, and the infantry attacked at 0530 hours. The Germans made good progress, but heavy rains hampered their advance on the night of the 6th. The attack ended when the Seventh Army reached the Ailette on 9 April. The Germans had shortened their line by some seven kilometers, at a cost of 1,900 casualties. By that date, twenty-two French infantry divisions and six cavalry divisions opposed the Germans between the Oise and the Somme.[270]

Assessment

The results

In sixteen days of fighting Operation MICHAEL penetrated the Allied positions to a depth of sixty kilometers, capturing 1,200 square miles of territory. (See Map 3.) The Germans also captured 90,000 Allied prisoners (75,000 British), 1,300 guns, and temporarily opened a wide gap between the British and the French. The British Fifth Army had been almost totally destroyed, and the BEF was on the verge of falling back on its Channel ports. The casualties on both sides were high. But while the Germans suffered slightly fewer casualties, they were losses that could not be replaced for the rest of the war. The arriving Americans more than made up the Allied losses.[271] See Table 6.9.

On the tactical level the results of MICHAEL appeared spectacular. They were far beyond anything that had been achieved in World War I so far. On the first day of the attack alone, the Germans had taken almost exactly as much territory as the British and French had needed 140 days to wrest from the Germans in 1916. Even so, on the first day of the attack the maximum advance was still four kilometers short of the assigned depth for that day. On 22 March the shortfall was seven kilometers. On 23 March, the shortfall was four kilometers, even though the Germans made their largest single-day advance that day. After French forces had arrived in the south in significant numbers by 28 March, the daily depths of the German advances declined sharply (see Table 6.10).

Of course, the impressive tactical results accomplished nothing operationally, much less strategically. By the time it was over, the Germans had committed ninety divisions, had consumed tons of precious supplies and ammunition, and had little to show for it. Nonetheless, Ludendorff would write in his memoirs:

> It was a brilliant feat of arms and will always stand as such in the history of the world. What the English and the French had not succeeded in, we had accomplished, and in the fourth year of the war.[272]

Table 6.9 Casualties from Operation MICHAEL[273]

German	
Seventeenth Army	81,200
Second Army	73,800
Eighteenth Army	84,800
Total	239,800
Allied	
British	177,739
French	77,000
Total	254,739

Source: *Der Weltkrieg*, Vol.14, p.255.

Table 6.10 MICHAEL daily advances[274]

Date	Maximum advance (kms)
21 March	5
22 March	5
23 March	16
24 March	6
25 March	10
26 March	8
27 March	6
28 March	4
29 March	1
30 March	3

Source: Pascal Lucas, *The Evolution of Tactical Ideas in France and Germany during the War of 1914–1918*, (Paris: 1923), (Manuscript translation in English by Major P.V. Kieffer, U.S. Army 1925), pp.137–138.

It may have been a brilliant feat of arms, but it was one that failed to pass the "So what?" test. Why did MICHAEL fail? Could it have succeeded? No general purposely goes into a battle intending to lose it, and my own thirty-eight years of military service—most of it in the operations and intelligence areas—make me extremely reluctant to try to second guess those who had to make the decisions, at the time, on the ground. On the other hand, this operation and the entire group of Ludendorff offensives taken together offer too many key points for a critical analysis of the modern concepts of the operational art. Therefore, the following assessment is conducted with that objective in mind.

Over-emphasis on the tactical level

One of the most common criticisms of MICHAEL is Ludendorff's obsession with the tactical level of warfare, at the expense of the operational and strategic levels. And to a large degree Ludendorff was a product of the institution he grew up in. As noted in previous chapters, the Germany Army and its General Staff had a tendency to ignore the strategic level of war, and their understanding of the operational level was deeply flawed, more resembling tactics on a very large scale. In one of the most widely quoted and criticized passages of his memoirs Ludendorff wrote: "It was necessary to place tactical considerations above pure strategy. The latter was not feasible without tactical success. A strategy that disregards it, is condemned to failure from the start."[275]

Yet there were solid tactical reasons to support the basic concept of MICHAEL, factors that could have been turned to operational advantage. MICHAEL was not as dependent on weather and terrain conditions to the extent GEORG was. And the terrain south of the Somme favored the attacker. Below the river the ground was mostly flat all the way to Amiens, and the only significant water obstacles were the Crozat Canal and the Canal du Nord. North of the Somme the terrain was more difficult, especially in the sector bounded by

Arras–Péronne–Amiens–Frevent. There the terrain elevation differences ran up to 150 meters, with water obstacles running through the valleys, most significantly the Canal du Nord, Omignon, Scarpe, and Ancre.

If tactical considerations reigned supreme, as Ludendorff so steadfastly maintained, then it is hard to understand why the main weight of the operation was not south of the Somme from the start, in the area where the terrain was most favorable and where the Allies were the weakest.

Failure to weight the main attack

The original intent was for the main effort to be north of the Somme. But on 21 March, the Seventeenth Army (minus the three corps allocated to Operation MARS) and the Second Army (minus XIV and LI Corps) started with thirty-two divisions north of the Somme. The Eighteenth Army and the XIV and LI Corps of Second Army started with thirty-five divisions south of the Somme.[276] The Seventeenth Army planners originally had estimated that they needed between thirty-two and forty-seven divisions for both MICHAEL I and MARS. They got twenty-five.[277] Even Kuhl noted: "All in all, it is safe to say that the Seventeenth Army was relatively weak for the task that had been assigned to it."[278]

Meanwhile, the Eighteenth Army, facing the weakest enemy, had more guns and more reserves. It had had twice as many guns per mile of front, and 50 percent more men than the Seventeenth Army. Writing immediately after the war, General Otto Fehr criticized Ludendorff's initial positioning of the reserve divisions as tending to support the concept of a main effort by the Eighteenth Army.[279] But the actual disposition of the reserves on 21 March (see order of battle table, Tables 6.1 and 6.3 above) does not really support Fehr's contention. If anything, it is difficult to see where the main effort was from the positions of the reserves on 21 March. What is clear is that as MICHAEL progressed, the commitment of reserves to the Eighteenth Army shifted the weight and direction of the main effort of the operation. The following table (Table 6.11) shows the

Table 6.11 Divisional reinforcements from OHL[280]

	Seventeenth	Second	Eighteenth
21–31 March			
Gain	+4	+ 8	+12
Loss	−5	− 1	−2
Net	−1	+ 7	+10
1–5 April			
Gain	0	+ 2	+ 7
Loss	−1	− 1	0
Net	−1	+ 1	+ 7
21 March–5 April			
Net	−2	+ 8	+17

Source: *Der Weltkrieg*, Vol.14, Appendix 35.

allocation of reserve divisions from OHL to the three armies for the periods 21–31 March, 1–5 April, and the combined totals for the entire operation.

Table 6.12 shows the total number of divisions committed to the Eighteenth Army and the two right-wing corps of Seventh Army at various points in the battle. When comparing the above and below tables, it is important to note that, as OHL fed divisions to Wilhelm's Army Group some were held in OHL reserve, while others were released to the operational control of the army group or the armies.

Some historians have argued that the attack should have extended to the Scarpe right from the start. The Seventeenth Army was bound to fail without it. The standard argument is that the Germans had sufficient divisions to extend the attack, but not sufficient artillery. But an analysis of the disposition of the OHL heavy artillery batteries (see order of battle table, Table 6.5, above) shows that the three attacking armies had only 598 out of the available 1,399 heavy batteries, or just 43 percent. If MICHAEL was really intended to win the war, the Germans should have been able to accept greater risks along other sectors of the Western Front, especially in the south, where "other army groups" had 149 of the heavy batteries. This is an echo of Moltke's unwillingness to accept risk in secondary sectors in order to weight overwhelmingly the main effort that in the end doomed his final variation of the Schlieffen Plan in 1914.

Table 6.13 shows the dispositions on 16, 23, and 30 March of the SCHWE-FLA batteries, the German Army's heaviest shooters. Note that on 23 March the

Table 6.12 Divisions committed in Crown Prince Wilhelm's Army Group[281]

Date	Time	OHL reserve divisions	Total divisions*
21 March	0940	1	27
22 March	0130	1	28
23 March	2330	3	29
24 March	Morning	2	30
24 March	2020	3	30
25 March	Evening	4	29
26 March	2010	5	33
28 March	0850	3	34
28 March	2210	2	35
**29 March	2345	4	42
30 March	Morning	4	42
30 March	2225	5	42
31 March	2300	9	46
3 April	1050	4	48
4 April	0715	3	51
5 April	1135	3	51

Source: Army Group German Crown Prince, War Diary Extracts, (21 March–5 April 1918), Bundesarchiv/Militärarchiv, File PH 5 I/29. *Der Weltkrieg*, Vol.14, Appendix 38.

Notes
*Includes Seventh Army's VIII Corps and VIII Reserve Corps.
**VIII Corps reassigned from Eighteenth Army to Seventh Army.

Table 6.13 SCHWEFLA batteries[282]

Army	16 March	23 March	30 March
Fourth	6	6	15
Sixth	7	6	10
Seventeenth	12	12	7
Second	8	8	0
Eighteenth	10	10	3
Seventh	7	7	13
First	1	1	2
Third	0	0	1
Fifth	4	4	2

Source: OHL, SCHWEFLA Staff Officer Reports, B7678, (16 March 1918), B7841, (23 March 1918), B8018, (30 March 1918), Bundesarchiv/Militärarchiv, File PH 3/503.

three MICHAEL armies had a total of twenty super-heavy batteries, but by 30 March they had only ten. By that date, many of those batteries had already been shifted north in preparation for GEORGETTE. This shortage of the heaviest artillery certainly reduced the power of any MICHAEL attacks launched after 30 March.

Unity of command

Many historians have correctly pointed to the lack of unity of command as one of MICHAEL's most serious flaws.[283] The fact that the command disjuncture occurred at the operational level, the army-group level, made it that much more serious. Ludendorff's justification for this command arrangement was his requirement to influence and control the battle personally.

> That would have been difficult, if only one group of armies had been in charge of the conduct of the operations. Any interference whatever by OHL would then have practically amounted to meddling on the part of a higher headquarters.[284]

In his memoirs Ludendorff issued a strong disclaimer that the decision was influenced by dynastic or political considerations. Judah Wallach, however, noted that by the start of 1918 Ludendorff was seriously considering forcing the Kaiser to abdicate in favor of his son, and it was therefore important for his candidate for the throne to get his share of the anticipated glory.[285] Rupprecht at the time noted: "For political reasons, especially after the fiasco at Verdun, it is desirable to give the German Crown Prince a chance to repair the damage."[286]

Ludendorff's method of command and control was exactly the opposite of Moltke's in 1914, but it was no more successful. The result was the unsynchronized army-group operations orders of 14 and 16 March, with their two very different concepts of the mission of the Eighteenth Army. Wilhelm's Army Group and the Eighteenth Army were clearly trying to go their own way, and in the end they did.

Artillery

One of the German Army's greatest advantages going into the battle was the innovative new artillery tactics based on neutralization, surprise, centralized planning, and decentralized execution. But the fragmentation at the army-group level of command did much to dilute that advantage which, if uniformly applied, could have contributed greatly to the operational results. When the Eighteenth Army was transferred to Wilhelm's Army Group, Bruchmüller went with it. Bruchmüller, of course, had the most experience with the new techniques. And although Kuhl was one of Bruchmüller's most ardent supporters, that apparently was not enough for the new techniques to be applied correctly and uniformly within Rupprecht's Army Group.

The artillery chiefs of the Second and Seventeenth Armies were not at all enthusiastic about having to follow the lead of the upstart from the Eastern Front. This was particularly true in the case of the Seventeenth Army, whose artillery chief, Lieutenant General Richard von Berendt, had been the German artillery chief at Caporetto, and had something of a reputation himself as a pioneer in artillery tactics. Berendt's had been one of the two major voices of dissent at the 26 January Artillery Planning Conference. It is quite possible that there was even some longer-standing animosity between Berendt and Bruchmüller, who were once lieutenants together in the 3rd Foot Artillery Regiment. As a lieutenant general, Berendt did not appreciate having to take suggestions from a mere lieutenant colonel. This resentment came through very clearly in Berendt's post-war writings.[287]

Thus there was a good deal of personal friction among the three army artillery chiefs. The Eighteenth Army's artillery followed the new concepts to the letter; the Seventeenth Army's artillery did not. A Seventeenth Army order issued on 3 February specifically required firing units to register.[288] Another order issued on 24 February spelled out the fire sequence for the preparation, which was to start with one hour of reinforced counter-battery fire. Then, all Seventeenth Army artillery, with the exception of the counter-battery units, was to cease firing for one half-hour.[289] After Ludendorff's message of 3 March, the Seventeenth Army issued revised fire plans on 6 March. That order was supposed to supercede the 24 February order, but it was little different from the original plan. It did drop the requirement for a precision registration, but it still included the half-hour break in the firing.[290] Finally, an order issued on 16 March noted that at 0640 hours on the morning of the attack there would be sufficient light and a "registration can be done."[291] By waffling on the whole issue of registrations, the final decision was left to the subordinate corps. In the event, many Seventeenth Army units did actually fire a precision registration, thereby compromising the surprise of the attack in the north. If that was not enough, the senseless half-hour pause in the preparation fire certainly telegraphed the attack to the British.[292]

There were other significant differences between the two army groups in artillery planning and execution. As previously noted in the discussion on order of battle, the Eighteenth Army started the battle with considerably more artillery assets than its supporting mission would have seemed to require. And on the first day of the attack Lieutenant Ernst Jünger bitterly complained about being held up by a standing barrage of German artillery fire that had reached its maximum range and then just continued to fire blindly. In the Eighteenth Army under Bruchmüller, once the guns firing in the creeping barrage reached their maximum range, they ceased firing. Then, those guns that could be supplied forward with ammunition were aggressively pushed up. Finally, only the Eighteenth Army used the complete Bruchmüller system of task-tailored artillery groupings. All of the Second and Seventeenth Army artillery orders for MICHAEL mention only super-heavy SCHWEFLA groups, but not counter-infantry IKA, counter-artillery AKA, or long-range FEKA groups and subgroups.

On 1 April 1918, Rupprecht's Army Group issued an analysis of the new artillery procedures that concluded: "The procedure gains complete surprise and had proved itself on 21 March."[293] In his post-war writings Kuhl continued to be a staunch supporter of Bruchmüller and his methods. Yet Kuhl never leveled any direct criticism at Berendt, and even defended his performance.[294] Ludendorff, on the other hand, was a little more direct in his post-war memoirs when he wrote of the Seventeenth Army's results: "the vitalizing energy that emanated from Colonel Bruchmüller was lacking."[295] Even more significantly, Ludendorff put Bruchmüller in complete charge of the artillery for the remaining four 1918 offensives and for the planning for HAGEN.

Condition of the German Army in 1918

Some historians have argued that MICHAEL never had a chance, under any circumstances, because the German Army at the start of 1918 had been burned out by more than three years of a grinding war of attrition. The troop morale, levels of training and leadership, and the resources were no longer there. Even Kuhl admitted, "The Army that stood ready to attack in March of 1918 was no longer the body of troops of 1914."[296]

On closer examination, however, this argument does not pass muster. The effects of the last three years were evenly distributed on all sides. The Allies were worn down too, and the national morale of the French was close to collapse. And while the Allies had the potential to be reinvigorated by thousands of fresh American troops, that potential in March 1918 was still several more months from full realization. The fact remains that after MICHAEL the Germans managed to muster the will and the resources to launch four more major offensives, and they were planning and actively preparing yet another one when the Allies finally counterattacked on 18 July. The Allies managed to contain Operations GNEISENAU and MARNESCHUTZ–REIMS fairly effect-ively, but during Operations GEORGETTE and BLÜCHER there was a real fear that the Germans could still win militarily. What would the results have been if the combined power of those five offensives had been focused in one properly designed sequence of operations?

The deficiencies in the German war economy and the German Army's logist-ics system are another element often used to bolster the "burn out" argument. And as noted above, many writers including Kuhl, Ludendorff, and the German official history have claimed that MICHAEL reached culmination because of supply failures. But while the German supply system was strained to its limits, and shortages of various classes of supplies plagued local commanders through-out the course of the battle, much the same can be said for many large-scale battles in the 20th century. The evidence for a complete breakdown in the German logistics system is just not there. As Colonel Jochim, the General Staff officer Ib of the Seventeenth Army, argued so forcefully in his manuscript: "The March offensive did not fail because the supplies did not come, as was said after the war sometimes."[297]

Operation MICHAEL reached culmination, but it did not culminate solely because of supply failures or because of any other single reason. It reached cul-mination because of a combination of factors, including supply problems, troop fatigue, length of lines of communications, lack of battlefield mobility, and most importantly, poor operational design and a series of bad decisions made during the execution of the operation.

Operational objective

Arguably the single greatest flaw in Operation MICHAEL was the lack of a clearly defined objective. Writing immediately after the war General Otto von Moser noted:

> We find that Ludendorff's plan of attack and first attack order for 1918, as opposed to the operations of 1914 and 1915 in the East, lacked not only the great, bold, clear, and simple outline, but also the idea intelligible to every-body that will kindle enthusiasm of both subordinate leaders and troops.[298]

And on 5 April, the date Operation MICHAEL was halted, Rupprecht wrote in his diary in frustration:

> It is obvious that one cannot discern a proper purpose in all OHL's direc-tives. They always mention certain landmarks which should be reached, and one gets the impression that OHL lives from hand to mouth, without acknowledging a fixed purpose.[299]

The initial MICHAEL plan did not call for a breakthrough of the British front on a large scale as far as the sea for the purpose of rolling up and destroying the enemy. Merely, it called for a breakthrough as far as the Somme and a drive on a wide front to the line of Bapaume–Péronne–Ham, with some vague form of exploitation to follow. The only clearly defined objective at the start was the first day's objective, which was to eliminate the Cambrai salient. As Ludendorff later wrote, "The crown of success was to be found in that operation in which we were able to develop our entire superiority of strength. To strive for that was our ultimate aim."[300] Whatever that meant to Ludendorff, it was hardly a crystal-clear concept for a war-winning operation. But as Kuhl also later wrote, "There is no doubt whatever that OHL intended to bring about a decision in the World War by means of this offensive, and not by a series of local attacks designed to wear out the enemy."[301]

For all the reasons already discussed, Amiens should have been the operational objective of MICHAEL right from the start. The failure to designate operational objectives in the beginning led the Germans to commit follow-on forces along the line of least resistance, which led away from the decisive point. Amiens finally did become a stated objective, but not until 26 March. That objective was clearly stated in all the post-operation analyses, but it was not clearly stated in the orders before 26 March. The German official history later imposed an ex-post facto operational objective. "Despite the superhuman efforts of men and horses, the operational objective (*operative Ziel*) of splitting the French and the British and then fighting each separately was not achieved."[302]

Ironically, some of the Allied leaders, most particularly Foch and Wilson, recognized the significance of Amiens long before Ludendorff did. On 18 April, the new commander of the British Fourth Army, Sir Henry Rawlinson, wrote to Wilson: "There can be no question that the Amiens area is the only one in which the enemy can hope to gain such a success as to force the Allies to discuss terms of peace."[303] Writing in his memoirs after the war Hindenburg said:

> The decision was therefore to be sought more and more in the direction of Amiens.... We ought to have shouted in the ear of every single man: "Press on to Amiens. Put in your last ounce. Perhaps Amiens means decisive victory. Capture Villers-Bretonneux whatever happens, so that from its height we can command it with masses of our heavy artillery."[304]

Things might have gone better for the Germans if Hindenburg had said that to Ludendorff well before 21 March.

The Germans ended up only seven miles from Amiens. The BEF's major forward marshaling and switching yards remained under artillery and air interdiction until the summer, and most rail traffic had to be routed through the much lower capacity station at Beauvais.[305] But the Germans apparently never fully exploited that advantage. On 7 April the Second Army sent OHL a telegram requesting the assignment of a 280 mm super-heavy battery specifically to shell the rail facilities around Amiens.[306] The following day OHL responded with a telegram signed by Ludendorff, curtly denying the request.[307]

Decision 21 March

By the end of the first day of Operation MICHAEL, less than sixteen hours after the German infantry had jumped off, the basic operational concept was already starting to come apart. The Cambrai salient had not been eliminated, and the inner wings of the Second and Seventeenth Armies were still separated. But rather than sticking to the original plan, Ludendorff followed the tactical principle of reinforcing success rather than failure. He committed six additional divisions to the Eighteenth Army, while committing none to the Second or Seventeenth. Nor did he order the shifting of the artillery north to support MARS. But he did order the Seventh Army to start moving forces into position, shifting even more weight to the south. Operationally, this all but killed the original MICHAEL plan, even though over the next several days Ludendorff attempted to waffle back to it.

Decision 23 March

Ludendorff's decisions on 23 March are completely glossed over in his memoirs. In ordering diverging attacks, northwest, west, southwest, he abandoned the original operational concept and enlarged the scope of the operation, without having yet separated the British and French. On 23 March the Cambrai salient had still not been taken, the British artillery was still mostly intact, and French forces in the south were starting to arrive in some numbers. Yet Ludendorff expanded the scope of the battle to three divergent main attacks, against two enemy forces, and involving a semicircular front of ninety miles. Ludendorff, in effect, started the exploitation phase of a battle not yet won. The three diverging attacks remind one of a larger-scale version of the U.S. 28th Infantry Division's disastrous attack in the Hürtgen Forest in November 1944.

In his post-war assessment of the operation, Kuhl maintained that Ludendorff should have stuck to the original operational plan by putting the left wing on the defensive along the Somme, and then shifting forces from the Eighteenth to the Second Army. This would have improved the Second Army's advance, and might possibly have carried along the Seventeenth Army as well.[308] Correlli Barnett, on the other hand, wrote that Ludendorff should have recognized the pattern of German success in the south as early as 22 March, and channeled all his forces into a single thrust to split the British and the French.[309]

Decision 26 March

By 26 March the three-pronged attack had given way to a two-pronged attack against the British and the French. But in deciding to launch the two MARS attacks and WALKÜRENRITT in the north two days hence, Ludendorff seemed to be trying to return to the original operational concept he abandoned late on 21 March. Those additional attacks in the north only further dissipated the main effort, and expended resources for no gain. Operationally they made no sense at all. MARS was originally supposed to facilitate the pivot of the Seventeenth Army. But the Seventeenth Army's direction of advance had already been changed from northwest to west, and its main effort was now supposed to be on its left wing. So just what was MARS supposed to accomplish? MARS was launched without forces sufficient for even a chance of its success. But what if the Germans had committed that nine-division and 1,250-gun force against Amiens?

In the south, the Eighteenth Army was given no direct role in the capture of Amiens, other than pivoting to block off the French—a movement away from Amiens itself. But directly in front of Amiens was a solid defensive position of wire systems and concrete bunkers. Built by the French in 1915, the Amiens line ran eight miles from Demuin on the Luce River to Sailly le Sec on the Somme.[310] The Eighteenth Army was supposed to pass just to the south of the Amiens defenses, and could have made a flanking attack against the British positions. Instead, the Second Army was given the mission of making a frontal attack, something that was supposed to be anathema to German tactical doctrine.

Decision 28 March

After the failure of MARS, Ludendorff all but shut down operations in the north and shifted back to the middle, but with his forces too dispersed to have any real effect. Just hours earlier, the path to Amiens had been wide open from the south, but by late on 28 March French forces under Fayolle were starting to shore up the British defenses. At a Fourth Army POW camp in late May, a British officer told Crown Prince Rupprecht:

> It would have been easy for the Germans to take Amiens on 29 March, if they had just pushed their attack farther. What did we have facing them? We were completely at the mercy of the Germans; but they stopped half way. God knows why.[311]

By not committing the Eighteenth Army to the drive for Amiens, Ludendorff had condemned the Second Army to a hopeless frontal attack across almost impossible terrain. Writing in the British official history, Edmonds speculated that the Germans did not exploit the success against the French at Montdidier because doing so would have lengthened the flanks of the salient already created, making them even more vulnerable. Yet taking Amiens then would have severed the rail link between the Allies, "and left the British on 'an island' so that they could have been dealt with at leisure without weakening the tactical situation."[312]

With the failure to take Amiens at that point, Operation MICHAEL had almost no hope of achieving any worthwhile operational results. Ironically, this is the point at which Amiens finally became a clear objective for Ludendorff. It remains questionable, however, whether he really finally understood Amiens' significance, or if it was just the last spot on the map he thought he had some sort of chance of taking.

Rupprecht thought it was a mistake to let up the pressure on the British at all. Several weeks later, as Operation GEORGETTE was dying, Rupprecht wrote to his father, the King of Bavaria:

> OHL, in view of their own not inconsiderable losses, decided to give up the attacks on the British and turn with strong forces against the approaching French, instead of staying on the defensive against the latter. The English, in consequence, were presented with the opportunity of being able to fortify their front anew.[313]

Decision 30 March

By 30 March it should have been clear to anyone that MICHAEL had reached culmination. In the case of culmination, the original plans had called for an immediate regrouping and shifting of forces, not wasting them in further costly and useless fighting. At this point the German Second and Eighteenth Armies had forty-one divisions (twenty-two in the front line), and four moving up. The British Fourth and French First and Third Armies had thirty-three infantry and six cavalry divisions (twenty in the front line), and five moving up.[314] And as noted above, by 30 March the three MICHAEL armies had only ten super-heavy batteries among them.

If Operation GEORGETTE had even the remotest chance of success, Ludendorff severely hurt that chance by deciding not to break off MICHAEL on 30 March. The resources squandered in the fighting after 30 March just might have tipped the balance in the follow-on Operation GEORGETTE, that in many ways was a closer-run thing than MICHAEL. To cite just the example of horses, one of the German Army's most critically scarce resources, more than one-third of the almost 29,000 horses were lost after 31 March (see Table 6.14).

Allied reactions

The competence and decisions of the enemy commanders is one thing a commander cannot directly control. The most he can hope to do is influence those decisions indirectly through a deception plan. Initially the German deception plan was successful, with the French believing the main German attack would

Table 6.14 Operation MICHAEL horse losses[315]

Army	21–31 March	1–10 April
Seventeenth	7,000	2,079
Second	5,987	3,201
Eighteenth	5,314	5,177
	18,301	10,457

Source: OHL, Ic 85444, (12 May 1918), Bundesarchiv/Militärarchiv, File PH 5 II/295.

come in Champagne and threaten Paris, and the British believing it would be toward their own Channel ports in the north. Thus, for the first six days of Operation MICHAEL, Pétain and Haig both saw themselves fighting completely different battles. The decisions of the two Allied commanders were doing almost as much to pull their two forces apart as the Germans were doing to drive them apart.

All that changed as the result of the Doullens Conference late on 26 March. One commander, Foch, was put in charge of the battle. Even the British official history admitted, "The appointment of General Foch to co-ordinate and control the Allied efforts prevented the disaster of the separation of the two Armies."[316] Nonetheless, the British did complain of communications problems that stemmed from Foch's inexperience at dealing with British commanders. Fortunately for the Allies, however, Foch saw the operational decisive point more clearly than either of his two primary subordinates, Haig and Pétain. He also saw that decisive point far more clearly than his key opponent, Ludendorff.

Alternatives

Was Operation MICHAEL the right attack, and could it have succeeded? Those two questions have been debated by historians and military analysts since almost immediately after Ludendorff broke off the attack. Some historians have argued that GEORG was the better of the two options, and that the same resources committed to GEORG would have produced greater results. A sixty-kilometer penetration northwest of Armentières would have reached the coast. The fallacy of that argument is that there is no way to assume that an attack in that sector with equal forces would have produced equal results on the ground. The terrain, the defenses, and the opposing forces were all very different.

Perhaps the greatest weakness of both MICHAEL and GEORG is that each was designed as a stand-alone decisive battle, rather than as a phase of a larger sequence of operations. And both were designed to attack directly and destroy the enemy's main force, rather than attacking an exploitable vulnerability, such as the BEF's very fragile and shallow logistics system. In other words, each was supposed to be a *Vernichtungsschlacht*. But if the two operations had been designed as phases of a larger operation to attack the enemy's center of gravity (the BEF itself) indirectly, then the decisive points of MICHAEL and GEORG should have been the rail centers at Amiens and Hazebrouck respectively. The loss of either one would have hurt the British severely; the loss of both would have been fatal. Once those two objectives were secure, follow-on objectives would be Abancourt, St. Pol, and then the Channel ports. This, of course, would have been a variation on the "skillful combination of multiple attacks having highly reciprocal effects" proposed by Wetzell on 12 December 1917, but in this case targeted for the BEF's logistics jugular vein.

If the operations had been designed as a sequenced set, MICHAEL was most likely the better one to start. An initial successful attack against Hazebrouck would have made it very clear that Amiens would be the next objective. At that point, the French would have been sure to push massive reinforcements to the Somme sector. A successful first attack against Amiens, on the other hand, would have partially sealed off the north and isolated the British forces there. The control of the north–south rail lines would have, temporarily at least, cut the movement of reinforcements to a trickle. Weather and terrain conditions at that time of year also favored an earlier attack in the south—although in the event, the late winter and early spring of 1918 were far drier than normal.

Amiens became the final objective for MICHAEL almost as an afterthought. If Amiens had been the clear operational objective right from the start, the operation would have looked completely different. For a focused drive on Amiens, MICHAEL would not necessarily have been as large an operation. The main attack should have been made by the Eighteenth Army, south of the Somme. The Allies were the weakest there, and the ground was some of the most favorable attack terrain on the Western Front. The attack would have been supported in the south by the Seventh Army, with a mission of blocking the French forces moving up and deceiving the French into thinking that Paris was the objective. That essentially was the Seventh Army's primary mission in Operation BLÜCHER in May 1918. To the north, the Second Army would have supported the attack by splitting the boundary between the British Third and Fifth Armies. The Cambrai salient could be fixed with a frontal holding attack, and later taken from the rear.

Once Amiens was taken, the Germans would have had to hold it with sufficient force to prevent the French from retaking it, while at the same time shifting sufficient artillery north as rapidly as possible to support the attack on Hazebrouck. Such a series of attacks would have been complex and difficult to orchestrate, but they would have been simpler than MICHAEL–MARS–GEORGETTE as those operations actually played out. A sequenced series of attacks specifically designed to take Amiens and Hazebrouck would have had a good to very good chance of succeeding. MICHAEL and GEORGETTE came very close to taking those respective objectives; and although GEORGETTE was designed to do that, MICHAEL was not.

7   Operation GEORGETTE
9–29 April 1918

One cannot help being struck by the contradiction which appears between Ludendorff's strong-willed character and the lack of perseverance in the directing idea which he had conceived.[1]

General Maxime Weygand

Command and staff work are quite different arts, and capacity for both is rarely combined in one individual.[2]

Brigadier-General James Edmonds

Plans (10 November 1917–18 April 1918)

Operation MICHAEL failed, but Ludendorff had not quite given up on it. Initially he thought it would be possible to resume MICHAEL in two or three weeks. On the other hand, he believed the British forces were shaken and off balance, and he wanted to resume offensive operations as quickly as possible to take advantage of the situation.[3] Soon after the termination of MICHAEL, Crown Prince Wilhelm recommended a focused attack on Amiens; but those preparations could not be completed before 17 April.[4] Rupprecht and Ludendorff also discussed the possibility of attacks against the British at Albert, Arras, and south of the Somme; but those attacks could not be ready to go until 16 April.[5] That was not fast enough for Ludendorff, so he reached for the old GEORG attack plan, which along the way had evolved into KLEIN-GEORG, and then GEORGETTE.

Wetzell had originally recommended an attack in the vicinity of St. Quentin, followed as soon as possible by an attack in Flanders—but for a very different purpose than what eventually became the GEORGETTE attack. Wetzell envisioned the St. Quentin offensive being conducted only up to a fixed line, and for the sole purpose of pulling the British reserves down from Flanders. Kuhl had also recognized the necessity for such a diversion in his original proposal. As Kuhl and Wetzell saw it, the main attack would be directed toward Hazebrouck, with the objective of rolling up the British front from the north. (See Map 4.) But Ludendorff had decided that the German Army did not have the necessary resources for a strong diversionary attack prior to the main attack, and OHL therefore rejected both Wetzell's and Kuhl's plans.[6]

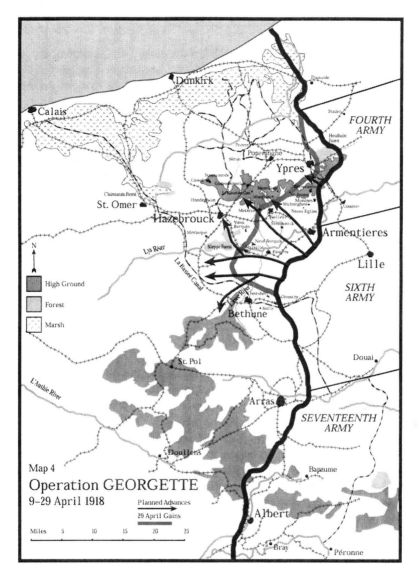

Map 4 Operation GEORGETTE (source: Map by Donald S. Frazier, Ph.D., Abilene, Texas, based on sketches and notes provided by David T. Zabecki).

On 20 November 1917 Crown Prince Rupprecht's headquarters issued its initial analytical study of the GEORG Operation:

> [GEORG's] objective must be to defeat the enemy. In the zone of the group of armies this objective would best seem to be attained by an attack near Armentières–Estaires against the flank and rear of the mass of the British Army assumed to be in the Ypres salient and west thereof. Furthermore, this attack is the best operation for thwarting the enemy offensive in Flanders and for ensuring the permanent security of our U-boat base.[7]

Rupprecht's planners had already identified the Portuguese sector as the weakest and therefore the best break-in point. Estaires–Hazebrouck was the "strategically most effective direction." The Sixth Army would make the main attack with twenty to twenty-five divisions, and the Fourth Army would conduct a supporting attack with twelve to fifteen divisions. With the attack's right flank anchored on the La Bassée Canal, the most serious problem would be the high ground on the right:

> Our primary effort must be to affect a wide envelopment on the left. In the case of an extension to the right, we must consider how the problem of the high ground near Kemmel will be handled.... We must avoid committing heavy forces in a stiff fight for this high ground.[8]

In a course of action analysis dated 15 December 1917, Rupprecht's planners warned that the Germans could no longer assume that the British would continue their offensive in Flanders. They recommended a supporting diversionary attack, either against Ypres or Cambrai, to tie down the British reserves. The subsequent main attack would collapse the British in the north, take their northern ports, and then roll them up to the south.[9] Six days later Rupprecht's staff issued another course of action analysis that recommended Cambrai rather than Ypres as the best place for the diversionary attack. Ypres, they argued, was too close to the main attack, which would give the British the advantage of operating on interior lines. The British might simply evacuate the Ypres salient and the British reserves could then be shifted against GEORG, which would reduce the attack's flank and rear effectiveness.[10]

On 3 January 1918 Rupprecht's Army Group issued the detailed planning guidance for its subordinate armies. The Sixth Army, now with thirty to forty divisions, would conduct the GEORG I main attack, creating a breakthrough in the direction of Hazebrouck, with the ports of Calais and Dunkirk as deep objectives. The Fourth Army would launch GEORG II, a supporting attack against the Ypres salient with an additional twelve to fifteen divisions.[11]

The final version of the original GEORG plan called for a frontal attack to fix the British First Army, followed by converging attacks against the British Second Army, with the objective of destroying it. If the Germans could secure the line of the Flanders Hills from Kemmel to Godewearsvedle, the British would be forced to evacuate the Ypres salient. Most of Rupprecht's planners saw this line of high ground in an otherwise flat plane as the key to the entire area. That line of high ground partially encircled Ypres, starting with the very low Passchendaele ridge just to the east-northeast of the town, continuing to the south-southwest through the Messines Ridge, and then hooking almost straight west through a line of relatively high peaks. Mount Kemmel (156 meters), some eight kilometers almost dead south of Ypres, was at the eastern end of that line. Mount des Cats (158 meters) near Godewearsvedle, south-southwest of Ypres, was at the western end. Farther to the west and separated from the Cats–Kemmel ridge by a stretch of flat ground, Mount Cassel (158 meters) was the last piece of high ground before the coast. Dunkirk could be observed directly from atop Mount Cassel. That piece of high ground was a key objective of the original GEORG plan.[12] (See Map 4.)

The original plan called for the Sixth Army to attack between the La Bassée Canal and Armentières. Once it broke through, it would attack the British forces to the north in the flank and rear. The right wing of the Sixth Army would envelope Armentières from the south. The center would take the high ground around Locre and Godewearsvedle. The left wing would screen the flank, but also be prepared to advance against British forces in the south. In the second phase of the attack, the Sixth Army would form into three groups. The right and strongest group would move against Dunkirk and Gravelines; the left group would screen the left flank; and the center group would follow in reserve to Aire. The artillery requirement for GEORG I was estimated at 620 field batteries and 588 heavy batteries.[13]

The Fourth Army would attack Messines Ridge and Mount Kemmel to cut off the British in the Ypres salient. GEORG II was divided into three subordinate attacks. HASENJAGD (RABBIT HUNT) would be the main effort to support GEORG I by driving northwest toward Poperinghe and taking Mount Kemmel. WALDFEST (FOREST FESTIVAL) would be an attack from the Houthulst Forest southwest against the northern flank of the Ypres salient, also converging on Poperinghe. FLANDERN III would be a diversionary attack from Dixmuide south-southwest toward Reninghelst, breaking through the Belgian positions and driving for the left flank of the British Second Army.

Ludendorff made the decision for the MICHAEL option at the 21 January Aresens Conference, but that decision was closely held for security purposes. At one of the meetings leading up to the Aresens Conference, Ludendorff made a point of noting that the GEORG II attack south of Ypres should advance in a northwest direction, bypassing the high ground around Mount Kemmel.[14] German planning would continue to waffle back and forth on the question of taking or bypassing the Flanders Hills. On 24 January OHL directed the Sixth and Fourth Armies to continue the GEORG I and II preparations, with a projected launch date in April. OHL cautioned, however, that it could allocate only thirty divisions for GEORG I.[15] At the subsequent planning conference held at Mons on 3 February, the GEORG attacks were downgraded from diversionary attacks to feints, and renamed KLEIN-GEORG I and II. Now OHL would only be able to provide twenty divisions for KLEIN-GEORG I, and twelve to fifteen divisions for KLEIN-GEORG II.[16]

Even though Kuhl continued to believe that GEORG was the best option, he had little enthusiasm for KLEIN-GEORG as a follow-up to MICHAEL. He argued that if large British reserves moved south from Flanders in response to MICHAEL, it would be very difficult to disengage German forces from MICHAEL, especially artillery, and shift them back north for KLEIN-GEORG. Kuhl thought instead that the Germans should launch strong diversionary attacks in Flanders in support of MICHAEL.[17] On 10 February Ludendorff sent a somewhat rambling telegram to Rupprecht's headquarters outlining the purpose and scope of any attacks in the north:

> In response to your message Ia 5459 (secret): OHL having decided on the MICHAEL offensive as the main operation, GEORG I and II will constitute merely the second phase, and on the contingency only that the MICHAEL offensive does not culminate in the expected great breakthrough, but instead comes to a standstill when encountering the British and French reserves that have moved up in response.
>
> From the general situation that results, it will be possible to execute the disposition of the units for the GEORG I and GEORG II offensives by regrouping the forces, especially the artillery that was used in the MICHAEL offensive. It will neither be possible nor necessary to execute the GEORG operations in the manner recommended by the Fourth and Sixth Armies and with the number of units required by them. We will not be able to make available the units these two armies have estimated for—not even the approximate numbers specified—nor, most importantly, will we be able to move them to the new front and commit them to action there in a short period of time. Thus it will be necessary to restrict materially or to abandon completely the operations on the left wing (the southern portion of GEORG I). The more than 20 divisions, excluding the trench divisions, cannot be made available in time for GEORG I; nor can the 12 to 15 divisions, not counting the trench divisions, be made available for GEORG II. It is, however, safe to assume that the GEORG operation considered as a second phase, will produce a decisive effect, inasmuch as we can count with absolute certainty on the British reserves being contained farther south by the MICHAEL offensive. It is most important, therefore, that GEORG I and HASENJAGD should advance on both sides of Armentières toward Hazebrouck. Simultaneously, WALDFEST should cut off the Ypres salient from the northeast.
>
> Therefore, I ask you to continue the GEORG preparations on this basis and forward the plans to OHL as soon as both armies have made their revisions.[18]

Rupprecht understood the message to mean that, although MICHAEL would be the main attack, GEORG would follow if necessary.[19] On 12 February

Rupprecht's headquarters informed the Fourth and Sixth Armies of that, noting, "The Sixth Army will conduct the main attack in the direction of Hazebrouck in order to take the English north wing from the rear." But now there was no mention of the Channel ports as deep objectives. The order also noted that the preparations for KLEIN-GEORG would constitute a major element of the deception plan for MICHAEL.[20]

On 17 February Rupprecht's Army Group approved the basic plans for KLEIN-GEORG I, but told the Sixth Army not to plan on more than twenty divisions.[21] It also ordered the Fourth Army to prepare, in order of priority, HASENJAGD, FLANDERN III, and WALDFEST, planning for twelve to fifteen divisions total.[22] When the plans were submitted to OHL, Rupprecht's staff pointed out that HASENJAGD was probably the only part of KLEIN-GEORG II that could be launched simultaneously with KLEIN-GEORG I. OHL approved the plans, stressing that the HASENJAGD attack against the Messines Ridge should not be too narrow. The artillery requirement for KLEIN-GEORG I was now reduced to 130 field batteries and 192 heavy batteries.[23]

On 9 March Rupprecht's Army Group issued plans for the regrouping of forces from MICHAEL to KLEIN-GEORG I. The Seventeenth Army would provide the Sixth Army with six divisions and 131 artillery batteries, and the Second Army would provide five divisions and 127 batteries. OHL would also provide two divisions and forty-five heavy artillery batteries.[24]

In the first days of Operation MICHAEL, when it appeared to be succeeding, OHL concluded that KLEIN-GEORG would not be needed. OHL figured it could accomplish the same objectives by extending MICHAEL farther to the north with MARS and WALKÜRENRITT.[25] On 23 March the Sixth and Fourth Armies were ordered to suspend all preparations for the attack.[26] The next day, however, KLEIN-GEORG was back on the table, with Wetzell telling Rupprecht that Ludendorff hoped to launch that offensive in about eight days. On 26 March Wetzell urged Ludendorff to cancel MARS and launch an upgraded Operation GEORG instead. Ludendorff rejected the recommendation.[27] That same day OHL ordered the Sixth Army to resume preparations for KLEIN-GEORG I and the Fourth Army to resume preparations for attacks against the Belgians.[28] With its resources reduced even more, the Sixth Army sent the plan for the operation now called GEORGETTE I to OHL.[29] The basic assumption was that the attack would be necessary only if the MARS and WALKÜRENRITT attacks failed.

The latest version of the plan called for the Sixth Army to make a ten-division attack with six fresh assault and four trench divisions. The main effort would be launched by four divisions against the Portuguese sector from Givenchy to Fromelles, driving northwest toward Hazebrouck. The immediate objective of that attack was to reach and cross the Lys on the first day, force the British back behind the river, and then facilitate the follow-on attack of the Fourth Army.[30] Two divisions had the mission of securing the left flank along the La Bassée Canal. Two divisions in the first echelon followed by two divisions in the second echelon would attack on the right flank to reach the Lys east of Sailly, and then prepare to exploit to the north. In addition to the ten initially attacking divisions, two divisions would follow behind the center as the army reserve.

The Fourth Army, initially launching only HASENJAGD, would attack to the west, with its left flank on Frelinghien. The sector between Fromelles and Frelinghien, which included Armentières, would be cut off and pinched out in conjunction with the right flank of the Sixth Army's attack. The success of the entire GEORGETTE operation depended on reaching the Lys between Estaires and Armentières in twenty-four to forty-eight hours and crossing in multiple places before the British could organize and move up a resistance.

Both MARS attacks failed on 28 March, and WALKÜRENRITT, which had been scheduled for the following day, was cancelled. On 29 March OHL issued orders for the conduct of further operations, and Rupprecht's Army Group issued a warning order for GEORGETTE.[31] The Sixth Army was now promised seven divisions from the Seventeenth Army, for a total plus-up of eleven divisions that would give it a total of seventeen. The Fourth Army was ordered to expand the FLANDERN III attack into FLANDERN IV, extending it from Dixmuide to the coast, with an objective of capturing the coastal area south of Nieuport. GEORGETTE and FLANDERN IV could not be executed simultaneously, however, because of insufficient forces. HASENJAGD would support GEORGETTE I initially, with WALDFEST and FLANDERN IV to follow based on the situation and the availability of forces.

It was difficult at that point for the Germans to provide more forces for GEORGETTE, because MICHAEL had added thirty-three miles to the length of the German front. OHL issued the orders for shifting and reassigning the artillery and special troops, but not on anywhere near the scale of the original GEORG plan. The Seventeenth Army would now provide the Sixth Army with fifty-six heavy batteries, and OHL would provide thirty-two heavy batteries.[32]

As it became more obvious that the Germans would not take Amiens, the importance of GEORGETTE grew for OHL. All the planners came to realize that it would actually constitute the second phase vaguely referenced in the MICHAEL operations order of 10 March. On 30 March OHL set 4 April as the start date for GEORGETTE, but only "if weather conditions permit."[33] Rupprecht's Army Group responded that the attacking divisions might not be available in time.[34]

On 1 April OHL ordered the resumption of Operation MICHAEL, supported in the north by Operation GEORGETTE on 8 April, and in the south by Operation ERZENGEL on 5 April.[35] On 3 April Ludendorff, Kuhl, and the chiefs of staff of the Fourth and Sixth Armies met in Tournai to review the GEORGETTE planning.[36] During the meeting Ludendorff only talked about initial objectives for the attacking forces and did not mention follow-on objectives.[37] Immediately following that meeting, Rupprecht's Army Group issued the final orders for GEORGETTE, which noted that, if the attack proved to be a major success, the remaining forces of the army group would be committed to exploit it.[38]

The Sixth Army was to attack with its right wing along the vector Armentières–Steenwerck–Bailleul to take the heights north of Bailleul (Mount Kemmel–Mount des Cats ridge), and then be prepared to advance beyond Godewearsvedle to Cassel. The center was to attack along the line Clairmarais Forest–Thiennes to take the Lys crossings. The left wing was to attack over the Canal d'Aire to secure the heights west and south of Béthune and the crossings at Béthune and La Bassée. The main effort was toward Hazebrouck. Both wings had to be deeply echeloned, and "objectives for follow-on attack [would] depend on the situation."

The Fourth Army was to be ready to launch HASENJAGD in the direction of Messines–Wulverghem as soon as the British front north of Armentières began to waver, but not until the right wing of the Sixth Army got across the Lys. The initial objective was Messines Ridge, then Mount Kemmel. HASENJAGD would then establish contact with right wing of GEORGETTE I in the vicinity of Neuve Eglise, then swing to the northwest. (See Map 4.) The Fourth Army would also be prepared to exploit on order with WALDFEST and FLANDERN IV.

The Germans broke off the attack on Amiens on 4 April, and officially terminated Operation MICHAEL the next day. On 6 April GEORGETTE I was pushed back one day, to 9 April.[39] At that point Rupprecht's Army Group estimated that there were six and $\frac{1}{3}$ British and two Portuguese divisions in the line opposite the Sixth Army.[40]

On 7 April Kuhl met at Tournai with the chiefs of staff of the Fourth and Sixth Armies.[41] Ludendorff now wanted the right wing of the Sixth Army and the left wing of the Fourth Army to attack simultaneously on 9 April, but Lossberg pointed out the available heavy artillery was insufficient to support both attacks. The decision was finally made for the Fourth Army to attack on 10 April.[42] The Fourth Army's WALDFEST attack from the Houthulst Forest against the north of the Ypres salient was split into two different options. One was a deliberate attack (*planmässigen Angriff*) called TANNENBERG; the other was a pursuit attack (*Verfolgungsangriff*) called BLÜCHER, to be launched if the British started to evacuate the salient voluntarily.[43]

In a telephone conversation on 8 April, Ludendorff told Kuhl that if GEORGETTE succeeded the Germans must then be prepared to follow-up with immediate attacks in the vicinities of Arras, Albert, and south of the Somme.[44] Rupprecht recorded in his diary that same day that the staff of the Second Army was irritated by Ludendorff's insistence on dictating such minor details as the times that rearward divisions would break camp.[45] As the period of intense combat of the 1918 offensives continued, Ludendorff increasingly interfered in lower level planning and execution details. Major Joachim von Stuelpnagel, a General Staff officer at the Seventeenth Army, also complained about being on the receiving end of many of Ludendorff's telephone calls about minutiae.[46]

Preparations

The preparations and buildup (*Aufmarsch*) for GEORGETTE were similar to those for MICHAEL, except on a smaller scale and on a far more compressed schedule.[47] OHL originally figured that, following a successful MICHAEL breakthrough, it would be possible to release some of the required artillery and trench mortar units, engineer units, labor forces, search light platoons, flamethrower companies, and visual signal platoons. It would not, however, be possible to transfer the bulk of the forces north until MICHAEL had been definitely terminated. Even after that point it would be necessary to leave most of the support columns with the MICHAEL armies until the local rail lines could be repaired and extended to the German advanced positions.[48]

OHL also had to determine which units could be shifted via the already overloaded rail net and which would have to march. Most of the units from the Seventeenth Army were nearer, so they would march. All marches would be conducted at night. The units from Second Army had the farthest to go, and they would go by rail whenever possible. The daily ammunition re-supply requirement was fourteen to fifteen trains just for the Sixth Army, and thirty to thirty-five trains for the whole of Rupprecht's Army Group. Even though MICHAEL had halted, the consolidation and defensive operations in the Second and Seventeenth Army sectors continued to consume unexpectedly high amounts of ammunition, and by 7 April Rupprecht's Army Group reported to OHL that the Sixth Army had received only half its total supply requirement.[49]

Ludendorff took no chances with the artillery preparations this time. The Sixth Army's artillery chief, General Huhn, had been one of the major dissenters at the 26 January artillery conference. At the end of March Huhn was sick. Possibly Kuhl asked for Bruchmüller first, but in the event Ludendorff decided to second Bruchmüller and his entire staff to the Sixth Army to make sure the firepower planning and execution were done right this time. Bruchmüller and his ARKO 86 staff were set up at a command post near Ham east of St. Quentin when he got the phone message to report personally to Ludendorff at OHL to receive his orders for GEORGETTE.[50]

Bruchmüller was not enthusiastic about the task he had been handed. He had only nine days to pull it all together. When he reached the Sixth Army headquarters he found almost no artillery planning had been started. A quick tour of the forward positions showed utter confusion among the artillery units. Reinforcing batteries transferred in from other sectors for the attack were just sitting around in the rear areas, and no one seemed to know what to do with them. Once more Marx and Pulkowski mounted a massive training effort, despite encountering stiff-necked skepticism.[51]

Allied actions

General Sir Henry Wilson clearly saw the most dangerous course of action to the British. In a telegram to Foch he wrote:

> In my opinion, the proper course for the enemy to pursue is as follows: place Amiens town and Amiens railway and junctions under his guns so as

to deny all serious traffic, then mass an attack of 40 to 50 divisions against the British between Albert and the La Bassée Canal. If the enemy does this and at the same time is prepared to give up ground in front of a French attack, I am quite certain the British line will not be able to sustain such an attack without the direct assistance of French divisions, or unless the French take over much more of the British line to enable Field-Marshal Haig to have many more troops than he now has in reserve.[52]

Haig agreed with Wilson and told Foch so, but the French declined to take over any more of the British line. Small French reserves were west of Amiens, but Haig wanted them moved farther north, to the vicinity of St. Pol. Foch felt very strongly that the Allies should attack as soon as possible south of the Somme to drive the Germans back from the Paris–Amiens rail line and the Amiens rail center. His two primary objectives at this point were to strengthen the connection between the British and the French and to "cover Amiens."[53]

By 2 April British intelligence estimated that the Germans would continue the attack in the Arras sector.[54] The British front line there was only fifty miles from the coast. At the southern end of the sector Vimy Ridge lay only three miles from the front. Control of that ridge would allow the Germans to exploit to the south. On the north end of the Arras sector lay that portion of the Béthune coalfields not already in German possession or under their guns. Even Pétain agreed that this was the most economically critical sector of the front.

At the Beauvais conference on 3 April, the Allies expanded Foch's mandate, giving him "strategic direction" of all Allied military operations, not just the response to MICHAEL. The commanders of the British, French, and American Armies in the field retained "full control of the tactical employment of their forces."[55] The Belgian King, however, flatly refused to recognize Foch's authority over Belgian forces.

By 5 April the Allied intelligence assessment noted the potential of a follow-on German offensive north of Arras.[56] Haig reorganized his reserves into two groups: one consisting of eight divisions (five fresh) between the Ancre and Doullens; and one of seven divisions (two fresh) northwest of Arras. Pétain also started shifting French forces north to Ailly sur Noye. Several days earlier, General Sir Henry Horne, the commander of the British First Army, had decided that the two weak Portuguese divisions should be withdrawn from their sector of the line in the vicinity of Neuve Chapelle. By 5 April the Portuguese 1st Division had been withdrawn, and the British 50th Northumbrian Division was scheduled to relieve the Portuguese 2nd Division on 9 April. But after the Portuguese 1st Division pulled out, the Portuguese 2nd Division merely extended to cover the gap, thus making that sector even weaker when the Germans struck.[57]

On 6 April Haig's intelligence chief, Brigadier-General E.W. Cox, reported that the Germans intended to capture Vimy Ridge by turning it on both flanks from Arras and Lens.[58] This essentially would have meant a resumption of the MARS and WALKÜRENRITT operations. On 8 April Horne reported to Haig that he had every indication he would be attacked the next day. The French, meanwhile, were planning in conjunction with the British Fourth Army to attack the German Eighteenth and Seventh Armies in the south, with a projected attack date of 12 April. Nonetheless, Foch on 7 April agreed to move four French infantry and three cavalry divisions west of Amiens.[59]

German order of battle

Only four of the Sixth Army's five corps participated in the GEORGETTE I attack. South of the La Bassée Canal, one corps held the line down to the Second Army's northern boundary. Both the Sixth and Fourth Armies had to attack with a high percentage of trench divisions which, with their very limited mobility, acted as a drag on the overall tempo of the attack. On the other hand, the Sixth Army was reinforced with six tank units, each with five tanks. Almost all were machines captured from the Allies.[60] When the attack jumped off, there were also three more trench divisions enroute to the Sixth Army sector as OHL reserve. See Tables 7.1 and 7.2.

The artillery order of battle for GEORGETTE shows the weighting of the main attack far more clearly than it did for MICHAEL. With a total of 1,686 German guns opposing 511 British, the Sixth Army started the battle with a tube superiority ratio of 3.3:1.

The weighting of the main effort is far less clear in the air order of battle. The two attacking armies had only 57 percent of the aviation squadrons of all types and only 50 percent of the bomber squadrons available to Rupprecht's Army Group. The Sixth Army, with four attacking corps, was supported by forty-three squadrons; while the Fourth Army, attacking with only two corps had thirty-three squadrons.

Table 7.1 German divisions on 9 and 10 April 1918[61]

	First line	Second line	Third line	Total divisions	Sector width
Fourth Army	1 Attack		2 Attack*	3 Attack	17 km
	3 Trench		2 Trench#	5 Trench	
Sixth Army	5 Attack	3 Attack	1 Attack#	9 Attack	27 km
	5 Trench	2 Trench	2 Trench§	9 Trench	
	6 Attack	3 Attack	3 Attack	12 Attack	44 km
	8 Trench	2 Trench	4 Trench	14 Trench	

Source: *Der Weltkrieg*, Vol.14, Appendices 35 and 38g.

Notes
*OHL reserve.
#Army reserve.
§1 each OHL and Army reserve.

Table 7.2 German corps on 9 and 10 April 1918[62]

	(North to south)		
	Corps	*Commander*	*Attacking*
Fourth Army		Sixt von Arnim	
	Naval Corps	Schroeder	No
	Guards Corps	Böchmann	No
	XVIII Reserve	Sieger	10 April
	X Reserve	Eberhardt	10 April
Sixth Army		Quast	
	II Bavarian	Stetten	9 April
	XIX	Carlowitz	9 April
	LV	Bernhardi	9 April
	IV	Kraewel	9 April
	XL	Litzmann	No

Source: *Der Weltkrieg*, Vol.14, Appendices 35 and 38g.

Table 7.3 German guns on 9 and 10 April 1918[63]

	Field guns	*Heavy guns*	*Super-heavy guns*	*Total guns*
Fourth Army	307	253*	11	571*
Sixth Army	892	765	29	1,686
	1,199	971	40	2,210

Source: *Der Weltkrieg*, Vol.14, Appendix 39b.

Note
*Includes forty-seven heavy guns transferred from Sixth Army on the night of 9 April.

Table 7.4 German squadrons on 10 April 1918[64]

	Observation	*Attack*	*Fighter*	*Bomber*	*Total*
Fourth Army	12	7	11	3	33
Sixth Army	16	10	14	3	43
GEORGETTE					
Total	28	17	25	6	76
Seventeenth Army	15	4	6	0	25
Second Army	16	4	8	6	33
Army group total	59	25	39	12	134

Source: AOK 6, Iad/koflieg 2656, (5 April 1918), Bayerisches Kriegsarchiv, File Hgr. Rupprecht, Bd. 168. AOK 4, Iae 238, (10 April 1918), Bayerisches Kriegsarchiv, File Hgr. Rupprecht, Bd. 96.

Allied order of battle

On the British side of the line, the First Army was spread especially thin, with each of the divisions having to cover a 6.7-kilometer sector on average. Between Switzerland and La Fére on the Oise, the French on 9 April had: forty-six divisions in the line; twelve divisions in reserve; three divisions in transit; and three American divisions. Between the Oise and the British the French had: eight divisions in the line; ten divisions in army and Army Group Reserve; ten divisions (one American) in GQG reserve; six cavalry divisions in GQG reserve; and four divisions in transit toward the sector[65] (see Table 7.5).

Execution (9–29 April)

9 April   As a lead-up to the GEORGETTE attack, the Germans on 7 and 8 April hit the British lines at Lens and Armentières with heavy mustard-gas barrages. On 9 April the Sixth Army launched its attack from Givenchy to Fromelles. The success of the operation depended on reaching the Lys between Estaires and Armentières in twenty-four to forty-eight hours and making multiple crossings before the British could bring up reinforcements. On the right, the Bavarian II Corps had to reach the Lys east of Sailly.[66]

The German artillery opened fire at 0415 hours. At 4.5 hours and with only four phases, the preparation was a streamlined version of the one Bruchmüller used at St. Quentin. Still not relying completely on the Pulkowski Method, the German guns firing against the British infantry positions verified their predicted registration data during the 2nd Phase of the preparation. The adjustment of the fire was accomplished by balloon observers wherever ground observers could not see the targets. The rate of advance of the creeping barrage was slower than at St. Quentin. The Sixth Army fired a total of 1.4 million artillery rounds that first day (see Table 7.6).[67]

At 0845 hours the German infantry surged forward, once again in heavy fog. The weak Portuguese division in the center disintegrated almost immediately. By 1500 hours the Germans reached the Lys at Bac St. Maur and soon reached it at Estaires. By that night their lead units reached the River Lawe at Petit Marais and Vielle Chapelle, a penetration of six miles. Once again the initial results

Table 7.5 British order of battle in the GEORGETTE sector 9–10 April 1918[68]

	Infantry divisions	Cavalry divisions	Army reserve	Heavy guns	Total guns	Sector width
Second Army	5	0	1 Inf	—	—	17 km
First Army	4*	0	2 Inf	200	511	27 km

Source: *Der Weltkrieg*, Vol.14, Appendices 38g, 39h.

Note
*Including one Portuguese division.

Table 7.6 Sixth army artillery preparation 9 April 1918[69]

1st Phase (120 minutes)
* Fire strike with *Buntkreuz* against enemy batteries, trench mortars, headquarters, communications centers, and depots.
* Trench mortars drop out after 20 minutes' firing.
* 50 minutes after the start, 10-minute saturation of the front infantry positions with no counter-battery fire.
* HE against the 1st line; Blue Cross against the 2nd and 3rd lines.

2nd Phase (30 minutes)
* Registration verification against the infantry positions.
* AKA continues counter-battery with gas.

3rd Phase (115 minutes)
* IKA attacks only those 1st infantry positions the mortars cannot reach.
* 2nd and 3rd positions attacked heavily, especially the break-in sector.
* AKA continues counter-battery.
* After 90 minutes, 10-minute fire strike against enemy artillery by IKA and AKA.

4th Phase (5 minutes)
* Saturation fire on the leading trenches of the 1st position.

Creeping barrage (*Feuerwalze*)
* 1st jump 300–400 meters.
* 200-meter subsequent jumps.
* 30 minutes per kilometer.

Source: AOK 6, Ia 2582, "Artillery Order Number 1," (31 March 1918), Bayerisches Kriegsarchiv, File AOK 6, Bd 7.

looked spectacular; but as on 21 March, the Germans had failed to achieve all their first-day objectives. On the extreme left wing of the attack, the Germans were held fast at Givenchy by stubborn resistance from the British 55th Division.[70]

One of the main difficulties was in getting the supporting artillery forward. Ironically, the tanks committed to GEORGETTE compounded that problem. With their notorious mechanical unreliability, more of the German tanks broke down under their own weight than were knocked out in combat. The soft, wet ground made the tanks, along with all other heavy equipment, road-bound. When the tanks started breaking down along the few and relatively narrow avenues of approach, they blocked the advance of the accompanying artillery. The stalled tanks had to be blown in place before the supporting guns could move up. That experience could not have done much to ameliorate Ludendorff's blind spot for the tank.[71]

That night Rupprecht's Army Group ordered the Sixth Army to resume attacking at 0600 hours the next morning and continue pushing over the Lys. The Fourth Army was ordered to launch its HASENJAGD phase of GEORGETTE II on 10 April. Sixth Army was ordered to leave the artillery it could not move forward behind its extreme right wing, to support the Fourth Army's attack.[72]

Foch happened to be visiting Haig at GHQ in Montreuil that day. When the reports of the attack began to come through, Haig immediately pressed Foch for French reinforcement divisions. Foch, however, refused, saying the attack was only a diversion and the real threat would come in the vicinity of Arras.[73]

10 April   At 0245 hours on 10 April, 522 field guns and 215 heavy and very heavy guns started the Fourth Army's artillery preparation. Two and a half hours later two corps moved forward with their left flank at Frelinghien. At 0600 hours the Sixth Army resumed its attack. Again, heavy fog worked to the overall advantage of the attackers. Shortly before noon the Fourth Army's XVIII Reserve Corps captured Messines and continued moving against the lower slopes of the Wytschaete Ridge. A little after noon the fog cleared. Encouraged by the initial success, Ludendorff planned to give the Fourth Army control of two more divisions plus the élite, division-sized Alpine Corps.

That afternoon an attack by a South African brigade retook Messines, only to lose it again quickly. Under pressure from both flanks, the British 34th Division started to evacuate Armentières, withdrawing to the north bank of the Lys. About 1645 hours Ludendorff told Lossberg that the Armentières–Bailleul road had to be taken by nightfall at all costs. An hour later the Sixth Army captured Steenwerck. By the end of 10 April the Germans had captured 11,000 prisoners and 146 guns. The Sixth Army had pretty much forced the line of the Lys, and in the south it crossed the Lawe and pushed as far as Lestrem. On the extreme left wing of the attack, however, the Germans were still held up by stubborn British resistance at Festubert and Givenchy.[74]

The Sixth Army issued orders for the Bavarian II Corps and XIX Corps to capture the high ground at Bailleul, Meteren, and Strazeele the next day. The two corps were also to link up with the Fourth Army in the vicinity of Nieppe and then pinch out Armentières. The two southern corps were to continue efforts to capture the crossings over the La Bassée Canal and eliminate the British at Festubert and Givenchy. The Fourth Army objective for the next day was to capture Wytschaete and push toward Wulverghem. The decision to move toward Kemmel or Dranoutre would be made only after Wulverghem was taken.[75]

Rupprecht at that point wanted to initiate the WALDFEST attack from the Houthulst Forest against the right flank of the Belgians, believing that only exhausted British divisions remained in the Ypres salient. The Fourth Army initially insisted that it needed three more divisions plus additional artillery, but finally agreed it could attack with only one extra division. Rupprecht believed that even if the attack did not achieve significant results on its own, it would do a great deal to reduce the resistance in front of the Fourth Army's main attack.[76]

That morning in Paris Wilson warned Clemenceau about the serious threat to the Channel ports and the consequences of their loss. Although Foch at that point still thought the attack in Flanders was a diversion, he nonetheless issued orders for the French Tenth Army to move north slightly, and for the French Fifth Army to move up behind it. Haig sent Foch a request for the French to relieve a sector of the British front in the south, but Foch ordered Pétain to move the French 133rd Division to Dunkirk by rail. In his memoirs Foch noted: "Our available railway lines had been reduced by the attack of March 21st, and the difficulty of moving troops was considerably increased."[77]

11 April   The Germans committed seven more divisions to GEORGETTE. The correlation of forces now stood at thirty-one German divisions against thirteen Allied. But ten of those German divisions had fought in MICHAEL. The Sixth Army took Armentières, but the British evacuated the town with few losses.[78] The Bavarian II Corps reached Steenwerck, but the IV Corps on the left wing still made little progress against Festubert and Givenchy. As Ludendorff laconically noted in his memoirs, "On the left, at Givenchy and Festubert, we were held up. The result was not satisfactory."[79] The Fourth Army, meanwhile, closed in on Wytschaete and Wulverghem and established contact with the Sixth Army near Le Romarin.[80] OHL pressured the Sixth Army to move more troops up to continue the attack. The Sixth Army resisted on the grounds that more troops in the area of operations would only add to the confusion, given the poor state of communications and the ground. It was more important, it argued, to move up supporting artillery and ammunition.[81]

By evening the Germans were almost to the Nieppe Forest, some nine miles from their starting line on 9 April. They were close to splitting the British First and Second Armies. In the orders for next day the Sixth Army was given the objectives of taking the high ground near Bailleul, Meteren, and Strazeele; the northern and western edges of the Nieppe Forest; the Aire–La Bassée Canal; and Mount Bernenchon before the Allies could reinforce.[82] The Fourth Army's XVIII Reserve Corps on the right was ordered to consolidate its gains until the X Reserve Corps on the left could make more progress in the direction of Neuve Eglise. Rupprecht's Army Group at that point still considered the priority for effort to be the attack toward Hazebrouck and then the far end of the Kemmel–Cats ridge at Godewearsvedle.[83]

Haig sent Foch a message that day requesting a minimum of four French divisions to support the Second Army. Foch finally began to recognize the threat to Hazebrouck and the Hazebrouck–Lille rail line, and he ordered the French Tenth Army to start moving toward the north to the line of Doullens–Vauchelles. Meanwhile, Pétain on his own initiative ordered the French Fifth Army farther north, up closer behind the Tenth Army.[84]

12 April   By the fourth day of GEORGETTE the Germans were on the verge of capturing Hazebrouck. They were less than five miles from that vital rail center. But the Sixth Army had not yet taken all its assigned objectives from 11 April. It was ordered to take them on 12 April.[85] About noon Ludendorff ordered a maximum effort drive on the approaches to Bailleul by the combined inner wings of the Fourth and Sixth Armies.[86] That, however, shifted the thrust of the main effort more to the north, away from Hazebrouck.

At 1315 hours the Fourth Army ordered the immediate capture of the high ground around Neuve Eglise, Wulverghem, and Wytschaete, then a push forward by the infantry to cover the concentration of the artillery to support the attack on Mount Kemmel. By that evening the Fourth Army was on the eastern edges of Wytschaete and Wulverghem. Its orders for the next day required it to attack with a strong left wing in the direction of Neuve Eglise.[87] Kuhl also told the Fourth Army that if the British started to withdraw from the Ypres salient, then the BLÜCHER pursuit attack should be launched immediately. The exact method of attacking Mount Kemmel, however, would be based on the outcome of the operations of 13 April. Ludendorff had earlier indicated that the attack should be executed from either the east or west, but not from the south.

Kuhl, Schulenburg, and Ludendorff also met in Avesnes on 12 April to consider a new attack by the Second Army against Amiens, projected for 20 April. Ludendorff considered it important to get "as close to Amiens as possible." At that meeting Kuhl also argued for a suspension of all operations south of the Somme. But Ludendorff was also considering an attack by the right wing of the Second Army, supported by the left wing of the Seventeenth Army—in other words, a renewed attack north of the Somme, which later would be designated NEU-MICHAEL.[88] Writing in his diary, Rupprecht noted that the Second Army attack south of the Somme should only be made if the attacks of the Sixth and Fourth Armies succeeded. If those attacks did not succeed, then it would be better for the Second Army to do nothing and consolidate its forces to support NEU-MICHAEL.

> The most important thing of all is to exhaust the British completely, in order to bring about their final collapse. Major Wetzell, the Chief of the Operations Section, agrees with this view, while Ludendorff seems to prefer a series of smaller attacks. These will only result in smaller successes— although with proportionately higher casualties—than large attacks. Moreover, in these smaller attacks the expenditure of ammunition is relatively greater than in larger attacks, owing to the necessity of protecting the flanks, and the regrouping of the artillery entails much work and fatigues the men and horses very much. Ludendorff is certainly a wonderful organizer, but not a great strategist. (*aber kein grosser Stratege*.)[89]

Haig issued his famous "Backs to the Wall" order of the day on 12 April: "Every position must be held to the last man."[90] Effective on noon that day, Plumer's Second Army assumed control of most of the battle as the boundary between Second Army and General Sir Henry Horne's First Army shifted south from just north of Armentières, to two miles north of the Lys at Merville. Foch, meanwhile, moved to establish a Franco–Belgian reserve groupment behind the British First Army, but under the command of Plumer. With French troops already starting to detrain at Dunkirk, Foch put the French II Cavalry Corps under Plumer to maintain contact between the British First and Second Armies.[91]

Recognizing the threat to the high ground of the Flanders Hills, Foch also ordered the French 28th Division to move north to the British sector. Foch then issued his plan for the defensive battle, which called for establishing two converging lines: one in the south from Béthune to St. Omer, facing the northeast; and one in the north from Mount Kemmel to Cassel, facing the south. Between these two solid converging lines Foch ordered the establishment of a series of successive lines facing east, to slow down and eventually stop the German advance. Those lines included in order: Bailleul–Nieppe Forest; Meteren–Caestre–Hazebrouck–Aire; Cassel–Ebblinghem; and Cassel–Clairmarais Forest.[92]

13 April   The German official history dourly noted, "The battle on 13 April was not fought under a lucky star."[93] The Sixth Army's objectives for the day were Bailleul, Meteren, Strazeele, the Nieppe Forest, and the La Bassée Canal crossings between Guarbecque and Mount Bernenchon.[94] Four divisions attacked the Nieppe Forest toward Hazebrouck, but made little progress. The Sixth Army also failed to take Bailleul and continued to be held fast at Festubert and Givenchy.

The Fourth Army attacked with only its X Reserve Corps to take the high ground between Neuve Eglise and Bailleul, while its XVIII Reserve Corps prepared to launch an envelopment against Wytschaete on 16 April.[95] Poor coordination on the inner flanks of the two corps resulted in elements of both corps firing on each other. Sixt von Arnim recommended launching the WALD-FEST attack from the Houthulst Forest north of Ypres to relieve the pressure in the south.[96]

The lead elements of the French II Cavalry Corps arrived in Flanders on 13 April. Foch, meanwhile, had ordered the defense of Hazebrouck to be conducted "as near as possible to the eastern edge of the Nieppe Forest."[97] The Australian 1st Division arrived in front of Hazebrouck and joined with the 4th Guards Brigade to form a solid barrier in front of the vital rail center. Although the original objective of GEORGETTE was now effectively screened, the German main effort had already shifted to the Mount Kemmel–Mount des Cats ridge.

14 April   By the sixth day of the battle the overall results were growing increasingly disappointing for the Germans. All committed units were ordered to continue the advance while preparations were made to launch the attack from the Houthulst Forest. The main effort was now against the line of low hills that included Bailleul and Neuve Eglise, well away from Hazebrouck. The deep objectives were Godewearsvedle for the Sixth Army and Poperinghe for the Fourth Army. All the emphasis was now focused on the inner wings of the two armies.[98]

The extreme left wing of the Sixth Army still made no progress against Festubert and Givenchy. The Sixth Army finally reported to OHL that its attack was stalling and the troops were exhausted. The Sixth Army chief of staff, Lieutenant Colonel von Lenz, recommended that the attack be halted until sufficient artillery and trench mortars could be brought up. Both Kuhl and Lossberg disagreed strongly, but Ludendorff accepted the recommendation.[99] As a result, new orders directed the Sixth Army to resume the attack on 17 April, north of the Nieppe Forest against Meteren and Strazeele. On the extreme left flank, however, the IV Corps had to continue attacking to take Festubert and Givenchy. The Fourth Army too would continue attacking.[100]

At noon the Fourth Army increased its frontage by assuming control of the three left flank divisions (117th, 32nd, and 10th Ersatz) of the Sixth Army. The units were assigned to the newly inserted Guards Reserve Corps. In the Sixth Army sector, the III Bavarian Corps replaced the II Bavarian Corps, which was considered to have failed. The IX Reserve Corps headquarters also was inserted between the LV and IV Corps.[101] The Sixth Army now had nineteen divisions under five corps headquarters committed to the battle. By the end of the day most German divisions were reporting officer losses exceeding 100 each.[102]

By the end of 14 April the French 28th and 133rd Divisions and the II Cavalry Corps were operating under Plumer's control. At an Allied conference at Abbeville, Haig pressed Foch to send more French forces to the Haze-brouck–Cassel area.[103] Foch, however, flatly refused to provide relief for any of the divisions fighting on the Lys. As he later wrote in his memoirs:

> To relieve units while the battle was in progress would immobilize both the relieving troops and those relieved during the time required for the operation, and at the very moment when the Allied reserves were scarcely sufficient to man the whole front.[104]

The British, meanwhile, continued to worry about the threat to the Channel ports. The Admiralty was especially concerned about the possibility of losing Calais and Boulogne. Because the potential substitute ports of Dieppe, Le Havre, Rouen, and Cherbourg were farther away, they were out of range for smaller ships. Using larger ships would slow down the flow of supplies, and would also make it almost impossible to continue to maintain the blockade at Dover, the key anchor in the antisubmarine defense.[105]

15 April   Rupprecht's Army Group issued the orders for the capture of Bailleul. Fourth Army was to encircle the town from the north and east, with follow-on objectives of St. Jans Cappel and Mount Noir. The Sixth Army was to attack from the south and west, with a follow-on objective of Berthen.[106] In the event, the Sixth Army postponed its attack, to allow for further preparations. The Fourth Army did take Bailleul and its XVIII Reserve Corps captured Wul-verghem. By end of day the Germans had pushed across the Bailleul–Wulverghem rail line.[107] The German main effort, however, was now clearly focused away from Hazebrouck, toward the high ground of the Flanders Hills.

Later that day OHL issued a wildly optimistic communiqué stating, "The break-in on both sides of Armentières has led to a new, great tactical success." Significantly, the message used the term break-in (*Einbruch*) rather than break-through (*Durchbruch*).[108] OHL also issued a warning order to the Second and Eighteenth Armies to start preparing an attack with their inner wings on both sides of Moreuil and also against Montdidier–Noyon.[109]

In order to free up forces for the fight in the Lys valley, that day the British made the agonizing decision to pull back their line north of Ypres. In the process they gave up all the territory won at the cost of almost a quarter of a million casualties during the previous year's Passchendaele offensive.[110] German intelligence that day reported two French divisions in vicinity of Doullens, thirty kilometers north of Amiens.[111]

16 April Sixth Army still stood fast, preparing to launch a renewed attack. But it did take advantage of the British evacuation of Bailleul to capture Meteren. The Fourth Army continued attacking with its three left flank corps between Bailleul and Wytschaete.[112] Kuhl, meanwhile, was trying to convince Ludendorff to authorize the TANNENBURG deliberate attack, arguing that even 19 April would be too late for that option.[113]

The Guards Corps, positioned between the Ypres Canal and the Houthulst Forest, was still unaware by afternoon of the British partial pull-back in the Ypres salient. By late afternoon its two left divisions (the 58th and 236th) unexpectedly broke into the former British positions. Upon receiving that information, Lossberg decided to execute the BLÜCHER pursuit attack option on 17 April. The Guards Corps would have four divisions in the first line, three in the second, and one in general reserve, and be supported by 180 batteries.[114] But now, the attackers would have to advance down two miles of an exposed ridge face, hauling their artillery pieces over open ground and through mud.

The first two French infantry divisions entered the battle on 16 April in support of the Second Army. At a meeting with Haig in Abbeville that day, Foch agreed to commit another infantry division and move up two more reserve divisions. The French now had twelve divisions behind the British.[115]

17 April The German Guards Corps launched BLÜCHER at 0900 hours. The objective was to separate the Belgians and British, but the attack was launched piecemeal. Of the four first-line divisions that were supposed to make the attack, two were already following the British. Two of the second echelon divisions had not completed detraining. The British partially neutralized the attack by pulling their line back even farther. At 0945 hours the Belgians launched a series of unexpectedly fierce counterattacks.[116]

At 1000 hours the left wing of the Fourth Army and right wing of the Sixth Army launched strong attacks. The Fourth Army's objective was to outflank Mount Kemmel by taking Mounts Noir and Rouge to the west. The Sixth Army attacked in the direction of Godewearsvedle. The objective of the combined attacks was now to cut off the Ypres salient by enveloping it from the north and by taking the high ground to the south. But the direction of those attacks led away from Hazebrouck.[117]

By evening it was clear that the German attacks had failed. North of Ypres the Belgians drove the attackers back almost to their starting positions. South of Ypres the commanders of the Fourth Army's X Reserve, Guards Reserve, and III Bavarian Corps all reported that they could not continue unless their exhausted front-line troops were relieved. The Sixth Army also halted its attacks in the Bailleul sector in the face of freshly arrived French reinforcements. On the Sixth Army's left wing, the IV Corps and IX Reserve Corps still made no progress against Festubert and Givenchy.

Between 1930 hours and midnight Ludendorff, Kuhl, and Lossberg discussed the situation in a series of phone conversations. Lossberg reported that the situation was very bad, and that the Fourth Army's left wing was in a poor tactical position, at the base of high ground held by the enemy. He recommended that all efforts to take Mounts Kemmel and Noir by direct attack on a broad front be abandoned, and the attack of the Guards Corps be halted. He also noted that the Fourth Army needed fresh divisions. Kuhl responded that it would be impossible to give the Fourth Army fresh divisions in the Bailleul area before 21 April. Kuhl instructed the Guards Corps to start preparing a line of defense in case their attack the next day failed. Ludendorff said he would not make any decisions until he saw how the Guards Corps' attack went the next day. If the attack went well, he would commit two more divisions to the Fourth Army. If the attack did not go well, he would withdraw the three uncommitted reserve divisions presently behind the Guards Corps.[118]

Even though the German offensive had every appearance of stalling, Foch noted that the British were still making contingency plans to destroy and evacuate the port of Dunkirk.[119] German intelligence, meanwhile, reported that French forces were "beyond doubt on the battlefield of Armentières."[120]

18 April   As the attacks resumed on the 18th, German morale continued to grind down. OHL General Staff officer Albrecht von Thaer noted in his diary: "The moral influence on the troops has passed to the company commanders and the troop leaders."[121] After conferring with Lossberg, Kuhl decided to halt the attack on both sides of Bailleul. On the extreme left, the Sixth Army again failed to take Festubert and Givenchy in the face of determined British counterattacks. On the extreme right, the Guards Corps' attack north of Ypres failed. That attack was suspended until 19 April. But after it later became clear that the Germans had not crossed the Steenebeeck and that the stream was held in force, the attack was further postponed until 20 April.[122]

About 1945 hours Ludendorff was conferring with Kuhl and Lossberg, still believing that the attack north of Ypres was going well. Ludendorff wanted the Guards Corps to continue attacking in the north, while the XVIII Reserve and X Reserve Corps attacked Mount Kemmel. Lossberg, however, was already recommending that GEORGETTE should be terminated and a new offensive should be launched on some other sector of the front.[123]

The Allies, meanwhile, continued to move up more forces. French units in Flanders were formed into "Army Detachment of the North."[124] Including the Tenth Army, the French now had nine infantry and three cavalry divisions north of the Somme.[125]

19 April   GEORGETTE had clearly reached culmination, although in the center the Sixth Army had pushed seventeen miles, to the line Bailleul–Merville.

Rupprecht's Army Group sent OHL a message arguing that GEORGETTE had turned into a battle of attrition and requesting permission to halt the attack and pass to the defensive.[126] Lossberg now insisted that the Fourth Army was no longer capable of conducting the TANNENBURG deliberate attack in the north. OHL cancelled the attack.[127] At 0800 hours the Fourth Army halted the Guards Corps' BLÜCHER attack. OHL immediately withdrew the three general reserve divisions and sent them south to support later operations anticipated in the Mount Kemmel sector.[128]

That same day Wetzell issued his first operational assessment since before the start of MICHAEL on 21 March. Noting the solidification of the British defenses in Flanders, supported by French and possibly American divisions, he concluded that all operations against the British should be suspended: "there no longer exists the probability of a great success in that region." He recommended instead, a new offensive to the south, in the sector of the German Seventh Army.[129] Ludendorff too was beginning to look elsewhere. Noting the relative weakness of the French forces opposite the German First, Third, and Fifth Armies, Ludendorff told Kuhl he wanted to launch an offensive in the Reims sector with the First and Third Armies.[130]

The Allies, meanwhile, put two French divisions into the line between Meteren and Wytschaete, with the French 28th Division assuming responsibility for Mount Kemmel. Five bloodied British divisions were withdrawn from the line, and sent south to the quiet sector along the Chemin des Dames.[131]

20–23 April OHL ordered the halt of the Sixth Army offensive, but still insisted on the capture of Festubert and Givenchy.[132] From that point on, the Sixth Army made some half-hearted efforts, but never did take the two British bastions. OHL also ordered a pause in the Fourth Army's attacks, with a renewed push scheduled for 25 April to take Mount Kemmel.[133]

Ludendorff held a meeting at X Reserve Corps headquarters on 21 April to plan the resumption of the attack against Mount Kemmel on 25 April. The final plan called for the left wing of the XVIII Reserve Corps to launch its attack fifteen minutes before the X Reserve Corps jumped off.[134] Both corps would attack with a combined seven divisions in the first line, four in the second line, and one in general reserve. They would be supported by 290 guns, six bomber squadrons, seventeen fighter squadrons, and sixteen attack squadrons. The attack's deep objective was the Poperinghe–Vlamertinghe road, north of the high ground of Mount des Cats, Mount Rouge, Mount Noir, and Mount Kemmel—in other words, to the northwest, away from Hazebrouck. North of Ypres, the Guards Corps was to be prepared to resume their attack.[135] Rupprecht's Army Group also issued a warning order that if the attack on Mount Kemmel went well, the inner flank corps of the two armies should be ready to advance immediately.[136]

German intelligence at this point had confirmed the presence of the French 133rd, 28th, and 34th Divisions in Flanders. It also estimated that fifty-one of the fifty-nine British infantry divisions had been committed to action since

21 March, and nineteen had gone into the line for a second time.[137] French intelligence, meanwhile, estimated that the Germans still had some sixty divisions available for another attempt at splitting the French and the British.[138]

24 April   One day before the resumption of the attack against Mount Kemmel, the Second Army launched an attack in front of Amiens. The initial plan had been developed between 8 and 11 April. The objective of the attack was Blangy Tronville, about halfway between Amiens and Villers-Bretonneux, with three corps attacking the first day, followed by another corps on the second day. Because of the general weakness of the Second Army's divisions, the plan was scaled back on 13 April to a three-corps attack on Cachy, just to the west of Villers-Bretonneux. Ten divisions (including five attack divisions) were committed to the first line, and four divisions were in the second line. They were supported by 1,208 guns, 710 aircraft, and thirteen tanks. The purpose of the operation was to make it possible to move up more forces and artillery to facilitate a follow-on attack on Amiens.[139] In his memoirs, Ludendorff merely noted that the attack was conducted by the Second Army "to improve its position."[140]

The artillery preparation against Villers-Bretonneux started at 0445 hours. The infantry jumped off at 0715 hours, and by just before noon Villers-Bretonneux was almost completely in German hands. The attackers pushed to the woods just beyond the town, but then started to get bogged down. Late that night at 2200 hours the Allies launched a strong counterattack with one British and two Australian brigades, driving the Germans almost back to their original line of departure. The Germans tried to take Villers-Bretonneux again the next day, but the defenders beat them back. In the end, the operation cost the Germans some 8,000 casualties with almost nothing to show for it. OHL finally halted the Second Army attack on 26 April.[141]

25 April   The German artillery preparation against Mount Kemmel started at 0330 hours and included high concentrations of Yellow Cross and *Buntkreuz*. Most of the French batteries were silenced or neutralized by 0830 hours. At 0645 hours the XVIII Reserve Corps on the left flank jumped off in thick fog, with visibility not more than fifty yards. Fifteen minutes later, as planned, the X Reserve Corps on the right flank jumped off. Three and a half German divisions hit six regiments in the French line, and within an hour French troops were falling back toward the rear. The attackers reached the summit of Mount Kemmel by 0810 hours. A few hours later, Lossberg called the commander of the Guards Corps northeast of Ypres and gave him a warning order to prepare to attack.

At 1100 hours Lossberg issued the orders for XVIII Reserve and X Reserve Corps to initiate the exploitation phase. The intent had been to take the hill indirectly from the east, but the frontal holding attack had been an unexpected success. With the loss of Mount Kemmel, a four-mile-wide gap opened up from Vierstraat to the point west of Mount Kemmel where the French 154th Division stood. The Allies had only three battalions in the gap. About noon the German main force swept over the summit and pushed down the north slope of Mount Kemmel, but then halted behind a defensive artillery barrage along the base of the hill at the Kemmelbeek. There the Germans waited until the artillery could be moved up to support the push on the final objectives.

Late that afternoon a still optimistic Lossberg told the commander of the Guards Corps that the British would almost certainly be forced to withdraw from the entire Ypres salient. The Guards Corps chief of staff, however, noted that all the local patrols sent out by the corps had encountered stiff resistance. As evening set in, mounting indicators of an Allied counterattack prompted Lossberg to order the XVIII Reserve and X Reserve Corps to move up their second echelon divisions in preparation. The German advance finally halted at Vierstraat. Late that day the British 25th Division moved into the area with orders to retake Mount Kemmel. It didn't, but it did close the gap, and the Germans missed the opportunity to take Mount des Cats and the entire ridge line from the rear.

After consulting with the chiefs of staff of the two attacking corps that evening, Lossberg ordered the resumption of the attack for 0800 hours the next morning, with the same divisions in the first and second lines. The new objective was the Reninghelst–Vlamertinghe line. Vlamertinghe was almost directly to the west of Ypres.[142]

26 April   Just as the Germans renewed their attack on 26 April, the first reports of strong Allied counterattacks started to reach Fourth Army headquarters. By 0900 hours the Germans were under heavy pressure in their center, and only the outer wings of the two corps attempted to advance. By mid-afternoon Lossberg decided that further attacks should be postponed until the following day, with the Fourth Army committing three fresh divisions from the army reserve. A little later Lossberg decided to postpone the resumption of the attack yet another day. Then about 1945 hours the chief of staff of the XVIII Reserve Corps recommended postponing the attack until 29 April, to provide adequate time to move up ammunition and relieve the divisions in the line. Reluctantly, Lossberg agreed.[143]

The British, meanwhile, pulled back another three kilometers north of Ypres, freeing up more reserves for the battle to the south. Foch ordered Pétain to send two regiments of field artillery and twelve heavy artillery groups to the Army Detachment of the North. The following day Foch ordered three more French divisions shifted to Flanders.[144]

27–28 April   The orders for the resumption of the attack on 29 April established the objective line Ypres–Vlamertinghe–Reninghelst–Westoutre–Mount Rouge. The plan called for seven divisions to attack in the first line, with six divisions in the second line, and two in army reserve. Lossberg asked for two fresh divisions from Rupprecht's Army Group. He was promised three, and two more if the Fourth Army succeeded.[145]

OHL was concerned about the potential for a major French attack in the south. German intelligence also estimated that there were now five French infantry divisions and one French cavalry division in Flanders, and more units from the French Tenth Army could be expected to move up.[146]

29 April–1 May   The Germans launched their final GEORGETTE effort on 29 April. The artillery preparation started at 0400 hours with the infantry jumping off at 0640 hours. The Allied artillery, which hardly responded during the preparation, opened with heavy fire as soon as the infantry advanced. At noon Lossberg called Ludendorff to report the heavy Allied resistance and the organization of their artillery in great depth. Lossberg, however, intended to press the attack on the left after a concentrated artillery preparation. But the German attacks made no progress, and around 2135 hours Lossberg finally advised Ludendorff to halt the attack. Kuhl and Ludendorff agreed at 2300 hours.[147]

At the end of the operation the Fourth Army had seventeen divisions facing twenty-five Allied divisions, and the Sixth Army had twenty-six divisions facing ten Allied divisions. The French had fourteen infantry and three cavalry divisions in Flanders. OHL estimated that more than half of the available French reserves were between Amiens and the coast. After analyzing the situation, Lossberg concluded that the Fourth Army would need ten to twelve fresh divisions in order to capture Poperinghe, Mount Noir, and Mount Rouge.[148] Operation GEORGETTE came to an official end on 1 May.[149] The Germans periodically made half-hearted attempts throughout May to take Mount Rouge and Mount Noir, but with little success.[150]

Assessment

The results

The German official history called Operation GEORGETTE "a skillful and effective operational chess move" (*operativer Schachzug*).[151] But despite the seemingly impressive tactical results, it was another operational failure. GEORGETTE failed to accomplish either of what were supposed to be its primary objectives at the various stages of the operation. Its initial objective was the vital BEF rail center at Hazebrouck. The Germans got within six kilometers of Hazebrouck, but they never made it. Midway in the battle the objective shifted to the line of the Flanders Hills. The control of that ground would have forced the British out of the Ypres salient. And although the loss of Mount Kemmel did force the British to abandon a major sector of the salient, they managed to hold fast just in front of Ypres. To the south, GEORGETTE did put the Germans within artillery range of the Béthune coal basin, which did affect for a time the output of the munitions factories and the railways that depended on Béthune.[152] But even that produced no long-term operational or strategic effect. In the forty days of fighting since the start of MICHAEL, the Germans sustained fewer casualties than they inflicted, but those were losses they could not recoup. Rupprecht, however, claimed that many of those casualties were lightly wounded who could be returned to duty in short order.[153] See Table 7.7.

Table 7.7 Casualties from Operations MICHAEL and GEORGETTE[154]

	MICHAEL	*GEORGETTE*	*Total*
German	239,800	86,000	325,800
British	177,739	82,040	259,779
French	77,000	30,000	107,000

Source: *Der Weltkrieg*, Vol.14, p.300. Edmonds, *1918*, Vol.II, pp.491–493.

Preparation time and strength

Without the seven weeks of elaborate preparations that MICHAEL had, GEOR-GETTE could not have been so well prepared. But Ludendorff felt that time was working against the Germans, as American forces continued to pour into Europe. Although some of the GEORGETTE preparations had already been accomplished as part of the GEORGEPLAN deception plan, the Germans really had only twelve days to carry out the preparations. They managed to accomplish a great deal in that short period, while at the same time maintaining an impressive level of operational security.

The major effect of the compressed schedule was the number of forces the Germans could move into the attack sector. With twenty-six divisions committed across a forty-four-kilometer front, GEORGETTE was less than half as strong as MICHAEL. Table 7.8 shows the various planning strengths as the operation evolved from GEORG to KLEIN-GEORG to GEORGETTE. Even after the force was increased by nine divisions in the final 29 March revision of the plan, the attackers still had only a superiority of about 2.2:1 over the defenders.

Mobility of the GEORGETTE divisions

The compressed preparation schedule also forced the Germans to use far too many trench divisions in GEORGETTE. Fourteen of the twenty-six divisions committed on 9 and 10 April were trench divisions, including eight of the

Table 7.8 Divisions allocated under the various GEORG plans*

Operation	*Plan date*	*Sixth Army*	*Fourth Army*
GEORG	20 Nov	20–25	12–15
GEORG	3 Jan	30–40	12–15
KLEIN-GEORG	3 Feb	20	12–15
GEORGETTE	26 Mar	10	4**
GEORGETTE	29 Mar	17	6**

Notes
*Not including OHL reserve divisions.
**HASENJAGD only.

fourteen divisions in the first line, and four of the seven divisions in either army or OHL reserve. Each trench division was 500 to 600 horses short, with especially critical shortages in the field artillery units, and they had no draft horses for the ammunition wagons for the infantry units.

Another problem was the state of the attack divisions transferred from the Second Army. Most had been committed to MICHAEL, and then had to march to the Sixth Army zone over poor roads and bad terrain. They arrived worn out, most at no better than half their normal level of strength.[155] Thus, even if GEORGETTE had achieved a breakthrough of the British lines, the Germans most likely did not have the necessary force capable of exploiting to operational depth.

Failure to weight the main effort

As in Operation MICHAEL, the weighting of the main effort in GEORGETTE was far from clear. The attack of the LX Corps toward Hazebrouck was supposed to be the main effort and, with four attack divisions in its first and second lines, it was the strongest of the four attacking corps. But in addition to the drive northwest toward Hazebrouck, part of the corps' force was supposed to branch off south of the La Bassée Canal and drive due west to support the IV Corps on its left. The XIX Corps to the right had the deepest assigned attack depth, yet it had only two trench divisions in its first line and one in its second line. On the far left flank of the attack, the IV Corps had two attack and one trench division in its first line, and one trench division in its second line for what was supposed

Table 7.9 Initial corps strengths and vectors[156]

Army	Corps	Divisional weight*	Direction	Attack depth	Vector line
Fourth	XVIII Res.	2 Trench	NW	4 km	Ypres
Fourth	X Res.	1 Attack 2 Trench	WNW	11 km	Messines–Kemmel (plus Armentières from the north)
Sixth	II. Bav.	2 Attack 2 Trench	NW	24 km	Steenwerck–Bailleul–Mount Cats (plus Armentières from the south)
Sixth	XIX	3 Trench	NW	29 km	Estaires–Steenvorde
Sixth	LV	4 Attack	NW	24 km	Merville–Nieppe Forest–Hazebrouck (also, hook WSW to the La Bassée Canal south of the Nieppe Forest)
Sixth	IV	2 Attack 2 Trench	W	15 km	Lawe–La Bassée Canal–high ground north of Béthune

Source: *Der Weltkrieg*, Vol.14, Appendices 12 and 38g.

Note
*Does not include army and OHL reserve divisions in the third line.

to be a supporting mission. As Tables 7.2 and 7.3 above show, the artillery this time was heavily weighted in favor of the Sixth Army, but the air assets were not as heavily weighted. As Table 7.9 shows, the six corps attacks diverged slightly, although not to the extent of the three army attacks in Operation MICHAEL.

As during Operation MICHAEL, OHL again fed reinforcements into the battle in driblets. In this case, however, the greatly compressed preparation period combined with the required transit times undoubtedly constrained what OHL could do. Up to the start of the battle, OHL moved ten divisions into the Sixth and Fourth Army sectors. During the twenty days of the battle itself, OHL moved in seventeen more divisions (see Table 7.10).

The army and OHL level reserves at the start and the end of the battle also show that the Germans had a very limited exploitation capability, especially at operational depth (see Table 7.11).

Finally, there was the Second Army's 24 April attack at Villers-Bretonneux, one day before the Fourth Army's attack at Mount Kemmel. Although the attack on Mount Kemmel was supposed to be the main German effort on the Western Front, the Villers-Bretonneux attack was weighted more heavily. The Second Army attacked with fourteen divisions (including five attack divisions) in its first and second lines; the Fourth Army attacked with eleven divisions in its first and second lines. The Second Army was supported by 1,208 guns (including 465 heavy); the Fourth Army was supported by only 290 guns (including 128 heavy). The Fourth Army, however, was far more heavily weighted with attack and fighter squadrons.

Table 7.10 Division reinforcements from OHL[157]

	Fourth Army	Sixth Army
1–10 April		
Gain	+5	+11
Loss	−4	−2
Net	+1	+9
11–20 April		
Gain	+12	+8
Loss	0	−4
Net	+12	+4
21–29 April		
Gain	+4	+1
Loss	0	−3
Net	+4	−2
1–29 April		
Net	+17	+10

Source: *Der Weltkrieg*, Vol.14, Appendix 35.

Table 7.11 GEORGETTE reserve divisions[158]

	9 April		29 April	
	Army	*OHL*	*Army*	*OHL*
Fourth Army	2 Trench	2 Attack	5 Trench	3 Attack
Sixth Army	1 Attack	1 Trench	4 Trench	2 Trench
	1 Trench			

Source: *Der Weltkrieg*, Vol.14, Appendices 15 and 38g.

Table 7.12 Army Group Rupprecht air order of battle 24 April 1918[159]

Army	Observation	Attack	Fighter	Bomber	Total squadrons
Fourth	14	16	17	6	53
Sixth	15	3	8	3	27
Seventeenth	14	2	4	0	20
Second	15	4	10	6	31

Source: Army Group Prince Rupprecht, "Air Order of Battle" (no document number), (24 April 1918), Bayerisches Kriegsarchiv, File Hgr. Rupprecht, Bd. 168.

Operational objective

As in Operation MICHAEL, the very objective of the attack changed in the middle of the operation. In the initial plans Hazebrouck was clearly identified as the direction of the main effort. In the early planning for the GEORG Operation, the Channel ports were the deep, follow-on objectives. GEORGETTE had no hope of reaching the Channel, but taking Hazebrouck and the western end of the Flanders Hills would put the Germans in a position to take the BEF from the rear. In their planning documents, the Germans clearly recognized the import-ance of the rail center; but, as with Amiens, that importance seemed to focus solely on Hazebrouck as a transfer point of forces, rather than as a logistical jugular vein.

After the Germans were stopped short of the Nieppe Forest on 13 April, the main effort shifted first to Bailleul, and then to Mount Kemmel, at the eastern end of the line of the Flanders Hills. They did finally take Mount Kemmel, but that brought them very little positional advantage at the operational level. As early as 20 November, Rupprecht's planners had warned of the dangers of getting bogged down in a protracted fight for Mount Kemmel, recommending instead that the Flanders Hills be outflanked. Right up until the start of GEOR-GETTE, however, various German planners waffled back and forth on the problem of Kemmel and a direct attack on the eastern end of the line of hills.

Thus in GEORGETTE, the Germans repeated the same mistake they had made in MICHAEL. When it became clear that they were not going to be able to achieve their original objective, they continued the attack in the hope of taking something to show for their efforts.

Decision 12 April

On 12 April the Germans were within five miles of Hazebrouck and on the verge of capturing the vital rail center. But Ludendorff's noontime order for a maximum effort against Bailleul by the inner wings of the two armies shifted the main effort away from Hazebrouck. That night the Sixth Army's orders for the next day assigned a spread of objectives, running from Bailleul on its right, through the Nieppe Forest in its center, to the La Bassée Canal crossings on its far left. Even with four divisions committed to the attack on the Nieppe Forest, the Sixth Army's combat and combat support power was spread too thinly across its twenty-seven-kilometer front. By the end of 13 April, the British had managed to move enough forces in front of Hazebrouck to establish a solid defensive barrier.

Decision 14 April

With the assignment of Godewearsvedle as the deep objective of the Sixth Army, and Poperinghe as the deep objective of the Fourth, the original GEOR-GETTE scheme of maneuver was dead. The objective at that point was the entire length of the Flanders Hills line, but the focus quickly shifted to the inner wings of the two armies, which in turn shifted the objective to Mount Kemmel and the eastern end of the line.

Decision 19–20 April

On 19 April the staff of Rupprecht's Army Group recognized that GEOR-GETTE had reached culmination and had turned into a battle of attrition. Rupprecht wanted to transition to the defensive all along the line. OHL agreed to suspending the operations of the Sixth Army, but still insisted that it take Festubert and Givenchy. There was no longer any purpose for that effort, however. OHL also ordered the Fourth Army to resume its attack against Mount Kemmel on 25 April, while at the same time ordering the Second Army's Villers-Bretonneux attack for 24 April. None of these widely separated and relatively weak attacks had much of a chance of accomplishing anything. At this point it appears that OHL was desperate to capture something, anything, that it could claim as a battlefield victory. But in so doing, it continued to expend its almost non-replenishable combat power for next to nothing in return. If the Germans had thrown all their power into one attack or the other, they might have accomplished something.

Decision 25 April

Despite the relatively low levels of fire support, the Fourth Army's attack on Mount Kemmel was a tactical success initially. Lossberg ordered the exploitation just before noon, but the German forces that swept over the hill to its base on the far side halted and waited for their fire support to move up. With the loss of Mount Kemmel, a four-mile-wide gap opened in the Allied lines and remained open for about eight hours, but the Germans lacked either the power or the will to exploit it. As Kuhl noted in his post-war analysis for the German government: "The storming of Kemmel was a great feat, but on the whole the objective set had not been attained."[160]

Allied reactions

One thing the Germans had not counted on was the stiff resistance put up by the British 55th Division at Festubert and Givenchy. In one of the most impressive defensive battles of the war, the 55th Division stubbornly held on and never gave way. This solid anchor on the left flank of the German attack diverted resources and combat power away from the main effort.

Another factor working against the Germans was the Allied Supreme Commander, General Foch, who kept a cooler head and had a far better grasp of the overall operational and strategic situation than did his primary opponent, Ludendorff. Writing in the British official history, Edmonds noted:

> [Foch] kept his main reserves near the junction of the Allied Armies and sent up reinforcements in driblets, divisions singly or in pairs, replacing those engaged by moving others up from the rear. His action in refusing to do more was justified by results, and this limitation of assistance to the absolute minimum may well be claimed as proof of the highest military judgement in relation to the Allied cause as a whole: he kept his head and declined to send his none too plentiful reserves in response to every call from General Pétain as well as from Sir Douglas Haig.[161]

Alternatives

GEORGETTE was far too weak to accomplish its intended objective. The only way it could have been made stronger was through more time to prepare and to move and build up forces. The best way to gain more preparation time for GEORGETTE would have been to terminate MICHAEL earlier. As reluctant as Kuhl was to criticize Ludendorff directly in any of his writings, he did note:

> One may ask the question whether it would not have been better to have broken off the MICHAEL offensive sooner, about 31 March; also whether it would not have been preferable to have dispensed with the subsequent Amiens attack on 4 April and the attack of the Seventh Army at Coucy le

Château on 6 April, designed to reduce the salient between the inner wings of the Seventh and Eighteenth Armies. In that case, it would have been possible to make the offensive near Armentières considerably stronger, so that it would have approached in scope the GEORG offensive as originally planned. Let it be admitted that that was the proper thing to do.[162]

Given that MICHAEL was allowed to run far beyond its culmination point, the only other way to gain more time would have been to push the start date farther back into April. Ludendorff believed he did not have that time. But after GEORGETTE failed he still managed to launch Operations BLÜCHER in May, GNEISENAU in June, MARNESCHÜTZ-REIMS in July, and he was planning HAGEN for August. Thus, if Ludendorff had given himself a few more weeks to build the Sixth and Fourth Armies back up to the levels approaching the original GEORG plan, the Germans would have had a far better chance of taking Hazebrouck. A delay of a few more weeks would have improved the ground conditions as well.

Such an operational pause naturally would have carried certain risks. Since Flanders was the next most likely target, the Germans would have had to screen the preparations with a far more extensive deception plan, supported by local diversionary attacks. But if the attack in Flanders succeeded in taking Hazebrouck, Ludendorff could then have turned his attention back toward Amiens. That too would have been an obvious follow-on objective, but the disruption to the British logistics system that would have been caused by the loss of Hazebrouck just might have given the Germans enough of a window of opportunity to shift forces south rapidly and push the few remaining kilometers to Amiens. This, of course, would have been the "skillful series of blows" originally proposed by Wetzell, and supported by Lossberg, Kuhl, and Rupprecht.

Finally, there remains the problem of the line of the Flanders Hills. Foch thought the control of this high ground was absolutely essential to any military success in Flanders. Commenting on the shift in objective during GEORGETTE, Foch wrote: "by continuing the advance west without having first captured the line of the Flanders Hills, [the enemy] would be exposing his right flank to serious risk. He therefore decided to attack that line before pursuing his march on Hazebrouck and Dunkirk."[163] And there is no question that the control of that high ground would be absolutely essential in a force-on-force operation—"to defeat the enemy" as the original 20 November estimate stated. But it would not necessarily be essential to control that high ground if the operational objective was not the main force, but rather a key vulnerability like the Hazebrouck rail junctions, or even deeper, the Channel ports.

8   Operations BLÜCHER, GOERZ, and YORCK

27 May–5 June 1918

In May 1918 it was our immediate business to try to separate the two allies in Flanders. England was easier to beat when France was far away.[1]

Field Marshal Paul von Hindenburg

Our previous objective could now be extended. New operational possibilities opened to us. All other considerations had to give way to the single idea of exploiting the extraordinary success of the first day.[2]

German Crown Prince Wilhelm

Plans (13 April–26 May)

With the failure of MICHAEL and then GEORGETTE, the Germans were on the verge of running out of time and resources. But the basic strategic imperative of defeating the British had not changed. As Hindenburg noted in his memoirs:

The attack against the British northern wing remained the focal point of our operations. I believed that the war would be decided if this attack was successful. If we reached the Channel coast, we could lay our hands directly on Britain's vital arteries. In so doing, we would not only be in the most favorable position conceivable for interrupting her maritime communications, but our heaviest artillery would be able to bring a segment of the south coast of Britain under fire. This technical marvel of science, which was even now sending shells into the French capital from the region of Laon, could be directed against Britain as well.[3]

Ironically, Hindenburg only seems to have grasped the importance of attacking Britain's lines of communications in his post-war writings. The operations orders issued at the time say nothing about such an objective. His "technical marvel of science," the Paris Guns positioned well in the sector of the Seventh Army, were already capable of hitting Britain's south coast if positioned in Flanders.

On 13 April, more than two weeks before GEORGETTE died out,

Rupprecht's Army Group issued planning guidance to develop courses of action for follow-on operations. The first option, called NEU-MICHAEL, was to be an attack between the Somme and Arras in the direction of Doullens. The second option, called NEU-GEORG, was to be a renewed attack in Flanders. The two operations were later re-designated WILHELM and HAGEN, respectively.[4]

The main operational problem for the Germans at this point was that in responding to the German attacks, the French had weakened their other sectors to support the British. As a result, Ludendorff and most of the German planners were now in agreement that the Allies were too strong north of the Somme. A decisive victory in Flanders would not be possible until the bulk of the French reserves were withdrawn from the sector. That meant the Germans would have to attack the French with enough force to threaten a vital point. As Ludendorff put it, "I was in hopes that it would consume enough enemy forces so as to permit us to resume our attack in Flanders."[5]

On 17 April Wilhelm's Army Group received a warning order to start preparing for an attack in the sector of General Hans von Boehn's Seventh Army. Ludendorff, however, did not want to make a final decision as long as there was some possibility that the Mount Kemmel phase of GEORGETTE might still lead to decisive results against the British. In its basic concept, the original objective of the new attack in the south was to be the line of the Aisne River, which required the capture of the Chemin des Dames ridge between the Ailette and the Aisne. During the subsequent planning, however, the objective was extended to the next ridge line, between the Aisne and the Vesle, and then to the Vesle itself. Just prior to the start of the attack, the objective was extended yet again to the high ground south of the Vesle (Map 5). Simultaneously, the planned frontage of the attack first narrowed, and then widened. Initially it was supposed to run from Brimont (a little west of Reims) to Soissons. Wilhelm's Army Group actually wanted to widen the attack from Reims on the east, to Compiègne (twenty-three miles west of Soissons) on the west. But Ludendorff didn't think he could free up the necessary infantry and artillery without weakening critical sectors in Crown Prince Rupprecht's area of operations.[6]

On 19 April, with GEORGETTE still hanging in the balance, Wetzell issued his first operational assessment since 25 December 1917. Wetzell noted that Foch appeared to be pursuing two objectives: to hold fast in the British sector, and especially in front of the Béthune coal fields; and also to relieve the pressure on British forces to allow them to reconstitute. Foch was able to pursue both objectives only by forgoing launching a major offensive himself. Thus, if the Germans wanted to retain the initiative, Wetzell argued, they had to attack again. The key question was where?

Wetzell went on to argue that another fifty-division attack on the scale of MICHAEL was no longer possible, because of the increased front line that resulted from MICHAEL and GEORGETTE. But by pulling divisions from Army Groups Gallwitz and Albrecht, a twenty-five- to thirty-division attack force could be assembled. Wetzell, therefore, recommended a penetration attack on the "southern front of the Seventh Army east of the Oise–Aisne canal and the

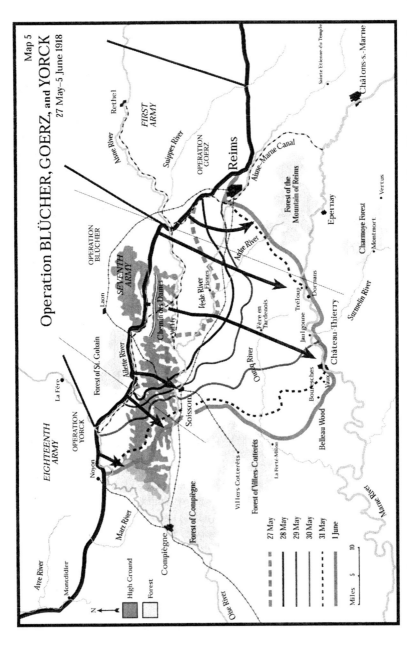

Map 5 Operations BLÜCHER, GOERZ, and YORCK (source: Map by Donald S. Frazier, Ph.D., Abilene, Texas, based on sketches and notes provided by David T. Zabecki).

refused right flank of the First Army." As a preliminary and supporting effort, he also recommended an attack toward the southwest through Montdidier by the Eighteenth Army. The objective of that attack would be to eliminate the flanking effect of the Arve bridgehead. The main purpose of the group of attacks would be to force the Allies to shift their reserves from Flanders.[7]

On 20 April, Crown Prince Wilhelm's Army Group issued a course of action analysis for what would become known as Operation BLÜCHER. The Seventh Army would conduct BLÜCHER I, attacking across the Chemin des Dames from Fort Malmaison to Berry au Bac, pushing to the Aisne. Simultaneously, General Fritz von Below's First Army on the left would conduct BLÜCHER II as far east as Brimont, and then prepare to exploit to the high ground between the Aisne and the Vesle in support of the Seventh Army. In the event that BLÜCHER failed, the Third Army should start making preparations to resurrect the ROLAND plan for an attack east of Reims.[8] Eventually, the Seventh Army's attack sector was extended to the left and absorbed BLÜCHER II. The First Army attack also shifted left to just west of Reims, and was re-designated GOERZ. Initially, that attack was planned as a single-corps effort. The First Army's XV Corps was told to plan on the minimum levels of artillery and to make maximum use of trench mortars and gas launchers. The VII Reserve Corps would support the attack by shelling the city of Reims.[9]

That same day (20 April) Ludendorff approved the basic concept proposed by Army Group German Crown Prince.[10] The terrain did not exactly favor the attackers. The Chemin des Dames was a twenty-four-mile long "hog's back" ridge, running east–west. It rose steeply from the Ailette River along the north, and then fell sharply to the Aisne River to the south. The top of the ridge was 300- to 400-meters wide and flat. The entire area between the Ailette and the Marne River consisted of a series of more or less parallel rivers with high ridge lines in between. South of the Aisne lay the Vesle, then the Ourcq, and finally the Marne. The French had taken the Chemin des Dames in 1917 and had held it lightly ever since. It was good defender's terrain, and the prevailing road network also ran east–west. Thus, the rivers, roads, and ridges almost all ran perpendicular to the axis of the German advance (see Map 5). As a Seventh Army operations order noted, "Of course, the very few roads running east–west prove difficult for this attack."[11] And even Hindenburg later wrote, "the ground was extremely unfavorable for attack."[12]

On 26 April the Seventh Army submitted its second version of the BLÜCHER plan to OHL. It recommended extending the first-day objectives beyond the Aisne to the high ground between the Vesle and the Aisne. The Seventh Army estimated its force requirements at seventeen divisions controlled by four corps headquarters. Twelve of those divisions would have to come from OHL. Two days later the Seventh Army started to consider adding another corps headquarters on the right flank of the attack.[13]

Wetzell issued another operational assessment on 28 April. He started out by stating the generally accepted notion: "In order to be able to strike another great blow against the British, the principal mass of the French reserves on the British front must first be withdrawn." This, he argued, could be accomplished by the Seventh Army's attack to the depth of the line Vauxaillon–Vailly–Aisne—the basic plan of the BLÜCHER attack. But Wetzell also recommended extending the right wing of the attack as far west as Malmaison. This extension would later be designated Operation YORCK. Wetzell went on to argue that if the Seventh Army attack succeeded, it would set up the conditions for "a really decisive blow" against the French reserves. This would entail a major thrust by the Eighteenth Army five or six days after the Seventh Army attack. The Eighteenth Army would attack in the direction of Compiègne to the line Domfort–Mery–Marsuil–Thiescourt. This attack would be supported by a further thrust of the Seventh Army in a westerly direction along both banks of the Aisne, through Soissons to create a giant pincer. Thus, contrary to his 19 April assessment, Wetzell was now advocating that the Eighteenth Army attack after the Seventh Army. This later attack came to be designated as Operation GNEISENAU and evolved into the fourth of Ludendorff's five major offensives. Wetzell concluded that after the extended BLÜCHER attack, followed by GNEISENAU, "a great blow could be struck against the British a few weeks later in the Seventeenth or Fourth Army sectors."[14]

At a meeting with the army group chiefs of staff on 29 and 30 April, Ludendorff made the final decision to proceed with the Chemin des Dames attack. The purpose of the operation was stated clearly as: "To disrupt the unity of the Allied front opposite Army Group Crown Prince Rupprecht, and create the possibility of renewing the offensive against the British." The attack was tentatively scheduled for 20 May, with the follow-up attack against the British being launched in mid-June.[15] Ludendorff directed Wilhelm's Army Group to expand the Seventh Army attack to the west as far as Pinon, and to start developing the plans for the possible follow-on attack by the Eighteenth Army from Montdidier to Lassigny that Wetzell had recommended.[16] To support the buildup, Rupprecht's Army Group was required to shift substantial artillery and some reserve divisions to Wilhelm's Army Group.

Wetzell issued another operational assessment on 2 May, now arguing: "Decisive results can only be achieved in the near future on the Montdidier–Reims front, and there we must strive for victory on a large scale." The best course of action, Wetzell noted, would be for the Seventh, First, and Eighteenth Armies to launch one massive coordinated attack. But since the Germans had insufficient artillery, the same results would have to be achieved through successive rather than simultaneous blows. Wetzell was convinced that, even if the Seventh Army attack was not completely successful, the French would overreact and mass their reserves in front of the center and left wing of the Eighteenth Army, thereby presenting a lucrative target. In such a situation, a strong Eighteenth Army attack would give further impetus to a renewed attack by the Seventh Army.[17]

Ludendorff essentially accepted Wetzell's recommendation. Ludendorff too would have preferred to attack simultaneously across the whole sector from Reims to Montdidier, but the forces were not available. Wilhelm's Army Group, nonetheless, did not want to conduct a split offensive. The Crown Prince's chief of staff, Schulenburg, pushed OHL several times for a single attack across the entire sector of the Seventh Army, and he recommended against the later attack of the Eighteenth Army. The wings of the Seventh Army attack had to be especially strong, he argued, with the right wing anchored along the Oise all the way to the Compiègne forest. Schulenburg also recommended a stronger effort by the First Army, extending that attack far enough to the east to take Reims and the high ground to the south. Schulenburg floated the idea of a push toward Paris, but Ludendorff rejected all his recommendations citing insufficient forces, especially in artillery.[18]

The same day that Wetzell issued the third of his recent string of operational assessments, Wilhelm's Army Group issued the operations order for BLÜCHER. With the army group staff still somewhat reluctant about the expanded operation, the order noted that the attack would not advance across the Aisne if the enemy succeeded in rapidly moving strong forces to the south of the river. On the other hand, if the right wing of BLÜCHER did prove successful, then the left wing of the Eighteenth Army (the XXXVIII Reserve Corps) would launch Operation YORCK as an enveloping attack between the Oise and the Aisne.[19]

The First Army's 5 May operations order for GOERZ expanded the scope of that attack. The First Army now had three missions. First, it was to push the enemy back over the Aisne–Marne Canal between Berry au Bac and Brimont; second, it was to take the high ground west of the canal as a line of departure for the next objective; and finally, it was to push the enemy across the Vesle between Prouilly and Reims in coordination with the Seventh Army. Confusingly, the exploitation phase in support of the Seventh Army was given the codename GNEISENAU. The First Army also strongly recommended the capture of Reims in the event that BLÜCHER reached the Vesle.[20]

The following day the Seventh Army sent the army group headquarters a new attack plan for BLÜCHER. The objective for the first day was extended to cross the Aisne and reach the Vesle. The Seventh Army emphasized that the attack had to cross the Aisne on the first day and continue pushing to the banks of the Vesle to deny the enemy the time to move reinforcements onto the high ground between the two rivers. "Higher headquarters must be prepared to halt the offensive if the line of the Vesle is not reached by the second day and if the enemy deploys a superior force on the high ground between the two rivers." On the afternoon of the first day of the attack the Seventh Army planned to shift about sixty field batteries and as many heavy batteries to the First Army sector; but a portion of the army's artillery also had to be shifted to the west to support the later YORCK attack.[21] OHL responded by designating 27 May as the start date for BLÜCHER.[22]

On 9 May the First Army sent a request to Wilhelm's Army Group for approval to launch the GOERZ attack one and a half hours after daybreak, rather than simultaneously with BLÜCHER.[23] That same day OHL issued orders stating that BLÜCHER and GOERZ must be launched simultaneously, but then later reversed itself and approved the First Army proposal. OHL also included the extremely cautious note: "Should the BLÜCHER attack encounter strong enemy resistance at or on the other side of the Aisne, the attack will be halted."[24]

On 16 May Ludendorff and the chiefs of staff met again at Avesnes. The objective of BLÜCHER remained the Vesle, but the west wing of the attack had to exploit its success until the enemy collapsed along the lower Ailette and the Oise toward the west. Three days after the main attack the inner wings of the Eighteenth and Seventh Armies were supposed to launch the YORCK attack across the Oise and the lower Ailette (see Map 5). The GNEISENAU attack of the Eighteenth Army, scheduled to follow a few days later between Montdidier and Lassigny, was reduced to a heavy stroke west of the Oise in the direction of Compiègne. It was not supposed to cross the general line Mery–Ressons–Matz, rather it was supposed to help the forces fighting in the Oise–Aisne angle move toward Compiègne.[25]

GOERZ would be a difficult attack at best. At the planned crossing point the Aisne–Marne Canal was thirty-five meters wide, and from there the attack would have to proceed uphill in wooded country. The initial plan called for the advance to be tied to the left wing of the Seventh Army. But on 17 May the First Army issued orders expanding GOERZ to include the capture of the high ground northeast of Cormicy.[26]

Ludendorff met with the chiefs of staff one last time at Marle on 21 May. As a result of that meeting, OHL extended the first day's objectives yet again, to across the Vesle and the high ground to the south.[27]

Preparations

On 1 May the Fourth and Sixth Armies in Flanders passed to the defensive and all army groups started issuing the orders to withdraw all "dispensable divisions," heavy and field artillery, engineers, trench mortars, communications units, and bridge units. The next day the Seventh Army issued generalized orders for preparations for a large-scale attack.[28]

Security, surprise, and deception

The buildup for BLÜCHER was another masterpiece of secrecy and operational security. As before, the Germans enforced stringent camouflage and concealment measures and light and noise discipline. One widely reported factor that supposedly helped mask the noise of the German night movements was the croaking of thousands of frogs in the Ailette and its surrounding marshy ground.[29] Special security officers down to the brigade level tested the security measures. Only the corps commanders and their chiefs of staff and operations officers knew of their activities.[30] During the buildup, the German trench divisions in the front lines of the attack sector were told that expended divisions were being rested to their rear.[31]

On 4 May OHL ordered the Fifth and Nineteenth Armies and Army Detachment C to initiate deception measures. Simultaneously, the thirty attack divisions left opposite the British in Flanders lit extra fires, marched their troops about behind their own lines, and conducted air attacks against the British rear areas. The Germans also planned a number of diversionary attacks, including Operation TARNOPOL, conducted by the inner wings of the Second and Eighteenth Armies from 27 May through 2 June; and Operation JOHANNISFEUER, conducted by Rupprecht's Fourth Army during the same dates.[32]

Right up until just before the attack, GHQ and GQG had no idea where the Germans would attack next. GHQ initially predicted that the Germans would resume the offensive between Albert and Arras. By 7 May the German deception measures seemed to indicate an attack astride the Scarpe. By 15 May, conspicuous radio silence farther north convinced the Allies the attack would be resumed in the area of the La Bassée Canal. By 18 and 19 May the thinking was back to the area between Albert and Arras. On 25 May, GQG thought the attack would come between the Oise and the sea. Finally, on 26 May Haig himself noted that an attack against the Chemin des Dames seemed likely.[33] The 26 May midday and evening reports of the German Crown Prince's Army Group noted that aerial reconnaissance showed that the three forward-most Allied trench lines opposite Seventh Army's VII Corps on the right and LXV Corps on the left were held normally.[34]

Ironically, the intelligence section of the American Expeditionary Force had accurately predicted the location of the next blow as early as 25 April. The assessment was based on German capabilities derived from order-of-battle and logistics realities. But the French and British rejected out of hand the assessment of the inexperienced Americans.[35]

Artillery and air preparations

As early as 20 April, the German Crown Prince's Army Group ordered Bruchmüller to report to the Seventh Army. The assigned artillery commander, Major General Meckel, was "placed at the disposal of other duties."[36] Bruchmüller and his staff had five weeks to work up the plans and position the guns without the Allies noticing. The first batteries with concealed firing positions started occupying those positions on 14 May, the last by 23 May. Only twenty of the more than 1,100 batteries were Category III, those that had to make their approach marches on the night of the attack. Two and a half days' ammunition basic load was positioned at the guns; one day's load on the battery wagons; one and a half days' load at the divisional ammunition point; and one day's load in the corps dumps. Each attacking corps was allocated 4,000 kilometers of communications wire, most of it for the artillery. About two-thirds of the trench mortars committed were used to substitute for the unavailable artillery in the First Army sector, where the attack zones were much narrower than in the Seventh Army. The Germans also prepared forward air fields, but did not occupy them until the day of the attack.[37]

Supply and transportation

The Germans made all movements larger than company-sized at night only. Because of the series of river lines running perpendicular to the attack, BLÜCHER had extensive bridging requirements. One corps, for example, had twenty-four specially constructed foot bridges in each of its divisional sectors for crossing the Ailette and the surrounding marshy ground, plus five additional heavy bridges for the entire corps sector. On 20 May the night approach marches of the attacking units began. By the night of 26 May all forces were in position.[38]

Allied actions

On 23 April, in accordance with Foch's *roulement* plan to rest tired divisions in order to build up the Allied general reserve, four British divisions under the headquarters of IX Corps were withdrawn from Flanders. They moved to the sector on the eastern end of the Chemin des Dames, and came under the command of the French Sixth Army.[39] Meanwhile, the rail lines from Paris south of Amiens and across the Somme were reinforced with two and three tracks, because the rail traffic was being interdicted by German long-range fire. Recognizing their key vulnerability apparently better than the Germans, the Allies used thirty-five rail construction companies and 20,000 workers to keep those lines open.[40]

On 17 May Haig ordered the British Fourth Army to wargame the possibility of a German attack east from Villers-Bretonneux in conjunction with an attack against the French. Three days later Foch issued his General Directive Number 3, which ordered the preparations for two offensive operations. The priority operation was between the Oise and the Somme, to relieve the pressure on Amiens and on the Paris–Amiens rail line, and the rail lines to the north. The other attack would be in the Lys sector, to take back the German-held part of the Béthune coalfields.[41]

Along the seemingly quite Chemin des Dames sector, the commander of the French Sixth Army, General Denis Duchêne, largely ignored Pétain's orders of 20 and 22 December 1917 mandating the adoption of defense-in-depth techniques. Foch supported Duchêne in his rigid forward defense approach.[42] On 19 April and again on 5 May Foch had issued directives that between the Oise and the sea, "no ground can be lost. . . . It is a matter of defense foot by foot."[43] Even after the start of BLÜCHER, the foot-by-foot defense was again emphasized in a 2 June memo from Foch to Pétain. The British IX Corps commander pleaded with Duchêne in vain for a flexible defense-in-depth, at least in his own sector. Along with the other French commanders, Duchêne scoffed at the American intelligence assessment and only began to take it seriously when two German prisoners captured the day before the attack provided detailed information.[44]

German order of battle

At start of MICHAEL, the Germans had 191 divisions on the Western Front. By mid-May, they had 207. The extra divisions were all late arrivals from the Eastern Front, but of low quality. For the combined BLÜCHER–GOERZ attack the Germans managed to mass twenty-nine attack divisions and ten trench divisions. Twenty-six of the attack divisions had participated in MICHAEL or MARS, but none had been in GEORGETTE. Eleven of the attack divisions were already in position at the start of the buildup, the remaining nineteen had to be provided by OHL (Table 8.1).

Again the Germans weighted the attack heavily with artillery. Facing the 1,422 French and British guns the Germans massed 1,158 batteries, including nine 240 mm railway guns. The fire-support assets also included 3,080 gas projector tubes and 1,233 trench mortars, of which 826 were medium or heavy. In the main attack zone for BLÜCHER the gun density averaged 110 tubes per kilometer. The resulting 3.7:1 tube superiority ratio was the highest the Germans achieved during any of the battles on the Western Front. All three first-line divisions of the LXV Corps also received a detachment of tanks. All were captured vehicles.[45] For air support for BLÜCHER and GOERZ the Germans massed some 500 aircraft, organized into at least fifty-four squadrons.

Allied order of battle

At the beginning of May the French had forty-seven divisions north of the Oise, with twenty-three in the line and twenty-four in reserve. They had fifty-five divisions between the Oise and the Swiss border, with forty-three in the line and

Table 8.1 German divisions on 27 May 1918[46]

	First line	Second line	Third line	Total divisions	Sector width
YORCK*	3	0	2 OHL 1 Army	6	25 km
BLÜCHER"	17	5	5 OHL 2 Army	29	43 km
GOERZ§	5	0	1 OHL 1 Army	7	32 km
	25	5	8 OHL 4 Army	42	100 km

Source: *Der Weltkrieg*, Vol.14, Appendix 38h. AOK 7, Ia 462, (22 May 1918), Combat Arms Reference Library, File: Operations Documents (BLÜCHER–GNEISENAU–GOERZ) from April 17 to May 20, 1918, Part I. AOK 1, Ia 2079 (5 May 1918), Combat Arms Reference Library, File: Operations Documents (BLÜCHER–GNEISENAU–GOERZ) from May 15 to 26, 1918, Part II.

Notes
*One corps each of Eighteenth and Seventh Armies.
"Five corps of Seventh Army.
§Two corps of First Army.

Table 8.2 German Corps on 27 May 1918[47]

| | *(West to east)* | | |
	Corps	Commander	Attack
Eighteenth Army		Hutier	
	XXXVIII Reserve	Hoffmann	YORCK II
Seventh Army		Boehn	
	VII	Francois	YORCK I
	LIV	Larisch	BLÜCHER
	VIII Reserve	Wichura	BLÜCHER
	XXV Reserve	Winckler	BLÜCHER
	IV Reserve	Conta	BLÜCHER
	LXV	Schmettow	BLÜCHER
First Army		Below	
	XV	Ilse	GOERZ
	VII Reserve	Wellmann	GOERZ

Source: *Der Weltkrieg*, Vol.14, Appendix 38h.

twelve in reserve.[48] Prior to BLÜCHER, German intelligence estimated that of the 58 divisions the BEF had in France, fifty-five had been committed since MICHAEL; twenty-nine had been committed twice; and six had been committed three times.[49] After the Mount Kemmel battle, the BEF had been forced to reduce ten of its divisions to cadre strength. But after April the British rushed 140,000 troops across the Channel, and by July all ten had been reconstituted.[50]

On 26 May Duchêne's French Sixth Army had only eleven divisions in the front line. Seven of those (four French and three British) were deployed along the Chemin des Dames ridge. Duchêne also had five divisions in reserve behind the ridge, including two French and one British. They were supported by fourteen squadrons of aircraft. German intelligence estimated that only six of the French divisions were fully combat-capable.

Execution (27 May–5 June)

27 May   At 0200 hours on 27 May 1918 the German artillery opened fire and caught the Allies almost completely by surprise.[51] This preparation was Bruchmüller's masterpiece. All firing was done using the Pulkowski Method. Because there was no adjustment of rounds, and therefore no need to observe, all the

Table 8.3 Guns supporting BLÜCHER and GOERZ[52]

Field	Heavy	Super-heavy	Total guns	Trench mortars
3,632	1,598	33	5,263	1,233

Source: *Der Weltkrieg*, Vol.14, Appendices 38h, 39c.

Table 8.4 Squadrons supporting BLÜCHER and GOERZ[53]

	Observation	Attack	Fighter	Bomber	Total
Seventh Army	24	8	10	?	42+
First Army	6	0	6	0	12
	30	8	16	?	54+

Source: AOK 7, Ia 242, (26 April 1918), AOK 1, Ia 2032, (20 April 1918), Combat Arms Reference Library, File: Operations Documents (BLÜCHER–GNEISENAU–GOERZ) from April 17 to May 20, 1918, Part I.

firing was done during darkness. After MICHAEL and GEORGETTE the German Army in the west had finally come to accept Bruchmüller's fire-support techniques. The fire lasted just two hours and forty minutes, the shortest of any of Bruchmüller's preparations.

Running concurrently with the preparation, the artillery of the units on the flanks of the main attack also laid down intensive fires to deceive the Allied commanders as to the precise sector of the main attack. The effect was accurate and devastating. The German gunners missed hardly a single forward position, communications trench, command post, or battery. The long-range units had been sited to enfilade the Aisne river valley on the backside of the Chemin des Dames. The super-heavy groups damaged the tracks behind the French railway guns. Unable to withdraw, fourteen were captured by the advancing Germans.[54]

The counter-battery fire was particularly effective. French Colonel J.P. Muller later wrote: "Our batteries, at first taken under fire by one enemy battery each firing gas shells, found themselves ten minutes later when they were ready to reply, subjected to the fire of three batteries each."[55]

The carnage was even worse than it should have been because of Duchêne's refusal to yield an inch of French soil. Duchêne packed all of his troops into the

Table 8.5 Allied order of battle in the BLÜCHER–GOERZ–YORCK sectors[56]

	Infantry divisions	Cavalry divisions	Reserve divisions	Heavy guns	Total guns	Sector width
*Third Army**	1	0	0	?	?	15 km
Sixth Army[#]	11	0	5 Inf	600	1,400	75 km
Fourth Army[§]	3	0	1 Inf 2 Cav	?	?	10 km
	15	0	6 Inf 2 Cav	600+	1,400+	100 km

Source: *Der Weltkrieg*, Vol.14, Appendices 38h, 39c. Foch, p.313.

Notes
*One corps of Third Army.
[#]Three corps (including British IX) of Sixth Army.
[§]One corps of Fourth Army.

Table 8.6 Seventh Army artillery preparation 27 May 1918[57]

1st Phase (10 minutes)
• Fire strike against enemy batteries, infantry positions, command posts, and communication centers.
• AKA guns fire Blue Cross.

2nd Phase (65 minutes)
• Reinforced counter-battery with all types of gas.
• Three-to-one ratio against the enemy batteries.
• Trench mortars did not fire.

3rd Phase (20 minutes)
• IKA fires against the crest of the Chemin des Dames and against the positions on the reverse slope using mixed Blue Cross and HE.
• AKA continues counter-battery with Blue Cross.
• FEKA and SCHWEFLA engage deep targets.
• Trench mortars fire on the front line.

4th Phase (20 minutes)
• Same as Phase 3, with slight variations in the targets.

5th Phase (45 minutes)
• IKA joins the trench mortars in attacking the front lines and in the last 10 minutes fires only HE.
• Trench mortars drop out in the last 10 minutes.
• AKA, FEKA, and SCHWEFLA continue as in Phases 3 and 4.

Creeping barrage (Feuerwalze)
• Double creeping barrage; first line with HE, second line with HE and Blue Cross.
• 4 to 5 minutes per 100 meters.
• High-angle fire up the north face of the Chemin des Dames

Source: AOK 7, Ia 235, (20 April 1918), Ia 242, (26 April 1918), Combat Arms Reference Library, File: Operations Documents (BLÜCHER–GNEISENAU–GOERZ) from April 17 to May 20, 1918, Part I.

most forward positions at an average density of one division for every eight kilometers.[58] The German artillery fired three million rounds on the first day of the battle. Fifty percent of that total was gas, their highest proportion of chemical rounds for any attack of the war.[59]

The German infantry assaulted at 0440 hours, twenty minutes before first light. Following behind a double creeping barrage, lead elements of the XXV Reserve Corps in the center reached the top of the ridge at 0535 hours. Five minutes later, the First Army on the left launched Operation GOERZ. At approximately 0900 hours lead elements of LXV Corps on the Seventh Army's far left reached the Aisne near Gemicourt, and the Germans closed in strength along the river's length within the next hour. The Germans moved so fast the French could not evacuate the large proportion of their own artillery on the north side of the river. The Germans captured some 650 guns as they swept along.[60] By 1100 hours the lead elements of IV Reserve Corps crossed both the Aisne and the Aisne–Marne canal at Oeuilly. Around 1800 hours elements of the First Army's XV Corps linked up with Seventh Army's LXV Corps on the left. Two hours later all three divisions of the IV Reserve Corps had reached the Vesle and elements crossed near Fismes. By 2200 hours elements of the XV Reserve Corps in the Seventh Army center crossed the Vesle at Courlandon.[61]

By the end of the first day the German infantry had advanced twenty-two kilometers, the largest single-day advance of any attack in World War I.[62] LIV Corps on the Seventh Army's right, however, had not reached its objective of the Aisne and the high ground south of Soissons. In a phone conversation at 2215 hours, Wetzell told the army group to continue the attack on the hills south of the Vesle on the 28th. Half an hour later OHL ordered the IV Reserve Corps to continue attacking throughout the night, to take the high ground south of the Vesle. The main effort was with the IV Reserve Corps, supported by the LXV and XXV Reserve Corps. The reserves were supposed to be concentrated behind those units. On the extreme left wing, the GOERZ attacking force had made it across the Aisne–Marne Canal, but then encountered stiff resistance from the British in front of Cormicy.[63]

On the first day the Allies committed five reserve divisions to the battle. Foch and Pétain conferred in the afternoon at Chantilly. Pétain immediately started moving forces toward the breakthrough area, including the Fifth Army with six infantry divisions and the I Cavalry Corps with three divisions. Three of the infantry divisions and two of the cavalry divisions were supposed to be committed to action by the 28th.[64]

Duchêne ordered that the German attack had to be stopped at the Allies' second position on the 28th. Unfortunately, Duchêne had helped the German advance by waiting too long to order the destruction of the bridges over the Aisne between Vailly and Pontavert.[65] He also threw his reserves into the battle piecemeal and too early, where they were consumed in the melee. Most of the French light and medium machine guns and field artillery had been as far forward as possible, and were swept over by the German infantry. As the War Diary of the Crown Prince's Army Group noted on the 27th, "It is remarkable that no hostile artillery appears in the district south of the Vesle and west of Fismes."[66]

28 May   On the 28th the Germans crossed the Vesle on a wide front. Most German units resumed operations at 0600 hours. By 1100 hours the Germans captured Fismes, and about 1215 hours they captured Breuil, on the boundary between the British IX Corps and the French XI Corps. But although the attack was making good progress in the center, the units on the flanks were starting to slow down.[67]

At 0800 hours Ludendorff met at Seventh Army headquarters with the army and army group chiefs of staff. Ludendorff was facing another decision point. So far the objective of the entire operation had been for the German center to cross the Vesle and take the high ground to the south. They were already past that, and Ludendorff now had two basic options. He could follow the original plan by slowing the pace of the BLÜCHER attack and then shift to the northern attack against the British; or he could continue to exploit the stunning and unexpected tactical success of BLÜCHER—but to what operational objective? No definite orders came out of that meeting, but at 1300 hours OHL apparently opted for the second course with the issuance of an order that effectively extended the BLÜCHER's objectives. In so doing, OHL also committed three additional divisions to the German Crown Prince's Army Group.[68]

> The group of armies must reach the general line: high ground southwest of Soissons–Fère en Tardenois–high ground south of Caulonges–south front (line of forts) of Reims. . . . Whether it will be of any advantage to advance in the direction of the line Compiègne–Dormans–Epernay, is still too early to say. Such action will receive consideration, however, in case the attack progresses favorably.[69]

Late that afternoon the army group issued an order to the Seventh and Eighteenth Armies to continue preparations for YORCK and GNEISENAU.[70] The army group also sent a message to the Eighteenth Army noting that Allied reserves were starting to move from Flanders and stressing that all rail lines leading south from Amiens had to be interdicted.[71]

Following OHL's orders to reach the high ground southwest of Soissons, LIV Corps' 5th Division crossed the Aisne east of Soissons about 2030 hours and sent four battalions into the town. A half hour later, however, a telephone message from the corps headquarters ordered the 5th Division to abandon Soissons and withdraw to the north of the Aisne. The basis for that order was supposed to be a large French force assembling south and southwest of the town.[72] Ludendorff later lamented the failure to exploit the situation at Soissons.[73] The German official historian, Theo von Bose, later suggested that the real reason for the withdrawal was the fear that German troops would go out of control if they got hold of the Allied supplies and rations in Soissons.[74] Late that evening OHL's orders stated: "Seventh Army must attack tomorrow at earliest possible hour."[75] At that point the Germans had captured more than 20,000 prisoners, and twenty-one German divisions were facing sixteen more or less stunned Allied divisions.[76]

Within twenty-four hours of the German breakthrough, Pétain had started moving sixteen divisions into position to block the road to Paris. He pulled four of those divisions from behind Amiens, without requesting approval from Foch. Most of those divisions were moved by truck and thrown into the battle by regiments, usually without their artillery.[77] During the 28th the French committed an additional four divisions (three infantry and one cavalry) to the battle, with eleven infantry and 3.5 cavalry divisions enroute.[78] Early morning German intelligence reports identified elements of the French 13th Division from Alsace in the vicinity of Fismes.[79] About 1000 hours, GQG ordered Army Group North to hold the line of the Vesle, but that order had been overcome by events before it was ever issued.[80] GQG also ordered the insertion of the Fifth Army headquarters into the line between the Fourth and Sixth Armies, on the east side of the salient, with an effective date of 2 June.[81]

Foch did not panic over the BLÜCHER attack. He saw almost right away that it could not lead to any decisive operational results, attacking as it did into the Allied depth. He correctly concluded it was a feint designed to draw off the Allied reserves. He therefore saw no need to shift large elements of the strategic reserves from the Flanders or Somme sectors.[82] The French at that point still had ten divisions from the Oise north to the Channel. The Germans, however, had forty-one divisions in reserve behind Rupprecht's Army Group.

29 May On the third day of BLÜCHER the German center extended its advance in the direction of Dormans. The two wings of the attack still trailed far behind. At that point the Germans again started to feel the heavy hand of "the tyranny of logistics." The only operable railway line into the salient ran east–west between Reims and Soissons. The former was still in French hands; the latter was effectively interdicted by French artillery. The only other major rail line into the sector was a single-track line that ran north–south from Soissons to German-held Laon. That line, however, was blocked at the tunnel at Vauxaillon—blown up by the Germans during their 1917 withdrawal to the *Siegfriedstellung*. German engineers estimated that it would take at least six weeks to reopen the tunnel.[83]

At 0045 hours OHL issued the warning order for the YORCK attack for the next day.[84] Several hours later, however, OHL postponed the start of YORCK until 31 May.[85] Later that morning OHL ordered the continuation of the offensive in the direction of the line Compiègne–Dormans–Epernay. The main effort continued in a southwesterly direction, but the left wing was ordered to shift to the east toward Reims, to capture the heights south of the city. That attack failed.[86] Ludendorff also ordered two attack divisions shifted from Rupprecht's Army Group, further disrupting the plans for the follow-on main attack against the British.[87]

About 2000 hours LIV Corps finally retook Soissons and the high ground to the west and southwest.[88] Several hours later Army Group German Crown Prince issued orders for the next day, designating the main effort for the Seventh Army between Soissons and Fère-en-Tardenois in the general direction of Château-Thierry. The lead elements of the advance were supposed to establish bridgeheads across the Marne, but not cross in force.[89]

At the end of the third day the Germans had twenty-two divisions in the battle, twenty in reserve, and one enroute. The apex of the German salient was near Fère-en-Tardenois, some twenty-five miles south of the German line of departure on the Ailette. But the frontage of the German line also had increased from thirty-six miles to almost sixty.[90] Another familiar problem began to surface. After German troops liberated the cellars of the villages in the Champagne region, Soissons that night was full of drunken *Landser*, confirming Bose's later assessment.[91]

Midday on 29 May Pétain asked Foch for control of the Tenth Army. Pétain also ordered a counterattack for 31 May, with the objective of pushing the Germans back across the Vesle, and then back over the Aisne.[92]

30 May   Mid-morning on 30 May OHL again enlarged the objective of BLÜCHER–GOERZ, hoping to capture Reims through a double envelopment.[93]

> The First Army will strengthen, at the expense of its center, its right wing south of the Vesle still further, in order to enable it to push forward vigorously within its zone of action in a southern and southeastern direction. The objective is to facilitate the envelopment of Reims, and not to impede the progress of the left wing of the Seventh Army. The possibility of cutting in on Reims from the east still farther should also be taken into consideration.[94]

The First Army now had six divisions committed to the attack. Although Wilhelm's Army Group dutifully passed the order along, an entry in its war diary expressed a note of serious skepticism: "The opinion that Reims will fall without serious fighting does not seem justified."[95] The skepticism, however, was justified. The XV Corps failed to take Reims, and the failure to gain control of the rail center resulted in serious ammunition shortages for the units committed to BLÜCHER.[96]

On the 30th Ludendorff also issued a reminder that the main purpose of BLÜCHER was to "threaten Paris," and in so doing draw large numbers of Allied reserves in from Flanders.[97] At 1510 hours the IV Reserve Corps' 231st Infantry Division reached the Marne near Tréloup. By the end of the day, German forces had closed along a twenty-kilometer stretch of the river, from Château-Thierry to Tréloup.[98] Late that night the German Crown Prince's Army Group ordered the First and Seventh Armies to continue attacking toward the Marne. To control the expanding battle, it inserted the headquarters of the VI Reserve Corps on the right of the First Army.[99] By the end of the fourth day of BLÜCHER the Germans had captured some 42,000 prisoners and 400 guns.[100]

On 29 and 30 May the French committed one cavalry and nine infantry divisions to the Sixth and Fifth Armies.[101] On the night of 30 May the U.S. 2nd and 3rd Divisions started moving toward Château-Thierry to reinforce the French. In a meeting with Foch that day, Pershing recommended an early counterattack against the flank of the new salient.[102] The French XXX Corps on the extreme western side of the attack zone, however, was starting to fall back, widening the base of the salient. Pétain, meanwhile, continued to pressure Foch for more reinforcements, asking for operational control of the divisions of the Army Detachment of the North, and some of the American divisions training in the British sector.[103]

31 May   On 31 May the Eighteenth Army's XXXVIII Reserve Corps and the Seventh Army's VII Corps launched YORCK, pushing south across the Oise–Aisne Canal, and extending the German attack between Pommiers and Noyon.[104] In the center, the Germans reached and crossed the Marne at Dormans and established a small bridgehead of 3.5 battalions at Jaulgonne. But they made precious little progress on the flanks. On the left they failed to take Reims, and on the right they failed to take the forest of Villers-Cotterêts.[105]

That afternoon OHL, Wilhelm's Army Group, and Seventh Army started to send out conflicting signals. At one point Ludendorff wanted to remove one OHL reserve division and one army-level reserve division from behind the IV Reserve and the LXV Corps, positioning those divisions behind the First Army's XV Corps. On OHL's orders, meanwhile, the Seventh Army shifted its main effort west, toward the Villers-Cotterêts–La Ferté-Millon line, turning the XXV Reserve Corps in that direction.[106] That evening, OHL ordered two more attack divisions from Rupprecht's Army Group and a division each from Army Groups Gallwitz and Duke Albrecht to be shifted to Wilhelm's Army Group. The BLÜCHER–GOERZ–YORCK attack continued to grow, but at the expense of what was supposed to be the subsequent main attack against the British. A Seventh Army order issued to LXV Corps stated it was of the highest importance "for the advance toward Paris" that the rail line through Reims be opened as soon as possible.[107] Late that night OHL ordered the control of the LXV Corps transferred from the Seventh Army to the First Army on the following day, to reinforce the attack on Reims.[108] Three corps were now attacking Reims from two directions. This is supposed to be the point at which the Germans shifted the main objective of BLÜCHER to Paris, but the disposition of forces and reserves on 31 May did not support such a decision. (See Table 8.8.)

At 1030 hours General Franchet d'Espérey authorized General Alfred Micheler, commander of the Fifth Army, to evacuate Reims to shorten the French front and reconstitute a reserve. Fortunately for the Allies, Micheler did not exercise that option.[109] At 1400 hours, the French Sixth Army counterattacked with four divisions north toward Soissons, and with three divisions northeast toward Fismes.[110] The French counterattacks against the German flanks that day miscarried, but their continual reinforcement of the units on the flanks of the salient prevented the Germans from gaining much more ground near Reims or Soissons.[111]

At Pétain's request, Foch ordered the French Tenth Army to shift south to the Marne sector from the rear of the British sector near Amiens.[112] Both Foch and Haig continued to believe that the Germans were still waiting for the right opportunity to launch the main attack against the BEF. British intelligence was reporting that only two divisions had been withdrawn from Rupprecht's Army Group, and he still had more than thirty divisions in reserve. Pétain, on the other hand, believed the German main thrust was against Paris.[113]

The British at that point were still making plans for the worst. Two days earlier the Chief of the Imperial General Staff, General Sir Henry Wilson, had issued orders to start the detailed planning for the evacuation of the BEF from the Continent.[114] That evening in Paris, Haig and Lloyd George discussed the potential evacuation of Dunkirk with Sir Eric Geddes, the First Lord of the Admiralty, and Admiral Sir Rosslyn Wemyss, the First Sea Lord. By the end of 31 May, thirty-two French and five British divisions had been committed to the battle. Seventeen of those were completely expended, and only fourteen more fresh divisions were available for commitment over the next ten days.[115]

1 June   On 1 June the Germans were only thirty-nine miles from Paris. The First Army attacked again on both sides of Reims with nine divisions. The Seventh Army thought its attack was still going well. That afternoon it asked the army group for three to four new divisions in order to exploit the situation. OHL provided a corps headquarters and another division from Army Group Rupprecht, as well as two divisions from Army Group Gallwitz. The last two were so weak that they could only be used in defensive positions along the Marne.[116] About 1500 hours Ludendorff sent a message to Rupprecht's Army Group:

> The operations of Army Group German Crown Prince are taking a favorable course. I therefore ask for further deception operations to continue in order to engage the enemy forces at the army group front there. Spoiling operations at places sensitive to the enemy also might be useful, but our infantry forces should not be wasted.[117]

OHL also informed Rupprecht's Army Group that HAGEN could not start before the middle of July.[118] Thus, the basic objective of drawing off the Allied reserves from the right wing of the German Army became subordinate to the objective of advancing the attack of the Seventh Army, turning it into an attempt at a decisive operation.

   Later that afternoon an OHL supplemental order noted with alarm: "It appears that the attack of the First Army is coming to a standstill."[119] The success of the First Army attack was critical because, without the opening of the rail connections through Reims, the logistics lifeline of the middle and the left wings of the Seventh Army could not be sustained in the long run. The bad news from the First Army prompted Ludendorff to telephone Army Group German Crown Prince at 1733 hours. In order to get the First Army attack moving again, he said, the Seventh Army would have to cross the Marne in the areas of Jaulgonne and Dormans and attack east toward Epernay. OHL would provide the necessary forces, including a corps headquarters, four divisions, and artillery. Reims had to be taken.[120]

   Wilhelm's Army Group did not like the plan. It argued instead that the First Army should regroup its right wing by pushing up two to three divisions that so far had been held back, and then should continue to attack toward Damery. The First Army should avoid a direct attack on Fort de la Pompelle east of Reims, in order to conserve forces. The main effort of the army group should be on the west wing of the Seventh Army, where the attack should advance as far as possible in order to draw in strong French forces, which in turn would facilitate the later GNEISENAU attack. Since the Seventh Army needed strong forces on its west wing, and since an attack south of the Marne toward Epernay would encounter heavy resistance and would also require strong forces, Wilhelm's Army Group recommended strongly against any move south of the Marne—even if the First Army failed. In the face of strong opposition, OHL dropped its plan.[121]

   That evening Ludendorff told Kuhl in a telephone conversation that the attack of the Seventh Army appeared to be grinding to a halt.[122] OHL's orders for 2 June stated: "The operational direction remains southwest."[123] The objective was to break the Allied defensive resistance between Soissons and Villers-Cotterêts, with the XXV Reserve Corps taking the latter town. The IV Reserve Corps was ordered to push west along the Marne to take Château Thierry.

The Allies, meanwhile, continued to rush forces into the area. The French inserted the II Cavalry Corps with two infantry and three cavalry divisions just south of Villers-Cotterêts, between the Sixth Army's XI and VII Corps. The U.S. 2nd Division took up defensive positions astride the Paris–Château-Thierry road. The Allies now had thirty-seven divisions, including five British and one American, committed to the battle.[124]

2 June At this point the Germans had eight fully fresh divisions behind the Seventh Army, and four more enroute, but BLÜCHER–GOERZ–YORCK had reached culmination. At a meeting in Rethel Ludendorff agreed to a pause in the First Army's operations to regroup. When operations did resume, however, the First Army had to take Reims first, and then take Fort de la Pompelle. A preliminary attack was scheduled for 6 June, with the main attack to follow on 8 June. The final objective line was Chatillon–Coulommes.[125]

That evening, the Seventh Army's orders for 3 June designated VII Corps on the far right of Operation YORCK as the main effort. The XXV Reserve Corps was ordered to take Villers-Cotterêts. The push southwest of Soissons was supposed to take the ground that would later facilitate the link-up with the Eighteenth Army's GNEISENAU attack, scheduled for 7 June. Just west of Reims, the First Army inserted the headquarters of the VI Reserve Corps between the LXV and XV Corps.[126]

3 June Since 27 May, the Germans had committed thirty-four divisions. Five divisions had been withdrawn from Rupprecht's Army Group.[127] But on the Seventh Army's far right, LIV Corps and Operation YORCK's VII Corps continued to make little progress, remaining north of the Aisne. Army Group German Crown Prince recommended halting the offensive until the Eighteenth Army could launch GNEISENAU. Ludendorff, however, issued instructions to continue operations by using well-prepared, limited objective attacks to minimize casualties.[128] For the following day the Seventh Army ordered the LIV and VIII Reserve Corps to continue attacking, while the VII, XXV Reserve, and IV Reserve Corps consolidated their positions.[129]

On the Allied side, the U.S. 3rd Division started taking up defensive positions near Château-Thierry. The French, meanwhile, eliminated the German bridgehead across the Marne at Jaulgonne.[130]

4–5 June The Germans made no significant advances on 4 June, either north of the Aisne or southwest of Soissons. The advance on both flanks, around Soissons and Reims, had ground to a standstill. With the approval of OHL, the Seventh Army decided to halt and regroup, with the intention of resuming operations on 8 or 9 June. The three right-wing corps, however (VII, LIV, and VIII Reserve) would continue to make local attacks. The follow-on attacks for the 8th or 9th were given the codenames BAUMFALLEN and HAMMER-SCHLAG.[131] Operations BLÜCHER, GOERZ, and YORCK were over. On 5 June the Seventh Army finally ordered all its corps to go on the defensive.[132]

On 4 June, Foch requested Haig to shift three divisions of the BEF's general reserve astride the Somme to the west of Amiens. Haig in turn requested the return of British IX Corps from west of Reims. Foch also convinced Haig and Pershing to release five U.S. divisions training behind the British front. Haig complied with all Foch's requests, but under protest.[133] Fayolle, meanwhile, had finally organized a defense-in-depth. The French Third Army now had seven divisions in the first line, five in the second line, and seven infantry and three cavalry divisions in the rear. At that point the Allies had committed thirty-five French infantry, six French cavalry, five British, two Italian, and two American divisions to the battle, with seven still moving up.[134]

Assessment

The results

On 5 June, OHL issued its own wildly pollyannaish assessment of BLÜCHER:

> One must resist the notion that the offensive did not result in a major break-through success, but stalled in the end. On the contrary, it advanced much farther than its original objective. The Allies suffered one of their heaviest defeats. For us it is the foundation for future successes.[135]

It is almost impossible to imagine what "future successes" the author of that paragraph could have had in mind. Rupprecht noted in his diary on 7 June that Luden-dorff was refusing to face reality.[136] The Germans were now bogged down south of the Somme in an operational quagmire that led nowhere, and the attack in the north against the British had been thrown off schedule beyond the point of recovery.

Yet the results seemed most impressive on the surface. The French had been caught almost totally by surprise, and the Germans had advanced an unbeliev-able sixty kilometers in just four days. In the process, they captured some 50,000 prisoners and 600 guns. But they also paid a heavy price in irreplaceable casual-ties (Table 8.7). Furthermore, OHL had pulled two corps headquarters, five

Table 8.7 Casualties from Operations BLÜCHER, GOERZ, and YORCK[137]

French	98,160
British	28,703
American	474
Allied total	127,337
German	105,370

Source: *Der Weltkrieg*, Vol.14, Appendix 42. Bose, *Wachsende Schwierigkeiten*, p.192. Edmonds, *1918*, Vol.III, p.160.

attack divisions, and huge numbers of laborers and support troops away from Rupprecht's Army Group—all to the determent of the coming main attack against the British.[138]

Battle management

As in MICHAEL and GEORGETTE, OHL once again lost control of the battle. What was supposed to be a diversion turned into an attempt at a decisive battle, with the original objectives being greatly exceeded. As with the two earlier offensives, the planning phase for BLÜCHER was characterized by what today would be called "mission creep," as the initial objective went from the Aisne, to the Vesle, to the high ground south of the Vesle. During the execution phase, the battle was characterized by the same old pattern of what might be called "mission leap," as the offensive expanded rather than concentrated, and in so doing dissipated its combat power. By 30 May, and perhaps even earlier, the offensive had again evolved into three diverging objectives. On the right it was trying to drive southwest, to "threaten Paris." In the center it was trying to drive south to the Marne. And on the left, it was trying to wheel to the southeast to take Reims.[139] But only Reims was a vital objective at that point, because of its critical rail center that controlled the only major rail line through the salient.

Forces and reserves

It is difficult to see any clear weighting of the main effort in either the commitment of first-line units, or the positioning of reserves throughout the battle. As Table 8.8 shows, the forces were more or less evenly distributed across the front on the first day of the battle. On 28 May, the IV Reserve Corps, just left of the German center, was designated as the main effort. Despite the stated intention to concentrate reserves behind the IV Reserve Corps and its supporting units on either side, it did not happen. As the battle progressed, the designated main effort increasingly shifted to the German right (west). If anything, the bulk of the OHL and army-level reserve divisions remained in the center, or even shifted to the left (east).

Logistics

As noted, the road, rail, and river network between the Chemin des Dames and the Marne ran predominantly east–west, perpendicular to the axis of attack. The only major east–west rail line into the area was closed at Reims, because the French held the city. The only north–south line, between Soissons and Laon, was blocked at the Vauxaillon tunnel. But Reims was not one of the attack's original objectives, because the Germans had not planned to advance any farther than the high ground south of the Vesle. Nor was Soissons an objective of the original plan, and the Germans apparently saw no need to get an early start on clearing the Vauxaillon tunnel. But once the limited objective attack expanded

Table 8.8 Forces and reserves 27 May to 4 June 1918[140]

	(Facing south)								
	XV	VIR	LXV	IVR	XXVR	VIIIR	LIV	VII	Total
27 May									
Front Line	3	—	3	3	3	4	2	2	20
Corps Res.	0	—	1	1	1	1	1	0	5
Army Res.	1	—	0	1	0	0	1	1	4
OHL Res.	1	—	1	1	1	1	1	2	8
28 May				**					
Front Line	3	—	3	4	3	3	3	2	21
Corps Res.	0	—	1	1	1	1	0	0	4
Army Res.	0	—	1	0	0	1	1	1	4
OHL Res.	0	—	1	1	1	2	1	0	6
29 May						**			
Front Line	4	—	3	3	3	4	3	2	22
Corps Res.	0	—	1	2	1	0	0	0	4
Army Res.	1	—	1	0	1	1	1	1	6
OHL Res.	1	—	1	1	1	3	2	1	10
31 May						**			
Front Line	5	—	3	5	3	4	4	3	27
Corps Res.	0	—	1	1	1	1	0	0	4
Army Res.	2	—	0	0	1	0	0	0	3
OHL Res.	0	—	0	2	3	3	0	0	8
2 June							**		
Front Line	2	3	5	4	3	5	3	5	30
Corps Res.	0	0	0	3	2	0	0	0	5
Army Res.	1	0	1	0	0	1	0	0	3
OHL Res.	2	0	1	0	3	2	0	0	8
4 June							**		
Front Line	2	4	4	5	4	4	3	5	31
Corps Res.	0	0	0	1	1	1	1	0	4
Army Res.	0	0	2	1	1	2	1	0	7
OHL Res.	3	1	0	1	2	1	0	1	9

Source: Army Group German Crown Prince, War Diary (27, 28, 29, 31 May, 2, 4 June 1918), Combat Arms Reference Library, File: Extracts from the War Diary of the Army Group German Crown Prince, May 27 to June 15, 1918.

Note

**Designated main effort for the day.

into a decisive attack, the logistics shortsightedness of the Germans came back to haunt them.

The Germans did make good use of the extensively stocked French depots they captured in the attack zone, using their limited road transport assets to move rations and ammunition forward.[141] And, once they captured Fismes and Soissons, they had use of the rail line between those two cities. But that was not enough. On 29 and 30 May the divisions of the LXV and IV Reserve Corps suffered serious ammunition shortages.[142] By the end of BLÜCHER, the Germans had another huge salient to hold. And largely because of inadequate lines of communications, that salient could not be held for any length of time. This was one of the major reasons why the Germans concluded they had to launch Operation MARNESCHUTZ–REIMS in July, to open the Reims–Soissons rail line into the BLÜCHER salient. MARNESCHUTZ–REIMS, of course, just pushed back the attack against the British even farther.

Decision 28 May

The order issued by OHL at 1300 hours, to advance to Fère en Tardenois on the Ourcq River and to the high ground southwest of Soissons, turned BLÜCHER from a diversion into an attempt at a decisive battle. But what was the decisive point? There was none, or at least there was not one the Germans could reach with their available forces and the logistics and mobility constraints in the area of operations. Thus, from that point on the attack could only run out to its culminating point. Ludendorff found himself in a difficult position on 28 May. Writing in his defense after the war, albeit in a somewhat muted tone, Kuhl noted:

> At the time, however, not one single soldier at the front would have understood the reasoning of OHL if it had failed to take advantage of the unexpectedly favorable situation, or had not endeavored to exploit the victory that had been gained by a complete surprise of the enemy, with a view to achieving a success as large as possible.[143]

But what was the definition of success? More ground captured? That just meant more ground to hold. More Allied troops killed, wounded, or captured? In the cold-blooded calculus of mid-1918 that was a price the Allies could afford to pay. The issue here is more complicated than saying Ludendorff simply committed the cardinal sin of command by grabbing for the easy wrong and the expense of the difficult right. The answer lies more in the deeply flawed German notion of the operational level of war, and in particular in Ludendorff's own fixation on the tactical level. At the tactical level, exploiting success is almost always the best course of action. This is not necessarily so at the operational level, as Operations MICHAEL, GEORGETTE, and BLÜCHER so clearly demonstrate.

Decision 30 May

Crown Prince Wilhelm's Army Group had wanted to include Reims in the scheme of attack from the very start. Ludendorff refused because he didn't want to shift more forces away from Rupprecht's Army Group. So long as BLÜCHER remained a limited attack to the line of the Vesle, the Germans figured they could get by without the rail line between Reims and Soissons.

Once the attack expanded, access to that rail line became critical, and OHL ordered the First Army to take the town and the rail center.

The attack on Reims, however, was handled as an ad hoc mission, cobbled together on the fly. Although some four corps eventually tried to take the city through a double envelopment, the First Army had started its GOERZ Operation critically short of artillery and with relatively low-quality divisions. Even after BLÜCHER and YORCK came to a halt on 4 June, the Germans were still planning to resume the attack on Reims four or five days later.

Decision 31 May

Some historians in describing Operation BLÜCHER suggest that the Germans made a specific decision on 30 or 31 May to shift the objective of the attack to Paris.[144] The French *Deuxième* Bureau at the time estimated that such a decision had been made as early as 28 May.[145] There is, however, no mention of such a decision in the surviving orders of either OHL or Crown Prince Wilhelm's Army Group. One of the last entries for 31 May in the army group's war diary notes: "The Seventh Army shifts the main effort now toward the west, and for that purpose, turns Group Winckler [XXV Reserve Corps] toward the west."[146] And OHL's orders of 2 June stated: "The operational direction remains southwest." Thus it appears that the Germans were really just following the path of least resistance, or at best trying to exploit a tactical opportunity, and that opportunity lay in the gap opening up between the French Third and Sixth Armies. On the other hand, a Seventh Army order issued that day mentioned "the advance toward Paris."[147]

The wording of the Seventh Army order might have been based on specific instructions in orders from higher headquarters; or it could have been based on an optimistic assumption; or it could have been based on Ludendorff's 30 May reminder about the main objective of BLÜCHER. A "threat" to Paris and an all-out attack toward Paris are not necessarily the same thing. The array of German front-line forces on 31 May (Table 8.8) does not indicate any weighting for an all-out drive on Paris; but the clear weighting of the OHL reserves in the center could. Nonetheless, the shift of the main effort toward Paris has become a widely accepted feature of the fifth or sixth day of BLÜCHER. In the final volume of the German official history, published in 1944, the writers suggested strongly that such a decision had not been made, as indicated by OHL's failure to commit strong reserves to the drive.[148] But even in the case of an appearance of a shift toward Paris, they tried to focus the blame away from Ludendorff.

> It is debatable whether or not the thought occurred to turn the offensive—since it was more successful than expected—into a major operation toward Paris. Ludendorff himself would not have had such an idea. He probably just wanted to make the enemy fear for his capital and draw attention away from Flanders. It is possible that Wetzell, Army Group German Crown

Prince, and the Seventh Army had been thinking about a main operation toward Paris.[149]

Decision 1 June

The events of 1 June reinforce that the Germans never really intended to attempt an all-out attack toward Paris. Although the day started on an optimistic note, it soon became clear that the First Army attack on Reims was a failure, and without Reims and control of the rail line to Soissons, the Germans could not hope to sustain a drive into any greater depth. As the day wore on, OHL had clear indicators that the Seventh Army attack was coming to a halt too, and Ludendorff told Kuhl as much in a phone conversation. BLÜCHER–GOERZ–YORCK was reaching culmination, yet OHL that day still pulled another division and a corps headquarters from Rupprecht's Army Group. That action contradicts what Ludendorff had to say about that point in the battle in his post-war writings: "I emphasized the need for not forgetting the necessary formation for defense, and of recognizing the moment when the attack must be stopped and the defense resumed. This must be felt by the systematic hardening of the enemy's resistance."[150]

Allied reactions

Once again, Ludendorff was out-generalled by Foch. Although the German attack was a stunning tactical surprise, Foch almost immediately recognized that it had to be a diversion at the operational level. Despite Pétain's insistence that Foch immediately release to him all forces available, Foch skillfully withdrew divisions from his reserve and fed them to Pétain slowly and methodically. Foch's management of the battle later received justified—if somewhat grudging—praise from Edmonds in the British official history. Foch understood that time and the numbers were on his side. Although Foch had serious shortcomings as a tactician, he was arguably the best the Allies had at the operational level on the Western Front.

Alternatives

BLÜCHER attacked right into the Allies' depth. It was the wrong attack in the wrong place. As Crown Prince Wilhelm noted in his post-war writings, "There was no strategic objective south of the Marne."[151] Many post-war critics, including French General Charles Mangin, thought the Germans should have renewed the attack against the British, or at least at the junction between the French and the British at Arras. Even small additional advances there, he argued, might have cut off the British Second Army and the Belgians.[152] Haig certainly thought his situation was desperate at the end of April.

Writing after the war, Kuhl agreed that a new attack against the British would have been the best course of action if the Germans had the available fresh forces to commit, but they did not. And after April the Allies assumed the German attack would continue against the British, with the initial objective of taking Amiens and separating the British and the French. Thus, the Allies massed their reserves on their own left flank, extending from the Oise to the northernmost part of Flanders. Any further German attack in that sector would have hit the Allied main strength.[153]

Kuhl's argument makes sense in the case of a force-on-force attack designed to destroy the enemy's main force—and these are the terms in which the German military habitually thought during the first half of the 20th century. After April 1918 the Germans almost certainly did not have the strength available for such an attack. They did, however, have enough strength to continue indirect attacks against a key vulnerability, the BEF's lines of communications with Amiens and Hazebrouck as the two choke points. The British clearly recognized their own vulnerability, and as late as 31 May Haig was still giving serious considerations to plans to evacuate Dunkirk.

If the Germans had continued focused attacks against the two rail centers after April, they still might have had a chance for some sort of military victory, although that became an increasingly longer shot day by day. But as soon as the Germans turned their attention away from the north and toward the Chemin des Dames, the war was effectively lost for them militarily. The Chemin des Dames sector may have been a softer target, but it was one that led nowhere, while at the same time giving the British in the north much-needed recovery time. In a certain sense, the whole thing was an eerie foreshadowing of the German decision on 7 September 1940 to shift their main effort during the Battle of Britain away from the RAF's air fields to the British cities. In the end, BLÜCHER turned into a quagmire for the Germans, one that led in a direct line to Operations GNEISENAU and MARNESCHUTZ–REIMS, and then to the Allied counterattack of 18 July and the British attack at Amiens on 8 August.

9 Operations GNEISENAU and HAMMERSCHLAG
9–15 June 1918

> The actions of the Eighteenth Army had not altered the strategic situation created by the attack of the Seventh Army, nor had it produced any tactical results.[1]
>
> General of Infantry Erich Ludendorff

Plans (31 March–14 June)

With the failure of Operation BLÜCHER, the Germans were caught in an operational bind of their own making. Ludendorff and all the planners at OHL believed the Allies were still too strong in the north for the final decisive attack against the BEF to have any real chance at success. On the other hand, the tactical advances made by BLÜCHER had created a huge salient that was difficult to defend, and even more difficult to supply. The large wooded areas on the western flank of the BLÜCHER salient, especially the forests of Villers-Cotterêts and Compiègne, provided ideal cover for an Allied counterattack force. Meanwhile, without gaining control of Reims or Compiègne, the Germans could make little use of the vital rail line that ran between those points and through Soissons. (See Map 6.)

The Germans at that point had no other real options but to attack in an attempt to improve their dangerously overextended position. Although Crown Prince Wilhelm later wrote about "our jumping off point for an attack on Paris,"[2] the German focus was certainly more limited in the early days of June. As Ludendorff himself noted:

> We wanted to gain more ground to the west, on account of the rail line that leads from the Aisne valley east of Soissons into that of the Vesle, and be in a position to give tactical support to the Eighteenth Army from the line Noyon–Montdidier.[3]

An attack east of Soissons would also give the Germans another advantage. The two huge salients created by MICHAEL and BLÜCHER roughly resembled a loose "M" on the map. By straightening the line between the points of the two salients, the Germans could reduce the length of the line they had to hold and thereby free up some forces.[4]

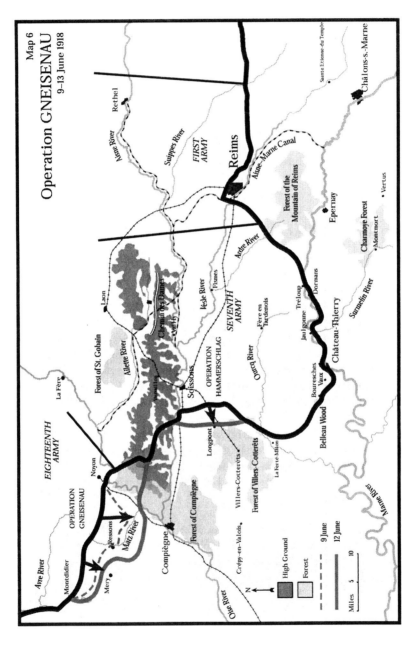

Map 6 Operation GNEISENAU (source: Map by Donald S. Frazier, Ph.D., Abilene, Texas, based on sketches and notes provided by David T. Zabecki).

As early as 31 March, Ludendorff had ordered the Eighteenth Army to make "a purely theoretical consideration" for an attack between Montdidier and Noyon that would be an exploitation of the Seventh Army's ERZENGEL attack. The initial objective of the new attack would be the line Domfort–Coivrel–Gournay.[5] After the failure of GEORGETTE, the Eighteenth Army's attack, now designated GNEISENAU, became an exploitation attack to follow BLÜCHER and YORCK, as Wetzell had proposed in his 28 April assessment. OHL planned to launch the Eighteenth Army's attack on 30 May between Montdidier and Lassigny, about twelve kilometers west of Noyon. The objective was to reach at least the line Montdidier–Compiègne. The attack would start several days after BLÜCHER, because of the time required to shift the necessary artillery. OHL also anticipated that by that point the French reserves in front of the Eighteenth Army would have been shifted to respond to BLÜCHER.[6]

The Eighteenth Army submitted its first attack plan on 3 May. The goal was to push the Allies back across the Montdidier–Compiègne main road and take the hills around Gury and Mareuil. The attack, echeloned in depth in the center and on the left wing, was supposed to reach the lower Matz on the first day. The base of the attack was also extended to the east as far as Noyon. The terrain in the attack sector was divided into three distinct areas. In the east, it was heavily wooded up to the Oise River. In the center, the ground was rolling and dotted with copses and farms. In the west, the ground was fairly open. The Matz creek itself was an insignificant barrier, only eight to ten feet wide, and not more than three feet deep.[7]

The Eighteenth Army's planners estimated the force requirements at twelve divisions (including three attack divisions), supported by 179 batteries. The planners at the German Crown Prince's Army Group, however, did not believe the necessary forces would be available, and suggested limiting the depth of the attack. OHL agreed and requested a re-calculation of the forces needed for an attack to the line Cuvilly–Ressons–Matz.[8]

A meeting of the chiefs of staff at Avesnes on 16 May confirmed that GNEISENAU would be a limited objective attack, and could only be launched after 1 June.[9] Subsequent orders from OHL, the German Crown Prince's Army Group, and the Seventh Army stressed that GNEISENAU would be a "heavy stroke west of the Oise in the direction of Compiègne." It would be a supporting attack for YORCK and BLÜCHER "to help the forces fighting in the Oise–Aisne angle move toward Compiègne."[10]

On 19 May the Eighteenth Army issued a new attack plan that established the Montdidier–Ressons road as the immediate objective, and the line Elincourt–Cambronne–Pipmrez on the Oise as the follow-on objective. As soon as the YORCK attack closed in on the Oise, GNEISENAU would then continue to the original objective of the Montdidier–Compiègne road. The artillery requirements were now calculated at 120 batteries. The entire artillery preparation was limited to only one hour. Both the army group and OHL agreed with the army's basic plan, but insisted on a much longer artillery preparation.[11]

Wetzell issued another operational assessment on 21 May, arguing that if the

French reserves in Flanders were not drawn off sufficiently by BLÜCHER–
YORCK, then GNEISENAU should be cancelled and the French should be
attacked again as soon as possible in a different sector. By not launching
GNEISENAU, he argued, the Germans could launch a significant attack against
Verdun without having to draw additional forces from Rupprecht's Army
Group. Even a small success at Verdun would produce a major psychological
blow against the French, who in turn could only draw reinforcements from the
Flanders sector. Thus the attack against Verdun would set up the conditions for
the final main attack in the north.[12]

During Operation BLÜCHER, OHL ordered the Seventh Army on 28 May to
advance with strong forces south of Soissons toward the west. Two days later
OHL designated 7 June as the start day for GNEISENAU. By 3 June, however,
BLÜCHER had reached culmination, and Army Group German Crown Prince
recommended halting the attack until the Eighteenth Army could launch
GNEISENAU. As long as the Seventh Army was making good progress, OHL
had figured that GNEISENAU would need only ten to twelve divisions.[13]

By 4 June Ludendorff decided that GNEISENAU was necessary to help the
right wing of the Seventh Army to advance. OHL also wanted to put heavy pressure on the Soissons–Crépy-en-Blois–Paris road. The problem at that point was
the time required to move the necessary supporting artillery. The completion of
the preparations by 7 June proved impossible, so OHL had to reschedule
GNEISENAU for 9 June. That two days, however, gave the Allies—who
anticipated the attack—extra time to move up their own reserves. The delay also
effectively severed any operational connection between BLÜCHER–YORCK
and GNEISENAU.[14]

On 4 June Hutier complained in his diary that Ludendorff had been
bothering him constantly over GNEISENAU's smallest tactical details. Hutier
also expressed the concern shared by many that Ludendorff's fixation on the
small picture obscured his ability to focus on the larger operational picture.[15]

The Seventh Army ordered all of its units to go on the defensive on 5 June.[16]
OHL, meanwhile, considered resuming the Seventh Army's attack with its three
right-wing corps to exploit whatever success GNEISENAU might achieve. At
that point, however, the original supporting nature of GNEISENAU had
changed. GNEISENAU was again extended eastward, this time over the Oise,
by including divisions of the Seventh Army's right-most VII Corps. In the first
stage of the attack the Eighteenth Army would push forward five miles to the
Matz, pivoting on Montdidier. For the second stage, no final objective was designated, but OHL hoped that the Eighteenth Army would at least be able to
reach the general line of Montdidier–Compiègne, which would put the army's
left wing six miles beyond the Matz.[17]

The Seventh Army now had the mission of setting the stage for GNEISE-
NAU by conducting local attacks with its three right-wing corps. Depending on
the results of GNEISENAU, the Seventh Army would then exploit about 11
June with westward attacks north and/or south of the Aisne. The northern
attack was codenamed BAUMFALLEN; the southern attack was codenamed

HAMMERSCHLAG. From the start, however, the Seventh Army's commander, General Hans von Boehn, only wanted to attack south of the river because of artillery shortages.[18]

The Seventh Army issued the orders on 6 June for the two right-most divisions of its right-wing VII Corps to attack on a twelve-kilometer front as part of GNEISENAU. The remaining divisions of the corps were ordered to support local deception measures.[19] The Seventh Army also issued the optimistic orders for HAMMERSCHLAG, stating, "When the progress of GNEISENAU begins to shake the enemy front, the [LIV] corps must be able to . . . attack immediately in the form of a pursuit."[20]

The following day OHL cancelled the plans for BAUMFALLEN. Instead of an exploitation attack north of the Aisne, OHL recommended that the Allied forces there be fixed in position with mortar and artillery fire. This was a questionable course of action, considering Boehn's concerns over artillery shortages. Crown Prince Wilhelm's Army Group, meanwhile, issued orders that HAMMERSCHLAG exploit GNEISENAU by attacking beyond tactical depth to the line Verberie–Crépy-en-Valois–Mareuil. That would give the Seventh Army the latitude to commit its entire VII Corps in direct support of GNEISENAU, rather than in support of HAMMERSCHLAG.[21]

OHL on 8 June approved the final GNEISENAU plans.[22] That same day OHL also issued a general directive to all German forces to "cause as much damage as possible, within the limits of the general situation, to the American units inserted in the front line, as they are to form the nucleus for the new [Allied] organizations."[23]

Preparations

This time the Germans were in a rush, and their hasty preparations cost them greatly in operational security. The German ammunition and gasoline supplies were very low. Their supply lines ran long distances to the railheads and the roads were in bad shape. The influenza pandemic, which previously had swept over the Allies, now hit the Germans—except much harder because of the inferior German diet and their strained medical system.[24]

Getting the 2,276 guns into position and supplied with ammunition proved a major problem. Bruchmüller was sick, but Ludendorff still pressed him back into service to plan the fire support. Bruchmüller was designated overall artillery chief, but only up through the first day of the attack. Joining the planning process late, he discovered that none of his usual methodical and painstaking measures to shape the battlefield had been initiated. Bruchmüller also encountered so much opposition from the Eighteenth Army's artillery staff that the normal artillery chief, a lieutenant colonel named Stuckenschmidt, had to be sent elsewhere.[25]

Any Allied commander who could read a map and knew something of the conditions of the rail lines in the sector could have pinpointed the location of the next German attack. Early in June French aerial observers started to report the troop movements. Greatly overestimating the enemy strength, French intelligence told Foch that the Germans had sixty divisions in reserve, and were capable of launching an attack of forty-five divisions between the Oise and the Somme. As the indicators of the coming German attack became almost too obvious, Allied intelligence thought they might be part of some grand deception plan.[26]

The indicators continued to grow. On 3 June the French code-breaker Georges Panvin decrypted a German radio transmission that detailed an attack scheduled for 7 June between Montdidier and Compiègne. Finally, on the night of 8 June a German deserter revealed the exact date and time of the attack, but the reported start time of the artillery preparation was off by ten minutes.[27]

As early as 3 June Pétain ordered the French Third Army to prepare to conduct a defensive battle west of the Oise. The following evening Foch sent Haig a message noting that intelligence indicators pointed to "the probability of an immediate attack extending from Noyon to Montdidier."[28] Pétain also reminded the Third Army commander, General Georges Humbert, of Directive Number 4 and ordered him to reduce drastically his front-line infantry strength and pull his guns back. Humbert's corps commanders were less than enthusiastic about carrying out that order and, when the attack came, the French still had nearly half their infantry within 2,000 meters of the front line.[29]

On 6 June, Foch sent Pétain a directive designating the Allied strategic objectives as the denial of the road to Paris and the covering of the northern ports, while at the same time maintaining control of the rail lines necessary to shift forces. Foch closed by again demanding a "foot-by-foot defense." That same day, the U.S. Marine's 4th Brigade of the U.S. Army's 2nd Division started its attack at Belleau Wood against the German Seventh Army's IV Reserve Corps.[30]

German order of battle

GNEISENAU was executed by four corps of Hutier's Eighteenth Army and the right-wing VII Corps of Boehn's Seventh Army (Table 9.1). The five corps had eight attack and sixteen trench divisions available for the first day. Two more corps in the Seventh Army were scheduled to launch the follow-up Operation HAMMERSCHLAG (see Table 9.2). The GNEISENAU units were supported by 625 artillery batteries and approximately 500 aircraft (see Table 9.3).

Allied order of battle

Humbert's Third Army had four corps facing the attackers. The defenders were supported by 146 field and 161 heavy batteries and 165 tanks in four groupments positioned behind the western-most XXXV Corps. The French were superior in the air, with four groupments plus the RAF's 9th Brigade, for a total of 1,200 aircraft, about half of which were bombers. Farther to the rear the French also had seven infantry and three cavalry divisions.[31] See Table 9.4.

Table 9.1 GNEISENAU divisions on 9 June 1918[32]

	First line	*Corps and army reserve*	*OHL reserve*	*Total divisions*	*Sector width*
Eighteenth Army	5 Trench	7 Trench	3 Trench	15 Trench	33 km
	6 Attack	—	—	6 Attack	
Seventh Army	—	1 Trench	—	1 Trench	12 km
	2 Attack	—	—	2 Attack	
	5 Trench	8 Trench	3 Trench	16 Trench	45 km
	8 Attack	—	—	8 Attack	

Source: *Der Weltkrieg*, Vol.14, p.397.

Table 9.2 German corps on 9 and 12 June 1918[33]

	(West to east)		
	Corps	*Commander*	*Attack*
Eighteenth Army		Hutier	
	III	Lüttwitz	No
	XXVI Reserve	Watter	No
	IX	Oetinger	GNEISENAU
	XVII	Webern	GNEISENAU
	VIII	Schoeler	GNEISENAU
	XXXVIII Reserve	Hoffmann	GNEISENAU
Seventh Army		Boehn	
	VII	Francois	GNEISENAU
	LIV	Larisch	HAMMERSCHLAG
	VIII Reserve	Wichura	HAMMERSCHLAG
	XXV Reserve	Winckler	No
	IV Reserve	Conta	No
	LXV	Schmettow	No

Source: *Der Weltkrieg*, Vol.14, p.397.

Table 9.3 Guns supporting GNEISENAU[34]

Field	*Heavy*	*Super-heavy*	*Total guns*	*Trench mortars*
1,492	774	10	2,276	1,000

Source: *Der Weltkrieg*, Vol.14, p.398, Appendix 39c.

Table 9.4 French order of battle in the GNEISENAU sector[35]

	Front-line divisions	*Rear divisions*	*Army group reserve divisions*	*Tank groups*	*Total guns*	*Sector width*
Third Army	9	5	1	4	1,058	33 km

Source: *Der Weltkrieg*, Vol.14, p.408, Appendix 39d.

Execution (9–15 June)

9 June   The German artillery preparation started at 0050 hours. Since Operation MICHAEL in March, the German Army on the Western Front had finally come to accept grudgingly Bruchmüller's and Pulkowski's predicted fire techniques, which meant the entire preparation could be fired in darkness with the infantry assault coming at first light. The French, believing that the German preparation was scheduled to start at 0100 hours, commenced firing their own counter-preparation at 0050 hours, believing they were starting ten minutes earlier than the Germans. Thus, the French counter-fire had only a limited effect, also because their guns were outnumbered more than two-to-one, and because Bruchmüller's fire plan was methodical and complete as usual. The German preparation had only three phases and lasted three hours and thirty minutes. The German gunners fired 1.4 million rounds that day, with one-third of that total being gas.[36]

The German first wave moved out at 0420 hours, but the start times were ragged because of the French counter-preparation. The main effort was with the Eighteenth Army's center-left VIII Corps. That unit had an especially difficult task, having to push through wooded and hilly terrain while crossing old defensive positions. By 0600 hours the XXXVIII Reserve Corps on the Eighteenth Army's far left reached the Oise River.[37]

At 1040 hours the Seventh Army issued the orders for operation HAMMERSCHLAG to begin on 11 June. The objective of that attack was to gain as much ground as possible north of Villers-Cotterêts, with the LIV and VIII Reserve Corps pushing forward without limits after reaching the initial objective line Vic–Coeuvres–Longpont. The main effort was with the LIV Corps, which was on the right of the attack and to the left of VII Corps, already fighting as part of GNEISENAU. The entire artillery of VII Corps, however, was to fire in support of LIV Corps.[38]

At 1100 hours Eighteenth Army units entered Ressons-sur-Matz, and an hour later they controlled the French second lines on a front of more than seven miles. By 1800 hours the Germans took Mareuil. On their left wing they had penetrated to a depth of 6.5 miles, reaching the north bank of the Matz. At that point the Germans estimated they had taken some 5,000 prisoners and had neutralized three French divisions. The German infantry halted for the night but the artillery fire continued. That same day the German First Army, supported by 400 guns, launched what turned out to be an abortive attack against Reims.[39]

The French on 9 June were not routed and fell back under pressure in an orderly manner. They actually managed to launch a small counterattack against the Seventh Army's VII Corps. Reserve Army Group commander, General Marie Fayolle, shifted one division from the Tenth Army's reserve to the Third Army, and he ordered another division to move from the Verdun sector to the junction of the Tenth and Third Armies. At 2030 hours Pétain asked Foch to let him have the British XXII Corps. Foch refused, citing the number of divisions remaining in Rupprecht's Army Group, but Foch did ask Haig to send Pétain one division from that corps.[40]

10 June The German attack resumed at 0500 hours, with the left wing moving to secure the Oise crossings. But with almost all of its artillery already either supporting the Eighteenth Army or moving south to support the coming HAM-MERSCHLAG attack, the VII Corps was incapable of moving fast enough. Nonetheless, as the Eighteenth Army units pushed forward on the left, the French 53rd Infantry Division collapsed, exposing Humbert's right flank. The French had planned to counterattack into both flanks of GNEISENAU, but now the attack in the east was impossible.[41]

By the end of the second day, the Germans had pushed well across the Matz in the center. The right wing of the attack, however, was making very little progress. Thirteen German divisions were opposing eleven French divisions in the front lines. The Eighteenth Army's intent for the next day was to push ahead to reach the Montdidier–Estrees St. Denis–Compiègne rail line, with the main effort being in the center. That evening, however, OHL postponed the HAM-MERSCHLAG attack until 12 June, because the necessary artillery ammunition was still not in place.[42]

About 1700 hours on the second day, the French put General Charles Mangin in charge of a five-division counterattack force on the French far left. That same day the Seventh Army's IV Reserve Corps also continued to encounter heavy American attacks in the Belleau Woods area.[43]

11 June The Seventh Army's VII Corps detected the French pulling back about 0600 hours on the third day. The two divisions of that corps started moving west into the former French positions, not really attacking so much as following. The Eighteenth Army, meanwhile, applied steady pressure along the entire GNEISENAU front. The center-right XVII Corps pushed west in order to take Tricot. The right wing of the center-left VIII Corps, which had been the main effort, pushed toward Compiègne.[44]

At 1230 hours Mangin's force of five divisions attacked into GNEISENAU's west flank on both sides of Mery, in the general direction of Ressons. Fayolle had originally planned to attack forty-eight hours later to give the French artillery time to plan and fire a preparation to neutralize the German artillery. Mangin, however, pushed for the earlier attack and received the backing of Foch. Thus the French attacked without artillery preparation, but preceded by a creeping barrage. Not all of his divisions were ready, but Mangin attacked anyway. The counterattack succeeded initially because it was supported by ground-attack aircraft and ten groups of tanks, operating in a coordinated manner similar to the British counterattack at Cambrai the preceding November. Within a few hours Mangin's force cleared the Aronde valley. German artillery eventually halted Mangin's counterattack, but the Eighteenth Army ordered its IX and XVII Corps on the right wing to halt and assume temporary defensive positions. A few hours later the Eighteenth Army ordered the insertion of the headquarters of the I Reserve Corps between the IX Corps and XVII Corps. At 2230 hours OHL ordered the IX and XVII Corps to cease offensive operations, with the exception of retaking Mery.[45]

12 June   The HAMMERSCHLAG artillery preparation began at 0330 hours and lasted only ninety minutes. Anticipating the attack, the French pulled most of their artillery back.[46] At 0500 hours the Seventh Army's LIV and VIII Reserve Corps attacked south of the Aisne in a westward direction toward Compiègne, with five divisions in the first line and three in the second. The artillery of the Seventh Army's VII Corps (not already committed to GNEISENAU) and XXV Reserve Corps fired in support of HAMMERSCHLAG's two attacking corps.[47]

At 0430 hours the French resumed their own counterattacks against the right wing of the Eighteenth Army. During the night the advance lines and the rear areas of all the German corps committed to GNEISENAU had suffered from heavy French artillery fire. OHL, nonetheless, repeated its order to retake Mery. The French counterattacks stalled by mid-morning after achieving only modest success, but they did succeed in completely disrupting the Eighteenth Army's plans for that day.[48]

By noon HAMMERSCHLAG had stalled on both its wings and was making only slow progress in the center. As the day dragged on, French artillery fire brought the attack to a halt. By evening OHL ordered the Eighteenth and Seventh Armies to halt temporarily both GNEISENAU and HAMMER-SCHLAG and assume defensive positions. The operational planners at Crown Prince Wilhelm's Army Group later concluded that HAMMERSCHLAG had been doomed from the start because of inadequate ammunition supplies.[49]

13–15 June   On 13 June the Germans only conducted local attacks. That morning Crown Prince Wilhelm's Army Group sent a recommendation to OHL to terminate HAMMERSCHLAG because of strong and organized enemy resistance. The following day, OHL ordered the end of both GNEISENAU and HAMMERSCHLAG. The Seventh Army's IV Reserve Corps did remain heavily engaged at Belleau Woods, and OHL still wanted the Eighteenth Army to retake Mery. That order, however, was rescinded on the afternoon of 15 June.[50]

The fourth of Ludendorff's 1918 offensives was over, but the Allies were still worried about the large and potentially dangerous force under the control of Rupprecht's Army Group opposite the BEF. The British also believed the French were close to cracking. On 5 June General Wilson and British Secretary of State for War, Lord Milner, had attended a meeting with the Prime Minister in London to discuss the possibility of evacuating the BEF should that happen. Milner followed up by sending a group to France on 13 June to evaluate the evacuation plans.[51]

Assessment

The results

Like its three predecessors, Operation GNEISENAU failed to produce any operationally significant gains that might have led to strategic results. But for the first time, one of Ludendorff's attacks had failed to produce any worthwhile tactical gains. The Germans had failed to reach any of the rail lines they needed to sustain their dangerously extended salient, so they were still faced with the same immediate problem they had had when GNEISENAU started. The five days of fighting cost the Germans some 25,000 casualties, and the French about 35,000. According to the German official history, Ludendorff was "disappointed:" "Strong German forces had been consumed, and the attack's objective of pulling enemy reserves out of Flanders had not been achieved."[52]

The objective

The above passage from the German official history betrays a general sense of confusion—at least in the post-war writings—over what the objective of Operation GNEISENAU really had been. While the official history talked about pulling the Allied reserves out of Flanders; Crown Prince Wilhelm talked about a "jumping off point for an attack on Paris;" and Ludendorff talked about gaining control of the "rail line that leads from the Aisne valley east of Soissons into that of the Vesle."[53] Clearly, with only twenty-four divisions supported by 2,276 guns, that third and very limited objective was the only one GNEISENAU had any hope of achieving. Yet, in reading the war diary entries and the morning, noon, and evening reports filed during the battle, one gets a strong sense of a German military leadership that was floundering, with no real clear sense of purpose at that point. Unlike the first three offensives, OHL did not completely lose control of the battle this time; but then, there had been no exploitable tactical opportunities to tempt the Germans to deviate from the plan.

Artillery

Artillery was the major pacing factor in the planning for both GNEISENAU and HAMMERSCHLAG. On 9 June GNEISENAU had already been postponed by two days because of the time required to shift the supporting artillery into position, and shortages in artillery guns and ammunition continued to handicap the operations of the Eighteenth and Seventh Armies between 9 and 13 June. Yet the same day that GNEISENAU started, the First Army's attack against Reims was supported by 400 guns.

On paper, at least, GNEISENAU did not appear to be an especially undergunned operation. Both GEORGETTE and GNEISENAU were roughly the same for the number of guns per division (eighty-five and ninety-five); the number of guns per kilometer of front (fifty and fifty-one); and the number of rounds fired on the first day (1.4 million for both). But the tactical situations were vastly different for the two operations. In June 1918 the Germans no longer had the advantage of even tactical surprise; they had no glaring weak point in the Allied line to attack; they did not have the advantage of a slow, methodical, and well-concealed buildup; and the Allies after the first three offensives were finally learning how to anticipate and counter the German attack tactics.

Perhaps the biggest difference between GEORGETTE and GNEISENAU was the lack of an operational objective at tactical depth in the latter case. If GEORGETTE had succeeded in capturing Hazebrouck, it would have crippled the BEF's logistics network. If GNEISENAU had succeeded in reaching the Montdidier–Estrees St. Denis–Compiègne rail line, it would only have partially relieved the German problems in supplying the BLÜCHER salient. Thus, the 400 guns committed to the First Army's failed attack against Reims could not have contributed to GNEISENAU becoming a decisive success, but those guns at least might have helped that operation achieve its limited objective.

Decision 10 and 12 June

On 10 June OHL decided to postpone HAMMERSCHLAG one day, until 12 June, because the required artillery ammunition could not be moved into position on time. That decision may have been sound on 10 June, but by 12 June the situation had changed completely, and HAMMERSCHLAG no longer made sense. On 11 June Mangin counterattacked, and the entire left wing of the Eighteenth Army had effectively come to a halt. By 12 June there was almost no operational linkage left between GNEISENAU and HAMMERSCHLAG. To reach Compiègne, the LIV and VIII Reserve Corps had to cover almost thirty kilometers, most of it through wooded terrain. Like MARS in relation to MICHAEL, HAMMERSCHLAG was too little, too late.

Allied reactions

Unlike the three previous offensives, the Allies anticipated GNEISENAU and took their first positive, if only marginally effective steps to counter the German offensive tactics. When GNEISENAU started the French still had too many of their forces packed into forward positions, and the artillery counter-preparation was too weak and started too late. Nonetheless, on the night of 11 June the planners at OHL reviewed the events of the past three days and could not decide whether or not the French had avoided the initial German attack by withdrawing their front-line forces.[54] The next day, it became quite clear that the French had done exactly that in response to HAMMERSCHLAG. Taken together, the French reactions to GNEISENAU and HAMMERSCHLAG, and especially Mangin's counterattack, were an ominous foreshadowing of how the Allies would react to the next major German offensive on 15 July.

On the political and strategic levels, the generally effective response to GNEISENAU was something of a psychological turning point for the French that may well have saved Clemenceau's government from collapse. And, Foch later wrote that the fact that none of Rupprecht's divisions could be identified in the 9 June attack led him to conclude that there was no need to draw forces away from Haig.[55]

Alternatives

GNEISENAU was once again the wrong attack in the wrong place, yet it was a direct and almost unavoidable result of Operation BLÜCHER and its failure. Writing after the war, Crown Prince Wilhelm argued that GNEISENAU would not have been necessary if BLÜCHER had been wide enough in the first place. OHL could have accomplished that by making "a modest draw on the forces being held to the rear of Rupprecht's Army Group."[56] Wilhelm also went on to argue that once BLÜCHER started achieving unexpected results, OHL should have exploited the situation to the fullest by "immediately moving up the large reserves earmarked for the Flanders offensive and concentrated behind Rupprecht's Army Group, and throwing them in without hesitation at the point where we had just broken through."[57]

Other post-war writers have suggested that, rather than launching GNEISE-NAU, the Germans should have continued to reinforce BLÜCHER, and that by building up the Eighteenth Army at the Seventh Army's expense, Ludendorff effectively killed BLÜCHER's momentum.[58] Those arguments, however, fail to account for the realities of the situation. With the limited battlefield mobility of the German Army and no operationally significant objectives at a realistically reachable depth, the withdrawal of the Allied reserves north of the Somme was the only thing the Germans could have hoped to achieve with BLÜCHER. When that failed, there was virtually nothing else that the Germans could have achieved operationally in the BLÜCHER sector.

Wetzell recognized that when he recommended in his 21 May assessment that if BLÜCHER failed to draw in the Allied reserves, then GNEISENAU should be cancelled and the French attacked in force at some other point, preferably Verdun.[59] But Wetzell's recommendation had been made before the unexpected territorial gains of BLÜCHER. Once the Germans wound up holding a huge, difficult-to-defend, and even more difficult-to-supply salient, their immediate operational options became very restricted.

For psychological and morale reasons, it was virtually impossible for the Germans to abandon the gains they had just achieved at such cost. Ludendorff at that point believed that he had no choice but to continue attacking—somewhere, anywhere. When prior to BLÜCHER some staff officers at OHL tried to argue that Germany could not continue launching large-scale offensives indefinitely, Ludendorff snapped at Lieutenant Colonel Albrecht von Thaer: "What do you expect me to do? Make peace at any price?"[60] Thus, Ludendorff was forced into a position of his own creation where he had to get control of the rail line that ran between Reims and Compiègne and through Soissons. His only two real options at the start of June were attacks toward Reims or Compiègne.

10 Operation MARNESCHUTZ–REIMS

15 July–3 August 1918

A real improvement to our supply system as well as our tactical situation was only possible if we captured Reims. In the battles of May and June we had not managed to get possession of that town. The capture of Reims must now be the object of a special operation, but the operation thus required fitted into the general framework of our plans.[1]

Field Marshal Paul von Hindenburg

We gave orders that [the French second] line should be prepared for assault by a fresh artillery preparation, but at the bottom of my heart I had to admit the bitter truth: the offensive had failed.[2]

German Crown Prince Wilhelm

Plans (5 June–14 July)

At the end of Operation GNEISENAU the German operational situation was no better than it had been following Operation BLÜCHER. If anything, it was worse. Crown Prince Wilhelm's Army Group now held a salient with a perimeter length of more than 100 kilometers, and a chord of some sixty kilometers. The position was vulnerable to attack from all sides, and almost impossible to supply. (See Map 7.)

The vital rail junction at Reims was still in French hands, and the only high-capacity, double-track rail line into the salient running from Laon to Soissons was still blocked at the Vauxaillon tunnel, and would not be back in operation until 7 July, and then with only a single track. The only other route was a single-tracked line that ran through the Aisne valley, branching off the main line between Laon and Reims. It was put into service on 16 June. Another connection from Vailly directly to Braisne was under construction, but was only scheduled for completion on 30 July.[3]

Although the strategic imperative of defeating the British remained, OHL was now in a situation where it had only two immediate alternatives—it could withdraw from the Marne salient, or it could try to enlarge it. For political and psychological reasons Ludendorff believed he could not order a withdrawal.

Ludendorff's fifth great offensive had its genesis in the planning leading up

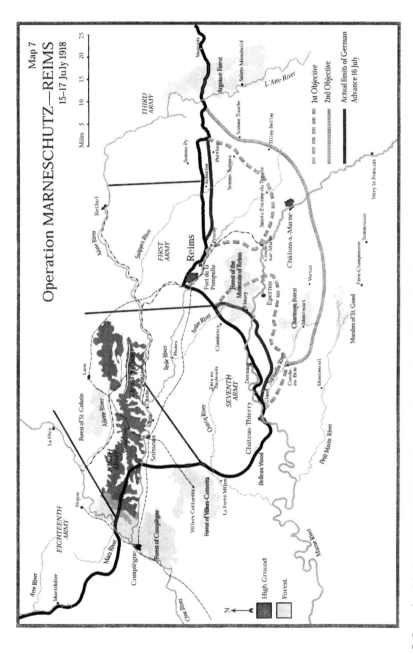

Map 7 Operation MARNESCHUTZ–REIMS (source: Map by Donald S. Frazier, Ph.D., Abilene, Texas, based on sketches and notes provided by David T. Zabecki).

to Operation MICHAEL. In January the German planners started work on Operation ROLAND by the Third Army east of Reims. It was developed as a contingency operation in case MICHAEL got bogged down in the south. On 5 June OHL resurrected ROLAND as a contingency operation in the event that GNEISENAU failed to draw the Allied reserves out of Flanders. ROLAND would be modified to take Reims from the east by an attack across the Vesle. Crown Prince Wilhelm's Army Group gave the order to start stockpiling the necessary ammunition for the operation. At the same time, OHL also scaled back the scope of the planned attacks directly against Reims by the First Army.[4]

Meanwhile, Crown Prince Wilhelm's Army Group on 1 June had sent OHL a recommendation for an operation to follow up GNEISENAU with an attack south of the Marne west of Reims, conducted by the inner wings of the Seventh and First Armies.[5] OHL initially rejected that proposal. On 6 June, Ludendorff, Wetzell, and Kuhl met in Avesnes with General Willi von Klewitz, the chief of staff of the Third Army, to try to decide whether to launch ROLAND or HAGEN after GNEISENAU. Although the general consensus was that any decision would be based on the outcome of GNEISENAU, Kuhl continued to argue that only HAGEN could produce decisive results.[6]

Wetzell argued that ROLAND would require fourteen to sixteen divisions, and take up to four additional weeks to prepare, which would push HAGEN back to the end of August. An offensive across the Marne with the objective of capturing Epernay and pinching out Reims was more feasible, because the French were weak in that sector and the attack would not require any HAGEN divisions. Thus Wetzell proposed an attack of six to eight divisions, which could be drawn from the Seventh and Eighteenth Armies. Such an attack could be ready for launch between 20 and 25 June. By taking Epernay, "the French front before Reims will lose the railway and roads which supply it." Wetzell also included a supporting attack by the First Army as far east as Prosnes, and he recommended that ROLAND continue to be prepared as a follow-on attack after HAGEN.[7]

The First Army was still planning a series of attacks against Reims through 13 June.[8] On 8 June, meanwhile, OHL in accordance with Wetzell's assessment prepared to replace ROLAND with the attack across the Marne and ordered Army Group German Crown Prince to have the Seventh Army quickly develop the plan for the attack. The planning guidance from the army group stated:

> The objective of the attack is to advance rapidly and with surprise south of the Marne against Epernay, to deprive the enemy of his most important route of communications in the Reims hills and to force him to abandon those hills.[9]

On 9 June the First Army attacked the high ground west of Reims, but the attackers were quickly driven back to their starting positions. OHL immediately canceled the planned supporting attacks of Seventh Army's LXV and VI Reserve Corps. As a result of the unsuccessful attacks, the First Army requested fresh divisions, with the army group concurring. Ludendorff, however, wanted to cancel all the local attacks against Reims for the time being.[10]

The following day General Bruno von Mudra assumed command of the First Army from Below, who had fallen ill. After conferring with OHL, Mudra issued orders placing the First Army on the defensive, and on 11 June he ordered the postponement of the attacks against Reims. Preparations for those attacks were supposed to continue, however. By this point too, GNEISENAU had failed and OHL finally began to confront the seriousness of the supply situation inside the Marne salient. OHL had previously rejected any suggestions of combining the attack by the Seventh Army across the Marne with an attack by the left wing of the First Army across the Vesle. OHL had believed that the German Army did not have the forces necessary for an attack on such a scale. But somehow the OHL planners now believed they could take Reims without the additional forces.[11]

On 11 June the Seventh Army estimated the force requirements for Wetzell's proposed attack across the Marne at ten divisions and 700 artillery batteries, with twenty days of preparation time.[12] Army Group German Crown Prince passed the preliminary plan on to OHL, but also recommended including a supporting attack by the right-wing corps of the First Army, "to prevent flanking from the north bank of the Marne, to hold the reserves there, and to capture the group of hills northwest of Damery."[13] On 12 June Wetzell issued another operational assessment. Noting that the conditions were still not right to launch Operation HAGEN, he continued to press for an attack south of the Marne.[14]

Ludendorff held another planning meeting in Roubaix on 14 June. He concluded that the failure of GNEISENAU, the heavy losses from BLÜCHER, and the shortage of replacements meant that ROLAND was unfeasible for the time being. Instead, the Germans would launch two attacks against Reims in one coordinated operation.[15] Following the meeting, OHL issued the preliminary orders to Army Group German Crown Prince. The Seventh Army would launch Operation MARNESCHUTZ (MARNE DEFENSE), crossing the Marne east of Château-Thierry and advancing to Epernay on both banks of the river. The First Army would launch Operation REIMS, attacking east of the city in the direction of Châlons. The inner wings of the two forces would meet at Epernay. The attack date was set for 10 July, with Rupprecht's Army Group to follow up with HAGEN on or about 20 July. The entire attack front was almost ninety kilometers, including the sector in front of the city that would not be attacked directly.[16] Wetzell's original attack force of six to eight divisions had now grown to more than twenty divisions.

On 16 June the First Army sent Army Group German Crown Prince an analysis recommending a significant expansion of the REIMS attack. In order to link up with the Seventh Army at Epernay, the planners argued, the First Army had to penetrate with its center to the Marne. Noting that the Seventh Army had advanced eighteen kilometers on the first day of the BLÜCHER attack,

> a similar advance by our army on the first day would bring us to the vicinity of les Garndes Loges–Vadenay. But in this case the terrain is far more

favorable than it was in the BLÜCHER attack, so that it is entirely probable that we will reach the Marne the very first day.

That would mean a first day advance of twenty-three kilometers. The First Army also recommended that it be given control of the right-wing corps of the Third Army. The expanded attack of the First Army would require some nine additional divisions supported by 600 batteries.[17]

Ludendorff approved the extension of the attack the next day.[18] That same day the Seventh Army submitted a refined plan and force estimate. "On the left wing, an advance against Epernay is possible only if we push forward north of the Marne simultaneously to at least the hills of Fleury la Riviere." That would require eighteen divisions controlled by four corps headquarters.[19]

The operation was again extended during a meeting between Ludendorff and the staff chiefs of Army Group German Crown Prince and the Seventh, First, and Third Armies in Rethel on 18 June. Klewitz argued that the Third Army should have a larger role in the operation. The Third Army was supposed to screen the flank of the attack against any counterattack from the east and the southeast. Schulenburg, the chief of staff of Army Group German Crown Prince, supported the Third Army recommendation as a means of reaching the Marne on as broad a front as possible, while maintaining a straight and strong front line. Ludendorff accepted the recommendation—over the objections of Wetzell, who pointed out that the expansion would delay the start of the attack and would require forces that were not available.[20] Nonetheless, OHL issued the order expanding operation REIMS to the east into Champagne, "as far as the Wetterecke."[21] The following day Ludendorff postponed MARNESCHUTZ–REIMS until 14 July.[22] As Hindenburg later explained the decision in his memoirs:

> After we had originally decided to limit our operation practically to the capture of Reims, our plan was extended in the course of various conferences by adding an attack eastward and right into Champagne. On the one hand our motive was an intention to cut off the Reims salient from the southeast also. On the other, we believed that in view of our recent experiences, we might perhaps reach Châlons-sur-Marne, attracted as we were by the prospect of great captures of prisoners and war material, if an operation on such a scale succeeded. We therefore *decided to risk the weakening of our forces at decisive points* for the sake of securing a broad front of attack.[23]
>
> (Emphasis added.)

Like Operations BLÜCHER and GNEISENAU, the overall front-line trace ran east and west in the MARNESCHUTZ–REIMS sector, which meant that the Germans would be attacking from north to south. West of Reims much of the line of departure ran along the Marne River. The German Seventh Army would have to start its attack with a deliberate river crossing. The Marne there was seventy to eighty meters wide and three to four meters deep. Both banks were firm, but 1 to 1.5 meters high. The hills of the valley rose to 170 meters in places. East of Reims, in Champagne, the Marne was anywhere from twenty to thirty kilometers south of the line of departure. The German First and Third Armies would have to attack over relatively open ground and then conduct a hasty crossing of the Marne. The Vesle was the only major water obstacle short of the Marne, but the flat, open ground gave the French good observation. The heavily cratered ground from previous battles also made it more difficult for the attacker, especially moving artillery and supplies forward. On 20 June the First Army issued its attack order for REIMS:

> The First Army will penetrate the enemy position between Prunay and the Suippe and will reach the Marne on the first day without stopping. In conjunction with the Seventh Army, it will annihilate the enemy in Reims and the Reims hills.... When the Marne is reached it should be crossed in a southwesterly direction.[24]

A follow-on order issued the next day filled in the details. The main effort of the First Army attack was to be XIV Corps which, after crossing the Marne would advance along both banks to link up with the Seventh Army at Epernay. The VII Reserve Corps north of the river would screen the right flank of the advance against any counterattack from the Reims hills.[25] But that same day Ludendorff also altered the basic plan of Army Group German Crown Prince.

> The question how the operation is to be continued depends on our own forces and very strongly on the enemy's resistance. The goal is to weaken the enemy in men and material.... The army group therefore can restrict itself toward the south with limited objectives and it must make major progress toward the southeast.[26]

The basic objective of MARNESCHUTZ–REIMS now had shifted from taking Reims to securing rail lines into the Marne salient, to the typical force-on-force battle that so dominated German military thinking. The total attack force had grown to thirty-nine divisions by that point. Ludendorff had convinced himself that another massive tactical victory in July in this otherwise non-decisive sector would collapse French morale and cause them to sue for peace. As he wrote later:

> A victory on 15 July was apt to undermine the morale of the enemy armies much more than any of the successes in the previous year. It alone could cause the peace germs found on the side of the Entente to bud forth and mature. Only a victory was able to tide us over our internal differences.[27]

On 21 June Army Group German Crown Prince issued revised orders for the operation. But the stated objective was not quite consistent with Ludendorff's message of the previous day.

The principle objective of the attack is to cut off the enemy forces in the Reims hills.

[Seventh Army] penetrates the enemy positions between Gland and Chambrecy, takes the crossings at Epernay and the hills southwest of the city, and disregarding limits, pushes forward on both banks of the Marne southeastward until contact is established with the First Army.

[First Army] penetrates the enemy position between Prunay and Auberive, pushes forward against Epernay with strong forces on both banks of the Marne, and establishes contact with the Seventh Army.

[Third Army] covers the left flank of the operation, taking the general line of the hills east of St. Etienne–southeastern slopes of the Piemont–Somme Suippes–hills southeast of Perthes ... so as to secure the Marne crossings for the First Army against the east.

Rapid execution of the attack is the prerequisite for success. The first two days of the attack and the first night will be decisive.[28]

On 23 June OHL ordered the insertion of the headquarters of the Ninth Army on the right flank of the Seventh Army. Assuming command of the weak VII, XXXIX Reserve, and XIII Corps effective 5 July, the Ninth Army's mission was to secure the right flank of the operation against an Allied counterattack from the west.[29] Two days later Ludendorff sent a message to the German senior commanders reiterating that the war could only be won by more large-scale attacks. He rejected completely any assumption of a defensive strategy.[30]

On 28 June the First Army modified its attack order of 21 June. The XIV Corps would still cross the Marne, but its mission was now to screen the southern flank of the VII Reserve Corps, which would now make the main effort and link up with the Seventh Army. "No daily objective will be established, but I expect that the center of the army will reach and cross the Marne on the first day." The XV Corps, directly in front of Reims would not attack the city frontally, but would be prepared to move forward as soon as any Allied retrograde movement was detected.[31] Two days later, however, Army Group German Crown Prince changed the First Army's 28 June operations order. XIV Corps was again ordered to advance on both sides of the Marne and make the main effort. In effect, the army group restored the scheme of maneuver established in the First Army's operations order of 21 June.[32]

Ludendorff approved the final plan of Army Group German Crown Prince on 1 July.[33] The army group also issued orders to the Ninth Army to secure the flank of the Seventh Army's MARNESCHUTZ attack by establishing "defensive positions in great depth and strong reserves." During the artillery preparation the Ninth Army was ordered to fire a deceptive preparation in its sector, to include the final saturation fire phase simultaneous with that of the Seventh Army.[34]

On 3 July OHL set Y-Day back one more day to 15 July.[35] The following day Crown Prince Rupprecht noted evidence of a British attack against the Sixth and Fourth Armies to take pressure off the coming attack around Reims.[36] On 6 July the First Army approved the plan of XV Corps to move into the city of Reims once the French started to withdraw. The objective remained to take the town without fighting. "The question will merely be to occupy the city gates with Landsturm sentries."[37]

On 7 July the Seventh Army issued specific orders to its attacking corps to dig in and establish defensive zones in depth upon reaching their attack objectives. The orders for all four previous major offensives of 1918 required the attacking units to continue moving forward, and not assume the defensive until specifically ordered to do so. The MARNESCHUTZ attack was different in this respect, at least.[38] Three days later, however, orders from Army Group German Crown Prince contradicted the 7 July orders to a certain extent, indicating an intent to exploit the attack beyond the Marne:

> When the Seventh and First Armies reach their initial objectives and link-up on the Marne, their interior wings will have to turn south and gain ground to defeat any enemy attempts at relief. This will guarantee the destruction of the enemy forces in the Reims hills.[39]

On 11 July the Ninth Army requested reinforcements of at least four fresh divisions to meet an anticipated French counterattack in their sector. Ludendorff refused, not wanting to divert forces from the main attack. But OHL did guarantee that the artillery and pioneer units of the Ninth Army that were tasked to support the initial stage of MARNESCHUTZ would be released back to the Ninth Army on the 15th, as soon as their assigned missions had been accomplished. The Ninth Army was also ordered to weaken its right wing significantly in order to reinforce its sector south of the Aisne, and to secure artillery flanking fire positions from the northern river boundary.[40]

About 2300 hours on the night of 14 July, Crown Prince Wilhelm went to a forward observation post to witness the artillery preparation. Upon his arrival the sector artillery commander reported that the German lines were receiving only normal harassing fire. The Crown Prince did not believe the report.

> I had, on the contrary, a decided impression that the French were keeping up a very lively fire on our rear areas. Many explosions were heard, and we could see several of our ammunition dumps on fire. My doubts increased.[41]

Preparations

Initially the operation south of the Marne was supposed to be a smaller-scale, hastily prepared attack for the sole purpose of cutting off Reims. As the attack grew in size and its objective shifted to inflicting a large-scale tactical defeat on the French, the preparations grew more complicated and required more time. Instead of the fourteen to nineteen days of preparation time Wetzell had first estimated, MARNESCHUTZ–REIMS required thirty-seven days of preparation from the time the Seventh Army received the initial warning order on 8 June. The Allies did not sit idle during that period.

Security, surprise, and deception

Like GNEISENAU, the Germans failed to achieve the same level of surprise they had for Operations MICHAEL, GEORGETTE, or BLÜCHER. They had sufficient time, but the conditions did not favor secrecy. The short, bright nights aided Allied observation, and the prevailing northeasterly winds carried the sounds from the German lines. The Germans tried to mask the preparation sounds with dummy activities, but with little success.[42]

Nonetheless, the Germans attempted to enforce stringent security precautions. Telephones in the front-line positions were not to be used prior to the start of the attack except to test the circuits using the buzzers.[43] Special security restrictions were imposed on German troops from Alsace and Lorraine, who were considered high security risks.[44] Generals and General Staff officers making personal reconnaissance in forward areas were required to wear privates' uniforms and carry rifles or spades.[45] Information was restricted, but one set of orders wisely noted that the number of officers with access to the plans should not be too low. "Those who do know . . . are far more cautious than those who merely suppose things."[46] In the Seventh Army, even the name of the MARNESCHUTZ operation was given the cover name of STRASSENBAU (ROAD CONSTRUCTION).[47]

Despite the stringent German security measures, most Allied commanders who could read a map could have predicted the general if not the exact area where the next blow would fall. Allied air superiority made it difficult for the Germans to conduct effective aerial reconnaissance, which in turn helped mask the Allied counter-preparations.[48] Right up until the start of the attack the senior German commanders worried that the Allies would detect their preparations. They did, of course, but they also effectively kept that knowledge from the Germans. An entry for 14 July in the Seventh Army War Diary noted that all indicators were that the French had not detected the German preparations, and the attack the next day would achieve surprise.[49] Writing in his memoirs after the war, Crown Prince Wilhelm noted, "As late as the evening of 14 July I rang up the chiefs of staff of the First and Third Armies . . . to make certain whether surprise was assured. Both were confident that the enemy had so far noticed nothing."[50]

Artillery and air preparations

Turning to his old artillery workhorse, Ludendorff put Bruchmüller in overall charge of the artillery for Army Group German Crown Prince.[51] This time, however, Bruchmüller did not get all the artillery he estimated he needed. The German Army was starting to run out of guns. The industrial base could no longer keep up with the rate of wear and tear from combat operations. Simultaneously, Ludendorff also ordered additional artillery moved north in preparation for a quick shift to HAGEN. To make up part of the shortage most of the training batteries inside Germany were stripped of their guns, which were sent to the Western Front to become the fifth and sixth guns for the batteries in place.[52]

The burden of the attack fell especially heavily on the artillery units. Some, like the 5th Field Artillery Regiment, were making their third major attack in four months.[53] One major problem was that the artillery ammunition could not be moved to the front as fast as it arrived at the forward-most railheads.[54] Much work was needed to prepare roads into the forward areas and the artillery positions. The ammunition supply problems made the buildup especially difficult to conceal. With a planned density of twenty-five batteries per kilometer of front, the huge amounts of artillery ammunition to be moved up required one route of approach every 125 meters.[55] The road network in the area was not sufficient, causing traffic jams of ammunition columns that Allied aerial reconnaissance spotted easily. In the Third Army's I Bavarian Corps alone, artillery ammunition supply transport required 2,000 wagons and 10,000 horses.[56]

The Germans also had to deal with the difficulty of ammunition supply after the start of the attack. A First Army order of 2 July addressed the problem of the chronic shortage of horses to support the advance. Guns and artillery vehicles that had to be left behind would be collected by special details. "Considering the difficulties of bringing up ammunition, it is better to leave a gun behind than a caisson."[57]

Despite the difficulties, Bruchmüller proceeded with his methodical preparations. The army and army group artillery orders made it clear that fire would open without registration or ranging shots. Corps headquarters were ordered to coordinate schools in the Pulkowski Method for their battalion and battery commanders.[58] Each newly arriving battery commander was handed a detailed list of instructions containing everything he needed to know. The Seventh Army ordered the artillery commanders of the attack divisions to give personally the Bruchmüller-type briefings to the divisions' infantry regiments, while Bruchmüller personally delivered a two-hour briefing to the staff of the Third Army at Vouziers.[59]

In the air, the Germans had lost the edge they had in the earlier offensives. On 17 June the Seventh Army estimated its air requirements as only thirteen observation squadrons and four fighter squadrons. Considering the more than forty-two squadrons that supported the Seventh Army during Operation BLÜCHER, that estimate must have been based on severely constrained resources.[60]

Organization, equipment, and training

The attacking MARNESCHUTZ units faced a more significant water barrier than in any of the previous four offensives, and the deliberate river crossing was vital to the success of the operation. On 21 June the Seventh Army issued the engineer orders for the crossing. All the necessary bridging material was to be pre-positioned as close as possible to the river. The initial crossings would be made with pontoon bridges, followed by the construction of footbridges. At least three pontoon bridges or ferries were required for each division sector. In some places it would be necessary to cut down the banks for the horses, but that could only be done on the night just before the start of the assault.[61]

A 5 July follow-on order specified that the bridge construction during the assault phase would be executed primarily by the engineers of the second- and third-line divisions. Because of transportation bottlenecks, the bridge trains were scheduled to arrive just before the start of the assault, which would require detailed and precise planning. The assault troops, meanwhile, rehearsed the crossing on the Vesle, near Fismes.[62]

Allied actions

Almost immediately after the failure of GNEISENAU the French started a series of local attacks between Soissons and Château-Thierry in an effort to push the Germans back. Between 6 June and 13 July the French launched some forty attacks against the west side of the Marne salient. Some of the attacks were as small as a few battalions; some were as large as several divisions. The French launched larger attacks on 15, 16, 18, 24, 25, 28, and 29 June, on 1 through 3 July, and again starting on 8 July. Their objective was to clear lanes in the high ground at Coeuvres against Soissons and in the woods at Villers-Cotterêts to secure the muddy area of the Savieres River (from Longpont via Faverolle to the Ourcq), which was a key obstacle for tanks.[63]

On 15 June Clemenceau, Pétain, and Weygand met at Foch's headquarters to consider the defense of Paris. Foch ordered Pétain to develop plans for an attack by the Tenth Army against the west side of the salient to seize the high ground west of Soissons. The Allied generalissimo clearly recognized Soissons for the communications and logistics choke point it was. If Soissons could be neutralized by Allied artillery fire, "any German offensive in the direction of Château-Thierry would be deprived of its lifeblood." On 20 June Mangin submitted his initial attack plan to Pétain.[64]

On 28 June the *Deuxième* Bureau estimated with great accuracy that the Germans would not be able to attack before 15 July. On 1 July Foch sent Pétain and Haig General Directive Number 4, concerning future operations. According to Foch, the two most dangerous directions the Germans could attack were toward Paris and Abbeville (Amiens). A major advance in any other direction would fail to produce any worthwhile operational results for the Germans. When the Germans did attack, therefore, the French would have the mission of covering Paris, and the British would cover Abbeville. Both armies had to be prepared to support each other.[65]

On 5 July Mangin recommended expanding the attack against the entire Château-Thierry salient. Three days later General Jean Degoutte's Sixth Army submitted an attack plan to support the Tenth Army by attacking the southern tip of the salient. At a meeting in Provins on 9 July, Foch ordered Pétain to coordinate the Tenth Army's attack with an attack by the Fifth Army against the eastern flank of the salient. Three days later Pétain issued his commander's intent for the coordinated attack against the entire Marne salient. The objective of the operation would be to eliminate the Château-Thierry pocket by lateral thrusts from the west and the east toward the high ground north of Fère-en-Tardenois.[66]

As Operation MARNESCHUTZ–REIMS was planned, the French Fifth and

Fourth Armies, west and east of Reims respectively, would bear the brunt of the German attack. The Tenth Army on the west side of the salient was not in the line of attack. Between the Tenth and the Fifth Armies, the center and right wing of the French Sixth Army was in the line of the attack. Initially French intelligence had estimated that the attack would be in the direction of Amiens, with the objective of separating the French and the British. As the indicators began to point to Reims, the *Deuxième* Bureau came to believe that the main attack would fall east of Reims, in the Champagne region. Finally, on 14 July French aerial observers reported large numbers of small parties moving in the German sector west of Reims, which now convinced French intelligence that the main blow would fall west of Reims.[67]

In the Fourth and Fifth Army sectors the French skillfully and secretly established defensive systems in great depth. The First (Red) Line consisted of thinly held observation posts. The Main Line of Defense (Yellow) was at least 2,000 meters from the German lines. Roughly two-thirds of the Allied infantry and three-quarters of the artillery were in this position. Behind the Yellow Line was the Second Line of Defense (Green). The reserves were to the rear of the Green Line. Overall, the defenses of the eastern-most Fourth Army were far better prepared than those of the Fifth Army.[68] With an accurate estimate of when and where the Germans would attack, Foch set 18 July as the counterattack date. Mangin's Tenth Army started to deploy on 14 July.[69]

German order of battle

French intelligence on 15 June estimated that the Germans had fifty-four divisions in reserve; sixty-one reserve divisions on 20 June; and seventy-five reserve divisions on 30 June—fifty-five of which were fresh.[70] While still holding a sizeable reserve in Flanders for the HAGEN attack, the Germans managed to assemble forty-eight divisions over the 119-kilometer front for MARNESCHUTZ–REIMS. The attacking divisions were organized into eleven corps, controlled by three armies. See Tables 10.1 and 10.2.

The MARNESCHUTZ–REIMS divisions, however, were not the same quality as those that executed MICHAEL, GEORGETTE, or even BLÜCHER. Allied intelligence rated ten of the twenty-seven divisions in the first line as 1st class; six as 2nd class; nine as 3rd class, and two as 4th class. Sixteen had fought in one of the previous offensives, and five had fought in two. Of the six completely fresh divisions, Allied intelligence rated four of them as 3rd class, and one each 2nd and 1st class.[71] The combat effectiveness ratings of Army Group German Crown Prince reported on 13 July were a bit more optimistic, but even that report showed the critical weakness of the divisions of the Ninth Army, which would absorb the main force of the Allied counterattack on 18 July (see Table 10.3).

Despite holding back a great deal of artillery in Flanders for HAGEN, by the start of the attack OHL had managed to mass 6,353 guns, with the Seventh Army getting about 45 percent of the total to support their difficult river-crossing operation (see Table 10.4). The Germans' overall tube superiority ratio,

Table 10.1 German divisions on 15 July 1918[72]

	First line	Second line	Third line	Total divisions	Sector width
*Seventh Army**	12	3	3 OHL 4 Army	22	33 km
First Army#	8	2	1 OHL 3 Army	14	54 km
Third Army§	7	1	2 OHL 2 Army	12	32 km
	27	6	6 OHL 9 Army	48	119 km

Source: *Der Weltkrieg*, Vol.14, Appendix 38i.

Notes
*Five of seven corps of the Seventh Army.
#Three of four corps of the First Army.
§Three corps of the Third Army.

Table 10.2 German Corps on 15 July 1918[73]

	(West to east)		
	Corps	Commander	Attacking on 15 July
Ninth Army		Eben	
	VII	Francois	No
	XXXIX	Staabs	No
	XIII	Watter	No
Seventh Army		Boehn	
	XXV Reserve	Winckler	No
	VIII	Schoeler	No
	XXIII Reserve	Kathen	Yes
	VIII Reserve	Wichura	Yes
	IV Reserve	Conta	Yes
	LXV	Schmettow	Yes
	VI Reserve	Borne	Yes
First Army		Mudra	
	XV	Ilse	No
	VII Reserve	Lindequist	Yes
	XIV	Gontard	Yes
	XXIV Reserve	Langer	Yes
Third Army		Einem	
	XII	Nidda	Yes
	I Bavarian	Enders	Yes
	XVI	Hohenvorn	Yes

Source: *Der Weltkrieg*, Vol.14, Appendix 38i.

Table 10.3 Reported combat effectiveness of German divisions 13 July 1918[74]

	Combat ready	2 to 3 weeks' rest and training	3 to 4 weeks' rest and training	Capable of holding positions
Ninth Army	3	3	8	2
Seventh Army	20	3	3	1
First Army	9	2	3	0

Source: Army Group German Crown Prince, Unnumbered Document, (13 July 1918), General Service Schools, *The German Offensive of July 15, 1918 (Marne Source Book)*, (Fort Leavenworth, Kansas: 1923), pp.402–403.

Table 10.4 Guns supporting MARNESCHUTZ–REIMS[75]

	Field	Heavy	Super-heavy	Total guns	Trench mortars
Seventh Army	1,908	895	4	2,807	?
First Army	1,158	561	32	1,751	?
Third Army	1,196	591	8	1,795	?
	4,262	2,047	44	6,353	2,200

Source: *Der Weltkrieg*, Vol.14, Appendices 38i, 39e.

however, was only 2:1, the lowest of any of the five major attacks. Despite their significant supply problems, the Germans did muster about 900 aircraft for the operation.

Allied order of battle

From east of Château-Thierry to east of Reims, the main German attack zone, the Allies had thirty-six divisions (including three American and two Italian) under the right wing of the French Sixth Army, and the French Fifth and Fourth Armies. West of Château-Thierry the main Allied counterattack force consisted of twenty-four infantry and three cavalry divisions (including four American), under the French Tenth Army and the left wing of the Sixth. To the rear of the Fourth and Fifth Armies, the general reserve consisted of the French Ninth Army, with ten infantry and three cavalry divisions. The ground forces were supported by forty-two French squadrons and nine British squadrons.[76] See Table 10.5.

Execution (15 July–3 August)

15 July At 0110 hours the Germans started firing the artillery preparation (Table 10.6) and the pioneer troops of the Seventh Army started assembling the pontoon bridges for the crossing. On the west side of Reims the preparation took

Table 10.5 Allied order of battle in the MARNESCHUTZ–REIMS sectors[77]

	First-line divisions	Second-line divisions	Third-line divisions	Heavy guns	Total guns	Sector width
Sixth Army*	3	3	2	?	?	25 km
Fifth Army#	8	5	0	789	1,440	40 km
Fourth Army§	7	6	2	?	?	54 km
	18	14	4	1,560	3,080	119 km

Source: *Der Weltkrieg*, Vol.14, Appendices 38i, 39e.

Notes
*Two corps of Sixth Army.
#Three corps of Fifth Army.
§Three corps of Fourth Army.

a slightly different form, to accommodate the Seventh Army's requirements to move into position for the river crossing. During the long fourth phase, the Seventh Army troops started crossing the river, and then the creeping barrage started from the far bank. German artillery fired 4.5 million rounds on the first day of the attack, including their first large-scale use of artillery-delivered smoke. Gas, however, made up only one-eighth of the total rounds fired, down significantly from the one-third average of the earlier attacks.[78]

Table 10.6 MARNESCHUTZ–REIMS artillery preparations[79]

Phase	Duration	Effect
First and Third Armies		
1	10 minutes	Surprise saturation with blue cross and high explosive.
2	75 minutes	Reinforced counter-battery fire with maximum gas.
3	90 minutes	IKA attacks infantry targets.
		AKA continues counter-battery fire.
		FEKA attacks deep targets.
4	15 minutes	Reinforced counter-battery fire.
5	30 minutes	IKA attacks close infantry targets.
		AKA continues counter-battery fire.
		FEKA attacks deep targets.
Seventh Army		
1	10 minutes	Surprise saturation fire.
2	60 minutes	Reinforced counter-battery fire.
3	30 minutes	Destruction fire against deep targets.
		AKA continues counter-battery fire.
4	120 minutes	IKA attacks close infantry targets.
		AKA continues counter-battery fire.
		FEKA attacks deep targets.

Source: Army Group German Crown Prince, Ia/Art 12968, (26 June 1918), Bundesarchiv/Militärarchiv, File PH 3/260. AOK 1, Ia/Art 2750/1113, (29 June 1918), Bundesarchiv/Militärarchiv, File PH 3/261.

Meanwhile, on the night of 14 July a French trench raid had netted twenty-seven German prisoners who divulged the attack was scheduled to commence the following morning, with the artillery preparation starting at 0110 hours. At 2400 hours the French artillery started an increased program of harassing and interdicting fire. At 0120 hours, ten minutes after the German opening time, the French artillery started a full-scale counter-preparation.[80] The fire was far more intense than anything the Germans could have thought possible. The I Bavarian Corps War Diary noted: "The activity of the enemy artillery during the period of preparation was uniformly strong, altogether contrary to previous experience in our offensive operations."[81] Since the French were outnumbered in guns they decided to forgo counter-battery fire and concentrate their counter-preparation on the German infantry. As a result, the German guns executed their own preparation relatively unhampered.[82]

At 0450 hours the German infantry moved forward behind a double creeping barrage, moving at the rate of forty to fifty minutes per thousand meters. The wind, however, was too strong and quickly dissipated the German gas. On the extreme left of the attack, the troops of the Third Army advancing into a strong wind from the south had to attack in gas masks.[83] Unlike the previous attacks, the French artillery continued to hit the German infantry as they moved forward. On each side of Reims the attackers encountered different situations.

East of Reims the First and Third Armies faced far heavier French artillery fire than anticipated, but almost no resistance on the ground. Despite taking stiff casualties, the German infantry advanced rapidly—at first. About 0730 hours the creeping barrage reached its maximum range and lifted. The attackers found themselves facing a fully manned zone defense that had hardly been touched by the preparation or the barrage. The German artillery fire had struck mostly empty ground.[84]

By not firing on the German guns the French artillery had taken a calculated risk that paid off. Long before the start of the attack the Germans had acquired most of the French divisional artillery in the line. But just prior to the attack the French divisional artilleries were reinforced by additional units that moved up in secrecy. Once in position they used meteorological calculations rather than registering. The 43rd Division's reinforcing artillery, for example, occupied their positions on 4 July and remained silent until the Germans attacked. When the attack came the 43rd Division's organic three direct support battalions and one general support battalion lost 25 percent of their guns to German counter-fire. Only two out of the division's nine reinforcing batteries took any German artillery fire at all.[85]

When the German First and Third Armies ran into the solid wall of French resistance they immediately called for additional artillery support. The fire requests had to be carried back by messenger and took hours to reach the guns. By that time many German batteries were already displacing forward and could not find suitable firing locations. Those units that were still in position and had the necessary range (heavies and super-heavies for the most part) were hesitant to fire based on requests that were several hours old. They feared with much justification that any subsequent changes in the tactical situation would greatly increase the risk of firing on their own troops.

As the advancing German direct support artillery units got closer to the front, they started to come under heavy fire from the French artillery. A large portion of the French guns occupied high ground 3,000 to 5,000 meters behind the main line of contact. From that position the moving German batteries were easy prey. Even though some of the heavier German guns were still in firing position, they were about 9,000 meters on the other side of the line of contact—too far back to reach the French guns.[86] The First Army War Diary recorded:

> Our batteries, which after the first infantry preparation followed up promptly, came under strong enemy artillery fire when crossing the shell crater situation on the open high ground of the Champagne hills. These batteries were compelled to unlimber under unfavorable conditions and suffered heavy losses. This deprived the infantry of artillery support.[87]

By noon the attack east of Reims had become pretty much bogged down. At 1300 hours the Third Army ordered a resumption of the attack, but that effort too ground to a halt within an hour. At 1530 hours the First Army also ordered resumption of the attack, but with little result. Only two divisions reached the Vesle near Prunay.[88]

West of Reims the French counter-preparation disrupted the Seventh Army's river crossing. Right from the start the French fire separated the attackers from their creeping barrage. The infantry stalled, but the barrage kept moving. The French fire played havoc with the bridging operation. Materiel failed to arrive at the river in the proper order and created traffic jams. As the bridges finally started going up, far behind schedule and under heavy fire, groups of infantry got across the Marne in small boats. For the most part they landed in the wrong locations and had little fire support because they could not get their artillery across.[89]

By mid-morning the Germans established a shallow bridgehead on either side of Dormans. The XXIII Reserve, VIII Reserve, and IV Reserve Corps crossed the river, and the LXV Corps north of the river pushed to the east. By noon most of the Seventh Army's forces reached the French second positions.[90] Although OHL wanted to increase the pressure on both sides of the Marne, the Allies subjected the German forces in the bridgehead to withering artillery fire and air attack. The heavy air strikes killed the Seventh Army's chief of engineers as he was observing bridge construction on the river.[91]

By that night the Germans had some six divisions on the south bank of the Marne, but hardly any artillery. The bridgehead was about twenty kilometers wide and five kilometers deep. (See Map 7.) At that point the French artillery, working in conjunction with their air force, started concentrating on the bridges to cut off the Germans on the south bank. By then it was clear that the German attack was going nowhere. As Hindenburg laconically noted, "The results certainly did not correspond to our high hopes."[92] There was, however, widespread agreement on what had gone wrong. The First Army War Diary recorded:

The general impression prevailed in the evening of the first day of battle that the enemy, in expectancy of our attack which had been communicated to him by prisoners as to the very day and hour, had organized his infantry and artillery in depth.[93]

In a phone conversation with Kuhl, Ludendorff complained of the poor results. Kuhl advised him to continue the First and Third Army attacks, but Ludendorff did not think he could risk the additional casualties.[94] OHL ordered the continuation of the operation, but with the more modest objective of cutting off the Reims salient—which had been Wetzell's original proposal. Incredibly, however, OHL did order the start of the planned transfer of forces north for HAGEN. Ludendorff still thought he could use the MARNESCHUTZ–REIMS operation to scare the Allies into shifting their reserves from Flanders.[95] The Seventh Army was ordered to continue the advance east along both banks of the Marne. The First and Third Armies had the mission of launching holding attacks to pin the Allied units to their front, and prevent them from being shifted against the Seventh Army.[96]

The Seventh Army, meanwhile, still believed it could accomplish its objectives, and ordered its corps to resume the attack in full force. According to the entry in its War Diary, "after the enemy second position had finally been taken, the attack could flow along smoothly as if we had not encountered any regular defense formed in great depth."[97] An entry in the War Diary of Army Group German Crown Prince was nowhere nearly as optimistic:

> It is now clear that the objective of the operation—to cut off the enemy in the Reims valley through a junction of the Seventh and First Armies in the vicinity of Epernay—cannot be achieved. We have to be satisfied with minor success.[98]

On the Allied side of the line, Pétain's initial reaction was to order Fayolle to place Mangin's attack on hold. Foch, however, told Pétain to launch Mangin's attack as planned. That afternoon, Foch and Haig met at Mouchy-le-Châtel, and Haig agreed to send his XXII Corps as reinforcements. Foch also suggested to Haig that he develop an attack east and southeast of Amiens. That would later become the 8 August attack, the "Black Day of the German Army."[99]

16 July   Just after midnight Army Group German Crown Prince ordered the Seventh Army to resume the advance on both sides of the Marne in the direction of Epernay. The heights at Igny le Jard, Boursault, and Pourcy were the next objective.[100] In the Third Army sector, meanwhile, the night had been relatively quiet. Einem issued orders at 0200 hours for the right wing of the army to advance in support of the First Army's attack. The rest of the army sector was supposed to go over to the defensive.[101]

On the second day of the operation the Germans made progress only north of the Marne. By the end of the day the Third Army terminated the attack of its right-wing XII Corps.[102] Now the best the Germans could hope to achieve was to cut off Reims at the base of the salient just south of the town.[103] The First and Third Armies ceased all offensive operations by the end of the day.[104] At 1945 hours Army Group German Crown Prince ordered the Seventh Army to halt its attacks south of the Marne, but to continue attacking the next day with their two corps north of the Marne against the Reims hills.[105]

Confident that the German offensive had been stopped, Pétain now believed that Mangin's counterattack could proceed as planned. About midday, the French resumed heavy artillery and air attacks against the German bridges. Three French divisions and elements of the American 28th Division counterattacked the western end of the bridgehead and drove the Germans back one mile.[106]

17 July   Early on the morning of 17 July OHL came to the conclusion that the MARNESCHUTZ–REIMS offensive had to be halted. The city of Reims, however, still had to be cut off and taken. A few hours later Army Group German Crown Prince issued the orders to continue the advance with the limited objective of taking Reims. The Seventh Army was to take the ridge west of Ville Dommange, and the First Army was to push its right wing south and turn west. Simultaneously, the First Army would also conduct a supporting attack against Fort de la Pompelle east of the city. The attacks would most likely start on 21 July. Almost immediately, OHL started shifting much of the reinforcing artillery away from the Seventh Army to support the planned attacks on Reims.[107]

That afternoon Ludendorff went to the headquarters of the First Army in Rethel to discuss the continued attack by the Seventh Army toward Reims, supported by the First Army attack toward the southwest. Ludendorff was dismayed when the First Army chief of staff told him that it would take several days of preparation "to continue even this purely local attack."[108] Following the meeting with Ludendorff, the Third Army issued the orders for all its units to go on the defensive.[109] The First Army issued the orders for VII Reserve, XIV, and XXIV Reserve Corps to go over to the defensive. The XV Corps in front of Reims, which previously had not attacked, was ordered to prepare to attack in conjunction with the Seventh Army. The VII Reserve Corps was ordered to prepare to seize Fort de la Pompelle.[110]

Immediately after the meeting in Rethel, Ludendorff left for Rupprecht's headquarters at Tournai for a planning meeting for HAGEN.[111] That same day, Lieutenant Colonel Hermann Mertz von Quirnheim, a General Staff officer in the OHL Operations Section, wrote in his diary: "I am convinced at this moment that neither Ludendorff nor Wetzell knows what further action they must take."[112] That afternoon, Lieutenant Colonel Walter Reinhardt, Seventh Army chief of staff, went forward to conduct a personal reconnaissance. At 1730 hours he telephoned his counterpart at Army Group German Crown Prince to recommend in the strongest terms that the three corps south of the Marne be pulled back immediately. According to Reinhardt, 70 percent of the bridge trains had been destroyed by Allied artillery fire and the Seventh Army could not continue to hold the south bank. Army Group German Crown Prince endorsed Reinhardt's assessment and forwarded it to OHL.[113]

At 1930 hours Boehn, acting on his own, halted the attacks and ordered the Seventh Army to go on the defensive.[114] By the night of the 17th the entire length of the German line was in a state of chaos. The Seventh Army's units south of the Marne were effectively cut off. Most of the bridges were down and French artillery and aircraft mercilessly pounded away at the trapped units. The First Army, meanwhile, desperately tried to organize the attack to cut off Reims.

About midnight OHL finally agreed to a withdrawal by echelon of the bridgehead.[115] The Seventh Army then issued the warning order to prepare for the withdrawal. The artillery minus the accompanying batteries wound cross back over on the night of the 18th and 19th, with the reserves coming back on the night of the 19th and 20th.[116] Apparently still not anticipating a major French attack, OHL sent a message to the Ninth Army stating:

> After the conclusion of the fighting near Reims, it will be necessary to affect a regrouping of the forces along the entire front of the group of armies. Not until then will it be possible to determine how the Ninth Army can be given positive assistance. For the time being, it is impossible to bring up fresh divisions, on account of the railroad situation alone.[117]

18 July During the night of the 17th German troops in the area of Cutry, southwest of Soissons, clearly heard the sounds of tank engines from the Allied lines. About 0415 in the morning of the 18th two French deserters revealed that the Allied attack would come between 0500 and 0600 hours. The information came too late to disseminate it up and then back down the chain of command across the sector. At 0535 hours the French Tenth Army attacked without artillery preparation (Map 8). The French Sixth Army launched its attack following a ninety-minute artillery preparation. More than 2,000 Allied guns fired along a forty-kilometer front to mask the exact attack sector.[118]

The Tenth Army forces came out of the wooded area of Villers-Cotterêts, advancing on Soissons. The Allied counterattack struck between the Aisne and the Marne, against the Ninth Army and the left flank of the Seventh Army. In that sector the Germans had ten divisions in the first line—of which only two were fully combat-capable—and six divisions in the second line. The sixteen German divisions were hit by twenty-four Allied divisions.[119] Mangin's Tenth Army had ten divisions in the first line—including the U.S. 1st and 2nd Divisions—and six infantry divisions and a cavalry corps in the second line. The Tenth Army was supported by 346 tanks, 1,545 guns, and 581 aircraft. Degoutte's Sixth Army had seven divisions in the first line—including one American—and one division in the second line. It also had on-call priority for three more of the huge American divisions. The Sixth Army was supported by 147 tanks, 588 guns, and 562 aircraft. Farther back, the Allies had ten more divisions—including two British—and 918 guns and approximately 800 aircraft

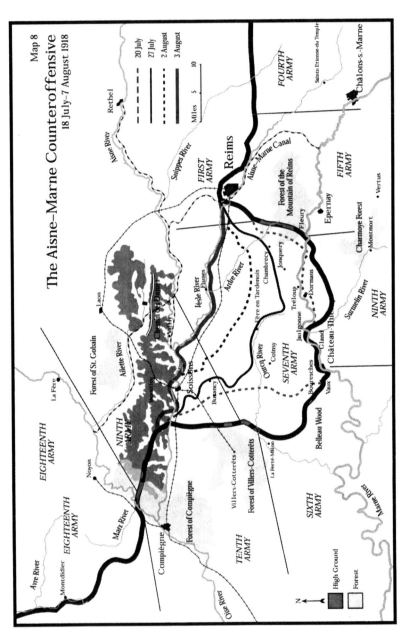

Map 8 The Aisne–Marne counteroffensive (source: Map by Donald S. Frazier, Ph.D., Abilene, Texas, based on sketches and notes provided by David T. Zabecki).

in army or army group reserve. Since the attack came in the same sector that OHL had stripped of most of its reinforcing artillery just the day before, the Allies had a tube superiority ratio of 2.3:1.[120]

Ludendorff, meanwhile, was at Tournai to plan the final details for HAGEN. He opened the conference by dismissing all the indicators that the French were massing for a counterattack from the forest of Villers-Cotterêts.

> Before we start our discussions on Operation HAGEN, I want to quell any rumors that the French have major reserves in the Villers-Cotterêts forest. OHL has a reliable intelligence system. The enemy cannot possibly have combat-ready reserves available. We know the casualty rates and decreases in strength in the French and British units. OHL can state categorically that any such rumors are unfounded.[121]

Almost as soon as he made those remarks the reports started coming in that the Allies were attacking in force. Ludendorff immediately ordered the 5th Infantry Division from the OHL reserve to be committed northeast of Soissons. Ludendorff ended the meeting and immediately returned to OHL, "in the greatest state of nervous tension."[122] Arriving about 1400 hours, he was met at the train station at Avesnes by Hindenburg, who briefed him on the overall situation. A few hours earlier OHL had ordered the Seventh Army to establish the main line of resistance as Soissons–Hartennes–Latilly—high ground north of Château-Thierry. At the same time the Seventh Army was ordered to organize a fallback line farther to the rear, but the divisions were not to retire to that line until so ordered.[123]

Late in the morning the French attack south of the Aisne started to run out of steam. At 1430 hours OHL ordered Army Group Crown Prince Rupprecht to transfer immediately two of its HAGEN attack divisions to Army Group German Crown Prince. The same order halted most of the transport then in progress for HAGEN, and placed all the resources in transit at the disposal of the Seventh Army.[124] About 1800 hours Army Group German Crown Prince transferred command of the Ninth Army's left-wing XIII Corps to the Seventh Army. At the same time, the command of the Seventh Army's left-wing VI Reserve Corps was transferred to the First Army.[125]

By the end of the day the Allies had advanced seven kilometers on a front of some twenty kilometers. The plan, however, had called for an advance of twelve to fourteen kilometers. French tank losses were greater than 80 percent, mostly from artillery direct fire.[126] Nonetheless, the German situation had become critical. The Soissons–Laon rail line was now within range of the Allied guns—including the only broad-gage bridge over the Aisne in German hands. By that afternoon the Allies were able to bring the Soissons–Laon line under fire at Crouy. By the end of the day the Allies were only thirteen kilometers away from the new spur from Sermoise to Missy, which was the rail connection through the Aisne valley to Fère-en-Tardenois.[127] Hindenburg summed up the situation nicely in his post-war memoirs.

Owing to hostile artillery fire from every side, the conduct of operations in the salient, which was still very deep, was extremely difficult. The enemy artillery had the critical section of our railway east of Soissons under fire. A regular hail of enemy airplane bombs descended upon it day and night. We were compelled to detrain the arriving reinforcements and reliefs in the neighborhood of Laon and far away from the salient. They then proceeded to the battlefield by forced marches, which took days.[128]

19 July   The Allies resumed the attack along the line at 0500 hours on 19 July. OHL was still trying to salvage HAGEN, but by the second day of the Allied counterattack the Germans had withdrawn four attack divisions from Rupprecht's Army Group. The situation on the Seventh Army's right was deteriorating rapidly. The lines of the XIII, XXV Reserve, and VIII Corps had all but caved in and those units were in the process of withdrawing to the general line from Billy to the high ground east of Courchamps. To shore up the situation the Seventh Army inserted the headquarters of the XVII Corps between XXV Reserve and XIII Corps.[129] Army Group German Crown Prince, meanwhile, ordered the Ninth Army to hold its forward-most positions.[130]

The fragile and shallow rail network hampered the German ability to shift reinforcements to the Seventh Army sector. Rail movement was all but impossible. Land march took too much time. The only workable alternative was to move the troops as far forward as possible by truck. Nonetheless, the troops arrived without their artillery and heavy equipment, and they were still exhausted from having to close the final distance on foot.[131]

About noon, Hindenburg uncharacteristically inserted himself into the operational planning process by suggesting that all the German reserves in Flanders should be moved south immediately, and committed across the Aisne against the left flank of the Allied attack. Ludendorff brushed off the idea. Later that evening Hindenburg brought it up again. In a fit of frustration Ludendorff dismissed the idea as "nonsense." At that point, Hindenburg called Ludendorff into his office, presumably to remind him who the commander was. Although Hindenburg did mention the basic operational idea, neither of them mentioned in his memoirs the blow-up between the two.[132]

Holding back the Allied attacks on its right flank, the Seventh Army continued to withdraw its forces across the Marne. But it was clear that the German position in the Marne salient would become increasingly untenable even after the evacuation of the south bank. About 1600 hours Army Group German Crown Prince ordered the Seventh Army to initiate reconnaissance operations in case it became necessary to pull back along the entire front. At the same time the order stressed that every voluntary withdrawal would have to be approved by higher headquarters.[133] About the same time, OHL sent a message requesting recommendations from the armies on a larger-scale withdrawal in the event of more major Allied attacks.[134] The Seventh Army's War Diary summed up their situation by the end of 19 July:

Even if the initial push of the attack has been stopped, resistance to continued attacks will have to be maintained until such time as the troops, equipment, and supplies have been withdrawn over the Vesle. This means in terms of the artillery of the approximately 40 divisions a total length of march of about 600 kilometers. If the defense, already weak and undermined, does not hold off the enemy during the withdrawal, a catastrophe could still occur.[135]

20 July   On the third day of the Allied counterattack the French Fifth and Ninth Armies joined the counterattack and hit the Germans on the eastern flank of the Marne salient. In back-and-forth fighting the Germans only managed to halt the attackers at the main line of resistance. The preparations for the First Army's attack against the Reims hills south of Virgny and against Fort de la Pompelle east of Reims—scheduled for 21 July—were completely disrupted and had to be postponed. The Germans were now defending along the entire Marne salient, from the Aisne almost to Reims.[136] Estimating that the next attack in its sector would come north of the Aisne, the German Ninth Army ordered a defense-in-depth and requested the insertion of two additional divisions into its line.[137]

That day Foch sent a message to Pétain reminding him that the objective of the operation was not merely to push the Germans back, but to cut off and destroy the German forces south of the Aisne and the Vesle. Ludendorff, meanwhile, had summoned to OHL General Fritz von Lossberg, chief of staff of the Fourth Army, and the German Army's acknowledged master of defensive operations. When Lossberg arrived at OHL he found Ludendorff in a near-panic state and openly blaming Wetzell for the German Army's failures. After studying the situation, Lossberg recommended an immediate general withdrawal behind the Aisne and the Vesle by the Seventh and Ninth Armies, to be followed three weeks later by a pull-back of all German forces on both sides of the Somme. That, of course, would have meant giving up the territory won at such a high price in the previous offensives. Lossberg also recommended that HAGEN be launched later in a reduced form, but that the withdrawals should be made without consideration of conserving supplies for HAGEN.

Ludendorff was growing increasingly despondent and talked about resigning. Lossberg talked him out of it, but later regretted doing so. Ludendorff ordered Lossberg to visit the Seventh and Ninth Armies and report back to him. Lossberg left for the front under the mistaken impression that Ludendorff would act immediately on his recommendations. Both army groups and Wetzell concurred with Lossberg's recommendations. Rupprecht believed that the turning point of the war had been reached and that the German Army had no choice but to go on the defensive. Ludendorff, however, had no intention of acting on Lossberg's recommendations.[138]

The Seventh Army, meanwhile, completed the last phase of the withdrawal across the Marne. With the flanks holding firm, the center pulled back. The Seventh Army's War Diary that day included the following wildly optimistic entry: "July 20th was a day of battles on a very large scale and a complete defensive victory for the Seventh Army."[139]

21 July–7 August   By dawn on 21 July the last elements of the Seventh Army were back on the north bank of the Marne, and by the end of the day the Allies recaptured Château-Thierry. With Soissons under Allied artillery fire, the supply situation inside the salient became impossible to sustain, and the Germans were slowly forced to the conclusion that they had no alternative but to withdraw. On 22 July Ludendorff tentatively agreed to a retirement, but only to the general line that ran through Fère-en-Tardenois. OHL also shortened the span of control of Crown Prince Wilhelm's Army Group by transferring command of the Eighteenth Army to Rupprecht's Army Group.[140]

For the next two weeks the Allies tried to cut off the German forces in the huge salient formed by Operation BLÜCHER, but the Germans managed to mount their trademark tenacious defense. On 28 July OHL ordered the withdrawal back across the Vesle.[141] By the afternoon of 2 August the final German forces pulled out of Soissons and all the Seventh Army's units completed crossing the Vesle that night. On 3 August the final elements of the Ninth Army withdrew to the north bank of the Aisne, and the Seventh Army blew all the remaining bridges over the Vesle.[142]

The Germans had been pushed back to roughly their line of advance at the end of the first day of the BLÜCHER offensive, but they had conducted a skillful fighting withdrawal that frustrated the Allied objective of cutting off and trapping large German forces in the pocket. On the other hand, the German Army was now at a serious operational disadvantage and completely off balance. Furthermore, German intelligence at that point completely failed to anticipate the Allies' next move. On 5 August Army Group German Crown Prince sent the Operations Section at OHL an assessment of the Allies' most probable courses of action.

> The enemy fully knows that his offensive will come to a stand on the Aisne. If he desires not to lose the initiative he has just gained, he will as soon as possible start a new attack with a more distant objective. That distant objective would be a shock against the Ninth Army. He could press against the flank of the Aisne position and simultaneously threaten the Eighteenth Army, which is bent forward. The other possibility, to envelop the front of the Seventh Army, lies in an attack against the First Army. According to reports from our agents, the enemy intends to attack via Reims in the direction of Berry au Bac.[143]

Both estimates were wrong. Just three days later the Allies launched their surprise attack on the German positions east of Amiens. On 7 August the Germans had sixty-seven divisions in reserve, only thirty-nine of them fresh. The Allies had seventy-seven infantry and ten cavalry divisions in reserve—and that number was growing.[144]

Assessment

The results

Although none of the 1918 offensives proved to be an operational success for the Germans, MARNESCHUTZ–REIMS was the first one that was a complete tactical failure as well. Fifty-nine Allied divisions (including seven American, four British, and two Italian) defeated sixty-five German divisions. In terms of raw numbers, the Germans inflicted more casualties than they sustained between 15 July and 3 August. The Allied casualties, dead, wounded, missing, and captured, amounted to 160,000.[145] The Germans estimated their own total casualties at about 110,000. But the Allied losses were being made up rapidly by American replacements, and the Germans also lost some 600 artillery pieces that they could not immediately replace.[146] Operationally, the Germans failed to take the rail center at Reims; they lost the one at Soissons; and the Allies regained control of the Paris–Châlons rail line. By that point, however, it made little difference, because the Germans had been pushed almost completely out of the salient they had taken during Operation BLÜCHER. Before much longer they would be pushed back across the Chemin de Dames as well.

How did it happen? Why was MARNESCHUTZ–REIMS such a failure compared to the other four offensives? (Even Operation GNEISENAU had been a minor tactical success.) In his analysis of the offensives conducted for the Reichstag after the war, Kuhl wrote: "The principal reason for our reverse must therefore be ascribed to the failure to achieve surprise."[147] While that answer is correct as far as it goes, there is much more behind it.

Predictability of the German tactics

The Allies had been stunned when the Germans used their new attack tactics for the first time on a large scale on the Western Front during the Cambrai counterattack in November 1917. The technical and tactical artillery innovations of the Germans were especially devastating against a linear, rigid, forward defense. Even as late as Operation GNEISENAU the Allies still made the mistake of packing far too many of their forces into their forward-most lines. By Operation MARNESCHUTZ–REIMS a little more than a month later, they had finally learned their hard lesson.

After the war the failure of MARNESCHUTZ–REIMS became a topic of long-running debate in German military circles. Bruchmüller in particular came under criticism for his handling of the artillery. In the June 1921 issue of the journal *Militär-Wochenblatt*, retired Major General Hans Waechter blasted Bruchmüller, calling him rigid and dogmatic. Waechter laid the blame for the failure of the entire attack on Bruchmüller, because he had used the same fire-support tactics for the fifth time in a row. Two months later in the same journal General Friedrich von Bernhardi came to Bruchmüller's defense. Bernhardi chided Waechter for merely criticizing Bruchmüller's plan, without suggesting what could have been done differently. Bernhardi dismissed the whole argument as a simple case of sour grapes, pointing out that Waechter had actually been a subordinate divisional artillery commander under Bruchmüller.[148] In his own defense Bruchmüller wrote: "No one objected to the contemplated scheme [of fire] for the attack, either verbally or in writing, and no one proposed a different plan."[149]

Kuhl was a staunch Bruchmüller supporter in this debate. Writing in the *Deutsches Offiziersblatt*, Kuhl defended the high degree of centralization in Bruchmüller's system as necessary for massing. But General Alfred Ziethen, who was generally a Bruchmüller supporter, later criticized the high degree of centralization as not being flexible enough to react to drastic changes in the tactical situation.[150]

The most severe condemnation came in the October 1925 issue of *Artilleristische-Rundschau*. Lieutenant General Richard von Berendt, who had been the Seventeenth Army artillery commander during Operation MICHAEL, echoed much of Waechter's earlier arguments, and then concluded that MARNESCHUTZ–REIMS had failed because of Bruchmüller's mishandling of the artillery—and the loss of that battle cost Germany the war. Wilhelm Marx, who was then a lieutenant colonel in the post-war Reichswehr, came to the defense of his old boss in the following issue. Taking the longer view of things, and including the experiences on the Eastern Front, Marx pointed out that Bruchmüller's techniques were being used for at least the thirteenth time by the MARNESCHUTZ–REIMS attack. They were well known by the time of Operation BLÜCHER, yet they worked during that attack. The reason for the failure in July 1918, then, must lay elsewhere. Marx gave the causes as the failure to maintain security, combined with the overall weakness of Germany's strategic position by mid-July.[151]

The debate continued almost up to the eve of World War II. Writing in *Der K.B. Feld-Artillerist* in 1936, Ferdinand Meier noted that in the Third Army there was a strong suspicion that the French were positioning their artillery in depth. As a result, four days before the start of the attack the Third Army issued orders for its own counter-artillery batteries to attack the French guns in depth. That caused a last-minute repositioning of German guns and shifting of ammunition forward—all of which could not have helped the Germans maintain secrecy.[152]

The truth probably contains elements of all these arguments. There can be little doubt that by July 1918 the Allies had finally developed enough of an understanding of the overall German attack techniques to begin to take effective counter-measures. The German Army even anticipated this to a degree. The German Third Army wargamed the possibility of a French withdrawal from their front lines, but gave the event only a 10 percent probability.[153]

Between 15 and 17 July Ludendorff had many telephone conversations with the subordinate chiefs of staff, particularly Kuhl, trying to come up with some new way the Germans could modify their offensive tactics to again take the Allies by surprise. On 22 July OHL issued a set of lessons learned from the recent debacle. The list included the need for a follow-on phase of reinforced counter-battery fire as soon as the infantry started their assault and the need to establish a positive technique to give the infantry control over the creeping barrage.[154] These, however, were little more than minor modifications to the existing tactics. A strong artillery preparation was the only reliable means the Germans had of achieving the initial disruption of the enemy's defensive positions. Without tanks in large numbers, the Germans had neither the speed nor the alternate means of firepower. Ludendorff at that point finally began to understand the seriousness of the lack of tanks.[155] Or as Kuhl later wrote, "At the time, we had found no new methods, nor were we able to adopt any new means of warfare. Unfortunately, we were in no position to obtain surprise effect with the aid of a tank attack."[156]

Allied reaction

Failure to achieve surprise is only fatal if the enemy exploits it properly, and this time the Allies did. By July 1918 the French had finally mastered the defense-in-depth tactics that were the basis of Pétain's Directive of December 1917. Because of the favorable terrain east of Reims, the French defense-in-depth there was far more effective, and essentially stopped the REIMS portion of the operation cold.

Anticipating the German move, Foch also shifted eight divisions from Flanders to counter the threat. The Allies' defense-in-depth allowed them to hold off the forty-eight German divisions with only thirty-six. That economy of force then allowed them to build up their counterattack force to twenty-four divisions, against only ten divisions on the German right flank.[157] The French counterattack force outnumbered the Germans in sector approximately two to one in infantry, and more than that in artillery. The Allies had air superiority and a powerful tank force against no German tanks. The attack was perfectly timed to strike the German attack precisely at its culminating point. The forward momentum of the MARNESCHUTZ portion of the attack had been exhausted, yet defense was not set. Off balance, the Germans were unable to shift smoothly to a retrograde movement. The Allied counterattack was even more critical because of the shallow proximity of Soissons and its vital rail junction. In the end, however, the counterattack never did achieve its primary objective of cutting off and destroying large German forces in the Marne pocket.

German failure to anticipate the Allied counterattack

The Germans did not completely fail to anticipate the Allied counterattack against the Ninth Army and the right flank of the Seventh Army. The indicators were there and they were strong. The Germans worked hard at ignoring and explaining them away. As early as 29 June an order from Army Group German Crown Prince to the Seventh Army stated: "We must count on the French continuing their attacks against the west front of the Seventh Army prior to and during MARNESCHUTZ."[158] The following day the Seventh Army responded with the assessment that the French would probably not strip their other sectors to muster the force for a large-scale attack. Seventh Army also noted that the most vulnerable area would be the vicinity of Soissons, which would threaten all lines of communications for the entire army.[159] On 1 July an OHL order even noted: "In case of enemy attacks on a large scale, we will have to reckon with numerous tank squadrons."[160]

On 9 July the Seventh Army's War Diary recorded intelligence reports indicating that the French would attempt to cut off the German salient between the Aisne and the Marne by simultaneous attacks on both flanks. The French national day of 14 July was seen as the most likely date of the attack. The following day the Seventh Army War Diary noted French efforts to seize good observation points that would support an offensive in the Soissons–Château-Thierry sector. The Ninth Army also reported that large-scale attacks were imminent in its sector.[161]

On 10 July Ludendorff telephoned Army Group German Crown Prince to order the formation of an integrated defense with the Eighteenth and Ninth Armies, and the right wing of the Seventh Army. As the indicators of a major Allied attack grew stronger, Army Group German Crown Prince issued orders on 11 July to the Ninth and Seventh Armies to assume defensive positions in the threatened sectors and to counter the enemy's infantry and artillery "with full power." The Ninth Army was supposed to weaken its right wing substantially in favor of the sector south of the Aisne.[162]

Once the German attack started on 15 July, the possibility of an Allied counterattack seemed to fade from the minds of the German commanders. That day Eben, the commanding general of the Ninth Army, withdrew the request for reinforcements he had made on 11 July. He noted: "The situation has since relaxed. The counterattack no longer seems probable. I therefore withdraw my request for four fresh divisions."[163] Army Group German Crown Prince agreed that there was no immediate danger in front of the Ninth Army for the moment. By 16 July, Ludendorff felt confirmed in his opinion that MARNESCHUTZ–REIMS had tied down enough of the French forces in order to relieve pressure on the front between the Oise and the Marne. During the meeting in Rethel on the afternoon of 17 July, Ludendorff told Army Group German Crown Prince to build up reserves rapidly for possible commitment in support of the Eighteenth Army and the right wing of the Ninth Army. At that point, therefore, he saw less of a threat to the sector directly east of Villers-Cotterêts than to the sector farther to the north.[164]

Nonetheless, there were still General Staff officers raising concerns about the indicators of a French counterattack from the forest of Villers-Cotterêts. Among them were General Hermann von Francois and Major Ludwig Beck.[165] For the most part, however, the Germans were genuinely caught by surprise when the Allied blow fell. On the night of 18 July the War Diary of the Seventh Army recorded an amazingly accurate assessment of the situation:

The enemy was fortunate in a certain sense in attaining operational surprise, although the concentration of his assault army in the woods of Villers-Cotterêts had not been concealed from us. However, it appeared now that we did not perceive the numbers of his troops to their fullest extent. And, in addition, we expected from our successful advance on Reims that it would compel French General Headquarters to commit the forces it had intended for the west front of the Seventh Army and the southern sector of the Ninth Army, immediately against the salient of Epernay–Châlons to prevent annihilation there. This assessment was based primarily on the assumption that our offensive would overrun with little resistance a weak and surprised enemy, and then all available enemy forces would be pulled into their catastrophe in the Reims salient. This first assumption was based on a second, that the number of divisions opposite Army Group German Crown Prince were so low that a concentration of them in the Villers-Cotterêts woods and simultaneous strong occupation of the Reims sector was out of the question. It was believed that the remainder of the enemy operational reserves would be held down by threatening Amiens. Both assumptions were wrong.

Finally, we had underestimated the value of the armored fighting vehicle. The November 1917 battles at Cambrai should have given us some indications what successes might be obtained by the surprise mass insertion of tanks in an attack. We now know that our enemies grasped that fact, improved their tanks technically, and augmented their numbers. On our part, we paid little attention to this auxiliary arm and did not think the enemy had done so either.

During our offensives in March and May 1918 tanks appeared but infrequently, as they are primarily an offensive arm and their forces could find little employment as our opponent in those days was strictly on the defensive. And our placing no high value on tanks as an auxiliary arm seemed justified. But 18 July taught us different for the first time. The tanks inserted in masses heretofore unknown, and technically highly developed, proceeded at their lumbering gait in long lines, connecting the infantry.[166]

Condition of German units

Despite all the previous estimates of the poor condition of the troops and the premature predictions of the death of the German Army, the *Landser* and their small-unit leaders did amazingly well in Operations MICHAEL, GEORGETTE, and BLÜCHER. But by July 1918 they were truly burned out. As previously noted, the Germans were hit much harder than the Allies by the influenza epidemic. Most divisions were reporting between 1,000 and 2,000 cases.[167] The trench strengths of some companies were down to sixty-five, and in some cases even down to forty and thirty. The prestigious 1st Guards Division, which had started the war with 1,000 soldiers in each of its twelve battalions, was now down to 750 soldiers in each of nine battalions. The 4th-class 86th Division averaged 525 men per battalion. The actual trench strengths were even lower than the reported field strengths. German commanders could not know from one day to the next what their unit strength would be on the day of the attack.[168]

Influenza and poor nutrition were not the German Army's only major health problems. On 15 and 24 May and again on 13 June the War Diary of Crown Prince Rupprecht's Army Group reported cases of typhus in the Sixth and Seventeenth Armies, and in the army group's carefully husbanded reserve divisions.[169] Rupprecht himself continually noted the bad condition of the troops in his diary. On 1 June he wrote:

> Reims probably would have fallen earlier if the advancing troops had not got drunk again on the wine they found in the suburbs. The lack of discipline of the troops is serious. Almost every time they take a town the troops look for food and wine. Since they are exhausted and without food, they get drunk fast.[170]

Ludendorff in his memoirs also complained about the condition of the German Army, especially the morale impact of disaffected troops from the east, the diet, and influenza. "I gave serious thought to the question whether, in view of the spirit of the Army and the condition of our reserves, it would not be advisable to adopt the defensive."[171] Ludendorff himself didn't do much to help troop morale. Although MARNESCHUTZ–REIMS was the operational codename for the offensive, as soon as it was launched it was given the name *Friedenssturm*— Peace Offensive. Ludendorff gave it that name to give the troops the impression this would be the last big push that would win the war—even though planners at OHL were busily working on HAGEN, and KURFÜRST after it. For the most part, the *Landser* were not fooled.

Lossberg called 18 July the "precise turning point in the conduct of the war." According to him, OHL's failure to understand that the combat strength of the German Army was shattered was the root of the failure, and that ultimately cost Germany the war.[172]

Mission creep

Like MICHAEL and BLÜCHER, and to lesser extents, GEORGETTE and GNEISENAU, MARNESCHUTZ–REIMS suffered from mission creep all throughout its planning. Wetzell had argued that the Germans did not have the fourteen to sixteen divisions necessary for Operation ROLAND, and the lead-time necessary to prepare it would be to the Allies' advantage. On 6 June, therefore, he recommended a six- to eight-division attack conducted by a single army. That attack could be ready to launch within fourteen to twenty days. By 11 June the operation had grown to ten divisions; by 14 June to twenty divisions; by 17 June to twenty-nine divisions; by 20 June to thirty-nine divisions; and by 15 July to forty-eight divisions controlled by three armies. Instead of two to three weeks' preparation time, Operation MARNESCHUTZ–REIMS was launched thirty-nine days after Wetzell proposed the original attack—time that the Allies used to good advantage.

The basic objective of the operation also expanded as the size of the force grew. Wetzell had proposed a limited objective attack to cut off Reims by taking the high ground to the south of the town, which in turn would give the Germans control of the rail center and ease the near catastrophic supply situation inside the Marne salient. By 15 July, the objective of the operation had expanded to include fixing and destroying large Allied forces east of Reims, as well as drawing large Allied reserves out of Flanders (which were original objectives of ROLAND). In the end, the Germans never seemed to know which objective had priority, taking Reims or drawing off the Allied reserves in Flanders.

Decision 15 July

In its basic design MARNESCHUTZ–REIMS was the most flawed of all the German offensives and the Allies were best prepared to react to it. The decisions made by OHL during its execution, therefore, had less to do with its failure than the other offensives. Those decisions did, however, contribute to the final collapse of the German Army.

By the end of the first day it was clear to all that the offensive was a total failure. Yet Ludendorff decided to continue the Seventh Army's attack, and to continue with HAGEN. But in deciding to continue with a reduced form of the MARNESCHUTZ–REIMS attack, Ludendorff and OHL failed to recognize that one of their key assumptions on why the Germans would not be counterattacked in force on the Seventh Army's right no longer had any basis whatsoever. Although the First and Third Armies were supposed to continue attacking east of Reims to fix the Allied forces there, it should have been clear that the Allies would have considerable freedom of maneuver behind their own lines in the coming days. It would appear that Ludendorff at that point was so fixated on HAGEN that he virtually lost interest in MARNESCHUTZ–REIMS as soon as it was clear that it had failed.

Decision 19 July

If Ludendorff did lose interest in MARNESCHUTZ–REIMS, the Allied counterattack of 18 July refocused his attention. He still, however, could not let go of HAGEN. Hindenburg's recommendation on 19 July to shift immediately all the German reserves in Flanders and to commit those forces across the Aisne against the left flank of the Allied attack just might have restored the German position in the Marne salient. But it also would have meant that HAGEN would never be launched and the German Army would have to assume the strategic and operational defensive. Ludendorff could not force himself to make the decision to go on the defensive, but in the end events forced the Germans to do just that. It is also interesting to note that the German Army of 1918 may well be the only army in modern history where the will of the chief of staff was able to override the will of the commander on a decision of this nature—despite the presumed dressing-down Ludendorff received.

Alternatives

The Germans really had no good alternatives in July 1918. After BLÜCHER and GNEISENAU they were in an untenable and overextended position in the Marne salient. Unable to defend or supply it, their only options were to attack further to improve it, or to withdraw. Ludendorff felt that he could never order a voluntary withdrawal for political and troop morale reasons, but that decision may have had more to do with Ludendorff's own psyche.

Even if MARNESCHUTZ–REIMS had succeeded, it would only have partially improved the Seventh Army's position. It would only have eased the threat to the eastern flank of the Seventh Army between the Marne and Reims; but it would not have eliminated the greater danger from the direction of the wooded ground in the area of Villers-Cotterêts. Control of the Reims rail center might have eased the supply situation in the salient, but the resulting rail network would still have been shallow and strained.

More than likely, MARNESCHUTZ–REIMS would also not have set up the conditions for HAGEN. Too long a pause was required to launch HAGEN in August. The British had been under no serious pressure since May, and German manpower at that point was so thin, that no matter how hard hit the Allied reserves would be by any diversionary attack, the effect on the Germans would be greater proportionally. As Kuhl pointed out in his post-war analysis:

> The offensive thrust in the direction of Reims constituted the last display of force that OHL was still able to make. Inasmuch as it did not aim at the final decision, OHL unconsciously abandoned the [HAGEN] plan definitely, even before Marshal Foch wrested the initiative from the Germans.[173]

But then on the same page Kuhl also went on to state:

> Yet abandoning the offensive would not have altered matters. How was the war to be continued then? To discontinue the offensive would have meant to pass to the defensive. OHL, being imbued with a strong determination, refused to entertain any such plan, and justly so.[174]

This was another example of the German General Staff tradition of seeking operational solutions for strategic problems

Was there any alternative to MARNESCHUTZ–REIMS? Kuhl also suggested that the operation might not have been necessary if HAGEN had been launched as early as possible, while at the same time the Seventh Army made preparations to fall back to the chord of the BLÜCHER salient if it was attacked.[175] It might have worked if Germany's manpower situation had been any better. Even at that late stage in the war the British were still worried about any threats to the Channel ports. The British Section of the Supreme War Council at Versailles continued to develop contingency plans. With the loss of Dunkirk, Calais, or Boulogne, British forces would have to be supplied through Dieppe, Rouen, and Le Havre, and the planners seriously questioned the capacity of those ports. An even greater threat for the Admiralty was the German use of Dunkirk as a naval base for operations in the Channel.[176] Fortunately for the Allies, the German Army and the German Navy seemed to be fighting two separate wars most of the time.

11 Operations HAGEN and KURFÜRST

My first objective is to achieve tactical success on a broad front in the sector of the Fourth Army. This objective can only be achieved by several days of fighting. Then we can go forward in God's name.[1]

Ludendorff's Planning Guidance for HAGEN

Plans (9 April–13 July)

Ludendorff envisioned Operation HAGEN as a resumption of the GEORGETTE offensive in Flanders that had come to a standstill in April.[2] When OHL ordered a halt to Operation MICHAEL on 5 April, Ludendorff asked the chiefs of staff of the Seventeenth, Second, and Eighteenth Armies when they would be ready to resume offensive operations. The Second and Seventeenth Armies replied that they needed three weeks to reconstitute. Ludendorff nonetheless ordered the Second Army to be prepared by 12 April to attack with its left wing south of the Somme to exploit the results of GEORGETTE.[3] On 9 April, the day GEOR-GETTE started, the staff of Rupprecht's Army Group recommended that if the operation got bogged down, follow-on operations against the British would be necessary. The precise point of the follow-on attack would depend on the results of GEORGETTE. Ludendorff agreed and ordered preparations for what essentially would be a continuation of MICHAEL on a broad front within two to three weeks.[4]

On 12 April Kuhl and Ludendorff met in Avesnes to consider the renewed attack by the Second Army.[5] The following day Rupprecht's Army Group issued an estimate of the situation listing two basic options for continuing operations. The first option was a resumption of the northern half of Operation MICHAEL, from the Somme to Arras, toward Doullens. This attack, called NEU-MICHAEL, would be executed by the inner wings of the Second and Seventeenth Armies. A supporting attack called HUBERTUS would be launched by the Sixth Army from Béthune toward St. Pol. The two attacks would have a fifty-five-kilometer front and require extensive forces. The second option was a renewed attack in Flanders by the inner wings of the Fourth and Sixth Armies. Called NEU-GEORG, the attack's initial objective would be the line Strazeele–Flêtre–Mount Noir–Reninghelst–northern edge of Ypres; and the final objective would be the line Borre–Godewearsvedle–Poperinghe–Boesinghe. (Borre is three kilometers east of Hazebrouck.) The purpose of NEU-GEORG was to cut off the British Second Army and the Belgians.[6] (See Map 9.) On 17 April Rupprecht's Army Group issued the initial planning order for NEU-MICHAEL, designating the Seventeenth Army as the main effort.[7]

On 28 April Wetzell issued one of his operational assessments, in which he argued, "In order to be able to strike another great blow against the British, the principal mass of the French reserves on the British front must first be withdrawn."[8] As noted in Chapter 8, this was the genesis of Operation BLÜCHER. The following day Ludendorff met with the army group chiefs of staff at Douai. After deciding to conduct an attack at the end of May with Army Group German Crown Prince along the Chemin des Dames, the discussion turned to the follow-up attack against the British. At that point Kuhl favored NEU-MICHAEL over NEU-GEORG. Ludendorff agreed with Kuhl. The Fourth Army was ordered to stand on the defensive, and the Seventeenth Army was ordered to start the preparations for an attack toward Doullens, supported by a Sixth Army attack toward St. Pol. The probable date of the attacks was mid-June.[9]

On 1 May, the same day GEORGETTE was terminated, OHL issued new planning guidance for the resumption of operations in the north. The overall operational objective of defeating the British remained unchanged, and the main attack would follow as soon as possible after the BLÜCHER diversion along the Chemin des Dames. "This attack is supposed to loosen the present solid front of the Entente opposite the Group of Armies of Crown Prince Rupprecht and thereby to restore the possibility for a successful resumption of the offensive against the British."[10]

OHL continued to support the assessment that NEU-MICHAEL would hit the weaker sector of the British front, and NEU-GEORG the stronger. But Rupprecht's staff was starting to develop serious doubts about NEU-MICHAEL, and sent a message back to OHL.

> The NEU-MICHAEL attack in the direction of Doullens is being prepared in conformity with the instructions received. This attack will have a comparatively narrow zone of action. Tactically, a widening is scarcely possible because on the right is the strong trench system of the Arras front, and on the left, the Ancre and Somme prevent any extension whatever. From the experience of our March offensive, we have learned that only a breakthrough on a wide front will yield great results. Accordingly, from NEU-MICHAEL we can hardly expect any more than a tactical success and a more or less large salient in the enemy line toward Doullens, unless specially favorable conditions obtain. If it is the intention to achieve a great strategic success, it will be necessary to combine NEU-MICHAEL with a second attack [HUBERTUS] on a large scale from the region of Béthune in the direction of St. Pol. The aim of both attacks must be to make a wide breach in the British front, to shake the British Arras front by means of an envelopment, and to push the British toward the sea in such a manner as to render their situation untenable.

Source: Based on map accompanying planning order Ia 7030 (1 May 1918).
ARMY GROUP PRINCE RUPPRECHT

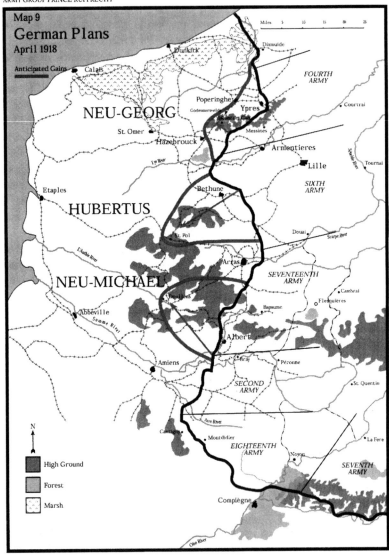

Map 9 German plans, April 1918 (source: Map by Donald S. Frazier, Ph.D., Abilene, Texas, based on sketches and notes provided by David T. Zabecki).

Both attacks, however, require very strong forces. (Roughly, the zone of action of both attacks will cover 55 kilometers in width.) It is very doubtful whether it will be possible to make these forces available.

If this should prove impracticable, it would be necessary, at least in conjunction with NEU-MICHAEL, to stage a limited diversion in the vicinity of Béthune and at the same time make a demonstration in Flanders. It is, however, doubtful whether this would suffice, to make NEU-MICHAEL a great, decisive victory.

The NEU-MICHAEL offensive will, moreover, prove very difficult inasmuch as it will hardly be possible to maintain secrecy regarding the preparations in the perfectly open terrain near Bapaume and Albert, with the result that surprise is likely to be lost.

Should the available forces prove insufficient for both the NEU-MICHAEL and HUBERTUS attacks, and should we therefore be compelled to practice economy with respect to our forces, it is recommended that NEU-GEORG be executed.

Even if our operations elsewhere have drawn away the French and our diversions and demonstrations fix the British reserves in other places, it is very probable that NEU-GEORG will merely constitute a new blow for the British and will create a salient of greater or lesser dimension in the direction of Poperinghe–Cassel. Yet, the political-military significance of such a success in Flanders must be valued much higher than a limited success in the region of Albert. Even assuming that NEU-GEORG turns out to be a limited success only, the British and the Belgians will be hard hit if we succeed in bombarding effectively the coast region as far as Dunkirk— including the valuable British supplies stored there—and in menacing Calais.[11]

Kuhl argued that Army Group Crown Prince Rupprecht lacked the fifty-five divisions necessary to execute both NEU-MICHAEL and HUBERTUS. NEU-GEORG offered the best chance of success. A precondition for its success would be the coming BLÜCHER attack against the French to draw their divisions out of Flanders. A feint attack against Doullens would also be necessary.[12]

That same day Rupprecht's Army Group issued another planning order to its subordinate armies. The objective of NEU-GEORG was to first attack in line from Ypres to Vieux Berquin in the direction Poperinghe–Cassel, and then to exploit north of Ypres. (Hazebrouck was not specified as an objective in this order.) The attack would be conducted on a front of twenty-four kilometers with eleven first-line divisions, fourteen follow-on divisions, and ten trench divisions in support. Then the attack front would narrow to six kilometers for the exploitation phase. The objective of NEU-MICHAEL was to attack along the line Ayette–Ville sur Ancre, northwest in the direction of Doullens. (Amiens was not specified as an objective in this order.) The attack would be conducted on a front of thirty kilometers with fifteen first-line divisions, fourteen follow-on divisions, and ten trench divisions in support. The objective of the HUBERTUS supporting attack was the line between St. Venant and Lens, southwest in the direction of St. Pol. The attack would be conducted on a front of twenty-seven kilometers with twelve first-line divisions, fifteen follow-on divisions, and eight trench divisions in support. Thus, the supporting attack for NEU-MICHAEL was almost as large as the main attack itself.[13]

OHL responded to Rupprecht's Army Group on 2 May, noting that the Allies had shifted the weight of their defenses to Flanders. NEU-MICHAEL, then, was still expected to strike the weaker position, and NEU-GEORG the stronger. But OHL did admit that the coming BLÜCHER offensive might alter that situation, and it would therefore be necessary to conduct full preparations for NEU-MICHAEL, while at the same time setting aside adequate labor forces to prepare for NEU-GEORG.[14]

Kuhl continued to argue that the HUBERTUS plan was extremely difficult, because it would involve an attack on the Loretto heights. It could only succeed if combined with NEU-MICHAEL, and the Germans had neither the manpower nor the artillery for both.[15] Wetzell also issued another operational estimate on 2 May, in which he unsuccessfully urged one large coordinated attack by the Eighteenth, Seventh, and First Armies in the south. That, he argued, would "give us the basis for a subsequent promising offensive in Army Group Rupprecht."[16]

Kuhl and Ludendorff continued to debate the relative merits of NEU-MICHAEL and NEU-GEORG at a chiefs of staff conference in Tournai on 4 May. NEU-MICHAEL, Kuhl argued, was too difficult, its zone of action was too narrow, and it was almost impossible to widen that zone. But if NEU-GEORG were launched from a line of departure running from northeast of Ypres to Neuf, the attack would have a definite and obtainable objective that could be accomplished with the forces available.[17] Ludendorff started to come around to Kuhl's way of thinking. Increasingly drawn by the smaller force requirement for NEU-GEORG, Ludendorff noted: "We have without doubt weakened our strength in the MICHAEL and GEORGETTE operations. We had very high losses. The losses are the reason we have to rethink our tactics."[18]

Further analysis of NEU-GEORG led to general discussion about the method of attack. Commenting on the Fourth Army's preliminary plan, the OHL planners suggested that the initial objective, the line Boesinghe–Poperinghe–Godewearsvedle–Borre, which was about ten kilometers from the line of departure, could only be reached by advancing in bounds. OHL, therefore, wanted to designate an intermediate objective line only a few kilometers deep, and then narrow the zone of action north of the line Ypres–Strazeele. The Fourth Army and Rupprecht's Army Group countered that the attack should be as broad as possible, extending to the right as far as the Flanders flood plain, and left to the Nieppe Forest. The objectives should also not be limited.[19]

The following day OHL reversed its previous position and gave NEU-GEORG precedence over NEU-MICHAEL for planning and preparations, but still withheld the final decision. Rupprecht's Army Group, however, maintained a close hold on that decision and did not inform its subordinate armies until 22 May. On 6 May OHL issued a directive designating the heights between

Poperinghe and Bailleul, as well as the high ground near Hazebrouck as the initial principal objectives. The operation was not to be extended until those objectives were secured.[20] Rupprecht's staff continued to protest the restrictive nature of the operation to OHL, also pointing out the Fourth Army's need for more artillery.[21]

The Fourth Army sent a memo to Rupprecht's Army Group on 11 May objecting to the restrictive nature of the OHL plan. The memo argued that an attack on a large scale had a better chance of succeeding with a wider zone of action. Arnim believed that if the attack extended only as far as Meteren or Strazeele, the left wing would come under flanking fire from the Nieppe Forest. He also objected to OHL's limited objectives and he argued that any initial tactical success should be aggressively exploited.[22] Kuhl sent a memo to OHL on 13 May concurring with Arnim's arguments.[23] OHL, meanwhile, had changed the names of the operations on 12 May. Operation NEU-MICHAEL became WILHELM. HUBERTUS was renamed FUCHSJAGD (FOX HUNT). Ironically, NEU-GEORG was re-designated HAGEN, after the character of German legend and Wagnerian opera who stabbed Siegfried in the back.[24]

On 15 May Ludendorff replied to Kuhl. He started by insisting that he agreed completely with Rupprecht's Army Group and the Fourth Army that broad and deep attacks were necessary. But then he concluded that the width and depth of the attack depended on the forces available. If the Germans had to restrict the width of the attack, as Ludendorff feared the forces available would dictate, then it was best to limit the northern sector. But Ludendorff did concur that an extension of the attack toward the south was a good idea, and he approved the initial preparations. The final decision, however, would be made later.[25]

Concerning the question of the advance by bounds, Ludendorff said that the depth of the thrust depended on the forces available as well as the anticipated resistance of the enemy and his reserves. Considering the current situation, the Fourth Army had to expect to encounter a strong initial resistance as well as strong enemy reserves. The initial strong resistance could be overcome by a heavy artillery preparation. The enemy reserves, which could come up later, could only be countered by redeploying the artillery forward. The attack, therefore, had to be made by bounds with large amounts of artillery and ammunition following. Ludendorff also worried about the potential high losses. "We cannot endure any more disappointments and losses. People are scarce, but we have enough munitions."[26]

The basic plans for HAGEN and WILHELM were essentially complete by 17 May, but OHL informed Rupprecht's Army Group that the attacks could not be launched before late June.[27] Three days later Ludendorff informed Rupprecht personally that the attack would start about 1 July, because of the time required to transfer the required artillery.[28] Rupprecht's Army Group sent OHL another course-of-action analysis on 19 May strongly recommending HAGEN over WILHELM.[29] Kuhl continued to push Ludendorff for a final decision, arguing that WILHELM was the more difficult operation and had no clear objective.

HAGEN was easier and had an achievable objective. In a meeting with Kuhl in Zeebrügge on 20 May, Ludendorff finally decided on HAGEN.[30]

On 21 May Wetzell issued his operational assessment recommending that if Operations BLÜCHER and YORCK did not draw sufficient French reserves out of Flanders, then Operation GNEISENAU should be cancelled and the French should be attacked at Verdun. By not launching GNEISENAU, the Germans could launch a significant attack in the Verdun sector without having to draw from the forces earmarked for HAGEN.[31] Commenting on Wetzell's recommendation, Rupprecht noted pessimistically in his diary:

> Ludendorff too expects that HAGEN will end with only a partial success, but he is hoping that under the circumstances more can be achieved even if HAGEN is not a breakthrough success. All other offensive actions would have to be halted for the rest of the year. The enemy too would not be able to counter with major offensive actions. Ludendorff's first adjutant told my adjutant "If the decision does not turn before the fall, the war can go on for years." Before the spring attack they were too optimistic and raised hopes back home that were not realized. The disappointment that will come if HAGEN fails will be all the worse.[32]

On 31 May OHL again renamed Operation WILHELM, previously NEU-MICHAEL, as ECKENBRECHER.[33] By the following day, Operation BLÜCHER was thirty-nine miles from Paris. The Germans had reached the Marne between Dormans and Château-Thierry, but had not crossed in force. At 1500 hours Ludendorff issued an order to Rupprecht's Army Group:

> Operations of Army Group German Crown Prince are taking a favorable course. I therefore ask for further deception operations to continue in order to engage the enemy forces on the front of your army group. Limited operations at places sensitive to the enemy might also be advantageous, but our infantry forces should not be wasted.
>
> Because of the heavy attrition, especially among the support columns, our preparations for HAGEN will be delayed accordingly. The attack won't be launched before mid-July. Since the enemy obviously still expects our attack, and the operations of Army Group German Crown Prince will be continued, we likewise will continue our deception measures beyond 2 June in order to tie down enemy forces.[34]

Thus, the original operational concept of drawing away the enemy reserves in front of the right wing of the German Army was now secondary to the objective of advancing the attack of the Seventh Army, and possibly turning it into the decisive operation it was never intended to be. On 2 June Rupprecht's Army Group also issued a revised version of the plans for follow-on operations. For Operation HAGEN the Fourth Army was to attack from the line Bultehoek–Wielje against and over the Yser Canal in the direction of

Boesinghe–Ypres on a thirty-seven-kilometer front with fifteen first-line and sixteen follow-on divisions. The Sixth Army would support the attack from the line Ypres–Bourre River in the vicinity of Merville in the direction of Poper-inghe–Cassel on a six-kilometer front with four first-line divisions and one follow-on division. The Seventeenth Army's ECKENBRECHER attack was reduced to a seventeen-kilometer front on both sides of Bucquoy, with five first-line and nine follow-on divisions. The supporting FUCHSJAGD attack would be launched on a 7.5-kilometer front to seize Festubert–Givenchy–Guinchy with three first-line and six follow-on divisions.[35]

By the time Army Group German Crown Prince on 3 June recommended halting the BLÜCHER offensive, five of the HAGEN reserve divisions had been withdrawn from Rupprecht's Army Group.[36] That day Rupprecht noted sourly in his diary: "My impression is that the attack of the Seventh Army has run its course, and that the [GNEISENAU] attack by the Eighteenth Army can hardly produce more success. The delay of HAGEN is a political decision."[37] The following day OHL informed Rupprecht's Army Group that if GNEISENAU failed and it became necessary to execute the ROLAND attack against Reims, then HAGEN would have to be postponed until 20 July.[38]

Ludendorff met with the chiefs of staff in Avesnes on 6 June to decide whether ROLAND or HAGEN would be the next major operation. Kuhl con-tinued to push for HAGEN as the only decisive option. Wetzell's Verdun opera-tion was not even discussed, but he did recommend that ROLAND become the follow-on attack after HAGEN. Ludendorff concluded that the final decision on HAGEN would be based on the outcome of GNEISENAU. OHL, however, started to look seriously at the possible courses of action if both the attacks against Reims and in Flanders produced only tactical but not decisive results.[39] At the meeting Ludendorff had told Kuhl: "HAGEN must bring the decision." Pessimistically, Kuhl later wrote in his diary: "That is not possible."[40] A couple of days later, Rupprecht, who as a commander was not at the Avesnes meeting, recorded in his diary:

> Today [Kuhl] told me that Ludendorff had said a little while ago in Avesnes that HAGEN should bring the decision. I don't believe that. We might be able to take the heights of Godewearsvedle, maybe even go all the way to Cassel and across Hazebrouck, push the British out of the Ypres salient, and the Belgians behind the Loos Canal; but we won't achieve more unless extraordinary good luck is with us. Then probably a month-long pause in the fighting will occur. Everything else depends on how many troops the Ameri-cans will be able to transport to Europe. The situation for the March offen-sive was more favorable than the one for HAGEN. If they [OHL] would have not turned from the British too soon in order to go toward the French, a major breakthrough success might have been achieved.[41]

By 10 June the operations in the south had drawn thirteen attack divisions and large numbers of support columns and artillery units away from Rupprecht's

Army Group. At that point in time, HAGEN was impossible with the forces available in the north.[42] Kuhl, meanwhile, complained in his own diary of having to put up for weeks with Ludendorff's "nervous excitement," his constant telephone calls, and his meddling in the most minute tactical details, all of which made careful planning and a logical orders process impossible.[43]

In his operational assessment of 12 June, Wetzell noted that the BLÜCHER offensive had "succeeded" because of three factors: it achieved surprise; it had struck a weakly held sector; and the Allied reserves were widely dispersed. All three of these conditions, he argued, were still lacking for HAGEN, whereas his recommended attack across the Marne and against Reims would establish those conditions.[44] Two days later Ludendorff held the planning session in Roubaix at which ROLAND evolved into MARNESCHUTZ–REIMS, scheduled for 10 July. HAGEN was scheduled to follow up on 20 July. Rupprecht's Army Group still wanted to widen the HAGEN attack by extending the Sixth Army's sector to the south by a division's width to the Bourre River. OHL, on the other hand, thought it was more important to precede HAGEN with the Seventeenth Army's ECKENBRECHER attack as a diversion. OHL noted that it would decide that question later.[45] Kuhl was unable at that point to convince Ludendorff that the Seventeenth Army attack was neither necessary nor feasible.[46]

Still lacking OHL concurrence, Rupprecht's Army Group on 15 June issued an order expanding the Sixth Army attack for planning purposes from a six- to a 9.5-kilometer front, with five instead of four divisions in the front line. The Fourth Army attack and the Seventeenth Army's ECKENBRECHER attacks remained essentially the same as in the 1 June order.[47] On 17 June OHL announced that the extension of the HAGEN attack south, as well as the ECK-ENBRECHER deception attack would not be approved because of shortages in available infantry and artillery. Ludendorff noted that he fully expected the coming MARNESCHUTZ–REIMS attack to pull not only the French reserves out of Flanders, but major British reserves as well. But since a large portion of the army-level artillery assets needed for HAGEN would have to be used for MARNESCHUTZ–REIMS, and since transportation to Flanders took eight to ten days, it might not be possible to launch HAGEN before 1 August. Rupprecht's Army Group was also short seven attack divisions at that point.[48]

OHL and Rupprecht's Army Group continued the debate over the width of HAGEN, exchanging memos on 18 June. The army group noted: "The capture of Hazebrouck is critical to the overall success of the attack." And, "The taking of Hazebrouck by a single envelopment from the north will be very difficult."[49] In his diary Rupprecht noted: "If we don't go farther south to the Lys, it will be very difficult for us to get all the way to Hazebrouck."[50] OHL, on the other hand, maintained that the main effort was on the left wing of the Fourth Army, and "it is only necessary to take the high ground north and south of Hazebrouck to dominate it." This was the first time that Hazebrouck was seriously discussed as a HAGEN objective. OHL also concluded that the ECKENBRECHER diversion was no longer possible because of the shortage of necessary infantry and artillery.[51]

On 19 June Ludendorff postponed MARNESCHUTZ–REIMS until 15 July, noting that the operation would require more support from HAGEN units. HAGEN was officially postponed until 1 August.[52] Ludendorff also sent a message to Rupprecht's Army Group agreeing in principle that a double envelopment would be the best way to take Hazebrouck, but still refusing to allow the addition of another division. He felt the additional division could be better used elsewhere than in the attack through the Nieppe Forest.[53] Kuhl, meanwhile, was becoming increasingly gloomy. Rupprecht's Army Group was losing 1,000 men per day in "wastage" from its trench divisions. The attack divisions could not remain in the rear and allow the trench divisions to absorb the losses. Kuhl thought that the war was at a turning point. HAGEN might produce tactical results, but no decision. He wrote cryptically in his diary, "Then the Americans."[54]

On 20 June the ECKENBRECHER diversionary attack was finally officially cancelled and replaced with a much smaller diversionary attack named NÜRN-BERG that was supposed to be launched by the Seventeenth Army two days before the start of HAGEN.[55] The following day Rupprecht's Army Group issued an order emphasizing the importance of the Sixth Army taking Haze-brouck.[56] The Sixth Army also stressed the importance of Hazebrouck in its own operations orders. The plan was to take the town at night, because "The British are not very good at operating in the dark."[57]

OHL, meanwhile, had been giving serious thought to the German Army's next move if HAGEN did not prove decisive. On 22 June Wetzell issued another operational assessment, which was based on a situation at the end of August if MARNESCHUTZ–REIMS and HAGEN "result as favorably as we hope." Wetzell believed that the British and French Armies would be badly shaken and unable to launch large-scale offensive operations, but still able to defend their positions with American support. The most logical direction for continued German operations would be the line Calais–St. Omer–Lens, but even with support from Austria-Hungary it would probably be impossible to mount another major attack in the late autumn.

After reconstituting during the winter, the French and British with American support would most likely launch an offensive. How then could the Germans prevent the Allies from taking the initiative? Wetzell recommended an attack in Italy. That would require OHL to shift twelve to fifteen reconstituted divisions from the Western Front, but Wetzell was "convinced that we should achieve an even greater success there than last year." German forces might even be able to advance to the Po plain as far as the Italian–French border. "It might make possible the complete destruction of the Italian Army." Wetzell argued that such an operation would draw off Allied, and especially American forces from the Western Front.[58]

Even though Wetzell was the chief of the OHL Operations Section, OHL that same day issued an order for follow-up operations after HAGEN that bore no resemblance to Wetzell's proposal. The order stated:

> After the conclusion of the offensive operations ordered on 14 June 1918
> [MARNESCHUTZ–REIMS and HAGEN], it is contemplated to stage an

attack between the Somme and the Marne. It will be executed with all available forces in the direction of Amiens *and* Paris. . . .

(Emphasis added.)

And: "Preparations will be pushed in such a manner as to make it possible to begin rail movements for the artillery, trench mortars, and divisions approximately in the second half of July."[59] The OHL order hit like a thunderbolt at the lower echelons. In his diary, Kuhl expressed the surprise and frustration of the entire staff of Army Group Rupprecht. Everyone thought it would be utterly impossible to launch an attack on such a scale after HAGEN.[60]

A 23 June message from OHL to Rupprecht's Army Group emphasized that the Germans could no longer expect to achieve surprise, and that the method of attack, therefore, had to take that reality into consideration. Ludendorff also thought that too much force was being concentrated in the Fourth Army.[61] In frustration, Rupprecht noted in his diary: "I don't believe that OHL gives any thought to the execution of HAGEN, since in their message they did not answer any one of the major points of our opposition against the weakening of the front of the Fourth Army. . . ." Rupprecht also complained that OHL seemed to be waffling on whether to launch HAGEN or the newly proposed attack toward Paris after MARNESCHUTZ–REIMS. Finally, OHL now completely dropped the notion of a deception preceding HAGEN. NÜRNBERG was no longer necessary because MARNESCHUTZ–REIMS would draw all the Allied reserves out of Flanders.[62]

On 25 June the chief of staff of the Naval Corps proposed an operation against Dixmuide simultaneous with HAGEN. As the northern-most corps in the Fourth Army, the Naval Corps was not scheduled to participate in HAGEN. The plan called for an advance along the line of dykes and the establishment of a bridgehead across the northern Flanders plain that had been intentionally flooded by the Allies. Rupprecht noted: "Since the Naval Corps will execute the operation with its own forces, there is nothing to be said against it." The plan, however, appears to have died a quick death.[63]

Army Group German Crown Prince issued the warning order for Operation KURFÜRST on 26 June. The Eighteenth Army (KURFÜRST I) would attack from the line St. Just-en-Chaussee–Verberie, securing the right flank of the attack from the west to the general line Clermont–Creil. The Ninth Army (KURFÜRST II) would attack from the line Verberie–Nanteuil-le-Haudoin to the line Creil–Senlis–Forêt d'Ermenonville. The main effort of the attack would be south of the Aisne, between the Compiègne Forest and the Soissons–Villers-Cotterêts–Nanteuil road. The Seventh Army (KURFÜRST III) would attack with its right wing beyond Nanteuil to the line Ver-le-Plessis–Bellville–Lizy. The depth and extension of the entire attack would depend on the situation in July and the available forces. OHL wanted to be ready to launch the attack suddenly about the end of July. Preliminary plans and force estimates were due by 5 July. "Troops will be used for preparatory work only in so far as training, recuperation, and the necessary harvest work does not suffer thereby."[64]

OHL sent Rupprecht's Army Group another HAGEN order on 27 June. In a change from the 18 June order, OHL now identified the main effort of the attack as the right wing of the Fourth Army. "The stronger the pressure of the enveloping attack can be made there, the more will the entire operation develop into a knock-out blow." OHL *hoped* that the effects of the operation would expand into the direction of Dunkirk–Calais and culminate in a decisive victory over the British.[65]

Wetzell on 27 June also issued another of his recently steady stream of operational assessments. Referring specifically to OHL order Ia 8895 issued on 22 June, Wetzell recommended that the Germans immediately follow up MAR-NESCHUTZ–REIMS and HAGEN with an attack toward Paris. Without citing the KURFÜRST plan of Army Group German Crown Prince submitted only the day before, Wetzell's proposal was similar, except that he placed the main effort with the left-wing Seventh Army. Wetzell also included a force estimate of forty-five to fifty-one attack divisions. Where this force would come from, Wetzell did not say. "Whether they can be assembled is a question which I shall not attempt to answer at present." Then he fell back on one of his favorite positions: "If we lack the strength for this blow, the Entente should be attacked in Italy."[66] It is difficult to escape the impression that, while appearing to support the KURFÜRST plan enthusiastically, Wetzell was really trying to show how impossible it was.

On 28 June Army Group German Crown Prince sent OHL a proposal to attack Verdun with the Third Army, following the conclusion of MAR-NESCHUTZ–REIMS. But the proposal also added the qualifier: "The direction toward the southeast, which is favorable operationally, will only be successful if at the same time a strong attack from the front of Army Group C can be made." The message went on to suggest that the forces earmarked for HAGEN should be committed to this operation instead. Ludendorff responded that the plan had great merit, but he said that no forces were available for a simultaneous attack by Army Group C.[67]

On 1 July Rupprecht's Army Group issued the final corps combat missions for Operation HAGEN (see Table 11.1). Although the Sixth Army's XIX Corps had the mission of taking the heights west and southwest of Hazebrouck, the town itself and its vital rail center were not listed as specific objectives (Map 10).

On 2 July OHL issued the orders to both army groups to start preparations for KURFÜRST. The main effort would be made by the Eighteenth Army and the right wing of the Ninth, attacking across the Aisne toward Bréteuil and Villers-Cotterêts. The enemy in front of the left wing of the Ninth and the Seventh Army would be rolled up, and then the Seventh Army would reinforce the continuing attack of the Ninth Army south of the Villers-Cotterêts woods. On the far right wing the attack of Army Group German Crown Prince would be extended by an attack of Rupprecht's Second Army in the direction of Amiens. Both army groups were ordered to coordinate closely the inner wings of the Second and Eighteenth Armies. OHL concluded the order by emphasizing that it

Table 11.1 Corps combat missions for Operation HAGEN[68]

Fourth Army

Guards Corps: (*Five divisions in the first line.*) The Guards Corps provides flanking support to the artillery of the XVIII Reserve Corps and attacks over the Yser Canal between Drie–Grachten and the southeastern edge of Ypres. The main effort of the attack will be along the canal line between the Staden–Boesinghe railway and the northern edge of Ypres. Along the northern edge of the line of attack the flanking effect of the enemy artillery group near Hazewind must be considered. Nonetheless, the enemy in that sector must be engaged in order to facilitate the envelopment from the south. In order to get our forces quickly into position, the artillery main effort must be in the sector north of Ypres. The town itself will be cut off from the north by the Guards Corps and from the west by the XVIII Reserve Corps.

XVIII Reserve Corps: (*Three divisions in the first line; two in the second line; one in the third line.*) The mission of the XVIII Reserve Corps is to push the enemy quickly into the flooded area north of Reiningen–Proven. The left wing of the corps must be strong in order to cross the Poperinghe–Ypres road. The follow-on mission of the corps is to cut off the town Ypres from the west and to prevent the enemy from defending along the Yser canal north of Ypres as he retreats westward.

X Reserve Corps: (*Two divisions in the first line; two in the second line; two in the third line.*) The X Reserve Corps has the mission of taking the heights of de Kleit, the Scherpenberg, and the eastern slopes of the Mount Rouge with an initial quick rush. The corps will then take the city of Poperinghe by enveloping it. The corps will then continue its attack toward the line Proven–Waten.

Guards Reserve Corps: (*Two divisions in the first line; two in the second line; two in the third line.*) The mission of the Guards Reserve Corps is to take the western slopes of the Mount Rouge, the heights of Vidaigne, Mount Noir, and the heights of Godewearsvedle. The main effort of the attack must be on the right wing in order to take the mountainous area from the east toward the north. Additional objectives of the corps attack are the heights north and northeast of Steenvorde.

III Bavarian Corps: (*Two divisions in the first line; two in the second line; two in the third line.*) The III Bavarian Corps has the mission of taking the heights of Cassel in a single rush, independent of the actions of the Guards Reserve Corps and the Sixth Army.

Sixth Army

XIX Corps: (*Two divisions in the first line; two in the second line.*) The XIX Corps will take the heights of Hondeghem and the heights west and southwest of Hazebrouck and the trench system in that sector before the enemy can organize a new defense. The corps will then consolidate its position and be prepared to push forward in support of an advance by the Fourth Army.

LV Corps: (*Three divisions in the first line.*) The LV Corps has the mission of ensuring freedom of maneuver for the XIX Corps by pivoting out from the baseline of the northern corner of Vieux Berquin–les Puresbeques southward, and advancing to the line Morbecque–le Pre a Vin–Bourre River. The corps will commit one division north of the woods of Aval toward Tir Anglais and la Motte au Bous, and another division south of the woods of Aval toward le Pre a Vin. In order to have enough combat power for the defensive flank near the woods, a trench division will be committed to rolling up the enemy position on the left attack wing.

Source: Army Group Crown Prince Rupprecht, Ia 8082, (1 July 1918), Bayerisches Kriegsarchiv: File Hgr. Rupprecht, Bd. 112.

SOURCE: BASED ON MAP ACCOMPANYING PLANNING ORDER IA 8082 (1 JULY 1918),
ARMY GROUP PRINCE RUPPRECHT

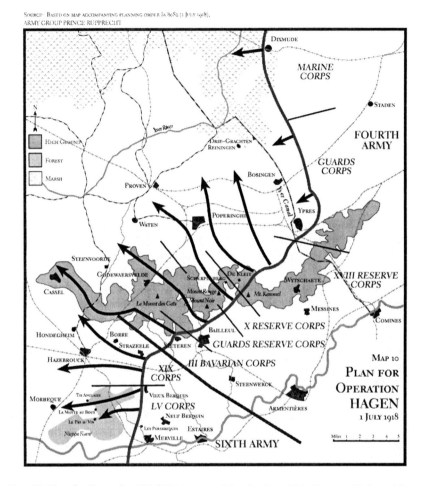

Map 10 Plan for Operation HAGEN (source: Map by Donald S. Frazier, Ph.D., Abilene, Texas, based on sketches and notes provided by David T. Zabecki. Based on map accompanying Planning Order Ia 8082, (1 July 1918), Army Group Prince Rupprecht).

was only preparatory in nature, and that it was not at all clear yet whether the necessary forces would be available.[69] Kuhl countered that even if all available forces were concentrated south of the Somme, they would still be insufficient. He continued to express doubts that either of the offensives, let alone both, would be possible to mount.[70]

OHL issued an order on 3 July stating conclusively that Operation KURFÜRST would be the follow-up to HAGEN.[71] Rupprecht's Army Group, meanwhile, remained unconvinced that a deception attack preceding HAGEN would not be necessary. On 6 July Kuhl and Lossberg went to OHL for further discussions on HAGEN. At the end of that meeting Ludendorff too seemed to favor a preliminary deception attack, but the forces were just not available.[72]

Wetzell on 6 July issued the last of his operational assessments. It was the most outlandish of the entire series. Wetzell proposed a follow-on offensive in Lorraine and Alsace by Army Group Duke Albrecht, estimating that the German Army can "without too great a hazard, employ about one-third of our total army reserves in divisions and artillery for an attack in Lorraine or Alsace." Wetzell proposed a main attack of twenty divisions, supported by a ten-division attack on the right, and a five-division attack on the left. The required artillery would total 1,960 batteries. Only 600 batteries were currently in sector, which meant OHL would have to come up with 1,360.[73] By this point, Wetzell seems to have lost Ludendorff's ear completely, and this recommendation was totally ignored.

On 9 July the Second Army submitted the force estimate for its KURFÜRST supporting attack south of the Somme, designated KURFÜRST-A. The army estimated ten fresh divisions in the first line and six in the rear lines. Rupprecht commented: "There won't be that many forces for that attack. The offensive is only on paper."[74] Army Group German Crown Prince issued its own estimate for KURFÜRST on 10 July, noting: "A simultaneous attack against Amiens and Paris would be difficult and hard to synchronize, because the directions of the main attacks toward the northwest and the southwest diverge, and the combat lanes correspondingly increase toward the enemy." It was also impossible to estimate if sufficient forces would be left for an attack on such a scale at the conclusion of the current operations. "The question will most likely be an attack toward Paris, or toward Amiens, but not both." The estimated requirement for the Paris attack was fifty divisions.[75]

By the second week in July the German Army was suffering heavily from the flu epidemic. Rupprecht feared that would force a delay in HAGEN.[76] On 11 July Rupprecht's Army Group sent a warning order to its armies alerting them that the British could be expected to launch an attack against the army group to provide relief to the French once MARNESCHUTZ–REIMS started. Any such attack had to be defeated without using the forces designated for HAGEN. Only if the British launched a major attack in the Cambrai sector would the HAGEN forces be committed.[77] Rupprecht's Army Group also issued its priority intelligence requirements for HAGEN. There were two principal questions. Following a successful German breakthrough, where would the strongest British resistance be? And, where would the British redeploy their artillery?[78]

Both army groups had serious doubts about KURFÜRST right from the start. On 12 July OHL told the army groups that they could not attack simultaneously in both directions, toward Amiens and Paris. The decision of which attack and to which extent it could be mounted could only be decided if there were enough forces after MARNESCHUTZ–REIMS and HAGEN, and based on the situation both operations would establish. There was no way to launch KURFÜRST before mid-September.[79] Rupprecht noted in his diary: "If HAGEN is executed then I'm convinced we'll hardly be able to let KURFÜRST follow that soon, if at all."[80]

As the launch date for MARNESCHUTZ–REIMS approached, it appeared that Rupprecht's Army Group would have between thirty-one and thirty-five attack divisions available for HAGEN. On 13 July the army group estimated that the British would almost certainly launch some sort of relief attack almost immediately. Patrols and aerial reconnaissance indicated that the British were on a high state of alert in front of the Fourth Army and the right wing of the Sixth—precisely the HAGEN sector.[81]

Preparations

On 1 May the entire northern sector of the German line passed to the defensive. Several days later the Fourth Army issued a warning order to start preparations immediately, with an emphasis on building the required roads and rail lines.[82] By the end of May the required labor forces had been transferred from the Second and Seventeenth Armies to the Fourth and Sixth Armies. All attacking units were to be supplied with four days of ammunition and two weeks of rations.[83]

Forces

As soon as the Germans went on the defensive in the north, thirty-two attack divisions were withdrawn from Rupprecht's Army Group to start reconstituting and training for HAGEN. Prior to the start of MARNESCHUTZ–REIMS, fourteen of those divisions had been given up to support other operations. OHL later made eight more attack divisions available, but Rupprecht Army Group had to fill the gaps with thirteen trench divisions to bring the attacking force up to the thirty-nine required. This greatly weakened the striking power of the HAGEN force. It also caused a large increase in the sector width of the trench divisions still in the line. The longer HAGEN was delayed, the greater the strain on the already paper-thin trench divisions.

By May most of Rupprecht's trench divisions were short between 2,000 to 3,000 troops. At the start of June, Rupprecht's Army Group requested permission from OHL to put some of the attack divisions back into the line to relieve the pressure on the trench divisions. On 3 June OHL rejected the request, claiming such a move would force the further postponement of HAGEN by several weeks. On 21 May the average battalion strength in Rupprecht's Army Group was 700. By 13 July it was down to 673.[84]

Artillery and air preparations

By the middle of 1918 the German Army was running short of artillery and the industrial base in Germany was falling farther and farther behind in its ability to replace the losses from combat operations. For the HAGEN attack the Fourth and Sixth Armies would have to use most of the heavy artillery that was being used for MARNESCHUTZ–REIMS. Bruchmüller, who after the war French General Freideric Herr called Ludendorff's "traveling salesman in methods of massed artillery command," was again designated as chief of artillery for

HAGEN.[85] Although Bruchmüller was heavily engaged in the MARNESCHUTZ–REIMS planning, he was able to influence the artillery planning in Rupprecht's Army Group through liaison officers and members of his own staff. With Kuhl himself being one of Bruchmüller's earliest and most ardent supporters, there was little risk his ideas would be ignored, as they had been by the Second and Seventeenth Armies in March. As early as 6 May the Sixth Army orders made it clear that all guns would be calibrated and the firing would be done using the Pulkowski Method.[86] Pulkowski himself shuttled back and forth between the army groups, conducting classes in his fire-direction system. According to the plan, the heavy guns and Bruchmüller along with them would start moving north to Rupprecht's Army Group as soon as the MARNESCHUTZ–REIMS preparation had been fired.[87]

The basic plan for the Sixth Army's artillery preparation (see Table 11.2) was issued on 4 July. Unlike the simpler and shorter preparations of the last three operations, this one was a bit longer. It had more phases, similar to the MICHAEL preparation, and unlike the other preparations this one included the creeping barrage as a phase. The main preparation itself was timed to last four hours, with the creeping barrage lasting another three. The ammunition allocation was 800 rounds for each field gun; 600 for each light field howitzer; 200 for each heavy field howitzer and 100 mm heavy gun; and eighty rounds for the heavy siege howitzers.

Table 11.2 Sixth Army HAGEN artillery preparation plan[88]

Phase	Duration	Effect
1	10 minutes	Surprise fire on the enemy HQs and communications centers. IKA fires against enemy observation posts. AKA fires counter-battery. FEKA and SCHWEFLA fire against deep targets.
2	110 minutes	Reinforced counter-battery with AKA and IKA. FEKA and SCHWEFLA engage deep targets. Trench mortars fire against enemy trench mortars.
3	20 minutes	Attack of enemy infantry positions. IKA fires against the enemy second positions. AKA fires counter-battery with gas. FEKA and SCHWEFLA fire deep. Trench mortars attack enemy first positions.
4	20 minutes	Like Phase 3, with fire on different enemy infantry positions.
5	20 minutes	Like Phase 3, with fire on different enemy infantry positions.
6	20 minutes	Like Phase 3, with fire on different enemy infantry positions.
7	20 minutes	Reinforced counter-battery, like Phase 2.
8	20 minutes	Like Phase 3, with fire on different enemy infantry positions.
9	180 minutes	IKA fires the creeping barrage. AKA continues to fire counter-battery. FEKA and SCHWEFLA continue firing deep.

Source: AOK 6, Ia/Art 3609/481, (4 July 1918), Bayerisches Kriegsarchiv: File AOK 6, Bd. 9.

On 1 May Rupprecht's Army Group estimated the artillery requirements for HAGEN at 772 batteries. By 16 May the estimate had increased to 960 batteries.[89] Over the course of the next two months the estimated requirements for artillery and air assets steadily increased. Then in the days immediately following the failure of MARNESCHUTZ–REIMS, the estimates dropped back sharply to the mid-May level, as the Germans desperately tried to find some way to continue with HAGEN (see Table 11.3).

Force transfers

From an operational standpoint, the biggest difficulty with the HAGEN attack was the transfer of massive amounts of artillery, air, and support assets from Army Group German Crown Prince to Rupprecht's Army Group. For the most part, the infantry forces were in place, with the exception of a few divisions that would be shifted within Rupprecht's Army Group at the last minute. Most of the support forces, on the other hand, were required in the south for MAR-NESCHUTZ–REIMS, and then had to be shifted north as fast as possible for HAGEN. According to the planners, the movement of all required assets from the Marne to Flanders would take two weeks. Most of the movements would be made by rail, which would put a strain on even the fairly robust rail network behind the German lines.[90]

On 26 May Rupprecht's Army Group issued the orders for the basic transportation plan for the forward deployment of the forces already within the command, including the approach marches of the attack divisions from the rear to their jumping-off positions. The few exceptions included a handful of assets from the Eastern Front and from Army Group German Crown Prince. The plan was also based on the assumption that the NÜRNBERG deception attack would still be mounted. With slight modifications the plan remained in force until 16 July (see Table 11.4).

Table 11.3 Artillery and air assets for HAGEN[91]

	1 June	*29 June*	*20 July*
Fourth Army			
Batteries	998	1,027	806
Attack squadrons	22	32	21
Fighter squadrons	28	32	26
Sixth Army			
Batteries	188	267	211
Attack squadrons	6	8	3
Fighter squadrons	8	13	10

Source: Army Group Crown Prince Rupprecht, Ia 7572, (1 June 1918), Bayerisches Kriegsarchiv: File Hgr. Rupprecht, Bd. 112. Army Group Crown Prince Rupprecht, Ia 8051, (29 June 1918), Bayerisches Kriegsarchiv: File Hgr. Rupprecht, Bd. 108. Army Group Crown Prince Rupprecht, Ia 8541, (20 July 1918), Bayerisches Kriegsarchiv: File Hgr. Rupprecht, Bd. 112.

Table 11.4 Operation HAGEN force transfer plan[92]

I Group (Latest arrival three weeks before the attack. [6–9 July])
- Trench-mortar companies and the artillery staffs of the attack divisions.
- Artillery park companies.
- Pioneer staff officers.
- Air squadron staffs.
- Elements of the horse columns.
- Staffs of the gas launcher battalions.
- Divisional communications units.

II Group (Arrival 21 to 17 days before the attack. [10–13 July])
- Attack division advanced parties.
- Lead elements of divisional staffs.
- Divisional signal battalions.
- Divisional engineer staffs.
- Military police units.
- Flak unit staffs.
- Munitions columns.
- Battery munitions columns.
- Pioneer battalions.
- Gas launcher battalions.
- Advance parties of the balloon units.
- Elements of the field bakeries.
- Traffic control field police.
  Fourth Army
  - Staffs of seven army-level artillery regiments.
  - Staffs of two foot artillery regiments.
  - Eleven light field howitzer battalions from *Oberost.*
  - Thirty-eight battery columns.
  Sixth Army
  - Staffs of three army-level artillery regiments.
  - Eleven foot artillery battery columns.

III Group (Arrival 16 to 14 days before the attack. [14–16 July])
- Remainder of the horse columns.
- Medical units.
- Flak units.
- Staffs of the fighter squadrons.
- Lead elements of the attack squadrons.
- Flamethrower companies.
- Remainder of the field bakeries.
  Fourth Army
  - Advanced parties of the 4th Guards Division and the *Jäger* Division.
  - Six foot artillery battalions.
  Sixth Army
  - Six foot artillery battalions.

IV Group (Arrival 13 to 10 days before the attack. [17–19 July])
- Elements of the fighter units.
- Balloon units.
- Remainder of the attack squadrons.

Table 11.4 Continued

Fourth Army
• 17th Infantry Division.
• Artillery of the 18th, 27th, 221st, and 2nd Guards Divisions.
• Artillery staffs and advanced parties of the 24th, 24th Reserve, and 50th Reserve Divisions.
• Six army-level artillery regiments.
Sixth Army
• Three army-level artillery regiments.

V Group (Arrival 9 to 6 days before the attack. [20–25 July])
• Infantry batteries.
• Remainder of the fighter units.
• Searchlight units.
• Army-level medical companies.
• Elements of the railroad units.
Fourth Army
• 18th, 24th, 27th, and 221st Divisions.
• Artillery of the 4th Guards and *Jäger* Divisions.
• Infantry of the 4th Guards and *Jäger* Divisions.
From Army Group German Crown Prince
• Eighteen field artillery battalions.
• Two foot artillery battalions.
• Two trench-mortar companies.

VI Group (Arrival 5 to 1 days before the attack. [26–30 July])
• Bridge trains.
• Bulk of the rail units.
• Collection companies.
Fourth Army
• Infantry of the 24th Reserve, 50th Reserve, and 54th Divisions.
• Reinforcing artillery from NÜRNBERG.
• Nine field and nine heavy battalions.
Sixth Army
• Reinforcing artillery from NÜRNBERG.
• Nine field and six heavy battalions.

Source: Army Group Crown Prince Rupprecht, Iab 7480, (26 May 1918), Bayerisches Kriegsarchiv: File Hgr. Rupprecht, Bd. 105. Army Group Crown Prince Rupprecht, Iad 8433, (16 July 1918), Bayerisches Kriegsarchiv: File Hgr. Rupprecht, Bd. 112.

On 28 June OHL issued the order establishing the priorities and sequencing of the transfer of air assets to Rupprecht's Army Group from the other army groups. The units would move in the following order: the observation detachments for the first-line divisions; the observation detachments for the super-heavy artillery units; one fighter wing; all the attack squadrons; the remainder of the observation detachments; the remainder of the fighter wings; and finally the bomber wings.[93] On 4 July Army Group German Crown Prince started the transfer of twenty-seven attack squadrons and thirty-eight fighter squadrons to Army Group Crown Prince Rupprecht for HAGEN. Since that was eleven days before the start of MARNESCHUTZ–REIMS, it can only be assumed those units were not needed for that operation.[94]

With the concurrence of OHL, Rupprecht's Army Group on 12 July issued the final plan for the movement of forces from Army Group German Crown Prince. All assets would move under the control of a special system designated *Y-Transport*. Y-Day was the start of the MARNESCHUTZ–REIMS attack. On order from OHL the movements would commence on the evening of Y + 1, and would be completed by Y + 12. The plan stressed the necessity of maintaining the security of the system. The receiving units included the Second and Seventeenth Armies, which were not making the HAGEN attack, but which had previously transferred like assets to the Fourth and Sixth Armies. On 14 July additional forces, including two divisions, were transferred to Rupprecht's Army Group from Army Group Duke Albrecht.[95]

German order of battle

Prior to the start of MARNESCHUTZ–REIMS, the British estimated that Rupprecht's Army Group had a total of 100 divisions. Sixty-three, including twenty-seven in reserve, were fit for action; twenty-two were regenerating and could be fit for action shortly; and fifteen were completely spent.[96] Despite OHL's 27 June order, the main effort of the Fourth Army was clearly reflected in the weighting of the left wing, rather than the right. The right-most Guards Corps had all five of its divisions in the first wave, and no divisions in follow-on waves. Three of the five were trench divisions. The left-wing III Bavarian Corps and the Guards Reserve Corps to its right both had two divisions in each of three waves. Only one of each corp's six divisions was a trench division. See Tables 11.5 and 11.6.

Allied order of battle

At the beginning of June 1918 the British had thirty-three divisions in the line, holding an average sector of three miles each; eight divisions in army

Table 11.5 HAGEN divisions on 14 July 1918[97]

	First line	Second line	Third line	Total divisions	Sector width
*Fourth Army**	9 Attack	6 Attack	5 Attack	20 Attack	37 km
	5 Trench	2 Trench	2 Trench	9 Trench	
Sixth Army#	4 Attack	2 Attack		6 Attack	9.5 km
	2 Trench		2 Trench	4 Trench	
	13 Attack	8 Attack	5 Attack	26 Attack	46.5 km
	7 Trench	2 Trench	4 Trench	13 Trench	

Source: AOK 4, Ia 1698, (12 July 1918), Bayerisches Kriegsarchiv: File Hgr. Rupprecht, Bd. 105. AOK 6, Ia 3844, (14 July 1918), Bayerisches Kriegsarchiv: File Hgr. Rupprecht, Bd. 108.

Notes
*Five of six corps.
#Two of four corps.

Table 11.6 German corps for HAGEN [98]

	Corps	Commander	Attacking
	(North to south)		
Fourth Army		Sixt von Arnim	
	Naval	Schröder	No
	Guards	Boeckmann	Yes
	XVIII Reserve	Sieger	Yes
	X Reserve	Gabain	Yes
	Guards Reserve	Marschall	Yes
	III Bavarian	Stein	Yes
Sixth Army		Quast	
	XIX	Lucius	Yes
	LV	Bernhardi	Yes
	IV	Kraewel	No
	XL	Litzmann	No

Source: Army Group Crown Prince Rupprecht, Ia 8082, (1 July 1918), Bayerisches Kriegsarchiv: File Hgr. Rupprecht, Bd. 112.

Table 11.7 Guns supporting HAGEN[99]

	Field	Heavy	Super-heavy	Total guns	Trench mortars
Fourth Army	2,052	788	35	2,875	?
Sixth Army	540	200	14	754	?
	2,592	988	49	3,629	?

Source: Army Group Crown Prince Rupprecht, Ia 8051, (29 June 1918), Bayerisches Kriegsarchiv: File Hgr. Rupprecht, Bd. 108.

Table 11.8 Allied order of battle in the HAGEN sector 1 August 1918[100]

	First-line divisions	Reserve divisions	Sector width
Belgian Army	10	2	42 km
British Second Army	11	11*	42 km
	21	13	84 km

Source: Edmonds, Vol.IV, p.7, Map 2.

Note
*1 cadre and 2 American divisions.

reserve; seven in GHQ reserve; five divisions with the French; and eight cadre divisions. North of the Oise the French still had two armies; the Third and the First, each with nine divisions in line and three in reserve.[101] See Table 11.8.

The decision to abort (15 July–6 August)

15–17 July   Despite the disappointing results on the first day of MARNESCHUTZ–REIMS, both OHL and Army Group German Crown Prince believed they had to press on, because aborting the attack would disrupt the entire operational plan. The consensus at that point was that halting MARNESCHUTZ–REIMS would kill HAGEN, because the Germans could not achieve surprise in Flanders, and it was therefore absolutely essential to draw off the Allied reserves. OHL issued the order to start the *Y-Transport* shifting forces to Rupprecht's Army Group.[102]

On 16 July Rupprecht's Army Group issued the order to initiate the forward deployment of its internal HAGEN forces based on the plan issued 26 May. Later that day the *Y-Transport* forces started moving by rail.[103] At that point the Germans still planned to launch deception attack NÜRNBERG with two divisions on a 4.5-kilometer front between Boiry-Becquerelle and Moyennville. OHL also agreed with the Fourth and Sixth Armies that they would need more artillery for HAGEN.[104]

Looking at the results of MARNESCHUTZ–REIMS so far, the HAGEN planners started to worry about the possibility of the British withdrawing their front-line forces in the same way the French had done opposite the German Third Army. They immediately recognized that would require the artillery to be pushed forward more rapidly. Rupprecht's planners concluded that the British had the depth to withdraw in front of the Sixth Army and the Fourth Army in the area north of Ypres, behind the Yser Canal, but not from that point south toward the left wing of the Fourth Army. A withdrawal in that critical middle sector would mean giving up the heights of Scherpenberg, Mount Rouge, and Mount Noir. Late on 16 July Rupprecht glumly recorded in his diary:

> According to the information we get this evening, there is little chance of continuing the attack east of Reims. That is not a good sign for the success of HAGEN, because if the attacks south of the Marne and east of Reims are finished already, no enemy reserves will be fixed there.[105]

Rupprecht's Army Group sent a message to its subordinate armies on 17 July informing them of the failure of the REIMS portion of the attack. The message described the withdrawal of the French first line, but also noted that the same technique was not used against the Seventh Army. The message concluded with two priority intelligence requirements. Would the British use the same technique against HAGEN? If so, where would they re-establish their main position?[106]

That same day Bruchmüller got the order to proceed to Rupprecht's Army Group to assume control of the artillery. Many of the heavy guns required to support HAGEN had also started moving north by that point. By the end of 17 July, four foot artillery battalions and one 170 mm-gun battery were already arriving in Rupprecht's sector. Four more foot artillery battalions, nine heavy trench mortar battalions, and three aerial observation detachments were in transit. Those movements did not escape the notice of Allied intelligence.[107]

Still determined to attack the British in Flanders, Ludendorff boarded a train that night for Rupprecht's headquarters at Tournai. The following day he would preside over a chiefs of staff planning conference for HAGEN. That night Rupprecht recorded in his diary that the Allies obviously knew from the start that MARNESCHUTZ–REIMS was a diversion and that the main attack would come in Flanders. He was convinced that the British had strengthened their defenses accordingly in the HAGEN sector.[108]

18 July   As described in Chapter 10, Ludendorff started the conference by dismissing any possibility of a major Allied counterattack in the south. The discussion then turned to the tactical options if the British attempted the same sort of defense the French had used against the Third Army. About noon the first reports of the Allied counterattack started coming into Rupprecht's headquarters. After the initial shock, Ludendorff closed the conference and made a hasty return to OHL.[109] At 1430 hours OHL ordered Rupprecht's Army Group to send two HAGEN divisions to Army Group German Crown Prince immediately. A few minutes later OHL issued another order to both army groups and the Seventh Army:

1   All transports from the Seventh Army destined for HAGEN (with the exception of the heavy artillery and trench mortars) must be halted and are at the disposal of the Seventh Army.
2   For the time being there will be no continuation of the REIMS attack. The attack divisions and artillery should be pulled back immediately. Further orders to follow.
3   The fighter squadrons and three observation detachments that were supposed to move to HAGEN will remain at the Eighteenth Army at the disposal of Army Group German Crown Prince.[110]

Although for the time being OHL kept the heavy artillery and the trench mortars moving, it was clear at that point that HAGEN would be affected and possibly postponed. Rupprecht wrote in his diary: "There is no doubt that we have passed the zenith of our success. Even if we take some territory in Flanders, it will be of no significance."[111] Ludendorff, on the other hand, told Kuhl in a phone conversation that night that OHL hoped to replace the HAGEN divisions as soon as the situation stabilized in the Ninth and Seventh Army sectors. Ludendorff was almost certain that HAGEN could still be executed.[112]

19 July   OHL still clung to the plan to execute HAGEN, although by 19 July four of the attack divisions had been transferred from Rupprecht's Army Group. That day OHL halted the remainder of the *Y-Transport* movements north, including the heavy artillery and heavy trench mortars.[113] Ludendorff asked Rupprecht's Army Group if HAGEN could be limited in scope if necessary. The army group answered that the attack was still possible with the remaining forces if the operation's objective was limited to breaking through toward Poperinghe–Cassel and pushing back the British north wing in the low area south of Dunkirk. The attack north of Ypres, however, was no longer possible. But if the situation at Army Group German Crown Prince or a British attack in the Seventeenth Army sector drew off any more HAGEN forces, then the objective would have to be limited even further. One option would be an attack to seize the line Deibruch–Mount Rouge–Mount Noir–Strazeele. The artillery and trench-mortar requirement would be about the same, but the number of divisions could be reduced.

Ludendorff initially concurred with that assessment, but he also said that the divisions of the third wave should not be committed if a major success did not appear achievable. Those units also had to be on alert for rapid deployment elsewhere. Ludendorff did not make a final decision at that point. Later that day, when Hindenburg suggested immediately moving the reserves of Army Group Rupprecht to the south for commitment against the flank of the French counterattack, Ludendorff dismissed that idea out of hand because it would have ended HAGEN on the spot.[114]

20 July   On 20 July Rupprecht's Army Group sent OHL a message recommending the postponement of HAGEN by "a few days." Noting that thirty-three batteries had already been transferred from the Fourth Army sector and another twenty-four from the Sixth Army, the staff still recommended the reduced version of HAGEN.[115] Later that afternoon Ludendorff called Kuhl and told him to transfer two more HAGEN divisions to the Seventh Army.[116] Meanwhile, Lossberg arrived at OHL and recommended an immediate withdrawal by the Seventh and Ninth Armies behind the Aisne and Vesle, followed by a deliberate withdrawal on both sides of the Somme.

But Lossberg also recommended executing HAGEN with all the divisions still available and in fighting condition. Because of their reduced number, however, only a limited tactical and not a major operational objective was now possible. If the limited HAGEN attack did not even achieve a tactical success, then Lossberg recommended that the Fourth and Sixth Armies should also be withdrawn to their original positions, and that the entire Western Front had to go on the defensive. The time gained by that move had to be used to reconstitute units. Simultaneously, the buildup of a strong defensive zone had been started to the Antwerp–Maas line, as well as the line Metz–Strasbourg–Rhine. The defensive lines had to be established behind areas that could be flooded.[117]

Lossberg made his recommendations in an attempt to salvage HAGEN. But Ludendorff could not bring himself to give up all the territory won since 21 March, nor could he accept the return to the defensive and the specter of attrition warfare.[118] Kuhl himself did not completely agree with Lossberg. He thought it would be a mistake to go completely on the defensive, but he did agree that a reduced form of HAGEN would prevent the Allies from wresting the initiative.

Kuhl continued to support a HAGEN attack with the more modest objective of taking the line of high ground from Dickebusch to Mount Rouge, Mount Noir, and Strazeele.[119] Rupprecht thought that "without the attack northeast of Ypres, the chances for a major success are so minimized that probably what gains would be made would not be in proportion to the forces committed."[120]

By the end of 20 July, seven of the HAGEN attack divisions had been withdrawn from Rupprecht's Army Group. That evening OHL issued the order signed by Ludendorff:

1 The HAGEN operation will not be executed because of the situation at Army Group German Crown Prince, which probably will require an even larger commitment of forces. Considering the possibility of British offensive actions, I might come back to the execution of HAGEN if the overall situation allows.
2 Army Group Crown Prince Rupprecht goes on the defensive on the HAGEN front.[121]

21–31 July Rupprecht's Army Group went on the defensive, with orders to hold sectors of the western banks of the Ancre and Avre in order to make the German intentions unclear to the Allies. The army group also had to alert five more divisions for possible immediate deployment south. Those divisions were to be positioned behind the left wing of the Second Army, from where they could reach Army Group German Crown Prince by land march.[122]

Kuhl went to Avesnes on 21 July to argue the case for a limited-objective HAGEN. Kuhl thought Ludendorff's swing to the other extreme was the result of the influence of Lossberg, who had argued that a limited-objective HAGEN attack would require as many forces as the full attack. Ludendorff, however, would not be swayed. Even if the Germans halted the French counterattack in the south, he argued, the situation would require counterattacks by Army Group German Crown Prince to consolidate its position. The five divisions being assembled behind the Second Army would most likely be committed to that.[123]

On the other side of the line, the Allies were slow to recognize that the power of Rupprecht's Army Group was being quickly eroded. Haig noted in his diary on 21 July: "In view of Rupprecht's large reserves, I cannot attack on the Kemmel front unless the enemy first attacks and is repulsed. If his reserves remain in my front, I will only carry out local attacks."[124]

On 22 July Rupprecht's Army Group sent Fourth and Sixth Armies a message indicating that HAGEN might still be executed.[125] The following day, however, the Sixth Army issued an order informing its subordinate units that HAGEN would not be executed.[126] Haig now seemed to have completely changed his assessment of the situation from only two days earlier:

As we are fairly well prepared to meet an attack by Rupprecht on my Second Army, it is most likely the attack won't be delivered. So I am preparing to take the offensive and have approved an operation taking place on Rawlinson's front. . . .[127]

Despite the 20 July order canceling the attack, various German headquarters continued to discuss the KLEIN-HAGEN option, with the objective of the Flanders hills of Scherpenberg, Mount Rouge, and Mount Noir. On 24 July Rupprecht recorded in his diary that such an attack was still possible. On 27 July, however, he said a major attack in any form was now out of the question.[128]

1–6 August On 2 August Ludendorff sent a personally drafted memo to the army groups of the Western Front, only for the eyes of the commanding generals, the chiefs of staff, and the operations officers (General Staff officers Ia). Ludendorff noted that while the immediate situation required the Germans to be on the defensive, they had to return to the offensive as soon as possible. After the heavy commitment of forces between the Vesle and the Marne, Ludendorff thought major enemy attacks in other sectors were unlikely for the immediate future—especially since the Allies still expected the Germans to launch a major attack.

But the longer the Germans waited, the more likely it was that the Allies would strike first. Ludendorff thought the most probable sectors were at Mount Kemmel against the Sixth Army; between the Somme and the Oise; toward Soissons; against the high ground at Moronvilliels in Champagne; against the southern front of Army Group C close to St. Mihiel; and finally against the Lorraine sector. Ironically, except for the general area south of the Somme, Ludendorff did not mention Amiens, where the British in fact attacked just six days later. Ludendorff ordered:

> While we organize the defensive, we prepare the attack at the same time. The options we must consider include:
> 1 A reduced form of HAGEN.
> 2 Operation KURFÜRST on both sides of the Oise, roughly between Montdidier and Soissons.
> 3 Smaller-scale attacks east of Reims, against Fort Pompelle, and at Vauquois, as well as in the sector of Army Group C.
> 4 Attacks from the sector of Army Group Duke Alberecht, in greater or lesser width.[129]

On 3 August Rupprecht's Army Group reported reduced enemy pressure in its sector, possibly because of the attacks against Army Group German Crown Prince. But the British also recognized that the Ancre and Avre bridgeheads were being withdrawn, and that the preparation activity for HAGEN had stopped. It was possible, therefore, that the British had sent more fresh reserves to support the French. British activity was now limited to local attacks and heavy patrolling.[130] That, of course, was a faulty intelligence assessment. The British at that point were preparing to mount their attack at Amiens.

In response to Ludendorff's 2 August message, Rupprecht's Army Group on 6 August submitted to OHL the preliminary attack plans of the Fourth Army for KLEIN-HAGEN, and of the Eighteenth Army for a limited KURFÜRST. (The Eighteenth Army had been transferred to Rupprecht's Army Group on 22 July.) But the army group no longer favored the HAGEN option. Since the Seventh Army had been pushed back so far, Rupprecht's planners now thought the best course of action was for the left wing of the Eighteenth Army to attack the Aisne in support of the Ninth Army. Two days later the British struck at Amiens.[131] Operations HAGEN and KURFÜRST had breathed their last.

Assessment

Could HAGEN have succeeded? There can be little doubt that the answer is no. As Wetzell accurately pointed out in his assessment of 12 June, none of the conditions of the previous tactical success were present. Surprise was unlikely; the British had almost three months to reconstitute their units and strengthen their defenses; and the Allied reserves were well positioned and concentrated. At best MARNESCHUTZ–REIMS could have altered the third condition in favor of the Germans, but not the first two. In addition, HAGEN would also have faced two more difficulties that contributed to the failure of MARNESCHUTZ–REIMS. The German Army was truly burned out by July 1918, and the Allies finally understood and were developing counter-measures for the new German infantry and artillery offensive tactics.

Objective

Like all of the 1918 offensives, HAGEN was designed as a force-on-force operation. The objective in this case was the defeat of the British Second Army and the Belgian Army. Beyond that, there was no clearly identified operational end-state. As early as the start of May, Rupprecht's planners admitted, "It is very probable that NEU-GEORG will merely constitute a new blow for the British and will create a salient of greater or lesser dimension in the direction of Poperinghe–Cassel." But then the longer-term results of the operation were couched in vague political and psychological terms: "Yet, the political-military significance of such a success in Flanders must be valued much higher than a limited success in the region of Albert."[132]

Throughout the German planning process there was little focus and very little evidence of any awareness of the vulnerability of the British logistics network. The early May assessment did conclude: "the British and the Belgians will be hard hit if we succeed in bombarding effectively the coast region as far as Dunkirk—including the valuable British supplies stored there—and in menacing Calais."[133] This is one of the few mentions of a logistics target in any of the surviving German documents. Even so, it was tacked onto the end as something of an afterthought, as if to say that the Germans would achieve that much if nothing else. Only as late as 9 July did one analysis produced by the Sixth Army really take a close look at Hazebrouck as a rail center.

> From Hazebrouck, two double lines run to Merville, and another double line to Isbergues. To the south a double line runs from St. Venant via Isbergues to Airs. Lines outside of Hazebrouck connect with double lines to Poperinghe, St. Omer, and Cassel. The Hazebrouck rail yards have 25 switch sidings and 15 loading platforms.[134]

During the early stages of the planning for NEU-MICHAEL and NEU-GEORG, Amiens and Hazebrouck with their critical BEF rail centers were not even identified as objectives. The original 1 May NEU-GEORG plan had the Fourth Army attack passing north of Hazebrouck.[135] The town did not figure in the HAGEN attack at all until the two right-wing corps of the Sixth Army were added to the operation in the 1 June operations order.[136] Following that, Rupprecht's Army Group and OHL between 18 and 21 June continued to debate the actual importance of taking Hazebrouck.[137] Even then the plan never called for securing the Nieppe Forest south of Hazebrouck, although the failure to take that objective had been one of the key reasons for the failure of GEORGETTE.

Mission creep

One of the recurring patterns of the 1918 German offensives is their tendency to expand rather than focus as the plans developed. HAGEN was no different. The original plan called for an attack by twenty-five divisions under the control of one army on a twenty-four-kilometer front. Between 1 May and 1 June the Fourth Army's attack zone increased from twenty-four to thirty-seven kilometers. The entire operation eventually grew to thirty-nine divisions controlled by two armies on a forty-seven-kilometer front. In early May OHL had been concerned about the ability of the attacking divisions to reach their initial objectives ten kilometers deep in a single bound. By 1 July the plan called for the III Bavarian Corps to reach Cassel in a single bound, a depth of sixteen-kilometers. Immediately after the Allied counterattack of 18 July, the HAGEN plan was scaled back to thirty-three divisions on a forty-kilometer front.

As in the previous operations, the impetus to expand the operations came from the armies and army groups, with OHL eventually acquiescing. This time was no different, but Rupprecht's Army Group was right to want to widen the operation to the south to include Hazebrouck. What was really not necessary in the original plan was the attack north of Ypres. As the HAGEN plan was scaled back after 18 July in an attempt to save the operation, that was the first element that dropped out.

Decision 18 July

Despite the initial failures of 15 and 16 July, Ludendorff decided to go ahead with HAGEN. He blamed Wetzell and the Seventh Army for the failure of

Table 11.9 HAGEN divisions and sector widths[138]

	1 May	*1 June*	*15 June*	*14 July*	*20 July*
Fourth Army	25	31	31	29	24
Sixth Army	0	5	8	10	9
Total sector	24 km	43 km	47 km	47 km	40 km

Source: Army Group Crown Prince Rupprecht, Ia 7034, (1 May 1918), Bayerisches Kriegsarchiv: File Hgr. Rupprecht, Bd. 112. Army Group Crown Prince Rupprecht, Ia 7567, (1 June 1918), Bayerisches Kriegsarchiv: File Hgr. Rupprecht, Bd. 105. Army Group Crown Prince Rupprecht, Ia 7883, (20 July 1918), Bayerisches Kriegsarchiv: File Hgr. Rupprecht, Bd. 112. AOK 6, Ia 3844, (14 July 1918), Bayerisches Kriegsarchiv: File Hgr. Rupprecht, Bd. 108. AOK 4, Ia 1698, (12 July 1918), Bayerisches Kriegsarchiv: File Hgr. Rupprecht, Bd. 105.

MARNESCHUTZ–REIMS, and convinced himself that it was just a local reverse. Even after the Allied counterattack of 18 July, Ludendorff still clung to the possibility of launching HAGEN in some form. Thus, he initially kept the heavy artillery and trench mortars moving north after he halted the rest of the *Y-Transport* movements. According to the German official history, OHL held out for HAGEN until the last possible moment, even though it was obvious that it could never produce decisive results, because the alternative was to yield the initiative to the Allies. "The continuation of the attacks was a risky game, but not more so than going over to the defense."[139]

Decision 20 July

By the end of 20 July, Ludendorff had no choice but to cancel HAGEN. With seven attack divisions having been withdrawn from Rupprecht's Army Group since 16 July, there were now only nineteen left, and five of those would shortly be placed on alert and moved south. It would have been impossible to mount HAGEN with the remaining fourteen attack divisions, especially considering the severe manpower shortages in Rupprecht's trench divisions that would have to fill the gaps. Even the various versions of KLEIN-HAGEN considered by OHL over the next two weeks were impossible.

Alternatives

The Germans had no real alternatives at that point. Many of the German commanders and planners approached the operations following BLÜCHER with a deep sense of pessimism and foreboding. The two principal army group commanders and their respective chiefs of staff were among the most pessimistic. Rupprecht, Kuhl, Crown Prince Wilhelm, and Schulenberg all believed that HAGEN was almost impossible and KURFÜRST was a pipe dream. And although it could not possibly produce decisive results, "In our opinion, the planned MARNESCHUTZ–REIMS offensive constituted, under compulsion of the dynamic law, the last great offensive effort of which we were capable."[140]

In contrast to the field headquarters, the planners at OHL seemed to be living increasingly in a dream world after the failure of BLÜCHER. The operational assessments of Wetzell, which at first had been so logical and penetrating, became increasingly bizarre as the German situation deteriorated and he fell increasingly out of favor with Ludendorff. (Ludendorff finally fired him in September.) Wetzell bounced back and forth between recommending major offensives at Verdun and in Italy, without ever explaining where the supporting artillery would come from. His completely unrealistic 6 July recommendation for a major offensive in Alsace never even attempted to suggest where the necessary thirty-five divisions and 1,360 batteries would come from. But Wetzell wasn't alone at OHL. The KURFÜRST plan was equally unrealistic. Just where would the German Army come up with fifty divisions capable of attacking after MARNESCHUTZ–REIMS, let alone after HAGEN? One is tempted here to draw parallels between the state of mind at OHL in July 1918 and the state of mind in Hitler's bunker in April 1945, with the Führer moving non-existent divisions around on the map.

Although Kuhl was a HAGEN skeptic from the start, he nonetheless continued to argue for mounting the operation, even after 18 July. As he explained it in his post-war analysis for the Reichstag:

> Yet abandoning the offensive would not have altered matters. How was the war to be continued then? To have discontinued the offensive would have meant to pass to the defensive. OHL, being imbued with a strong determination, refused to entertain any such plan, and justly so.[141]

This is a classic example of the German Great General Staff tradition of seeking operational solutions for strategic problems. Kuhl also wrote:

> In summing up, one can say with regard to our offensive in July that considerable objections militated against it. Still, it might have succeeded. In that event, it would probably have been possible to execute also the HAGEN offensive.[142]

When he was chief of staff of the United States Army in the early 1990s, General Gordon Sullivan once famously said, "Hope is not a method." Hope was about the only method OHL had left in July 1918.

12 Conclusions

OHL failed in 1918 because it disregarded one of the most important lessons of military history—the interrelationship of politics and war.[1]

Hans Delbrück

Nothing could illustrate more the mindlessness of the efficiency and power of the German empire than this great military offensive within a political vacuum.[2]

Correlli Barnett

At the end of Ludendorff's offensives in July 1918, the greatest string of tactical successes in World War I had failed to produce any significant operational advantage, much less strategic victory. Quite the contrary, Germany in August 1918 found itself in a far weaker strategic position than it had been in at the start of the year. The German Army in the west was weaker than its opponents in manpower and equipment—both qualitatively and quantitatively—and its once impressive morale and esprit de corps were on the verge of collapse. Operationally, the German Army was overextended, exposed, and vulnerable to counterattack along more than one sector of the front. Reasons for this failure can be found on all three levels of warfare.

The operational–strategic disconnect

On the strategic level Ludendorff's grand scheme was doomed from the start. An absolute military victory was impossible for the Germans to achieve in 1918. As Hans Delbrück reported to the German Reichstag in 1925, Germany at the start of 1918 had only a slight numerical superiority and was inferior in reserves. Much of its equipment was inferior and worn out; fuel was in short supply; and the supply system was inadequate. Delbrück strongly criticized OHL for rationalizing away these shortcomings.[3]

Delbrück and Hermann von Kuhl argued that with its strong position based on interior lines, the German Army might have been able to convince its enemies that it could not be defeated militarily. The objective of the 1918 offensives, they argued, should have been a negotiated peace that Germany could have entered into from a position of strength by achieving a limited military victory.[4] But the precondition for such a negotiated peace in the west was German willingness to give up claims to Belgium, which Ludendorff would not do. Along with this as the strategic objective, the operational goal should have been to orchestrate a series of major tactical successes by attacking at the points where success would be easiest. This was basically how the Allies won after July 1918.

If the 1918 offensives had been better designed operationally (as discussed below), the Germans more than likely could have split the British from the French. They probably could have pushed the BEF off the Continent. The Germans might even have been able to put enough pressure on the French to collapse their government. But then what? If Britain had been defeated on the Continent it almost certainly would have continued the fight so long as the Germans controlled the Belgian coast. The British still held an overwhelming superiority at sea, and the blockade had already come close to bringing Germany to its knees at home. The American forces streaming toward France could have been redirected to Britain to form a large military base for an eventual counterattack. This essentially is the scenario that played out in World War II, and in 1940 the Germans were relatively far stronger than they were in 1918.

When an inherent linkage to a strategic objective is not the dominant force in the planning process, operational and tactical considerations begin to determine strategy. Ludendorff launched a series of major operations without a clear strategic vision of what was to be accomplished, or the specific aims required to provide the necessary operational and tactical linkages. The early tactical success and gains in territory in March through May created an illusion that the offensives might lead to victory, and that in turn strengthened the political position of the annexationists in Germany.[5] Instead, the strategic incoherence that undermined the campaign became a major factor in the German Army culminating before any real operational success could be achieved. The offensives were also an example of the German General Staff's propensity to attempt operational solutions for strategic problems. As Correlli Barnett pointed out, the 1918 offensives were "an attempt by purely military means to decide on the battlefield a war involving total national economic, military, social, and technical power, a war that Germany was losing."[6]

Compounding these problems was Ludendorff's own blind spot—phobia even—against the operational level of war, and his stunning strategic and political ineptitude. Herbert Rosinski pointed out that, considering all the political activity of OHL, it is difficult to find an instance in which its interference in German internal, economic, or foreign policy did not have an exact opposite effect than that intended.[7] Even Ludendorff's own contemporaries were harshly critical of his political incompetence. Writing in his diary, Bavarian Crown Prince Rupprecht noted: "[Ludendorff] lacks any psychological understanding of foreign or domestic politics."[8] And Fritz von Lossberg wrote: "Ludendorff undoubtedly was inwardly convinced of the correctness of his decisions at that time, but he had underrated the breakdown of the larger part of the German people at home and very much overrated the remaining strength of the German Army."[9]

The operational–tactical disconnect

The Germans were responsible for a disproportionately large percentage of the tactical innovations to come out of World War I. They won four of the five battles between March and July, but they still lost the spring 1918 campaign and the war. As Liddell Hart pointed out, Ludendorff's tactical success was his own undoing. He had pushed too far and too long, depleting his reserves in the process. By the end of June, he had driven in three large wedges, but in no place to operational depth. All the Germans had to show for the tremendous expenditure of manpower and resources was an extended front with vulnerable salients.[10] And as Martin Van Creveld noted, once initial tactical success was achieved it became irrelevant, because the entire German strategic posture collapsed within five months.[11]

On the tactical level, the Germans were formidable opponents. Their discipline, training, leadership, and tactical doctrine produced units that were almost impossible to beat in anything approaching evenly matched force-on-force encounters, either on the defense or the offense. Their innovations in infantry tactics especially changed the way infantry fought for most of the remainder of the 20th century. Their artillery innovations too cast a long shadow over modern warfare, but the Germans adopted the new fire-support methods unevenly. During Operation MICHAEL only the Eighteenth Army used the full range of Bruchmüller/Pulkowski techniques, and they did not become standard practice across the German Army until Operation BLÜCHER. During Operation MICHAEL the Germans failed to weight the designated main attack with artillery. They never made that mistake again, after Bruchmüller was put in complete charge of the fire-support planning for all of the subsequent offensives. From mid-July until the end of the war, the Allies themselves increasingly adopted the German fire-support tactics.[12]

The German Army's greatest tactical handicap was in its mobility, which limited its ability to maneuver to operational depth. During World War I mechanical power replaced muscle power as the primary source of battlefield mobility, but the Germans were slower to adapt than the Allies. Ludendorff certainly had a blind spot for the tank; but armored fighting vehicles in World War I were not the wonder weapons some thought them to be. Despite having an overwhelming advantage in tanks at the end of the war, the Allies never achieved tactical gains on the levels of MICHAEL or BLÜCHER, or even GEORGETTE. Nor did the Allies completely dismount their own cavalry divisions. The Germans did on the Western Front, but not necessarily because they recognized that the days of horse cavalry were over. Rather, the Germans needed the manpower and the horses for other things. Because of the inept management of their war industry, the Germans were chronically short of trucks and other motor vehicles. Thus the horses, which were also in short supply, were needed for battlefield transportation forward of the railheads. Yet, some histor-ians have suggested that dismounting all the cavalry divisions was a major mistake, no matter how badly the horses were needed elsewhere. If one or two cavalry divisions had been available in the Eighteenth Army sector on 26 and 27 March, they just might have been able to exploit the gap at Montdidier to capture Amiens.

Operational design assessment and alternatives

The single greatest flaw in the 1918 offensives was the lack of clearly defined strategic and operational objectives. Neither Hindenburg nor Ludendorff in their post-war books offered a vision of a concrete military objective or a concrete political objective to be gained from the offensives.[13] None of the contemporary operations orders offer any such objective. The orders do contain vague refer-ences to the BEF's Channel ports, but no clear roadmap or series of intermediate objectives on how to get there. Given the German Army's lack of reach and operational mobility, this is not too surprising. Ludendorff clearly understood that he wanted to knock the BEF out of the war, but he wasn't quite sure how. Throughout the first half of 1918 he seems more concerned with holding onto the military initiative in the absence of any other concrete objective. As he wrote after the war, "I expected my own Army to be weakened and I hoped it would be less so than the enemy. By continuing the attack, we would still retain the initiative. More I could not aim at."[14]

By retaining the initiative without any clear objective Ludendorff was in effect attempting to develop the situation in the hope of exploiting any opportun-ities that might arise. He admitted as much when he wrote: "Since I had been able hitherto, to find the proper strategic remedy in the most serious situations, I had no reason to believe that I would not succeed this time."[15] While such an approach can be useful in certain tactical situations, it is almost always a recipe for failure at the operational level.

In the end, Ludendorff's offensives only managed to gain ground. As Richard Simpkin noted, ground is seldom a viable operational objective except when it holds a geographically fixed enemy resource, like a governmental center, air base, navy base, bridge, or a topographical feature that provides access to or control of a key resource.[16] There were such key pieces of ground in the Allied sector and within German reach, but the Germans never really seemed to recognize their significance. The Allies did.

Center of gravity

At the start of 1918 the BEF was clearly the operational center of gravity of the Allied coalition. Although recovering from the mutinies of 1917, the French Army was still shaky, and the Americans had not yet arrived in significant numbers to tip irrevocably the strategic balance. Despite the fatal flaw in Luden-dorff's strategic goal—total military victory as opposed to negotiated peace from a position of strength—the operational center of gravity remained the same. True centers of gravity are almost always very difficult to attack directly, but that is exactly what the Germans tried to do. Operations MICHAEL, GEORGETTE, and HAGEN were designed as classic force-on-force encounters to produce the battle of annihilation that was so central to German military thinking. Operations BLÜCHER, GNEISENAU, and MARNESCHUTZ–REIMS were large-scale diversions to set up the conditions for the success of HAGEN. At least, that was the intent behind BLÜCHER before Ludendorff and OHL lost control of the operation. Operation KURFÜRST was a half-baked, muddled plan to follow up against the French after the success of HAGEN. The plan had almost no grounding in reality, and is yet another example of the progressive loss of touch at OHL.

A force-on-force attack against the BEF was a long shot at best. Although the Germans could still muster impressive force ratio superiorities locally, they did not have the battlefield mobility, the necessary speed, or the reserves to achieve the large-scale *Vernichtungsschlacht* they so desperately sought. Nor did they have the logistics system and resources to sustain it. But there was a way to defeat the BEF without necessarily attacking it head-on. The shallow and fragile British logistics system was a crucial vulnerability that might have yielded far greater results if the Germans had subjected it to a coordinated and sustained attack throughout its depth. By the spring of 1916 the BEF's logistics system was on the verge of collapsing under its own weight. On 1 September 1916 the British brought in the civilian expert Sir Eric Geddes to rationalize the system. He largely succeeded, but the system remained fragile and strained until the end of the war.[17]

Almost everything that sustained the British Army in the field entered the Continent through three major and four minor ports in the north, and three major ports in the south. The BEF's Q-Staff organized the logistics flow into northern and southern lines of communications, with Amiens being the dividing point. The southern ports were the BEF's main first-class base ports.[18] In February 1917, for example, the ports handled 168,599 tons of supplies, with 56.2 percent of the total coming through the northern ports, and 43.7 percent coming through the southern ports. See Table 12.1.

Although the various operations orders for MICHAEL, GEORGETTE, and HAGEN made vague references to the BEF's Channel ports as long-range or follow-on objectives, they were generally too deep for the Germans to reach. Nor were the ports necessarily the key vulnerabilities in the British logistics system. The actual capacity of a port is based on throughput, not on the amount of tonnage that can be unloaded at a given time. A ship can always be discharged on the quay faster than the quay itself can be cleared. The quay can be cleared much faster than the transit sheds can be cleared. Thus, actual port capacity was linked to rail capacity, and British ports in France generally had too many berths and not enough railways.[19]

Rail was the primary means of moving supplies from the ports. Rail had to be used to move all supplies to destinations more than thirty miles from the ports.

Table 12.1 Supply flow through BEF Channel ports in February 1917[20]

	Percentage of total
Northern ports	
Dunkirk	17.5
Calais	10.1
Boulogne	17.3
Small ports	11.3
Etaples	
St. Valery	
Tréport	
Fécamp	
Southern ports	
Rouen	22.9
Le Harve	14.9
Dieppe	5.9

Source: A.M. Henniker, *Transportation on the Western Front, 1914–1918*, (London: 1937), pp.235–236.

Because of the poor conditions and low capacity of the roads of the time, this was the maximum distance for motorized or horse-drawn supply columns. It took 150 trucks to equal one train.[21] In September 1916 it took 1,934 tons of supplies per mile of front per day to sustain the BEF.[22] By the close of 1917 the BEF was using 6 million gallons of petrol per month, and had to feed 449,880 horses. In April 1918 the British ran 725 ammunition trains to the front—almost as many as during the entire five-month period of the battle of the Somme in 1916. By the end of the war, the BEF was operating 1,486 locomotives in its sector with 18,500 personnel.[23]

   Generally, it is difficult to close down, or even temporarily neutralize a rail network. While it is relatively easy to destroy signaling and switching equipment, that only slows down but does not stop rail movement. The roadbeds and track are much harder to destroy. The key vulnerabilities in a rail network are its choke points: tunnels, bridges, switching yards, and rail junctions. If a rail network is dense, like the one behind most of the German sector in 1918, single choke points may have little military significance, because the system has ample bypasses and workarounds. But the British sector was shallow to begin with, and the rail network in that sector was not robust and had two significant choke points—its two major forward marshaling and switching yards at Amiens and Hazebrouck. Amiens formed the hub of almost all of the BEF's forward railway operations. Anything that needed to run between railheads had to go through Amiens, or be taken back to the regulating stations near the base ports.[24]

   There can be no doubt that in March and April 1918 the British feared for their logistics infrastructure. Around 25 March Q-Staff planners started developing contingency plans (Scheme X and Scheme Y) based on having to abandon their northern line of communications. Then they developed Scheme Z to abandon the southern ports and line of communications.[25] On 18 April Rawlinson wrote to General Sir Henry Wilson: "There can be no question that the Amiens area is the only one in which the enemy can hope to gain such a success as to force the Allies to discuss terms of peace."[26] The value the British placed on Amiens is also indicated by the fact that they counterattacked there first on 8 August 1918.

Foch too understood very clearly the significance of Amiens, but for some reason the Germans never seemed to recognize this key vulnerability. Amiens was never one of the original primary objectives of Operation MICHAEL, and only became an objective as something of an afterthought after the original plan had fallen apart beyond recovery. Even after the end of MICHAEL Ludendorff would not allocate heavy artillery assets to the Second Army to bring the rail yards under heavier interdiction fire. Hazebrouck was an original objective of the GEORGETTE plan, but then a few days into the battle Ludendorff shifted the main effort away from Hazebrouck and toward Mount Kemmel.

All the operations orders for and the message traffic during Operations MICHAEL and GEORGETTE focus on using deep attack assets to hit the rail lines and rail centers primarily to prevent the Allies from shifting reinforcements. Until the planning for Operation HAGEN was well developed, there was not even a hint of attacking rail centers for the main purpose of strangling the British logistically. Ironically, the Germans found themselves in just such a situation after Operation BLÜCHER, when the rail center at Soissons was the choke point on their only major rail line into the new salient. This condition forced the Germans to launch Operations GNEISENAU and MARNESCHUTZ–REIMS to improve the logistics flow into the salient. It is about this time, when the attention of the Germans operational planners was focused on rail centers, that Hazebrouck was added as a key objective in the HAGEN plan. The Allies clearly recognized the German vulnerability at Soissons, which was one of the principal objectives in the 18 July counteroffensive.

Decisive points

As discussed above, any German offensive operation in which first Amiens and then Hazebrouck were the decisive points would have had dire consequences for the British Army on the Continent. These should have been the objectives of Operations MICHAEL and GEORGETTE, respectively. If the Germans had taken Amiens, the British would have been forced to attack to retake it almost immediately. That in turn would have forced the British to weaken their forces in the north, making Hazebrouck that much more vulnerable, and GEORGETTE more likely to succeed. Decisive points for follow-on operations could possibly have been the secondary rail centers at Abbeville and St. Omer, but holding on to Amiens, or better Amiens and Hazebrouck, for any extended period of time would have made the British position on the Continent very tenuous, if not untenable.

Not all the German staff officers were blind to the significance of Amiens. Writing after the war, Major General Max Hoffmann, the chief of staff of the Eastern Front, noted that Amiens should have been the decisive point of

MICHAEL, although he did not necessarily identify its importance as a logistics choke point.

> The attack was not made solely at the point that was considered the most favorable for a breach in the line to be made, and it was not made with the whole of the forces that could be disposed of. The point that was considered as the most favorable was the southern wing of the English Army to the north of the Somme. All available forces should have been thrown at that one point. Instead of which, attacks were made both to the north and the south of the Somme.
>
> However, we did not succeed in taking Amiens, and thus separating the English and French armies—we almost succeeded, we did not win the victory.[27]

Culmination

Strategically the Germans probably reached culmination in World War I with the failure of the unrestricted U-boat campaign and the entry of America into the war. On the tactical level, each of the five offensives culminated before they achieved any significant objective. MICHAEL, GEORGETTE, and BLÜCHER all reached culmination after achieving large-scale but irrelevant tactical gains, and then not along the lines of their original plans. GNEISENAU and MAR-NESCHUTZ–REIMS both ran out of steam before they accomplished much of anything, especially the REIMS attack to the east of the city that ran into a well-prepared defense-in-depth.

Considering the five offensives as a single integrated campaign, it is a little harder to pinpoint just where the Germans culminated on the operational level. Certainly they were well beyond their culminating point after Ludendorff tried to exploit the initial successes of BLÜCHER, and then the operation ground to a halt leaving the Germans holding a large, exposed, and almost impossible-to-supply salient. From that point on HAGEN had no chance of accomplishing anything except more attrition. Max Hoffmann argued rather emphatically that the Germans reached their culminating point when they failed to take Amiens, even though that was not one of MICHAEL's objectives in the original plan.

> At the very moment when OHL saw that they would not get Amiens, that they had not been able to break through the enemy's front, they ought to have realized that a decisive victory on the Western Front was no longer to be expected. If this first attempt, which had been made with the best forces they possessed, had failed, every succeeding attack that could only be made with ever diminishing forces, would likewise have no chance of success.[28]

After the end of March, however, the Germans just might have had one or two chances to recover. One option was a renewed push on Amiens, which was only ten kilometers away. Crown Prince Wilhelm recommended such a course of action, but that attack could not be prepared and launched before 17 April. Ludendorff wanted to attack sooner, so he reached for the radically reduced GEORG plan and launched GEORGETTE on 9 April. But GEORGETTE was too weak, and in the end it was little more than a waste of resources, time, and initiative. When the Germans did try to take Amiens again, on 24 April when GEORGETTE was clearly stalling, it was another waste of resources, too little, too late—just like MARS and HAMMERSCHLAG.

Even as light as GEORGETTE was, it just might have succeeded in taking Hazebrouck if Ludendorff on 12 April had not shifted the main effort toward the approaches to Bailleul. The loss of Hazebrouck would not have hurt the British as badly as the loss of Amiens, but it would have knocked their entire logistics system off balance enough to buy the Germans some breathing space and more time to mount a stronger push against Amiens. By the end of 13 April, however, the British and Australians had formed a defense in front of Hazebrouck—one solid enough that the Germans probably could not have overcome it with the resources they had immediately at hand. At that point, the Germans most likely reached culmination on the operational level. Ludendorff, however, refused to accept that either strategic or operational culmination had been reached right up until 8 August, the "Black Day of the German Army." According to Kuhl: "General Ludendorff, who before 8 August still had faith in the possibility of a strategic remedy, lost after this date all hope of consolidating the situation in our favor by means of a strategic expedient."[29]

Lines of operations

Strategically the Germans were operating on interior lines. With their robust and deep rail network in their rear areas, they had a greater ability to shift forces and resources to various points along their own front than did the Allies. (This, of course, did not apply to the German forces in the BLÜCHER salient after May 1918.) Tactically, each of the offensives was somewhat different. MICHAEL advanced on divergent lines, clearly to its detriment as the operation proceeded. GEORGETTE generally converged—perhaps too much at the end. BLÜCHER diverged, especially after it crossed the Vesle. GNEISENAU tried to converge, but never really accomplished much. MARNESCHUTZ and REIMS diverged, and even within itself MARNESCHUTZ diverged. HAGEN, as it was planned, was to advance along converging lines.

Generally, but not necessarily always, it is better for an attacking force to converge, so that combat power increases as the forces near the objective. Too great a degree of convergence, however, can cause congestion and confusion, with too many forces in too little space. This is what happened to some degree in the later phases of GEORGETTE at the junction of the Sixth and Fourth Armies. MICHAEL, on the other hand, clearly diverged too rapidly, especially in the Eighteenth Army sector, as too few forces covered too much space and combat power dissipated. In his 1925 report to the Reichstag, Delbrück was especially critical of the way Operation MICHAEL diverged.

In order to attain the strategical goal—the separation of the English Army from the French and the consequent rolling up of the former—the attack would have to be so arranged so that it followed the course of the Somme. Ludendorff, however, had stretched the offensive front some four miles farther to the south because the enemy seemed especially weak there.

The supporting wing of the attack under Hutier broke through at this point, and it outpaced the wing of the main attack under Below. Thus, it threw the entire operation off balance. The result was ultimately to follow through with Hutier's success, which resulted in a dispersal of the effort.[30]

Considering the campaign as a whole, the operations advanced along diverging lines at the operational level. The focus of the main effort was always supposed to be in the north against the British, with the Germans attacking generally from east to west. MICHAEL was supposed to start out toward the west, and then wheel to the northwest. Instead, it shifted to the southwest. The three offensives in the south threw far too much force into the north-to-south attacks, which further dissipated the German ability to project combat power from east to west. BLÜCHER and MARNESCHUTZ–REIMS were supposed to be diversionary attacks, but they were both far larger than GEORGETTE or even HAGEN as planned. They were 63 and 72 percent as large respectively as MICHAEL in divisions, and 80 percent and 96 percent as large respectively in artillery.

During MICHAEL, GEORGETTE, and BLÜCHER, Ludendorff shifted the main effort in mid-operation. That can be done at the tactical level by committing the reserve, but it is nonetheless difficult. At the operational level it is even more difficult, because it means shifting not only the entire logistical tail, but also the critical combat-support forces, to include artillery, engineers, and air. Delbrück concluded that by following the tactical line of least resistance, Ludendorff violated his own stated primary principle of annihilation warfare: "A strategy that intends to force the decision must do so at the point of the first successful blow."[31]

Depth

The Germans in 1918 had an understanding of depth more advanced than most of their opponents. They had pioneered the concept of defense-in-depth, and in the offense their storm troop units and their long-range FEKA artillery units had specific deep attack roles—at least at the tactical level. The decision to attack in the north against the British was based partly on the shallow Allied depth in the area, with the British having their backs almost against the sea. On the other hand, when Ludendorff decided to push Operation BLÜCHER beyond the Vesle, he made the mistake of attacking into the Allies' depth, a sector where they could more easily fall back and absorb the attack—even if it was in the direction of Paris. Foch was quick to recognize that BLÜCHER would lead nowhere. Operation MARNESCHUTZ and the extreme western arm of REIMS made some sense because the Germans needed the rail center at Reims, but the extension of REIMS to the east made no sense at all. There was no place for that attack to go.

Depth has both a spatial and a time component. An enemy's combat and support systems can also be attacked in depth. While the Germans probably would have accomplished more if they had focused their attacks on the Amiens and Hazebrouck rail centers, a simultaneous and sustained attack throughout the entire depth of the BEF's logistics system would have produced even greater results. As previously noted throughout this study, such an attack would have brought the full weight of the German Navy to bear on the sea-lanes and the ports on both sides of the Channel. This would have included the naval batteries on the north Flanders coast, and the *Wilhelmgeschütze* (the so-called Paris Guns that were actually manned by navy crews), which could have been used to shell the Channel ports or even Dover if they were in the right position. Such an attack would not have been decisive in itself, but it would certainly have increased pressure on the British logistics system, especially if one or both of the key forward rail centers fell.

Timing, tempo, and sequencing

The Germans had little choice in the timing of the campaign. They knew they had only a very narrow window of opportunity, and they had to strike before the arriving Americans tipped the balance. That combined with the time required for the buildup and the training, and the weather and the condition of the ground in the attack zone, all pointed to no later than the end of March for the start of offensive operations. Despite the basic flaws in the operational plan itself and Ludendorff's constant meddling and micro-management, the planning, organization, and execution of the preparations and training for Operation MICHAEL constituted one of the modern masterpieces of military staff work.

Sequencing and sequential effects are two of the key elements of the operational art that distinguish it from tactics. Yet as noted in the introduction to this study, Ludendorff started out rejecting the sequential operations that Wetzell recommended. Ludendorff's original rationale was that the German Army only had the manpower and resources for one major decisive attack. Yet this was clearly not the case. Ludendorff's initial rejection of sequential operations had more to do with his intention to achieve a decisive victory through a *Vernichtungsschlacht*.

As events played out, the Germans launched five large-scale attacks within a four-month period and were still planning two more attacks when the Allies went on the offensive. As the following table shows, the Germans launched a total of 235 divisional attacks on the initial days of Operations MICHAEL through MARNESCHUTZ–REIMS. Many divisions, of course, attacked in two of the operations, and some attacked in three. After the start of the various operations, OHL committed at least twenty-five more divisions to MICHAEL; twenty-three more to GEORGETTE; fifteen more to BLÜCHER; five more to

Table 12.2 First-day force distributions

	Total divisions	Total guns	Sector width	Kilometers per division	Guns per division	Guns per kilometer
MICHAEL	67	6,608	103 km	1.5	99	64
GEORGETTE	36	2,210	44 km	1.2	61	50
BLÜCHER	42	5,263	100 km	2.4	125	53
GNEISENAU	24	2,276	45 km	1.9	95	51
MARNESCHUTZ–REIMS	48	6,353	19 km	2.5	132	53
HAGEN	39	3,629	47 km	1.2	93	77
KURFÜRST	50	—	—	—	—	—

GNEISENAU; and six more to MARNESCHUTZ–REIMS.[32] OHL was also planning for a combined total of eighty-nine more divisional attacks in HAGEN and KURFÜRST.

In the end, the German offensives were only haphazardly linked. GEORGETTE was a response to the failure of MICHAEL, not a well-planned and coordinated follow-up. HAGEN was a response to the combined failure of MICHAEL and GEORGETTE. BLÜCHER was designed to set the conditions for HAGEN. It not only failed to do that, it caused other major problems for the Germans. Despite what Ludendorff and others said in their post-war writings, GNEISENAU and MARNESCHUTZ–REIMS had far more to do with relieving problems with the lines of communications into the BLÜCHER salient than they had to do with setting up the conditions for HAGEN. Even after MARNESCHUTZ–REIMS had failed to take the rail center at Reims or to draw off significant Allied reserves from the north, Ludendorff still intended to go ahead with HAGEN within a few weeks' time. What would the results have been if the five large offensives, totaling at least 309 divisional attacks between mid-March and mid-July 1918, had been conducted as a single, integrated, synchronized, and sequential campaign?

Many historians, including Richard Simpkin, have said that the 1918 offensives failed because their overall tempo was too slow. The long pauses between each of the attacks gave the Allies the opportunity to recover and prepare for the next blow.[33] Although the Germans were stretched to the limit on manpower, artillery was really the major pacing factor. Because of the inept management of the war industries, the German Army was short on artillery throughout the war. Some batteries took part in three and even four of the offensives; and some of the heavy and long-range batteries that made up the vaunted "Battering Train" were committed to all five and were in the process of moving north for HAGEN on 18 July.

Given the need to commit resources to multiple operations and the transportation times required, the tempo, or the time between attacks was a balancing act that required tradeoffs. GEORGETTE was launched only four days after the end of MICHAEL. Although it achieved surprise, it was too light. BLÜCHER came twenty-nine days after GEORGETTE. The long delay allowed the Germans to build up a sizeable force, but the attack still achieved surprise. Four days after BLÜCHER Operation GNEISENAU was neither a surprise nor heavily weighted enough to achieve much. MARNESCHUTZ–REIMS came thirty days after GNEISENAU. Although it was the second largest of the five attacks, it achieved neither surprise nor any worthwhile results. HAGEN was scheduled to start about twelve days after MARNESCHUTZ–REIMS, and would certainly not have been a surprise to the British. Not only did MARNESCHUTZ–REIMS fail to draw off any significant Allied reserves in Flanders, the Allied counterattack of 18 July actually drew off HAGEN divisions.

When the Allies went on the offensive from 18 July 1918 on, they operated within the limitations of the speed of a marching infantryman or a horse team pulling a field gun. Rather than launching deep-penetration battles in an attempt to reach the ever-elusive open warfare, the Allies conducted a series of limited objective but logistically sustainable and sequenced attacks on a broad front designed to push the German Army steadily back while inflicting heavy losses.[34] It was one of history's first successful operational campaigns in the modern sense.

Reach

Reach and depth are closely related concepts. The armies of World War I, and especially the German Army, had limited operational reach because of their limited mobility technology. The ability to reach to operational depth, however, is not necessarily rigidly tied to mobility and a given linear distance. If the BEF's Channel ports had been the designated objectives of MICHAEL, GEORGETTE, or HAGEN, then the Germans certainly did not have the reach to achieve those objectives in a single attack. If on the other hand Amiens and Hazebrouck had been the designated objectives, then the German Army did have the operational reach to achieve those objectives—in March and April at least. The two key rail centers were at what normally would be considered tactical depth in terms of linear distance. But in terms of the consequences that would have resulted from the British losing either or both of the rail centers, they were—or should have been—operational targets. In this specific case, then, the Germans in March and April 1918 had operational reach, albeit one that was very situationally dependent.

The influence of 1918

Volumes have been written about how the German Army following World War I transformed itself first into the 100,000-man *Reichswehr* of the Weimar Republic, and then into the *Wehrmacht* of World War II. A complete review of that story is far beyond the scope of this study, but a few observations about the German approach to the operational level of war are in order. Immediately following World War I and the drastic reduction of the German Army under the terms of the Versailles Treaty, General Hans von Seeckt initiated an exhaustive and comprehensive analysis of the German Army's performance in the war. Based on the recommendations of the many study commissions he formed, Seeckt oversaw the transformation of the *Reichswehr* into a force based on an organization and doctrine for future mobile warfare. Seeckt also structured the *Reichswehr* into a *Führerheer*—literally a leader army—a cadre army upon which a greatly expanded German Army could be built in a short period of time.

Seeckt broke with the traditional German reliance on numbers and mass armies. He believed that future wars would be decided by mobile armies, small but of high quality. He also rejected the absolute primacy given to the envelopment by the pre-war Schlieffen School. Recognizing the technical weakness of the Germans in World War I, as identified in the Theobeck Report (see Chapter 3), Seeckt placed increased emphasis on technical training for officers. He also saw the air force as primarily a ground-support weapon, rather than a strategic offensive arm.[35]

The most important product of the Seeckt reforms was the new manual for tactical doctrine, *Heeresdienstvorschrift 487, Führung und Gefecht der verbundenen Waffen* [*Command and Combat of the Combined Arms*—universally called "*Das FuG*"]. Published in 1921 (Part 1) and 1923 (Part 2), it was a remarkable piece of work. Unlike the post-World War I doctrinal manuals of almost every other country, *Das FuG* completely disregarded positional, or trench warfare (*Stellungskrieg*). Instead, it focused on mobile warfare (*Bewegungskrieg*), while at the same time adopting many of the tactical techniques the Germans had developed between 1914 and 1918.

Ten years after the appearance of *Das FuG*, the German Army issued an updated version titled *Heeresdienstvorschrift 300, Truppenführung* [*Unit Command*]. The manual, published in 1933 (Part 1) and 1934 (Part 2), was written primarily by Generals Ludwig Beck, Werner von Fritsch, and Otto von Stuelpnagel. It updated the basic concepts in *Das FuG* to bring them into line with the rapidly emerging potentials of motorized warfare, aviation, and electronic communications. The underlying mobile and offensive focus of *Das FuG* remained unchanged, and entire paragraphs and sections were carried over into *Truppenführung*, which remained the German Army's capstone doctrinal manual right up until 1945.

Seeckt reversed Ludendorff's influence and restored the balance between tactics and operations in German military thinking.[36] German operational thinking, however, did not advance between the World Wars as nearly as fast as it did in the Soviet Union. German operational thinking remained firmly rooted in the pre-World War I concepts of Moltke and Schlieffen. The Germans continued to shun sequential operations and cumulative effects, associating such an approach with the attritional warfare (*Materialschlacht*) they feared and abhorred. The focus of *Das FuG* and *Truppenführung*, therefore, was almost exclusively tactical. As noted in Chapter 2 of this study, many historians have argued that what passed for operational art in the German Army was really little more than tactics on a grand scale.

This thinking also contributed to a major blind spot in the German approach to logistics. Because sustainment requirements increase with time, the inadequacies in an army's logistical system cause far greater problems at the operational level of war than at the tactical. Although the Germans were masters of using railway systems for large-scale troop movements, most other elements of their logistics system were not robust. This hurt the Germans severely in both World Wars. Two of *Truppenführung*'s twenty-three chapters deal with logistics matters, but many of those who managed these functions on a divisional staff were not even soldiers; rather, they were military civil servants (*Wehrmachtsbeamten*). Captain Harlan N. Hartness attended the *Kriegsakadamie* from 1935 to 1937 as an American exchange officer. In his after-action report to the U.S. Army he noted that the instructor-to-student ratio at the school was 1:20 for tactics, but only 1:120 for supply and 1:240 for transportation.[37] Without the robust supply and transportation systems to support it, true operational maneuver is impossible. The Germans learned that lesson with a vengeance on the Eastern Front in World War II.

In another sense, the 1918 offensives cast a long shadow over German military operations in World War II. German strategy in 1939–1945 was certainly no better than it had been in World War I, yet, unit for unit the *Wehrmacht* was tactically superior to any of its opponents.[38] On the operational level the Germans still had problems, continuing to approach operations as tactics writ large. The Soviets, on the other hand, had a far better-developed sense of the operational art, and that was their primary means of defeating their tactically superior opponent on the Eastern Front. As the German strategic situation progressively deteriorated, they fell back into their old familiar pattern of attempting operational solutions for strategic problems.

The parallels between Operation MICHAEL in March 1918 and Operation WACHT AM RHEIN in December 1944 are hard to miss. Both operations were last-ditch gambles; both aimed to split two enemies along their boundary and collapse the alliance; and the Germans did not have the operational mobility in either case to make it work. Both operations featured long-range firepower attacks that were only haphazardly linked to the main operations. In 1918 it was the Gotha raids on London and the *Wilhelmgeschütze* shelling Paris. In 1944 it was the V-1 and V-2 attacks on London and Antwerp. Both operations were followed up immediately with another large-scale, desperate operation that only wasted more precious resources—GEORGETTE in April 1918 and NORDWIND in January 1945. As General Günther Blumentritt later said about the Ardennes Offensive, "When the documents of this period are carefully studied, it seems likely that Hitler will be seen to have been thinking in terms of the great March offensive of 1918 in the First World War."[39]

Some concluding thoughts on generalship

No general, as the old saying goes, ever wakes up in the morning and decides that he is going to lose a battle that day. Yet for every general who wins a battle, there is another one who loses it. Although the "Great Man School of History" has been largely discredited for many years, there can be no doubt that the competence, motivation, and decision making on the part of the most senior commander on either side of a battle or a campaign are major factors in the outcome. It is impossible, therefore, to analyze the 1918 German offensives without considering the generalship of Ludendorff—or for that matter, his primary opponent Foch.

Second guessing a general's decisions—in either peace or war—is one of the great spectator sports of military life. Since becoming a general officer myself I am only too well aware of this. Yet as a military historian, I would be remiss in not offering my conclusions at the end of this study. I do so, however, fully aware that what may seem perfectly clear to me more than eighty-five years after the fact, and after more than six years of researching and studying this nine-month period of German military history, looked totally different to those who were there on the spot, on the ground, as events were unfolding. I am not so naive as to think I could have done any better, or even as well, in their positions. It is with that qualification that I offer these concluding comments.

As discussed at length in Chapter 4 and summarized at the start of this chapter, Ludendorff was clearly out of his element when dealing with strategic and especially political, social, and economic matters. But as also noted in Chapter 2, the German officer-education system of the time and up through the end of the first half of the 20th century was not designed to train officers to think and operate on these levels. Though well beyond the scope of this study, I think a strong argument can be assembled to show that Hindenburg and Ludendorff expanded their influence into the political, social, and economic spheres more by default than anything else, as the weak internal institutions of Wilhelmine Germany collapsed under the strain of the world's first industrialized war. Nonetheless, Ludendorff bears a major responsibility for the decisions that doomed Germany on the strategic level, especially the unrestricted U-boat campaign and the Belgian policy.

On the tactical level, Ludendorff presents a far more complex picture. He was a gifted, if not a truly great tactician, despite his blind spot for the potential of the tank and his general disregard for many—but not all—aspects of emerging military technology. Although he could be a petty tyrant and a micro-manager, he nonetheless presided over one of the most brilliant and innovative sets of tactical reforms in the history of warfare. In accordance with the best traditions of the German General Staff, he allowed and even encouraged vigorous debate among relatively junior staff officers, resulting in a give-and-take that produced first the new defensive doctrine based on flexible defense-in-depth, and then the new offensive doctrine, based on non-linear infiltration tactics. When Fritz von Lossberg produced a pamphlet highly critical of the new defensive tactics, Ludendorff even had OHL reproduce that pamphlet for distribution within the German Army.[40]

In many ways, however, the vaunted German General Staff system began to work against itself as the war progressed. Herbert Rosinski noted the tendency in the German Army throughout the war for commanders to become marginalized, as the chiefs of staff and the General Staff officers in the subordinate units gained more real power through their own network. The commanders, on the other hand, tended to be far better in touch with actual conditions among their own troops. Thus, when the final breakdown came in the fall of 1918, Ludendorff and OHL were caught by surprise.[41] Ludendorff himself was one of the worst offenders, routinely interfering directly in the business of the armies over the heads of the army group commanders—usually in response to some communication from a junior General Staff officer down in the units.[42]

Albrecht von Thaer in his memoirs paints a stark picture of the loss of contact with tactical and operational reality at OHL as the offensives progressed. Thaer was a General Staff officer who in 1904–1905 had worked under Major Ludendorff at the Great General Staff. When Thaer was transferred from the field to OHL at end of April 1918, he made a point of telling Hindenburg, Ludendorff, and Wetzell about the real conditions in the front lines. Hindenburg patronizingly pointed out that Thaer's personal experience of only twelve miles of the front was not representative of the bigger picture. Since OHL got reports from the front every day, it obviously had a better understanding of the overall situation. Hindenburg was sure that Thaer's attitude would soon improve in the more optimistic air at OHL. Ludendorff told Thaer bluntly, "If the troops are getting worse, if discipline is slipping, then it is your fault and the fault of all the commanders at the front for not being tough enough." Thaer also noted that right until the very end the operational planners at OHL continued to regard all divisions shown on the map as equal. Wetzell, for example, refused to believe that a division that had been committed in a recent attack in Thaer's sector was down to an average strength of thirty riflemen per company.[43]

As discussed throughout this study, the German Army in World War I recognized the existence of a level of warfare between the tactical and the strategic, but its understanding of the operational level was distorted by their fear of the *Materialschlacht* and their overriding emphasis on the *Vernichtungsschlacht*. Ludendorff himself, however, had a major prejudice against the operational level and operations (*Operativ*) as opposed to tactics. This prejudice comes through again and again in his own words and his writings. Each of the six great offensives he planned aimed to produce a large-scale tactical breakthrough, with the follow-on actions being ad hoc and determined by the situation. This is the very antithesis of the operational art.

Ludendorff is also open to criticism for his management of the various battles. Time and again he shifted the main effort to exploit short-term opportunities at the expense of long-term objectives. When the course of the action started to turn against him, he repeatedly made erratic and sometimes even irrational decisions. After the Allied counterattack on 18 July, Ludendorff was close to a state of psychological collapse. As Richard Simpkin pointed out, command decision at the operational level rarely requires physical courage. Moral courage is needed to keep judgement unclouded when forced to accept short-term setbacks for the sake of long-term gains. An operational-level commander needs moral courage to make the big decisions and to stick to them.[44] One can only wonder what might have happened without the steadying influence of Hindenburg to shore up Ludendorff from crisis to crisis.

Ludendorff was not the German Army's only gifted tactician. Others were at least as good, and may not have had his blind spot for the operational level—at least to quite the same debilitating degree. Again, one can only speculate how the spring 1918 campaign would have turned out if someone else had been the First Quartermaster General. Officers who come immediately to mind include Kuhl, Lossberg, Seeckt, and Hoffmann. In a July 1919 letter to Seeckt, Wetzell speculated that Ludendorff might have been talked into a more logical and rational approach if Seeckt had been at OHL.[45]

Although the focus of this study is German operational art in the planning and execution of the 1918 offensives, it is impossible to ignore completely the responses of the Allied forces and commanders in contributing to the German defeat. And while a detailed analysis of Allied operational art, decision making, and generalship are the subjects of a completely separate study, it is impossible to escape the conclusion that time after time Foch simply out-generaled Ludendorff because the Allied generalissimo had a far better understanding of the strategic and operational realities and dynamics during the first half of 1918.

In my final assessment on Ludendorff, I have to conclude that in many ways he was a reflection of the German Army as a whole in the first half of the 20th century: tactically gifted, operationally flawed, and strategically bankrupt.

Notes

1 Introduction

1 Richard M. Swain, "Reading about Operational Art," in *On Operational Art*, Clayton R. Newell and Michael D. Krause (eds.), Center of Military History, (Washington: 1994), p.199.

2 Gary Sheffield, *Forgotten Victory: The First World War, Myths and Realities*, (London: 2001), p.221.

3 See Paul Fussell, *The Great War in Modern Memory*, (Oxford: 1975).

4 Brian Bond, *The Unquiet Western Front: Britain's Role in Literature and History*, (Cambridge: 2002), p.vii.

5 Tim Travers, *The Killing Ground: The British Army, the Western Front and the Emergence of Modern Warfare, 1900–1918*, (London: 1987), pp.xvii–xxii.

6 Jonathan Bailey, *The First World War and the Birth of the Modern Style of Warfare*, Strategic and Combat Studies Institute, (Camberley: 1996), p.3. Writing for the Strategic Studies Institute of the U.S. Army War College, E.H. Tilford argued in 1995 that World War I was a Military Technical Revolution that did not become a true RMA until after it ended.

7 Steven Metz and James Kievit, *Strategy and the Revolution in Military Affairs: From Theory to Policy*, Strategic Studies Institute, U.S. Army War College, (Carlisle Barracks, Pennsylvania: 1995), p.v.

8 Bailey, p.3, n.1.

9 Bailey, p.3.

10 Bailey, pp.7, 37.

11 Bailey, p.32.

12 Harry P. Ball, *Of Responsible Command: A History of the U.S. Army War College*, (Carlisle Barracks, Pennsylvania: 1994), pp.190–193.

13 Lewis S. Sorley, *Some Recollections*, unpublished memoir, (December 1957), pp.118–129.

14 Carl von Clausewitz, *On War*, Michael Howard and Peter Paret (eds. and trans.), (Princeton, New Jersey: 1976), p.12.

15 Thomas E. Griess, "A Perspective on Military History," in *A Guide to the Study and Use of Military History*, John E. Jessup and Robert W. Coakley (eds.), U.S. Army Center of Military History, (Washington, D.C.: 1978), p.28.

2 The operational art

1 Quoted in Rupprecht, Crown Prince of Bavaria, *Mein Kriegstagebuch*, Vol.II, (Munich: 1929), p.372.

2 See Christopher Bellamy, *The Evolution of Modern Land Warfare: Theory and Practice*, (London: 1990); A.S.H. Irwin, *The Levels of War, Operational Art, and*

Campaign Planning, The Occasional Number 5, Strategic and Combat Studies Institute, (Camberley: 1993); B.J.C. McKercher and Michael A. Hennessy (eds.), *The Operational Art: Developments in the Theories of War*, (Westport, Connecticut: 1996); and Clayton R. Newell and Michael D. Krause (eds.), *On Operational Art*, Center of Military History, (Washington, D.C.: 1994).

3 Glenn K. Otis, "The Ground Commander's View," in Newell & Krause, p.31.
4 Shimon Naveh, *In Pursuit of Military Excellence: The Evolution of Operational Theory*, (London: 1997), p.7.
5 Cited in Irwin, p.10.
6 United States, *Field Manual 100-5, Operations*, (Washington, D.C.: 1993), p.6-2.
7 Richard Simpkin, *Race to the Swift: Thoughts of Twenty-first Century Warfare*, (London: 1985), p.xi.
8 Naveh, p.13.
9 James J. Schneider, "Theoretical Implications of Operational Art," in Newell & Krause, p.18.
10 Naveh, p.22.
11 Simpkin, p.24.
12 United States, *Joint Publication 3-0, Doctrine for Joint Operations*, (Washington, D.C.: 9 September 1993), p.II-4.
13 Quoted in Peter G. Tsouras, *The Greenhill Dictionary of Military Quotations*, (Stackpole, Pennsylvania: 2000), p.363.
14 Irwin, p.8.
15 Arthur F. Lykke, *Military Strategy: Theory and Application*, U.S. Army War College, (Carlisle, Pennsylvania: 1989), pp.6–8.
16 Irwin, p.8.
17 Simpkin, p.24.
18 McKercher & Hennessy, p.3.
19 Naveh, pp.xiii–xvii.
20 Schneider in Newell & Krause, p.20. Bruce W. Menning, "Operational Art's Origins," *Military Review*, (September 1997), pp.33–34.
21 Menning, p.33. John English, "Operational Art: Developments in the Theory of War," in McKercher & Hennessy, p.7.
22 Friedrich von Bernhardi, *How Germany Makes War*, (New York: 1914), p.41.
23 Antoine Jomini, *The Art of War*, (reprint), (Westport, Connecticut: 1972), p.162.
24 Carl von Clausewitz, *On War*, Michael Howard and Peter Paret (eds. and trans.), (Princeton, New Jersey: 1976), p.128.
25 Clausewitz, p.379.
26 Bradley J. Meyer, "The Operational Art: The Elder Moltke's Campaign Plan for the Franco-Prussian War," in McKercher & Hennessy, p.45.
27 Naveh, pp.40–41.
28 Naveh, p.91.
29 Clausewitz, p.285.
30 Bellamy, p.68.
31 Schneider in Newell & Krause, p.21.
32 Naveh, p.56.
33 Martin van Creveld, *Command in War*, (Cambridge, Massachusetts: 1985), p.151. Hew Strachan, *The First World War: Volume I: To Arms*, (New York: 2001), p.298.
34 Van Creveld, pp.152–158.
35 Menning, pp.34–35.
36 Jacob Kipp, "Two Views of Warsaw: The Russian Civil War and Soviet Operational Art," in McKercher & Hennessy, p.65.
37 Richard M. Swain, "Reading about Operational Art," in Newell & Krause, p.205.
38 Menning, p.35.

39 David Glantz, "The Intellectual Dimension of Soviet (Russian) Operational Art," in McKercher & Hennessy, p.128.
40 Irwin, p.7. J.F.C. Fuller, *The Foundations of the Science of War*, (London: 1926), p.71.
41 Fuller, pp.107–109.
42 Fuller, p.110.
43 Menning, p.37.
44 Kipp in McKercher & Hennessy, pp.53, 75.
45 Chris Bellamy, *Red God of War: Soviet Artillery and Rocket Forces*, (London: 1986), p.45.
46 Menning, p.37. McKercher & Hennessy, p.2. Bellamy, *Evolution of Modern Land Warfare*, p.65.
47 Kipp in McKercher & Hennessy, p.69.
48 David T. Zabecki, *Steel Wind: Colonel Georg Bruchmüller and the Birth of Modern Artillery*, (Bridgeport, Connecticut: 1994), pp.128–129.
49 V.K. Triandafillov, *The Nature of the Operations of Modern Armies*, William A. Burhans, (trans.), (London: 1994), pp.127–158.
50 Glantz in McKercher & Hennessy, p.130. Menning, p.40.
51 Naveh, pp.xvii, 105–150.
52 Menning, p.39.
53 Bellamy, *Evolution of Modern Land Warfare*, pp.63–64.
54 Germany, *Heeresdienstvorschrift 300, Truppenführung*, (Berlin: 1933), pp.46–49. See also the modern English translation: *On the German Art of War: Truppenführung*, (Bruce Condell and David T. Zabecki, eds. and trans. and eds.), (Boulder, Colorado: 2001).
55 Ludwig Beck, *Studien*, Hans Speidel (ed.) (Stuttgart: 1955), p.67.
56 Naveh, p.116.
57 For example, the term *operative Aufklärung* was translated as "strategical reconnaissance."
58 Newell in Newell & Krause, p.4.
59 Menning, pp.42–43.
60 Newell in Newell & Krause, p.13.
61 Swain in McKercher & Hennessy, p.161.
62 United States, *Field Manual 100-5, Operations*, (Washington, D.C.: 1982), p.7–13.
63 United States, *Field Manual 100-5, Operations*, (Washington, D.C.: 1986), pp.19–20.
64 *Joint Warfare Publication 0-01: British Defence Doctrine*, (London: 2001), pp.1-2–1-4. Irwin, pp.4–6. English in McKercher & Hennessy, p.17.
65 Herbert Rosinski, *The German Army*, (New York: 1966), pp.127–130, 301.
66 McKercher & Hennessy, p.2.
67 Rosinski, p.127.
68 Roland G. Foerster, *Operatives Denken bei Clausewitz, Moltke, Schlieffen und Manstein*, (Freiburg: 1989), pp.28–29. Bellamy, *Evolution of Modern Land Warfare*, p.60.
69 Michael D. Krause, "Moltke and the Origins of Operational Art," *Military Review*, (September 1990), p.42.
70 English in McKercher & Hennessy, p.8.
71 Simpkin, p.14.
72 Meyer in McKercher & Hennessy, p.43.
73 Meyer in McKercher & Hennessy, p.29.
74 Bradley Meyer, *Operational Art and the German Command System in World War I*, dissertation, (Ohio State University: 1988), p.228.
75 Cited in Meyer in McKercher & Hennessy, p.45.
76 Michael Geyer, "German Strategy in the Age of Machine Warfare, 1914–1945," in

Peter Paret (ed.), *Makers of Modern Strategy from Machiavelli to the Nuclear Age*, (Princeton, New Jersey: 1986), p.532. Antulio J. Echevarria, II, *After Clausewitz: German Military Thinkers before the Great War*, (Lawrence, Kansas: 2000), pp.188–197.

77 Strachan, pp.172, 288.
78 Meyer (1988), pp.87–88.
79 Jehuda L. Wallach, *The Dogma of the Battle of Annihilation: The Theories of Clausewitz and Schlieffen and Their Impact on the German Conduct of Two World Wars*, (Westport, Connecticut: 1986), pp.41–46, 72.
80 Naveh, pp.40–48.
81 Echevarria, p.226.
82 Clausewitz, p.90.
83 Simpkin, p.xix.
84 Simpkin, p.14.
85 Wallach, pp.14, 24.
86 Bernhardi, p.136.
87 Erich Ludendorff, *Kriegsführung und Politik*, (Berlin: 1922), p.24.
88 Rosinski, pp.92–96, 119. Wallach, p.77.
89 Gary Sheffield, *Forgotten Victory: The First World War, Myths and Realities*, (London: 2001), pp.115–116. Strachan, pp.171, 1009. Echevarria, pp.183–188.
90 Menning, p.37. Bellamy, *Evolution of Modern Land Warfare*, p.63. Schneider in Newell & Krause, pp.25–26. Strachan, p.178.
91 Bernhardi, p.160.
92 Bernhardi, p.183.
93 Walter Görlitz, *History of the German General Staff, 1657–1945*, (New York: 1953), p.188.
94 Meyer, (1988), pp.389–390.
95 Meyer, (1988), p.391.
96 Robert B. Asprey, *The German High Command at War: Hindenburg and Ludendorff Conduct World War I*, (New York: 1991), p.305.
97 Rupprecht, pp.95–98. Rupprecht had objected to the massive destruction during the withdrawal.
98 Army Group Bavarian Crown Prince Rupprecht, War Diary, "Minutes of a Conference held with Ludendorff, 18–21 January 1918—Recorded by Thilo," (23 January 1918), Bundesarchiv/Militärarchiv, File PH 5 I/45.
99 Robert M. Citino, Professor of History, Eastern Michigan University, Email to the author, 26 July 2001.
100 See for example, AOK 2 Ia 220, "Contributions to the Development of a Doctrine for Offensive Operations in Trench Warfare," (7 December 1917), Bundesarchiv/Militärarchiv, File PH 3/452.
101 Erich Ludendorff, *Meine Kriegserinnerungen 1914–1918*, (Berlin: 1919), p.474.
102 *FM 100-5*, (1993), p.6-7.
103 *Joint Publication 3-0*, p.III-27.
104 *FM 100-5*, (1993), p.6-7.
105 Naveh, p.19.
106 Clausewitz, pp.194–195.
107 Clausewitz, p.196.
108 Jomini, p.63.
109 *FM 100-5*, (1986), pp.179–180.
110 *Truppenführung*, (1933), pp.13–14, 123.
111 *FM 100-5*, (1993), p.6-8.
112 British doctrine recognizes centers of gravity at the strategic and the operational levels.
113 Clausewitz, p.528.

114 *FM 3-0*, (2001), pp.5-9–5-10.
115 *FM 100-5*, (1993), p.6-8.
116 *Joint Publication 3-0*, p.III-22.
117 Jomini, p.93.
118 *Joint Publication 3-0*, p.III-14.
119 Simpkin, p.148.
120 Naveh, p.258.
121 Zabecki, pp.41–42.
122 *Joint Publication 3-0*, p.III-19.
123 Simpkin, pp.106–107.
124 *Joint Publication 3-0*, p.III-24/27.
125 *Joint Publication 3-0*, p.III-21.
126 *FM 100-5*, (1993), p.2-10/11.
127 United States, *Field Manual 3-0, Operations*, (Washington, D.C.: 2001), p.4-10.
128 Simpkin, pp.81–87.
129 Irwin, p.21.
130 *Joint Publication 3-0*, p.IV-13.
131 Naveh, pp.49–55.
132 *Oberkommando des Heeres, Der Weltkrieg 1914 bis 1918*, Volume 12, (Berlin: 1939), Appendix 28b, pp.2–11. *Oberkommando des Heeres, Der Weltkrieg 1914 bis 1918*, Volume 14, (Berlin: 1944), Appendix 35, pp.2–17.
133 Irwin, p.19.
134 Bellamy, *Red God of War*, p.47.
135 Naveh, pp.20–21.
136 *FM 3-0* (2001), p.4-6.
137 *Joint Publication 3-0*, p.III-29.
138 Simpkin, p.225.
139 Barton Whaley, "Toward a General Theory of Deception," *Journal of Strategic Studies*, (March 1982), pp.178–192. Simpkin, pp.189–194.
140 Cited in Simpkin, p.182.

3 The tactical realities of 1918

1 William Balck, *Development of Tactics: World War*, Harry Bell (trans.), (Fort Leavenworth, Kansas: 1922), p.8.
2 Cited in Correlli Barnett, *The Swordbearers: Supreme Command in the First World War*, (Bloomington, Indiana: 1964), p.33.
3 Christopher Bellamy, *The Evolution of Modern Land Warfare: Theory and Practice*, (London: 1990), p.78.
4 Balck, p.16.
5 J.B.A. Bailey, *Field Artillery and Firepower*, (Oxford: 1989), pp.128–129.
6 Jan Bloch, "The Wars of the Future," in *Jean de Bloch: Selected Articles*, (Fort Leavenworth, Kansas: 1993), pp.1–40.
7 Hew Strachan, *The First World War: Volume I: To Arms*, (New York: 2001), pp.1005–1014. Holger Herwig, "Germany and the 'Short-War' Illusion: Toward a New Interpretation?," *The Journal of Military History*, (July 2002), pp.681–693.
8 Erich Ludendorff, *Urkunden der Obersten Heersleitung über ihre Tätigkeit 1916–1918*, (Berlin: 1921), p.14.
9 Timothy T. Lupfer, *The Dynamics of Doctrine: Changes in German Tactical Doctrine during the First World War*, Leavenworth Papers Nr. 4, (Fort Leavenworth, Kansas: July 1981), p.2.
10 Michael Howard, "Men against Fire: The Doctrine of the Offensive in 1914," in *Makers of Modern Strategy: From Machiavelli to the Nuclear Age*, Peter Paret (ed.), (Princeton, New Jersey: 1986), pp.512–515.

11 Pascal Lucas, *The Evolution of Tactical Ideas in France and Germany during the War of 1914–1918*, P.V. Kieffer, (trans.) (Fort Leavenworth, Kansas: 1925), p.65. French publication Berger-Levrault, (Paris: 1923).

12 Lucas, p.6. Griffith argues that the French tactical failure in 1914 was despite Grandmaison's theory of the defensive, rather than because of it. The main shortcoming of Grandmaison's theory was that it was too complex for ordinary soldiers to understand and execute. Paddy Griffith, *Forward into Battle: Fighting Tactics from Waterloo to the Near Future*, (Novato, California: 1991), pp.84–94.

13 Richard Holmes, *The Western Front*, (London: 1999), pp.30–35.

14 Tim Travers, *The Killing Ground: The British Army on the Western Front, and the Emergence of Modern Warfare, 1900–1918*, (London: 1987), pp.48–55, 62–78.

15 Lucas, p.87.

16 In the French Army the regiment had three battalions, but all higher echelons had only two sub-units. That meant that all echelons above brigade either had to attack with half their force and the other half in reserve, or had to attack with the entire force and no reserve. Griffith, pp.92–93.

17 John Ellis, *Eye-Deep in Hell: Trench Warfare in World War I*, (Baltimore, Maryland: 1976), pp.33–38.

18 Lucas, p.105.

19 Graeme C. Wynne, *If Germany Attacks*, (London: 1940), pp.57–58. Lucas, pp.38, 109.

20 Jonathan M. House, *Toward Combined Arms Warfare: A Survey of 20th Century Tactics, Doctrine, and Organization*, (Fort Leavenworth, Kansas: 1984), p.12.

21 Lucas, p.136.

22 John Terraine, *White Heat: The New Warfare 1914–1918*, (London: 1982), p.286.

23 Lucas, p.170.

24 Friedrich von Bernhardi, *How Germany Makes War*, (New York: 1914), p.141.

25 Gary Sheffield, *Forgotten Victory: The First World War Myths and Realities*, (London: 2001), p.98.

26 Balck, p.54.

27 Lucas, p.6.

28 House, pp.22–25. Balck, pp.55–56.

29 Lucas, pp.123–126.

30 Ellis, pp.24–25.

31 Erich Ludendorff, *Meine Kriegserinnerungen 1914–1918*, (Berlin: 1919), p.461.

32 Ellis, pp.77–79.

33 Thomas E. Griess, *Definitions and Doctrine of the Military Art*, The West Point Military History Series, (Wayne, New Jersey: 1985), pp.116, 158. These diseases far outweighed battle casualties as killers and incapacitators of World War I soldiers.

34 James S. Corum, *The Roots of Blitzkrieg: Hans von Seeckt and German Military Reform*, (Lawrence, Kansas: 1992), p.18.

35 House, pp.7–8.

36 Trevor N. Dupuy, *A Genius for War: The German Army and General Staff, 1807–1945*, (Falls Church, Virginia: 1977), p.169.

37 Holger Herwig, "The Dynamics of Necessity: German Military Policy during the First World War," in Alan R. Millett and Williamson Murray, *Military Effectiveness*, Volume I: *The First World War*, (Boston: 1988), pp.94–95.

38 Eric Dorn Brose, *The Kaiser's Army: The Politics of Military Technology in Germany during the Machine Age, 1870–1918*, (New York: 2001), pp.4–6, 101–108, 182.

39 Balck, p.129.

40 Kurt Theobeck, *Erfahrungen und Lehren des Weltkriegs 1914 bis 1918 auf Waffentechnichem und Taktischem Gebit*, (12 April 1920), Bundesarchiv/Militärarchiv, Freiburg, Germany, File RH 12-2/94.

41 A.A. Goschen, "Artillery Tactics," *Journal of the Royal Artillery*, Vol.LII (1925), p.259. Vincent Meyer, "Evolution of Field Artillery Tactics during and as a Result of the World War," *Field Artillery Journal*, (March 1932), p.209.
42 Ian V. Hogg, *The Guns, 1914–1918*, (New York: 1971), p.8.
43 Alan F. Brooke, "The Evolution of Artillery in the Great War," Part 1, *Journal of the Royal Artillery*, (November 1924), pp.250–267.
44 Balck, pp.330–333.
45 David T. Zabecki, "The Guns of Manchuria," *Field Artillery Journal*, (April 1988), p.22.
46 Lucas, pp.9–10, 26, 39–40
47 Shelford Bidwell and Dominick Graham, *Firepower: British Army Weapons and Theories of War, 1904–1945*, (London: 1982); pp.17, 90.
48 In most armies artillery is classified as light, medium, and heavy. These classifications refer both to the weight of the gun, and the weight of the shell it fires. Generally, light artillery fires projectiles up to 105 mm in diameter; medium artillery up to 155 mm, and heavy artillery anything over 155 mm.
49 David T. Zabecki, "The Dress Rehearsal: Lost Artillery Lessons of the 1912–1913 Balkan Wars," *Field Artillery Journal*, (August 1988), p.22.
50 David T. Zabecki, *Steel Wind: Colonel Georg Bruchmüller and the Birth of Modern Artillery*, (Bridgeport, Connecticut: 1994), pp.8–9.
51 Bailey, p.132.
52 Brose, p.35.
53 United States, War Department, *German and Austrian Tactical Studies: Translations of Captured Documents*, (Washington, D.C.: 1918), p.157. The German Foot Artillery used $\frac{1}{16}$ of a degree as their smallest unit of angular measurement. The German Field Artillery used the mil (6,400 mils to a circle). On 25 December 1916 the Foot Artillery was ordered to convert to the mil, which is used by most artilleries of the world to this day.
54 Colonel Maitre, "Evolution of Ideas in the Employment of Artillery during the Great War," (translation of a lecture given at the Centre d'Etudes Tactiques d'Artillerie at Metz), *Field Artillery Journal*, (January 1922), p.3.
55 Alfred Muther, "Organization, Armament, Ammunition, and Ammunition Expenditure of the German Field Artillery during the World War, Part 1," *Field Artillery Journal*, (May 1935), p.201. Heinrich Rohne, "Artillery Statistics from the World War," *Field Artillery Journal* (translated from an article in the January 1924 issue of *Artilleristche Monatshefte*), (September 1924), pp.451–454. Balck, pp.315–317.
56 Martin Farndale, *History of the Royal Regiment of Artillery: Western Front 1914–18*, (Dorchester: 1986), pp.341–342. James E. Edmonds, *Military Operations, France and Belgium 1914*, Vol.II, (London: 1937), p.164.
57 Brooke, Part 6, (July 1925), pp.236–237.
58 This quote is frequently attributed to Pétain.
59 Farndale, pp.184, 260.
60 Bailey, pp.131–132. Farndale, p.92. Sheffield, pp.106–107.
61 House, p.26. Balck, p.352.
62 In early 1916 the British introduced the Model 106 artillery fuze that produced super-quick detonations and proved relatively efficient in cutting enemy wire. Sheffield, p.117.
63 Farndale, p.144. Bailey, p.134.
64 Bidwell & Graham, p.14.
65 The modern study of Bruchmüller and his tactics is Zabecki, *Steel Wind*.
66 Max Hoffmann, *Der Krieg der versäumten Gelegenheiten*, (Munich: 1923), p.136.
67 Ludendorff, *Kriegserinnerungen*, p.487.
68 Georg Bruchmüller, *Die Deutsche Artillerie in den Durchbruchschlachten des Weltkriegs*, 2nd ed., (Berlin: 1922), p.80.

69 Georg Bruchmüller, *Die Deutsche Artillerie in den Durchbruchschlachten des Weltkriegs*, 1st ed., (Berlin: 1921), pp.34–40.
70 Charles E. Heller, *Chemical Warfare in World War I: The American Experience, 1917–1918*, Leavenworth Papers, Nr. 10, (Fort Leavenworth, Kansas: 1984), p.15. Bruchmüller (1922), pp.20–21. Balck, pp.190–192.
71 Bruchmüller, *Durchbruchschlachten* (1922), pp.74–75.
72 Georg Bruchmüller, *Die Artillerie beim Angriff im Stellungskrieg*, Verlag Offene Worte, (Berlin: 1926), pp.52–55. Bruchmüller, *Durchbruchschlachten* (1921), pp.16–20.
73 Bruchmüller, *Durchbruchschlachten* (1921), p.30. Bruchmüller, *Durchbruchschlachten* (1922), pp.93–97. Bruchmüller, *Stellungskrieg*, p.122.
74 Corum, p.15.
75 Herwig, p.96. Corum, p.15.
76 Corum, pp.13–15.
77 AOK 17, "Overview of the Air Forces," Iad 624, (24 Feb 1918), Bayerisches Kriegsarchiv, File Hgr. Rupprecht, Bd. 168.
78 Oberste Heeresleitung, "Der Angriff im Stellungskrieg," (Sections 81–102), in Ludendorff, *Urkunden*, pp.661–664.
79 Randal Gray, *Kaisersschlacht 1918: The Final German Offensive*, Osprey Campaign Series, (London: 1991), pp.21, 24.
80 AOK 2, "Army Order: Employment of Flyers during MICHAEL," Iad 616 (9 March 1918), National Archives and Records Administration, RG165, Entry 320, Box 42, Folder 3.
81 Bernhardi, p.82.
82 Albrecht von Thaer, *Generalstabsdienst an der Front und in der O.H.L.*, (Göttingen: 1958), p.220.
83 Ludendorff, *Kriegserinnerungen*, p.462.
84 Balck, p.132.
85 Ludendorff, *Kriegserinnerungen*, p.462.
86 Hermann von Kuhl, *Entstehung, Durchführung und Zusammenbruch der Offensive von 1918*, (Berlin: 1927), p.82.
87 Kuhl, pp.72–75.
88 Corum, p.23.
89 J.F.C. Fuller, *Tanks in the Great War*, (London: 1920), p.171.
90 Kuhl, p.70.
91 Ludendorff, *Kriegserinnerungen*, p.461.
92 Hubert Essame, *The Battle for Europe 1918*, (London: 1972), p.2.
93 Terraine, p.303.
94 Balck, pp.134–137.
95 Balck, pp.135–136.
96 Lucas, p.68.
97 Bradley J. Meyer, *Operational Art and the German Command System in World War I*, dissertation, (Ohio State University: 1988), pp.123–163.
98 Bernhardi, p.115.
99 Meyer, pp.112–117.
100 Antulio J. Echevarria, II, *After Clausewitz: German Military Thinkers before the Great War*, (Lawrence, Kansas: 2000), pp.38–42, 95–103, 214.
101 Christian O.E. Millotat, *Understanding the Prussian-German General Staff System*, (Carlisle, Pennsylvania: 1992), pp.23–24.
102 Carl von Clausewitz, *On War*, Michael Howard and Peter Paret (eds. and trans.), (Princeton, New Jersey: 1984), Book I, Chapter 7, pp.119–120.
103 Clausewitz, pp.119–120.
104 Richard E. Simpkin, *Race to the Swift: Thoughts on Twenty-first Century Warfare*, (London: 1985), pp.79–80, 83, 85, 92.

105 J.F.C. Fuller, *The Foundations of the Science of War*, (London: 1926), p.269.
106 Trevor N. Dupuy, *Numbers, Predictions, and War: Using History to Evaluate Combat Factors and Predict the Outcome of Battles*, (New York: 1979), pp.148–150.
107 Dupuy (1979), pp.158–162.
108 Dupuy (1977), pp.7–11. Dupuy, however, does not establish a precise definition of what constitutes a war.
109 Travers, p.261.
110 Norman Stone, "General Erich Ludendorff," in Sir Michael Carver (ed.), *The War Lords: Military Commanders of the Twentieth Century*, (London: 1976), p.79.
111 Michael Geyer, "German Strategy in the Age of Machine Warfare, 1914–1945," in Peter Paret (ed.), *Makers of Modern Strategy, from Machiavelli to the Nuclear Age*, (Princeton, New Jersey: 1986), p.542.
112 Lupfer, p.55.
113 Corum, p.xv.
114 Cited in Lupfer, p.33.
115 Rupprecht, Crown Prince of Bavaria, *Mein Kriegstagebuch*, Vol.II, (Berlin: 1919), p.270.
116 Lupfer, p.55.
117 Lucas, pp.75–76.
118 Wynne, pp.88–89.
119 Fritz von Lossberg, *Meine Tätigkeit im Weltkriege 1914–1918*, (Berlin: 1939), p.131.
120 Lupfer, p.19.
121 Wynne, pp.125–126, 160.
122 Oberste Heeresleitung, "Grundsätze für die Abwehrschlacht im Stellungskrieg," in Ludendorff, *Urkunden*, pp.604–640. Ludendorff, *Kriegserinnerungen*, p.306.
123 Oberkommando des Heeres, *Der Weltkrieg 1914 bis 1918*, Vol.12, (Berlin: 1939), pp.53–54.
124 Griffith, p.98. Balck, pp.153–160.
125 Lucas, p.91.
126 Bruce I. Gudmundsson, *Stormtroop Tactics: Innovation in the German Army, 1914–1918*, (New York: 1989), pp.151–152.
127 Gudmundsson, pp.47–53. Samuels, pp.17–20.
128 Gudmundsson, pp.77–79, 96. Lupfer, p.43.
129 House, p.35.
130 Wynne, p.295. Corum, p.9.
131 Laszlo M. Alfoldi, "The Hutier Legend," *Parameters*, No.2, (1976), pp.69–74.
132 Oberste Heeresleitung, "Der Angriff im Stellungskrieg," in Ludendorff, *Urkunden*, pp.641–666.
133 Gudmundsson, p.149. Sheffield also points out that many of the elements of the new German doctrine were essentially the same as those contained in two British doctrinal pamphlets issued eleven months earlier in February 1917, *SS143, Instructions for the Training of Platoons for Offensive Action*, and *SS144, The Normal Formation for the Attack*. Sheffield, p.151.
134 Lucas, pp.132, 138. Balck, p.266.
135 Travers, p.260. Balck, p.264.
136 Lucas, pp.43, 102. Balck, pp.62, 81, 91. Ludendorff, *Kriegserinnerungen*, pp.465–466.
137 *Heeresdienstvorschrift 300, Truppenführung*, Parts 1 and 2, (Berlin: 1933, 1934).
138 Ludendorff, *Urkunden*, p.642. This passage is echoed in *Truppenführung* Paragraph 15.
139 Ludendorff, *Urkunden*, p.643. This passage is echoed in *Truppenführung* Paragraph 6.
140 Oberkommando des Heeres, *Der Weltkrieg 1914 bis 1918*, Vol.14, (Berlin: 1944), pp.41–42.

141 *Der Weltkrieg*, Vol.14, p.59.
142 Ludendorff, *Kriegserinnerungen*, p.468.

4 The strategic reality

1 Carl von Clausewitz, *On War*, Michael Howard and Peter Paret (eds. and trans.), (Princeton, New Jersey: 1976), pp.194, 196.
2 Erich Ludendorff, *Kriegsführung und Politik*, (Berlin: 1922), p.24.
3 Clausewitz, pp.605–610.
4 Jehuda L. Wallach, *The Dogma of the Battle of Annihilation: The Theories of Clausewitz and Schlieffen and Their Impact on the German Conduct of Two World Wars*, (Westport, Connecticut: 1986), p.14.
5 Michael Geyer, "German Strategy in the Age of Machine Warfare, 1914–1945," in *Makers of Modern Strategy from Machiavelli to the Nuclear Age*, Peter Paret (ed.), (Princeton, New Jersey: 1986), pp.527–528.
6 Hans Hitz, "Taktik und Strategie," in *Wehrwissenschaftliche Rundschau*, (November 1956), pp.615–617.
7 Geyer, "German Strategy," pp.531–532.
8 Hew Strachan, *The First World War: Volume I: To Arms*, (New York: 2001), pp.164–166.
9 Holger H. Herwig, "The Dynamics of Necessity: German Military Policy during the First World War," in *Military Effectiveness*, Vol.I: *The First World War*, Allan R. Millett and Williamson Murray (eds.), (Boston: 1988), p.93. Wallach, p.71. Strachan, pp.168–169, 179.
10 Georg Wetzell, *Der Bündniskrieg: Eine militärpolitisch operativ Studie des Weltkrieges*, (Berlin: 1937). Strachan, pp.176, 288–289, 293, 697.
11 Herwig, "Dynamics of Necessity," pp.87–90.
12 Reinhard Scheer, *Germany's High Seas Fleet in the World War*, reprint, (Nashville, Tennessee: 2002), p.19.
13 Geyer, "German Strategy," p.533.
14 Herwig, "Dynamics of Necessity," p.81.
15 Herwig, "Dynamics of Necessity, pp.81–82.
16 See Timothy T. Lupfer, *The Dynamics of Doctrine: Changes in German Tactical Doctrine during the First World War*, Leavenworth Papers Nr. 4, (Fort Leavenworth, Kansas: July 1981).
17 Holger Herwig, *The First World War: Germany and Austria-Hungary, 1914–1918*, (London: 1997), p.420.
18 Erich Ludendorff, *Meine Kriegserinnerungen 1914–1918*, (Berlin: 1919), p.474. Otto Fehr, *Die Märzoffensive 1918 an der Westfront: Strategie oder Taktik?*, (Leipzig: 1921), pp.1–7.
19 Geyer, "German Strategy," p.537.
20 Ernst von Wrisberg, *Wehr und Waffen, 1914–1918*, (Leipzig: 1922), pp.95–96, 284–288.
21 Gerald D. Feldman, *Army, Industry, and Labor in Germany, 1914–1918*, (Princeton, New Jersey: 1966), pp.154, 301. Ludendorff, *Kriegserinnerungen*, p.263.
22 Herwig, "Dynamics of Necessity," p.105. Wrisberg, p.99.
23 Robert B. Asprey, *The German High Command at War: Hindenburg and Ludendorff Conduct World War I*, (New York: 1991), p.285. Walter Görlitz, *History of the German General Staff, 1657–1945*, (New York: 1953), p.184.
24 Feldman, pp.190–196.
25 Feldman, pp.197–249.
26 Erich Ludendorff, *Urkunden der Obersten Heersleitung über ihre Tätigkeit 1916–1918*, (Berlin: 1921), pp.107–109.
27 Ludendorff, *Urkunden*, pp.77, 127.
28 Ludendorff, *Kriegserinnerungen*, p.262.

29 John Dan Buckelew, *Erich Ludendorff and the German War Effort 1916–1918: A Study in the Military Exercise of Power,* dissertation, (University of California, San Diego: 1974), p.198.
30 Hans W. Gatzke, *Germany's Drive to the West: A Study of Germany's Western War Aims during the First World War,* (Baltimore, Maryland: 1950), pp.290–291.
31 Gatzke, p.289.
32 Herwig, *First World War,* pp.378, 382–383.
33 Georg Wetzell, "The Future Concentration and Present Peace Aims," (30 September 1917), Bundesarchiv/Militärarchiv, File PH 3/267.
34 Hermann von Kuhl, *Personal War Diary of General von Kuhl,* (1 November 1917) Bundesarchiv/Militärarchiv, File: W-10/50652.
35 Hans von Haeften, "Ludendorff and the Question of a Sacrificial Peace," Bundesarchiv/Militärarchiv, File N 35/8, Nachlass Haeften.
36 Görlitz, p.191.
37 Basil H. Liddell Hart, *The Real War 1914–1918,* (Boston: 1930), p.204.
38 Friedrich von Bernhardi, *Von Kriege der Zukunft, nach den Erfahrungen des Weltkriegs,* (Berlin: 1920), p.ix.
39 Correlli Barnett, *The Swordbearers: Supreme Command in the First World War,* (Bloomington, Indiana: 1964), p.274.
40 Holger H. Herwig, *"Luxury" Fleet: The Imperial German Navy, 1888–1918,* (London: 1980), p.4.
41 Eugene L. Rasor, "Blockade, Naval, of Germany," in *The European Powers in the First World War: An Encyclopedia,* Spencer C. Tucker (ed.), (New York: 1996), pp.132–133.
42 Liddell Hart, p.202.
43 Herwig, "Dynamics of Necessity," pp.90, 98.
44 Herwig, *Luxury Fleet,* p.222.
45 Herwig, *Luxury Fleet,* pp.263, 267.
46 Herwig, *Luxury Fleet,* p.111.
47 Gary E. Wier, *Building the Kaiser's Navy,* (Annapolis, Maryland: 1988).
48 Geyer, "German Strategy," pp.546–547.
49 Ludendorff, *Kriegserinnerungen,* pp.245–251.
50 Ludendorff, *Urkunden,* pp.301–369.
51 Asprey, p.513n.
52 Herwig, *Luxury Fleet,* p.243.
53 Oberkommando des Heeres, *Der Weltkrieg 1914 bis 1918,* Vol.13, (Berlin: 1942), p.319.
54 Ludendorff, *Kriegserinnerungen,* p.430. Herwig, "Dynamics of Necessity," p.104.
55 Terraine, John, *White Heat: The New Warfare 1914–1918,* (London: 1982), p.262.
56 Sheffield, p.75.
57 Eberhard Rössler, *U-Boat: The Evolution and Technical History of German Submarines,* (Annapolis, Maryland: 1999), pp.329–332.
58 Paul Kemp, *U-Boats Destroyed: German Submarine Losses in the World Wars,* (London: 1997), pp.9–59. Herwig, *Luxury Fleet,* p.291.
59 Scheer, pp.314–317.
60 Ferdinand Foch, *The Memoirs of Marshall Foch,* (New York: 1931), p.299.
61 OHL, Heavy Artillery Staff Officer Weekly Reports B7678, B7841, and B8018, (16, 23, and 30 March 1918), Bundesarchiv/Militärarchiv, File PH 3/504.
62 Gerald V. Bull and C.H. Murphy, *Paris Kanonen—The Paris Guns (Wilhelmgeschüzte) and Project HARP,* (Herford: 1988), pp.35–36.
63 Görlitz, p.183.
64 Ludendorff, *Kriegserinnerungen,* p.440.

65 Rupprecht, Crown Prince of Bavaria, *Mein Kriegstagebuch*, Vol.II, (Munich: 1929), p.178.
66 Herwig, *First World War*, p.382.
67 Ludendorff, *Kriegserinnerungen*, pp.526, 554–555.
68 Ludendorff, *Urkunden*, p.162.
69 Reichsarchiv, "Historical Study on Air Forces 1918," (12 April 1926), Bundesarchiv/Militärarchiv, File RH 2/2195.
70 Herwig, "Dynamics of Necessity," p.100.
71 Eric and Jane Lawson, *The First Air Campaign: August 1914–November 1918*, (Norwalk, Connecticut: 1996), p.221.
72 *Der Weltkrieg*, Vol.14, (Berlin: 1944), Appendix 40. For the week of 5–11 August 1918, the Royal Air Force claimed 177 German aircraft shot down against 150 losses. Between 4 and 10 November 1918, the last intense aerial combat of World War I, the RAF claimed sixty-eight kills against sixty losses.
73 James S. Corum, *The Roots of Blitzkrieg: Hans von Seeckt and German Military Reform*, (Lawrence, Kansas: 1992), pp.16–17.
74 James S. Corum, *The Luftwaffe: Creating the Operational Air War, 1918–1940*, (Lawrence, Kansas: 1997), p.36.
75 David T. Zabecki, *Steel Wind: Colonel Georg Bruchmüller and the Birth of Modern Artillery*, (Bridgeport, Connecticut: 1994).
76 Hermann von Kuhl, *Entstehung, Durchführung und Zusammenbruch der Offensive von 1918*, (Berlin: 1927), pp.77–78.
77 Hubert Essame, *The Battle for Europe 1918*, (London: 1972), p.27.
78 A.M. Henniker, *Transportation on the Western Front, 1914–1918*, (London: 1937), pp.232–233.
79 OHL, Chef des Feldeisenbahnwesens, Nr.1264, (1 June 1917), Bundesarchiv/Militärarchiv, File PH 3/387.
80 OHL, Chef des Feldeisenbahnwesens, Nr. 929, (no date), Bundesarchiv/Militärarchiv, File PH 3/387.
81 Herwig, *First World War*, p.392.
82 Great Britain, War Office, General Staff, *Handbook of the German Army in the War, April 1918*, reprint (London: 1977), pp.129–131.
83 Fritz von Lossberg, *Meine Tätigkeit im Weltkriege 1914–1918*, (Berlin: 1939), p.317.
84 Data extracted and extrapolated from *Der Weltkrieg*, Vol.14, Appendix 35.
85 Essame, pp.24–25.
86 Ian Malcolm Brown, *British Logistics on the Western Front, 1914–1919*, (Bridgeport, Connecticut: 1998), pp.109–138.
87 Brown, p.189.
88 Henniker, pp.398–400.
89 Henniker, pp.404–411.
90 Randolph Y. Hennes, *The March Retreat of 1918: An Anatomy of a Battle*, dissertation, (University of Washington: 1966), pp.107–108, n.58.
91 Douglas Haig, *The Private Papers of Douglas Haig, 1914–1919*, Robert Blake (ed.), (London: 1952), p.279.
92 Foch, pp.262–263.
93 Cited in Brown, p.191.
94 Michael Stone, "General Erich Ludendorff," in *The War Lords: Military Commanders of the Twentieth Century*, Sir Michael Carver (ed.), (Boston, Massachusetts: 1976), p.74.
95 Kuhl, *Offensive von 1918*, p.78.
96 Brown, pp.124, 145.
97 Kuhl, *Offensive von 1918*, pp.75–76.
98 Strachan, pp.173–174, 176.
99 Ingrid P. Westmoreland, "Casualties," in Tucker, *European Powers*, pp.172–173.

100 Kuhl, *Offensive von 1918*, p.58.
101 Kuhl, *Offensive von 1918*, p.64.
102 Ludendorff, *Kriegserinnerungen*, p.470.
103 *Der Weltkrieg*, Vol.14, p.666. Ludendorff, *Urkunden*, p.560.
104 Görlitz, p.185.
105 Kuhl, *Offensive von 1918*, p.6.
106 *Der Weltkrieg*, Vol.14, Appendix 28a.
107 Giordan Fong, "The Movement of German Divisions to the Western Front, Winter 1917–1918," *Stand To! The Journal of the Western Front Association*, (September 2002), p.24. Kuhl, *Offensive von 1918*, p.6 cites slightly different numbers.
108 Kuhl, *Offensive von 1918*, p.66.
109 United States, War Department Document No.905, *Histories of Two Hundred and Fifty-one Divisions of the German Army Which Participated in the War, 1914–1918*, (1920), reprint, (London: 1989).
110 Department of the Army, *United States Army in the World War 1917–1919: Military Operations of the American Expeditionary Force*, Vol.13, reprint, (Washington, D.C.: 1991), p.178.
111 The level of statistical significance is determined by a test of hypothesis using the *t* distribution.
112 Asprey, p.374.
113 Haig, pp.289–290.
114 Kuhl, *Offensive von 1918*, p.8.
115 Kuhl, *Offensive von 1918*, p.55.
116 Kuhl, *Offensive von 1918*, pp.53–56.
117 *Der Weltkrieg*, Vol.14, Appendix 42.
118 OHL, "The Military Situation of the Entente, Winter 1917–1918," Ic 6730a, (December 1917), Bundesarchiv/Militärarchiv, File PH 5 II/111.
119 Görlitz, p.186.
120 Asprey, pp.316, 402.
121 Kuhl, *Offensive von 1918*, p.10.
122 Feldman, p.442.
123 *Der Weltkrieg*, Vol.14, p.31.
124 Rupprecht, *Kriegstagebuch*, Vol.II, p.410.
125 Feldman, pp.442–458.
126 Görlitz, p.193.
127 Feldman, p.459.
128 Kuhl, *Offensive von 1918*, pp.19, 28.
129 Kuhl, *Offensive von 1918*, p.27. Ludendorff, *Kriegserinnerungen*, p.500.
130 Herwig, *First World War*, p.384.
131 Herwig, *First World War*, p.393.
132 *Der Weltkrieg 1914 bis 1918*, Vol.12, (Berlin: 1939), pp.560–589.
133 Ludendorff, *Kriegserinnerungen*, pp.434–435.
134 Ludendorff, *Kriegserinnerungen*, pp.240–257.
135 Rupprecht, *Kriegstagebuch*, Vol.II, p.336.
136 Friederich von der Schulenburg, "The Military Situation at the End of 1917," Bundesarchiv/Militärarchiv, File N58/1, Nachlass Schulenburg, pp.168–169.
137 Wilhelm, Crown Prince of Germany, *Meine Erinnerungen aus Deutschlands Heldenkampf*, (Berlin: 1923), pp.292–293.
138 Lossberg, p.316.
139 Kuhl, *Offensive von 1918*, pp.74, 89.
140 Kuhl, *Diary*, (6 November 1917).
141 Max Hoffmann, *Der Krieg der versäumten Gelegenheiten*, (Munich: 1923), p.245.
142 Schulenburg, Nachlass File N58/1.
143 *Der Weltkrieg*, Vol.13, pp.323–324.

144 Georg Wetzell, "In Consideration of Our Situation in the Spring of 1918, How Are our Operations in the Winter of 1917–18 to Be Conducted, and What Preparations Are to Be Made in the Spring of 1918?," (23 October 1917), Bundesarchiv/Militärarchiv, File PH 3/267.
145 Herwig, *First World War*, p.393.
146 Georg Wetzell, "How Is a Decisive Offensive to Be Conducted on the Western Front in the Spring of 1918 in Case the Necessary Infantry and Artillery Forces Are Available?," (9 November 1917), Bundesarchiv/Militärarchiv, File PH 3/267.
147 Barnett, p.281.
148 Kuhl, *Offensive von 1918*, p.89.
149 Hans von Haeften, "The Political Offensive," Bundesarchiv/Militärarchiv, File N 35/8, Nachlass Haeften. Ludendorff, *Urkunden*, pp.473–478.
150 Gatzke, pp.251–259.
151 Rupprecht, *Kriegstagebuch*, Vol.II, pp.399–400.
152 Görlitz, p.195.
153 Hoffmann, p.240.
154 Kuhl, *Offensive von 1918*, p.89.
155 Wilhelm, *Erinnerungen*, p.293.
156 Paul von Hindenburg, *Aus meinem Leben*, (Leipzig: 1920), p.298.

5 The operational decision

1 Paul von Hindenburg, *Aus meinem Leben*, (Leipzig: 1920), p.327.
2 Oberkommando des Heeres, *Der Weltkrieg 1914 bis 1918*, Vol.14, (Berlin: 1944), pp.51–55. Hermann von Kuhl, *Entstehung, Durchführung und Zusammenbruch der Offensive von 1918*, (Berlin: 1927), pp.101–103.
3 Hermann von Kuhl, *Personal War Diary of General von Kuhl*, (11 November 1917), Bundesarchiv/Militärarchiv, File W-10/50652.
4 Wilhelm, Crown Prince of Germany, *Meine Erinnerungen aus Deutschlands Heldenkampf*, (Berlin: 1923), p.294.
5 Quoted in Kuhl, *Offensive von 1918*, p.103.
6 *Der Weltkrieg*, Vol.14, pp.57–58.
7 OHL, Ia 5299, (21 November 1917), Bundesarchiv/Militärarchiv, File PH 3 I/33. Initially the operations were dubbed ST. MICHAEL and ST. GEORGE, but the German planning documents and operations orders soon dropped the "ST."
8 Rupprecht, Crown Prince of Bavaria, *Mein Kriegstagebuch*, Vol.II, (Munich: 1929), p.303.
9 Correlli Barnett, *The Swordbearers: Supreme Command in the First World War*, (Bloomington, Indiana: 1964), p.278.
10 Army Group German Crown Prince, "Considerations on a Major Offensive to Be Launched against the British and French in 1918," Ia 2194, (12 November 1917), Bundesarchiv/Militärarchiv, File PH 3/278.
11 Army Group German Crown Prince, Ia 2196, (16 November 1917), Bundesarchiv/Militärarchiv, File PH 5 I/33.
12 Army Group German Crown Prince, Ia 2191, (19 November 1917), Bundesarchiv/Militärarchiv, File PH 5 I/33.
13 Fritz von Lossberg, *Meine Tätigkeit im Weltkriege 1914–1918*, (Berlin: 1939), pp.315–320.
14 Army Group Crown Prince Rupprecht, "Analytical Study of the GEORG Operation and Attack in the Sector of the Second Army," Ia 4501, (20 November 1917), Bundesarchiv/Militärarchiv, File PH 3/278.
15 Army Group Crown Prince Rupprecht, "Analytical Study of the GEORG Operation and Attack in the Sector of the Second Army," Ia 4501, (20 November 1917), Bundesarchiv/Militärarchiv, File PH 3/278.

16 Sir Douglas Haig, *The Private Papers of Douglas Haig, 1914–1919*, Robert Blake (ed.), (London: 1952), p.289.

17 Martin Middlebrook, *The Kaiser's Battle*, (London: 1978), p.25.

18 Georg Wetzell, "The Offensives in the West and Their Prospects of Success," (12 December 1917), Bundesarchiv/Militärarchiv, File PH 3/267.

19 James E. Edmonds (ed.), *Military Operations: Belgium and France 1918*, Vol.I, (London: 1935), p.142.

20 Army Group Crown Prince Rupprecht, Ia 4835, "Concerning the GEORG Operations in 1918," (15 December 1917), Bundesarchiv/Militärarchiv, File PH 3/278. Kuhl, *Diary*, (19 December 1917).

21 David T. Zabecki, *Steel Wind: Colonel Georg Bruchmüller and the Birth of Modern Artillery*, (Bridgeport, Connecticut: 1994), pp.64–66, 70.

22 Army Group Crown Prince Rupprecht, Ia 4872, (19 December 1917), Bayerisches Kriegsarchiv, File Hgr. Rupprecht, Bd. 80.

23 Army Group Crown Prince Rupprecht, "1918 Operations—Attack in the Zone of the Second and Eighteenth Armies (MICHAEL),"Ia 4922, (21 December 1917), Bundesarchiv/Militärarchiv, File PH 3 I/278.

24 Georg Wetzell, "Offensive of 1918 against the English or the French," (25 December 1917), Bundesarchiv/Militärarchiv, File PH 3/267.

25 Army Group Crown Prince Rupprecht, Ia 4929, (25 December 1917), Bundesarchiv/Militärarchiv, File PH 3/278.

26 *Der Weltkrieg*, Vol.14, pp.68–69. Rupprecht, *Kriegstagebuch*, Vol.II, pp.305–309. Kuhl, *Offensive von 1918*, p.115.

27 OHL, "1918 Operations in the West," Ia 5905, (27 December 1917), Bundesarchiv/Militärarchiv, File PH 3/278.

28 Rupprecht, *Kriegstagebuch*, Vol.II, p.308.

29 *Der Weltkrieg*, Vol.14, p.69.

30 Army Group Crown Prince Rupprecht, "Operations in the West 1918," Ia 5002, (3 January 1918), Bundesarchiv/Militärarchiv, File PH 3/278.

31 *Der Weltkrieg*, Vol.14, p.73.

32 Army Group Crown Prince Rupprecht, Ia 5050, (9 January 1918), *United States Army in the World War 1917–1919 Military Operations of the American Expeditionary Force*, Vol.11, Center of Military History (reprint), (Washington, D.C.: 1991), p.249.

33 Army Group Crown Prince Rupprecht, Ia 5063, (10 January 1918), Bundesarchiv/Militärarchiv, File PH 3/278.

34 Haig, p.273.

35 Army Group Crown Prince Rupprecht, Iab 5111, (15 January 1918), National Archives and Records Administration, Record Group 165, Entry 320, Box 42, Folder 3.

36 Thilo, "Meeting Minutes with Excellency Ludendorff, 19 January 1918," (19 January 1918), Bundesarchiv/Militärarchiv, File PH 5 II/199.

37 Thilo, "Meeting Minutes with Excellency Ludendorff, 20 January 1918," (21 January 1918), Bundesarchiv/Militärarchiv, File PH 5 II/199.

38 *Der Weltkrieg*, Vol.14, pp.76–77. Kuhl, *Offensive von 1918*, p.116.

39 Thilo, "Meeting Minutes with Excellency Ludendorff, 21 January 1918," (23 January 1918), Bundesarchiv/Militärarchiv, File PH 5 I/45.

40 Erich Ludendorff, *Meine Kriegserinnerungen 1914–1918*, (Berlin: 1919), p.474.

41 Thilo, (23 January 1918).

42 Ludendorff, *Kriegserinnerungen*, p.474.

43 Friederich von der Schulenburg, "Preparation of the Great Attack," p.180, Schulenburg Nachlass, Bundesarchiv/Militärarchiv, File N58/1.

44 Rupprecht, *Kriegstagebuch*, Vol.II, p.322.

45 *Der Weltkrieg*, Vol.14, pp.76–77.

46 Rupprecht, *Kriegstagebuch*, Vol.II, p.321. Lossberg, p.321.

344 *Notes*

47 AOK 18, Ia5, (16 January 1918), Bundesarchiv/Militärarchiv, File PH 3/278.
48 *Der Weltkrieg*, Vol.14, pp.80–81.
49 Rupprecht, *Kriegstagebuch*, Vol.II, pp.322–324.
50 Ferdinand Foch, *The Memoirs of Marshall Foch*, (New York: 1931), pp.235–244.
51 Edmonds, *1918*, Vol.I, pp.93–94.
52 Edmonds, *1918*, Vol.I, p.258.
53 Timothy Travers, *The Killing Ground: The British Army on the Western Front and the Emergence of Modern Warfare*, (London: 1987), pp.221–222.
54 Travers, pp.222–223.
55 Randal Gray, *Kaisersschlacht 1918: The Final German Offensive*, (London: 1991), p.33.
56 Middlebrook, p.105.
57 Middlebrook, p.71.
58 Middlebrook, pp.71–73.
59 Travers, pp.224–226.
60 Edmonds, *1918*, Vol.I, p.97.
61 Hindenburg, p.327.

6 Operations MICHAEL and MARS

1 Rupprecht, Crown Prince of Bavaria, *Mein Kriegstagebuch*, Vol.II, (Munich: 1929), p.307. Rupprecht wrote this comment in his diary immediately after the Krueznach Conference on 27 December 1917.
2 Albrecht von Thaer, *Generalstabsdienst an der Front und in der O.H.L.*, (Göttingen: 1958), pp.150–151. Thaer wrote this comment in his diary on 31 December 1917.
3 Otto Fehr, *Die Märzoffensive 1918 an der Westfront: Strategie oder Taktik?*, (Leipzig: 1921), pp.25–26. Oberkommando des Heeres, *Der Weltkrieg 1914 bis 1918*, Vol.14, (Berlin: 1944), p.83.
4 AOK 18, Ia5, (16 January 1918), Bundesarchiv/Militärarchiv, File PH 3/278.
5 Army Group Crown Prince Rupprecht, Ia 5135, (19 January 1918), Bundesarchiv/Militärarchiv, File PH 5 I/43.
6 OHL, Ia 6205, (24 January 1918), Bundesarchiv/Militärarchiv, File PH 5 I/31.
7 OHL, Ia 6213, (24 January 1918), Bundesarchiv/Militärarchiv, File PH 2/278.
8 *Der Weltkrieg*, Vol.14, pp.77–78.
9 AOK 7, Ia 200, (29 January 1918), Bundesarchiv/Militärarchiv, File PH 2/279.
10 Army Group Crown Prince Rupprecht, Ia 5243, (26 January 1918), Bundesarchiv/Militärarchiv, File PH 3/278.
11 AOK 2, Ias 51, (29 January 1918), National Archives and Records Administration, RG 165, Entry 320, Box 42, Folder 3.
12 AOK 2, Ias 69, (1 February 1918), Bundesarchiv/Militärarchiv, File PH 3/279.
13 OHL, "Mons Conference Minutes by Major Thilo," (4 February 1918), Bundesarchiv/Militärarchiv, File PH 5 I/45.
14 Hermann von Kuhl, *Personal War Diary of General von Kuhl*, (3 February 1918), Bundesarchiv/Militärarchiv, File: W-10/50652.
15 Rupprecht, *Kriegstagebuch*, Vol.II, p.327.
16 Kuhl, *Diary*, (8 February 1918).
17 *Der Weltkrieg*, Vol.14, pp.80–82.
18 OHL, "Maubeuge Conference Minutes by Major Thilo," (4 February 1918), Bundesarchiv/Militärarchiv, File PH 5 I/45.
19 OHL, Ia 6205, (8 February 1918), Bundesarchiv/Militärarchiv, File PH 5 I/32.
20 Army Group German Crown Prince, Ia 2299, (8 February 1918), Bundesarchiv/Militärarchiv, File PH 5 II/204.
21 OHL, Ia 6435, (10 February 1918), Bundesarchiv/Militärarchiv, File PH 3/279.
22 Erich Ludendorff, *Meine Kriegserinnerungen 1914–1918*, (Berlin: 1919), p.472.

23 Army Group Crown Prince Rupprecht, Ia 5581, (14 February 1918), Bundesarchiv/ Militärarchiv, File PH 5 I/49.
24 OHL, Ia 6562, (16 February 1918), Bundesarchiv/Militärarchiv, File PH 3 I/280.
25 OHL, "Meeting Minutes," (n.d.), Bundesarchiv/Militärarchiv, File PH 5 II/204.
26 Army Group Crown Prince Rupprecht, Ia 5887, (26 February 1918), Bundesarchiv/ Militärarchiv, File PH 5 I/45.
27 Army Group Crown Prince Rupprecht, Ia 5884, (26 February 1918), Bundesarchiv/ Militärarchiv, File PH 3/280.
28 Rupprecht, *Kriegstagebuch*, Vol.II, p.343.
29 Fehr, pp.28–29.
30 Army Group German Crown Prince, Ia 2364, (6 March 1918), *United States Army in the World War 1917–1919 Military Operations of the American Expeditionary Force*, Vol.11, Center of Military History (reprint), (Washington, D.C.: 1991), pp.262–263. Wilhelm, Crown Prince of Germany, *Meine Erinnerungen aus Deutschlands Heldenkampf*, (Berlin: 1923), p.300.
31 AOK 18, Ia 844, (2 March 1918), Bundesarchiv/Militärarchiv, File PH 5 I/30.
32 *Der Weltkrieg*, Vol.14, p.82.
33 AOK 2, Ia 540, (6 March 1918), National Archives and Records Administration, RG 165, Entry 320, Box 42, Folder 3.
34 AOK 2, Ia 591, (7 March 1918), National Archives and Records Administration, RG 165, Entry 320, Box 42, Folder 3.
35 Army Group Crown Prince Rupprecht, Ia 6072, (6 March 1918), Bundesarchiv/ Militärarchiv, File PH 3/281.
36 Army Group Crown Prince Rupprecht, Ia 6072, (6 March 1918), Bundesarchiv/ Militärarchiv, File PH 3/281.
37 *Der Weltkrieg*, Vol.14, pp.83–84.
38 Rupprecht, *Kriegstagebuch*, Vol.II, pp.335–336
39 AOK 2, Iad 616, (9 March 1918), National Archives and Records Administration, RG 165, Entry 320, Box 42, Folder 3.
40 OHL, Ia 7070, (10 March 1918), Bundesarchiv/Militärarchiv, File PH 3/281.
41 Hermann von Kuhl, *Entstehung, Durchführung und Zusammenbruch der Offensive von 1918*, (Berlin: 1927), p.118.
42 Rupprecht, *Kriegstagebuch*, Vol.II, p.338.
43 *Der Weltkrieg*, Vol.14, p.89.
44 Army Group Crown Prince Rupprecht, Ia 6202, (12 March 1918), Bundesarchiv/ Militärarchiv, File PH 5 I/49.
45 OHL, Ia 7069, (12 March 1918), *United States Army in the World War 1917–1919 Military Operations of the American Expeditionary Force*, Vol.11, Center of Military History (reprint), (Washington, D.C.: 1991), p.265.
46 Army Group German Crown Prince, Ia 2377, (14 March 1918), Bundesarchiv/ Militärarchiv, File PH 3/281.
47 AOK 18, Ia 1121, (15 March 1918), Bundesarchiv/Militärarchiv, File PH 3/281.
48 Kuhl, *Der Offensive von 1918*, p.132.
49 Army Group Crown Prince Rupprecht, Ia 6263, (16 March 1918), Bundesarchiv/ Militärarchiv, File PH 3/281.
50 Army Group Crown Prince Rupprecht, War Diary, (20 March 1918), Bayerisches Kriegsarchiv, File Hgr. Rupprecht, Bd. 80. *Der Weltkrieg*, Vol.14, pp.88–89.
51 OHL, Ia 7240, (20 March 1918), Bundesarchiv/Militärarchiv, File PH 3/268.
52 Kuhl, *Der Offensive von 1918*, pp.132–133. Rupprecht, *Kriegstagebuch*, Vol.II, p.343.
53 Army Group Crown Prince Rupprecht, Ia 4929, (25 December 1917), Bundesarchiv/ Militärarchiv, File PH 3/287. Kuhl, *Der Offensive von 1918*, pp.123–124.
54 *Der Weltkrieg*, Vol.14, pp.167–168.
55 AOK 2, Ias 23, (22 January 1918), National Archives and Records Administration, RG 165, Entry 320, Box 42, Folder 3.

56 Kuhl, *Der Offensive von 1918*, pp.121–124. *Der Weltkrieg*, Vol.14, p.101.
57 OHL, Ic 14926, (5 February 1918), Bundesarchiv/Militärarchiv, File F-12655.
58 OHL, Ia 6620, (18 February 1918), Bundesarchiv/Militärarchiv, File PH 3/280.
59 OHL, Ia 65317, (14 February 1918), Bundesarchiv/Militärarchiv, File F-12655.
60 Army Group Crown Prince Rupprecht, Ia 5921, (28 February 1918), Bundesarchiv/ Militärarchiv, File PH 3/281.
61 OHL, Ia 6925, (4 March 1918), Bundesarchiv/Militärarchiv, File PH 3/281.
62 Georg Bruchmüller, *Die Deutsche Artillerie in den Durchbruchschlachten des Weltkriegs*, 2nd ed., (Berlin: 1922), pp.88–89.
63 Hermann von Kuhl, "Das Deutsche Angriffsverfahren bei der Offensive in Jahre 1918," *Deutsches Offiziersblatt*, (21 September 1921), p.534.
64 OHL, "Unnumbered Memo from Geyer to Bruchmüller on the Pulkowski Method," (22 January 1918), Bundesarchiv/Militärarchiv, File PH 5 II/204.
65 OHL, II 6645, (25 January 1918), Bundesarchiv/Militärarchiv, File PH 3/454.
66 Army Group Crown Prince Rupprecht, Ia 5305, (29 January 1918), Bayerisches Kriegsarchiv, File AOK 6, Bd. 279.
67 OHL, II 6815, (28 February 1918), Bundesarchiv/Militärarchiv, File PH 3/281.
68 Ludendorff, *Kriegserinnerungen*, p.464.
69 Georg Wetzell, "Michael, die Grosse Schlacht in Frankreich," *Militär-Wochenblatt*, (28 May 1935), p.1945.
70 Georg Bruchmüller, *Die Artillerie beim Angriff im Stellungskrieg*, (Berlin: 1926), p.97.
71 Bruchmüller, *Artillerie beim Angriff*, p.118.
72 Bruchmüller, *Artillerie beim Angriff*, p.96.
73 AOK 18, War Diary: Narrative Summary, Bundesarchiv/Militärarchiv, File PH 5 I/29.
74 Bruchmüller, *Durchbruchschlachten*, (1922), pp.63–66.
75 AOK 18, Ia/Art 15/61, "Artillery Order Nr. 1," (31 January 1918), Bundesarchiv/ Militärarchiv, File PH 5 II/99.
76 Reichsarchiv, "Historical Study of Air Forces 1918," (12 April 1926), Bundesarchiv/Militärarchiv, File RH 2/2195. AOK 18, Fl N 21 "Army Order: Commitment of Air Units on the Attack Day," Bundesarchiv/Militärarchiv, File RH 2/2195.
77 OHL Ia 7517, (5 April 1918), Bayerisches Kriegsarchiv, File Hgr. Rupprecht, Bd. 80. Also quoted in *Der Weltkrieg*, Vol.14, p.253.
78 Colonel Jochim, Untitled Manuscript about Seventeenth Army Logistics for MICHAEL, (29 April 1930), Bundesarchiv/Militärarchiv, File PH 2/203, pp.65–67.
79 Kuhl, *Der Offensive von 1918*, p.125.
80 AOK 18, War Diary: Narrative Summary, Bundesarchiv/Militärarchiv, File PH 5 I/29.
81 Jochim, pp.12, 60.
82 AOK 2, Ias 719, (12 March 1918), National Archives and Records Administration, RG 165, Entry 320, Box 42, Folder 3.
83 Jochim, pp.55–58.
84 AOK 2, Ias 695/18, (11 March 1918), National Archives and Records Administration, RG 165, Entry 320, Box 42, Folder 3.
85 Jochim, p.39.
86 Kuhl, *Der Offensive von 1918*, pp.1256–1228.
87 Georg Bruchmüller, *Die Deutsche Artillerie in den Durchbruchschlachten des Weltkriegs*, 1st ed., (Berlin: 1921), p.30.
88 Reichsarchiv, "Historical Study of Air Forces 1918," (12 April 1926), Bundesarchiv/Militärarchiv, File RH 2/2195.
89 Correlli Barnett, *The Swordbearers: Supreme Command in the First World War*, (Bloomington, Indiana: 1964), pp.293–296.

90 James E. Edmonds (ed.), *Military Operations: Belgium and France 1918*, Vol.I, (London: 1935), pp.41–42.
91 Barrie Pitt, *1918: The Last Act*, (New York: 1963), pp.78–79.
92 Tim Travers, *How the War Was Won: Command and Technology in the British Army on the Western Front, 1917–1918*, (London: 1992), p.31.
93 Ferdinand Foch, *The Memoirs of Marshall Foch*, (New York: 1931), p.253.
94 Edmonds, *1918*, Appendices, pp.45–47.
95 Edmonds, *1918*, Vol.I, pp.48–50.
96 Edmonds, *1918*, Vol.I, pp.51–52.
97 Edmonds, *1918*, Vol.I, p.105.
98 Sir Douglas Haig, *The Private Papers of Douglas Haig, 1914–1919*, Robert Blake (ed.), (London: 1952), p.291.
99 Edmonds, *1918*, Vol.I, pp.106–108.
100 Edmonds, *1918*, Vol.I, pp.109–110. The divisions were the 20th and the 50th.
101 *Der Weltkrieg*, Vol.14, Appendix 38a.
102 Frederic Herr, *Die Artillerie in Vergangenheit, Gegenwart, und Zukunft*, (translation of *L'Artillerie, ce qu'elle a été, ce qu'elle est, ce qu'elle doit être*, (Paris: 1923)) (Charlottenburg: 1925), p.126.
103 H.A. Bethell, "The Modern Attack on an Entrenched Position," *Journal of the Royal Artillery*, (July 1918), p.122.
104 *Der Weltkrieg*, Vol.14, Appendix 38a.
105 *Der Weltkrieg*, Vol.14, Appendix 38a.
106 *Der Weltkrieg*, Vol.14, Appendices 38a and 39a.
107 OHL, II 78685, "OHL Heavy Batteries in Position by 20 March," (26 February 1918), Bundesarchiv/Militärarchiv, File PH 3/259.
108 Reichsarchiv, "Historical Study of Air Forces 1918," (12 April 1926), Bundesarchiv/Militärarchiv, File RH 2/2195.
109 Randal Gray, *Kaisersschlacht 1918: The Final German Offensive*, (London: 1991), p.19.
110 Ludendorff, *Kriegserinnerungen* pp.479–480. OHL, Ia 7240, (20 March 1918), Bundesarchiv/Militärarchiv, File PH 3/268.
111 Edmonds, *1918*, Vol.I, pp.114–115.
112 Georg Bruchmüller, Letter to Georg Wetzell, (18 July 1935), Bruchmüller Nachlass, Bundesarchiv/Militärarchiv, Folder N275/36.
113 Bruchmüller, *Die Artillerie beim Angriff*, (1926), pp.101–103.
114 *Der Weltkrieg*, Vol.14, Appendix 39a.
115 Army Group Crown Prince Rupprecht, Ia 6384, (21 March 1918), War Diary, Bayerisches Kriegsarchiv, File Hgr. Rupprecht, Bd. 80.
116 Edmonds, *1918*, Vol.I, p.208.
117 Rupprecht, *Kriegstagebuch*, Vol.II, pp.345–346.
118 Wilhelm, *Erinnerungen*, p.304.
119 Ludwig Beck, *Studien*, (ed. Hans Speidel), (Stuttgart: 1955), p.217.
120 *Der Weltkrieg*, Vol.14, p.114.
121 *Der Weltkrieg*, Vol.14, pp.121–122.
122 *Der Weltkrieg*, Vol.14, pp.128–130.
123 Ludendorff, *Kriegserinnerungen*, p.481.
124 Ernst Jünger, *The Storm of Steel: From the Diary of a German Storm-Troop Officer on the Western Front*, (New York: 1985), p.266.
125 Edmonds, *1918*, Vol.I, pp.249–250.
126 Pitt, p.99.
127 *Militär-Wochenblatt*, "Die deutsche Offensive im März 1918," Part 4, (11 March 1928), p.1291.
128 Kuhl, *Der Offensive von 1918*, p.131.
129 *Der Weltkrieg*, Vol.14, Appendix 35. Army Group German Crown Prince, War Diary Extracts, (21 March 1918), Bundesarchiv/Militärarchiv, File PH 5 I/29.

130 AOK 17, Ia 1368, (21 March 1918), Bundesarchiv/Militärarchiv, File PH 5 II/202. Rupprecht, *Kriegstagebuch*, Vol.II, p.345.
131 Army Group German Crown Prince, War Diary Extracts, (21 March 1918), Bundesarchiv/Militärarchiv, File PH 5 I/29.
132 Army Group German Crown Prince, Ia 2387, (21 March 1918), Bundesarchiv/Militärarchiv, File PH 3/268.
133 Edmonds, *1918*, Vol.I, p.261.
134 Timothy Travers, *The Killing Ground: The British Army on the Western Front and the Emergence of Modern Warfare*, (London: 1987), p.227. Martin Middlebrook, *The Kaiser's Battle*, (London: 1978), pp.207–208.
135 Foch, p.255.
136 Martin Kitchen, *The German Offensives of 1918*, (Stroud, Gloucestershire: 2001), p.72.
137 Foch, p.266.
138 Travers, p.232.
139 *Der Weltkrieg*, Vol.14, p.145.
140 Pitt, p.109.
141 *Der Weltkrieg*, Vol.14, p.142.
142 Travers, p.235.
143 AOK 18, Ia 1461, (22 March 1918), Bundesarchiv/Militärarchiv, File PH 5 I/29. *Der Weltkrieg*, Vol.14, p.145.
144 OHL, Ia 7280, (22 March 1918), Bundesarchiv/Militärarchiv, File PH 3/268. *Der Weltkrieg*, Vol.14, p.148.
145 Army Group Crown Prince Rupprecht, Ia 6380, (22 March 1918), Bundesarchiv/Militärarchiv, File PH 3/268.
146 Rupprecht, *Kriegstagebuch*, Vol.II, pp.348–349. *Der Weltkrieg*, Vol.14, pp.134–135, 138–139.
147 Edmonds, *1918*, Vol.I, p.322.
148 Haig, p.296.
149 AOK 2, War Diary, (23 March 1918), Bundesarchiv/Militärarchiv, File PH 5 II/121. Kuhl, *Diary*, (23 March 1918).
150 Ian V. Hogg, *The Guns 1914–1918*, (New York: 1971), pp.134–135. Rupprecht, *Kriegstagebuch*, Vol.II, p.352.
151 Edmonds, *1918*, Vol.I, p.322.
152 OHL, Ia 7288, (23 March 1918), Bundesarchiv/Militärarchiv, File PH 3/268. *Der Weltkrieg*, Vol.14, p.166.
153 Rupprecht, *Kriegstagebuch*, Vol.II, pp.351–352.
154 AOK 17, Ia 1400, (23 March 1918), Bundesarchiv/Militärarchiv, File PH 5 II/202. *Der Weltkrieg*, Vol.14, p.170.
155 Kuhl, *Der Offensive von 1918*, p.133.
156 Wilhelm, *Erinnerungen*, p.307.
157 *Der Weltkrieg*, Vol.14, pp.162–163.
158 Army Group German Crown Prince, Ia 2394, (23 March 1918), Bundesarchiv/Militärarchiv, File PH 5 I/31. *Der Weltkrieg*, Vol.14, p.175.
159 Edmonds, *1918*, Vol.I, p.368.
160 *Der Weltkrieg*, Vol.14, pp.172–173, 180.
161 Army Group Crown Prince Rupprecht, Ia 6406, (24 March 1918), Bundesarchiv/Militärarchiv, File PH 5 II/202. *Der Weltkrieg*, Vol.14, p.180.
162 OHL, Ia 7299, (24 March 1918), Bundesarchiv/Militärarchiv, File PH 5 II/202. *Der Weltkrieg*, Vol.14, p.180. Rupprecht, *Kriegstagebuch*, Vol.II, p.353.
163 *Der Weltkrieg*, Vol.14, p.181. Rupprecht, *Kriegstagebuch*, Vol.II, pp.353–354.
164 *Der Weltkrieg*, Vol.14, Appendix 35. Army Group German Crown Prince, War Diary Extracts, (24 March 1918), Bundesarchiv/Militärarchiv, File PH 5 I/29.
165 *Der Weltkrieg*, Vol.14, pp.175–177.

166 AOK 18, War Diary: Narrative Summary, (24 March 1918), Bundesarchiv/Militärarchiv, File PH 5 I/29.
167 Travers, p.237.
168 James B. Ord, *The German Offensive of March 21–April 8, 1918*, Unpublished Paper, (U.S. Army War College: 1922), p.37.
169 Foch, p.257.
170 Haig, p.297.
171 Kitchen, p.79. Edmonds, *1918*, Vol.I, p.449.
172 Army Group Crown Prince Rupprecht, Ia 6427, (25 March 1918), Bundesarchiv/ Militärarchiv, File PH 3/268. Rupprecht, *Kriegstagebuch*, Vol.II, p.354. Kuhl, *Diary*, (26 March 1918).
173 Army Group German Crown Prince, War Diary Extracts, (25 March 1918), Bundesarchiv/Militärarchiv, File PH 5 I/29.
174 OHL, Ia 7320, (25 March 1918), Bundesarchiv/Militärarchiv, File PH 3/268.
175 *Der Weltkrieg*, Vol.14, p.186.
176 Wilhelm, *Erinnerungen*, p.308.
177 Ord, p.41.
178 Ludendorff, *Kriegserinnerungen*, p.482.
179 *Der Weltkrieg*, Vol.14, Appendix 38c.
180 Ord, p.40.
181 Travers, p.237.
182 A.M. Henniker, *Transportation on the Western Front, 1914–1918*, (London: 1937), p.402. Ian Malcolm Brown, *British Logistics on the Western Front, 1914–1919*, (Bridgeport, Connecticut: 1998), p.186.
183 Foch, pp.257–258.
184 *Der Weltkrieg*, Vol.14, p.189.
185 Rupprecht, *Kriegstagebuch*, Vol.II, p.356.
186 AOK 2, War Diary, (26 March 1918), Bundesarchiv/Militärarchiv, File PH 5 II/121.
187 *Der Weltkrieg*, Vol.14, p.193.
188 *1918*, pp.125–126.
189 Rupprecht, *Kriegstagebuch*, Vol.II, p.357.
190 Ludendorff, *Kriegserinnerungen*, p.481.
191 Foch, p.256.
192 *Der Weltkrieg*, Vol.14, pp.201, 210–211, Appendix 38e.
193 OHL, Ia 7341, (26 March 1918), Bundesarchiv/Militärarchiv, File PH 3/268. Army Group Crown Prince Rupprecht, Ia 6438, (26 March 1918), Bundesarchiv/ Militärarchiv, File PH 5 II/202. *Der Weltkrieg*, Vol.14, pp.199–202.
194 Army Group Crown Prince Rupprecht, War Diary, (26 March 1918), Bayerisches Kriegsarchiv, File Hgr. Rupprecht, Bd. 80.
195 Kuhl, *Der Offensive von 1918*, p.135.
196 Edmonds, *1918*, Vol.I, p.537.
197 Ludendorff, *Kriegserinnerungen*, p.481.
198 *Der Weltkrieg*, Vol.14, p.201.
199 Army Group Crown Prince Rupprecht, Ia 6442, (26 March 1918), Bundesarchiv/ Militärarchiv, File PH 5 II/202. *Der Weltkrieg*, Vol.14, p.206.
200 *Der Weltkrieg*, Vol.14, pp.196–199.
201 Wilhelm, *Erinnerungen*, p.309. *Der Weltkrieg*, Vol.14, pp.196–198.
202 Foch, pp.262–263.
203 Foch, p.266.
204 *Der Weltkrieg*, Vol.14, pp.211–212.
205 Army Group German Crown Prince, War Diary Extracts, (27 March 1918), Bundesarchiv/Militärarchiv, File PH 5 I/29.
206 AOK 18, War Diary: Narrative Summary, (27 March 1918), Bundesarchiv/Militärarchiv, File PH 5 I/29.

207 Wilhelm, *Erinnerungen*, pp.310–311.
208 *Der Weltkrieg*, Vol.14, p.208.
209 Rupprecht, *Kriegstagebuch*, Vol.II, p.359.
210 *Der Weltkrieg*, Vol.14, pp.206–207.
211 Army Group Crown Prince Rupprecht, Ia 6458, (27 March 1918), Bundesarchiv/ Militärarchiv, File PH 5 II/202. AOK 17, Ia 1556, (27 March 1918), Bundesarchiv/Militärarchiv, File PH 5 II/202.
212 Rupprecht, *Kriegstagebuch*, Vol.II, p.359.
213 AOK 2, War Diary, (27 March 1918), Bundesarchiv/Militärarchiv, File PH 5 II/121.
214 *Der Weltkrieg*, Vol.14, Appendix 8.
215 Ord, p.48.
216 Army Group German Crown Prince, War Diary Extracts, (27 March 1918), Bundesarchiv/Militärarchiv, File PH 5 I/29.
217 Army Group German Crown Prince, War Diary Extracts, (27 March 1918), Bundesarchiv/Militärarchiv, File PH 5 I/29.
218 Army Group German Crown Prince, War Diary Extracts, (27 March 1918), Bundesarchiv/Militärarchiv, File PH 5 I/29.
219 Ord, p.47.
220 Army Group German Crown Prince, War Diary Extracts, (28 March 1918), Bundesarchiv/Militärarchiv, File PH 5 I/29.
221 Rupprecht, *Kriegstagebuch*, Vol.II, p.360.
222 Georg Wetzell, "Michael," p.1946.
223 Rupprecht, *Kriegstagebuch*, Vol.II, p.358. *Der Weltkrieg*, Vol.14, p.214.
224 *Der Weltkrieg*, Vol.14, pp.215–216.
225 Wilhelm, *Erinnerungen*, p.310. *Der Weltkrieg*, Vol.14, p.223.
226 *Der Weltkrieg*, Vol.14, p.214.
227 Brown, p.186.
228 *Der Weltkrieg*, Vol.14, pp.216–220.
229 AOK 2, War Diary, (28 March 1918), Bundesarchiv/Militärarchiv, File PH 5 II/121.
230 Rupprecht, *Kriegstagebuch*, Vol.II, p.361. *Der Weltkrieg*, Vol.14, p.226.
231 Wilhelm, *Erinnerungen*, p.311.
232 OHL, Ia 7373, (28 March 1918), Bundesarchiv/Militärarchiv, File PH 3/268. *Der Weltkrieg*, Vol.14, p.228.
233 *Der Weltkrieg*, Vol.14, Appendix 35.
234 Ludendorff, *Kriegserinnerungen*, p.481.
235 OHL, Ia 7380, (28 March 1918), Bundesarchiv/Militärarchiv, File PH 3/268. Army Group Crown Prince Rupprecht, Ia 6479, (29 March 1918), Bundesarchiv/Militärarchiv, File PH 5 II/202. Army Group Crown Prince Rupprecht, Ia 6486, (29 March 1918), Bundesarchiv/Militärarchiv, File PH 5 II/202. *Der Weltkrieg*, Vol.14, pp.226–227.
236 Army Group Crown Prince Rupprecht, Ia 6483, (29 March 1918), Bundesarchiv/ Militärarchiv, File PH 3/281.
237 Army Group German Crown Prince, War Diary Extracts, (28 March 1918), Bundesarchiv/Militärarchiv, File PH 5 I/29. *Der Weltkrieg*, Vol.14, p.228, Appendix 35.
238 *Der Weltkrieg*, Vol.14, p.229.
239 Ord, pp.45, 47.
240 Army Group German Crown Prince, Ia 2406, (29 March 1918), Bundesarchiv/Militärarchiv, File PH 3/268. OHL, Ia 7390, (29 March 1918), Bundesarchiv/Militärarchiv, File PH 3/268.
241 Rupprecht, *Kriegstagebuch*, Vol.II, p.363. *Der Weltkrieg*, Vol.14, p.234.
242 Brown, pp.188–189.
243 Rupprecht, *Kriegstagebuch*, Vol.II, p.362. *Der Weltkrieg*, Vol.14, p.235.
244 *Der Weltkrieg*, Vol.14, Appendix 35.

245 OHL, Ia 7389, (29 March 1918), Bundesarchiv/Militärarchiv, File PH 3/268. Rupprecht, *Kriegstagebuch*, Vol.II, p.364. *Der Weltkrieg*, Vol.14, pp.235–236.
246 James E. Edmonds, *Military Operations: Belgium and France 1918*, Vol.II, (London: 1937), p.86.
247 AOK 2, War Diary, (29 March 1918), Bundesarchiv/Militärarchiv, File PH 5 II/121.
248 *Der Weltkrieg*, Vol.14, pp.234, 236.
249 Army Group German Crown Prince, War Diary Extracts, (29 March 1918), Bundesarchiv/Militärarchiv, File PH 5 I/29.
250 Foch, p.270.
251 *Der Weltkrieg*, Vol.14, Appendix 38f.
252 Army Group German Crown Prince, War Diary Extracts, (18 May 1918), Bundesarchiv/Militärarchiv, File PH 5 I/29.
253 OHL, Ia 7408, (30 March 1918), Bundesarchiv/Militärarchiv, File PH 3/268. OHL, II 81943, (30 March 1918), Bundesarchiv/Militärarchiv, File PH 3/259.
254 AOK 2, War Diary, (30 March 1918), Bundesarchiv/Militärarchiv, File PH 5 II/121. Army Group German Crown Prince, Ia 2410, (30 March 1918), Bundesarchiv/Militärarchiv, File PH 3/268. *Der Weltkrieg*, Vol.14, pp.242–243.
255 Wilhelm, *Erinnerungen*, p.311.
256 Edmonds, *1918*, Vol.II, p.107.
257 OHL, Ia 7414, (31 March 1918), Bundesarchiv/Militärarchiv, File PH 3/268.
258 OHL, Ia 7416, (31 March 1918), Bundesarchiv/Militärarchiv, File PH 3/268. AOK 18, War Diary: Narrative Summary, (31 March 1918), Bundesarchiv/Militärarchiv, File PH 5 I/29. Rupprecht, *Kriegstagebuch*, Vol.II, pp.366–367. *Der Weltkrieg*, Vol.14, p.244.
259 Army Group German Crown Prince, War Diary Extracts, "Notes of Discussion with Ludendorff," (1 April 1918), Bundesarchiv/Militärarchiv, File PH 5 I/29. Army Group Crown Prince Rupprecht, War Diary, (1 April 1918), Bayerisches Kriegsarchiv, File Hgr. Rupprecht, Bd. 80. According to the War Diary of Rupprecht's Army Group, the meeting was held in Avesnes. *Der Weltkrieg*, Vol.14, pp.245–246.
260 OHL, Ia 7438, (1 April 1918), *United States Army in the World War 1917–1919 Military Operations of the American Expeditionary Force*, Vol.11, Center of Military History (reprint), (Washington, D.C.: 1991), pp.280–281. Army Group Crown Prince Rupprecht, Ia 6543, (1 April 1918), Bundesarchiv/Militärarchiv, File PH 5 I/45. Army Group German Crown Prince, Ia 2406, (1 April 1918), Bundesarchiv/Militärarchiv, File PH 5 I/31.
261 AOK 2, War Diary, (2 April 1918), Bundesarchiv/Militärarchiv, File PH 5 II/121.
262 AOK 2, War Diary, (3 April 1918), Bundesarchiv/Militärarchiv, File PH 5 II/121.
263 Gray, pp.76–78.
264 Rupprecht, *Kriegstagebuch*, Vol.II, p.370. *Der Weltkrieg*, Vol.14, p.251.
265 *Der Weltkrieg*, Vol.14, pp.251–252.
266 Rupprecht, *Kriegstagebuch*, Vol.II, p.372.
267 Kuhl, *Diary*, (4 April 1918).
268 Rupprecht, *Kriegstagebuch*, Vol.II, p.371. *Der Weltkrieg*, Vol.14, p.252.
269 OHL, Ia 7515, (5 April 1918), *United States Army in the World War 1917–1919 Military Operations of the American Expeditionary Force*, Vol.11, Center of Military History (reprint), (Washington, D.C.: 1991), p.282.
270 Ord, p.18. Kitchen, pp.96–97.
271 *Der Weltkrieg*, Vol.14, pp.254–259.
272 Ludendorff, *Kriegserinnerungen*, p.482.
273 *Der Weltkrieg*, Vol.14, p.255.
274 Pascal Lucas, *The Evolution of Tactical Ideas in France and Germany During the War of 1914–1918*, (Paris: 1923), (manuscript translation in English by Major P.V. Kieffer, U.S. Army 1925), pp.137–138.

275 Ludendorff, *Kriegserinnerungen*, p.474.
276 *Der Weltkrieg*, Vol.14, Appendix 38a.
277 Jochim, p.11.
278 Kuhl, *Der Offensive von 1918*, p.119.
279 Fehr, p.46.
280 *Der Weltkrieg*, Vol.14, Appendix 35.
281 Army Group German Crown Prince, War Diary Extracts, (21 March–5 April 1918), Bundesarchiv/Militärarchiv, File PH 5 I/29. *Der Weltkrieg*, Vol.14, Appendix 38.
282 OHL, SCHWEFLA Staff Officer Reports, B7678, (16 March 1918), B7841 (23 March 1918), B8018 (30 March 1918), Bundesarchiv/Militärarchiv, File PH 3/503.
283 Friederich von der Schulenberg, "Preparation of the Great Attack," p.180, Schulenberg Nachlass, Bundesarchiv/Militärarchiv, File N 58/1. Edmonds, *1918*, Vol.I, pp.146–149. Kitchen, pp.37–38.
284 Ludendorff, *Kriegserinnerungen*, p.475.
285 Jehuda L. Wallach, *The Dogma of the Battle of Annihilation: The Theories of Clausewitz and Schlieffen and Their Impact on the German Conduct of Two World Wars*, (Westport, Connecticut: 1986), p.190.
286 Rupprecht, *Kriegstagebuch*, Vol.II, p.322.
287 Richard von Berendt, "Die Artillerie beim Angriff im Stellungskrieg," *Artilleristische Rundschau*, (April 1927), pp.17–23. Richard von Berendt, "Schiessübungen," *Artilleristische Rundschau*, (October 1935), pp.193–196.
288 AOK 17, Ia/Art 145/112, (3 February 1918), Bundesarchiv/Militärarchiv, File PH 5 II/199.
289 AOK 17, Ia/Art 615/220, (24 February 1918), Bundesarchiv/Militärarchiv, File PH 5 II/199.
290 AOK 17, Ia/Art 924/112, (6 March 1918), Bundesarchiv/Militärarchiv, File PH 5 II/199.
291 AOK 17, Ia/Art 1216, (16 March 1918), Bundesarchiv/Militärarchiv, File PH 5 II/199.
292 Bruchmüller (1926), pp.118–120, 178–180.
293 Army Group Crown Prince Rupprecht, Ic 6598, (1 April 1918), *United States Army in the World War 1917–1919 Military Operations of the American Expeditionary Force*, Vol.11, Center of Military History (reprint), (Washington, D.C.: 1991), pp.281–282.
294 Kuhl, "Das Deutsche Angriffsverfahren," p.535.
295 Ludendorff, *Kriegserinnerungen*, p.487. In a letter to Bruchmüller after the war, Ludendorff wrote: "I enjoyed your book. I especially appreciate that the record has finally been set straight on the situation at the Seventeenth Army." Bruchmüller Papers, Bundesarchiv/Militärarchiv, Folder N 275/2.
296 Kuhl, *Der Offensive von 1918*, p.130.
297 Jochim, pp.63–69.
298 Otto von Moser, *Kurzer strategischer Überblick über den Weltkrieg 1914–1918*, (Berlin: 1921), p.100.
299 Rupprecht, *Kriegstagebuch*, Vol.II, p.372.
300 Ludendorff, *Kriegserinnerungen*, p.472.
301 Kuhl, *Der Offensive von 1918*, p.120.
302 *Der Weltkrieg*, Vol.14, p.255.
303 Cited in Brown, p.191.
304 Hindenburg, pp.320–321.
305 Kitchen, p.79.
306 AOK 2, Ia/Art (no number), (7 April 1918), Bayerisches Kriegsarchiv, File Hgr. Rupprecht, Bd. 38.

307 OHL, II 82923, (8 April 1918), Bayerisches Kriegsarchiv, File Hgr. Rupprecht, Bd. 38.
308 Kuhl, *Der Offensive von 1918*, p.134.
309 Barnett, p.317.
310 *Der Weltkrieg*, Vol.14, pp.207–208.
311 Rupprecht, *Kriegstagebuch*, Vol.II, pp.402–403.
312 Edmonds, *1918*, Vol.II, p.464.
313 Rupprecht, *Kriegstagebuch*, Vol.III, p.23.
314 *Der Weltkrieg*, Vol.14, Appendix 38f.
315 OHL, Ic 85444, (12 May 1918), Bundesarchiv/Militärarchiv, File PH 5 II/295.
316 Edmonds, *1918*, Vol.I, p.486.

7 Operation GEORGETTE

1 Cited in James E. Edmonds, *Military Operations: Belgium and France 1918*, Vol.II, (London: 1937), p.465.
2 Edmonds, *1918*, Vol.II, p.465.
3 Oberkommando des Heeres, *Der Weltkrieg 1914 bis 1918*, Vol.14, (Berlin: 1944), p.261.
4 *Der Weltkrieg*, p.303.
5 Rupprecht, Crown Prince of Bavaria, *Mein Kriegstagebuch*, Vol.II, (Munich: 1929), p.394.
6 Hermann von Kuhl, Entstehung, *Durchführung und Zusammenbruch der Offensive von 1918*, (Berlin: 1927), p.147.
7 Army Group Crown Prince Rupprecht, Ia 4501, (20 November 1917), Bundesarchiv/Militärarchiv, File PH 3/278.
8 Army Group Crown Prince Rupprecht, Ia 4501, (20 November 1917), Bundesarchiv/Militärarchiv, File PH 3/278.
9 Army Group Crown Prince Rupprecht, Ia 4835, (15 December 1917), Bundesarchiv/Militärarchiv, File PH 3/278.
10 Army Group Crown Prince Rupprecht, Ia 4877, (21 December 1917), Bundesarchiv/Militärarchiv, File PH 3/278.
11 Army Group Crown Prince Rupprecht, Ia 5002, (3 January 1918), Bundesarchiv/Militärarchiv, File PH 3/278.
12 Army Group Crown Prince Rupprecht, Ia 5243, (26 January 1918), Bundesarchiv/Militärarchiv, File PH 3/278.
13 Rupprecht, *Kriegstagebuch*, Vol.III, p.279.
14 OHL, "Meeting Minutes with Excellency Ludendorff, by Major Thilo, 21 January 1918," (23 January 1918), Bundesarchiv/Militärarchiv, File PH 5 I/45.
15 OHL, Ia 6213, (24 January 1918), Bundesarchiv/Militärarchiv, File PH 3/278.
16 OHL, "Mons Conference Minutes by Major Thilo," (4 February 1918), Bundesarchiv/Militärarchiv, File PH 5 I/45.
17 Hermann von Kuhl, *Personal War Diary of General von Kuhl*, (9 February 1918), Bundesarchiv/Militärarchiv, File: W-10/50652.
18 OHL, Ia 6435, (10 February 1918), Bundesarchiv/Militärarchiv, File PH 3/279.
19 Rupprecht, *Kriegstagebuch*, Vol.II, p.327.
20 Army Group Crown Prince Rupprecht, Ia 5537, (12 February 1918), Bundesarchiv/Militärarchiv, File PH 3/279.
21 Army Group Crown Prince Rupprecht, War Diary, Ia 5676, (17 February 1918), Bayerisches Kriegsarchiv, File Hgr. Rupprecht, Bd. 80.
22 Army Group Crown Prince Rupprecht, War Diary, Ia 5681, (17 February 1918), Bayerisches Kriegsarchiv, File Hgr. Rupprecht, Bd. 80.
23 Rupprecht, *Kriegstagebuch*, Vol.III, p.280.
24 Army Group Crown Prince Rupprecht, Ib 6116, (9 March 1918), Bayerisches Kriegsarchiv, File Hgr. Rupprecht, Bd. 100.

25 Kuhl, *Offensive von 1918*, p.150.
26 Army Group Crown Prince Rupprecht, Ia 6395, (23 March 1918), Bundesarchiv/ Militärarchiv, File PH 3/277. *Der Weltkrieg*, Vol.14, p.265.
27 Rupprecht, *Kriegstagebuch*, Vol.II, pp.354–355.
28 OHL, Ia 7341, (26 March 1918), Bundesarchiv/Militärarchiv, File PH 3/268.
29 AOK 6, Ia 2503, (26 March 1918), Bundesarchiv/Militärarchiv, File PH 3/281.
30 *Der Weltkrieg*, Vol.14, p.273.
31 Army Group Crown Prince Rupprecht, Ia 6485, (29 March 1918), Bundesarchiv/ Militärarchiv, File PH 3/281. Army Group Crown Prince Rupprecht, Ia 6486, (29 March 1918), Bundesarchiv/Militärarchiv, File PH 5 II/202.
32 Army Group Crown Prince Rupprecht, Ia 6483, (29 March 1918), Bundesarchiv/ Militärarchiv, File PH 3/281.
33 OHL, Ia 7408, (30 March 1918), Bundesarchiv/Militärarchiv, File PH 3/268.
34 Army Group Crown Prince Rupprecht, Ia 6491, (30 March 1918), Bundesarchiv/ Militärarchiv, File PH 3/281.
35 Army Group Crown Prince Rupprecht, Ia 6543, (1 April 1918), Bundesarchiv/Militärarchiv, File PH 5 I/45.
36 According to the German Official History, the meeting took place in St. Amand. *Der Weltkrieg*, Vol.14, pp.266–268.
37 Rupprecht, *Kriegstagebuch*, Vol.II, p.371.
38 Army Group Crown Prince Rupprecht, Ia 6587, (3 April 1918), Bayerisches Kriegsarchiv, File AOK 6, Bd. 7. AOK 6, Ia 2628, (3 April 1918), Bayerisches Kriegsarchiv, File AOK 6, Bd. 7.
39 OHL, Ia 7536, (6 April 1918), Bayerisches Kriegsarchiv, File Hgr. Rupprecht, Bd. 80.
40 Army Group Crown Prince Rupprecht, Ia 6618, (6 April 1918), Bundesarchiv/Militärarchiv, File PH 3/277.
41 *Der Weltkrieg*, Vol.14, p.269.
42 Army Group Crown Prince Rupprecht, War Diary, Ia 6657, (8 April 1918), Bayerisches Kriegsarchiv, File Hgr. Rupprecht, Bd. 80.
43 *Der Weltkrieg*, Vol.14, p.276.
44 Kuhl, *Diary*, (8 April 1918), Bundesarchiv/Militärarchiv, File: W-10/50652.
45 Rupprecht, *Kriegstagebuch*, Vol.II, pp.373–374.
46 Joachim von Stuelpnagel Papers, Bundesarchiv/Militärarchiv, File N 27, p.125.
47 *Der Weltkrieg*, Vol.14, p.270.
48 Kuhl, *Offensive von 1918*, p.149.
49 Kuhl, *Offensive von 1918*, p.154.
50 Georg Bruchmüller Papers, "Der Feldherr in meinem Blickfeld," (Unpublished Reminiscence of Ludendorff), Bundesarchiv/Militärarchiv, File N 275/2.
51 Georg Bruchmüller Papers, "Bemerkung zu der mir vom Reichsarchiv zugesandten Bearbeitung der Georgette Operation," (Unpublished memo to the Reichsarchiv), Bundesarchiv Militärarchiv, File N 275-34.
52 Edmonds, *1918*, Vol.II, pp.142–143.
53 Ferdinand Foch, *The Memoirs of Marshall Foch*, (New York: 1931), pp.274, 278.
54 Edmonds, *1918*, Vol.II, pp.138–139.
55 Barrie Pitt, *1918: The Last Act*, (New York: 1963), pp.129–130.
56 James B. Ord, *The German Offensive of March 21–April 8, 1918*, Unpublished Paper, (U.S. Army War College: 1922), p.53.
57 Pitt, pp.133–134. Edmonds, *1918*, Vol.II, p.147.
58 Edmonds, *1918*, Vol.II, p.141.
59 Foch, p.283. Edmonds, *1918*, Vol.II, p.142.
60 *Der Weltkrieg*, Vol.14, p.270.
61 *Der Weltkrieg*, Vol.14, Appendices 35 and 38g.
62 *Der Weltkrieg*, Vol.14, Appendices 35 and 38g.

63 *Der Weltkrieg*, Vol.14, Appendix 39b.
64 AOK 6, Iad/koflieg 2656, (5 April 1918), Bayerisches Kriegsarchiv, File Hgr. Rupprecht, Bd. 168. AOK 4, Iae 238, (10 April 1918), Bayerisches Kriegsarchiv, File Hgr. Rupprecht, Bd. 96.
65 Edmonds, *1918*, Vol.II, p.146.
66 "Die Fortführung der deutschen Grossoffensive in April 1918," *Militär-Wochenblatt*, 11 May 1928, p.1618. *Der Weltkrieg*, Vol.14, p.273.
67 *Der Weltkrieg*, Vol.14, p.272.
68 *Der Weltkrieg*, Vol.14, Appendices 38g, 39h.
69 AOK 6, Ia 2582, "Artillery Order Number 1," (31 March 1918), Bayerisches Kriegsarchiv, File AOK 6, Bd. 7.
70 Rupprecht, *Kriegstagebuch*, Vol.II, pp.375–376. *Der Weltkrieg*, Vol.14, pp.272–275.
71 Bruchmüller (1922), pp.33–34. Rupprecht, *Kriegstagebuch*, Vol.II, p.375.
72 Army Group Crown Prince Rupprecht, War Diary, Ia 6691, (9 April 1918), Bayerisches Kriegsarchiv, File Hgr. Rupprecht, Bd. 80. AOK 6, Ia 2722, (9 April 1918), Bayerisches Kriegsarchiv, File AOK 6, Bd. 7.
73 Haig, p.302.
74 Fritz von Lossberg, *Meine Tätigkeit im Weltkriege 1914–1918*, (Berlin: 1939), p.326. *Der Weltkrieg*, Vol.14, pp.275–276.
75 AOK 6, Ia 2737, (10 April 1918), Bayerisches Kriegsarchiv, File AOK 6, Bd. 7. Lossberg, p.328.
76 Rupprecht, *Kriegstagebuch*, Vol.II, pp.376–378. Lossberg, pp.328–329. In his diary Rupprecht stated that he wanted to order the BLÜCHER option of WALDFEST, which was the pursuit variation. There was no indication at that point, however, that the British had started to pull forces out of the Ypres salient.
77 Foch, pp.285–286, 293.
78 Edmonds, *1918*, Vol.II, p.252.
79 Erich Ludendorff, *Meine Kriegserinnerungen 1914–1918*, (Berlin: 1919), p.488.
80 Lossberg, p.328.
81 Rupprecht, *Kriegstagebuch*, Vol.II, p.379.
82 AOK 6, Ia 2749, (11 April 1918), Bayerisches Kriegsarchiv, File AOK 6, Bd. 7.
83 Rupprecht, *Kriegstagebuch*, Vol.II, pp.378–379. *Der Weltkrieg*, Vol.14, pp.277–278.
84 Foch, pp.287, 289.
85 *Der Weltkrieg*, Vol.14, p.278.
86 Army Group Crown Prince Rupprecht, War Diary, Ia 6738, (12 April 1918), Bayerisches Kriegsarchiv, File Hgr. Rupprecht, Bd. 80.
87 AOK 6, Ia 2764, (12 April 1918), Bayerisches Kriegsarchiv, File AOK 6, Bd. 7. Lossberg, p.329.
88 Kuhl, *Diary*, (13 April 1918). *Der Weltkrieg*, Vol.14, p.305.
89 Rupprecht, *Kriegstagebuch*, Vol.II, pp.379–381.
90 Edmonds, *1918*, Vol.II, p.512.
91 Edmonds, *1918*, Vol.II, pp.255, 277.
92 Foch, pp.288–290. Edmonds, *1918*, Vol.II, p.280.
93 *Der Weltkrieg*, Vol.14, p.282.
94 AOK 6, Ia 2782, (13 April 1918), Bayerisches Kriegsarchiv, File AOK 6, Bd. 7.
95 Army Group Crown Prince Rupprecht, War Diary, Ia 6748, (13 April 1918), Bayerisches Kriegsarchiv, File Hgr. Rupprecht, Bd. 80.
96 *Der Weltkrieg*, Vol.14, pp.280–282.
97 Foch, p.290.
98 *Der Weltkrieg*, Vol.14, p.282. Lossberg, p.330.
99 Rupprecht, *Kriegstagebuch*, Vol.II, p.382. Lossberg, pp.330–331. Kuhl, *Diary*, (14 April 1918).

100 AOK 6, Ia 2800, (14 April 1918), Bayerisches Kriegsarchiv, File AOK 6, Bd. 7.
101 AOK 6, Ia 2770, (14 April 1918), Bayerisches Kriegsarchiv, File AOK 6, Bd. 7. Rupprecht, *Kriegstagebuch*, Vol.III, p.315. Lossberg, p.329.
102 *Der Weltkrieg*, Vol.14, p.284.
103 Haig, p.303.
104 Foch, p.291.
105 Martin Kitchen, *The German Offensives of 1918*, (Stroud, Gloucestershire: 2001), p.111.
106 Army Group Crown Prince Rupprecht, War Diary, Ia 6778, (15 April 1918), Bayerisches Kriegsarchiv, File Hgr. Rupprecht, Bd. 80.
107 Rupprecht, *Kriegstagebuch*, Vol.II, pp.383–384.
108 *Der Weltkrieg*, Vol.14, p.284.
109 OHL, Ia 7720, (15 April 1918), Bayerisches Kriegsarchiv, File Hgr. Rupprecht, Bd. 100.
110 Pitt, p.140.
111 Army Group German Crown Prince, Ic 9649, (16 April 1918), Combined Arms Reference Library, "Extracts from the War Diary of the Army Group of the German Crown Prince, April 15 to 30, 1918."
112 AOK 6, Ia 2833, (15 April 1918), Bayerisches Kriegsarchiv, File AOK 6, Bd. 7.
113 Kuhl, *Diary*, (16 April 1918).
114 Lossberg, pp.333–334. *Der Weltkrieg*, Vol.14, p.286.
115 Kitchen, p.114.
116 Lossberg, p.334.
117 Army Group Crown Prince Rupprecht, War Diary, Ia 6831, (17 April 1918), Bayerisches Kriegsarchiv, File Hgr. Rupprecht, Bd. 80.
118 Rupprecht, *Kriegstagebuch*, Vol.II, pp.385–386. Lossberg, pp.334–335. *Der Weltkrieg*, Vol.14, pp.286–287.
119 Foch, p.294.
120 Army Group German Crown Prince, Ic 9709, (18 April 1918), Combined Arms Reference Library, "Extracts."
121 Albrecht von Thaer, *Generalstabsdienst an der Front und in der O.H.L.*, (Göttingen: 1958), pp.181–182.
122 Rupprecht, *Kriegstagebuch*, Vol.II, p.386. Lossberg, p.337. *Der Weltkrieg*, Vol.14, pp.287–288. Kuhl, *Diary*, (18 April 1918).
123 Lossberg, p.335.
124 Foch, p.295.
125 *Der Weltkrieg*, Vol.14, p.306.
126 Army Group Crown Prince Rupprecht, War Diary, Ia 6852, (19 April 1918), Bayerisches Kriegsarchiv, File Hgr. Rupprecht, Bd. 80. *Der Weltkrieg*, Vol.14, p.286.
127 Kuhl, *Diary*, (19 April 1918).
128 Rupprecht, *Kriegstagebuch*, Vol.II, pp.386–387.
129 Georg Wetzell, "Situation on April 20. How Is the Offensive in the West to Be Continued?," (19 April 1919), Bundesarchiv/Militärarchiv, File PH 3/267.
130 Kuhl, *Diary*, (19 April 1918).
131 Pitt, pp.141–144.
132 OHL, Ia 7777, (20 April 1918), Army Group Crown Prince Rupprecht, War Diary, Bayerisches Kriegsarchiv, File Hgr. Rupprecht, Bd. 80. AOK 6, Ia 2896, (20 April 1918), Bayerisches Kriegsarchiv, File AOK 6, Bd. 7.
133 *Der Weltkrieg*, Vol.14, p.289. Hermann von Kuhl, *Der Weltkrieg 1914–1918*, (Berlin: 1929), Vol.II, p.348.
134 *Der Weltkrieg*, Vol.14, p.289. Rupprecht, *Kriegstagebuch*, Vol.II, pp.387–388.
135 AOK 6, Ia 2912, (22 April 1918), Bayerisches Kriegsarchiv, File AOK 6, Bd. 7. *Der Weltkrieg*, Vol.14, p.294. Edmonds (*1918*, Vol.II, p.428) reports that the Germans

were supported by 191 field and 129 heavy batteries, but *Der Weltkrieg* (Vol.14, p.294) reports the total number of guns as 290, with 128 of those being heavy.

136 Army Group Crown Prince Rupprecht, Ia 6905, (23 April 1918), Bayerisches Kriegsarchiv, File AOK 6, Bd. 7.

137 Army Group German Crown Prince, Ic 9784, (22 April 1918) and Ic 9800, (22 April 1918), Combined Arms Reference Library, "Extracts."

138 Foch, p.296.

139 *Der Weltkrieg*, Vol.14, pp.289–309. Rupprecht, *Kriegstagebuch*, Vol.II, pp.389–390.

140 Ludendorff, *Kriegserinnerungen*, p.482.

141 OHL, Ia 7875, (26 April 1918), Army Group Crown Prince Rupprecht, War Diary Bayerisches Kriegsarchiv, File Hgr. Rupprecht, Bd. 80. *Der Weltkrieg*, Vol.14, p.310.

142 *Der Weltkrieg*, Vol.14, pp.296–297. Rupprecht, *Kriegstagebuch*, Vol.II, pp.390–391. Lossberg, pp.338–339.

143 *Der Weltkrieg*, Vol.14, p.297. Rupprecht, *Kriegstagebuch*, Vol.II, pp.391–392.

144 Foch, pp.298–299.

145 *Der Weltkrieg*, Vol.14, p.298. Rupprecht, *Kriegstagebuch*, Vol.II, pp.391–392.

146 Army Group Crown Prince Rupprecht, Ia 6965, (27 April 1918), Bundesarchiv/Militärarchiv, File PH 3/277.

147 Army Group Crown Prince Rupprecht, War Diary, Ia 7010, (29 April 1918), Bayerisches Kriegsarchiv, File Hgr. Rupprecht, Bd. 80. Rupprecht, *Kriegstagebuch*, Vol.II, p.392.

148 *Der Weltkrieg*, Vol.14, p.301. Rupprecht, *Kriegstagebuch*, Vol.II, pp.392–393.

149 OHL, Ia 7952, (1 May 1918), Bayerisches Kriegsarchiv, File Hgr. Rupprecht, Bd. 80.

150 Foch, p.299.

151 *Der Weltkrieg*, Vol.14, p.299.

152 Foch, p.300.

153 Rupprecht, *Kriegstagebuch*, Vol.II, p.394.

154 *Der Weltkrieg*, Vol.14, p.300. Edmonds, *1918*, Vol.II, pp.491–493.

155 Kuhl, *Offensive von 1918*, p.153.

156 *Der Weltkrieg*, Vol.14, Appendices 12 and 38g.

157 *Der Weltkrieg*, Vol.14, Appendix 35.

158 *Der Weltkrieg*, Vol.14, Appendices 15 and 38g.

159 Army Group Crown Prince Rupprecht, "Air Order of Battle," (no document number), (24 April 1918), Bayerisches Kriegsarchiv, File Hgr. Rupprecht, Bd. 168.

160 Kuhl, *Offensive von 1918*, p.155.

161 Edmonds, *1918*, Vol.II, p.487.

162 Kuhl, *Offensive von 1918*, p.155.

163 Foch, p.292.

8 Operations BLÜCHER, GOERZ, and YORCK

1 Paul von Hindenburg, *Aus meinem Leben*, (Leipzig: 1920), p.328.

2 Wilhelm, Crown Prince of Germany, *Meine Erinnerungen aus Deutschlands Heldenkampf*, (Berlin: 1923), p.320.

3 Hindenburg, p.327.

4 Hermann von Kuhl, Entstehung, Durchführung und Zusammenbruch der Offensive von 1918, (Berlin: 1927), pp.158–160. Oberkommando des Heeres, *Der Weltkrieg 1914 bis 1918*, Vol.14, (Berlin: 1944), pp.317–318. Rupprecht, Crown Prince of Bavaria, *Mein Kriegstagebuch*, Vol.III, (Munich: 1929), pp.318–319.

5 Erich Ludendorff, *Meine Kriegserinnerungen 1914–1918*, (Berlin: 1919), p.495.

6 Theo von Bose, *Deutsche Siege 1918, Das Vorbringen der 7. Armee über Ailette, Aisne, Vesle, und Ourcq bis zur Marne (27. Mai bis 13. Juni): Schlachten des*

Weltkriegs, Vol.32, (Berlin: 1929), pp.9–10. *Der Weltkrieg* Vol.14, p.312. Ludendorff, *Kriegserinnerungen*, p.495.

7 Georg Wetzell, "Situation on 20 April. How Is the Offensive in the West to Be Continued?," (19 April 1918), Bundesarchiv/Militärarchiv, File PH 3/267.

8 Army Group German Crown Prince, Ia 2444, (20 April 1918), Combat Arms Reference Library, File: Operations Documents (BLÜCHER–GNEISENAU–GOERZ) April 17 to May 20, 1918, Part I.

9 AOK 1, Ia 2041, (24 April 1918), Combat Arms Reference Library, File: Operations Documents (BLÜCHER–GNEISENAU–GOERZ) April 17 to May 20, 1918, Part I.

10 OHL, Ia 7792, (20 April 1918), Combat Arms Reference Library, File: Operations Documents (BLÜCHER–GNEISENAU–GOERZ) April 17 to May 20, 1918, Part I.

11 AOK 7, Ia 371, (12 May 1918), Combat Arms Reference Library, File: Operations Documents (BLÜCHER–GNEISENAU–GOERZ) May 15 to 26, 1918, Part II.

12 Hindenburg, p.328.

13 AOK 7, Ia 240, (26 April 1918); Ia 242, (26 April 1918); Ia 248, (28 April 1918); Ia 328, (7 May 1918) Combat Arms Reference Library, File: Operations Documents (BLÜCHER–GNEISENAU–GOERZ) April 17 to May 20, 1918, Part I.

14 Georg Wetzell, "Offensive against the French" (28 April 1918), Bundesarchiv/Militärarchiv, File PH 3/267.

15 *Der Weltkrieg*, Vol.14, p.317. Kuhl, *Offensive von 1918*, p.158.

16 OHL, Ia 7936, (30 April 1918), Combat Arms Reference Library, File: Operations Documents (BLÜCHER–GNEISENAU–GOERZ) April 17 to May 20, 1918, Part I.

17 Georg Wetzell, "How to Continue the Attack," (2 May 1918), Bundesarchiv/Militärarchiv, File PH 3/267.

18 *Der Weltkrieg*, Vol.14, p.325. Wilhelm, *Erinnerungen*, p.315.

19 Army Group German Crown Prince, Ia 2474, (2 May 1918), Combat Arms Reference Library, File: Operations Documents (BLÜCHER–GNEISENAU–GOERZ) April 17 to May 20, 1918, Part I.

20 AOK 1, Ia 2082, Ia 2084, (2 May 1918), Combat Arms Reference Library, File: Operations Documents (BLÜCHER–GNEISENAU–GOERZ) April 17 to May 20, 1918, Part I. *Der Weltkrieg*, Vol.14, p.326.

21 AOK 7, Ia 326, (6 May 1918), Combat Arms Reference Library, File: Operations Documents (BLÜCHER–GNEISENAU–GOERZ) April 17 to May 20, 1918, Part I.

22 OHL, Ia 8064, (8 May 1918), Combat Arms Reference Library, File: Operations Documents (BLÜCHER–GNEISENAU–GOERZ) April 17 to May 20, 1918, Part I.

23 AOK 1, Ia 2108, (9 May 1918), Combat Arms Reference Library, File: Operations Documents (BLÜCHER–GNEISENAU–GOERZ) April 17 to May 20, 1918, Part I.

24 OHL, Ia 8060, (9 May 1918), Combat Arms Reference Library, File: Operations Documents (BLÜCHER–GNEISENAU–GOERZ) April 17 to May 20, 1918, Part I. *Der Weltkrieg*, Vol.14, p.347.

25 OHL, Ia 8153, (16 May 1918), Army Group German Crown Prince, Ia 2505, (16 May 1918); AOK 7, Ia 400, (16 May 1918), Combat Arms Reference Library, File: Operations Documents (BLÜCHER–GNEISENAU–GOERZ) May 15 to 26, 1918, Part II. *Der Weltkrieg*, Vol.14, pp.326, 338–339.

26 AOK 1, Ia 2186, (17 May 1918), Combat Arms Reference Library, File: Operations Documents (BLÜCHER–GNEISENAU–GOERZ) May 15 to 26, 1918, Part II.

27 AOK 7, Ia 478, (23 May 1918), Combat Arms Reference Library, File: Operations Documents (BLÜCHER–GNEISENAU–GOERZ) May 15 to 26, 1918, Part II. *Der Weltkrieg*, Vol.14, p.339.

28 AOK 7, Ia 291, (2 May 1918), Combat Arms Reference Library, File: Operations Documents (BLÜCHER–GNEISENAU–GOERZ) April 17 to May 20, 1918, Part I. Kuhl, *Offensive von 1918*, p.163.

29 Hindenburg, p.329. Wilhelm, *Erinnerungen*, p.322.

30 Bose, *Deutsche Siege*, p.70. At the start of World War I a German division had two infantry brigades of two regiments each, plus a field artillery brigade of two regiments. By 1918 the German division had only three infantry regiments, but they were still under the administrative control of a single brigade headquarters. The field artillery brigade had been replaced by an artillery command (Arko) that had both field and foot artillery units.

31 Richard Holmes, "The Ludendorff Offensives Phase 3: The Aisne," *The Marshall Cavendish Illustrated Encyclopedia of World War I*, Vol.IX, (New York: 1984), p.2780.

32 *Der Weltkrieg*, Vol.14, p.319. Bose, *Deutsche Siege*, p.12. Wilhelm, *Erinnerungen*, p.319. Rupprecht, *Kriegstagebuch*, Vol.II, p.398.

33 James E. Edmonds, *Military Operations: Belgium and France 1918*, Vol.III, (London: 1939), pp.17–21.

34 Army Group German Crown Prince, War Diary, (26 May 1918), Combat Arms Reference Library, File: Extracts from the War Diary of the Army Group German Crown Prince, May 1 to 26, 1918.

35 John J. Pershing, *My Experiences in the World War*, (New York: 1931), Vol.2, pp.61–62. Edmonds, *1918*, Vol.III, pp.17–18.

36 Army Group German Crown Prince, Ia 2444, (20 April 1918), Combat Arms Reference Library, File: Operations Documents (BLÜCHER–GNEISENAU–GOERZ) April 17 to May 20, 1918, Part I.

37 *Der Weltkrieg*, Vol.14, p.332. Bose, *Deutsche Siege*, pp.16–18.

38 *Der Weltkrieg*, Vol.14, p.330. Bose, *Deutsche Siege*, pp.12, 72.

39 Holmes, "The Aisne," p.2779.

40 *Der Weltkrieg*, Vol.14, pp.335–336.

41 Ferdinand Foch, *The Memoirs of Marshall Foch*, (New York: 1931), pp.310–311. Douglas Haig, *The Private Papers of Douglas Haig, 1914–1919*, Robert Blake (ed.), (London: 1952), p.311.

42 *Der Weltkrieg*, Vol.14, p.348.

43 Edmonds, *1918*, Vol.III, p.175.

44 Foch, p.321. Edmonds, *1918*, Vol.III, pp.30–46.

45 *Der Weltkrieg*, Vol.14, pp.331, 343, Appendix 39c. AOK 1, Ia 2258, (23 May 1918), Combat Arms Reference Library, File: Operations Documents (BLÜCHER–GNEISENAU–GOERZ) May 15 to 26, 1918, Part II.

46 *Der Weltkrieg*, Vol.14, Appendix 38h. AOK 7, Ia 462, (22 May 1918), Combat Arms Reference Library, File: Operations Documents (BLÜCHER–GNEISE-NAU–GOERZ) April 17 to May 20, 1918, Part I. AOK 1, Ia 2079, (5 May 1918), Combat Arms Reference Library, File: Operations Documents (BLÜCHER–GNEISENAU–GOERZ) May 15 to 26, 1918, Part II.

47 *Der Weltkrieg*, Vol.14, Appendix 38h.

48 Foch, p.301.

49 *Der Weltkrieg*, Vol.14, p.333.

50 Barrie Pitt, *1918: The Last Act*, (New York: 1963), p.183.

51 *Der Weltkrieg*, Vol.14, p.340.

52 *Der Weltkrieg*, Vol.14, Appendices 38h, 39c.

53 AOK 7, Ia 242, (26 April 1918), AOK 1, Ia 2032, (20 April 1918), Combat Arms Reference Library, File: Operations Documents (BLÜCHER–GNEISENAU–GOERZ) April 17 to May 20, 1918, Part I.

54 Georg Bruchmüller, *Die Artillerie beim Angriff im Stellungskrieg*, (Berlin: 1926), pp.71–94, Appendix IV.

55 J.P. Muller, "The German Artillery at Chemin des Dames in 1918," *Field Artillery Journal*, [translated from *Revue d'Artillerie* (March 1922)], March 1922, p.159.

56 *Der Weltkrieg*, Vol.14, p.337, Appendices 38h, 39c. Foch, p.313.

57 AOK 7, Ia 235, (20 April 1918), Ia 242, (26 April 1918), Combat Arms Reference

Library, File: Operations Documents (BLÜCHER–GNEISENAU–GOERZ) April 17 to May 20, 1918, Part I.

58 Frederic Herr, *Die Artillerie in Vergangenheit, Gegenwart, und Zukunft*, [translation of *L'Artillerie, ce qu'elle a été, ce qu'elle est, ce qu'elle doit être*, (Paris: 1923)], (Charlottenburg: 1925), p.132.

59 *Der Weltkrieg*, Vol.14, Appendix 39c.

60 William Balck, *Entwicklung der Taktik im Weltkriege*, (Berlin: 1922), p.373.

61 *Der Weltkrieg*, Vol.14, pp.341–343. Bose, *Deutsche Siege*, pp.59, 64, 69, 95.

62 Archer Jones, *The Art of War in the Western World*, (Chicago, Illinois: 1987), p.477.

63 Army Group German Crown Prince, War Diary, (27 May 1918), Combat Arms Reference Library, File: Extracts from the War Diary of the Army Group German Crown Prince, May 27 to June 15, 1918. *Der Weltkrieg*, Vol.14, p.344.

64 *Der Weltkrieg*, Vol.14, p.349. Bose, *Deutsche Siege*, p.130. Foch, p.315.

65 Foch, p.313.

66 Army Group German Crown Prince, War Diary, (27 May 1918), Combat Arms Reference Library, File: Extracts from the War Diary of the Army Group German Crown Prince, May 27 to June 15, 1918. *Der Weltkrieg*, Vol.14, p.349. Holmes, "The Aisne," p.2785.

67 Army Group German Crown Prince, War Diary, (28 May 1918), Combat Arms Reference Library, File: Extracts from the War Diary of the Army Group German Crown Prince, May 27 to June 15, 1918. Bose, *Deutsche Siege*, pp.115, 121, 124.

68 Army Group German Crown Prince, War Diary, (28 May 1918), Combat Arms Reference Library, File: Extracts from the War Diary of the Army Group German Crown Prince, May 27 to June 15, 1918. *Der Weltkrieg*, Vol.14, p.351. Foch, p.317.

69 OHL, Ia 8408, (28 May 1918), Combat Arms Reference Library, File: Operations Documents (BLÜCHER–GNEISENAU–GOERZ), May 27 to June 9, 1918.

70 Army Group German Crown Prince, Ia 2545, (28 May 1918), Combat Arms Reference Library, File: Operations Documents (BLÜCHER–GNEISENAU–GOERZ), May 27 to June 9, 1918.

71 Army Group German Crown Prince, Ia/b 2547, (28 May 1918), Combat Arms Reference Library, File: Operations Documents (BLÜCHER–GNEISENAU–GOERZ), May 27 to June 9, 1918.

72 Army Group German Crown Prince, War Diary, (28 May 1918), Combat Arms Reference Library, File: Extracts from the War Diary of the Army Group German Crown Prince, May 27 to June 15, 1918. *Der Weltkrieg*, Vol.14, pp.345–346.

73 Ludendorff, *Kriegserinnerungen*, (Berlin: 1919), p.508.

74 Bose, *Deutsche Siege*, pp.104–205.

75 OHL, Ia 8415, (28 May 1918), Combat Arms Reference Library, File: Operations Documents (BLÜCHER–GNEISENAU–GOERZ), May 27 to June 9, 1918.

76 Bose, *Deutsche Siege*, p.131.

77 OHL, Ia 8509, (2 June 1918), Combat Arms Reference Library, File: Extracts from the War Diary of the Army Group German Crown Prince, May 27 to June 15, 1918. Foch, p.315.

78 *Der Weltkrieg*, Vol.14, pp.350–351. Bose, *Deutsche Siege*, p.130.

79 Army Group German Crown Prince, War Diary, (28 May 1918), Combat Arms Reference Library, File: Extracts from the War Diary of the Army Group German Crown Prince, May 27 to June 15, 1918.

80 Holmes, "The Aisne," p.2786.

81 Bose, *Deutsche Siege*, p.131.

82 Edmonds, *1918*, Vol.III, p.24.

83 Theo von Bose, *Wachsende Schwierigkeiten: Vergebliches Ringen vor Compiegne, Villers-Cotterets, und Reims: Schlachten des Weltkriegs*, Vol.33, (Berlin: 1930), p.92.

84 OHL, Ia 8418, (29 May 1918), Combat Arms Reference Library, File: Operations Documents (BLÜCHER–GNEISENAU–GOERZ), May 27 to June 9, 1918.

85 OHL, Ia 8431, (29 May 1918), Combat Arms Reference Library, File: Operations Documents (BLÜCHER–GNEISENAU–GOERZ), May 27 to June 9, 1918.
86 *Der Weltkrieg*, Vol.14, pp.356–357. Bose, *Deutsche Siege*, p.161. Kuhl, *Offensive von 1918*, p.169.
87 Rupprecht, *Kriegstagebuch*, Vol.II, p.404.
88 *Der Weltkrieg*, Vol.14, p.360. Bose, *Deutsche Siege*, p.135.
89 Army Group German Crown Prince, Ia 2557, (29 May 1918), Combat Arms Reference Library, File: Operations Documents (BLÜCHER–GNEISENAU–GOERZ), May 27 to June 9, 1918.
90 Edmonds, *1918*, Vol.III, p.134.
91 Rupprecht, *Kriegstagebuch*, Vol.III, p.326.
92 *Der Weltkrieg*, Vol.14, p.362. Foch, p.317.
93 OHL Ia 8441, (30 May 1918), Combat Arms Reference Library, File: Operations Documents (BLÜCHER–GNEISENAU–GOERZ), May 27 to June 9, 1918. *Der Weltkrieg*, Vol.14, p.364. Kuhl, *Offensive von 1918*, p.169.
94 Army Group German Crown Prince, Ia 2559, (30 May 1918), Combat Arms Reference Library, File: Operations Documents (BLÜCHER–GNEISENAU–GOERZ), May 27 to June 9, 1918.
95 Army Group German Crown Prince, War Diary, (30 May 1918), Combat Arms Reference Library, File: Extracts from the War Diary of the Army Group German Crown Prince, May 27 to June 15, 1918.
96 *Der Weltkrieg*, Vol.14, p.364.
97 Hermann von Kuhl and Hans Delbrück, *Ursachen des Zusammenbruchs: Entstehung, Durchführung und Zusammenbruch der Offensive von 1918*, (Berlin: 1923), p.168.
98 Army Group German Crown Prince, War Diary, (30 May 1918), Combat Arms Reference Library, File: Extracts from the War Diary of the Army Group German Crown Prince, May 27 to June 15, 1918. Bose, *Deutsche Siege*, p.195.
99 Army Group German Crown Prince, Ia 2562, (30 May 1918), Combat Arms Reference Library, File: Operations Documents (BLÜCHER–GNEISENAU–GOERZ), May 27 to June 9, 1918.
100 *Der Weltkrieg*, Vol.14, p.363.
101 *Der Weltkrieg*, Vol.14, p.363.
102 Pershing, Vol.II, pp.62–65.
103 Foch, p.320.
104 Army Group German Crown Prince, War Diary, (31 May 1918), Combat Arms Reference Library, File: Extracts from the War Diary of the Army Group German Crown Prince, May 27 to June 15, 1918.
105 *Der Weltkrieg*, Vol.14, pp.365–366.
106 Army Group German Crown Prince, War Diary, (31 May 1918), Combat Arms Reference Library, File: Extracts from the War Diary of the Army Group German Crown Prince, May 27 to June 15, 1918.
107 *Der Weltkrieg*, Vol.14, p.368.
108 OHL, Ia 8474, (31 May 1918), Army Group German Crown Prince, Ia 2567, (31 May 1918), Combat Arms Reference Library, File: Operations Documents (BLÜCHER–GNEISENAU–GOERZ), May 27 to June 9, 1918. *Der Weltkrieg*, Vol.14, p.371.
109 Edmonds, *1918*, Vol.III, p.146.
110 *Der Weltkrieg*, Vol.14, p.365.
111 Edmonds, *1918*, Vol.III, pp.144–245.
112 Foch, p.320.
113 Edmonds, *1918*, Vol.III, pp.143–246.
114 Martin Kitchen, *The German Offensives of 1918*, (Stroud, Gloucestershire: 2001), p.143.

115 Edmonds, *1918*, Vol.III, p.147.
116 AOK 7, Ia 598, (1 June 1918), Combat Arms Reference Library, File: Extracts from the Diary of the Commander-in-Chief of the Seventh Army, June 1 to August 21, 1918. Bose, *Wachsende Schwierigkeiten*, p.75. *Der Weltkrieg*, Vol.14, p.372.
117 Rupprecht, *Kriegstagebuch*, Vol.III, p.326.
118 Rupprecht, *Kriegstagebuch*, Vol.III, p.325.
119 OHL, Ia 8485, (1 June 1918), Combat Arms Reference Library, File: Operations Documents (BLÜCHER–GNEISENAU–GOERZ), May 27 to June 9, 1918.
120 *Der Weltkrieg*, Vol.14, p.373.
121 Army Group German Crown Prince, Ia 2573, (2 June 1918), Combat Arms Reference Library, File: Operations Documents (BLÜCHER–GNEISENAU–GOERZ), May 27 to June 9, 1918. *Der Weltkrieg*, Vol.14, pp.373–374. Wilhelm, *Erinnerungen*, p.324.
122 Rupprecht, *Kriegstagebuch*, Vol.II, p.405.
123 *Der Weltkrieg*, Vol.14, p.374.
124 Rupprecht, *Der Weltkrieg*, Vol.14, pp.379–380.
125 Bose, *Wachsende Schwierigkeiten*, p.90. *Der Weltkrieg*, Vol.14, pp.375, 386.
126 AOK 7, Ia 607, (2 June 1918), Combat Arms Reference Library, File: Extracts from the Diary of the Commander-in-Chief of the Seventh Army, June 1 to August 21, 1918. Bose, *Wachsende Schwierigkeiten*, p.128. *Der Weltkrieg*, Vol.14, p.376.
127 Bose, *Wachsende Schwierigkeiten*, p.151. *Der Weltkrieg*, Vol.14, pp.376–377.
128 Army Group German Crown Prince, War Diary, (3 June 1918), Combat Arms Reference Library, File: Extracts from the War Diary of the Army Group German Crown Prince, May 27 to June 15, 1918. Wilhelm, *Erinnerungen*, p.325.
129 Army Group German Crown Prince, Ia 2575, (3 June 1918), Combat Arms Reference Library, File: Operations Documents (BLÜCHER–GNEISENAU–GOERZ), May 27 to June 9, 1918. AOK 7, Ia 609, (3 June 1918), Combat Arms Reference Library, File: Extracts from the War Diary of the Army Group German Crown Prince, May 27 to June 15, 1918.
130 *Der Weltkrieg*, Vol.14, p.377.
131 Army Group German Crown Prince, Ia 670, (5 June 1918), Combat Arms Reference Library, File: Army Group German Crown Prince, Operations Documents, BLÜCHER–GNEISENAU–GOERZ, May 27 to June 9, 1918. Army Group German Crown Prince, War Diary, (4 June 1918), Combat Arms Reference Library, File: Extracts from the War Diary of the Army Group German Crown Prince, May 27 to June 15, 1918. Bose, *Wachsende Schwierigkeiten*, p.157.
132 Army Group German Crown Prince, Ia 675, (5 June 1918), Combat Arms Reference Library, File: Army Group German Crown Prince, Operations Documents, BLÜCHER–GNEISENAU–GOERZ, May 27 to June 9, 1918.
133 Edmonds, *1918*, Vol.III, pp.161–163. Haig, p.313.
134 Paul Greenwood, *The Second Battle of the Marne, 1918*, (Shrewsbury: 1998), p.54. *Der Weltkrieg*, Vol.14, p.381.
135 Rupprecht, *Kriegstagebuch*, Vol.II, p.407.
136 Rupprecht, *Kriegstagebuch*, Vol.II, p.407
137 *Der Weltkrieg*, Vol.14, Appendix 42. Bose, *Wachsende Schwierigkeiten*, p.192. Edmonds, *1918*, Vol.III, p.160.
138 Hermann von Kuhl, *Personal War Diary of General von Kuhl*, (31 May and 2 June 1918), Bundesarchiv/Militärarchiv, File: W-10/50652.
139 *Der Weltkrieg*, Vol.14, p.357.
140 Army Group German Crown Prince, War Diary, (27, 28, 29, 31 May, 2, 4 June 1918), Combat Arms Reference Library, File: Extracts from the War Diary of the Army Group German Crown Prince, May 27 to June 15, 1918.
141 Edmonds, *1918*, Vol.III, p.134.

142 *Der Weltkrieg*, Vol.14, p.364.
143 Kuhl, *Offensive von 1918*, p.172.
144 Robert B. Asprey, *The German High Command at War: Hindenburg and Luden-dorff Conduct World War I*, (New York: 1991), p.416. Holger H. Herwig, *The First World War: Germany and Austria-Hungary, 1914–1918*, (London: 1997), pp.415–416. Pitt, pp.167–168, 178.
145 Kitchen, p.166.
146 Army Group German Crown Prince, War Diary, (31 May 1918), Combat Arms Reference Library, File: Extracts from the War Diary of the Army Group German Crown Prince, May 27 to June 15, 1918.
147 *Der Weltkrieg*, Vol.14, p.368. The order was cited in the German official history, but the order itself apparently no longer exists.
148 *Der Weltkrieg*, Vol.14, pp.391–392.
149 *Der Weltkrieg*, Vol.14, p.371.
150 Ludendorff, *Kriegserinnerungen*, p.494.
151 Wilhelm, *Erinnerungen*, p.323.
152 Kuhl, *Offensive von 1918*, p.165.
153 Kuhl, *Offensive von 1918*, p.166.

9 Operations GNEISENAU and HAMMERSCHLAG

1 Erich Ludendorff, *Meine Kriegserinnerungen 1914–1918*, (Berlin: 1919), p.510.
2 Wilhelm, Crown Prince of Germany, *Meine Erinnerungen aus Deutschlands Heldenkampf*, (Berlin: 1923), p.328.
3 Ludendorff, *Kriegserinnerungen*, p.508.
4 Barrie Pitt, *1918: The Last Act*, (New York: 1963), p.179.
5 Oberkommando des Heeres, *Der Weltkrieg 1914 bis 1918*, Vol.14, (Berlin: 1944), p.393.
6 Army Group German Crown Prince, Ia 2466, (30 April 1918), OHL, Ia 7736, (30 April 1918), Combat Arms Reference Library, File: Operations Documents (BLÜCHER–GNEISENAU–GOERZ) April 17 to May 7, 1918, Part I. *Der Weltkrieg*, Vol.14, p.394.
7 *Der Weltkrieg*, Vol.14, p.396.
8 Army Group German Crown Prince, Ia 2505, (16 May 1918), Combat Arms Reference Library, File: Operations Documents (BLÜCHER–GNEISENAU–GOERZ) May 15 to 26, 1918, Part II. *Der Weltkrieg*, Vol.14, pp.394–395.
9 OHL, Ia 8153, (16 May 1918), Combat Arms Reference Library, File: Operations Documents (BLÜCHER–GNEISENAU–GOERZ) May 15 to 26, 1918, Part II.
10 Army Group German Crown Prince, Ia 2505, (16 May 1918), AOK 7, Ia 400, (16 May 1918), Combat Arms Reference Library, File: Operations Documents (BLÜCHER–GNEISENAU–GOERZ) May 15 to 26, 1918, Part II. *Der Weltkrieg*, Vol.14, pp.326–327, 338–339.
11 *Der Weltkrieg*, Vol.14, pp.394–395.
12 Georg Wetzell, "The BLÜCHER and HAGEN Attacks," (21 May 1918), Bundesarchiv/Militärarchiv, File PH 3/267. *Der Weltkrieg*, Vol.14, pp.321–322.
13 Wilhelm, *Erinnerungen*, p.325. *Der Weltkrieg*, Vol.14, pp.395–396.
14 Ludendorff, *Kriegserinnerungen*, p.509. *Der Weltkrieg*, Vol.14, pp.395–396.
15 Oskar von Hutier, *Private Diary of General von Hutier*, (4 June 1918), Bundesarchiv/Militärarchiv File: W-10/50640.
16 AOK 7, Ia 675, (5 June 1918), Combat Arms Reference Library, File: Extracts from the Diary of the Commander-in-Chief of the Seventh Army, 1 June to 21 August, 1918.
17 Theo von Bose, *Wachsende Schwierigkeiten: Vergebliches Ringen vor Compiegne, Villers-Cotterets, und Reims: Schlachten des Weltkriegs*, Vol.33, (Berlin: 1930),

p.124. OHL, Ia 8536, (5 June 1918), Combat Arms Reference Library, File: Army Group German Crown Prince, Operations Documents BLÜCHER–GNEISENAU–GOERZ, May 17 to June 9, 1918. *Der Weltkrieg*, Vol.14, pp.395–396.

18 AOK 7, Ia 670, (5 June 1918), Ia 679, (6 June 1918), Combat Arms Reference Library, File: Army Group German Crown Prince, Operations Documents BLÜCHER–GNEISENAU–GOERZ, May 17 to June 9, 1918. *Der Weltkrieg*, Vol.14, pp.383–384.

19 *Der Weltkrieg*, Vol.14, pp.382–383.

20 AOK 7, Ia 679, (6 June 1918), Combat Arms Reference Library, File: Army Group German Crown Prince, Operations Documents BLÜCHER–GNEISENAU–GOERZ, May 17 to June 9, 1918.

21 Army Group German Crown Prince, Ia 2591, (7 June 1918), Combat Arms Reference Library, File: Army Group German Crown Prince, Operations Documents BLÜCHER–GNEISENAU–GOERZ, May 17 to June 9, 1918.

22 OHL, Ia 8588, (8 June 1918), AOK 7, Ia 696, (8 June 1918), Combat Arms Reference Library, File: Army Group German Crown Prince, Operations Documents BLÜCHER–GNEISENAU–GOERZ, May 17 to June 9, 1918.

23 OHL, Ia 8584, (8 June 1918), AOK 7, Ia 696, (8 June 1918), Combat Arms Reference Library, File: Army Group German Crown Prince, Operations Documents BLÜCHER–GNEISENAU–GOERZ, May 17 to June 9, 1918.

24 Army Group German Crown Prince, Ia 2545, (28 May 1918), Combat Arms Reference Library, File: Army Group German Crown Prince, Operations Documents BLÜCHER–GNEISENAU–GOERZ, May 17 to June 9, 1918. Theo von Bose, *Deutsche Siege 1918, Das Vorbringen der 7. Armee über Ailette, Aisne, Vesle, und Ourcq bis zur Marne (27. Mai bis 13. Juni): Schlachten des Weltkriegs*, Vol.32, (Berlin: 1929), pp.99–131. *Der Weltkrieg*, Vol.14, pp.344–348, 382.

25 Georg Bruchmüller, *Die Deutsche Artillerie in den Durchbruchschlachten des Weltkriegs*, 1st ed., (Berlin: 1921), p.116. Georg Bruchmüller, *Die deutsche Artillerie in den Durchbruchschlachten des Weltkriegs*, 2nd ed., (Berlin: 1922), p.91. Hutier, *Diary*, (5 June 1918).

26 Ferdinand Foch, *The Memoirs of Marshall Foch*, (New York: 1931), p.371. James E. Edmonds, *Military Operations: Belgium and France 1918*, Vol.III, (London: 1939), p.172.

27 Martin Gilbert, *The First World War: A Complete History*, (New York: 1994), p.24. Edmonds, *1918*, Vol.III, p.172.

28 Foch, p.324.

29 Edmonds, *1918*, Vol.III, pp.165, 175.

30 Edmonds, *1918*, Vol.III, p.177. *Der Weltkrieg*, Vol.14, pp.382–383.

31 Edmonds, *1918*, Vol.III, p.179. Foch, p.324.

32 *Der Weltkrieg*, Vol.14, p.397.

33 *Der Weltkrieg*, Vol.14, p.397.

34 *Der Weltkrieg*, Vol.14, p.398, Appendix 39c.

35 *Der Weltkrieg*, Vol.14, p.408, Appendix 39d.

36 AOK 18, War Diary, (9 June 1918), Bundesarchiv/Militärarchiv, File PH 5 II/219. Army Group German Crown Prince, War Diary, (9 June 1918), Combat Arms Reference Library, File: Extracts from the War Diary of the Army Group German Crown Prince, May 27 to June 15, 1918. Frederic Herr, *Die Artillerie in Vergangenheit, Gegenwart, und Zukunft*, (translation of *L'Artillerie, ce qu'elle a été, ce qu'elle est, ce qu'elle doit être*, (Paris: 1923)), (Charlottenburg: 1925), p.135. *Der Weltkrieg*, Vol.14, Appendix 39d.

37 *Der Weltkrieg*, Vol.14, p.399.

38 AOK 7, Ia 702, Ia 710, (9 June 1918), Combat Arms Reference Library, File: Army Group German Crown Prince, Operations Documents BLÜCHER–GNEISENAU–GOERZ, May 17 to June 9, 1918. *Der Weltkrieg*, Vol.14, pp.383–384.

39 *Der Weltkrieg*, Vol.14, pp.388, 399–401.
40 Edmonds, *1918*, Vol.III, p.179. *Der Weltkrieg*, Vol.14, p.399.
41 Army Group German Crown Prince, War Diary, (10 June 1918), Combat Arms Reference Library, File: Extracts from the War Diary of the Army Group German Crown Prince, May 27 to June 15, 1918. *Der Weltkrieg*, Vol.14, pp.401–402.
42 Army Group German Crown Prince, War Diary, (10 June 1918), Combat Arms Reference Library, File: Extracts from the War Diary of the Army Group German Crown Prince, May 27 to June 15, 1918. *Der Weltkrieg*, Vol.14, pp.383–384, 402.
43 Edmonds, *1918*, Vol.III, p.180. Foch, p.329.
44 Army Group German Crown Prince, Morning and Noon Reports, (11 June 1918), Combat Arms Reference Library, File: Extracts from the War Diary of the Army Group German Crown Prince, May 27 to June 15, 1918. *Der Weltkrieg*, Vol.14, pp.382–383.
45 Army Group German Crown Prince, War Diary, (11 June 1918), Combat Arms Reference Library, File: Extracts from the War Diary of the Army Group German Crown Prince, May 27 to June 15, 1918. Foch, pp.329–330. *Der Weltkrieg*, Vol.14, pp.403–404.
46 Martin Kitchen, *The German Offensives of 1918*, (Stroud, Gloucestershire: 2001), p.157.
47 Army Group German Crown Prince, War Diary and Morning Reports, (12 June 1918), Combat Arms Reference Library, File: Extracts from the War Diary of the Army Group German Crown Prince, May 27 to June 15, 1918. *Der Weltkrieg*, Vol.14, pp.384–385. Bose, *Wachsende Schwierigkeiten*, pp.164–166. In the LIV Corp's 34th Infantry Division, the 2nd Battalion, 24th Infantry Regiment was commanded by Captain Cordt von Brandis, who had been awarded a dubious *Pour le Mérite* for the capture of Fort Douamount at Verdun, when in fact he had merely carried the message of the fort's capture back to his higher headquarters.
48 *Der Weltkrieg*, Vol.14, p.404. Edmonds, *1918*, Vol.III, p.181.
49 Army Group German Crown Prince, Noon and Evening Reports, (12 June 1918), Combat Arms Reference Library, File: Extracts from the War Diary of the Army Group German Crown Prince, May 27 to June 15, 1918. Bose, *Wachsende Schwierigkeiten*, p.176.
50 Army Group German Crown Prince, Morning Reports, (13 June 1918), Combat Arms Reference Library, File: Extracts from the War Diary of the Army Group German Crown Prince, May 27 to June 15, 1918. *Der Weltkrieg*, Vol.14, pp.385, 405.
51 Edmonds, *1918*, Vol.III, p.170. Kitchen, p.154.
52 *Der Weltkrieg*, Vol.14, p.405.
53 Wilhelm, *Erinnerungen*, p.328. Ludendorff, *Kriegserinnerungen*, p.508.
54 *Der Weltkrieg*, Vol.14, pp.403–404.
55 Foch, p.328.
56 Hermann von Kuhl, *Entstehung, Durchführung und Zusammenbruch der Offensive von 1918*, (Berlin: 1927), p.168. Wilhelm, *Erinnerungen*, p.316.
57 Wilhelm, *Erinnerungen*, p.328.
58 Robert B. Asprey, *The German High Command at War: Hindenburg and Ludendorff Conduct World War I*, (New York: 1991), pp.421, 423.
59 Wetzell, "The BLÜCHER and HAGEN Attacks," Bundesarchiv/Militärarchiv, File PH 3/267.
60 Albrecht von Thaer, *Generalstabsdienst an der Front und in der O.H.L.*, (Göttingen: 1958), p.192.

366   *Notes*

10 Operation MARNESCHUTZ–REIMS

1 Paul von Hindenburg, *Aus meinem Leben*, (Leipzig: 1920), p.339.
2 Wilhelm, Crown Prince of Germany, *Meine Erinnerungen aus Deutschlands Heldenkampf*, (Berlin: 1923), p.336.
3 Oberkommando des Heeres, *Der Weltkrieg 1914 bis 1918*, Vol.14, (Berlin: 1944), p.466.
4 OHL, Ia 8536, (5 June 1918), Combat Arms Reference Library, File: Army Group German Crown Prince, Operations Documents BLÜCHER–GNEISENAU–GOERZ, May 17 to June 9, 1918. *Der Weltkrieg*, Vol.14, pp.78, 387, 414.
5 Army Group German Crown Prince, Ia 2573, (1 June 1918), Combat Arms Reference Library, File: Army Group German Crown Prince, Operations Documents BLÜCHER–GNEISENAU–GOERZ, May 17 to June 9, 1918.
6 Hermann von Kuhl, *Personal War Diary of General von Kuhl*, (7 June 1918), Bundesarchiv/Militärarchiv, File: W-10/50652. *Der Weltkrieg*, Vol.14, pp.414–415.
7 Georg Wetzell, "How Are Operations in the West to Be Conducted after GNEISENAU?" (6 June 1918), Bundesarchiv/Militärarchiv, File PH 3/267.
8 AOK 1, Ia 2456, (7 June 1918), Combat Arms Reference Library, File: Army Group German Crown Prince, Operations Documents BLÜCHER–GNEISENAU–GOERZ, May 17 to June 9, 1918.
9 Army Group German Crown Prince, Ia 2593, (8 June 1918), Bundesarchiv/Militärarchiv, File PH 3/262.
10 OHL, Ia 8613, (9 June 1918), Combat Arms Reference Library, File: Army Group German Crown Prince, Operations Documents BLÜCHER–GNEISENAU–GOERZ, May 17 to June 9, 1918. *Der Weltkrieg*, Vol.14, pp.388–389.
11 *Der Weltkrieg*, Vol.14, pp.389–390.
12 AOK 7, Ia 726, (11 June 1918), Combat Arms Reference Library, File: Army Group German Crown Prince, Operations Documents BLÜCHER–GNEISENAU–GOERZ, May 17 to June 9, 1918.
13 Army Group German Crown Prince, Ia 2593, (12 June 1918), Combat Arms Reference Library, File: Army Group German Crown Prince, Operations Documents BLÜCHER–GNEISENAU–GOERZ, May 17 to June 9, 1918.
14 Georg Wetzell, "Estimate of Our Tactical Situation after the BLÜCHER-GNEISENAU Attack," (12 June 1918), Bundesarchiv/Militärarchiv, File PH 3/267.
15 Kuhl, *Diary*, (14 June 1918).
16 OHL, Ia 8685, (14 June 1918), Combat Arms Reference Library, File: Operations Documents, Headquarters, Army Group German Crown Prince, 1918, BLÜCHER–GNEISENAU–GOERZ, June 14 to July 15, 1918.
17 AOK 1, Ia 2510, (16 June 1918), Bundesarchiv/Militärarchiv, File PH 3/260.
18 OHL, Ia 8720, (16 June 1918), Bundesarchiv/Militärarchiv, File PH 3/260.
19 AOK 7, Ia 773, (17 June 1918), Bundesarchiv/Militärarchiv, File PH 3/262.
20 *Der Weltkrieg*, Vol.14, pp.334–335.
21 OHL, Ia 8777, (18 June 1918), Combat Arms Reference Library, File: Operations Documents, Headquarters, Army Group German Crown Prince, 1918, BLÜCHER–GNEISENAU–GOERZ, June 14 to July 15, 1918.
22 Kuhl, *Diary*, (19 June 1918).
23 Hindenburg, p.342.
24 AOK 1, Ia 2573, (20 June 1918), Combat Arms Reference Library, File: Operations Documents, Headquarters, Army Group German Crown Prince, 1918, BLÜCHER–GNEISENAU–GOERZ, June 14 to July 15, 1918.
25 AOK 1, Ia 2605, (21 June 1918), Bundesarchiv/Militärarchiv, File PH 5 II/409.
26 *Der Weltkrieg*, Vol.14, pp.436–437.
27 Erich Ludendorff, *Kriegsführung und Politik*, (Berlin: 1922), p.221.

28 Army Group German Crown Prince, Ia 2622, (21 June 1918), Bundesarchiv/Militärarchiv, File PH 5 II/129.
29 Army Group German Crown Prince, Ia 5967, (23 June 1918), Bundesarchiv/Militärarchiv, File PH 5 I/40.
30 OHL, Ia 8950, (25 June 1918), *United States Army in the World War 1917–1919: Military Operations of the American Expeditionary Force*, Vol.11, (Washington, D.C.: 1991), p.318.
31 AOK 1, Ia 2740, (28 June 1918), Bundesarchiv/Militärarchiv, File PH 5 II/409.
32 Army Group German Crown Prince, Ia 2622, (30 June 1918), Combat Arms Reference Library, File: Extracts from the War Diary of the Army Group of the German Crown Prince, Operations REIMS–MARNE Protection 1918, and Operations West 1, June 18, 1918.
33 OHL, Ia 9058, (1 July 1918), Combat Arms Reference Library, File: Operations Documents, Headquarters, Army Group German Crown Prince, 1918, BLÜCHER–GNEISENAU–GOERZ, June 14 to July 15, 1918.
34 Army Group German Crown Prince, Ia 2644, (1 July 1918), Combat Arms Reference Library, File: Operations Documents, Headquarters, Army Group German Crown Prince, 1918, BLÜCHER–GNEISENAU–GOERZ, June 14 to July 15, 1918.
35 Army Group German Crown Prince, Ia 2643, (4 July 1918), Bundesarchiv/Militärarchiv, File PH 3/263.
36 Hermann von Kuhl, *Entstehung, Durchführung und Zusammenbruch der Offensive von 1918*, (Berlin: 1927), pp.158–160. Oberkommando des Heeres, *Der Weltkrieg 1914 bis 1918*, Vol.14, (Berlin: 1944), pp.317–318. Rupprecht, *Kriegstagebuch*, Vol.II, p.421.
37 AOK 1, Ia 2925, (6 July 1918), Combat Arms Reference Library, File: Operations Documents, Headquarters, Army Group German Crown Prince, 1918, BLÜCHER–GNEISENAU–GOERZ, June 14 to July 15, 1918.
38 AOK 7, Ia 957, (7 July), Bundesarchiv/Militärarchiv, File PH 5 II/163.
39 Army Group German Crown Prince, Ia 2666, (10 July 1918), Bundesarchiv/Militärarchiv, File PH 3/261.
40 AOK 9, Ia 289, (11 July 1918), Combat Arms Reference Library, File: Extracts from Archives—Army Group German Crown Prince, 1918, First Army, June 16 to July 31, 1918. *Der Weltkrieg*, Vol.14, pp.467–468, 474.
41 Wilhelm, *Erinnerungen*, p.334.
42 Wilhelm Marx, "Die Artillerievorbereitung beim Angriff beiderseits Reims am 15. Juli 1918," *Artilleristische Rundschau*, (December 1925), pp.260–261.
43 AOK 7, Ia/Art 415/18, (20 June 1918), Bundesarchiv/Militärarchiv, File PH 5 II/163.
44 AOK 1, Ia 2532, (18 June 1918), Bundesarchiv/Militärarchiv, File PH 3/260.
45 AOK 7, Pi 144, (21 June 1918), Combat Arms Reference Library, File: Extracts from the War Diary, Army Group German Crown Prince, Operations 1918, REIMS–MARNE DEFENSE, June 6 to 20, 1918.
46 AOK 1, Ia/Art 2556/1002, (19 June 1918), Bundesarchiv/Militärarchiv, File PH 5 II/407.
47 AOK 7, Ia 797, (19 June 1918), Combat Arms Reference Library, File: Operations Documents, Headquarters, Army Group German Crown Prince, 1918, BLÜCHER–GNEISENAU–GOERZ, June 14 to July 15, 1918.
48 James E. Edmonds, *Military Operations: Belgium and France 1918*, Vol.III, (London: 1939), p.240.
49 AOK 7, War Diary, (14 July 1918), Combat Arms Reference Library, File: Extracts from the Diary of the Commander-in-Chief of the Seventh Army, June 1 to August 21, 1918.
50 Wilhelm, *Erinnerungen*, p.334.
51 Alfred Stenger, *Schlachten des Weltkriegs: Der letzte deutsche Angriff: Reims 1918:*

Schlachten des Weltkriegs, Vol.35, (Berlin: 1930), p.35. Erich Ludendorff, *Meine Kriegserinnerungen 1914–1918*, (Berlin: 1919), p.533.

52 Georg Bruchmüller, *Die Deutsche Artillerie in den Durchbruchschlachten des Weltkriegs*, 2nd ed., (Berlin: 1922.), pp.32–33. Stenger, *Letzte Deutsche Angriff*, p.34. OHL, Ia 8728, (18 June 1918), Bayerisches Kriegsarchiv, File Hgr. Rupprecht, Bd. 80.

53 Herbert Sulzbach, *Zwischen zwei Mauern: 50 Monate Westfront*, (Berg am See: 1986), p.266.

54 AOK 7, Ia 773, (17 June 1918), Bundesarchiv/Militärarchiv, File PH 3/262.

55 Stenger, *Letzte Deutsche Angriff*, p.34.

56 Ferdinand Meier, "Die Artillerie des Kgl. Bayer. I. A-K. bei der Juli-Offensive 1918," Part 2, *Der K.B. Feld-Artillerist*, August 1936, p.91. Marx (1925), pp.266–267.

57 AOK 1, Ia/Art 2846/1175, (2 July 1918), Bundesarchiv/Militärarchiv, File PH 3/261.

58 AOK 7, Ia/Art 415/18, (20 June 1918), Bundesarchiv/Militärarchiv, File PH 5 II/163.

59 Ferdinand Meier, "Die Artillerie des Kgl. Bayer. I.A.-K. bei der Juli-Offensive 1918," Part 1, *Der K.B. Feld-Artillerist*, July 1936, pp.76–77. AOK 1, Ia/Art 2575/1010, (20 June 1918), Bundesarchiv/Militärarchiv, File PH 5 II/407.

60 AOK 7, Ia 773, (17 June 1918), Bundesarchiv/Militärarchiv, File PH 3/262.

61 AOK 7, Pi 144, (21 June 1918), General Service Schools, *The German Offensive of July 15, 1918 (Marne Source Book)*, (Fort Leavenworth, Kansas: 1923), pp.122–127.

62 AOK 7, Pi 151, (24 June 1918), General Service Schools, *The German Offensive of July 15, 1918 (Marne Source Book)*, (Fort Leavenworth, Kansas: 1923), pp.148–151.

63 AOK 7, War Diary, (13 July 1918), Combat Arms Reference Library, File: Extracts from the Diary of the Commander-in-Chief of the Seventh Army, June 1 to August 21, 1918. *Der Weltkrieg*, Vol.14, p.473.

64 Ferdinand Foch, *The Memoirs of Marshall Foch*, (New York: 1931), pp.310–311. Edmonds, *1918*, Vol.III, p.190.

65 Foch, pp.337–338. Edmonds, *1918*, Vol.III, pp.190–191, 217–219.

66 Foch, pp.354–355. Edmonds, *1918*, Vol.III, pp.215, 238.

67 John Keegan, "The Second Battle of the Marne: 2. The Allied Counter Attack," *The Marshall Cavendish Illustrated Encyclopedia of World War I*, Vol.IX, pp.2876–2880, (New York: 1984), p.2879. Edmonds, *1918*, Vol.III, p.232.

68 Edmonds, *1918*, Vol.III, p.280.

69 Foch, p.355. *Der Weltkrieg*, Vol.14, p.476.

70 Foch, p.333.

71 United States, War Department Document No. 905, *Histories of Two Hundred and Fifty-one Divisions of the German Army Which Participated in the War (1914–1918)*, (London: 1989).

72 *Der Weltkrieg*, Vol.14, Appendix 38i.

73 *Der Weltkrieg*, Vol.14, Appendix 38i.

74 Army Group German Crown Prince, Unnumbered Document, (13 July 1918), General Service Schools, *The German Offensive of July 15, 1918 (Marne Source Book)*, (Fort Leavenworth, Kansas: 1923), pp.402–403.

75 *Der Weltkrieg*, Vol.14, Appendices 38i, 39e.

76 Edmonds, *1918*, Vol.III, pp.228–229.

77 *Der Weltkrieg*, Vol.14, Appendices 38i, 39e.

78 Army Group German Crown Prince, Ia/Art 12968, (26 June 1918), Bundesarchiv/Militärarchiv, File PH 3/260. *Der Weltkrieg*, Vol.14, Appendix 39e.

79 Army Group German Crown Prince, Ia/Art 12968, (26 June 1918), Bundesarchiv/

Militärarchiv, File PH 3/260. AOK 1, Ia/Art 2750/1113, (29 June 1918), Bundesarchiv/Militärarchiv, File PH 3/261.

80 Frederic Herr, *Die Artillerie in Vergangenheit, Gegenwart, und Zukunft*, (translation of *L'Artillerie, ce qu'elle a été, ce qu'elle est, ce qu'elle doit être*, (Paris: 1923)), (Charlottenburg: 1925), p.136. J. Goubard, "Defensive Employment of the French Artillery in 1918: The Artillery of the 21st Corps in the Battle of the 15th of July," *Field Artillery Journal*, (translation of an article from the August 1921 issue of *Revue d'Artillerie*), (November 1921), p.572.

81 I Bavarian Corps, War Diary, (15 July 1918), *United States Army in the World War 1917–1919: Military Operations of the American Expeditionary Force*, Vol.5, (Washington, D.C.: 1991), pp.208–209.

82 Conrad H. Lanza, "The German XXIII Reserve Crosses the Marne," *Field Artillery Journal*, (July 1937), p.308.

83 AOK 7, War Diary, (15 July 1918), Combat Arms Reference Library, File: Extracts from the Diary of the Commander-in-Chief of the Seventh Army, June 1 to August 21, 1918. AOK 3, War Diary, (15 July 1918), Bundesarchiv/Militärarchiv, File PH 5 II/129.

84 Conrad H. Lanza, "Five Decisive Days: The Germans in the Reims Offensive," *Field Artillery Journal*, January 1937, p.42.

85 Goubard, pp.574–575.

86 Lanza, (January 1937), pp.43–44, 64.

87 AOK 1, War Diary, (15 July 1918), *United States Army in the World War 1917–1919: Military Operations of the American Expeditionary Force*, Vol.5, (Washington, D.C.: 1991), p.185.

88 *Der Weltkrieg*, Vol.14, pp.449–450.

89 Army Group German Crown Prince, War Diary, (15 July 1918), Combat Arms Reference Library, File: Extracts from the War Diary, Army Group German Crown Prince, July 15 to August 3, 1918, 15 July. Pascal Lucas, *The Evolution of Tactical Ideas in France and Germany during the War of 1914–1918*, (Paris: 1923), (manuscript translation in English by Major P.V. Kieffer, U.S. Army: 1925), p.142. Lanza, (January 1937), pp.45–49.

90 AOK 7, War Diary, (15 July 1918), Combat Arms Reference Library, File: Extracts from the Diary of the Commander-in-Chief of the Seventh Army, June 1 to August 21, 1918.

91 Army Group German Crown Prince, Seventh Army Evening Report, (15 July 1918), Combat Arms Reference Library, File: Extracts from the War Diary, Army Group German Crown Prince, July 15 to August 3, 1918, 15 July.

92 Hindenburg, p.345.

93 AOK 1, War Diary, (15 July 1918), *United States Army in the World War 1917–1919: Military Operations of the American Expeditionary Force*, Vol.5, (Washington, D.C.: 1991), p.184.

94 Kuhl, *Diary*, (16 July 1918).

95 OHL, Ia 9304, (15 July 1918), Bundesarchiv/Militärarchiv, File PH 3/264.

96 Army Group German Crown Prince, War Diary, (15 July 1918), Combat Arms Reference Library, File: Extracts from the War Diary, Army Group German Crown Prince, July 15 to August 3, 1918, 15 July.

97 AOK 7, War Diary, (15 July 1918), Combat Arms Reference Library, File: Extracts from the Diary of the Commander-in-Chief of the Seventh Army, June 1 to August 21, 1918.

98 Army Group German Crown Prince, War Diary, (15 July 1918), Combat Arms Reference Library, File: Extracts from the War Diary, Army Group German Crown Prince, July 15 to August 3, 1918, 15 July.

99 Martin Kitchen, *The German Offensives of 1918*, (Stroud: Gloucestershire: 2001), pp.183, 186. Foch, p.369.

100 Army Group German Crown Prince, Ia 2670, (16 July 1918), Bundesarchiv/Militärarchiv, File PH 5 II/409. AOK 7, Ia 1023, (16 July 1918), Bundesarchiv/Militärarchiv, File PH 5 II/163.
101 AOK 3, War Diary, (16 July 1918), Bundesarchiv/Militärarchiv, File PH 5 II/129. *Der Weltkrieg*, Vol.14, p.453.
102 AOK 3, Ia 7695, (16 July 1918), Combat Arms Reference Library, File: The Army Records, Army Group of the German Crown Prince, MARNE, 1918 Campaign. AOK 3, War Diary, (16 July 1918), Bundesarchiv/Militärarchiv, File PH 5 II/129.
103 OHL, Ia 9325, (16 July 1918), Combat Arms Reference Library, File: Extracts from Archives—Army Group German Crown Prince, 1918, First Army, June 16 to July 31, 1918.
104 AOK 7, War Diary, (16 July 1918), Combat Arms Reference Library, File: Extracts from the Diary of the Commander-in-Chief of the Seventh Army, June 1 to August 21, 1918.
105 Army Group German Crown Prince, Ia 2672, (16 July 1918), General Service Schools, *The German Offensive of July 15, 1918 (Marne Source Book)*, (Fort Leavenworth, Kansas: 1923), pp.568–570.
106 AOK 7, War Diary, (16 July 1918), Combat Arms Reference Library, File: Extracts from the Diary of the Commander-in-Chief of the Seventh Army, June 1 to August 21, 1918. Kitchen, p.187. Edmonds, *1918*, Vol.III, p.234.
107 Army Group German Crown Prince, Ia 2674, (17 July 1918), General Service Schools, *The German* Offensive of July 15, 1918 (Marne Source Book), (Fort Leavenworth, Kansas: 1923), p.578. Stenger, *Letzte Deutsche Angriff*, p.200.
108 Ludendorff, *Kriegserinnerungen*, p.536.
109 AOK 3, War Diary, (17 July 1918), Bundesarchiv/Militärarchiv, File PH 5 II/129.
110 AOK 1, Ia 3101, (17 July 1918), Bundesarchiv/Militärarchiv, File PH 5 II/409. *Der Weltkrieg*, Vol.14, p.455.
111 Rupprecht, *Kriegstagebuch*, Vol.II, pp.421–422.
112 Cited in Wolfgang Foerster, *Ludendorff: Der Feldherr im Unglück*, (Wiesbaden: 1952), p.17. Hermann Mertz von Quirnheim was the father of Colonel Albrecht Mertz von Quirnheim, a close friend and fellow conspirator of Claus von Stauffenberg in the July 1944 assassination attempt against Hitler.
113 AOK 7, Unnumbered Reinhardt Report, (17 July 1918), Combat Arms Reference Library, File: Extracts from Archives—Army Group German Crown Prince, 1918, First Army, June 16 to July 31, 1918.
114 AOK 7, Ia 1031, (17 July 1918), Bundesarchiv/Militärarchiv, File PH 5 II/163.
115 Army Group German Crown Prince, Ia 2678, (17 July 1918), General Service Schools, *The German Offensive of July 15, 1918 (Marne Source Book)*, (Fort Leavenworth, Kansas: 1923), p.599.
116 AOK 7, Ia 1039, (17 July 1918), Bundesarchiv/Militärarchiv, File PH 5 II/163.
117 Hermann von Kuhl, *Entstehung, Durchführung und Zusammenbruch der Offensive von 1918*, (Berlin: 1927), p.179.
118 Foch, p.363.
119 Alfred Stenger, *Schicksalswende, von der Marne bis zur Vesle 1918: Schlachten des Weltkriegs*, Vol.35, (Berlin: 1930), p.32. *Der Weltkrieg*, Vol.14, p.478.
120 Stenger, *Letzte Deutsche Angriff*, p.200. *Der Weltkrieg*, Vol.14, Appendix 39h. Edmonds, *1918*, Vol.III, p.239.
121 Kuhl, *Diary*, (2 August 1918).
122 Ludendorff, *Kriegserinnerungen*, pp.537, 539.
123 Army Group German Crown Prince, Ia 2689, (18 July 1918), Bundesarchiv/ Militärarchiv, File PH 5 I/40.
124 Rupprecht, *Kriegstagebuch*, Vol.II, p.422. *Der Weltkrieg*, Vol.14, p.471.
125 Army Group German Crown Prince, Ia 2684, (18 July 1918), Bundesarchiv/Militärarchiv, File PH 5 I/40.

126 Lucas, p.134. Keegan, p.2880.
127 *Der Weltkrieg*, Vol.14, p.480.
128 Hindenburg, pp.350–351.
129 AOK 7, War Diary, (19 July 1918), Combat Arms Reference Library, File: Extracts from the Diary of the Commander-in-Chief of the Seventh Army, June 1 to August 21, 1918. *Der Weltkrieg*, Vol.14, p.481.
130 Army Group German Crown Prince, Ia 2690, (19 July 1918), Combat Arms Reference Library, File: Extracts from the War Diary, Army Group German Crown Prince, July 15 to August 3, 1918.
131 Army Group German Crown Prince, War Diary, (19 July 1918), Combat Arms Reference Library, File: Extracts from the War Diary, Army Group German Crown Prince, July 15 to August 3, 1918.
132 Foerster, pp.18–19. Hindenburg, p.349. *Der Weltkrieg*, Vol.14, p.484.
133 *Der Weltkrieg*, Vol.14, p.484.
134 OHL, Ia 9373, (19 July 1918), *United States Army in the World War 1917–1919: Military Operations of the American Expeditionary Force*, Vol.11, (Washington, D.C.: 1991), p.337.
135 AOK 7, War Diary, (19 July 1918), Combat Arms Reference Library, File: Extracts from the Diary of the Commander-in-Chief of the Seventh Army, June 1 to August 21, 1918.
136 *Der Weltkrieg*, Vol.14, pp.482, 487. Edmonds, *1918*, Vol.III, p.244.
137 AOK 9, Ia 617, (20 July 1918), Combat Arms Reference Library, File: Extracts from Operations Documents from July 1 to August 6, 1918, Pertaining to Army Group German Crown Prince: The Defensive in July 1918.
138 Fritz von Lossberg, *Meine Tätigkeit im Weltkriege 1914–1918*, (Berlin: 1939), pp.344–347. *Der Weltkrieg*, Vol.14, pp.487–488. Rupprecht, *Kriegstagebuch*, Vol.II, pp.424–427.
139 AOK 7, War Diary, (20 July 1918), Combat Arms Reference Library, File: Extracts from the Diary of the Commander-in-Chief of the Seventh Army, June 1 to August 21, 1918.
140 OHL, Ia 9420, (22 July 1918), Bundesarchiv/Militärarchiv, File PH 3/264.
141 OHL, Ia 9541, (28 July 1918), *United States Army in the World War 1917–1919: Military Operations of the American Expeditionary Force*, Vol.11, (Washington, D.C.: 1991), pp.348–349.
142 Army Group German Crown Prince, War Diary, (1–3 August 1918), Combat Arms Reference Library, File: Extracts from the War Diary, Army Group German Crown Prince, July 15 to August 3, 1918.
143 Army Group German Crown Prince, Ia 2756, (5 August 1918), Combat Arms Reference Library, File: Extracts from Operations Documents from July 1 to August 6, 1918, Pertaining to Army Group German Crown Prince: The Defensive in July 1918.
144 Paul Greenwood, *The Second Battle of the Marne, 1918*, (New York: 1998), pp.194–195.
145 Greenwood, p.196.
146 Stenger, *Schicksalswende*, pp.218–219.
147 Kuhl, *Offensive von 1918*, p.185.
148 Friedrich von Bernhardi, "Die Deutsche Artillerie in den Durchbruchschlachten des Weltkrieges," *Militär-Wochenblatt*, (20 August 1921), pp.157–158. Hermann Kuhl, "Das Deutsche Angriffsverfahren bei der Offensive in Jahre 1918," *Deutsches Offiziersblatt*, (21 September 1921), pp.533–535. Weachter's June 1921 article is cited by both Kuhl and Bernhardi.
149 Georg Bruchmüller, *Die Deutsche Artillerie in den Durchbruchschlachten des Weltkriegs*, 2nd ed., (Berlin: 1922), p.38.
150 Franz Nikolas Kaiser, *Das Ehrenbuch der Deutschen Schweren Artillerie*, Vol.I, (Berlin: 1931), p.64. Kuhl, *Deutsches Offiziersblatt*, p.534.

151 Richard von Berendt, "Schiessübungen," *Artilleristische Rundschau*, (October 1925), pp.193–196. Wilhelm Marx, "Die Artillerievorbereitung beim Angriff beiderseits Reims am 15. Juli 1918," *Artilleristische Rundschau*, (December 1925), pp.257–268.

152 Meier, "Die Artillerie," Part 2, pp.88–92.

153 Meier, pp.91–92. Bruchmüller (1922), pp.34–35.

154 Lucas, p.143.

155 *Der Weltkrieg*, Vol.14, p.463.

156 Kuhl, *Offensive von 1918*, p.185.

157 Kitchen, p.188.

158 Army Group German Crown Prince, Ia 2639, (29 June 1918), Combat Arms Reference Library, File: Extracts from Archives—Army Group German Crown Prince, 1918, First Army, June 16 to July 31, 1918.

159 AOK 7, Ia 893, (30 June 1918), Bundesarchiv/Militärarchiv, File PH 5 II/163.

160 OHL, Ia 9038, (1 July 1918), Combat Arms Reference Library, File: The Army Records, Army Group of the German Crown Prince, MARNE, 1918 Campaign.

161 AOK 7, War Diary, (9 July 1918), Combat Arms Reference Library, File: Extracts from the Diary of the Commander-in-Chief of the Seventh Army, June 1 to August 21, 1918. AOK 7, Ia 988, (11 July 1918), Bundesarchiv/Militärarchiv, File PH 3/264. AOK 9, Ia 289, (11 July 1918), Combat Arms Reference Library, File: Extracts from Archives—Army Group German Crown Prince, 1918, First Army, June 16 to July 31, 1918.

162 *Der Weltkrieg*, Vol.14, pp.467, 474.

163 Kuhl, *Offensive von 1918*, p.180.

164 *Der Weltkrieg*, Vol.14, pp.469–470, 475.

165 Kuhl, *Diary*, (2 August 1918).

166 AOK 7, War Diary, (18 July 1918), Combat Arms Reference Library, File: Extracts from the Diary of the Commander-in-Chief of the Seventh Army, June 1 to August 21, 1918.

167 Edmonds, *1918*, Vol.III, p.215.

168 Keegan, p.2878.

169 Army Group Crown Prince Rupprecht, War Diary, (15 May, 24 May, and 13 June 1918), Bayerisches Kriegsarchiv, File Hgr. Rupprecht, Bd. 80.

170 Rupprecht, *Kriegstagebuch*, Vol.II, p.326.

171 Ludendorff, *Kriegserinnerungen*, p.516.

172 Lossberg, p.351.

173 Kuhl, *Offensive von 1918*, p.182.

174 Kuhl, *Offensive von 1918*, p.182.

175 Kuhl, *Offensive von 1918*, p.182.

176 Kitchen, p.180.

11 Operations HAGEN and KURFÜRST

1 OHL, Ia 8154, (15 May 1918), Bayerisches Kriegsarchiv, Munich, Germany: File Hgr. Rupprecht, Bd. 105.

2 Erich Ludendorff, *Meine Kriegserinnerungen 1914–1918*, (Berlin: 1919), p.537.

3 Oberkommando des Heeres, *Der Weltkrieg 1914 bis 1918*, Vol.14, (Berlin: 1944), p.302. OHL, Ia 7515, (5 April 1918), *United States Army in the World War 1917–1919: Military Operations of the American Expeditionary Force*, Vol.11, (Washington, D.C.: 1991), p.282.

4 *Der Weltkrieg*, Vol.14, p.304.

5 Army Group Crown Prince Rupprecht, War Diary, (12 April 1918), Bayerisches Kriegsarchiv: File Hgr. Rupprecht, Bd. 80.

6 Hermann von Kuhl, *Entstehung, Durchführung und Zusammenbruch der Offensive*

von 1918, (Berlin: 1927), pp.158–164. The German official history reports Rupprecht's Army Group sending similar recommendations to OHL on 1 May. *Der Weltkrieg*, Vol.14, pp.317–318. Crown Prince Rupprecht in his diary notes such a report being sent to OHL on 3 May. Rupprecht, Crown Prince of Bavaria, *Mein Kriegstagebuch*, Vol.III, (Munich: 1929), pp.318–319.

7 Army Group Crown Prince Rupprecht, Ia 6822, (17 April 1918), Bayerisches Kriegsarchiv: File Hgr. Rupprecht, Bd. 112.

8 Georg Wetzell, "Offensive against the French" (28 April 1918), Bundesarchiv/Militärarchiv, File PH 3/267.

9 Hermann von Kuhl, *Personal War Diary of General von Kuhl*, (30 April 1918), Bundesarchiv/Militärarchiv, File: W-10/50652. Rupprecht, *Kriegstagebuch*, Vol.II, p.392. Army Group Crown Prince Rupprecht, Ia 7010, (29 April 1918), Bayerisches Kriegsarchiv: File Hgr. Rupprecht, Bd. 80.

10 Army Group Crown Prince Rupprecht, Ia 7030, (1 May 1918), Bayerisches Kriegsarchiv: File Hgr. Rupprecht, Bd. 80.

11 Kuhl, *Offensive von 1918*, pp.158–159.

12 Kuhl, *Diary*, (1 May 1918).

13 Army Group Crown Prince Rupprecht, Ia 7034, (1 May 1918), Bayerisches Kriegsarchiv: File Hgr. Rupprecht, Bd. 112.

14 OHL, Ia 7960, (2 May 1918), Bayerisches Kriegsarchiv: File Hgr. Rupprecht, Bd. 80. *Der Weltkrieg*, Vol.14, p.318.

15 Kuhl, *Diary*, (2 May 1918).

16 Georg Wetzell, "How to Continue the Attack" (2 May 1918), Bundesarchiv/Militärarchiv, File PH 3/267.

17 Kuhl, *Diary*, (4 May 1918).

18 *Der Weltkrieg*, Vol.14, p.315.

19 Kuhl, *Offensive von 1918*, pp.160–161. *Der Weltkrieg*, Vol.14, p.319.

20 OHL, Ia 8018, (6 May 1918), Bayerisches Kriegsarchiv: File Hgr. Rupprecht, Bd. 80.

21 Army Group Crown Prince Rupprecht, Iaf 7100, (5 May 1918), Bayerisches Kriegsarchiv: File Hgr. Rupprecht, Bd. 112.

22 Kuhl, *Offensive von 1918*, p.159.

23 Kuhl, *Offensive von 1918*, p.161.

24 Army Group Crown Prince Rupprecht, Ia 7207, (12 May 1918), Bayerisches Kriegsarchiv: File Hgr. Rupprecht, Bd. 80.

25 *Der Weltkrieg*, Vol.14, p.320.

26 OHL, Ia 8154, (15 May 1918), Bayerisches Kriegsarchiv: File Hgr. Rupprecht, Bd. 105.

27 Kuhl, *Diary*, (17 May 1918).

28 Rupprecht, *Kriegstagebuch*, Vol.III, p.323.

29 Army Group Crown Prince Rupprecht, Ia 7355, (19 May 1918), Bayerisches Kriegsarchiv: File Hgr. Rupprecht, Bd. 80.

30 Kuhl, *Diary*, (21 May 1918). *Der Weltkrieg*, Vol.14, p.321.

31 Georg Wetzell, "The BLÜCHER and HAGEN Attacks," (21 May 1918), Bundesarchiv/Militärarchiv, File PH 3/267.

32 Rupprecht, *Kriegstagebuch*, Vol.III, pp.323–324.

33 Army Group Crown Prince Rupprecht, War Diary, (31 May 1918), Bayerisches Kriegsarchiv: File Hgr. Rupprecht, Bd. 80.

34 Rupprecht, *Kriegstagebuch*, Vol.III, p.325.

35 Army Group Crown Prince Rupprecht, Iaf 7567, (1 June 1918), Bayerisches Kriegsarchiv: File Hgr. Rupprecht, Bd. 105.

36 Theo von Bose, *Wachsende Schwierigkeiten: Vergebliches Ringen vor Compiegne, Villers-Cotterets, und Reims: Schlachten des Weltkriegs*, Vol.33, (Berlin: 1930), p.151.

37 Rupprecht, *Kriegstagebuch*, Vol.II, p.407.
38 OHL, Ia 8500, (4 June 1918), Bayerisches Kriegsarchiv: File Hgr. Rupprecht, Bd. 80.
39 Kuhl, *Diary*, (7 June 1918). Georg Wetzell, "How Are the Operations in the West to Be Continued after GNEISENAU?," (6 June 1918), Bundesarchiv/Militärarchiv, File PH 3/267. *Der Weltkrieg*, Vol.14, pp.414–415, 429.
40 Kuhl, *Diary*, (11 June 1918).
41 Rupprecht, *Kriegstagebuch*, Vol.III, p.327.
42 *Der Weltkrieg*, Vol.14, p.422.
43 Kuhl, *Diary*, (9 June 1918).
44 Georg Wetzell, "Estimate of the Situation after the BLÜCHER–GNEISENAU Attack", (12 June 1918), Bundesarchiv/Militärarchiv, File PH 3/267.
45 OHL, Ia 8685, (14 June 1918), Bayerisches Kriegsarchiv: File Hgr. Rupprecht, Bd. 80.
46 Kuhl, *Diary*, (14 June 1918).
47 Army Group Crown Prince Rupprecht, Ia 7767, (15 June 1918), Bayerisches Kriegsarchiv: File Hgr. Rupprecht, Bd. 112.
48 *Der Weltkrieg*, Vol.14, pp.423–424.
49 Army Group Crown Prince Rupprecht, Ia 7814, (18 June 1918), Bayerisches Kriegsarchiv: File Hgr. Rupprecht, Bd. 105.
50 Rupprecht, *Kriegstagebuch*, Vol.III, p.330.
51 OHL, Ia 8727, (18 June 1918), Bayerisches Kriegsarchiv: File Hgr. Rupprecht, Bd. 80.
52 OHL, Ia 8792, (19 June 1918), Bayerisches Kriegsarchiv: File Hgr. Rupprecht, Bd. 105.
53 OHL, Ia 8800, (19 June 1918), Bayerisches Kriegsarchiv: File Hgr. Rupprecht, Bd. 80.
54 Kuhl, *Diary*, (19 June 1918).
55 Army Group Crown Prince Rupprecht, Ia 7872, (20 June 1918), Bayerisches Kriegsarchiv: File Hgr. Rupprecht, Bd. 80.
56 Army Group Crown Prince Rupprecht, Ia 7883, (21 June 1918), Bayerisches Kriegsarchiv: File Hgr. Rupprecht, Bd. 80.
57 AOK 6, Iab 3458, Iab 3463, (22 June 1918), Bayerisches Kriegsarchiv: File Hgr. Rupprecht, Bd. 105.
58 Georg Wetzell, "How Is the War to Be Carried on after the Battles in the West in July–August?," (22 June 1918), Bundesarchiv/Militärarchiv, File PH 3/267.
59 OHL, Ia 8895, (22 June 1918), Combat Arms Reference Library, File: Operations Documents, Headquarters, Army Group German Crown Prince, 1918, BLÜCHER–GNEISENAU–GOERZ, June 14 to July 13, 1918.
60 Kuhl, *Diary*, (23 June 1918).
61 OHL, Ia 8876, (23 June 1918), Bayerisches Kriegsarchiv: File Hgr. Rupprecht, Bd. 105.
62 Rupprecht, *Kriegstagebuch*, Vol.III, pp.331–332.
63 Rupprecht, *Kriegstagebuch*, Vol.III, pp.333–334.
64 Army Group German Crown Prince, Ia 2629, (26 June 1918), General Service Schools, *The German Offensive of July 15, 1918 (Marne Source Book)*, (Fort Leavenworth, Kansas: 1923), pp.172–174.
65 Kuhl, *Offensive von 1918*, pp.185–186.
66 Georg Wetzell, "The Attack on Paris," (27 June 1918), Bundesarchiv/Militärarchiv, File PH 3/267.
67 *Der Weltkrieg*, Vol.14, pp.423–424.
68 Army Group Crown Prince Rupprecht, Ia 8082, (1 July 1918), Bayerisches Kriegsarchiv: File Hgr. Rupprecht, Bd. 112.
69 *Der Weltkrieg*, Vol.14, p.432.

70 Kuhl, *Diary*, (12 July 1918).
71 OHL, Ia 8994, (3 July 1918), Combat Arms Reference Library, File: Operations Documents, Headquarters, Army Group German Crown Prince, 1918, BLÜCHER–GNEISENAU–GOERZ, June 14 to July 13, 1918.
72 Rupprecht, *Kriegstagebuch*, Vol.II, p.419.
73 Georg Wetzell, "Attack in Alsace and Lorraine," (6 July 1918), Bundesarchiv/Militärarchiv, File PH 3/267.
74 Rupprecht, *Kriegstagebuch*, Vol.III, p.335.
75 Army Group German Crown Prince, Ia 2629, (10 July 1918), Combat Arms Reference Library, File: Operations Documents, Headquarters, Army Group German Crown Prince, 1918, BLÜCHER–GNEISENAU–GOERZ, June 14 to July 13, 1918.
76 Rupprecht, *Kriegstagebuch*, Vol.II, p.420.
77 Army Group Crown Prince Rupprecht, Ia 8313, (11 July 1918), Bayerisches Kriegsarchiv: File Hgr. Rupprecht, Bd. 112. *Der Weltkrieg*, Vol.14, p.427.
78 Army Group Crown Prince Rupprecht, Ia 8302, (11 July 1918), Bayerisches Kriegsarchiv: File Hgr. Rupprecht, Bd. 112.
79 *Der Weltkrieg*, Vol.14, p.432.
80 Rupprecht, *Kriegstagebuch*, Vol.III, p.335.
81 *Der Weltkrieg*, Vol.14, pp.427–428.
82 AOK 4, Ia 763, (7 May 1918), Bayerisches Kriegsarchiv: File Hgr. Rupprecht, Bd. 105.
83 Kuhl, *Offensive von 1918*, p.186.
84 Kuhl, *Offensive von 1918*, p.187.
85 Frederic Herr, *Die Artillerie in Vergangenheit, Gegenwart, und Zukunft*, (translation of *L'Artillerie, ce qu'elle a été, ce qu'elle est, ce qu'elle doit être*, (Paris: 1923)), (Charlottenburg: 1925), p.141.
86 AOK 6, Ia/Art 3122/390, (16 May 1918), Bayerisches Kriegsarchiv: File AOK 6, Bd. 9.
87 Georg Bruchmüller, *Die Deutsche Artillerie in den Durchbruchschlachten des Weltkriegs*, 2nd ed., (Berlin: 1922.), pp.32–33.
88 AOK 6, Ia/Art 3609/481, (4 July 1918), Bayerisches Kriegsarchiv: File AOK 6, Bd. 9.
89 Army Group Crown Prince Rupprecht, Ia 7090, (1 May 1918), Bayerisches Kriegsarchiv: File Hgr. Rupprecht, Bd. 105. Army Group Crown Prince Rupprecht, Ia 7308, (16 May 1918), Bayerisches Kriegsarchiv: File Hgr. Rupprecht, Bd. 105.
90 Kuhl, *Offensive von 1918*, p.186.
91 Army Group Crown Prince Rupprecht, Ia 7572, (1 June 1918), Bayerisches Kriegsarchiv: File Hgr. Rupprecht, Bd. 112. Army Group Crown Prince Rupprecht, Ia 8051, (29 June 1918), Bayerisches Kriegsarchiv: File Hgr. Rupprecht, Bd. 108. Army Group Crown Prince Rupprecht, Ia 8541, (20 July 1918), Bayerisches Kriegsarchiv: File Hgr. Rupprecht, Bd. 112.
92 Army Group Crown Prince Rupprecht, Iab 7480, (26 May 1918), Bayerisches Kriegsarchiv: File Hgr. Rupprecht, Bd. 105. Army Group Crown Prince Rupprecht, Iad 8433, (16 July 1918), Bayerisches Kriegsarchiv: File Hgr. Rupprecht, Bd. 112.
93 OHL, Ia 8963, (28 June 1918), Bayerisches Kriegsarchiv: File Hgr. Rupprecht, Bd. 112.
94 Army Group Crown Prince Rupprecht, Iab 8130, (4 July 1918), Bayerisches Kriegsarchiv: File Hgr. Rupprecht, Bd. 112.
95 Army Group Crown Prince Rupprecht, Iab 8377, (14 July 1918), Bayerisches Kriegsarchiv: File Hgr. Rupprecht, Bd. 112.
96 James E. Edmonds, *Military Operations: Belgium and France 1918*, Vol.III, (London: 1939), p.166.
97 AOK 4, Ia 1698, (12 July 1918), Bayerisches Kriegsarchiv: File Hgr. Rupprecht, Bd. 105. AOK 6, Ia 3844, (14 July 1918), Bayerisches Kriegsarchiv: File Hgr. Rupprecht, Bd. 108.

98 Army Group Crown Prince Rupprecht, Ia 8082, (1 July 1918), Bayerisches Kriegsarchiv: File Hgr. Rupprecht, Bd. 112.
99 Army Group Crown Prince Rupprecht, Ia 8051, (29 June 1918), Bayerisches Kriegsarchiv: File Hgr. Rupprecht, Bd. 108.
100 Edmonds, *1918*, Vol.IV, p.7, Map 2.
101 Edmonds, *1918*, Vol.IV, (London: 1947), p.4. Edmonds, Vol.III, pp.165–166.
102 OHL, Ia 9305, (15 July 1918), Bundesarchiv/Militärarchiv, File PH 3/264. *Der Weltkrieg*, Vol.14, p.463.
103 Army Group Crown Prince Rupprecht, Ia 8433, (16 July 1918), Bayerisches Kriegsarchiv: File Hgr. Rupprecht, Bd. 112. *Der Weltkrieg*, Vol.14, pp.451–452.
104 Army Group Crown Prince Rupprecht, Ia 8422, (16 July 1918), Bayerisches Kriegsarchiv: File Hgr. Rupprecht, Bd. 112.
105 Rupprecht, *Kriegstagebuch*, Vol.III, p.337.
106 Army Group Crown Prince Rupprecht, Iaf 8441, (17 July 1918), Bayerisches Kriegsarchiv: File Hgr. Rupprecht, Bd. 112.
107 Barrie Pitt, *1918: The Last Act*, (New York: 1963), p.202.
108 Rupprecht, *Kriegstagebuch*, Vol.II, p.421.
109 *Der Weltkrieg*, Vol.14, pp.470–471.
110 *Der Weltkrieg*, Vol.14, p.471.
111 Rupprecht, *Kriegstagebuch*, Vol.II, p.422.
112 Kuhl, *Diary*, (18 July 1918).
113 Army Group Crown Prince Rupprecht, Ia 8484, (19 July 1918), Bayerisches Kriegsarchiv: File Hgr. Rupprecht, Bd. 80.
114 *Der Weltkrieg*, Vol.14, pp.484, 531. Paul von Hindenburg, *Aus meinem Leben*, (Leipzig: 1920), p.328.
115 Army Group Crown Prince Rupprecht, Ia 8514, (20 July 1918), Bayerisches Kriegsarchiv: File Hgr. Rupprecht, Bd. 108.
116 Kuhl, *Diary*, (20 July 1918).
117 Fritz von Lossberg, *Meine Tätigkeit im Weltkriege 1914–1918*, (Berlin: 1939), pp.344–346.
118 *Der Weltkrieg*, Vol.14, pp.531–532.
119 Kuhl, *Diary*, (20 July 1918).
120 Rupprecht, *Kriegstagebuch*, Vol.II, p.424.
121 OHL, Ia 9388, (20 July 1918), Bayerisches Kriegsarchiv: File Hgr. Rupprecht, Bd. 105. *Der Weltkrieg*, Vol.14, p.534.
122 Army Group Crown Prince Rupprecht, Ia 8542, (20 July 1918), Bayerisches Kriegsarchiv: File Hgr. Rupprecht, Bd. 105. Army Group Crown Prince Rupprecht, Ia 8564, (21 July 1918), Bayerisches Kriegsarchiv: File Hgr. Rupprecht, Bd. 80. Rupprecht, *Kriegstagebuch*, Vol.II, p.425.
123 Kuhl, *Diary*, (20–21 July 1918). *Der Weltkrieg*, p.534.
124 Sir Douglas Haig, *The Private Papers of Douglas Haig, 1914–1919*, Robert Blake, ed., (London: 1952), p.320.
125 Army Group Crown Prince Rupprecht, Ia 8578, (22 July 1918), Bayerisches Kriegsarchiv: File Hgr. Rupprecht, Bd. 80.
126 AOK 6, Ia 3978, (23 July 1918), Bayerisches Kriegsarchiv: File AOK 6, Bd. 414.
127 Haig, p.320.
128 Rupprecht, *Kriegstagebuch*, Vol.III, pp.338, 340.
129 *Der Weltkrieg*, Vol.14, p.537.
130 *Der Weltkrieg*, Vol.14, p.538.
131 *Der Weltkrieg*, Vol.14, p.540.
132 Kuhl, *Offensive von 1918*, pp.158–159.
133 Kuhl, *Offensive von 1918*, pp.158–159.
134 AOK 6, Iad 3748, (9 July 1918), Bayerisches Kriegsarchiv: File AOK 6, Bd. 9.

135 Army Group Crown Prince Rupprecht, Ia 7034, (1 May 1918), Bayerisches Kriegsarchiv: File Hgr. Rupprecht, Bd. 112.
136 Army Group Crown Prince Rupprecht, Ia 7567, (1 June 1918), Bayerisches Kriegsarchiv: File Hgr. Rupprecht, Bd. 105.
137 Army Group Crown Prince Rupprecht, Ia 7814, (18 June 1918), Bayerisches Kriegsarchiv: File Hgr. Rupprecht, Bd. 105. OHL, Ia 8727, (18 June 1918), Bayerisches Kriegsarchiv: File Hgr. Rupprecht, Bd. 80. OHL, Ia 8727, (18 June 1918), Bayerisches Kriegsarchiv: File Hgr. Rupprecht, Bd. 80. Army Group Crown Prince Rupprecht, Ia 7883, (21 June 1918), Bayerisches Kriegsarchiv: File Hgr. Rupprecht, Bd. 80.
138 Army Group Crown Prince Rupprecht, Ia 7034, (1 May 1918), Bayerisches Kriegsarchiv: File Hgr. Rupprecht, Bd. 112. Army Group Crown Prince Rupprecht, Ia 7567, (1 June 1918), Bayerisches Kriegsarchiv: File Hgr. Rupprecht, Bd. 105. Army Group Crown Prince Rupprecht, Ia 7883, (20 July 1918), Bayerisches Kriegsarchiv: File Hgr. Rupprecht, Bd. 112. AOK 6, Ia 3844, (14 July 1918), Bayerisches Kriegsarchiv: File Hgr. Rupprecht, Bd. 108. AOK 4, Ia 1698, (12 July 1918), Bayerisches Kriegsarchiv: File Hgr. Rupprecht, Bd. 105.
139 *Der Weltkrieg*, Vol.14, p.684.
140 Wilhelm, Crown Prince of Germany, *Meine Erinnerungen aus Deutschlands Heldenkampf*, (Berlin: 1923), p.372.
141 Kuhl, *Offensive von 1918*, p.182.
142 Kuhl, *Offensive von 1918*, p.185.

12 Conclusions

1 Hans Delbrück and Hermann von Kuhl, "*Die Ursachen des Deutschen Zusammenbruchs im Jahre 1918*," Vol.3, *Entstehung, Durchführung und Zusammenbruch der Offensive von 1918*, (Berlin: 1923), p.253.
2 Correlli Barnett, *The Swordbearers: Supreme Command in the First World War*, (Bloomington, Indiana: 1964), p.282.
3 Delbrück and Kuhl, Vol.3, p.246.
4 Delbrück and Kuhl, Vol.3, p.253.
5 Hans W. Gatzke, *Germany's Drive to the West: A Study of Germany's Western War Aims during the First World War*, (Baltimore, Maryland: 1950), p.262.
6 Barnett, p.303.
7 Herbert Rosinski, *The German Army*, (New York: 1966), p.144.
8 Rupprecht, Crown Prince of Bavaria, *Mein Kriegstagebuch*, Vol.II, (Munich: 1929), p.399.
9 Fritz von Lossberg, *Meine Tätigkeit im Weltkriege 1914–1918*, (Berlin: 1939), p.359.
10 Basil Liddell Hart, *Strategy*, (New York: 1967), p.212.
11 Martin van Creveld, *Command in War*, (Cambridge, Massachusetts: 1985), p.168.
12 David T. Zabecki, *Steel Wind: Colonel Georg Bruchmüller and the Birth of Modern Artillery*, (Bridgeport, Connecticut: 1994), pp.105–126.
13 Barnett, p.281.
14 Erich Ludendorff, *Meine Kriegserinnerungen 1914–1918*, (Berlin: 1919), p.472.
15 Cited in Hermann von Kuhl, *Entstehung, Durchführung und Zusammenbruch der Offensive von 1918*, (Berlin: 1927), p.191.
16 Richard Simpkin, *Race to the Swift: Thoughts on Twenty-first Century Warfare*, (London: 1985), p.22.
17 Ian Malcolm Brown, *British Logistics on the Western Front, 1914–1919*, (Bridgeport, Connecticut: 1998), pp.109–134.
18 Brown, p.184.
19 Brown, p.149.
20 A.M. Henniker, *Transportation on the Western Front, 1914–1918*, (London: 1937), pp.235–236.

21 Brown, pp.143, 145.
22 Henniker, p.157.
23 Brown, pp.126, 144, 165, 189.
24 Brown, p.191.
25 Henniker, pp.402–410.
26 Cited in Brown, p.191.
27 Max Hoffmann, *Der Krieg der versäumten Gelegenheiten*, (Munich: 1923), pp.238–239
28 Hoffmann, pp.236–240.
29 Kuhl, *Offensive von 1918*, p.196.
30 Delbrück and Kuhl, Vol.3, pp.246–247.
31 Delbrück and Kuhl, Vol.3, pp.250–251.
32 Oberkommando des Heeres, *Der Weltkrieg 1914 bis 1918*, Vol.14, (Berlin: 1944), Appendix 35.
33 Simpkin, p.30.
34 Gary Sheffield, *Forgotten Victory: The First World War, Myths and Realities*, (London: 2001), p.206.
35 James S. Corum, *The Roots of Blitzkrieg: Hans von Seeckt and German Military Reform*, (Lawrence, Kansas: 1992), pp.30–33.
36 Rosinski, p.301.
37 Harlan N. Hartness, *Report No. 15,260, Report on German General Staff School, Staff Methods, and Tactical Doctrine*, 3 May 1937, p.7 (National Archives and Records Administration, Record Group 165, Box 1113).
38 See Martin van Creveld, *Fighting Power: German and U.S. Army Performance, 1939–1945*, (Westport, Connecticut: 1982).
39 Cited in Paul Fussell, *The Great War in Modern Memory*, (Oxford: 1975), p.317.
40 Graeme Wynne, *If Germany Attacks: The Battle in Depth in the West*, (London: 1940), pp.131, 249. Timothy T. Lupfer, *The Dynamics of Doctrine: Changes in German Tactical Doctrine during the First World War*, (Fort Leavenworth, Kansas: July 1981), pp.9–11.
41 Rosinski, pp.145–146.
42 Lossberg, pp.326–327.
43 Albrecht von Thaer, *Generalstabsdienst an der Front und in der O.H.L.*, (Göttingen: 1958), pp.194–198.
44 Simpkin, p.217.
45 Georg Wetzell, Letter to Hans von Seeckt, (24 July 1919), Seeckt Papers, Bundesarchiv/Militärarchiv, Folder N247/175.

Bibliography

Unpublished sources

Bundesarchiv/Militärarchiv, Freiburg, Germany

PH 2/203
PH 2/278
PH 2/279
PH 3/52
PH 3/259
PH 3/260
PH 3/261
PH 3/262
PH 3/263
PH 3/264
PH 3/267
PH 3/268
PH 3/269
PH 3/277
PH 3/278
PH 3/279
PH 3/280
PH 3/281
PH 3/409
PH 3/452
PH 3/453
PH 3/454
PH 3/455
PH 3/456
PH 3/503
PH 3/504
PH 3 I/33
PH 3 I/278
PH 3 I/280
PH 3 I/287
PH 5 I/29
PH 5 I/29

PH 5 I/30
PH 5 I/31
PH 5 I/32
PH 5 I/33
PH 5 I/40
PH 5 I/43
PH 5 I/44
PH 5 I/45
PH 5 I/46
PH 5 I/49
PH 5 I/50
PH 5 II/99
PH 5 II/111
PH 5 II/117
PH 5 II/121
PH 5 II/122
PH 5 II/123
PH 5 II/128
PH 5 II/129
PH 5 II/134
PH 5 II/163
PH 5 II/169
PH 5 II/189
PH 5 II/195
PH 5 II/199
PH 5 II/200
PH 5 II/202
PH 5 II/203
PH 5 II/204
PH 5 II/205
PH 5 II/207
PH 5 II/209
PH 5 II/215
PH 5 II/218
PH 5 II/219
PH 5 II/295
PH 5 II/351
PH 5 II/407
PH 5 II/409
PH 5 II/418
PH 5 II/502
PH 6 II/21
PH 6 V/9
RH 61/38
RH 2/2195
RH 12-2/94
F-12655
N 27-5   (von Stuelpnagel Papers)
N 35-8/12/15 (von Haeften Papers)

N 58-1   (von Schulenburg Papers)
N 221-25/29   (Geyer Papers)
N 247-175   (von Seeckt Papers)
N 275-2/34   (Bruchmüller Papers)
W-10/50652   (von Kuhl Diary)
W-10/50640   (von Hutier Diary)

Bayerisches Hauptstaatsarchiv, Kriegsarchiv, Munich, Germany

Hgr. Rupprecht, Bd. 38.
Hgr. Rupprecht, Bd. 80.
Hgr. Rupprecht, Bd. 96.
Hgr. Rupprecht, Bd. 100.
Hgr. Rupprecht, Bd. 105.
Hgr. Rupprecht, Bd. 108.
Hgr. Rupprecht, Bd. 112.
Hgr. Rupprecht, Bd. 168.
AOK 6, Bd. 7.
AOK 6, Bd. 8.
AOK 6, Bd. 9.
AOK 6, Bd. 279.
AOK 6, Bd. 414.

National Archives and Records Administration, College Park, Maryland

Record Group 165, Entry 320, Box 2, Folder 1.
Record Group 165, Entry 320, Box 3, Folder 12.
Record Group 165, Entry 320, Box 12, Folder 8.
Record Group 165, Entry 320, Box 35, Folder 8.
Record Group 165, Entry 320, Box 42, Folders 2 and 3.
Record Group 165, Box 1113, Report No. 15, 260.

Combat Arms Research Library, U.S. Army Command and General Staff College, Fort Leavenworth, Kansas

Operations Documents (BLÜCHER–GNEISENAU–GOERZ) April 17 to May 20, 1918, Part I.
Operations Documents (BLÜCHER–GNEISENAU–GOERZ) May 15 to 26, 1918, Part II.
Army Group German Crown Prince, Operations Documents BLÜCHER–GNEISENAU–GOERZ, May 17 to June 9, 1918.
Extracts from Operations Documents from July 1 to August 6, 1918, pertaining to Army Group German Crown Prince: The Defensive in July 1918.
Extracts from War Diary of the Army Group German Crown Prince, May 1 to 26, 1918.
Extracts from the War Diary of the Army Group German Crown Prince, May 27 to June 15, 1918.
Extracts from War Diary, Army Group German Crown Prince, July 15 to August 3, 1918.
Operations Documents, Headquarters, Army Group German Crown Prince, 1918, BLÜCHER–GNEISENAU–GOERZ, June 14 to July 15, 1918.

Extracts from the Diary of the Commander-in-Chief of the Seventh Army, June 1 to August 21, 1918.

Extracts from Archives—Army Group German Crown Prince, 1918, First Army, June 16 to July 31, 1918.

Extracts from the War Diary, Army Group German Crown Prince, Operations 1918, REIMS–MARNE DEFENSE, June 6 to 20, 1918.

Attack Orders, First Army, REIMS, July 1918.

The Army Records, Army Group of the German Crown Prince, MARNE, 1918 Campaign.

Extracts from the War Diary of the Army Group of the German Crown Prince, Operations REIMS–MARNE Protection 1918, and Operations West 1, June 18, 1918.

Extracts from War Diary of the Army Group German Crown Prince, April 15 to 30, 1918.

War Diary, Army Group German Crown Prince, Volume I, June 14 to July 14, 1918: Daily Reports of Operations; Important Operation Orders; Intelligence Summary.

Dissertations and Unpublished Monographs

Buckelew, John Dan, *Erich Ludendorff and the German War Effort 1916–1918: A Study in the Military Exercise of Power*, University of California, San Diego: 1974.

Hennes, Randolph Y., *The March Retreat of 1918: An Anatomy of a Battle*, University of Washington: 1966.

Meyer, Bradley, *Operational Art and the German Command System in World War I*, Ohio State University: 1988.

Ord, James B., *The German Offensive of March 21–April 8, 1918*, U.S. Army War College: 1922.

Sorley, Lewis S., *Some Recollections*, unpublished memoir, December 1957.

Venohr, Wolfgang, *Die operative Führung General Ludendorffs im Spiegel der · Deutschen Fachkritik*, University of Berlin: 1954.

Official histories

Germany

Bose, Theo von, *Deutsche Siege 1918, Das Vorbringen der 7. Armee über Ailette, Aisne, Vesle, und Ourcq bis zur Marne (27. Mai bis 13. Juni): Schlachten des Weltkriegs*, Volume 32, Gerhard Stalling, Berlin: 1929.

Bose, Theo von, *Wachsende Schwierigkeiten: Vergebliches Ringen vor Compiegne, Villers-Cotterets, und Reims: Schlachten des Weltkriegs*, Volume 33, Gerhard Stalling, Berlin: 1930.

Bose, Theo von, *Die Katastrophe des 8. August 1918: Schlachten des Weltkriegs*, Volume 36, Gerhard Stalling, Berlin: 1930.

Deutschen Reichstages, *"Die Ursachen des deutschen Zusammenbruchs im Jahre 1918,"* Volume 3, Hermann von Kuhl and Hans Delbrück, *Entstehung, Durchführung und Zusammenbruch der Offensive von 1918*, Deutsche Verlagsgesellschaft für Politik und Geschichte, Berlin: 1925.

Oberkommando des Heeres, *Der Weltkrieg 1914 bis 1918*, Volume 10, *Die Operationen des Jahres 1916 bis zum Wechsel in der Obersten Heeresleitung*, Mittler und Sohn, Berlin: 1936.

Oberkommando des Heeres, *Der Weltkrieg 1914 bis 1918*, Volume 12, *Die Kriegs-führung im Frühjahr 1917*, Mittler und Sohn, Berlin: 1939.
Oberkommando des Heeres, *Der Weltkrieg 1914 bis 1918*, Volume 13, *Die Kriegs-führung im Sommer und Herbst 1917*, Mittler und Sohn, Berlin: 1942.
Oberkommando des Heeres, *Der Weltkrieg 1914 bis 1918*, Volume 14, *Die Kriegs-führung an der Westfront im Jahre 1918*, Mittler und Sohn, Berlin: 1944.
Stenger, Alfred, *Der Letzte Deutsche Angriff: Reims 1918: Schlachten des Weltkriegs*, Volume 34, Gerhard Stalling, Berlin: 1930.
Stenger, Alfred, *Schicksalswende, von der Marne bis zur Vesle 1918: Schlachten des Weltkriegs*, Volume 35, Gerhard Stalling, Berlin: 1930.
Strutz, Georg, *Die Tankschlacht bei Cambrai, 20.–29. November 1917: Schlachten des Weltkriegs*, Volume 31, Gerhard Stalling, Berlin: 1929.

Great Britain

Edmonds, James E., *Military Operations: Belgium and France 1918*, Volume I, Macmillan & Co., Ltd., London: 1935.
Edmonds, James E., editor, *Military Operations: Belgium and France 1918*, Volume I Appendices, Macmillan & Co., Ltd., London: 1935.
Edmonds, James E., *Military Operations: Belgium and France 1918*, Volume II, Macmillan & Co., Ltd., London: 1937.
Edmonds, James E., Military *Operations: Belgium and France 1918*, Volume III, Macmillan & Co., Ltd., London: 1939.
Edmonds, James E., *Military Operations: Belgium and France 1918*, Volume IV, Macmillan & Co., Ltd., London: 1947.
Edmonds, James E., *Military Operations: Belgium and France 1918*, Volume V, Macmillan & Co., Ltd., London: 1949.
Falls, Cyril, *Military Operations: Belgium and France 1917*, Volume I, Macmillan & Co., Ltd., London: 1940.
Henniker, A.M., *Transportation on the Western Front, 1914–1918*, Macmillan & Co., Ltd., London: 1937.

United States

Department of the Army, *United States Army in the World War 1917–1919: Military Operations of the American Expeditionary Force*, Volume 4, Center of Military History (reprint), Washington, D.C.: 1989.
Department of the Army, *United States Army in the World War 1917–1919: Military Operations of the American Expeditionary Force*, Volume 5, Center of Military History (reprint), Washington, D.C.: 1989.
Department of the Army, *United States Army in the World War 1917–1919: Military Operations of the American Expeditionary Force*, Volume 11, Center of Military History (reprint), Washington, D.C.: 1991.
Department of the Army, *United States Army in the World War 1917–1919: Military Operations of the American Expeditionary Force*, Volume 13, Center of Military History (reprint), Washington, D.C.: 1991.

General histories

Ball, Harry P., *Of Responsible Command: A History of the U.S. Army War College*, Carlisle Barracks, Pennsylvania: 1994.

Bond, Brian, *The Unquiet Western Front: Britain's Role in Literature and History*, University of Cambridge Press, Cambridge: 2002.

Carver, Sir Michael, ed., *The War Lords: Military Commanders of the Twentieth Century*, Little, Brown & Company, Boston, Massachusetts: 1976.

Cron, Hermann, *Geschichte des deutschen Heeres im Weltkriege 1914–1918*, Militärverlag Karl Siegismund, Berlin: 1937.

Falls, Cyril, *The Great War*, Putnam Publishing Group, New York: 1959.

Farndale, Martin, *History of the Royal Regiment of Artillery: Western Front 1914–18*, Brassey's, Dorchester: 1986.

Fussell, Paul, *The Great War in Modern Memory*, Oxford University Press, Oxford: 1975.

Gilbert, Martin, *The First World War: A Complete History*, Henry Holt, New York: 1994.

Griess, Thomas E., *Definitions and Doctrine of the Military Art*, Avery Publishing Group, Wayne, New Jersey: 1985.

Herwig, Holger H., *The First World War: Germany and Austria-Hungary, 1914–1918*, Arnold, London: 1997.

Holmes, Richard, *The Western Front*, BBC Books, London: 1999.

Keegan, John, *The First World War*, New York: 1998.

Jessup, John E. and Coakley, Robert W., eds., *A Guide to the Study and Use of Military History*, U.S. Army Center of Military History, Washington, D.C.: 1978.

Kuhl, Hermann von, *Der Weltkrieg 1914–1918*, Verlag Tradition Wilhelm Holt, Berlin: 1929.

Liddell Hart, Basil H., *The Real War 1914–1918*, Little, Brown and Company, Boston, Massachusetts: 1930.

Sheffield, Gary, *Forgotten Victory: The First World War Myths and Realities*, London: Headline Book Publishing, 2001.

Strachan, Hew, *The First World War: Volume I: To Arms*, Oxford University Press, New York: 2001.

Tsouras, Peter G., *The Greenhill Dictionary of Military Quotations*, Stackpole, Harrisburg, Pennsylvania: 2000.

Tucker, Spencer C., ed., *The European Powers in the First World War: An Encyclopedia*, Garland, New York: 1996.

Memoirs

Foch, Ferdinand, *The Memoirs of Marshall Foch*, Doubleday, New York: 1931.

Haig, Sir Douglas, *The Private Papers of Douglas Haig, 1914–1919*, (Robert Blake, ed.), Eyre & Spottiswoode, London: 1952.

Hindenburg, Paul von, *Aus meinem Leben*, Hirzel, Leipzig: 1920.

Hoffmann, Max, *Der Krieg der versäumten Gelegenheiten*, Verlag für Kulturpolitik, Munich: 1923.

Jünger, Ernst, *The Storm of Steel: From the Diary of a German Storm-Troop Officer on the Western Front*, Zimmermann & Zimmermann, New York: 1985.

Lossberg, Fritz von, *Meine Tätigkeit im Weltkriege 1914–1918*, Mittler und Sohn, Berlin: 1939.

Ludendorff, Erich, *Meine Kriegserinnerungen 1914–1918*, Mittler und Sohn, Berlin: 1919.

Ludendorff, Erich, *Urkunden der Obersten Heersleitung über ihre Tätigkeit 1916–1918*, Mittler und Sohn, Berlin: 1921.

Ludendorff, Erich, *Kriegsführung und Politik*, Mittler und Sohn, Berlin: 1922.

Pershing, John J., *My Experiences in the World War*, Frederick A. Stokes Company, New York: 1931.

Rupprecht, Kronprinz von Bayern, *Mein Kriegstagebuch*, Deutscher National Verlag, Munich: 1929.

Sulzbach, Herbert, *Zwischen zwei Mauern: 50 Monate Westfront*, Kurt Vowincker-Verlag, Berg am See: 1986.

Thaer, Albrecht von, *Generalstabsdienst an der Front und in der O.H.L.*, Vandenhoeck & Ruprecht, Göttingen: 1958.

Wilhelm, Kronprinz von Deutschland, *Meine Erinnerungen aus Deutschlands Heldenkampf*, Mittler und Sohn, Berlin: 1923.

Ludendorff

Asprey, Robert B., *The German High Command at War: Hindenburg and Ludendorff Conduct World War I*, William Morrow, New York: 1991.

Beck, Ludwig, *"Der 29. September 1918,"* in *Studien*, Hans Speidel, ed., K.F. Koehler Verlag, Stuttgart: 1955.

Foerster, Wolfgang, *Ludendorff: Der Feldherr im Unglück*, Limes Verlag, Wiesbaden: 1952.

Goodspeed, D.J., *Ludendorff: Genius of World War I*, Houghton Mifflin Company, Boston, Massachusetts: 1966.

Haeften, Hans von, *Hindenburg und Ludendorff als Feldherren*, Mittler und Sohn, Berlin: 1937.

Stone, Norman, "General Erich Ludendorff," in *The War Lords: Military Commanders of the Twentieth Century*, Field Marshal Sir Michael Carver, ed., Weidenfeld and Nicolson Ltd, London: 1976, pp.73–83.

Venohr, Wolfgang, *Ludendorff: Legende und Wirklichkeit*, Ullstein Verlag, Berlin: 1993.

Wetzell, Georg, *Von Falkenhayn zu Hindenburg-Ludendorff*, Mittler und Sohn, Berlin: 1921.

German army

Benary, Albert, ed., *Das Ehrenbuch der deutschen Feldartillerie*, Verlag Tradition Wilhelm Holt, Berlin: 1930.

Brose, Eric Dorn, *The Kaiser's Army: The Politics of Military Technology in Germany during the Machine Age, 1970–1918*, Oxford University Press, New York: 2001.

Cron, Hermann, *Die Organisation des deutschen Heeres im Weltkriege*, Mittler und Sohn, Berlin: 1932.

Dupuy, Trevor N., *A Genius for War: The German Army and the General Staff, 1807–1945*, Nova, Falls Church, Virginia: 1977.

Echevarria, Antulio J., II, *After Clausewitz: German Military Thinkers before the Great War*, University Press of Kansas, Lawrence, Kansas: 2000.

Görlitz, Walter, *History of the German General Staff, 1657–1945*, Praeger, New York: 1953.

Great Britain, War Office, General Staff, *Handbook of the German Army in the War, April 1918*, (reprint), Arms & Armour Press, London: 1977.

Great Britain, War Office, General Staff, *The German Forces in the Field: 7th Revision, 11th November 1918*, (reprint), Battery Press, Nashville, Tennessee: 1995.

Kaiser, Franz Nikolas, *Das Ehrenbuch der deutschen Schweren Artillerie*, Volume I, Verlag Tradition Wilhelm Holt, Berlin: 1931.

Millotat, Christian O.E., *Understanding the Prussian-German General Staff System*, Strategic Studies Institute, U.S. Army War College, Carlisle, Pennsylvania: 1992.

Rosinski, Herbert, *The German Army*, Praeger, New York: 1966.

United States, War Department Document No. 905, *Histories of Two Hundred and Fifty-one Divisions of the German Army Which Participated in the War (1914–1918)*, 1920, (reprint), London Stamp Exchange, London: 1989.

Military manuals

Germany, *Heeresdienstvorschrift 300, Truppenführung*, Mittler und Sohn, Berlin: 1933.

Germany, *Heeresdienstvorschrift 487, Führung und Gefecht der verbunden Waffen*, Mittler und Sohn, Berlin: 1923.

Germany, Kriegsministerium, *Exerzier-Reglement für die Feldartillerie*, Mittler und Sohn, Berlin: 1907.

Germany, Kriegsministerium, *Exerzier-Reglement für die Fussartillerie*, Mittler und Sohn, Berlin: 1908.

United Kingdom, *Joint Warfare Publication 0-01, British Defence Doctrine*, London: 2001.

United States, *Field Manual 100-5, Operations*, Washington, D.C.: 1976.

United States, *Field Manual 100-5, Operations*, Washington, D.C.: 1982.

United States, *Field Manual 100-5, Operations*, Washington, D.C.: 1986.

United States, *Field Manual 100-5, Operations*, Washington, D.C.: 1993.

United States, *Field Manual 3-0, Operations*, Washington, D.C.: 2001.

United States, *Joint Publications 3-0, Doctrine for Joint Operations*, Washington, D.C., 9 September 1993.

Strategic level

Books

Bloch, Jan, *Jean de Bloch: Selected Articles*, (reprint), United States Army Command and General Staff College, Fort Leavenworth, Kansas: 1993.

Clausewitz, Carl von, *On War*, Michael Howard and Peter Paret, eds., Princeton University Press, Princeton, New Jersey: 1976.

Feldman, Gerald D., *Army, Industry, and Labor in Germany, 1914–1918*, Princeton University Press, Princeton, New Jersey: 1966.

Foerster, Wolfgang, *Der deutsche Zusammenbruch 1918*, Verlag Eisenschmidt, Berlin: 1925.

Gatzke, Hans W., *Germany's Drive to the West: A Study of Germany's Western War Aims during the First World War*, Johns Hopkins University Press, Baltimore, Maryland: 1950.

Gehre, Ludwig, *Die deutsche Kräfteverteilung während des Weltkrieges: Eine Clausewitzstudie*, Mittler und Sohn, Berlin: 1928.

Herwig, Holger H., *"Luxury" Fleet: The Imperial German Navy, 1888–1918*, Ashfield Press, London: 1980.

Jomini, Antoine H., *The Art of War*, (reprint), Praeger, Westport, Connecticut: 1972.

Kemp, Paul, *U-Boats Destroyed: German Submarine Losses in the World Wars*, Arms and Armour Press, London: 1997.

Kuhl, Hermann von, *Entstehung, Durchführung und Zusammenbruch der Offensive von 1918*, Deutsche Verlagsgesellschaft für Politik und Geschichte, Berlin: 1927.

Kuhl, Hermann von and Hans Delbrück, *Ursachen des Zusammenbruchs: Entstehung, Durchführung und Zusammenbruch der Offensive von 1918*, Verlag von Reimar Hobbing, Berlin: 1923.

Liddell Hart, Sir Basil H., *Strategy*, Praeger, New York: 1967.

Lykke, Arthur F., *Military Strategy: Theory and Application*, U.S. Army War College, Carlisle Barracks, Pennsylvania: 1989.

Metz, Steven and James Kievet, *Strategy and the Revolution in Military Affairs: From Theory to Policy*, Strategic Studies Institute, U.S. Army War College, Carlisle Barracks, Pennsylvania: 1995.

Moser, Otto von, *Kurzer strategischer Überblick über den Weltkrieg 1914–1918*, Mittler und Sohn, Berlin: 1921.

Paret, Peter, (ed.), *Makers of Modern Strategy from Machiavelli to the Nuclear Age*, Princeton University Press, Princeton, New Jersey: 1986.

Rössler, Eberhard, *U-Boat: The Evolution and Technical History of German Submarines*, U.S. Naval Institute Press, Annapolis, Maryland: 1999.

Scheer, Reinhard, *Germany's High Seas Fleet*, (reprint), Battery Press, Nashville, Tennessee: 2002.

Wetzell, Georg, *Der Bündniskrieg: Eine militärpolitisch operativ Studie des Weltkrieges*, Mittler und Sohn, Berlin: 1937.

Wier, Gary, *Building the Kaiser's Navy*, U.S. Naval Institute Press, Annapolis, Maryland: 1988.

Wiest, Andrew A., *Passchendaele and the Royal Navy*, Greenwood Press, Westport, Connecticut: 1995.

Wrisberg, Ernst von, *Wehr und Waffen, 1914–1918*, Koehler Verlag, Leipzig: 1922.

Journal and periodical articles

Herwig, Holger, "Germany and the 'Short-War' Illusion: Toward a New Interpretation?," *The Journal of Military History*, July 2002, pp.681–693.

Hitz, Hans, "Taktik und Strategie," *Wehrwissenschaftliche Rundschau*, November 1956, pp.611–628.

Operational level

Books

Bailey, J.B.A., *The First World War and the Birth of the Modern Style of Warfare*, The Occasional, Number 22, British Staff College, Camberley: 1996.

Bellamy, Christopher, *The Evolution of Modern Land Warfare: Theory and Practice*, Routledge, London: 1990.

Bernhardi, Friedrich von, *How Germany Makes War*, George Doran Company, New York: 1914.

Barnett, Correlli, *The Swordbearers: Supreme Command in the First World War*, Indiana University Press, Bloomington, Indiana: 1964.

Brown, Ian Malcolm, *British Logistics on the Western Front, 1914–1919*, Praeger, Bridgeport, Connecticut: 1998.

Corum, James S., *The Roots of Blitzkrieg: Hans von Seeckt and German Military Reform*, University Press of Kansas, Lawrence, Kansas: 1992.

Corum, James S., *The Luftwaffe: Creating the Operational Air War, 1918–1940*, University Press of Kansas, Lawrence, Kansas: 1997.

Corum, James S. and Richard R. Muller, *The Luftwaffe's Way of War: German Air Force Doctrine, 1911–1945*, Naval and Aviation Publishing Company, Baltimore, Maryland: 1997.

Foerster, Roland, *Operatives Denken bei Clausewitz, Moltke, Schlieffen und Manstein*, MGFA, Freiburg, Germany: 1989.

Fuller, J.F.C., *The Foundations of the Science of War*, Hutchinson & Co., London: 1926.

Fuller, General J.F.C., *War and Western Civilization: 1832–1932*, Duckworth, London: 1932.

Fuller, J.F.C., *The Conduct of War: 1789–1961*, Rutgers University Press, Rutgers, New Jersey: 1961.

Gooch, John, (ed.), *The Origins of Contemporary Doctrine*, The Occasional Number 30, Strategic & Combat Studies Institute, Camberley: 1997.

Irwin, A.S.H., *The Levels of War, Operational Art, and Campaign Planning*, The Occasional Number 5, Strategic & Combat Studies Institute, Camberley: 1993.

Jones, Archer, *The Art of War in the Western World*, University of Illinois Press, Chicago, Illinois: 1987.

McKercher, B.J.C. and Michael A. Hennessy (eds.), *The Operational Art: Developments in the Theories of War*, Praeger, Westport, Connecticut: 1996.

Naveh, Shimon, *In Pursuit of Military Excellence: The Evolution of Operational Theory*, Frank Cass, London: 1997.

Newell, Clayton R. and Michael D. Krause (eds.), *On Operational Art*, Center of Military History, Washington, D.C.: 1994.

Samuels, Martin, *Command or Control? Command, Training, and Tactics in the British and German Armies, 1888–1918*, Frank Cass, London: 1995.

Schlieffen, Alfred von, *Cannae*, (third reprint), United States Army Command and General Staff College, Fort Leavenworth, Kansas: 1992.

Simpkin, Richard, *Race to the Swift: Thoughts on Twenty-first Century Warfare*, Oxford University Press, London: 1985.

Triandafillov, V.K., *The Nature of the Operations of Modern Armies*, (William A. Burhans, trans.), Frank Cass & Co., Ltd., London: 1994.

van Creveld, Martin, *Command in War*, Harvard University Press, Cambridge, Massachusetts: 1985.

Wallach, Jehuda L., *The Dogma of the Battle of Annihilation: The Theories of Clausewitz and Schlieffen and Their Impact on the German Conduct of Two World Wars*, Greenwood Press, Westport, Connecticut: 1986.

Journal and periodical articles

Fong, Giordan, "The Movement of German Divisions to the Western Front, Winter 1917–1918," *Stand To! The Journal of the Western Front Association*, September 2002, pp.23–28.

Krause, Michael D., "Moltke and the Origins of Operational Art," *Military Review*, September 1990, pp.28–44.

Meier-Welcker, Hans, "Die deutsche Führung der Westfront im Frühsommer 1918," *Die Welt als Geschichte*, Volume XXI, Number 3, 1961, pp.164–184.

Menning, Bruce W., "Operational Art's Origins," *Military Review*, September 1997, pp.32–47.

Schneider, James J. and Lawrence L. Izzo, "Clausewitz's Elusive Center of Gravity," *Parameters*, September 1987, pp.46–57.

Whaley, Barton, "Toward a General Theory of Deception," *The Journal of Strategic Studies*, March 1982, pp.178–192.

Tactical level

Books

Bailey, J.B.A., *Field Artillery and Firepower*, Military Press, Oxford: 1989.

Balck, William, *Entwicklung der Taktik im Weltkriege*, Eisenschmidt, Berlin: 1922 (*Development of Tactics: World War*, Harry bell, trans.).

Bellamy, Chris, *Red God of War: Soviet Artillery and Rocket Forces*, Brassey's Defence Publishers, London: 1986.

Bernhardi, Friedrich von, *Von Kriege der Zukunft, nach den Erfahrungen des Weltkriegs*, Mittler und Sohn, Berlin: 1920.

Bidwell, Shelford and Graham Dominick, *Firepower: British Army Weapons and Theories of War, 1904–1945*, Allen & Unwin, London: 1982.

Bruchmüller, Georg, *Die Deutsche Artillerie in den Durchbruchschlachten des Weltkriegs*, 1st ed., Mittler und Sohn, Berlin: 1921.

Bruchmüller, Georg, *Die Deutsche Artillerie in den Durchbruchschlachten des Weltkriegs*, 2nd ed., Mittler und Sohn, Berlin: 1922.

Bruchmüller, Georg, *Die Artillerie beim Angriff im Stellungskrieg*, Verlag Offene Worte, Berlin: 1926.

Bull, G.V. and C.H. Murphy, *Paris Kanonen—The Paris Guns (Wilhelmgeschütze) and Project HARP*, E.S. Mittler & Sohn, Herford: 1988.

Chasseaud, Peter, *Topography of Armageddon: A British Trench Map Atlas of the Western Front, 1914–1918*, Mapbooks, Lewes, East Sussex, 1991.

Curti, Paul, *Umfassung und Durchbruch*, Huber & Co., Frauenfeld: 1955.

Dupuy, Trevor N., *Understanding War: History and the Theory of Combat*, Paragon House, New York: 1987.

Dupuy, Trevor N., *Numbers, Predictions and War: Using History to Evaluate Combat Factors and Predict the Outcome of Battles*, Bobbs-Merrill, New York: 1979.

Ellis, John, *Eye-deep in Hell: Trench Warfare in World War I*, Johns Hopkins University Press, Baltimore, Maryland: 1976.

Fuller, J.F.C., *Tanks in the Great War*, John Murray, London: 1920.

Fuller, J.F.C., *Armament and History*, London: 1946.

Griffith, Paddy, *Forward into Battle: Fighting Tactics from Waterloo to the Near Future*, Presidio, Novato, California: 1991.

Griffith, Paddy, *Battle Tactics of the Western Front: The British Army's Art of the Attack, 1916–1918*, Yale University Press, New Haven, Connecticut: 1994.

Gudmundsson, Bruce I., *Stormtroop Tactics: Innovation in the German Army, 1914–1918*, Praeger, New York: 1989.

Heller, Charles E., Chemical Warfare in World War I: The American Experience, 1917–1918, Leavenworth Papers, Nr. 10, U.S. Army Command and General Staff College, Combat Studies Institute, Fort Leavenworth, Kansas: 1984.

Herr, Frederic, *Die Artillerie in Vergangenheit, Gegenwart, und Zukunft*, (translation of *L'Artillerie, ce qu'elle a été, ce qu'elle est, ce qu'elle doit être*, (Paris: 1923)), Offene Worte, Charlottenburg: 1925.

Hogg, Ian V., *Barrage: The Guns in Action*, Ballantine Books, New York: 1970.

Hogg, Ian V., *The Guns 1914–1918*, Ballantine Books, New York: 1971.

Hogg, Ian V., *Gas*, Ballantine Books, New York: 1975.

House, Jonathan M., *Toward Combined Arms Warfare: A Survey of 20th Century Tactics, Doctrine, and Organization*, U.S. Army Combat Studies Institute, Fort Leavenworth, Kansas: 1984.

Lawson, Eric and Jane, *The First Air Campaign: August 1914–November 1918*, MBI, Inc., Norwalk, Connecticut: 1996.

Lucas, Pascal, *The Evolution of Tactical Ideas in France and Germany during the War of 1914–1918*, Berger-Levrault, Paris: 1923, (manuscript translation in English by Major P.V. Kieffer, U.S. Army, 1925).

Lupfer, Timothy T., *The Dynamics of Doctrine: Changes in German Tactical Doctrine during the First World War*, Leavenworth Papers Nr. 4, U.S. Army Combat Studies Institute, Fort Leavenworth, Kansas: July 1981.

Marx, Wilhelm, *Artillerie im Kampf*, Ludwig Voggen Reiter Verlag, Potsdam: 1936.

Millett, Alan and Williamson Murray, (eds.), *Military Effectiveness*, Volume I: *The First World War*, Unwin Hyman, Boston, Massachusetts: 1988.

Rawling, Bill, *Surviving Trench Warfare: Technology and the Canadian Corps 1914–1918*, University of Toronto Press, Toronto: 1992.

Samuels, Martin, *Doctrine and Dogma: German and British Infantry Tactics in the First World War*, Greenwood, Westport, Connecticut: 1992.

Seesselberg, Frederich, *Der Stellungskrieg 1914–1918*, Mittler und Sohn, Berlin: 1926.

Terraine, John, *White Heat: The New Warfare 1914–1918*, Sidgwick & Jackson, London: 1982.

Travers, Tim, *The Killing Ground: The British Army on the Western Front and the Emergence of Modern Warfare, 1900–1918*, Allen and Unwin, London: 1987.

Travers, Tim, *How the War Was Won: Command and Technology in the British Army on the Western Front, 1917–1918*, Allen and Unwin, London: 1992.

United States, Department of War, *A Survey of German Tactics, 1918*, Monograph No. 1, Government Printing Office, Washington, D.C.: 1918.

United States, Department of War, *German and Austrian Tactical Studies: Translations of Captured Documents*, Government Printing Office, Washington, D.C.: 1918.

van Creveld, Martin, *Fighting Power: German and U.S. Army Performance, 1939–1945*, Greenwood, Westport, Connecticut: 1982.

Zabecki, David T., *Steel Wind: Colonel Georg Bruchmüller and the Birth of Modern Artillery*, Praeger, Bridgeport, Connecticut: 1994.

Zabecki, David T. and Bruce Condell, *Truppenführung: On the German Art of War*, Lynne Rienner Publishers, Boulder, Colorado: 2001.

Journal and periodical articles

Alfoldi, Laszlo M., "The Hutier Legend," *Parameters*, Volume 5, Number 2, 1976, pp.69–74.

Altmayer, Rene, "The German Military Doctrine," *Field Artillery Journal*, (translation of an article in the July 1934 issue of *Revue Militaire Française*), March 1935, pp.181–191.

Berendt, Richard von, "Mit der Artillerie durch den Weltkrieg," *Wissen und Wehr*, 1924, pp.185–197.

Berendt, Richard von, "Die Artillerie beim Angriff im Stellungskrieg," *Artilleristische Rundschau*, April 1927, pp.17–23.

Berendt, Richard von, "Schiessübungen," *Artilleristische Rundschau*, October 1925, pp.193–196.

Bernhardi, Friedrich von, "Die Deutsche Artillerie in den Durchbruchschlachten des Weltkrieges," *Militär-Wochenblatt*, 20 August 1921, pp.157–159.

Bethell, H.A., "The Modern Attack on an Entrenched Position," *Journal of the Royal Artillery*, July 1918, pp.121–129.

Birch, Sir Noel, "Artillery Development in the Great War," *Field Artillery Journal*, (reprint from the October 1920 issue of *The Army Quarterly*), July 1921, pp.356–366.

Brooke, Alan F., "The Evolution of Artillery in the Great War: Part I," *Journal of the Royal Artillery*, November 1924, pp.250–267.

Brooke, Alan F., "The Evolution of Artillery in the Great War: Part II," *Journal of the Royal Artillery*, January 1925, pp.359–372.

Brooke, Alan F., "The Evolution of Artillery in the Great War: Part III," *Journal of the Royal Artillery*, April 1925, pp.37–51.

Brooke, Alan F., "The Evolution of Artillery in the Great War: Part IV," *Journal of the Royal Artillery*, October 1925, pp.369–387.

Brooke, Alan F., "The Evolution of Artillery in the Great War: Part V," *Journal of the Royal Artillery*, April 1926, pp.76–93.

Brooke, Alan F., "The Evolution of Artillery in the Great War: Part VI," *Journal of the Royal Artillery*, July 1926, pp.232–249.

Brooke, Alan F., "The Evolution of Artillery in the Great War: Part VII," *Journal of the Royal Artillery*, October 1926, pp.320–329.

Brooke, Alan F., "The Evolution of Artillery in the Great War: Part VIII," *Journal of the Royal Artillery*, January 1927, pp.469–482.

Brooke, Alan F., "Does Radio Telephony Offer a Possible Solution to the Main Artillery Problem of the Day?," *Journal of the Royal Artillery*, January 1929, pp.438–452.

Corda, H., "Evolution in Offensive Methods—Part I," *Field Artillery Journal*, (translation of an article in the April 1921 issues of *Revue Militaire Suisse*), May 1922, pp.248–264.

Corda, H., "Evolution in Offensive Methods—Part II," *Field Artillery Journal*, (translation of an article in the May 1921 issues of *Revue Militaire Suisse*), July 1922, pp.292–307.

Culmann, Frederic, "The Artillery Preparation for Attacks and the Rupture of Defensive Zones," *Field Artillery Journal*, (translation from a French journal), May 1933, pp.254–267.

Culmann, Frederic, "Cooperation between Artillery and Tanks," *Field Artillery Journal*, (translation from a French journal), September 1937, pp.325–332.

Curry, M.L., "Artillery in the Elastic Defense," *Field Artillery Journal*, July 1940, pp.296–299.

Drees, L., "Das Anwachsen der Artillerie im Weltkriege," *Artilleristische Rundschau*, August 1926, pp.139–149.

Field Artillery Journal, "Organization of a Rolling Barrage in the German Army: Translation of a German Document," July 1918, pp.417–421.

Field Artillery Journal, "Accompanying and Infantry Batteries," July 1918, pp.422–426.

Field Artillery Journal, "Notes on Tactical Organization of German Artillery," July 1918, pp.432–435.

Field Artillery Journal, "Artillery in Recent Attacks," July 1918, pp.437–439.

Field Artillery Journal, "Measures Taken by the German Artillery for Attack without Betraying the Intentions of the Command," October 1918, pp.504–512.

Field Artillery Journal, "The Scientific Preparation of Fire in the German Artillery," October 1918, pp.527–534.

Field Artillery Journal, "German Artillery: Batteries of Infantry Guns: Translation of a German Document," October 1918, pp.578–585.

Field Artillery Journal, "Notes on Tactical Employment of Field Artillery (Extract of A.E.F. Doc. 1348, 5 Sept. 1918)," October 1918, pp.586–592.

Field Artillery Journal, "Artillery Fire of Protection: Extracts from a German Document," January 1919, pp.104–106.

Field Artillery Journal, "German Field Artillery in the War," (translation of an article from the January 1920 issue of *Artilleristische Monatshefte*), July 1920, pp.412–434.

Field Artillery Journal, "Remarks on the Organization of German Artillery," (translation of an article from the April 1921 issue of *Revue d'Artillerie*), January 1923, pp.66–73.

Goschen, A.A., "Artillery Tactics," *The Journal of the Royal Artillery*, Volume LII, 1925, pp.254–260.

Isbert, General, "The French and German Field Artillery at the Start of the War," *Field Artillery Journal*, (translation of an article in the February 1920 issue of *Artilleristische Monatshefte*), September 1920, pp.527–538.

Journal of the Royal Artillery, "Artillery Fire," (reprinted from the March 1924 issue of the *Coast Artillery Journal*), 1924–1925, Volume LI, Number 3, pp.123–135.

Kunh, *General der Artillerie*, "Die deutsche Artillerie in den Durchbruchschlachten des Weltkriegs," *Militär-Wochenblatt*, 14 May 1921, pp.1007–1008.

Lanza, Conrad H., "The Start of the Meuse-Argonne Campaign," *Field Artillery Journal*, January 1933, pp.57–71.

Maitre, Colonel, "Evolution of Ideas in the Employment of Artillery during the War," *Field Artillery Journal*, (translation of a lecture delivered at the Centre d'Etudes Tactiques d'Artillerie at Metz, France), January 1922, pp.1–18.

Merz, H., "Truths from the German Front," *Journal of the United States Artillery*, (translation of an article from the 29 October 1921 issue of *Allgemeine schweizerische Militärzeitung*), 1922, pp.346–356.

Muther, Alfred, "Organization, Armament, Ammunition, and Ammunition Expenditure of the German Field Artillery during the World War—Part 1," *Field Artillery Journal*, May 1935.

Oldfield, L.C.L., "Artillery and the Lessons We Have Learnt with Regard to It in the Late War," *The Journal of the Royal Artillery*, 1923, Volume XLIX, pp.462–482.

Rohne, Heinrich, "Technical Training of Artillery Officers," *Field Artillery Journal*, (translation of an article from the June 1919 issue of *Artilleristische Monatshefte*), May 1921, pp.303–310.

Rohne, Heinrich, "Die deutsche Artillerie in den Schlachten des Stellungskriegs," *Artilleristische Monatshefte*), July 1921, pp.145–154.

Rohne, Heinrich, "Observed and Unobserved Artillery Fire," *Journal of the Royal*

Artillery, (translation of an article from a 1922 issue of *Artilleristische Monatshefte*), 1923, Volume L, pp.123–129.

Rohne, Heinrich, "Artillery Statistics from the World War," *Field Artillery Journal*, (translation of an article from the January 1924 issue of *Artilleristische Monatshefte*), September 1924, pp.451–454.

Zabecki, David T., "The Guns of Manchuria," *Field Artillery Journal*, (April 1988).

Zabecki, David T., "The Dress Rehearsal: Lost Artillery Lessons of the 1912–1913 Balkan Wars," *Field Artillery Journal*, August 1988.

1918 Battles

Books

Essame, Hubert, *The Battle for Europe 1918*, Batsford, London: 1972.

Fehr, Otto, *Die Märzoffensive 1918 an der Westfront: Strategie oder Taktik?*, Verlag Koehler, Leipzig: 1921.

General Service Schools, *The German Offensive of July 15, 1918 (Marne Source Book)*, General Service Schools Press, Fort Leavenworth, Kansas: 1923.

Goes, Gustav, *Chemin des Dames*, Berlin: 1938.

Gray, Randal, *Kaisersschlacht 1918: The Final German Offensive*, Osprey Campaign Series, London: 1991.

Greenwood, Paul, *The Second Battle of the Marne, 1918*, Airlife, New York: 1998.

Holmes, Richard, "The Ludendorff Offensives Phase 3: The Aisne," *The Marshall Cavendish Illustrated Encyclopedia of World War I*, Volume IX, pp.2778–2787, Marshall Cavendish, New York: 1984.

Kabisch, Ernst, *Michael: Die grosse Schlacht in Frankreich*, Berlin: 1936.

Kabisch, Ernst, *Um Lys und Kemmel*, Berlin: 1936.

Keegan, John, "The Second Battle of the Marne: 2. The Allied Counter Attack," *The Marshall Cavendish Illustrated Encyclopedia of World War I*, Volume IX, pp.2876–2880, Marshall Cavendish, New York: 1984.

Kitchen, Martin, *The German Offensives of 1918*, Tempus Publishing Ltd., Stroud, Gloucestershire: 2001.

Macdonald, Lyn, *To the Last Man: Spring 1918*, Penguin Books, London: 1999.

Middlebrook, Martin, *The Kaiser's Battle*, Penguin, London: 1978.

Paschall, Rod, *The Defeat of Imperial Germany, 1917–1918*, Algonquin Books, Chapel Hill, North Carolina: 1990.

Pitt, Barrie, *1918: The Last Act*, Ballantine Books, New York: 1963.

Wynne, Graeme, *If Germany Attacks: The Battle in Depth in the West*, Faber and Faber, London: 1940.

CD-ROM

Captured German Trench and Operations Maps from the National Archives, Naval and Military Press in association with Imperial War Museum, Uckfield, East Sussex: 2003.

Journal and periodical articles

Bergmann, General, "Bei einer deutschen Angriffsdivision während dreier Offensiven des Jahres 1918," *Wissen und Wehr*, Volume XVI, 1936, pp.289–319, 400–416, 463–487.

Goubard, J., "Defensive Employment of the French Artillery in 1918: The Artillery of the 21st Corps in the Battle of 15th July," *Field Artillery Journal*, (translation of an article from the August 1921 issue of *Revue d'Artillerie*), November 1921, pp.565–575.

Kuhl, Hermann von, "Das Deutsche Angriffsverfahren bei der Offensive in Jahre 1918," *Deutsches Offiziersblatt*, 21 September 1921, pp.533–535.

Kuhl, Hermann von, "Die Schlachten im Sommer 1918 an der Westfront," *Militär-Wochenblatt*, 1921, pp.673–674.

Lanza, Conrad H., "Five Decisive Days: The Germans in the Reims Offensive," *Field Artillery Journal*, January 1937, pp.37–66.

Lanza, Conrad H., "The German XXIII Reserve Crosses the Marne," *Field Artillery Journal*, July 1937, pp.305–316.

Marx, Wilhelm, "Die Artillerievorbereitung beim Angriff beiderseits Reims am 15. Juli 1918," *Artilleristiche Rundschau*, December 1925, pp.257–268.

Meier, Ferdinand, "Die Artillerie des Kgl. Bayer. I. A.-K. bei der Juli-offensive 1918," Part 1, *Der K.B. Feld-Artillerist*, July 1936, pp.73–77.

Meier, Ferdinand, "Die Artillerie des Kgl. Bayer. I. A.-K. bei der Juli-offensive 1918," Part 2, *Der K.B. Feld-Artillerist*, August 1936, pp.88–92.

Militär-Wochenblatt, "Die deutsche Offensive im März 1918," Part 1, 18 February 1928, pp.1161–1167.

Militär-Wochenblatt, "Die deutsche Offensive im März 1918," Part 2, 25 February 1928, pp.1208–1210.

Militär-Wochenblatt, "Die deutsche Offensive im März 1918," Part 3, 4 March 1928, pp.1251–1257.

Militär-Wochenblatt, "Die deutsche Offensive im März 1918," Part 4, 11 March 1928, pp.1289–1295.

Militär-Wochenblatt, "Die Fortführung der deutschen Grossoffensive in April 1918," 11 May 1928, pp.1617–1622.

Muller, J.P., "The German Artillery at Chemin des Dames in 1918," *Field Artillery Journal*, (translated from the March 1922 edition of *Revue d'Artillerie*), March 1922, pp.154–162.

Raicer, Ted S., "Storm in the West," *Command Magazine*, May–June 1992, pp.16–33.

Solger, Dr., "Der Durchbruchsangriff dargetan an den Kämpfen in Jahre 1918," *Militär-wissenschaftliche Rundschau*, March 1939, pp.204–228.

Waechter, Hans, "Das Artillerie-Angriffsverfahren beim Durchbruch im Weltkriege," *Militär-Wochenblatt*, 11 June 1921, pp.1093–1097.

Wetzell, Georg, "Michael, die grosse Schlacht in Frankreich," *Militär-Wochenblatt*, 28 May 1935, pp.1944–1946.

Index

Eastern Front xxi, 43, 54, 56, 89, 94, 126, 272, 297, 317
Ebblinghem 191
Eben, General *258,* 274
Eberhardt, General *185*
Echevarria, Antulio 25
Edmonds, James 2, 110–1, 151, 156, 170, 204, 231, 357n135
Einbruch see break-in
Einem, General *258*
Elincourt 235
Ellis, John 2
encirclement 24, 25
Enders, General *258*
English, John 23
English Channel 77, 221, 279, 321
Entente Powers 81–2, 88, 95
Entscheidungsstelle see decisive point
Envelopment 24, 26, 324
Epehy 131
Epernay 220–1, 224, 248–52, 263, 275
Equancourt 117–18, 143
Ermattungsstrategie see strategy
Essame, Hubert 60
Essen 92
Estaires 104, 176, 180, 186, *200*
Estrees St. Denis 241, 244
Etaples *316*
Etray 117
Eu 86
exploitation 41

Falkenhayn, Erich von 27, 66, 69, 93
Fassbender, General *136*
Faverolle 255
Fayolle, Marie 147, 152, 158, 170, 226, 241, 263
Fécamp *316,*
Fehr, Otto 162
Fère en Tardenois 220–1, 229, 255, 267, 270
Festubert 188–9, 191–5, 203–4, 287
Feuerwalze see artillery, creeping barrage
Field Manual 3–0, *Operations* 22, 35
Field Manual 100–5, *Operations* 12, 21–2, 30, 31, 35
Fins 131
firepower xx, 3, 23, 27, 42, 43; *see also* artillery; operational fires 37–8, 40, 56
Fismes 219–20, 223, 227, 255
flamethrowers 47
Flanders 98, 102–3, 105, 110–11, 115, 133, 174, 176, 178, 188, 191, 194–5, 202, 205, 206–7, 209, 212–13, 220–2, 230, 232, 236, 243, 245, 248, 256, 268, 273, 277, 280, 283–3, 286–8, 290, 297, 302–3, 307, 321
Flanders Hills 176–7, 190, 192, 198, 202–3, 205, 306
Flesquières Salient *see* Cambrai Salient
Flêtre 280

Fleury la Riviere 250
flexible defense 34, 66, 67–8, 110
Foch, Ferdinand 43, 149, 152, 154–5, 168, 182–4, 187–94, 197, 204–5, 207, 220–3, 226, 231, 238, 240–1, 244, 255–6, 263, 269, 273, 278, 320, 326, 328; General Directive Number 3 214; General Directive Number 4 255; *Roulement* plan 214
Foerster, Roland 22
follow-on-forces attack (FOFA) 21, 33
Fontaine lez Croisilles 123
force protection 35
Foreign Office, German 72
Forester, C.S. 1
Forêt d'Ermenonville 290,
Fort de la Pompelle 224–5, 264, 269, 306
Fort Malmaison 209
forward defense 45, 214
Fourteen Points, Wilson's 81–2
Francois, Hermann von *216, 239, 258,* 274
Franco-Prussian War (1870–71) 23
Frederick the Great 26, 73, 81
Frelinghien 180, 188
French Army 50, 51, 91, 95, 137, 146, 186, 334n16; cult of the offensive 43; *Deuxième* Bureau 230, 255–6; *Grand Quartier Général* (GQG) xx, 147, 220, 275; mutinies of 1917 314
French army groups: Army Detachment of the North 194, 197, 222; Army Group Center 91; Army Group East 91; Army Group North 91, 220; Army Group Reserve 147, 158, 186, 240
French corps: I Cavalry Corps 219; II Cavalry Corps 190–2, 219, 225; VII Corps 225; XI Corps 219, 225; XXX Corps 222
French divisions: 13th Division 220; 28th Division 190, 192, 195; 34th Division 195; 43rd Division 261; 53rd Division 241; 133rd Division 188, 192, 195; 154th Division 196
French field armies: First Army 147–8, 150, 153–4, 156–7, 301; Third Army 133, 147–9, 153, 157, 226, 238, *239,* 240, 301; Fourth Army 259, *260;* Fifth Army 156, 188–9, 219, 222–3, 255–6, 259, *260,* 269; Sixth Army 150, 214–15, 222–3, 225, 255–6, 259, *260,* 265; Ninth Army 269; Tenth Army 60, 156, 188–9, 194, 198, 221, 223, 240, 255–6, 259, 265
Frevent 162
Freytag-Loringhoven, Hugo von 20
friction xx, 32
Fritsch, Werner von 324
Fromelles 179, 186
Frunze reforms, Soviet 19
Führung und Gefecht der verbundenen Waffen (Heeresdienstvorschrift 487) 324
Fuller, J.F.C. 18–20, 39, 60, 64

Galicia 115, 126

Lightning Source UK Ltd.
Milton Keynes UK
UKOW05f1209160414

230075UK00007B/281/P